## DATE DUE

|  |  |  |  |
|---|---|---|---|
|  |  |  |  |
|  |  |  |  |
|  |  |  |  |
|  |  |  |  |
|  |  |  |  |
|  |  |  |  |
|  |  |  |  |
|  |  |  |  |
|  |  |  |  |
|  |  |  |  |
|  |  |  |  |
|  |  |  |  |
|  |  |  |  |
|  |  |  |  |
|  |  |  |  |
|  |  |  |  |
|  |  |  |  |
|  |  |  |  |
|  |  |  | PRINTED IN U.S.A. |

# PHILOSOPHY

## An Introduction to the
## ART of WONDERING

### Sixth Edition

# PHILOSOPHY

## An Introduction to the
## ART *of* WONDERING

### Sixth Edition

JAMES L. CHRISTIAN

*Rancho Santiago College, Santa Ana, California*

HARCOURT BRACE COLLEGE PUBLISHERS

*Fort Worth   Philadelphia   San Diego   New York   Orlando   Austin   San Antonio*
*Toronto   Montreal   London   Sydney   Tokyo*

*Publisher* TED BUCHHOLZ

*Acquisitions editor* DAVID TATOM

*Developmental editor* JOHN HALEY

*Project editor* KATHERINE V. LINCOLN/STEVE NORDER

*Production manager* JANE TYNDALL PONCETI

*Art director* NICK WELCH

*Permissions editor* SHEILA SHUTTER

Cover image created by John Fry, Dallas
Biographical portraits created courtesy of Scott Baker

ISBN: 0-15-500373-9

Library of Congress Catalog Card Number: 92-75744

Address for Editorial Correspondence:
*Harcourt Brace College Publishers, 301 Commerce Street, Suite 3700,
Fort Worth, TX 76102*

Address for Orders:
*Harcourt Brace & Company, 6277 Sea Harbor Drive, Orlando, FL 32887
1-800-782-4479, or 1-800-433-0001 (in Florida)*

Copyright acknowledgments begin on page 635, which constitutes a continuation of
this copyright page.

Printed in the United States of America

3 4 5 6 7 8 9 0 1 2   0 6 9   9 8 7 6 5 4 3 2 1

# PRELUDE

*The following pages
may cause you to wonder.
That's what philosophy is.
Wondering.*

*To philosophize
is to wonder about life—
about right and wrong,
love and loneliness,
war and death,
about freedom, truth, beauty, time . . .
and a thousand other things.*

*To philosophize
is to explore life.
It means breaking free
to ask questions.
It means resisting
easy answers.
To philosophize
is to seek in oneself
the courage to ask
painful questions.*

*But if, by chance,
you have already asked
all your questions
and found all the answers—
if you're sure you know
right from wrong,
and whether God exists,
and what justice means,
and why men fear and hate and pray—
if indeed you have done your wondering
about freedom and love and loneliness
and those thousand other things,
then the following pages
will waste your time.*

*Philosophy is for those
who are willing to be distrubed
with a creative disturbance.*

*Philosophy is for those
who still have the capacity
for wonder.*

## EDWIN PRINCE BOOTH

*Thank you for showing me why we must tirelessly seek out the profoundly human element in all historic events since only therein can their meaning be found. . . .*

## ARNOLD TOYNBEE

*In memorium: October 22, 1975*

*Thank you for the passion to see all existence as a single phenomenon without losing sight of the most minute details—this cave painting, this foot-note, this flower in this crannied wall. . . .*

## HERMAN AND ANNE

*In memorium: April 22 and 27, 1987*

*Thank you each for a parent's love and more. There are no words to express my appreciation of you both. . . .*

## BARBARA

*Thank you for your faith in our work, and for the relentless reminders that we must relate helium-filled abstractions to realities. . . .*

## LORI

*Thank you for teaching me that survival is one thing, living is quite another. . . .*

# CREDIT ✦ BLAME ✦ ACKNOWLEDGMENTS

*From the Preface to the First Edition ✦ February 1973*

I have written this book for my philosophy students . . . and for all who are caught up in the wonderment of life—its mystery, its enormity, its diversity.

All of us wonder, sometime or often, about our place in the world. What we are asking is how we can relate most happily to ourselves, to others close about us, to fellow creatures with whom we share our delicate planet, and to our mind-boggling universe. We burn with an urgency to know and understand, but we often despair of finding a way to turn our knowledge into insight and wisdom.

A philosophy text should offer cautious counsel to all who would seek intelligent, nonpartisan guidance on the life-and-death questions of human existence.

Eliot Aronson notes that so many of our students ask us what time it is, and we respond by presenting to them the history of time-keeping from waterclocks to wristwatches. By the time we finish, they have turned elsewhere to ask their questions.

And J. B. Priestley hurts when he reminds us that the man who shouts "My house is on fire!" may not be able to define precisely what he means by *my* and *house* and *is* and *on* and *fire,* but he may still be saying something very, very important.

*From the Preface to the Second Edition ✦ January 1977*

This book is a teaching instrument, a collection of teaching materials which, at one point or another, raises most of the classical problems of philosophy as well as many contemporary and relatively new philosophical questions. All materials in this book can be employed analytically and synoptically, to perform the numerous tasks required by classroom philosophic activity.

Some chapters include empirical data that we would normally subsume under Psychology, Biology, Chemistry, and the like. It helps enormously, I have found, if philosophy students have a fund of shared information, however brief, on a few specific problems before they plunge into a philosophic discussion of them.

*From the Preface to the Third Edition ✦ January 1981*

My gratitude continues to the many individuals acknowledged in the first and second editions. Now, I'm indebted to many more.

To Dr. Robert W. Smith for being a travel-guide in many worlds and co-conspirator in this one; and for strength and friendship.

Lastly, and firstly, to my wife Barbara, an enormous debt that remains unpaid and unpayable. . . . For a full decade now substantial portions of this book have been enriched by the depth and breadth of her intellect, so that, in its final form, this book stands as a joint labor of love.

*From the Preface to the Fourth Edition ✦ August 1985*

Each evening one of our local television stations plays its off-the-air theme containing the words "The world has gone through a lot today." This is my sentiment as the years pass and new revisions of this textbook are published. I am astounded at how much the world has gone through during each interim, how much it has changed, how many new world-views are in the offing, how much new knowledge has been gained, and how much new understanding has been made possible. It's bewildering, of course, but very exciting.

Each new edition of this book attempts to incorporate some of these new understandings. Unhappily, the Nuclear Winter scenario is included this time, along with—more happily—the future vision of the space artist Robert McCall. Twelve new biographies of Western philosophers have been added in an attempt (1) to supply the student with some historical roots in the Western philosophical tradition; and (2) to make a select few of the great thinkers come to life as human beings.

*From the Preface to the Fifth Edition ✦ January 1990*

My gratitude continues to numerous individuals who gave time and strength to previous editions of this book, and I would like to say thank you once again to them: Court Holdgrafer, Robert Putman, Ray Bradbury.

To a special group of people—perplexing innocents all, but wise; changing but never changing: Cathy, Dane, Carla, Marcia, Sherrie, Reinar, Laurie, Shawn, Shannon, Linda. I love you all.

To Peter Angeles, Robert and Louise McCall—from a distance, thank you, still.

*Sixth Edition ✦ Moreover . . .*

Most of us today don't like the world very much and would like to reiterate Plato's conviction that there can be no peace until statesmen become philosophers, or vice versa.

We would like to say to the world, "Look, there are better ideas to live by." For instance, Voltaire said he might disagree with others' ideas but that he would fight to the death for their right to express them. Aristotle reminds us that the function of government is to provide safe environment so that we can all work to achieve *eudaimonia*, a state of well-being in which we can grow as human persons and actualize our creative energies.

Marcus Aurelius warns us not to worry about the perceptions of others, but to tend to our own honesty and integrity. Chuang-tzu gently chides us for worrying so much about what others think of us that we forget who we are. Thoreau reflected, "If I am not I, who will be?"

The Jains of India tell us there are 353 perspectives on every issue and not to think we've found the truth until we have explored all 353 viewpoints. Symmachus reminds us that we will never find the truth by following one road only, and Thomas Merton shows us that there are many paths to the top of the mountain.

Bergson spent his life telling us we must learn to be compassionate in our empathetic concern for others. Francis of Assisi exhorts us to sense the pain we inflict on the animals with whom we share our planet; and Schweitzer insists that a truly ethical individual will extend his compassion to all living creatures, not just to members of his own tribe.

There *are* better ideas than we hear on the networks and, like Plato, we become impatient. But then Toynbee suggests we remember that it wasn't our parents who made the world; Caesar admonishes us to make haste slowly—*festina lente;* and Joseph Campbell tells us that this life can be wonderful just as it is when we discover that we are all on the Hero's journey. Nietzsche reassures us that the human race will become nobler, fret not; and Ray Bradbury urges us to dream of great futures and, with courage and imagination, to work for them and make them happen.

My gratitude deepens to friends and foes alike who have criticized, inspired, prodded, cajoled, and praised, and who have become a part of this book: Fred Hills, Jeff Stebbins, Elaine Farina, Robert Davidson, Gerald Ghelfi, Reza Ganjavi, Eva Armstrong-Gooneratne, Robert Badra, George Kinnamon, Greg Pezzetti (my computer guru), Diane Alatorre, Myron Yeager, Robin Wilkes, John Velasquez. Thank you!

At Harcourt Brace, John Haley, Katherine Lincoln, and steve Norder: Thank you for your patience, dedication, artistic sensitivity, and technical expertise.

# CONTENTS

**THE
FINE ART
OF
WONDERING**

THE
CONDITION
AND THE
ODYSSEY

ii

COEXISTENCE:
MAN'S LOVE /
HATE
CONDITION

V

MICROCOSM /
MACROCOSM /
COSMOS

vii

## BIOGRAPHIES

# WHAT DO YOU MEAN PHILOSOPHY??

*For man, the unexamined life is not worth living.*

SOCRATES

*Life does not cease to be funny when people die; any more than it ceases to be serious when people laugh.*

GEORGE BERNARD SHAW

Sometime, at your leisure—if you want to know what philosophy is—go into a large bookstore and browse. Check a variety of books in psychology, anthropology, physics, chemistry, archeology, astronomy, and other nonfiction fields. Look at the last chapter in each book. In a surprising number of cases, you will find that the author has chosen to round out his work with a summation of what the book is all about. That is, having written a whole book on a specialized subject in which he is probably an authority, he finds that he *also* has ideas about the larger meaning of the facts that he has written about. The final chapter may be called "Conclusions," "Epilogue," "Postscript," "My Personal View," "Implications," "Comments," "Speculations," or (as in one case) "So What?" But in every instance, the author is trying to elucidate the larger implications of his subject matter and to clarify how he thinks it relates to other fields or to life. He has an urge to tell us *the meaning* of all his facts *taken together*. He wants to share with us the *philosophic implications* of what he has written.

When he does this, the author has moved beyond the role of a field specialist. He is a philosopher.

This is a textbook in synoptic° philosophy. It is an invitation to ponder, in the largest possible perspective, the weightier, more stubborn problems of human existence. It is an invitation to think—to wonder, to question, to speculate, to reason, even to fantasize—in the eternal search for wisdom. In a word, synoptic philosophy is an attempt to weave interconnecting lines of illumination between all the disparate realms of human thought in the hope that, like a thousand dawnings, new insights will burst through.

°Synoptic.
From the Greek *sunoptikos*, "seeing the whole together" or "taking a comprehensive view." The attempt to achieve an all-inclusive overview of one's subject matter. See Chapter 1-4 and glossary.

By its very nature, philosophy is a do-it-yourself enterprise. There is a common misunderstanding that philosophy—like chemistry or history—has a content to offer, a content that a teacher is to teach and a student is to learn. This is not the case. There are no facts, no theories, certainly no final truths that go by the name of "philosophy" and that one is supposed to accept and believe. Rather, philosophy is a skill—more akin to mathematics and music; it is something that one *learns to do.*

Philosophy, that is, is a *method.* It is *learning how* to ask and reask questions until meaningful answers begin to appear. It is *learning how* to relate materials. It is *learning where* to go for the most dependable, up-to-date information that might shed light on some problem. It is *learning how* to double check fact-claims in order to verify or falsify them. It is *learning how* to reject fallacious fact-claims—no matter how prestigious the authority who holds them or how deeply one would personally like to believe them.

Ever since Socrates spent his days in the marketplace engaging the Athenian citizens in thoughtful conversations, the message of philosophy has been that ordinary everyday thinking is inadequate for solving the important problems of life. If we are serious about finding solutions, then we need to learn to think more carefully, critically, and precisely about the issues of daily life.

It is often said that philosophers engage in two basic tasks: "taking apart"—*analyzing* ideas to discover if we truly know what we think we know (and we don't)—and "putting together"—*synthesizing* all our knowledge to find if we can attain a larger and better view of life (we can). That is, philosophers try very hard to dig deeper and fly higher in order to solve problems and achieve a modicum of wisdom on the question of life and how to live it.

To accomplish all this philosophers talk a lot. They carry on dialogues with anyone who comes within range. And they argue a great deal. Not the usual kinds of argument in which egos fight to win, but philosophical arguments in which the participants attempt to clarify the reasoning that lies behind their statements; and no one cares about winning since, in philosophical arguments, everyone wins.

Philosophers also ask one another for definitions to be sure they're thinking clearly, and they push one another to pursue the implications of their ideas and statements. They prod themselves and others to examine the basic assumptions upon which their beliefs and arguments rest.

Philosophers are persistent explorers in the nooks and crannies of human knowledge that are commonly overlooked or deliberately ignored. It is an exciting but restless adventure of the mind.

Philosophers, however, do not engage in this critical task just to make nuisances of themselves. Indeed, the central aim of philosophers has always been . . . to construct a picture of the whole of reality, in which every element of man's knowledge and every aspect of man's experience will find its proper place. Philosophy, in short, is man's quest for the unity of knowledge: it consists in a perpetual struggle to create the concepts in which the universe can be conceived as a *uni*verse and not a *multi*verse. The history of philosophy is the history of this attempt. The problems of philosophy are the problems that arise when the attempt is made to grasp this total unity. . . .

*Understanding man and his place in the universe is perhaps the central problem of all science.*

Dunn and Dobzhansky

*A life not put to the test is not worth living.*

Epictetus

*The meaning of life is arrived at . . . by dark gropings, by feelings not wholly understood, by catching at hints and fumbling for explanations.*

Alfred Adler

*"We're lost, but we're making good time."*

*City Slickers*

*There is an old saying that philosophy bakes no bread. It is perhaps equally true that no bread would ever have been baked without philosophy. For the act of baking implies a decision on the philosophical issue of whether life is worthwhile at all. Bakers may not have often asked themselves the question in so many words. But philosophy traditionally has been nothing less than the attempt to ask and asnwer, in a formal and disciplined way, the great questions of life that ordinary men put to themselves in reflective moments.*

*Time, January 7, 1966*

It cannot be denied that this attempt stands without rival as the most audacious enterprise in which the mind of man has ever engaged. Just reflect for a moment: Here is man, surrounded by the vastness of a universe in which he is only a tiny and perhaps insignificant part—and he wants to *understand* it. . . .

WILLIAM HALVERSON

The student should be aware that philosophy has never been just one kind of activity with a single approach to a single task. Rather, there have been many kinds of philosophy: the quiet philosophy of the sage who sees much but speaks little because language cannot hold life; the articulate, noisy dialectics of Socrates; the calm, logical apologetics of Aquinas; the mystical philosophy of Plotinus and Chuang-tzu; the mathematical philosophy of Russell and Wittgenstein.

*God gave us memories so that we may have roses in December.*

**JAMES M. BARRIE**

Each school of philosophy has concentrated upon some aspect of man's knowledge. Logical/analytical philosophy has worked long and hard on the confusion that vitiates so much of our thinking and communicating. Pragmatism has concentrated on finding solutions to problems of man's social existence. Existential philosophy has been concerned with making life meaningful to each, unique individual. Activist schools argue that philosophers spend too much time trying to make sense of the world and too little time trying to change it. Several schools of philosophy, Eastern and Western, challenge the individual to turn away from an alienating society and to seek harmony with Nature or Ultimate Reality.

*Out yonder there was this huge world . . . which stands before us like a great eternal riddle. . . .*

**ALBERT EINSTEIN**

Each kind of philosophy has made an immense contribution to its area of concern. Each was doubtless a part of the *Zeitgeist*—"the spirit of the age"— that gave it birth and to which it spoke.

**PEANUTS®**                                            **By Charles M. Schulz**

The present unhappy condition of human knowledge calls for the application of a synoptic methodology. We now possess vast accumulations of specialized knowledge in countless fields, but these fields remain isolated from one another. Yet it is increasingly clear that many of our urgent problems can be understood only when specialized information from a variety of these separate fields is integrated and "seen together"—synoptically. Only then can we develop realistic solutions to these complex problems.

*"The truth, huh. It's worth a shot."*
**Room for Two (TV)**

In one respect, philosophic material can be deceptive. Since it deals with life by examining the sort of questions we ask every day, some of the subject matter will have an easy, familiar ring.

The fact is that synoptic philosophy must be as diligently studied as any other subject, not to remember data, but to set the mind in motion toward developing larger concepts, connecting ideas, and seeing through and beyond mere words and facts.

In a sense, intellectual growth *happens to us;* it is not really something that we do. But it happens to us only when our minds are given a chance to operate on their terms. They take their own time to process information and to begin developing a web of interconnecting lines of illumination among their materials. This undertaking is partly conscious, of course; but largely it is an unconscious process. This is why much philosophic insight just happens, as though the light moves from the depths upward and not from the rational conscious downward.

*Man's concern about a meaning of life is the truest expression of the state of being human.*
**VIKTOR FRANKL**

Only disciplined study with an open mind will produce philosophic awareness. Insight and consciousness still come only with relentless labor. In this age of instant everything, there is still no instant wisdom, unfortunately.

*Morally, a philosopher who uses his professional competence for anything except a disinterested search for truth is guilty of a kind of treachery.*
**BERTRAND RUSSELL**

No two of us possess precisely the same information, or see things from the same viewpoint, or share the same values. Therefore, each of us must do

*I don't ask questions, I just have fun!*

**"Bugs Bunny"**
***Bugs Bunny/Roadrunner Show***

*Most men spend their days struggling to evade three questions, the answers to which underlie man's every thought, feeling and action, whether he is consciously aware of it or not: Where am I? How do I know it? What should I do?*

**Ayn Rand**

*There is but one Moon in the heavens, yet it is reflected in countless streams of water.*

**Amritabindu Upanishad**

*"Don't think about it. Just do it!"*

***Total Recall***

synoptic philosophy in his own unique and personal way. A student entering upon the activity of philosophizing may need to be on guard against developing a world-view that resembles, a bit too closely, the prepackaged philosophy of life belonging to someone else or to some institution. Most of us are philosophically lazy, and it is easy to appropriate another's thoughts and rationalize our theft. The British logician Wittgenstein warned us that "a thought which is not independent is a thought only half understood." Similarly, a philosophy of life that is not the authentic product of one's own experience is a philosophy only half understood.

Nor will any of us succeed in developing a finished philosophy; for as one changes with life, so does one's thinking. A philosophy *of life* must change *with life*. Doing philosophy is an endless activity.

For this reason, this textbook is merely an example of synoptic philosophy. This is the way I have had to do it because of *my* perspectives, *my* interests, *my* areas of knowledge, *my* personal concerns, and *my* limitations. But *your* world-view will be different because it will be *yours,* and *yours alone.*

This is why my attempt to do synoptic philosophy is, at most, a guideline showing how it might be done; at least, the expression of a hope that, someday, in your own way, you will resolve the contradictions of your own existence—both of knowing and of being—and proceed to see life in a larger, more fulfilling way.

Uno itinere non potest perveniri ad tam grande secretum.

*"The heart of so great a mystery can never be reached by following one road only."*

Q. AURELIUS SYMMACHUS
*Relatio Tertia*

THEAETETUS: *Yes, Socrates, I stand in amazement when I reflect on the questions that men ask. By the gods, I do! I want to know more and more about such questions, and there are times when I almost become dizzy just thinking about them.*

SOCRATES: *Ah yes, my dear Theaetetus, when Theodorus called you a philosopher he described you well. That feeling of wonder is the touchstone of the philosopher, and all philosophy has its origins in wonder. Whoever reminded us that Iris (the heavenly messenger) is the offspring of Thaumas (wonder) wasn't a bad genealogist.*

PLATO
*Theaetetus*

A sense of wonder started men philosophizing, in ancient times as well as today. Their wondering is aroused, first, by trivial matters; but they continue on from there to wonder about less mundane matters such as the changes of the moon, sun, and stars, and the beginnings of the universe. What is the result of this puzzlement? *An awesome feeling of ignorance.* Men began to philosophize, therefore, to escape ignorance. . . .

ARISTOTLE
*Metaphysics*

# THE FINE ART OF WONDERING

*To grow into youngness is a blow. To age into sickness is an insult. To die is, if we are not careful, to turn from God's breast, feeling slighted and unloved. The sparrow asks to be seen as it falls.*

*Philosophy must try, as best it can, to turn the sparrows to flights of angels, which, Shakespeare wrote, sing us to our rest.*

RAY BRADBURY

1

## JUST IN CASE . . .

Shortly before a solar eclipse was to occur in central India, an Indian physicist—who was also a member of the Brahmin caste—was lecturing to his students at the university. He told them precisely when the event would begin and described in detail how the moon's orbit would take it between the sun and the earth. In their city there would be only a partial eclipse, but on a wall map he pointed out the path of total eclipse as it moved across the terrestrial globe to the north of them. They discussed such things as the corona, the solar flares, the beauty of annular rings, and the appearance of Bailey's beads during that rare total eclipse. Some of the students from the rural villages had heard stories about a Giant Dragon that swallowed the sun, but their teacher's lucid presentation of celestial mechanics had dispelled any fears they might have felt.

Having dismissed his class, the professor returned to his village and, since he was a Brahmin, assumed his duties as a priest. Around his shoulders he draped the vestments of his office and began counting through his string of beads, calling aloud the names of the gods. A goat was beheaded in sacrifice to Kali, the Black Goddess, the cause and controller of earthquakes, storms, and other evil things, and the archenemy of demons. Prayers were offered to her that she might frighten away the Dragon. "Glory to Mother Kali," the priest and people chanted.

While in the classroom there was nothing illogical about describing the solar eclipse in terms of celestial mechanics, neither was there anything wrong in offering a gift to the Black Goddess—*just in case. . . .*

*Every culture has devised its own way of responding to the riddle of the Cosmos. . . . There are many different ways of being human.*

CARL SAGAN

*We are what we think, having become what we thought.*

THE DHAMMAPADA

*One can tell for oneself whether the water is warm or cold.*

*I Ching*

## THE HUMAN CONDITION

To sensitive spirits of all ages, life is filled with cruel contradictions and bitter ironies. Human experience is capricious, and our finite minds are not able to see enough of life *at one time* for us to know for sure what is going on. We see only fragments of life, never the whole. We are not unlike children struggling with a cosmic picture puzzle made up of pieces that won't fit together.

Just under the surface of the entire human enterprise, implicit in all we think and do, there lies the eternal question: *What is the meaning of existence?* It is the ultimate question of all Mankind, yet it must be reopened by each of us in our turn. If we refuse to take the contradictions of life for granted; if we can't accept prepackaged solutions; if we can't persuade ourselves to accept a mere fragment of life as the whole of life—then for all of us, the question persists. We may have great difficulty finding satisfactory answers to it, but we also know that there is no escape from it.

On the real-life scene where the human tragicomedy plays itself out, our question splits into two further practical questions. Stated positively: How can we make life worth living? Stated negatively: How can we prevent life from turning into tragedy?

Through the ages, man has sought clues to life's meaning through his religions and philosophies. To date they have given us immense help, but a contemporary overview of Mankind's quest supplies us with a superabundance of answers, so many answers in fact that we can't decide among them.

Furthermore, after a more critical reexamination, we discover that most of man's religions and many of his philosophies have concluded that, in the final analysis, life-in-this-world is *not* worth living. At best it's but a time of troubles to be endured until we can reach something better. That's not much help to those of us still dedicated to the assumption that life may be worth living.

In Alexei Panshin's *Rite of Passage* the heroine, a young girl, states candidly: "If you want to accept life, you have to accept the whole bloody universe." She may be right. But how can we really "accept" a universe of wild and destructive contradictions? After all, we seem to be as ambivalent about ultimate realities as the Indian physicist/priest.

The natural world is not the mystery today that it was some four centuries ago, before the birth of the New Science. We are fairly secure in our general mathematical descriptions of the physical universe. To be sure, at the quantum level anomalous and unpredictable events seem to occur; and it appears that there was a time following the Big Bang when our mathematical and physical formulas, as we know them, did not apply. But there is so much mathematical consistency to our experience of nature's operations that we have arrived at the point of accepting a naturalistic world-view *for nature*. We have, more or less, made our peace. With the physical universe—from galaxies and gravity fields to microchips and laser beams—the cosmos that challenged the existence of ancient thinkers and eluded their understanding is no longer a bewildering problem to us.

Our serious problems, therefore, lie buried somewhere within the biological realm, within the protoplasmic venture we call *life.* To borrow a phrase from

Buckminster Fuller, the puzzlement seems to be that this protoplasmic experiment came without an instruction manual.

Long before the birth of modern psychology, there were perceptive individuals who felt stirrings from the depths of the human organism, but it was left to Sigmund Freud to launch a depth probe into the inner world. As the Viennese doctor shook loose the secrets of the human psyche, it was no longer deniable that the subconscious mind, quite without our conscious permission, pushes us headlong into all forms of irrational behavior. The subconscious mind is a vast depository for emotionally charged experience that, for one reason or another, we cannot face; and these repressed elements determine to a large extent how we feel, think, and behave.

*There is a coherent plan in the universe, though I don't know what it's a plan for.*
**Sir Fred Hoyle**

To realize that we do countless things without understanding why—this can be, for rationalists, a soul-jarring discovery. We are manipulated, like puppets on a string, by inner forces over which we have little control. We scurry about in frenzied activity, accomplishing little else than satisfying the whims of the shadowy slavedriver. Not knowing our motivations, we don't understand what we do; and much of the time our strivings bring little fulfillment.

Perhaps here is one source of the meaninglessness of our lives. We have no clear notion of what we are after, but we plunge blindly ahead anyway, in search of something.

"Good morning," said the little prince.
"Good morning," said the railway switchman.
"What do you do here?" the little prince asked.
"I sort out travelers, in bundles of a thousand," said the switchman. "I send off the trains that carry them: now to the right, now to the left."
And a brilliantly lighted express train shook the switchman's cabin as it rushed by with a roar like thunder.
"They are in a great hurry," said the little prince. "What are they looking for?"
"Not even the locomotive engineer knows that," said the switchman.
And a second brilliantly lighted express thundered by, in the opposite direction.
"Are they coming back already?" demanded the little prince.

Paul Gauguin. *D'où venons-nous? Que sommes-nous? Où allons-nous? 1897.* "Where do we come from? What are we? Where are we going?"

*Tompkins Collection. Courtesy, Museum of Fine Arts, Boston.*

"These are not the same ones," said the switchman. "It is an exchange."

"Were they not satisfied where they were?" asked the little prince.

"No one is ever satisfied where he is," said the switchman.

And they heard the roaring thunder of a third brilliantly lighted express.

"Are they pursuing the first travelers?" demanded the little prince.

"They are pursuing nothing at all," said the switchman. "They are asleep in there, or if they are not asleep they are yawning. Only the children are flattening their noses against the windowpanes."

"Only the children know what they are looking for," said the little prince. "They waste their time over a rag doll and it becomes very important to them; and if anybody takes it away from them they cry . . ."

"They are lucky," the switchman said.

SAINT-EXUPÉRY
*The Little Prince*

In Freud's world, life is at once a blessing and a curse, for *eros* (the life-force) is pitted in mortal combat against *thanatos* (the death wish).

On the one hand, we possess drives toward self-preservation that countermand almost all other impulses. We fear the cessation of breath and sense. "Let me not see the death which I ever dread!" cried the hero of the Gilgamesh Epic three thousand years ago. While alive, we dream our dreams, work toward our goals, and feel the joyous pain of activity and growth. All this indicates the depth of our hunger for life; we will fight to the death in order to live. *Eros.*

On the other hand, "To exist is to suffer," taught the Buddha, and we have devised ingenious ways of escaping existence. We sense a futility in our dreams; an inner voice chides us for yearning for goals we can't achieve. We often have an empty feeling when we hold in our hands something we have fought for, wondering why we wanted it. All around we see loneliness, surd hatreds, and pointless sadisms. Mephistopheles speaks for many: Hell is no fable, for *this life IS hell.* Away from all this, we are pulled toward death, as though it would be a blessing to have done with it. *Thanatos.*

Out of frustration, perhaps we ought to ask whether the essential implication of so many of man's religions and philosophies might be correct after all—the implication that the human condition is uninhabitable. Perhaps there really is something inherently wrong. Perhaps Norman Brown is close when he calls man a "disease." It's not inconceivable that self-destruction, in some sense, is already an accomplished fact.

Albert Schweitzer once wrote that he remained optimistic because hope is an indispensable ingredient of daily life, but that when he took a long look at human history he could not escape the gloom of pessimism.

When asked if he was "optimistic these days about the state of the world," Alan Watts replied: "I have to be. There is no alternative. For if I were to bet, I would bet that the human race will destroy itself by 2000. But there's nowhere to place the bet."

## THE SEARCH FOR MEANING

Modern men are caught in an "existential vacuum," writes Viktor Frankl, a feeling of the total and ultimate meaninglessness of their lives. They lack the awareness of a meaning worth living for. They are haunted by the experience of their inner emptiness, a void within themselves. . . .

The existential vacuum is a widespread phenomenon of the twentieth century. This is understandable; it may be due to a twofold loss that man had to undergo since he became a truly human being. At the beginning of human history, man lost some of the basic animal instincts in which an animal's behavior is embedded and by which it is secured. Such security, like Paradise, is closed to man forever; man has to make choices. In addition to this, however, man has suffered another loss in his more recent development: the traditions that had buttressed his behavior are now rapidly diminishing. No instinct tells him what he has to do, and no tradition tells him what he ought to do; soon he will not know what he wants to do.

The search for life, if it is to succeed, must be an aggressive individual odyssey. Each of us is caught in the philosophical enterprise. There is not one of us who is not trying to make sense of his existence, and at some level of our being each is seeking fulfillment. Our experiences come pouring into us in endless variety, and they do not come neatly packaged and labeled. Each one of us must select and assimilate, organize and arrange, value and apply. So we are all philosophers by default, not by choice.

To be sure, we must seek the guidance of others who have searched; we can listen to those who have found answers that work *for them*. But in the last analysis, no one else can give us insight. It has to be indigenous, grown from native soil.

Nor is our quest for meaning a quixotic tilting after windmills. There are many who find, to some degree, what they are seeking; they find the clues that set them in the right direction. When we listen to their recounting of what has happened to their lives, we cannot doubt the depth of meaning to which their insights have led them.

Each of the following men, at some point in his search, found an answer, or at least a perspective, that affected the quality of his entire existence.

After working through the long hot days with his patients at the Lambaréné hospital, Albert Schweitzer would retire to his cluttered study in the evening and take up again the problem from which he could not escape. He was attempting to discover a positive ethical principle upon which civilization could be securely grounded.

For months on end I lived in a continual state of mental excitement. Without the least success I let my thought be concentrated, even all through my daily work at the hospital, on the real nature of world- and life-affirmation and of ethics, and on the question of what they have in common. I was wandering about in a thicket in

*Castle of the Pyrenees* by René Magritte (1959)

*I have one longing only: to grasp what is hidden behind appearances, to ferret out that mystery which brings me to birth and then kills me, to discover if behind the visible and unceasing stream of the world an invisible and immutable presence is hiding.*

NIKOS KAZANTZAKIS

Albert Schweitzer (1875-1965)

Abraham Maslow (1908-1970)

which no path was to be found. I was leaning with all my might against an iron door which would not yield.

While in this mental condition I had to undertake a longish journey on the river. . . . Slowly we crept upstream, laboriously feeling—it was the dry season—for the channels between the sandbanks. Lost in thought I sat on the deck of the barge, struggling to find the elementary and universal conception of the ethical which I had not discovered in any philosophy. Sheet after sheet I covered with disconnected sentences, merely to keep myself concentrated on the problem. Late on the third day, at the very moment when, at sunset, we were making our way through a herd of hippopotamuses, there flashed upon my mind, unforeseen and unsought, the phrase, "Reverence for Life." The iron door had yielded: the path in the thicket had become visible. Now I had found my way to the idea in which world- and life-affirmation and ethics are contained side by side! . . .

The world-view of Reverence for Life follows from taking the world as it is. And the world means the horrible in the glorious, the meaningless in the meaningful, the sorrowful in the joyful. However it is looked at it remains to many a riddle.

But that does not mean that we need stand before the problem of life at our wits' end because we have to renounce all hope of comprehending the course of world-events as having a meaning. Reverence for Life brings us into a spiritual relation with the world which is independent of all knowledge of the universe. . . . It renews itself in us every time we look thoughtfully at ourselves and the life around us.

*Reverence for Life.* "In that principle," Schweitzer writes, "my life has found a firm footing and a clear path to follow."

The editors of *Psychology Today* wrote a brief note after the death of Dr. Abraham Maslow. In it they remarked that he had "a joyful affirmation of life that surged through the long tapes he often dictated for us, encouraging *Psychology Today* to explore questions that have no easy answers. Much as we loved this beautiful man, we did not understand the source of his courage—until the last cassette came in."

On that tape, they say, Dr. Maslow

talked with intense introspection about an earlier heart attack that had come right after he completed an important piece of work. "I had really spent myself. This was the best I could do, and here was not only a good time to die but I was even willing to die. . . . It was what David M. Levy called the 'completion of the act.' It was like a good ending, a good close. I think actors and dramatists have that sense of the right moment for a good ending, with a phenomenological sense of good completion—that there was nothing more you could add. . . .

"My attitude toward life changed. The word I used for it now is the post-mortem life. I could just as easily have died so that my living constitutes a kind of an extra, a bonus. It's all gravy. Therefore I might just as well live as if I had already died.

"One very important aspect of the post-mortem life is that everything gets doubly precious, gets piercingly important. You get stabbed by things, by flowers and by babies and by beautiful things—just the very act of living, of walking and breathing and eating and having friends and chatting. Everything seems to look more beautiful rather than less, and one gets the much-intensified sense of miracles.

"I guess you could say that post-mortem life permits a kind of spontaneity that's greater than anything else could make possible.

"If you're reconciled with death or even if you are pretty well assured that you will have a good death, a dignified one, then every single moment of every single day is transformed because the pervasive undercurrent—the fear of death—is removed. . . . I am living an end-life where everything ought to be an end in itself, where I shouldn't waste any time preparing for the future, or occupying myself with means to later ends."

Abe's message ended there.—The Editors.

Dr. Gordon Allport has written in the preface to Viktor Frankl's book *Man's Search for Meaning:*

> As a longtime prisoner in bestial concentration camps [Viktor Frankl] found himself stripped to naked existence. His father, mother, brother, and his wife died in camps or were sent to the gas ovens, so that, excepting for his sister, his entire family perished in these camps. How could he—every possession lost, every value destroyed, suffering from hunger, cold and brutality, hourly expecting extermination—how could he find life worth preserving?. . .
>
> From [Frankl's] autobiographical fragment the reader learns much. He learns what a human being does when he suddenly realizes he has "nothing to lose except his so ridiculously naked life." Frankl's description of the mixed flow of emotion and apathy is arresting. First to the rescue comes a cold detached curiosity concerning one's fate. Swiftly, too, come strategies to preserve the remnants of one's life, though the chances of surviving are slight. Hunger, humiliation, fear and deep anger at injustice are rendered tolerable by closely guarded images of beloved persons, by religion, by a grim sense of humor, and even by glimpses of the healing beauties of nature—a tree or a sunset.
>
> But these moments of comfort do not establish the will to live unless they help the prisoner make larger sense out of his apparently senseless suffering. It is here that we encounter the central theme of existentialism: to live is to suffer, to survive is to find meaning in the suffering. If there is a purpose in life at all, there must be a purpose in suffering and in dying. But no man can tell another what this purpose is. Each must find out for himself, and must accept the responsibility that his answer prescribes. If he succeeds he will continue to grow in spite of all indignities. Frankl is fond of quoting Nietzsche, "He who has a *why* to live can bear with almost any how."

Viktor Frankl

*"Realistic people" who pursue "practical aims" are rarely as realistic or practical, in the long run of life, as the dreamers who pursue their dreams.*

HANS SELYE

*The idea that so much suffering can be in vain is intolerable to me, it kept me awake all night: I'm awake now. . .*

ANDRÉ GIDE

*"There is no hope."
"We're both alive. And for all I know, that's hope."*

*"Henry II"*
**The Lion in Winter**

## WHY-QUESTIONS

Our urge to ask "Why?" seems irresistible. If, for example, an avalanche plunges down the mountainside, burying sixty schoolchildren in a few seconds, is it humanly possible for the families of the children not to ask *why* it happened?

Nor is a naturalistic answer satisfying, even though a scientifically adequate one may be possible. "The avalanche was produced by a week of especially warm days alternating with cold nights. Much snow melted during those days, and when the water refroze at night the expanding ice gradually loosened the snowbank. The slide occurred during the daytime because melting snow finally produced enough water to dissolve the surfaces where friction was holding the snowbank to the mountainside. The snow gave way and cascaded down the slope."

Such an explanation is scientifically sound, is it not? However, at the mass funeral service for the children, imagine in your mind the presiding clergyman presenting the scientific explanation for the tragedy—and stopping there.

Does this not prove Frankl's thesis that, above all else, man must find meaning in his living and, finally, in his dying?

It would be comforting to know that life has meaning; it would feel good to know that "nothing happens without a purpose." But our need for meaning leads us to find easy and absurd answers to our why-questions.

For instance, in the year A.D. 410 when the city of Rome fell to Alaric the Goth, the "pagans" blamed the Christians for having abandoned the true gods of Rome; but Saint Augustine spent a dozen years writing *The City of God* to show that the fall of Rome was a part of God's plan to vanquish paganism and establish the Reign of God.

In November 1755 a terrible earthquake struck Lisbon. In a few minutes, more than thirty thousand people were killed or injured. The event occurred on All Saints' Day when churches throughout the land were filled with worshipers. The French philosopher Jean-Jacques Rousseau suggested that the people of Lisbon suffered because they were stacked up in multistoried dwellings; had they been living in the open countryside or woodlands, few would have been killed.

But French clergymen interpreted the disaster as punishment for the sins of the Portuguese. Protestants blamed the event upon the tyranny of the Catholics, while the Roman clergy laid the event to the fact that there were so many Protestant heretics in Catholic Portugal. In England John Wesley, the founder of Methodism, in a sermon entitled "The Cause and Cure of

*The story of Eden is a greater allegory than man has ever guessed. For it was truly man who, walking memoryless through paths of sunlight and shade in the morning of the world, sat down and passed a wondering hand across his heavy forehead. Time and darkness, knowledge of good and evil, have walked with him ever since. . . .*

LOREN EISELEY

*The young man who has not wept is a savage, and the old man who will not laugh is a fool.*

CONFUCIUS

ZORBA: Why do the young die? Why does anybody die, tell me?
SCHOLAR: I don't know.
ZORBA: What's the use of all your damn books? If they don't tell you that, what the hell do they tell you?
SCHOLAR: They tell me about the agony of men who can't answer questions like yours.

NIKOS KAZANTZAKIS
*Zorba the Greek*

Earthquakes," blamed original sin as "the moral cause of earthquakes, whatever the natural cause may be. . . ."

In April 1970, after the near-tragic *Apollo XIII* lunar mission was aborted, an American political leader stated on national television that mission failure was a warning from God that man is not to attempt further ventures into space. "A warning," he said; man's next attempt would result in tragic consequences.

## THE WORLD-RIDDLE

In a hotel in East Africa, weary hunters relax from their safaris into the veld. In the hotel lounge one finds a comfortable set of sofas covered with zebra skins, and on one wall hang several lion skins separated by a dozen or so Masai spears spread out as a fan. Higher up, on all four walls of the lounging area, are mounted heads of game animals. One looks up at the heads of the great African antelopes: elands with long, straight horns; kudus with screw-twisted spires; dainty gazelles; stately sables with long, back-curving horns; and wildebeests with short, upturned hooks. Other sentinels looking down upon visitors include the legendary African buffalo, whose horns cover its forehead and spread widely on either side; a rhinoceros with double-horns rising from its snout; and a warthog with ivory tusks coming out of either side of its lower jaw and curling over its nose. Various smaller game animals are mounted between the larger heads.

Down through evolutionary time, each animal has developed a means of defense and/or killing. The overwhelming and singular thrust of evolution seems to have been to produce some mechanism of survival against attackers: horns to hold predators at bay; spiked tusks to rip apart and kill; fangs, claws, sharp hooves; thick skins; powerful jaws; sleek, strong legs for running and jumping.

*Life is the life of life.*
BHAGAVATA PURANA

Each animal must exist in unending competition with other creatures that would kill it. Species prey upon species. Nature is, after all, "red in tooth and claw."

No single animal had anything to say about this. It possessed no "freedom" to choose a "life-style." Its place in the scheme of nature is entirely determined for it. What a strange, impertinent thought—that any single, individual animal *could* have had freedom to *choose* its own life-style or to determine its "role" in life.

*Life is a comedy to those who think, a tragedy to those who feel.*
HORACE WALPOLE

What forces would design creatures to prey upon one another and, at the same time, instill into each creature the capacity for intense pain and suffering?

And what an unbelievable, ironic condition: In this "deadly feast of life," each of us, to exist, must *eat* living things that harbor the same life-drive we possess. *Life feeds upon itself!*

Desmond Morris is quite sure that our problems are genetic in origin. In *The Naked Ape* he refers to the "deep-seated biological characteristics of our species" and contends that certain patterns of social behavior "will always be with us, at least until there has been some new and major change in our makeup."

*As soon as man does not take his existence for granted, but beholds it as something unfathomably mysterious, thought begins.*
ALBERT SCHWEITZER

"Species that have evolved special killing techniques for dealing with their prey seldom employ these when dealing with their own kind." But man's trouble, writes Konrad Lorenz, "arises from his being a basically harmless omnivorous creature, lacking in natural weapons with which to kill big prey, and, therefore, also devoid of the built-in safety devices which prevent 'professional' carnivores from abusing their killing power to destroy fellow members of their own species. . . ."

The "Law of the Jungle," writes Morris, is that you don't kill your own kind. "Those species that failed to obey this law have long since become extinct."

It was in early spring when Captain Jacques Cousteau's oceanographic vessel *Calypso* anchored off the shore of a southern California island. One night his crewmen noticed a churning of the waters, and the ship's lights were turned on. In the water were millions of squid, six to ten inches long. Cousteau and his men had accidentally discovered the breeding ground of the sea arrows. These small squid returned here in cycles of two or three years to mate, lay their eggs, and die. Arriving on the scene by the millions, they milled around, waiting.

Then a frenzy of mating began. The females had developed their eggs in tubular egg-cases. Now as the sea arrows darted about, males would grab females and hold them fast in their arms. A special tentacle was used to insert a capsule of sperm under the mantle of the female. The mating continued for days.

Then the females extracted the elongated egg-cases from their bodies and attached them in clusters to the rocks below, where the cases slowly swayed, like fingers covering the bottom of the ocean. Each female would carefully place six to eight egg-cases in position. With the last case attached, her time was finished; she went limp and died. The males, fertilization completed, had already died.

A few days later Cousteau's divers scoured the bottom for signs of life. Of the millions of squid that had made the waters alive, nothing survived. As though covered with snow, the ocean bottom was white with the bodies of the squid. They had fulfilled their purpose, and it was all over. All that the divers found were acres of egg-cases, now covered with a leathery skin to protect them. Inside each egg-case another generation of sea arrows waited to be born. They would come singly out of their eggs, begin to grow, move out to sea, and continue the cycle of life. Then at their appointed time, they would return to the breeding ground as their parents had done to meet their destiny and die.

In the last days of the squid's life, two of the *Calypso's* crewmen, swimming the bottom, came upon a female trying to push the last egg-case from her body. Gently they helped her by pulling out the case and attaching it to a rock. Then, joining the rest of her sea arrow family, she too died.

The instinct to fulfill the breeding cycle is so deep that no single sea arrow could thwart or change it. The "meaning of existence" for the squid is species-wide; it is provided by its instinctual makeup.

Is it conceivable that man has been totally separated from that evolutionary past when the instincts determined all significant behavior? If our problems

*Let us confess it: evil strides the world.*

**VOLTAIRE**

*The world has always been ruled by Lucifer. The world is evil. Call his name, my love. Call the name of Lucifer.*

**Ritual of Evil**
**NBC-TV**

*The world's a failure, you know. Someone, somewhere, made a terrible mistake.*

**Mission Impossible**
**CBS-TV**

### "Childhood's End"

From what is presently known, Homo sapiens—the modern form of man—has existed on earth for approximately a hundred thousand years in numbers large enough to constitute a population. Barring catastrophic accidents, it can be expected that man will continue living on earth for many millions of years. Using a somewhat fanciful kind of arithmetic, it can be calculated from these figures that the present age of humanity corresponds to very early childhood in the life of a human being. Pursuing still further the same farfetched comparison, reading and writing were invented a year ago; Plato, the Parthenon, Christ, date from but a few months; experimental science is just a few weeks old, and electricity a few days; mankind will not reach puberty for another hundred thousand years. In this perspective, it is natural that so far mankind should have been chiefly concerned with becoming aware of the world of matter, listening to fairy tales, and fighting for pleasure or out of anger. The meaning of life, the problems of man and of society, become dominant preoccupations only later during development. As mankind outgrows childhood, the proper use of science may come to be not only to store food, build mechanical toys, and record allegories, myths, and fairy tales, but to understand, as well as possible, the nature of life and of man in order to give more meaning and value to human existence.

René Dubos
*The Torch of Life*

are species-wide, is it not possible that there also exist impulses-to-meaning—goal-directed instincts—that are species-wide? Might there not be such left-over urges moving in us, pulsing in the dimmest reaches of our being so that we are unaware of them, yet determining still our most basic behavioral patterns?

As a psychologist, Abraham Maslow believed he had discerned such drives. He was convinced that

the human being has within him a pressure (among other pressures) toward unity of personality, toward spontaneous expressiveness, toward full individuality and identity, toward seeing the truth rather than being blind, toward being creative, toward being good, and a lot else. That is, the human being is so constructed that he presses toward fuller and fuller being.

[There is] a single ultimate value for mankind, a far goal toward which all men strive. This is called variously by different authors self-actualization, self-realization, integration, psychological health, individuation, autonomy, creativity, productivity, but they all agree that this amounts to realizing the potentialities of the person, that is to say, becoming fully human, everything that the person *can* become. . . .

It is still not out of the question that man, unique among living things, lies free and lost. Perhaps Sartre is right in saying we are "condemned to be free." Perhaps there is no God, no Goddess, no Spirit, no Fate, no Moral Law, no phylogenetic urge-to-life, no instinct—and no meaning.

Perhaps Kierkegaard was right: "There is no truth, except truth *for me.*"

The nihilistic existentialists have consistently held that the cosmos is depressingly meaningless and human society absurd. Our lives can achieve meaning

*In this world, the only thing that is important is being human.*

**Robert W. Smith**

*Christina's World* by Andrew
Wyeth (1948)

only if we boldly grasp the choices before us and make whatever meaningful
responses we can.

To be sure, many of us wake up each morning—and wonder why.

Richard Strauss composed the great tone poem *Also Sprach Zarathustra* in
the spring and summer of 1896, basing it on passages from Nietzsche's book of
the same title, written a dozen years earlier. Strauss himself wrote:

> I meant to convey by means of music an idea of the development of the human race
> from its origin, through various phases of its development, religious and scientific,
> up to Nietzsche's idea of the Superman. The whole symphonic poem is intended as
> an homage to Nietzsche's genius. . . .
>
> Will the mind of man ever solve the riddle of the world? A few calm introduc-
> tory bars, and already the trumpet sounds, *pp*, their solemn motto C-G-C, the so-
> called World-Riddle theme which, in various rhythmic guises, will pervade the
> whole symphonic poem through its very end. The simple but expressive introduction
> grows quickly in intensity and ends majestically on the climactic C major chord of
> the organ and full orchestra. . . .
>
> And then comes the mystical conclusion which, ending in two different keys,
> aroused much controversy when the work was first performed. While the trombones
> stubbornly hold the unresolved chord C-E-F-sharp, the violins and upper wood-
> winds carry upward the Theme of the Ideal to higher register in B major. . . . the
> pizzicati of the basses all the while sounding repeatedly the C-G-C of the World-
> Riddle. *Evidently the great problem remains unsolved.*

*Wise men come ever
promising
The riddle of life to know,
Wise men come . . . Ah, but
over the sands,
The silent sands of time
They go. . . .*
  **Kismet**
  ***From "The Sands of Time,"***
  ***Robert Wright and George Forest.***
  ***© 1953 by Frank Music Corp.***
  ***Used by permission.***

Nil desperandum
*There's no cause for despair.*
                    **HORACE**

## REFLECTIONS

1  The Indian physicist/priest seems to be involved in a contradiction. (It's
   difficult to sympathize with him, of course, because you and I never let our

selves get caught in such dilemmas.) How would you characterize his contradiction? What philosophic assumptions might we infer from his behavior? Would you call him a hypocrite? Can he believe, logically and simultaneously, in *both* world-views implied by his actions?

2 "To sensitive spirits of all ages, life is filled with cruel contradictions and bitter ironies." List some of the contradictions and ironies that you have come across in your own experience.

3 When we ask whether life has meaning, what precisely are we asking? What is "meaning"? Is our question essentially logical or psychological? (Or both?) What might be the source(s) of meaning? How would we *know* if life has meaning?

4 What do you understand to be meant by the term *why-question?* In your opinion, why do we have such a deep impulse to ask why-questions? What assumptions must we make to render such questions meaningful? Do you think why-questions are asked universally by all men, or are they asked more in our Western tradition because of specific religious assumptions about "the meaning" of events?

5 Ponder the implications of Schweitzer's "Reverence for Life," Maslow's "post-mortem life," and Frankl's conviction that the search for meaning is the key to life. Is there a common *ethic* implied in these three convictions? Would they all lead to a common goal or to a similar kind of experience?

6 Imagine that among the millions of squid, one of the sea arrows became a philosopher. If you could ask it (in Squidanese) about "the meaning of life," what do you think it might reply? Ask the same question—as vividly as your imagination will allow—of the Saturn V moon rocket (see Prelude) and Marcus Aurelius (pp 16–20).

7 The fact that "life feeds upon itself" strikes some as being a puzzling *theological* contradiction. Why might it be considered a theological problem and not merely a philosophical problem?

8 What if you decide that life is without meaning—what would this mean to you personally? Do you think your life would be worth living? (Why, incidentally, are you attempting to answer this question?)

# MARCUS AURELIUS

## *Philosopher-King*

When Plato wrote that "philosophers must become kings or kings must become philosophers before the world will have peace," he was dreaming of a science fiction world in some utopian state. His words exquisitely describe the life and thoughts of Marcus Aurelius, the fourteenth emperor of Rome. He reigned from A.D. 161 to 180. Marcus was a visionary statesman and legislator and a powerful commander of the Roman legions that held the empire's borders against persistent invasions, but he is best remembered in Western history for the sort of personal qualities that transform otherwise mundane souls into saints.

What was great about Marcus was that he succeeded in living-in-the-world while refusing to compromise his ideals with the petty obsessions of lesser men; and what made this possible was his philosophy of life: a set of convictions, rationally derived, about how *his life* should be run *by him*. His only writing—random reflections commonly called *Meditations* but which he referred to as *Things Written to Himself*—is an exercise in self-discovery. It is one man's instruction manual for living.

He was born in Rome of an old Spanish family and named Marcus Annius Verus. While still a child he lost both parents, but he remembers them gratefully. From his father, he writes, "I learned modesty and manliness"; and from his mother, a woman of talent and culture, he learned "religious piety, generosity, and not only refraining from wrongdoing but even from thoughts of it." He dearly loved his mother—who was enormously wealthy—and from her he learned, he says, "to be far removed from the ways of the rich."

Marcus was given the best education possible. It began with a thorough grounding in reading, writing, and arithmetic. Marcus was always grateful for his education; he was fortunate, he tells us, "to have enjoyed good teachers at home and to have learned that it is a duty to spend liberally on such things."

At twelve he commenced his secondary education with the study of geometry, music, mathematics, painting, and literature. In the Roman world to be educated meant to be thoroughly acquainted with Greek language and literature, so he was placed in the hands of one Greek and two Latin masters and became fluent in both languages. At fourteen he assumed the *toga virilis,* a plain white garment signifying he was an adult and a full citizen of Rome. The third stage of his education began, and he concentrated on the study of oratory, which included further study of Greek and Latin literature, and philosophy. He had three tutors in Greek oratory, one in Latin oratory, and one in law. All together this gave him a full university education in the liberal arts.

In January, A.D. 138, momentous events began to happen. The emperor Hadrian chose Marcus's uncle Antoninus to succeed him to power; Hadrian chose Antoninus on the condition that Antoninus in turn adopt Marcus as his successor. Thus Marcus became frightfully aware, at the age of sixteen, that someday—the Fates permitting—he would have to assume the awesome responsibilities of running the empire. On the night of his adoption, he had a dream in which his shoulders seemed to be made of ivory, and he feared that he would not be able to bear the burden of governing the empire, but he awoke from the dream reassured that his shoulders would be strong enough.

At seventeen, therefore, Marcus was heir apparent to the imperial throne. He was designated a quaestor with responsibility for public finance, a consul of Rome, and Caesar. He was enrolled in the college of priests and moved into the imperial palace. "Life," he later wrote, "is possible in a palace, so it should be possible to live the *right kind* of life in a palace."

In the spring of A.D. 145 Marcus, then twenty-four, married a cousin, Annia Galeria, known to history as Faustina II. In his later reflections Marcus thanks the gods for a wife "so obedient, so warmhearted, so without affectations." All told, fourteen children were born to them, including two sets of twins.

Marcus had to deal with the pain of death all his life. In A.D. 149 Faustina bore twin sons, and Marcus celebrated the event by issuing a coin showing busts of two small boys and bearing the incription *Temporum felicitas,* "What a happy time!" Soon the coins show Marcus and Faustina with one tiny girl and one baby boy, and, still later that year, new coins show them, standing, with only a little girl. Several times in his *Meditations,* Marcus refers to grief caused by the loss of children. He wrote that too often we pray, "Please, may I not lose my little child;" rather we should pray, "May I not be afraid when I lose him." Another son was born to Marcus and Faustina in A.D 152, and the story is repeated. Coins first show two little girls and an infant boy; but by A.D. 156 they depict only two small girls with their parents. Little wonder that Marcus reflects so often on man's mortality.

At twenty-five Marcus vowed his full devotion to the study of Stoic philosophy—for as long as the world would let him. Throughout the rest of his life he alternated between carrying his worldly obligations—which he met energetically, resourcefully, and with common sense—and nourishing his spiritual life. When his duties became oppressive, he would return to his thoughts in stolen hours, late at night, in a tent pitched beside a battlefield, and there, by candlelight, continue his reflections.

Marcus became emperor at thirty-nine (in March, A.D. 161) and was entitled Imperator Caesar Marcus Aurelius Antoninus Augustus. Uncomfortable with power and bored with the perfunctory public rituals of his office, he warned (himself): "Don't be dipped into the purple dye!" He was terribly afraid, he wrote, that he might be "turned into a Caesar." But all who knew him testify that in his personal qualities—sincerity, discipline, morality, simplicity Marcus was the same man as emperor that he was as a private citizen.

Marcus's likeness is familiar from coins and inscriptions. He had a

*As emperor, Rome is my city and my country; but as a human being I belong to the world.*

*If you want to stop wasting your time in vain fantasies, perform every act in life as though it were your last.*

*The human beings with the shortest life and the longest life, when they come to die, lose one and the same thing.*

*Never esteem anything as of advantage to you that will make you break your word or lose your self-respect.*

*Our life is what our thoughts make it.*

*All that is harmony for you, my Universe, is in harmony with me as well. Nothing that comes at the right time for you is too early or too late for me. Everything is fruit to me, Nature, that your seasons bring. All things come of you, have their being in you, and return to you.*

*Time is a sort of river of passing events, and strong is its current; no sooner is a thing brought to sight than it is swept by and another takes its place, and this too will be swept away.*

*Look beneath the surface, and don't let the specialness of a thing, or its unique worth, escape you.*

*It is man's peculiar duty to love even those who wrong him.*

*Remember this, that very little is needed to make a happy life.*

*A wrongdoer is often a man who has left something undone, not always one who has done something.*

handsome face, deep-set brooding eyes, black curly hair, and a heavy beard. Physically he was not strong; he suffered from chest pains, digestive troubles, and ulcers that resulted in prolonged bouts with illness; he was under doctors' care most of his life. He slept irregularly or not at all and frequently worked deep into the night. He enjoyed boxing, fencing, and wrestling, both as participant and spectator. He was a talented painter.

Those who knew him saw a modest, reserved, and serious man, thorough in all he did; he paid great attention to detail, almost to the point of perfectionism. His biographer Cassius Dio says that "he never said, wrote, or did anything as if it were an unimportant matter." His lifetime concern for the condition of slaves, orphans, and minors tells us much about the man.

His presentiments of weighty responsibilities more than came true. Most of his ruling years were spent fighting back invasions in Britain, Italy, Spain, Syria, and Egypt. It was during the last ten years of his life, while battling the Germanic tribes along the Rhine-Danube frontier, that Marcus wrote his *Things Written to Himself,* a very private journal in eloquent Greek. It is divided into twelve books. The first book—though the last to be written—is his tribute to family, friends, and teachers who meant much to him. He thanks them all and tells us what he learned from each. The other eleven books are his attempt to summarize the lessons he has learned from life.

◆

Marcus had to work out a philosophy to live by. His notebook shows just how desperately he needed the strength and support of meaningful philosophic beliefs. He had been well acquainted with Stoic philosophy since he was twelve, but the ideas lay dormant; during the earlier stages of life he had little use for them.

But sooner or later life makes philosophers of us all. In time he came to

need a coherent set of ideas to render life intelligible, to help him accept what he must accept and change what he could change; and he must accomplish this without losing his integrity or his sanity. So what is important to Marcus is not whether he could find answers to Life— there may not be any—but whether *he* could find answers that would work *for him.*

Marcus might have asked, first, whether one really has to live in the world. It's rough out there. Maybe there are gentler paths to follow.

Not for Marcus. In another lifetime, he would surely have chosen some other life-path so that he could meditate, reflect, paint, write poetry, compose music—so that he could tend to his spiritual life. Since the Fates chose to birth Marcus in second-century Rome and endow him with Stoic ideas, this meant accepting the conditions and responsibilities assigned to him.

He wrote: "Men seek all sorts of escape for themselves—houses in the country, by the seashores, in the mountains; and you too will probably want such things very much. But this is altogether a mark of the most common sort of men." By contrast, wise men are called to live "the life of the social animal" and be responsible to their fellow human beings, to whom they belong.

So, as Marcus saw it, *the problem* was finding a way to live in the world and not be destroyed by it.

The *answer,* Marcus reasons, lies in making a deep and permanent distinction between what you can take charge of and what you can't, a distinction, that is, between the inner world over which we can exercise a modicum of control, and the real world "out there" over which we have little or no control at all.

Clearly, we are not in charge of the grand events that constitute human history. The world of events is merely a stage, provided for us by the Fates, on which we play out our lives. "All the world's a stage," Shakespeare would later write, "And all the men and women merely players . . ." But we must understand, clearly, that we have little choice of the roles we must play. The Fates have cast us in our roles. Marcus, for instance, did not *choose* to be emperor or to marry Faustina; he did not *choose* to fight the Parthians or Quadi. There are no tryouts or callbacks. Such events are the acts and scenes in the playing out of the drama, and while a few individuals are selected to play lead roles, most of us are merely spear-carriers. Once cast, we all have a sacred duty to play our roles and to play them well, for this is how history will judge us. Furthermore, quite a few of the stage-props supplied for our roles are also given, and are quite beyond our control. We cannot change the time and place of our birth, or our parents, or the fact of aging and death, or our genetic makeup. So why fret and fume and struggle over what you cannot change?

We should all be method actors playing our roles with consummate skill but without ever being caught up in the destructive passions of the dramatic plot. The Stoics had a word for it: *apatheia*, which we rather mistranslate as "apathy." It derives from the Greek *a*, meaning "not," and *pathos*, "suffering," implying an indifference to painful events.

What we must do, Marcus reasons, is to turn to our inner world and take charge. Marcus sees the self metaphorically as a cherished plot of ground, and each of us as the caretaker of his garden plot. Each must look after the garden, tend it, not let weeds grow, and keep the plants protected, watered, and nourished.

This is the goal of life for Marcus: to guard and protect the well-being of the self. The tranquility of our spiritual/emotional life should be a normal, natural ground-state that never leaves us. The wise man "will not go against the Divinity that is planted in his breast; but rather he will preserve his deepest inner self in tranquility. He will, above all, preserve his own autonomy and integrity, and not let anything alienate him

from himself." How does one go about maintaining this ground-state? For one thing, we practice. We recondition ourselves. No one is totally depraved or totally good; all of us can grow, step by step, but it takes practice.

Marcus organized his practice into a set of four virtues which he never stopped practicing. *Wisdom*—learn what is good and bad, which involvements are beneficial and which are damaging, which concerns are enobling and which are degrading. *Justice*—be honest and fair so that you can always respect yourself; do not be arrogant, thinking you are more than you are; but do not think less of yourself either, thinking you are worth nothing. *Fortitude*—develop the strength to withstand courageously "the slings and arrows of outrageous fortune," as Shakespeare later phrased it. And *temperance*—develop control of one's passions, resist excesses, and learn to strike a balance in all of life.

Marcus writes: "Do you see me unhappy because thus-and-so has happened to me? Not at all. Rather, I am happy *despite* its happening to me. Why? Because I continue on, free from pain, neither crushed by the present nor fearing the future. For events such as this happen to every human being."

"This then remains"—Marcus reminds himself—"Remember to retire into this little territory of the inner self—your own world (which is all there is)—and there be free, and, as a human being, observe the world passing by. . . ."

◆

While encamped in Vienna in the nineteenth year of his reign, Marcus was stricken ill; he sensed that death, an old invader long stayed, was near. He beckoned Commodus to his bedside and outlined strategies for holding off the Germanic invaders. He abandoned further food and drink. On the sixth day he rose from his couch, led Commodus outside his tent, and presented him to his armies as their new emperor. Then he returned to his tent, lay down, covered his head as if to sleep, and died. He was almost fifty-nine. The date was March 17 of the year A.D. 180.

Earlier he wrote: "Don't act as if you are going to live ten thousand years. Death always hangs over you. While you are alive and while it is still in your power, be good."

He bore the burdens of empire, the loss of wife and children, the betrayal of trusted friends, the degradation of war, the boredo of empty speeches and meaningless ceremonials, personal illnesses, and the ever-present shadow of death—yet through it all he maintained his sensitivity, his decency, his humanity.

His body was returned to Rome in a final triumphal march.

1 2

## THE LOVE OF WISDOM

The word *philosophy* comes from two Greek words: *philein* ("to love") and *sophia* ("wisdom"), implying that a philosopher is (or should be) a "lover of wisdom." Among countless definitions of *philosophy*, this is still one of the simplest and best.

And so, the would-be philosopher unabashedly admits that he wants to become wise. The wisdom he seeks, however, is not merely the acquisition of facts to dispel ignorance. Rather "wisdom" is the antonym of (and antidote for) "foolishness." It is indeed the "fool" who may acquire volumes of information yet not know how to use it. To be "wise" is to possess the understanding and skill to make mature judgments about the use of human knowledge in the context of daily life.

But this sort of wisdom is elusive. It dissolves when desired too desperately, and in times of need it can become paralyzed. Wisdom is not unlike the Tao: if defined too precisely, it will lose its essence; if sought too diligently, it will be missed.

Nevertheless, the philosopher at least knows what he is looking for: *wisdom.*

"Wisdom! What wisdom? . . . I certainly have no knowledge of such wisdom, and anyone who says that I have is a liar and wilful slanderer." Thus Socrates began his defense when brought to trial in Athens in 399 B.C.

You know Chaerephon, of course. . . . Well, one day he actually went to Delphi and asked this question of the god [Apollo]. . . . He asked whether there was anyone wiser than myself. The priestess replied that there was no one. . . .

When I heard about the oracle's answer, I said to myself "What does the god

*"Then you believe in an afterlife?"*

*"Slow up! I don't 'believe' anything. I know certain things—little things, not the Nine Billion Names of God— from experience. But I have no beliefs. Belief gets in the way of learning."*

ROBERT HEINLEIN
**Time Enough for Love**

*The word philosophy means the love of wisdom. And the love of wisdom, I suppose, is like any other sort of love— the professionals are the ones who know least about it.*

ABRAHAM KAPLAN

Socrates (469-399 B.C.)

mean? Why does he not use plain language? I am only too conscious that I have no claim to wisdom, great or small; so what can he mean by asserting that I am the wisest man in the world?" . . .

After puzzling about it for some time, I set myself at last with considerable reluctance to check the truth of it in the following way. I went to interview a man with a high reputation for wisdom. . . . Well, I gave a thorough examination to this person—I need not mention his name, but it was one of our politicians that I was studying when I had this experience—and in conversation with him, I formed the impression that although in many people's opinion, and especially in his own, he appeared to be wise, in fact he was not. . . . I reflected as I walked away: "Well, I am certainly wiser than this man. It is only too likely that neither of us has any knowledge to boast of; but he thinks that he knows something which he does not know, whereas I am quite conscious of my ignorance. At any rate it seems that I am wiser than he is to this small extent, that I do not think that I know what I do not know."

From that time on I interviewed one person after another. I realized with distress and alarm that I was making myself unpopular. . . . After I had finished with the politicians I turned to the poets, dramatic, lyric, and all the rest. . . . It seemed clear to me that the poets were in much the same case; and I also observed that the very fact that they were poets made them think that they had a perfect understanding of all other subjects, of which they were totally ignorant. So I left that line of inquiry too with the same sense of advantage that I had felt in the case of the politicians.

Last of all I turned to the skilled craftsmen. I knew quite well that I had practically no technical qualifications myself, and I was sure that I should find them full of impressive knowledge. . . . But, gentlemen, these professional experts seemed to share the same failing which I had noticed in the poets; I mean that on the strength of their technical proficiency they claimed a perfect understanding of every other subject, however important. . . .

The effect of these investigations of mine, gentlemen, has been to arouse against me a great deal of hostility. . . . This is due to the fact that whenever I succeed in disproving another person's claim to wisdom in a given subject, the bystanders assume that I know everything about that subject myself. But the truth of the matter, gentlemen, is pretty certainly this: that real wisdom is the property of [Apollo], and this oracle is his way of telling us that human wisdom has little or no value. It seems to me that he is not referring literally to Socrates, but has merely taken my name as an example, as if he would say to us "The wisest of you men is he who has realized, like Socrates, that in respect of wisdom he is really worthless."

PLATO
*The Apology*

## THE GREEK MIRACLE

The birth date of philosophy and science is usually taken to be 585 B.C., for about that time a philosopher named Thales of Miletus made an assumption that broke with the world-view of his day. He assumed that all things were made of a single substance (Thales thought it might be water) and that the processes of change come from within the substance itself. Thales seems to have thought that the principle of motion and change was inherent in the basic material of which the universe is made.

Now why is this assumption significant? Before Thales, physical events were explained by supernatural causes. Since the cosmos was inhabited by all sorts of gods and goddesses, godlets, demigods, demons, ancestral ghosts, and a host of other spirits good and bad, it was reasonable to conclude that all events of human experience occurred *because they had been willed.*

If lightning struck, Zeus had hurled another thunderbolt. When the sun moved through the heavens, all knew that Apollo was driving it in his fiery chariot. If the Greeks lost the battle of Troy, or if Jason's ship slipped safely between the rocks of Scylla and the whirlpool of Charybdis, then the Olympians were playing games again.

And so, before the time of these first philosophers, all *natural* events were attributed to *supernatural* causes. G. K. Chesterton once remarked that for those holding the ancient world-view, the sun moved across the sky each day only because God got up before the sun and said to the sun, "Sun, get up and do it again."

The first philosophers were not quite satisfied with all this. Perhaps they realized that if, to every question you can ask, you get but a single answer ("The gods willed it"), then in fact you know nothing meaningful or useful. So the Milesian philosophers (Thales and his pupils Anaximander and Anaximenes) sought a different *kind* of explanation: When they asked about the cause of events, *they made the assumption* that the answer might be found in "nature" or within matter itself. In other words, they deliberately ignored the unpredictable wills of the anthropomorphic Greek deities.

This assumption marks the beginning of knowledge in the West. This is the breakthrough that has been called "the Greek miracle."

Only two centuries passed from the emergence of philosophy at Miletus to its zenith in the works of Plato and Aristotle. Yet in that time, using new instruments of inquiry, vast amounts of knowledge had been acquired.

Mathematics in the Greek world had a nebulous beginning with the first philosophers, notably the Eleatics (Parmenides and Zeno) and Pythagoras, but it was at Plato's Academy that mathematics flourished. This "exact science" was Plato's first love and became the model for his metaphysics. Over the entrance to the Academy was the inscription: "Let no one without geometry enter here."

Aristotle approached philosophy through the empirical sciences and was enthralled with every aspect of learning. He founded his Lyceum in 334 B.C. and initiated the first coordinated research into the history of the sciences. His pupil and successor Theophrastus worked on the history of the natural philosophers (the *physici*), while Menon studied the history of medicine and Eudemus recorded the history of arithmetic, geometry, and astronomy. Within a half-century after the death of Aristotle, this synoptic approach to learning came to an end. By the beginning of the third century B.C., almost every branch of learning had been freed from philosophy to go its own way.

Scientific inquiry—being incompatible with religious dogmatism—died out in the West during the Dark Ages (c. A.D. 500–1000), and the entire corpus of Greek philosophic and scientific knowledge was passed on to the Arabs. After they had made considerable contributions, this body of knowledge, still essentially Greek, made its way to the Latin West, eventually giving birth to the Renaissance and the New Science.

Thales (fl. 585 B.C.)

*Love is a strong word, but not, I think, too strong for a passion which scorns the harlotry of fantasy and demands that those dedicated to an austere beauty should be faithful even unto death. The love of truth—which must not be confused with love of certainty—has seldom made much appeal to religious minds.*

**HECTOR HAWTON**

Aristotle (385-322 B.C.)

*Faith can move mountains, or lead a man endlessly down a blind path. . . .*

JAMES E. GUNN

*It would not do for a student to answer every question in history by saying that it was the finger of God. Not until we have gone as far as most in tidying up mundane events and the human drama are we permitted to bring in wider considerations.*

EDWARD HALLETT CARR

From the great period of Greek science (roughly 300–100 B.C.) to the present day, various branches of inquiry have split off from philosophy and established themselves as independent disciplines, including the natural sciences, mathematics and geometry, and astronomy. With the rise of the universities and the development of science, such new fields as physiology, anatomy, and medicine proliferated, but the most recent offspring of philosophic question-asking (the "baby sciences," which, significantly, are the *human* sciences) have been psychology, anthropology, sociology, and political science.

The history of philosophy is the history of asking questions—better and better questions. The history of science is the history of specialization in question-asking, plus the accumulated fund of answers which *all* this question-asking has produced.

## FREEDOM TO WONDER AND TO ASK QUESTIONS

Philosophy and freedom of inquiry were born together. Neither has ever existed without the other. If we possess freedom, we inquire. But if our freedom to inquire is too limited, freedom, which is rightly a condition, becomes itself the goal for which we are willing to fight and die.

Throughout Western history, of course, religious sentiment has resisted critical inquiry into certain questions the final answers to which were allegedly known. The question of God's existence, for example, was not considered debatable. In more recent times there has been opposition to investigation into the nature of man, especially his evolutionary origin and the operations of his inner world. The possibility of synthesizing life in the laboratory has also been feared and fought. In such areas scientists have long since probed where others feared to search and have reduced the *mysterium* to quantitative analysis.

For the philosopher, as for the scientist, there is no holy ground—unless indeed *all* is holy ground.

Despite our background of Greek rationalism, reason in the Western world has had a difficult time. In the Judeo-Christian tradition it is made clear that we are saved by faith and not by our rational intellects or academic credentials.

The epitome of the righteous man was Abraham, who was willing to go so far as to kill his son Isaac *to obey* the word of his God, Yahweh. He assumed no right (according to the story in Genesis 22) to question the command; there was no chance of his debating with Yahweh the morality of the order. (However, read Genesis 18:20-33, where Abraham—yes, Abraham—carried on a running argument with God about a similar moral issue—and won!) In sacrificing Isaac, absolute obedience was required, and because of his submission Abraham has been held up as the ideal "Man of Uprightness" for more than three thousand years. Salvation is the reward of faith and obedience.

In the gospel tradition, Thomas is the example of what we are not to be, if we can help it. Thomas doubted. He wanted better evidence than he had before believing something reported to him by others, that is, before he *could* believe emotional second-hand reports of an event which, at first glance, seemed extremely improbable. Eventually "doubting Thomas" was told to place his hands in the wound in Jesus' side so that then he too might believe. But this skepticism is not commendable, for Jesus is reported to have said, "Blessed be those who have not seen me and yet believe!" (John 20:29).

Similarly, Saint Paul had grave misgivings about human wisdom and those who seek it. It appears that he had a rather sour experience with some Stoic and Epicurean philosophers in Athens. "Where now is your philosopher? Your scribe? Your reasoner of today?" he wrote to the Corinthian Christians. "Has not God made a fool of the world's wisdom?" A similar word of caution was sent to his friends in the Lycus Valley: "Take care that nobody exploits you through pretensions of philosophy. . . ."

Time and again, Paul found that philosophers were the hardest minds to sway, and, despairing of their lack of understanding, he moved on to the towns where he could find people who had the capacity for faith.

Reason and knowledge are of little value in achieving salvation, according to orthodox Western theology. On the contrary, they can be a positive hindrance. We are saved by *faith*. Redemption is for the illiterate as much as for the educated. For in Christ, Paul reminds us, there is neither Jew nor Gentile, male nor female, slave nor free. "In union with Christ, all men are one." In matters of salvation, that is, all men of faith are equal.

The Church Fathers and Scholastic philosophers, of course, followed Paul's lead. Saint Augustine (A.D. 354–430) always asserted the primacy of faith: *Fides proecedit intellectum*, "Faith must exist before one can understand." Augustine "never abandoned or depreciated reason," writes a church historian, "he only subordinated it to faith and made it subservient to the defense of revealed truth. Faith is the pioneer of reason, and discovers the territory which reason explores."

> *I do not seek to understand in order that I may believe, but I believe in order that I may understand, for this I feel sure, that, if I did not believe, I would not understand.*
>
> ST. ANSELM

Saint Anselm of Canterbury (1033–1109) took the same position. *Credo ut intelligam*, "I believe in order to understand." Revealed truth must first be accepted, and in the light of that certainty one can then know how to interpret all else. The revealed truth cannot itself be subject to doubt.

Peter Abelard (1079–1142) disagreed and stoutly declared it was the other way around. Understanding comes first, and only then can one decide what to believe. Abelard was not afraid of questions and doubts: "For by doubting we come to inquiry, by inquiry we discover the truth."

Needless to say, Augustine and Anselm won, and Abelard lost. We speak of *Saint* Augustine and *Saint* Anselm, but we do not say "Saint" Abelard.

## A WESTERN DILEMMA

Time and again, when we want to understand ourselves, we find that we must return to the two great traditions that together make up our Western heritage. Like intellectual archeologists, we have to chip at the clay and brush away the dust from the remains of our buried past.

Countless ideas inherited from our two ancestral worlds—the Greco-Roman and the Judaic—have been harmonized into a fairly coherent

*The Ancient of Days* by
William Blake (1794)

world-view, and Western life has been richer for it. But like a dissonant undercurrent, a few Greek and Judeo-Christian beliefs have remained stubbornly
incompatible, and thinkers have tried in vain to work out some sort of coexistence.

We have now, in this chapter, encountered basic assumptions about life,
involving ultimate commitments, which are logically and psychologically
incompatible. For almost two millennia we have been torn by the conflict.

Despite all healing attempts by some of the West's greatest minds, we are still intellectually dichotomized.

The Greek commitment is to reasoned inquiry into the nature of existence. This commitment has enabled us to understand the natural world we live in and to lay the foundations for an understanding of man.

On the other hand, the Judeo-Christian commitment has been to religious beliefs that lie beyond human understanding. What has been revealed by the Infinite Mind cannot be comprehended by finite minds; the "mysteries of faith" will remain beyond our grasp, for "we see through a glass, darkly." Our purpose in life should not be to analyze the Infinite or synthesize life's fragments. Rather, our goal should be "to get into a right relationship with God," to do his will through faith, and to look forward to an eternity which will transcend this mortal existence.

This is a Western dilemma, and for many, it is either/or. Here the road forks and one may be forced to choose the road he will travel. Many have tried to blaze a way between them, but no clear path has yet been found.

In this dichotomy, the philosopher generally chooses the company of Socrates. The philosopher has no doubt about the transforming power and the pragmatic virtue of religious belief, but he believes that courageous inquiry, and growth from the knowledge thereby gained, hold out greater hope for both personal fulfillment and the future of Mankind.

"I have said some things," Socrates once remarked, "of which I am not altogether confident. But that we shall be better and braver and less helpless if we think that we ought to inquire, than we should have been if we indulged in the idle fancy that there was no knowing and no use in seeking to know what we do not know—that is a theme upon which I am ready to fight, in word and deed, to the utmost of my power."

*Development means dealing with experience in increasingly sophisticated and complex ways and being able to integrate this complexity into stable structures. . . . Development occurs when the individual is confronted with novel perspectives and events that he cannot account for with his usual assumptions.*

NORBERT RALPH

*Almost all the spiritual traditions recognize that there is a stage in man's development when belief—in contrast to faith—and its securities have to be left behind.*

ALAN WATTS

## BELIEF, DOUBT, CRITICAL THINKING, AND FAITH

In our reflections to this point, we have dealt with several varieties of faith and belief without precisely defining our terms. Faith and belief are not the same, so careful distinctions need to be made. Believing, having faith, and doing critical thinking are different mental activities that complement, enrich, and balance one another.

Let's begin with belief. The word "belief" will be used in this book to refer to "blind belief," the unthinking acceptance of an idea or system of ideas *(credentia)*—as in "I believe it, I believe it, don't confuse me with facts!" Belief is the process of making a commitment to an idea in order to make that idea work for you. The idea may be inherited, derived from authority, or freely chosen. In any case, we think about the idea, identify with it, invest ourselves in it, condition ourselves with it, find ways of applying it. Belief is the complex psychic process by which we make ideas work for us; it is the process of making ideas true.

All of us are believers; to live by an idea requires commitment to it. There are many forms of commitment. The deepest belief—and the most rigid

*The real tragedy that may occur in any of our lives is not the losing of our faith. . . . The real tragedy is not to lose our faith . . . to be satisfied, to be smug and content, to have arrived . . .*

BERT C. WILLIAMS

Paul Tillich (1886-1965)

*The passion for truth is silenced by answers which have the weight of undisputed authority.*

PAUL TILLICH

belief—is when we hold on to an idea come hell or high water; we maintain our commitment even though the idea may have outlived its usefulness. We do this out of loyalty to the person(s) or institutions from whom we acquired the idea, or out of fear of an authoritarian source ("It's true [for me]; therefore it had better be true for you!"), or because the idea has become closely identified with one's self—for a variety of reasons other than the inherent worth of the idea itself. We often try to keep ideas alive long after they have died.

The emotional stance of the individual who engages in blind belief is one of defense. Stockades are built around the idea and he stands guard to ward off any perceived attack. Such a defensive stance encapsulates one in his own egocentric predicament, interferes with the acquisition of further knowledge, and effectively blocks empathy with other people. A rigid believer generally fails to understand others' moral values, ethnic customs, religious beliefs, and philosophic journeys. Growth is inhibited, and rich sources of insight, understanding, and adventure are lost.

There are, however, other forms of commitment that don't preclude learning and growth. The American theologian Paul Tillich preferred to use the word "faith" to describe a form of belief that is open to new ideas yet permits us to commit ourselves to ideas for daily living. Tillich writes:

> The most ordinary misinterpretation of faith is to consider it an act of knowledge that has a low degree of evidence. . . . If this is meant, one is speaking of belief rather than of faith. . . . Almost all the struggles between faith and knowledge are rooted in the wrong understanding of faith as a type of knowledge which has a low degree of evidence but is supported by religious authority. One of the worst errors of theology and popular religion is to make statements which intentionally or unintentionally contradict the structure of reality. Such an attitude is an expression not of faith but of the confusion of faith with belief.

Authentic faith is always based on doubt. Faith is the act of committing oneself to an idea after having "processed" it, that is, after raising doubts about it, analyzing it, applying it. The idea, having been tested in the trenches, continues to stay alive; what one does with it then is to have faith in it. It may not be "proven"; it may be only temporarily useful—who knows?; and more evidence may be needed to determine its truth-status. Despite all these hesitations, you continue to invest in the idea and work with it. That's faith.

Further, "faith" refers to a kind of courage that enables one to act upon the best facts and ideas that are available, although they are incomplete and there is no signed guarantee of satisfactory results. In a general sense, then, faith is the courage to proceed to live in terms of possibilities and probabilities rather than absolutes and certainties.

*The surest way to corrupt a young man is to teach him to esteem more highly those who think alike than those who think differently.*

FRIEDRICH NIETZSCHE

Every act of faith, writes Tillich, involves risk, and all risk is accompanied by doubt. Authentic doubt "is always present as an element in the structure of faith. . . . There is no faith without an intrinsic 'in spite of' and the courageous affirmation of oneself in the state of ultimate concern. . . . If doubt appears, it should not be considered as the negation of faith, but as an element which was always and will always be present in the act of faith."

A philosopher engages in doubt as a normal modus operandi, insisting upon doubting a fact-claim to force it to defend itself. A historian once remarked that *all* knowledge begins with a "good, healthy doubt." The works of seventeenth-century rationalist René Descartes typify the productive role that doubt plays in acquiring knowledge. Descartes doubted everything he could in the hope of arriving at some "fact" that he could not further doubt. When he discovered such a datum (*Cogito, ergo sum;* "I think, therefore I exist"), he began to build deductively upon that clear first principle. This brand of doubt has played a major role in all the knowledge-gathering sciences.

In his *Meditations,* Descartes shares his first steps toward productive doubt:

> Some years ago I came to realize that from my youth onwards I had been accepting as true many opinions that were really false, and that consequently the beliefs which I based upon such infirm grounds must themselves be doubtful and uncertain. Thereupon I became convinced that I need to make, once in my life, a clean sweep of my formerly held opinions and to begin to rebuild from the bottom up, if I wished to establish some kind of firm and assured way of thinking in the sciences. . . .
>
> Today then . . . I shall apply myself earnestly and freely to the task of eradicating all of my formerly held opinions. To this end it will not be necessary to show that the old opinions are false. . . . Rather, since my reason persuades me that I ought to withhold belief from whatever is not entirely certain and indubitable, quite as much as from what is manifestly false, I shall be sufficiently justified in rejecting any belief if only I can find in each case some reason to doubt it.

Does all this render human existence a little less certain, a little less secure, and demand of us a little more courage and a willingness to face adventure? *Yes!* "Flight from insecurity is catastrophic to any kind of human growth," wrote the personalist philosopher Peter Bertocci. "To flee from insecurity is to miss the whole point of being human." Alan Watts made a similar observation: "Almost all the spiritual traditions recognize that there is a stage in man's development when belief—in contrast to faith—and its securities have to be left behind."

In his investigations of what he terms the "self-actualizing" personality, Abraham Maslow made a significant discovery.

*Flight from insecurity is catastrophic to any kind of human growth. To flee from insecurity is to miss the whole point of being human. It is to miss, at any rate, the whole point of religion.*

PETER BERTOCCI

Our healthy subjects are uniformly unthreatened and unfrightened by the unknown, being therein quite different from average men. They accept the unknown, they are comfortable with it, and often are even attracted by it. To use Frenkel-Brunswick's phrase, "they can tolerate the ambiguous." . . . Since for healthy people, the unknown is not frightening, they do not have to spend any time laying the ghost, whistling past the cemetery, or otherwise protecting themselves against danger. They do not neglect the unknown, or deny it, or run away from it, or try to make believe it really is known, nor do they organize, dichotomize, or rubricize it prematurely. They do not cling to the familiar, nor is their quest for truth a catastrophic need for certainty, for safety, for definiteness, and order. The fully functioning personality can be, when the objective situation calls for it, comfortably disorderly, anarchic, vague, doubtful, uncertain, indefinite, approximate, inexact, or inaccurate.

The person of faith, therefore, is fully as committed to ideas as any blind believer, but he has made a decision to take charge of the selection of the ideas that he will live by. This, by definition, is what the philosophic venture is all about: Critical thinking is nothing more, and nothing less, than taking a good look at the ideas that we are thinking and then making a commitment to live by the best ideas we can come up with.

## THE FOUR PASSIONS

It is commonly thought that philosophers, scientists, and others who attempt to be precise are people without passion, dull and lifeless, since, after all, the search for "objective facts" requires a calm, *dis*passionate mind. Not so. The philosophic mind is a passionate mind, passionate because its commitments must be strong enough to override all sorts of pressures from within—our own needs—and from without—the push and pull of all those who would make us think differently. The philosophic/critical mind is characterized by at least four passions, all necessary for getting the work done.

A PASSION FOR FREEDOM "My trade is to say what I think," said Voltaire. We can add that the philosopher's vocation is to think what he pleases and then speak and write what he thinks. He cannot in good faith accept any restraint upon his professional calling. For economy and efficiency, of course, he will choose how he limits himself and how he articulates his questions, but he will resist any external threat to his freedom of inquiry.

In this spirit, he will grant to all others the same freedom he insists upon for himself. To turn again to Voltaire, to whom a well-known, but little-heeded, line is attributed: "I do not agree with a word that you say, but I will defend to the death your right to say it."

A PASSION FOR INFORMATION The philosophic mind wants knowledge, facts, data. Why? To have something to think with! We don't think very well with vacuums, though too often we try, and we all know individuals who specialize in talking when they don't know very much about their subject. We also know the experience of needing desperately to think productively about a problem and yet not having sufficient information to think our way to a solution. So the prime purpose of gaining knowledge is to have information to think with.

*I have had to experience so much stupidity, so many vices, so much error, so much nausea, disillusionment and sorrow, just in order to become a child again and begin anew.*

HERMANN HESSE
*Siddhartha*

The philosophic mind is a question-asking mind. We want to know about all kinds of things. "What does it all mean, Alf?" "Where did the moon come from?" "What makes the planets round?" "Is there life on other planets?" Alf's response is appropriate: "How else are you going to learn?"

Are birds really decendants of dinosaurs? What was Stravinsky attempting to express with his *Rite of Spring?* How could the Rain Man know there were 246 toothpicks in the box? How do genes work? Why does every living thing share the same amino acid code? Why do some flowers last but a day? What is time? Why do we remember some painful events and forget others? How old is the human race? Where did we come from? Why so many races? Do dolphins think? How do mollusks create those beautiful shells always with the same design?

How can I know right from wrong? Why do I have such trouble doing the right thing? Which is the right religion? Is there a better form of government? What is justice? What is truth, beauty, art? Why do we fight wars? What is evil? Why is there sex? Why are there only two sexes? Why should we be concerned for whales, seals, and rhinos?

And a thousand other questions. The philosophic mind will not accept, will not tolerate, any stifling of this natural curiosity that is the gift of childhood and a source of continual excitement.

One who has a passion for knowledge never stops asking questions, never stops gathering, never stops growing. All this for the joy of learning, of course; but more, so we don't come up running on empty when we are required to think creatively in our problem solving.

**A PASSION FOR THE TRUTH** The critical mind has a passion for the truth, not merely a passion for saccharine ideas that temporarily help us feel better. The philosopher shares this longing with Oedipus the king: Tell me about myself—who I am, what I am, what I have done. "I will not stop until I know everything that is to be known about myself."

The philosopher turns to the field specialists—or anyone else—who can help him find and face the truth. To the sociologist or anthropologist: Tell me the truth about the hidden assumptions of my society that have shaped my life without my knowing it. To the psychologist: Tell me the truth about why I behave the way I do, about why I get angry and feel guilt and self-doubt; tell me the truth about my own past, and who I really am. To the paleontologist: Tell me the truth about my human origins, about my genetic connections, and, perhaps, about why I am here. To the political scientist and social psychologist: Tell me the truth about corporate ethics, about political power, about tribal loyalties, about why we fight wars. To the environmentalist: Tell me the truth about the degradation of our planet; can we save our environment and ourselves?

Whatever the truth, whatever its source, whatever its impact—it is to be sought and accepted. To be sure, this takes courage, but then, consider thoughtfully the alternatives.

**A PASSION FOR UNDERSTANDING** This is the final passion of the philosophic spirit. Understanding is the goal and purpose of acquiring knowledge. We acquire knowledge, not for knowledge's sake, but to nourish the mind's fundamental need to understand. The mind naturally makes connections, but it must have data and ideas to connect.

*The strongest principle of growth lies in human choice.*
GEORGE ELIOT

*I do not agree with a word that you say, but I will defend to the death your right to say it.*
**Attributed to VOLTAIRE**

*It is only charlatans who are certain . . . Doubt is not a very agreeable state, but certainty is a ridiculous one.*
VOLTAIRE

*A point of view can be a dangerous luxury when substituted for insight and understanding.*
MARSHALL MCLUHAN

Understanding—not the accumulation of masses of unconnected data—should be the fundamental goal of education. Dr. Matthew Lipman, a leader in the critical thinking movement, takes the educational system to task for failing to develop in us the mental habits of creative connecting. In a "Good Morning America" interview, he stressed that understanding can't develop when the educational process is mechanical and indoctrinational: "The whole aim of education should not just be to learn a discipline, to learn a body of knowledge, but *to learn to think in that discipline—to think* in music, *to think* in mathematics. That's the goal of education."

In his play *Doctor Einstein before Lunch*, Ernest Kinoy shows a supernatural visitation to the great physicist shortly before his death. The visitor—with formidable side-whiskers and the heavy cutaway coat of the pre-turn-of-the-century German professional man—offers Einstein the formula he had spent his last thirty years searching for. "One last great 'ahah'! *That* would interest you . . . The last equation? The One Theory? Suppose . . . suppose Respected Doctor . . . I could offer you that? . . . Would you like to . . . know it?"

Einstein asks how he derived this formula—from some new mathematics, something new in wave mechanics, some new experimental evidence. "No . . . no . . . no . . . you don't understand! I can make you *know!* . . . I offer you . . . knowledge! . . . One moment you will doubt . . . you will yearn for the answer . . . and the next moment . . . Ahah you will KNOW!"

Einstein slowly shakes his head.

EINSTEIN: No thank you.

VISITOR: I beg your pardon.

EINSTEIN: No thank you.

VISTIOR: But Doctor . . . I offer you the . . . answer of your soul's question. I offer you the . . . confirmation of your faith.

EINSTEIN: Any fool can KNOW! The point is . . . to understand! To follow the thought . . . to build a structure of theory and mathematics which is . . . True! That is science . . .

VISTIOR: (Taking out a wallet) I have it here . . . (Peeking in the wallet as if he had within the soul of Miser Stevens) A very lovely equation.

EINSTEIN: But would I understand? Would I be able to make it so clear that any scientist would have to agree?

VISITOR: (Shrugs) *You* would know! (Einstein shakes his head again . . . 'No.' The visitor looks again in his wallet.) Oh, with very interesting Greek letters . . . (Einstein still shakes his head 'no.')

VISITOR: Come Doctor . . . time approaches zero. You will not find what you are looking for . . . your way. Try mine . . . (Holding out the wallet) Know . . . accept the gift! (Einstein is still shaking no) Perhaps what you are looking for cannot be found?

EINSTEIN: But the important thing is never to stop questioning. Curiosity has its own reason for existence. One cannot help but be in awe when one contemplates the mysteries of eternity, of life, of the marvelous structure of reality. It is enough if one tries merely to comprehend a little of this mystery each day.

VISITOR: (Still looking down at his hidden formula) No?

EINSTEIN: No. My God cannot be understood by . . . miracles and blind faith.

*Why is the Universe as it is and not something else? Why is the Universe here at all? It is true that at present we have no clue to the answers to questions such as these. . . . But throughout the history of science, people have been asserting that such and such an issue is inherently beyond the scope of reasoned inquiry, and time after time they have been proved wrong. . . . All experience teaches us that no one has yet asked too much.*

FRED HOYLE

*What we need is not the will to believe, but the wish to find out, which is exactly the opposite.*

BERTRAND RUSSELL

## REFLECTIONS

1   Socrates came to some clear conclusions after he had investigated several men who laid claim to being wise. Do you think his observations were accurate about the claims we make? In the last analysis, according to Socrates, what makes a person wise?

2   Summarize in your own words the philosophic breakthrough that has been called the "Greek miracle." Why is this naturalistic methodology so important in the gathering of information? Or, conversely, what would happen to human knowledge if the naturalistic assumption were not followed?

3   Summarize in your own way the nature of the "Western dilemma" regarding human knowledge. Is it "either/or" for you personally, or have you discovered a pathway between the two traditions?

4   Without attempting a precise definition of religion at this point, do you think it possible for a philosopher who insists upon the freedom to inquire into *everything* (including religious axioms and "revealed truths") to also be religious?

5   Suppose a philosopher inquires into the existence of God (and all do, sooner or later). If he concludes, after the most honest inquiry, that God exists, is he still a philosopher? If he concludes, after his most honest investigation, that God doesn't exist, does he cease to be religious? Do one's philosophic credentials depend upon the questions he asks or the answers he arrives at?

6   After reading this chapter, contrast *faith* and *belief,* and write definitions of each. (See glossary.) Are you a "faith-full" person? Are you a "belief-full" person?

7   Note the famous comment attributed to Voltaire ("I do not agree with a word that you say . . . "). Do you agree? If not, why? If you do agree, how well do you practice it?

# RENÉ DESCARTES

## *"I think, therefore I exist!"*

Two events in the life of René Descartes are peculiarly intriguing: one has to do with a dream by a warm stove on a cold winter night; the other is his encounter with one of history's really weird women—Queen Christina of Sweden.

The date of the first incident was November 10, 1619. In his lodging on the bank of the Danube in Neuberg, Germany, Descartes retreated to a warm room to think about some disturbing problems. For years he had been obsessed with the uncertain state of what he knew—an age-old problem that has bothered every philosopher since Thales. "I always had an excessive desire to learn to distinguish the true from the false," he tells us, "in order to see clearly in my actions and to walk with confidence in this life." He was frustrated, agitated, disconsolate, discouraged, and probably angry that the bits and pieces of information floating disparately in his mind wouldn't quite come together.

Hovering by a tile stove, he dreamed three dreams. In one he felt that he was trying to escape from something; he was lame, apparently running, and he sought sanctuary in a church. In another dream he heard thunder and saw sparks of fire. In a third there appeared before his dreaming eyes a line from a poem by Ausonius: *Quid vitae sectabor iter?* "What way of life shall I follow?"

When he awakened, the answers—or at least a method for seeking answers—stood clear in his mind. What he had sought was a method for seeing the truth of things and a guideline for building a system of knowledge on secure foundations. At last he saw the answers to both problems: he would apply the rules of geometry to all knowledge of the world and build a complete system of understanding with reason alone.

By his own testimony, this experience was interpreted as a mystical experience, and he was grateful to God for the assurance that he was moving in the right direction.

René Descartes (pronounce it "day-kart") was born March 31, 1596, in the Touraine, France. His mother, Jeanne Brochard, had tuberculosis and died of it a year later. René was frail from birth and suffered from dry coughs all his life.

His father was Joachim Descartes, a lawyer and a councillor of the parlement in Rennes.

What quality of nurturance René received during these formative years is not known. What we do know is that his bright mind was evident very early and that he fell in love with learning before he went away to school. Already his father referred to him as "my little philosopher."

At the age of eight he was sent to the Jesuit school of La Flèche in Anjou. He spent eight years there, and his passion for learning burned ever brighter. He performed brilliantly in all his studies, especially mathematics and physics, and received a good grounding in classical languages and literature. Because of his delicate health he was permitted a unique privilege: rather than being shocked awake at the crack of dawn with the other students, he was allowed to linger in bed till noon. To be sure, he didn't sleep in. He awakened early, then spent the morning reading, taking notes, and reflecting. This became a routine that he followed for the rest of his life.

He left La Flèche at sixteen and spent the next four years at the University of Poitiers, graduating in 1616 with a degree in civil and canon law. He spent considerable time in Paris sampling the city's excitements, but, on the whole, we are told, he behaved fairly well. He made friends, played the tables at the casinos, spent his money, and became bored with it all. Soon he abandoned the roulette wheels and salons and returned to the excitements of the mind. Geometry and mathematics were his true friends.

After graduation he joined the army, not to fight, but to travel. He managed to have considerable leisure time for reading and studying mathematics. With the escalation of the Thirty Years' War he joined the forces of Maximilian, Duke of Bavaria; and it was while traveling with this army that he found himself in Neuberg and had the mystical experience that gave his life direction and purpose. For the next eight years he traveled widely, finally settling in Holland, where an atmosphere of intellectual freedom encouraged a creative flow of ideas.

More tired than ever of the social scene, Descartes sought a place where he could be quiet and develop his ideas systematically. He lived in a small château, alone except for some servants. He entertained few visitors, thereby avoiding both his polemical enemies and his fawning friends. He picked up his mail at stations other than where he lived so that the world couldn't find him. He spent much time walking in his garden, reflecting.

He never married. In 1634 a servant girl by the name of Hélène became his lover, and they had a daughter, who was christened Françine Descartes. When, at the age of five, the little girl died of scarlet fever, Descartes wept for his loss and wrote the story of his daughter in his own small cursive handwriting on the flyleaf of one of his books.

In appearance, Descartes was nondescript, of medium build and height, slightly balding (he wore a full black wig almost day and night), with wide-set gray-black eyes, and a fashionable mustache and goatee. His dress was proper, almost immaculate; he usually wore a black suit complete with a scarf, a sword, and a feather in his hat.

He was modest and gentle, courteous and kind. With friends he was quiet (not aggressive) and thoughtful (he listened well). He felt considerable pride and could anger easily. He ate abstemiously, stayed far away from drugs and doctors, and was almost never ill. He drank a little wine, but never got drunk (he feared all vices, and carefully cultivated good habits that would serve him well).

Descartes had one of the clearest of minds. (In retrospect he is judged to have had an IQ of 180, though it seems appropriate to add that IQs are notoriously irrelevant for judging very creative individuals.) Balzac once urged him to

*The chief cause of our errors is to be found in the prejudices of our childhood . . . principles of which I allowed myself in youth to be persuaded without having inquired into their truth.*

*Cogito, ergo sum. Je pense, donc je suis. I think, therefore I am.*

*No more useful inquiry can be proposed than that which seeks to determine the nature and scope of human knowledge.*

*No opinion, however absurd and incredible, can be imagined, which has not been maintained by some one of the philosophers.*

*The principal effect of the passions is that they incite and persuade the mind to will the events for which they have already prepared the body.*

*Except our own thoughts, there is nothing absolutely in our own power.*

*The greatest minds are capable of the greatest vices as well as of the greatest virtues. . . .*

*It is not enough just to have a superior mind. The important thing is that we use it well.*

"write the story of your mind." He was relentless in his intellectual pursuits, literate, and highly original. He had an inner detachment, keen perception and subtle discernment of others, and lots of common sense.

Descartes was one of the world's great mathematicians; he invented analytical geometry. His restless intellect explored countless fields of knowledge: geometry, mathematics, and physics were his first loves; but also astronomy, physiology, anatomy, psychology, all branches of philosophy—epistemology, ethics, metaphysics—theology, and more. As he put it, he dedicated himself to study *le grand livre du monde*—"the great book of the world."

He published four works during his lifetime. Most influential was the *Discourse on Method*, written in elegant French—*Discours de la méthode*. His other important works were written in Latin: *Meditations on First Philosophy* (which was placed on the Roman Church's Index of Prohibited Books in 1662); and *Principles of Philosophy*, published in 1646. A much earlier work, dealing mostly with physics and finished in 1633, was entitled *The World;* it was about to be published when Descartes was told of the Inquisition's persecution of Galileo for supporting the Copernican theory. Since Descartes had written similar ideas, he decided to withdraw his book from publication.

◆

Descarte's philosophy is dominated by his personal quest for certainty. This is not a preoccupation unique to Descartes or to his age. There seem to be traumatic transition periods in the history of understanding when it becomes more painfully obvious that our old assumptions don't work any more. They no longer fit our experience of the world. At such times philosophic minds like Descartes's are driven to critical reassessment of the very foundations of

what we know.

Descartes was a geometrician. He found only in mathematics and geometry the certainty that he required. Therefore, he used the methods of geometry to think about the world. Now, in geometry one begins with a search for axioms, simple undeniable truths—for example, the axiom that a straight line is the shortest distance between two points. On the foundations of such "self-evident" propositions, whole geometrical systems can be built.

Following his geometrical model, Descartes proceeds to doubt everything—*de omnibus dubitandum*. He will suspend belief in the knowledge he learned from childhood, all those things "which I allowed myself in youth to be persuaded without having inquired into their truth." Doubt will be his method, a deliberate strategy for proceeding toward certainty. (Descartes is a doubter not by nature, but by necessity. What he really wants is secure understanding so he can *stop* doubting.)

Descartes finds that he has no trouble doubting the existence of real objects/events—our senses too easily deceive us. And we can doubt the existence of a supernatural realm of reality—figments and fantasies are too often conjured by our native imaginations. But now his geometrical model pays off: in trying to doubt everything, he discovers something that he can't doubt. What he can't doubt is that he is doubting. Obviously, I exist if I doubt that I exist. My doubt that I exist proves that I exist, for I have to exist to be able to doubt. Therefore, I can't doubt that I exist. Hence, there is at least one fact in the universe that is beyond doubt. "I am, I exist, is necessarily true each time that I pronounce it, or that I mentally conceive it."

Descartes thus becomes the author of the most famous phrase in Western philosophy: *Cogito ergo sum*, or, in his original French, *Je pense, donc je suis*— "I think, therefore I exist!" With roots in

Saint Augustine, this is certainly one of the catchiest ideas yet created by the human mind.

This secure anchor now becomes the basis of Descartes's philosophical system, and he proceeds to infer the rest of his "truths." From here on his journeys of the mind are more questionable, and his answers raise serious problems. His intent was honorable, and his methodology was promising; but we might wish that he had doubted a bit more. From the *cogito* he next tried to prove that God exists using a revised version of Anselm's Ontological Argument, but his argument is filled with fallacies. His next step is to attempt to prove the existence of the real world by contending that a perfect God would not have endowed us with a deceiving sensor system. This argument, also, doesn't seem to do justice to what we know empirically about the senses.

Descartes arrived at an all-inclusive dualism—subsequently called "Cartesian dualism" in Western philosophy. We can have knowledge of only two things: mind and matter. Each is a separate order of reality, a different world, and follows different laws of operation. Minds don't occupy space; they are not "extended" (Descartes's term). Since they are not material, they are not subject to the causal laws and the formulas of physics. Minds are free; they can think what they want to think. By contrast, the material world operates according to the laws of physics. Therefore, the *structure* of the material world is easily apprehended by a rational mind, since the laws by which it operates are rational (that is, mathematical).

Descartes was attempting to work out a coherent system that would support traditional human values—free thinking and free willing—and also do full justice to the natural world, where the laws of physics reign. This way of looking at the world endures even now. Many of us today are Cartesian dualists without our

knowing it: we still think of the two worlds of spirit and body as two quite different orders of reality.

◆

Finally, there is the encounter with Queen Christina.

Christina became queen of Sweden at the age of six. The only child of King Gustavus Adolphus, she had bright intellectual gifts that were soon the talk of Sweden. But so were her bizarre sexual inclinations and eccentric lifestyle. She refused to marry—to the despair of her countrymen; and she converted to Catholicism—to the horror of Swedish Protestants.

Whatever her motives, in February of 1649 Christina invited Descartes to come to Stockholm to organize an academy of science. He was reluctant to go. He had a premonition that, should he bury himself "in the land of bears, amid rocks and snows," something terrible might happen. So instead of going to the Queen, he wrote a treatise on love and sent it to her; but it only whetted her appetite for the author. Christina—who always had her way—persisted; and finally Descartes relented. In September he embarked from Amsterdam for the four-week trip to Stockholm.

The young queen (she was twenty-two) gave Descartes a glorious reception. She excused him from attendance at court functions and suggested he travel to get acquainted with the country. Shivering, Descartes was not impressed by what he saw. "Men's minds seem to freeze as the water freezes." Then, to his horror, he found that Christina wanted him to give her philosophy lessons three times a week at five o'clock in the morning. Descartes valiantly complied—for two months. He lighted his way through the drifting snows to the queen's library, warmed up, taught philosophy, then plodded back through the cold to his lodging. He wished he had never left Holland.

*If you would be a real seeker after truth, it is necessary that at least once in your life, you doubt, as far as possible, all things.*

*I always had an excessive desire to learn to distinguish the true from the false, in order to see clearly in my actions and to walk with confidence in this life.*

On February 1, 1650, he caught a cold that turned into pneumonia. His strength had been exhausted. The doctors were summoned. All his life Descartes despised medicines and refused the common practice of being bled. He declined treatment. He rallied briefly, got up and sat for a few hours by the fire. Then he relapsed and was twice bled by the doctors. *"Messieurs, épar-gnez le sang français!,"* he cried in vain: "Spare the French blood!" On February 11, 1650, at four o'clock in the morning, Descartes passed away in the arms of Father Viogué. He was given the last rites of the Roman Catholic Church.

His body now rests in the church of St. Germain-des-Prés in the Latin Quarter of Paris.

# How to Philosophize
## Critical Analysis

1 3

Aristotle gave wings to philosophy, and defined it wisely, out of the depths of his own sense of wonderment. He beheld a world of infinite variety and complexity, and he was profoundly curious about everything. We know he spent time studying the tidepool creatures in Mytilene's big lagoon, and that he dissected fishes, thought about rainbows, followed the stars, pondered the cause of seasons, and reflected on a thousand other things. At some point in this adventure of the mind he wrote

> A sense of wonder started men philosophizing, in ancient times as well as today. Their wondering is aroused, first, by trivial matters; but they continue on from there to wonder about less mundane matters such as the changes of the moon, sun, and stars, and the beginnings of the universe. What is the result of this puzzlement? *An awesome feeling of ignorance.* Men began to philosophize, therefore, to escape ignorance. . . .

This wonderment is the origin of philosophy. Since the beginning of human consciousness two or three million years ago, we humans have wondered about the world we live in. Huddled at night under the acacia trees, the first humans undoubtedly pondered the stars, listened to night-sounds of animals stalking their prey, loved, fought, fled, bled—and wondered what life is all about.

All our wondering can be subsumed under two all-embracing questions to which we humans *must* find answers. (1) How does the world work? (2) What is our place in it? These are the two ultimate questions addressed by mankind's religions. Every great religious tradition has developed a full, complete set of answers to these two questions, and this was accomplished centuries or millennia before any data-gathering disciplines came along. But no matter: Whatever the place and whenever the time we happen to be born, just so that our souls can rest a little easier, there must be lodged within the psyche of each of us a

*It began when I was in the fifth grade. I came home from school one day, and my mother said to me, "What did you do in school today—think or believe?"*

**RALPH NADER**

*All philosophy begins—as the ancient Greeks so well knew—with astonishment and wonder.*

**KURT REINHARDT**

*The General shook his head. "You've been out of school all these years, and what have you learned? Don't you know raw ability will never take you to the top?"*

*"I'd rather be myself than be at the top," said Beller. "I like to know what I think when I go to bed at night."*

**CHRISTOPHER ANVIL**

*If the only tool you have is a hammer, you tend to treat everything as if it were a nail.*

ABRAHAM MASLOW

clear understanding of what sort of universe we live in and what it demands of us.

From its beginnings in the 6th century B.C., philosophy, too, has addressed just these questions; and it does this by looking at the world, very carefully, to find out what is really there. Philosophers, by definition and passion, want to find answers to these questions about "the changes of the moon, sun, and stars, and the beginnings of the universe" and to find out who we are, where we came from, and how we should live. This is the first and final goal of philosophy—*to understand the world and our place in it.*

## THE PHILOSOPHIC MIND

*Pythagoras was the first person who invented the term "Philosophy," and who called himself a philosopher.*

DIOGENES LAERTIUS

*It is impossible for a man to learn what he thinks he already knows.*

EPICTETUS

*"There's no use trying," said Alice: "one can't believe impossible things."*

*"I dare say you haven't had much practice," said the Queen. "When I was your age I always did it for half an hour a day. Why sometimes I've believed as many as six impossible things before breakfast."*

LEWIS CARROLL

*History is the story of the defiance of the unknown and of what happens when man tries to extend his reach. Such defiance is necessary because conventional wisdom has never been good enough to run a civilization.*

NORMAN COUSINS

*When you know all the answers, you haven't asked all the questions.*

HAROLD LEVITT

All knowledgeable individuals experience that awesome feeling of ignorance that Aristotle is describing; only the ignorant are exempt. If one does not know very much, he does not know what he does not know; but if he knows a great deal, he becomes aware of how much more there is that he still does not know.

How does one go about dispelling that feeling of ignorance and moving toward the truth of things? The first step is to ask questions. (See p. 31.)

The mind that genuinely wants to understand what is going on in the world—the philosophic mind—is a question-asking mind. When we ask questions, what we are doing, of course, is honoring that wonderful sense of curiosity we possessed in childhood but which, in so many of us, was repressed because it proved bothersome to adults. Our latent interest in the world and everything in it lay dormant and undeveloped. For many of us learning to ask questions about things involves the recovery of that curiosity and the formulation of the million questions that never got asked.

To a thoughtful mind, however, not just any answers will do; they must be honest answers that enable us to better apprehend the stubborn realities of the world we live in. The answers must be the product of critical thought. Over the centuries, and especially during the twentieth century, philosophers have developed a wide array of critical skills designed to help us get at the truth and therefore to better understand the world. These technical skills are eminently practical and productive; with them we can dissolve controversies, go to the heart of issues, have a meeting of minds, and be honest with ourselves and others.

The notion of being critical can be misleading. Admittedly, in our society "criticism" has a negative connotation. "Don't criticize me!" usually means "Don't find fault with me." And "He's critical of others" means he is judgmental, that he has a habit of evaluating others negatively (and probably letting them know what he thinks).

This is not what the word originally meant and not the way it is used in philosophy. Our words "criticize," "criticism," and "critic" all derive from the Greek word *krino,* which means "I judge." To criticize means "to place [something] under judgment," implying that, in philosophy, one looks at an idea, thinks about it, judges it (both positively and negatively) for its validity and worth, and then decides what to do with it. Critical thinking is a discriminating process for deciding which ideas are good ones and which are bad. Becoming

## WONDER/CONFUSION/PATIENCE/WISDOM

"Confusion" is an initial phase of all knowledge, *without which one cannot progress to clarity.* The important thing for the individual who truly desires to think is that he not be overly hurried but be faithful at each step of his mental itinerary to the aspect of reality currently under view, that he *strive to avoid disdain for the preliminary distant and confused aspects* due to some snob sense of urgency impelling him to arrive immediately at the more refined conclusions.

JOSE ORTEGA Y GASSET
*The Origin of Philosophy*

The teacher's obligation is to be patient enough to permit deliberation and decision by each of those he is trying to help. If his students do not choose, each in the light of his own contingent existence and his own limitations, they will not become ethical beings; if they are not ethical beings—in search of their own ethical reality—they are not individuals; if they are not individuals, they will not learn.

SØREN KIERKEGAARD
*The Point of View*

Philosophy, as Plato and Aristotle said, begins in wonder. This wonder means a dim awareness of the useless talent, some sense that antlikeness is a betrayal. . . .

Philosophy means liberation from the two dimensions of routine, soaring above the well known, seeing it in new perspectives, arousing wonder and the wish to fly. Philosophy subverts man's satisfaction with himself, exposes custom as a questionable dream, and offers not so much solutions as a different life.

A great deal of philosophy, including truly subtle and ingenious works, was not intended as an edifice for men to live in, safe from sun and wind, but as a challenge: don't sleep on! there are so many vantage points; they change in flight: what matters is to leave off crawling in the dust.

WALTER KAUFMANN
*Critique of Religion and Philosophy*

critical means that each of us takes responsibility for the truthfulness and validity of the ideas we live by.

## CRITICAL SKILLS

There are three broad families of critical skills. They are (1) fact-claim verification, (2) concept clarification, and (3) inference validation.

1  FACT-CLAIM VERIFICATION A fact-claim is any idea submitted for consideration as an item of knowledge. In epistemology, a fact-claim becomes a fact only after it has been carefully checked with the truth-tests (see chapter 3-4) and has passed muster. If it passes critical examination, then it can validly be called a "fact."

Fact-claim: **It's raining outside.**

*Never accept a fact until it is verified by a theory!*

SIR ARTHUR EDDINGTON

*The things which exist around us, which we touch, see, hear and taste, are regarded as interrogations for which an answer must be sought. . . .*
**JOHN DEWEY**

This seems like a relatively simple fact-claim, and it is. How do I go about verifying or falsifying it? All I need to do is step outside and look. If I perceive with my senses that it is raining, then I can conclude that the idea in my mind corresponds sufficiently to what my senses tell me about real events, and I can accept the fact-claim as true. If it is not raining, then the fact-claim is false. In this example we are making use of two of the three truth-tests, the correspondence truth-test and the pragmatic truth-test (see pp. 227 and 229.)

Fact-claim: **Water freezes at 32° F.**

At first this is merely an abstract idea floating in our minds, but what we want to know is whether it's true. So how do we find out if it is true? We go find some water, put it outside in the winter weather or otherwise lower its temperature to 32° or below, and see what happens. If it freezes when the temperature drops to 32°, then the idea is true; if it does not, then the idea is false. The American philosopher William James argued that the idea-in-the-abstract is neither true nor false until it has been applied to a real event, and that the idea *becomes* true when it is applied and found to work (or becomes false when so applied and found not to work, that is, does not describe accurately a real event). In the case of water freezing at 32°, the idea is true, of course; and the idea has been applied and has worked enough times for us to have confidence that it will continue to work whenever so applied. (Note that truth exists only as a quality of an idea that works, and as a quality of the sentence used to express that idea.) This is another example of the application of both the pragmatic and correspondence truth-tests.

*There is not a philosophical method, though there are indeed methods, like different therapies.*
**LUDWIG WITTGENSTEIN**

Fact-claim: **In the year A.D. 451 Attila the Hun defeated the forces of the Saracens at the battle of Châlons and turned back the invading Muslims who might otherwise have conquered Europe and converted it into an Islamic empire.**

True statement or false? How can these fact-claims be verified or falsified? I cannot go somewhere and apply the idea to any actual events now taking place; the year A.D. 451 is very long gone. What I must do is go to the historical records and find references to Attila, the Huns, the Saracens (Muslims) and Islam, the Battle of Châlons, and whatever else seems relevant. If I find historical data that support the above fact-claims, then I can accept the statement as true; but if no such historical facts can be found, then I must consider the statement questionable (that is, I must suspend making a final judgment about its truth status); or if I find historical facts that contradict any of the above fact-claims, then I must conclude that the statement is false.

So, is the statement true or false? (Perhaps you want to go look up the historical sources before you read on.)

What I find in the records is that there was indeed a Battle of Châlons fought in the year A.D. 451, and that Attila the Hun was the victor. But I find that Attila was battling the Roman legions, not the Saracens. In fact, when I look up Saracens, Moslems, and Islam, I discover that the Islamic religion did not come into existence until the seventh century A.D. (Mohammad, the prophet and founder of Islam, was born in A.D. 570, died in 632). The fact-claims stated about the Saracens do not cohere with (are not consistent with) known historical facts. Conclusion, therefore: The statement is false. This is an application of the coherence truth-test (see pp. 228-229).

The three truth-tests (outlined more fully in chapter 3-4) can be used to determine the truth status of *all* fact-claims. If we care about thinking clearly, then making sure that the data we are working with are sound is vitally important. What is the point of investing our time and energy building on an idea if it can be shown up front to be untrue? Aristotle was the first critical philosopher to make this point; we must be sure, he said, that the "facts" we begin to think with (the *archai*, "starting points," "first principles") are true. When they are, then our subsequent thinking stands a better chance of being accurate and productive.

**2   CONCEPT CLARIFICATION** We rarely think and say anything that does not have within it hidden assumptions and implications. These are meanings that sneak into our thoughts uninvited, so that our statements don't say what we think we are saying, or they don't say what we want to say; in fact we may be saying what we don't want to say. Too often there are hidden agendas and logical fallacies in our reasoning that render our arguments invalid. But if we are to be honest in our thinking—if honest only with ourselves—then clarification is always in order. Consider, for example, the following account.

A young bank employee was indicted for embezzlement, and the evidence all seemed to point to a conviction. But *he* knew he was innocent, and his wife believed him. She was soon informed by another bank employee that he knew the whereabouts of documents that would reveal the real embezzler and prove that her husband was innocent. But her informant also made it clear he would give out with the evidence only if she made herself sexually available. The couple were devout Catholics, but to clear her husband of almost certain conviction she quickly made the decision to get whatever information at whatever cost. So she spent several nights with the other bank employee. Eventually the documents were forthcoming, her husband was exonerated, and the real embezzler was indicted and convicted.

Now, why is clarification urgently needed in this case? Because the woman claimed (adamantly) that she had done nothing morally wrong while the church authorities held (adamantly) that she had deliberately violated the Seventh Commandment and was therefore very morally wrong. Arguments could be (and were) advanced to support each point of view; but before we proceed to defend either perspective, a good deal of clarification of hidden assumptions and implications is needed. (For a more extended treatment of the ethical criteria we use in making moral judgments see pp. 368-372.)

First, note that what we are doing here is classified as ethics, the branch of philosophy that deals with *evaluations* of certain kinds of events—human intents and actions—events that we commonly evaluate as good or bad, right or wrong, sinful or virtuous, moral or immoral. The aim of ethics is to establish how we humans should ideally feel, think, and behave toward other human beings (and other living creatures, according to some ethicists). (Note also that evaluations are not fact-claims, though we commonly make numerous fact-claims to

*If I told you, you would not know; you simply would have been told. Study it thoroughly and . . . I will ask you. You will answer and then you will know.*

**"DR. HARTLEY BALDWIN"**
**in ROBERT HEINLEIN**
*Friday*

*Give to the intellect, wisdom to comprehend that one thing; to the heart, sincerity to receive this understanding; to the will, purity that wills only one thing.*

**SØREN KIERKEGAARD**

*It is much easier to bury a problem than to solve it.*

**LUDWIG WITTGENSTEIN**

*Science is the attempt to make the chaotic diversity of our sense-experience correspond to a logically uniform system of thought. . . . The sense-experiences are the given subject-matter. But the theory that shall interpret them is manmade. . . . hypothetical, never completely final, subject to question and doubt.*

**ALBERT EINSTEIN**

support our ethical judgments. No *facts* are involved in my statement "You shouldn't do thus-and-so"; it's a judgment call based on what I think and feel about what people should or should not do.)

So, is the woman in this account—we'll call her Rita—to be judged moral or immoral? The Catholic church uses formal criteria for making moral judgments. In this case, the criterion or abstract rule by which the value-judgment is made is: "You shall not commit adultery" (*Exodus* 20:14 in the Old Testament). This rule is intended to have universal application; as the Roman church interprets it, it is supposed to apply equally to all human beings. It is a God-given law, and every human being should be acquainted with it ahead of time and be ready to apply it to any appropriate occasion. It is an apodictic law—not to be argued with, negotiated, modified, or violated. In this case Rita knew about the rule ahead of time, she knowingly broke the rule, and she is therefore to be judged guilty of immoral behavior. The logic is valid, and the judgment of the church is sound.

But Rita argued that the decision she made was the loving, compassionate thing to do. She found herself in a moral predicament in which she was forced to choose from several courses of action, all painful; she could see no real option that would not lead to devastating consequences. So what is one to do when forced to choose and only bad choices are possible—follow the abstract rule or do the loving thing? In this case Rita elected to save her husband from "almost certain conviction" and a heavy jail term. She sacrificed herself ("I went through hell to get the information I needed") for someone she cared for; she chose, she believed, the best option available to her in a terribly traumatic predicament. According to contextual ethics, if one chooses the best option that one can see with the well-being of another (or others) in mind, then that person is to be judged moral in the fullest sense. Using contextual criteria, Rita's actions were compassionate, her logic is valid, and her moral judgment is sound. (For more on contextual ethics see pp. 368-372.)

So, was Rita moral or immoral in her behavior? She can validly be judged either way. Our *evaluation* of her conduct depends entirely on which criterion we select for making the judgment. Both criteria can be given strong defense, and countless volumes have been written in support of each position. Such an indecisive answer is not satisfying to many of us; we do not like ambiguity. The next step, therefore, is to try to decide which criterion is the better one, or the right one; but this is another story for another time.

There are many more assumptions and implications in this actual episode that need to be clarified and made explicit; just note that we have attempted here to clarify one thing only—the criteria used in this case for making moral evaluations. From this brief treatment, however, three ethical axioms can be inferred. (1) No evaluation, including ethical judgment, is intelligible unless the criterion used to make the judgment is made explicit and clearly understood. (2) Any action or event, including all human behavior events, can logically be evaluated as good or bad, right or wrong, depending on the criterion selected for making the judgment. (3) The ethically informed individual is aware that different and distinct criteria exist and are used in daily life by all us human beings who are trying, as best we can, to deal with life's moral dilemmas; and this awareness should help us to better understand the passionate disagreements that seem to be an inherent part of our social existence.

*Eastern and Western epistemology are united in reminding us that when we are thinking we are not experiencing outside ourselves.*

WILLIAM W. BLAKE

*Understanding the world for a man is reducing it to the human, stamping it with his seal. . . . The truism "All thought is anthropomorphic" has no other meaning. Likewise, the mind that aims to understand reality can consider itself satisfied only by reducing it to terms of thought.*

ALBERT CAMUS

## "THE UNEXAMINED LIFE"

Men of Athens, I know and love you, but I shall obey God rather than you, and while I have life and strength I shall never cease from the practice and teaching of Philosophy. . . . I am that gadfly which God has attached to the state, and all day long and in all places am always fastening upon you, arousing and persuading and reproaching you. . . . I tell you that to do as you say would be a disobedience to God, and therefore I cannot hold my tongue. Daily to discourse about virtue, and about those other things about which you hear me examining myself and others is the greatest good of man. The unexamined life is not worth living. . . . In another world I shall be able to continue my search into true and false knowledge. . . . In another world they do not put a man to death for asking questions: assuredly not.

PLATO
*The Apology*

The trial of Socrates represents something more than a mere historical event that could not possibly happen again. The trial of Socrates is a charge leveled at the type of intellectual questioning that seeks out the true problems lying outside everyday mediocrity. When Socrates tormented the Athenians like a gadfly, he prevented them from sleeping peacefully, from relaxing with their ready-made solutions to moral and social problems. By astonishing us, Socrates prevents us from thinking along the old lines that have been handed down to us and have become habits. Thus Socrates stands at the very opposite end of the scale from intellectual well-being, easy conscience, and beatific serenity. For all who think that the evidence of authority ought to prevail over the authority of evidence, that order and stability cannot permit the crimes of nonconformity and "lèse-société," Socrates could only have been the enemy. . . .

JEAN BRUN
*Socrates*

**3   INFERENCE VALIDATION** A third family of critical skills involves the fundamental rules of reasoning invented by Aristotle and known as Aristotelian or classical logic. Logic can be defined as the science of valid inference, and it is used to clarify the relationships of ideas. It includes both inductive and deductive reasoning.

We can work with "the problem of evil" (or "theodicy") to illustrate what is meant by valid inference. This problem, given extensive treatment in all the great religions, has been the source of an enormous amount of anger, bitterness, and agonized questioning by believers caught in the devastating tragedies of everyday life.

The *Book of Job* contains the classic statement of the problem of evil. In the prose prologue to the book, Job is portrayed as a prosperous man who had lived a long and righteous life. One day the God Yahweh and the Satan (literally "the Adversary," a sort of prosecuting attorney at this point in Judaic thought, not the supreme Evil One of later theology) fell to discussing Job and his profound devotion to his God. God praised Job's unwavering loyalty, but the Satan began to argue that Job was loyal only because, as Yahweh's protégé, he had been

*The world we have made as a result of the level of thinking we have done thus far creates problems we cannot solve at the same level at which we created them.*

**ALBERT EINSTEIN**

*You see me as an atheist. God sees me as the loyal opposition.*

**WOODY ALLEN**

INTERLANDI ©1976 Los Angeles Times

"Yes, there is a God . . . yes, there is a God . . . yes, there is a God . . ."

showered with abundant blessings and that, if he had suffered like other men, he would forsake his pious stance and curse God. So they agreed to a test of Job's faith. The ground rules: The Satan could afflict Job in any way he pleased but he mustn't take his life. So Job was subjected to a series of devastating disasters. He lost all his worldly goods, his possessions, his family, and finally his health. When Job's misery reached unbearable depths, three of his friends appear to comfort him. But Job curses the day he was born and will not be comforted. His friends assail Job with the standard Judaic belief that suffering is the result of sin, and Job's suffering proves that he has sinned mightily. If he will confess his sin and repent, then his suffering will cease. Through three cycles of exquisite poetry, Job reiterates his innocence and protests that his suffering is absurd and meaningless and that God is monstrously unfair in making him suffer this way.

The "problem of evil" can be summarized: If God is all-powerful, and if God is compassionate, then why are we humans made to suffer? This problem is our agonized attempt to justify the ways of God to ourselves. By the end of the Book of Job a variety of possible solutions to the problem of theodicy are explored.

Numerous assumptions and implications are hidden in this story of Job. Using some of the critical guidelines of classical logic, and putting some of the above arguments in syllogistic form, we can make a search for some of these hidden meanings.

The late Judaic version of this moral law which caused such pain to Job can be stated:

Sin (and only sin) causes suffering
Job is suffering

---

Therefore, Job has sinned

Note also the validity of the following belief which is explicit in the *Book of Job:*

The degree of one's suffering is proportional to the degree of one's sinning
If one sins much, then he will suffer much
If one sins little, then he will suffer little
Job is suffering much

---

Therefore, Job has sinned much

The doctrine also assumes that sin and suffering are causally related, and if one alters the cause he will then alter the effect:

Sin (and only sin) causes suffering
If you stop sinning, then you'll stop suffering
You, Job, have not stopped suffering

---

Therefore, you Job, have not stopped sinning

Since there could be a time-lag between cause and effect (between the sinning and the suffering), then perhaps an after-the-fact recognition and confession of one's sins would reinstate the sinner in God's favor:

If you recognize and confess your sins, then you'll stop suffering
You're still suffering

---

Therefore, you haven't recognized and confessed your sins

On the other hand, when we reflect on this argument from Job's side, we begin to see why the doctrine produced so much spiritual (and intellectual) anguish. Job might say: "My friends all agree that—"

Sin (and only sin) causes suffering
I am suffering

---

Therefore, I have sinned.

"But they're wrong! I maintain that I'm innocent of any wrongdoing, of any blasphemy, and that I have not sinned. I'm sure—"

I have not sinned
I am suffering

---

Therefore, suffering is not caused (solely) by sin

"Then why am I suffering? Why?"

A just God would not allow an innocent person to suffer
God is just

---

Therefore, God would not allow me to suffer

"But he *is* allowing me to suffer! Therefore, maybe—"

A just God would not allow an innocent person to suffer
I am innocent
I am suffering

---

Therefore, God is unjust

"But how could that be? God—if he be God—must necessarily be just. What, then, is the answer?"

I must conclude (from belief and definition) that God is just
I must conclude (from experience and logic) that God is unjust

---

Therefore, God is both just and unjust (God is both A and not-A in the same sense at the same time)

"But this is impossible! Then, why, oh Lord, why? Is there no way out?"

One can sense Job's anguish—and that of countless other believers who have found themselves caught in this very human puzzlement and are attempting to make sense of it. There is really no way out, and having wrestled deeply

*It is a terrible thing, Tolstoi said, to watch a man who doesn't know what to do with the incomprehensible, because generally he winds up playing with a toy named God. Pasteur saw nothing particularly terrifying or unsatisfying about this situation, saying that the only thing to do in the face of the incomprehensible is to kneel before it. But that which is most incomprehensible of all is not a distant planet but the human mind itself; kneeling under these circumstances may represent the ultimate vanity.*

**NORMAN COUSINS**

with the problem, the authors of the *Book of Job* fail to resolve it. A logical contradiction is involved which, given his premises and his limited data, Job (or the authors of Job) could not have solved. Since we readers are privileged to be outside observers to the story, we are let in on the secret from the beginning: we know that the painful drama was planned as a test of Job's faith. God and the Satan good-naturedly agree to do a number on Job to see how far he can be pushed before he breaks and curses God for his misfortunes.

This doctrine of a "moral law" has been a headache for theologians and philosophers for thousands of years. For our purposes, just note the role of logical analysis as used here: placing the arguments into logical form helped us to make valid inferences from the Judaic doctrine of a moral law. Logic did not solve the problem; it merely clarified a few aspects of our thinking about the problem; and for some it may have partially dissolved it. Some method other than deductive logic—perhaps an inductive investigation of the immediate causes of human suffering—could suggest a solution to the problem (see pp. 185-186).

You might be interested in the answer(s) which the writer(s) of the *Book of Job* seem to offer. One answer is found in chapters 40:6-42:6—the statement of Yahweh out of the whirlwind. However, if this answer leaves you intellectually empty, then read the prose prologue to the book (chapters 1:1-3:1) along with the prose epilogue (chapter 42:7-16). Quite a different answer is offered. These different solutions merely illustrate the challenge of the problem if taken seriously and treated within the parameters of the given premises.

## BRIEF SKIRMISHES / EXAMPLES OF CRITICAL THINKING

Here are some brief examples of how critical thinking might be done using the critical skills surveyed above. In each case, how would you respond to the quoted statement? What are the first questions you would ask about it? What about the definitions involved? the hidden assumptions? the reasoning employed in the statement?

### 1  "Enquiring minds want to know."

This statement is from a TV commercial for *The Enquirer,* the weekly tabloid found at our check-out stands. What questions would you begin asking about the statement? And how would you go about critically evaluating it?

Here are just a few critical comments of many that might be made. As the statement stands, it is true, of course, by definition. What is the definition of "enquiring minds"? Answer: those minds that "want to know." But this is a commercial sales pitch, and therefore I know that they want to sell me something; so I have to be on guard. As with all commercials, I must decide if I really want what they want me to buy.

In this case what do they want to sell me? *The Enquirer,* of course. They are trying to persuade me that if I have an inquiring mind—which they know I will claim to have; an inquiring mind is still a respected commodity in our society— then I will want to buy their paper which will tell me what my mind, an inquiring mind, wants to know.

But I have news for them. I don't want to know what they have to tell me. I am not merely not interested; I am strongly disinterested. I have better things to do with my mind, for three reasons: (1) Virtually all the material in the paper I would label gossip, the worst kind, since it deals with the sensational, the personal and private, and the morbid. (2) It caters to my prurient passions and wastes my time. It gives me almost no ideas or information that I can grow on, knowledge that will make me a better-informed human being. (3) I cannot trust the information it purports to convey. Its fact-claims are relayed to me uncritically and without verification. What I want is the truth, so I will have to turn elsewhere.

2 **"Call us now! The number is 1-900-555-2823 and your call will be answered by a member of the Psychic Network who can accurately predict your future. The future does not have to be unknown. We don't just predict the future, we change it!"**

Wouldn't it be wonderful if we could know the future! It would have so much survival value: we could see what is coming and try to get out of the way! So strong is our desire to look ahead that whole religions have grown up to minister to this very human need. Every society has had its tea leaves, psychics, seances, astrology, tortoise shells, palm reading, tarot cards, and crystal balls.

But the idea that the future can be known needs very careful critical evaluation. If the future has not yet happened, then it cannot now be known; and if it can now be known, then it has already happened. And if it has already happened, it cannot now be changed. So there are some contradictions in such claims that have to be thought through.

Knowing the future might be broken down under (1) soft prediction and (2) hard prediction. With soft prediction, we can predict the future based on present knowledge and experience. Economists will predict that the third quarter will see an increase in unemployment, a lowering of interest rates, a slowdown in production, and fewer housing starts. I can also predict that Christmas will arrive before New Year's Day, and that if you are in your late thirties then you will likely face a midlife crisis before too long. But such soft predictions as these may or may not happen; they don't *have* to happen just because I, or an "expert," predicts them. They are not logically necessary events. They are all "if-then" predictions: *if* the economy continues as it has been going, and follows past trends, *then* there will be more unemployment, and so on. But the economy may not follow past trends; it does seem to have a mind of its own sometimes. It might do wild, erratic, unpredictable things this year.

Hard prediction is another story. In this case someone—such as a prophet, diviner, a psychic, or one's self (in dreams, perhaps)—*foresees* future events exactly as they will take place; and, since they are *foreseen*, and because they may have an element of divine revelation in their interpretation, then they *must* take place exactly as foreseen. This is properly called precognition. A famous case is the dream episode of Abraham Lincoln of his own funeral. A few days

*Beginning to think is beginning to be undermined.*

ALBERT CAMUS

*Lord Russell tells us that he once received a letter from a well-known logician, a Mrs. Franklin, admitting that she was herself a solipsist and was surprised that no one else was. Russell comments: "Coming from a logician, this surprise surprised me."*

J. MILLER

*We do not want a thing because we reason; we find reasons for a thing because we want it. Mind invents logic for the whims of the will.*

G.W.F. HEGEL

before his assassination Lincoln dreamed that he saw a funeral service held in one wing of the White House. The mourners, some of whom he recognized, were all dressed in black. When, in the dream, he asked whose funeral it was, he was told "the president has been shot." This dream certainly looked like a case of genuine precognition, and it had a considerable impact on Lincoln. He shared the dream with several close friends and members of his cabinet.

The problem is that, while such episodes are rampant in popular mythology, there isn't a shred of evidence that such predictions have any validity beyond sheer (and not uncommon) coincidence. Lincoln's dream, which on the surface appears to be a classic example of precognition, belongs to a class of experiences easily explained psychologically. Lincoln was quite aware of the degree to which he was hated by sympathizers of the South; he had received numerous death threats. Even if he had repressed his awareness and his fears from consciousness, his subconscious mind confronted these fears and acted upon them symbolically in the dream sequence. The Swiss depth psychologist, Carl Jung, developed the theory that the subconscious mind, not being absorbed with the mediation of present realities as is the conscious mind, can connect feelings and events and foresee with thoughtful accuracy events that the conscious mind cannot see. But even this is a kind of soft prediction, symbolically represented, and not an authentic hard prediction.

[Note: The ABC television network program "PrimeTIME Live" conducted an investigation of the psychic industry and found widespread fraud. But note that a critical analysis of their claims by any one of us shows essentially the same thing. Revealing their fallacious claims does not prove fraud, of course; we are not here passing judgment on their honesty or intent. But what an epistemological analysis of the nature of time does show is that their claims cannot possibly be true, whatever their intent may be.]

### 3 "Mommy, Ginny told me . . . [crying] Ginny said that I was adopted. Mommy, am I adopted?"

The word "adopt" has several distinct meanings, and is used in different societies in a variety of senses. First, it's a legal term that, in some societies, refers to . . .

Whoa . . . wait a minute! Let's be very careful. There's a time and a place for everything, and this may not be the time for critical analysis. With children—with all of us—there is so much more to listen to than what the words denote; or better, words always carry far more meanings than narrow definition can capture. Obviously, in this case, a mere intellectual response seems woefully off the mark. It is not always easy to discern what responses are appropriate, but we can be sure that we daily encounter such decision times. The plaint of Tevya to his wife, "After twenty-five years I've never asked you before: Do you love me?" or the cry of the woman screaming "My house is on fire!"—in all such cases the appropriate response just may not be critical analysis. This is not to say that the rational intellect could not help us decide *what kind* of response is most appropriate. It certainly can. But critical analysis, as a response, may be the last thing called for.

*Men talk because men have the capacity for speech, just as monkeys have the capacity for swinging by their tails. For philosophers, as for other human caddis flies, talk passes the time away that would otherwise hang like a millstone about a man's neck. Tellurians in general, and philosophers in particular, swing from day to day by their long prehensile tongues, and are finally hurled headlong into their silent tombs or flaming furnaces.*

**Herman Tennessen**

*Philosophy is at once the most sublime and the most trivial of human pursuits. It works in the minutest crannies and it opens out of the widest vistas. . . . No one of us can get along without the far-flashing beams of light it sends over the world's perspectives.*

**William James**

**4   It was a fever of the gods, a fanfare of supernal trumpets and a clash of immortal cymbals. Mystery hung about it as clouds about a fabulous unvisited mountain. . . .**

I'm confused by such a passage. How can the gods have a fever? or what is immortal about cymbals? or how can mystery hang "about it as clouds"? After all, mystery is a subjective experience, not a thing "out there." And what is "it"?

But . . . I'm off the mark—again. This is *poetry!* If I approach this passage with the assumption that the author intends to convey precise meanings to my intellect, then I will miss the intent of the passage. These words by H. P. Lovecraft, the early and great science-fiction writer, represent his loving, creative wordplay—which is what poetry is all about. In deciding what sort of response is appropriate, the nature of the material and the intent of the creator must always be taken into account.

**5   "I hate broccoli. It tastes awful! I'm president now, and I'll never eat broccoli again!"**

(Or words to that effect.) This episode, for many Americans, was a delightful interlude between the weighty problems of Mr. Bush's tenure. It possessed a fairly high level humor, and we had the feeling that, for a brief moment, the president had dropped his public persona and was just being himself; in his light candor we found him charming and believable. We liked that, and we liked ourselves in a relaxed, unguarded moment with the president.

Should we decide to be analytical, however, we might note that the above broccoli-pronouncement is made up of four separate and rather interesting statements. (1) Bush makes a private fact-claim: "I hate broccoli!" is a statement of a private fact, and if he is reporting accurately, it stands as a non-debatable datum. To this statement I would be foolish to reply, "No you don't. You like broccoli!" The fact-claim is true if he says it is, and that's the end of the matter; only he can report on what he is experiencing, and only he knows, finally, whether the statement is true or not.

*Facts are the raw material for thinking.*

ROBERT E. SPARKS

(2) Bush makes an evaluation involving a fallacy: "It tastes awful!" should be qualified to read "It tastes awful to me!" so that it is clear that he is not placing the bad-taste experience onto the object: Broccoli doesn't taste; we taste. Our taste-buds do the tasting, not the broccoli. All such qualities (such as beauty, sounds, tastes, smells) should properly be located within the experiencing self, not in the real world.

(3) Bush makes a simple fact-claim—"I'm president now"—to which there can be little argument since it can be easily verified. And (4) he makes a soft prediction that includes an intended commitment: "I'll never eat broccoli again!" Predictions are neither fact-claims nor evaluations of events. A prediction is a statement of a personal expectation, or a statement of a hoped-for goal toward which one will devote some effort to achieving, or a political statement to affect the actions of others toward a goal. In this case, Bush's statement is probably of the second kind: he is telling us that he intends to devote some considerable energy and effort toward not ever eating the green stuff again.

*You will never succeed in getting at the truth if you think you know, ahead of time, what the truth ought to be.*

MARCHETTE CHUTE

**6 . . . Time had a beginning at the big bang. Many people do not like the idea that time has a beginning, probably because it smacks of divine intervention.**

This idea of time is to be found in Stephen Hawking's best-selling book *A Brief History of Time* (Bantam Books, 1988, page 46). And yes, he is right that a lot of people do not like the idea that time has a beginning, but not for the reason he gives. Rather it is because Hawking makes the assumption that time is real and, like any real object, could have a beginning and an end. It is seriously to be doubted that time is real, even though this is a common assumption made by physicists and cosmologists.

In the first place, how could one write a "brief history of time"? We can only write a history of something that has endured, that is, has had a continued existence *in time.* That is what the word "history" means, does it not? There could be a history of time only if it endured in time, which also had endured in another time, which had endured in still another time, and so on, ad infinitum. So unless physicists want to plead some special definition, the notion of time having a beginning and an end leads to an absurd concept of time. Almost certainly, time is an experience, not a real thing (see pp. 267-270).

*The Real is one though sages speak of it in many ways.*

**Rig-Veda** 1.164.46

Yet many modern-day physicists treat their formulas as though they were real, just as many mathematicians tend to think of numbers as real. The fundamental reason for this fallacy is because virtually all the objects of physics (atoms, molecules, organisms, rocks, trees, planets, galaxies, black holes, pulsars, and so on) involve motion; and it takes time for things to move. Furthermore, things always move in space. It follows that the formulae and equations employed by physicists to describe moving entities therefore *assume* both space and time; motion makes no sense, and could not be measured, without such an assumption. But because the assumption is necessary to make our equations work, it does not follow that space and time are real, though the assumption is a natural one. Physicists commonly speak of the "space-time continuum" as though "it" is a real thing, but this involves another fallacy: treating time as if it were space, when, in fact, they are separate and distinct entities that must not be confused; that is, we must be critically on guard not to spatialize time or temporalize space. It just may be that the foundations of modern physical theory are laid on a conceptual fallacy which, someday, will have to be reviewed and reevaluated.

*In his ignorance of the whole truth, each person maintains his own arrogant point of view.*

**THE BUDDHA**

**7   The swastika is the hated symbol of Nazi horror.**

Well, yes and no. In the minds of millions the swastika is a symbol of Hitler, the Nazis, the Holocaust, the Axis during World War II; and it certainly is hated. But it is important to remind ourselves of a semantic fact: symbols have no meaning. Symbols are meaning-*less.* Symbols, that is, don't *have* meaning; they are *given* meaning. They are given meaning by us meaners; and the semanticists are forever reminding us that we humans can make anything stand for anything. Meaning is not a property of symbols, but is an experience located in the minds of us meaners.

It is an historical fact that Hitler adopted the swastika to stand for the Third

Reich, and because of his actions this symbol has come to mean monstrous and terrible things. But it is also an historical fact that the swastika has been for more than three thousand years a symbol of good fortune and divine favor in Indian religion, and for the Jains it has long meant salvation. It is the central symbol on the Jain flag. Thus the swastika, like all symbols, can be given different meanings; and the meanings of all symbols, including words, must be determined from the living contexts in which they are used.

### 8 "Who discovered America—Columbus or the Vikings? Watch TLC Monday night at 8:00—on THE LEARNING CHANNEL."

"Columbus discovered America," so the claim goes. Besides the problem of defining "America," the key word that renders such a statement problematical is "discover." What does it mean to discover? Do you go to the refrigerator and "discover" that someone has finished off the apple pie? This "discovery" gave you a bit of new information which you did not have before; so yes, it was a discovery. Did Admiral Peary "discover" the North Pole when he reached it in 1909? Geographers had known that a North Pole must exist ever since theorists figured out that the Earth is round and rotates on an axis; Peary was the first human being to make the journey to where the real pole was calculated to be, find it, and plant a flag there; so in a precise sense we can say "Peary discovered the North Pole."

Let us define the word: "To discover" means "to be the first to find, to learn of, or to observe." Only individuals discover, though several individuals can "discover" at about the same time. So "to discover" means to come across something that the discovering individual did not previously know. Did Columbus and his crew "discover" a new land-mass with people living there? Yes, of course. It was something new for them; and since Columbus was, in his mind, making the voyage to a new world on behalf of Spain (a big idea) and "European civilization" (an even bigger idea), then he made his "discovery" on their behalf and returned home to share his new knowledge of this previously (to them) unknown land and people. To Europeans it was meaningful and valuable new knowledge; and the "discovery" is a part of the European experience.

To the native peoples of this new land-mass, to find that there were people living across the sea to the east was also a discovery—a new item of knowledge they did not previously possess. The claim to some discovery always requires the stipulation of the perspective from which the discovery is made. The intrepid Henry M. Stanley traipsed across Africa to find the great missionary doctor, David Livingstone, and announced to the world back home that he had "discovered" him; but Livingstone announced that he was not lost and that he had very mixed feelings about his being "discovered." Likewise, the "native Americans" could inform Columbus that they were not lost. Columbus could rightly claim that he had "discovered" them for himself and European Christendom, and if Columbus wanted to claim that that was all that really mattered, the Indians could well retort, "I'm glad you 'discovered' us since that is what you set out to do. Now go home and leave us alone!" Later generations of native Americans would have evaluated this "discovery" event quite differently since Columbus brought bigotry, slavery, disease, and death, as well as pigs,

*It is wrong always, everywhere, and for everyone to believe upon insufficient evidence.*

**W. K. CLIFFORD**
***(19th century mathematician)***

*The greatest single achievement of science in this most scientifically productive of centuries is the discovery that we are profoundly ignorant; we know very little about nature and understand even less. . . .*

**LEWIS THOMAS**

citrus fruit, and sugarcane; that such a man could be dubbed a hero would have baffled them.

Because of his destructive impact many today still want to deny Columbus the honor of having discovered the New World; to praise him for it is felt to be insulting. The honor, they feel, should go to Leif Erickson and his Vikings or to Huishin the Chinese Buddhist monk blown off course in the fifth century A.D., or to someone else. Some of the feeling that drives this denial is from individuals and groups who do not share the Euro-centric perspective in which Columbus is essentially a hero, or who feel that this perspective is denigrating to other points of view, which are not then given full value.

Our conclusion must be that the general claim "Columbus discovered America" is really a political statement and not the precise statement of an historian. It betrays a Euro-centric bias which, today, is no more acceptable than any other bias, such as the bias of a WASP, white supremacist, anti-feminist, anti-Catholic, anti-Muslim, anti-Semite, or whatever. If the statement were to read "Columbus discovered some new islands and their native inhabitants, none of which were previously known to Europeans," then most of the confusion could be avoided. But since the claim seems to carry with it the implication that Columbus discovered a gigantic land-mass whose existence had never been known to anybody important, then the statement is offensive and should have no status as a description of an historical event.

> At the heart of science is an essential tension between two seemingly contradictory attitudes—an openness to new ideas, no matter how bizarre or counterintuitive they may be, and the most ruthless skeptical scrutiny of all ideas, old and new. This is how deep truths are winnowed from deep nonsense. . . .
> CARL SAGAN

## PRELIMINARY STEPS TO CRITICAL ANALYSIS

Making one's way into philosophic analysis is a bit like altering one's consciousness (Eastern style): take three deep breaths, relax, and let the mind do its work. To move into a critical mode of consciousness, it helps to follow a sequence of four steps.

> The essence of Zen is to learn to do just one thing at a time.
> WILLIAM W. BLAKE

1.   First, *stop-the-world.* Our minds are continually flooded with meaning-events—too many events, too much meaning. Ongoing conversations are difficult to slow down; politicians and preachers and talkshows on TV just roll on; any good discussion will cover too many meaning-events to be focused on and carefully analyzed.

So, we must stop-the-world. The real world will not slow down for us. In fact, it tries to race onward, demanding that we keep up and that we *not* pause to really see what is going on. But each of us can slow things down inwardly and say, "I want to see. And *I will* the world to stop *until I see.*"

2.   Next, decide *what* and *how.* Having stopped-the-world, we can then decide *what* meaning-events we want to focus on, and *how* to deal with them. Whether we are analyzing written material, live conversations, TV news reports, commercials, or political speeches, specific ideas will come to our attention and strike us as being in serious need of critical work.

3.   Then *zero in on an idea.* The proverbial definition of a scientist as the specialist "who knows more and more about less and less" suggests also the stance of the critical analyst. One's subject matter is delimited by gazing long

and intently at specific ideas; then we zero in on an idea, give it full attention, and, by living with it for a time, begin to see the hidden meanings involved in the idea. Given the chance, the deeper intuitive levels of our minds can become allies in the analytic process.

4. *Think about it.* Having focused on an idea, critical analysis begins by thinking about it. To get our thinking processes started, one of the starter-games we can play on ourselves (or others) is to ask questions about the idea. Is the idea ambiguous? Does it need a context to be made intelligible? Do words need defining? Does the idea involve fact-claims? Does it make value judgments? How can I decide if it is true? Whether true or not, is it valid? And so on. There is no end to the questions that can be asked about even the simplest meaning-event.

## A Special Kind of Listening

A critical thinker engages in a special kind of listening. In most of our idea exchanges, we listen to what others say, but a philosopher listens not only to what you say but even more to the implicit thought processes that got you there.

You may say, "I have concluded that . . ." and the philosopher will respond, "Fine. Tell me how you arrived at your conclusion."

You may say, "In my opinion . . ." and the philosopher will listen to your opinion and then ask, "How did you arrive at your opinion?"

You may say, "I believe . . ." and the philosopher will say, "I'm pleased that you believe that. How did you arrive at that belief?"

Someone may tell you, "I think thus-and-so is morally wrong," and as a philosopher you will say, "I understand what you're saying. Now tell me how you arrived at that evaluation."

Someone may retort, "I disagree with you." As a philosopher you will say, "Thank you. Now tell me about the sequence of thoughts that led you to that disagreement. Do that, and we can talk."

*I never saw an instance of one of two disputants convincing the other by argument. I have seen many, on their getting warm, becoming rude, and shooting one another.*

**Thomas Jefferson**

## Reflections

1 According to this chapter, the role of philosophy in our lives is to deal with meaning. How many different kinds of meaning can you list? As for "the meaning of life," would you still define the phrase about the same way you did after reflecting on chapter 1-1?

2 By way of summary, recast in your own thoughts what is intended by *analysis* and *synthesis*. How do we go about analysis? How do we go about synthesis? What are the goals in each case?

3 Most of the time we plunge spontaneously into our mental tasks, so this chapter suggests some preliminary steps to doing philosophy. In your case, would they work? What do you think of the idea that we must "stop-the-world" before we can zero in on ideas because the world—like a speeded-up movie film—is buzzing too rapidly for us to deal with the

(*Continued on p. 60*)

# PLATO

## *The First Educator*

His name was Aristocles, and he was born in Athens on the seventh of Thargelion in the first year of the LXXXVIII Olympiad—May 29, 427 B.C. His father, Ariston, traced his lineage to Codrus, the last king of Athens, and his mother, Perictione, traced hers to Solon, Athen's greatest lawgiver. His was an illustrious heritage, and he moved with statesmen, playwrights, artists, and philosophers all his life.

We call him Plato because his coach so nicknamed him, from the Greek word *platon,* meaning "broad-shouldered"; he excelled in sports and wrestled in the Isthmian games at Corinth. Multitalented, he distinguished himself in every field. He fought in three battles during the Peloponnesian War and was decorated for bravery.

At twenty-one, Plato was caught up by the charismatic brilliance of Socrates and dedicated himself to philosophy, which he called "a precious delight"; and though he was to be Socrates's pupil for only eight years, their association would set the course of Western thought for the next two thousand years.

Socrates didn't operate in a school with buildings and a campus. He conducted his teachings entirely in the agora, the open marketplace of Athens, where everyone gathered to exchange goods, carry on their political life, have their clothes made and sandals fixed in the cobbler's shop on the Street of the Leather-Workers, bid for furniture and order inscribed tablets and statuettes from stone-carvers on the Street of the Marble-Workers, carry on religious rites as around the Altar to the Twelve Gods, and do business at the tables of the money-changers. The whole life of Athens was lived here in the agora. Above all, the Athenians loved to talk, and they wandered among the covered colonnades, talking and listening to teachers, political orators, preachers of mystery cults, poets, and playwrights.

Plato would have stayed close to his teacher during the entire time he was in Athens as a student. He probably lived and spent his nights in private homes near the agora. He would have taken his meals and passed most of his days in the company of fellow students, watching and listening to Socrates, exchanging with bystanders—talking and examining ideas. Plato was born, lived most of his long life, and died within the immediate environs of the Acropolis in Athens.

When Athens was finally garrisoned by the Spartans in 404 B.C., Plato—already horrified at the inhumanity of war, the tyranny of the oligarchs, and the bestiality of mobs—saw the Athenians further degraded by their own ruthlessness and greed. He wrote: "Whereas at first, I had been enthusiastic about a political career, now all that I could do is watch, helplessly, this chaotic world about me." This experience of the Absurd turned personal when, at twenty-nine, he witnessed the trial and execution of his teacher. Socrates was convicted on trumped-up charges of impiety and corrupting youth and was put to death with a cup of poison hemlock. "This is the end of our comrade," Plato later wrote, "a man, as we would say, of all then living we had ever met, the noblest and the wisest and the most just."

Plato seems to have made a serious attempt to put the Athenian nightmare behind him. He traveled for a dozen years, visited Italy and Sicily—where he absorbed Pythagorean metaphysics—possibly sailed to Cyrene and Egypt, and returned home to Athens about 388 B.C. He was forty. Within the year he established the school that would occupy him the rest of this life: the Academy, the first institution of higher learning in the Western world. (The Academy endured for more than nine hundred years. In the year A.D. 529 it was closed by the Byzantine emperor Justinian because, in his eyes, it was a stronghold of paganism.)

At the age of sixty Plato was invited back to Syracuse to educate the new king, Dionysius II. He also hoped to field-test the theories of social psychology he had described in *The Republic*. But the young king proved ineducable, and political intrigues drove the philosopher back to Athens.

After another failed mission to Syracuse when he was sixty-seven, Plato attended the Olympic games in July, then came home to Athens to settle for the rest of his life, teaching and writing. His greatest works, in which he used Socrates as his literary hero, were written before he was forty; they include *The Apology, Crito,* and *The Republic.* During this last period he wrote *Parmenides, Theaetetus,* the *Laws,* and others. He was by this time universally admired and honored.

On his eightieth birthday one of his pupils invited the master to a wedding feast. He attended, and the tale is told that he danced at the party, into the night. Eventually he took leave of his students and withdrew to rest. He died in his sleep. According to tradition, it was the first year of the CVIII Olympiad—347 B.C.

◆

Plato's life is marked by two supreme achievements: the establishment of the Academy and the immortalizing of Socrates in writing. Both have profoundly influenced the Western world.

The Academy was located on several acres of public park on the outskirts of Athens, about a mile northwest of the Dipylon Gate. The site contained olive trees, statues, and temples named for the legendary Greek hero Academus—hence its name. Also on the grounds were lecture halls, classrooms, and a shrine of learning—a sort of chapel, built by Plato himself, dedicated to the worship of the Muses, those nine daughters of Zeus who were the inspiring spirits of all the arts and sciences. Adjacent to the grounds was a large sports gymnasium. The land was purchased for Plato by his friends.

Here Plato gathered about him a circle of serious students and organized them into a disciplined educational community. Young men and women came from all parts of the Greek world and dedicated themselves to a demanding program of study that included literature, history, music, mathematics and geometry, and philosophy. They were to be educated, not trained. Through intellectual and moral development they were to become qualified leaders of the state. They lived close by, off campus. They paid no fees, but their parents gave

*Until philosophers are kings, or the kings and princes of this world have the spirit and power of philosophy, and political greatness and wisdom meet in one . . . cities will never have rest from their evils—no, nor the human race.*

ON PLATO: *Plato is philosophy, and philosophy Plato.*
RALPH WALDO EMERSON

ON PLATO: *The safest general characterization of the European philosophical tradition is that it consists of a series of footnotes to Plato.*
ALFRED NORTH WHITEHEAD

*Democracy—a charming form of government, full of variety and disorder, and dispensing a sort of equality to equals and unequals alike.*

*Let us suppose that in the mind of each man there is an aviary of all sorts of birds . . . [These] birds are kinds of knowledge, and when we were children, this receptacle was empty; whenever a man has gotten and detained in the enclosure a kind of knowledge, he may be said to have discovered the thing which is the subject of this knowledge: this is what it means to know.*

*Behold! human beings living in an underground den . . . Like ourselves . . . they see only their own shadows, or the shadows of one another, which the fire throws on the opposite wall of the cave.*

generous gifts so that, after a few years, the school was heavily endowed. The students were Hellas's finest youth, and they stayed on for years, or even a lifetime, engaged in rigorous study and research.

Today the search for Plato's Academy is disappointing. One can follow the Panathenaic Way down from the Propylaea of the Acropolis northward past the Stoa of Attalos for less than a kilometer. Then the way is blocked by a swath of railroad tracks and the fume-filled streets of modern Athens. Where the Academy once stood there is only an open field of weeds dotted with yellow daisies and patches of blood-red paparumas, a few marble drums, friezes, and late Roman sarcophagi. The site awaits excavation to bring to light whatever secrets are to be found about the institution that was the glory of Hellas.

◆

Plato had a fiercely clear vision of what he wanted to do: educate young men and women to seek the truth, with the hope that they will be qualified to assume positions of leadership in the world where they can put that truth to work.

By the time Plato started his school, he had already witnessed a lifetime of tragedy. Human beings, he observed, have an unfortunate tendency to see everything through the narrow slits of their defensive armor. We operate from a reduced point of view, while claiming little less than omniscience. Out of irrationality, or on the basis of false or inadequate information, or because of myths and fallacies, we draw lines of separation, erect fortresses, and go to war.

While lies and limited information can alienate people, a clear understanding of universal truth would bring men together. Plato believed that truth—if it *is* truth—must be universal. There can be but one truth—or one set of truths—for all men. It follows that if men understand things as they really are—that is, if they possess the truth—then they could

no longer divide themselves into parochial encampments, and, out of ignorance and arrogance, so bitterly fight with one another, with words and/or swords.

Over the entrance to the Academy Plato had inscribed the words *MEDEIS AGEOMETRETOS EISITO*, "Let no one without geometry enter here." This inscription implies more than its literal meaning. Geometry (which includes mathematics) is *the* universal science. It is Plato's metaphor for the search for universal truth.

Thus, Plato is the founder of rational philosophy, and philosophy, Plato would say, is the art and science of developing universal ideas.

What are universal ideas?

An idea is an abstract concept manufactured by the mind to enable it to handle a large number of particular observations. For instance, my experience of one lonely meadowlark singing from a fencepost is a single direct perception; but my notion of bird (that is, bird-in-the-abstract, "birdness"—what all birds have in common) is an idea—a universal idea. The first is my *perception* of a real object (meadowlark); the latter is my *conception* of an idea (bird).

How do we develop universal ideas?

Suppose I have actually seen only six crows and ten turkeys. I will indeed have an idea of bird (that will include only whatever characteristics crows and turkeys have in common); but my ideas can't be very accurate (or very useful) because I haven't experienced enough birds. It's a beginning, but it's too limited.

Now, say that I add to my repertoire a hundred finches, a thousand gulls, and a pair of pelicans. Having experienced *more* birds, I have a *more accurate* idea of bird. Suppose that I have actually seen millions of birds of countless species during my lifetime. My idea of bird will be more inclusive, more accurate, more universal—and more useful.

In daily life, our misuse of ideas is

a calamity. What happens is this. Athenians have seen only seagulls and terns; still, they will tell you that they have a clear idea of bird. Alexandrians have seen vultures, kites, and ibises; they too have a clear notion of bird, so they say. Latins from Italy have just as clear an idea of bird, too, for they have seen finches, sparrows, and sanderlings. Each has a clear notion of bird. But what is likely to happen when Athenians, Alexandrians, and Latins get together to discuss birds? They will all have different *ideas* of what bird is, and, since they're only human—and if they don't take time out to clarify and define their ideas—they will soon be arguing and fighting because each knows that the others' bird-idea is wrong.

Going to battle over something as trivial as our different ideas of bird seems silly. But what about our (similarly incomplete) ideas of justice, virtue, morality, decency, right, wrong, sin, evil, pleasure, happiness, loyalty, selfishness, pride, human nature—and countless other ideas, including Faith, Hope, and Love . . . and Goodness, Truth, and Beauty? Plato observed that we all seem to be possessed by a diabolical drive to fight over our differences before trying to discover the root and cause of those differences.

Plato is convinced that men will stop fighting only when they understand the truth about things. This is the task of philosophy and the goal of education. To philosophize is to exchange and refine ideas by talking about them—through dialogue. If Athenians and Spartans could have talked over their ideas of honor and justice, perhaps they would never have had to fight over them.

"Until philosophers are kings, or the kings and princes of this world have the spirit and power of philosophy . . . cities will never rest from their evils—no, nor the human race. . . ."

*The feeling of wonder is the touchstone of the philosopher, and all philosophy has its origins in wonder.*

*Astronomy compels the soul to look upward and leads us from this world to another.*

*Our object in the construction of the state is the greatest happiness of the whole, and not that of any one class.*

*It is a human being's goal to grow into the exact likeness of a God.*

meaning-events taking place around us? How would you stop *your* world to deal with it meaning-fully?

4    There is an essential difference in the psychology of learning between adversary dialogue and supportive dialogue. What is the goal of adversary dialogue? Of supportive dialogue? Do these two modes of operation make good clear sense to you? Could you alternate from one to the other, depending upon the requirements of the situation?

5    General philosophic analysis is a very practical kind of activity; so before the mood and method fade away, practice this kind of analysis in the first appropriate conversations that present themselves. Remembering the preliminary steps, practice until you acquire a feel for it and it begins to work for you.

1
4

## AND HE WANTS TO UNDERSTAND IT

The goal of synoptic philosophy is what the Greek words imply: *sun-optikos,* "seeing (everything) together," and *philein-sophia,* "to love wisdom." Put these root-words together and the message comes out clear: synoptic philosophy is the love of the wisdom that comes from achieving a coherent picture of everything seen together—a vision of the whole of life.

"A vision of the whole of life"—! Could any human undertaking be grander, or more grandiose? William Halverson writes that "this attempt stands without rival as the most audacious enterprise in which the mind of man has ever engaged. Just reflect for a moment: Here is man, surrounded by the vastness of a universe in which he is only a tiny and perhaps insignificant part—and he wants to *understand it. . . .*"

We want to understand it, of course, because we must. Being what we are, it isn't a matter of choice. If we have eyes to see, then we must see; if we have ears, then we must hear. There are at least three reasons for this necessity, and all are ontological.

First, seeing life holistically is a matter of survival. Imagine some animal at home in its environmental niche with all the normal, routine life-and-death events going on around it. The more it can perceive of these events, and *the more accurately it can perceive them,* then the better it can adjust. Developing a realistic sense of priorities—to be able to distinguish between significant and insignificant events, between the dangerous and the benign—means survival. This is just as true for abstract man as for the wild fox and the wallaby. Investing our energies in consequential events rather than trivialities requires a wisdom born of perspective.

*Learning is not the* accumulation *of scraps of knowledge. It is a* growth, *where every act of knowledge develops the learner. . . .*

EDMUND HUSSERL

*He who knows does not speak; He who speaks does not know.*

TAO TEH CHING

*When a speculative philosopher believes he has comprehended the world once and for all in his system, he is deceiving himself; he has merely comprehended himself and then naively projected that view upon the world.*

C.G. JUNG

But man has a need that (we think) goes beyond the deer and the dolphin: the need for meaning. For man a meaning-less existence is a contradiction. Intuitively we have known that the well-lived life—the meaning-full life—results from what we humans call wisdom. By definition wisdom *is* the understanding of life and how to live it; and for as long as men have sought wisdom it has been apparent that wisdom is correlated to our capacity to *perceive more* and *understand more*.

Lastly, this drive to create a personal universe has still deeper origins. Each of us harbors within a pressure to achieve psychological wholeness, and our passion for wholeness in knowledge is a part of this drive. Unity of personality and unity of knowledge are two aspects of the same goal. What do we feel if we see on a table a jigsaw puzzle half finished or a painting left undone? We assume—we *know*—that any enterprise, once begun, ought to be completed. An unfinished story nags at us. An unfinished letter haunts us. An unfinished sentence, left dangling in mid-air, leaves us waiting, and when

## LIFE ON A PICTURE-PUZZLE

Think of life as a jigsaw puzzle with an enormous number of pieces, and think of synoptic philosophy as our attempt to fit the puzzle together. This puzzle didn't come to us sealed in a cardboard box with an illustration on the cover, so we really don't know what the picture on the puzzle will turn out to be.

To be sure, we have been told what the picture is. But this is the problem. So many people have told us, on the best authority, what picture is *really* on the puzzle, and they describe different pictures. We must draw the logical conclusion that they, too, have not yet attained a glimpse of the whole picture.

Our ultimate goal is clear: to fit *all* the pieces together so we can attain a clear look at the picture. But it's an incredibly complex puzzle, and we may never succeed in getting the whole picture pieced together. Attempts thus far have failed, though many have been able to assemble scattered clusters. You and I may succeed in filling a few random spaces or joining together a small group of pieces here and there. Still, for all of us, at this point in the progress of human understanding, the total picture is diffuse, with light and dark shades that don't yet make sense. The task requires endless patience. If, in the meantime, we can enjoy just working the puzzle, that might be a sufficiently rewarding compromise.

So, the goal of synoptic philosophy is to see the picture on the puzzle—the whole picture, nothing less—and to see it clearly, unmistakably, and realistically.

The metaphor of the picture-puzzle helps to clarify several characteristics of synoptic philosophy.

The first, of course, is that the goal of synoptic synthesis is to see the whole picture. It will not settle for a fragmented view of scattered designs; nor will it allow itself to be seduced into believing that any mere fragment is really the whole picture. The mandate of synoptic philosophy is to keep working with the jigsaw pieces until the picture is seen and the puzzle is resolved.

The philosopher of history Arnold Toynbee has written that, as of the latter part of the twentieth century, we are collectively in transition to a new worldview in which our dominant perception will be that of being meaningful parts of a larger universe. These new ties contrast sharply with the old world we are now leaving, in which the dominant sense of consciousness was for each of us to believe we were complete, self-contained universes within ourselves.

To use the puzzle metaphor, most of us have heretofore taken up residence on a single piece of the jigsaw puzzle. We lived out our lifetimes on this small picture plot; we put down roots and became intimately familiar with the design of one small bit of reality. Eventually we came to believe that our cardboard square was the most important piece in all the puzzle; the rest of the vast scene was to be judged from the perspective of our own mini-puzzle. The final illusion followed close behind: we convinced ourselves that our single puzzle-piece was in fact the whole of reality—the total picture.

To escape this predicament, synoptic philosophy encourages each of us to wander over the puzzle, visiting neighboring parts and trying to see how the pieces of the puzzle all fit together. It urges us to travel from square to square

*One thing, at least, seems clear: the quest for "the total picture," the struggle to discern the unity that we instinctively believe must somehow lie behind the apparent inconsistencies of our little fragments of knowledge . . . will go on, with or without the cooperation of professional philosophers. It may turn out that those philosophers who of late have found their profession somewhat sterile and unchallenging will find a renewed interest in their work if the quest for unity comes once again to be accepted as the* raison d'être *of the philosophical enterprise.*

**WILLIAM HALVERSON**

*Knowledge of the world demands more than just seeing the world. One must know what to look for in foreign countries.*

**IMMANUEL KANT**

until it becomes clear that no single part is in fact the whole. Only by wandering over the puzzling terrain restlessly and observantly—like itinerant flat-landers—can we arrive at an honest conclusion as to what the whole of reality is like.

The way in which philosophic analysis and philosophic synthesis work together is also implicit in the picture-puzzle analogy.

Although a synoptist wants to stand back and ponder the whole picture, he finds that he must spend much of his time close-up working with singular pieces of the puzzle—turning them, scrutinizing them, studying them. Philosophic analysis works with each microscopic area of the giant puzzle until it is clearly understood.

Analysis generally precedes synthesis. We must first make sure each piece really belongs in the puzzle. (Ever work on a jigsaw puzzle where someone had mixed in pieces from another puzzle?) The analyst familiarizes himself with each fragment so that, at some later time, he stands a good chance of recognizing where it fits in.

Leaving aside the puzzle analogy, what we find is that "the bugs" must be worked out of so many of our ideas before we can confidently put them to use. What is the point in wasting time trying to synthesize an idea into our philosophy of life if in fact it is false, or involves a fallacy, or is a trivial value judgment?

These are factual matters, they are what-is-really-the-case kinds of problems. Factual questions usually requiring analytical assistance are: Does God exist? How could we know? Is there personal immortality? What makes religious beliefs "right" or "wrong"? How can subjective selves "know" the objects/events of the real world? In terms of freedom and determinism, should I be held personally responsible for everything I do?

Equally confusing, and in need of analysis, are value-questions: Can we ever justify the deliberate killing of another human being (as in self-defense, or when an individual goes berserk; in euthanasia or capital punishment; in war, in a "wrong" war, in a revolution against oppression)? Can we justify the deliberate killing of animals (a species nearing extinction, our pets, dolphins, whales)? Can we justify abortion, the nonpayment of taxes, disobeying unjust laws or disobeying just laws under special circumstances? Or, more broadly, what makes any action "right" or "wrong"?

Philosophic analysis becomes especially useful in our very personal dilemmas. Was I justified in lying to someone who trusts me? Should I feel guilty about having sex (or enjoying sex) at the "wrong" time and place? (And exactly what makes the time and place "wrong"?) Is cheating on exams ever justified (not rationalizable, but justifiable)? If I do not love someone whom I "should" love—a child, a husband or wife, a parent—am I a "bad" person (or ungrateful, or neurotic, or immoral)?

Only after analysis has been performed on such questions—all of which hide a multitude of complexities—can synoptic philosophy go to work fitting the pieces into the whole puzzle.

The history of philosophy is the record of men and women who were caught up in just such problems. Many of them invested life/times in the same

*My young men shall never work. Men who work cannot dream, and wisdom comes in dreams. . . .*

SMOHALLA (INDIAN PROPHET)

*From the cowardice that shrinks from new truth, From the laziness that is content with half-truths, From the arrogance that thinks it knows all truths, O God of Truth, deliver us.*

ANCIENT PRAYER

questions we face today. After all, they shared "the cruel contradictions and bitter ironies" of the human condition, and their guidance can be of enormous help to us.

But the philosophers of the past can't do our work for us. They moved within the possible world-views of their times. Given the data-limitations and the conceptual schemes within which they had to think, they phrased questions and found answers as best they could; and we honor their accomplishments when we draw upon their work.

By contrast, we have at our service vast quantities of empirical data and pragmatic concepts not available to those of past ages. Our lives overflow with an abundance of knowledge that would have made Aristotle and Bacon and Spinoza ecstatic, and we are self-defeating philistines if we take this wealth of knowledge for granted.

You and I face the all-too-human temptation to become dependent upon thinkers of the past for answers to our philosophic inquiries, and with scarcely half an effort we can rationalize our dependence: these were great intellects, after all; they had special gifts; they had leisure time to reflect upon such problems—and so on. We can easily kid ourselves into believing that the great problems of life have long been solved.

Recall Wittgenstein's warning that when we repeat another's thought it indicates a failure to think it for ourselves, and that dependence on the think-

*Continuel Lumière Mobile, 1963* by Julio Le Parc

ing of others "at best hinders independent thought, and at most, prevents it. And a thought which is not independent is a thought only half understood. . . ."

Synoptic philosophy is a *now* philosophy. We live in the present, not in the past. It is the meaning of *our* lives we must live, not the meaning of the great lives of the past, and not "the Meaning of Life" as others believed they saw it. History serves us; we are not here to serve history. We must make use of the best facts and ideas available to us *now* in assembling our own jigsaw puzzles.

By and large, the pensive minds of the past were wise. They would be content to have us use their ideas when we can and let us lay them to rest, appreciatively, when they are no longer serviceable.

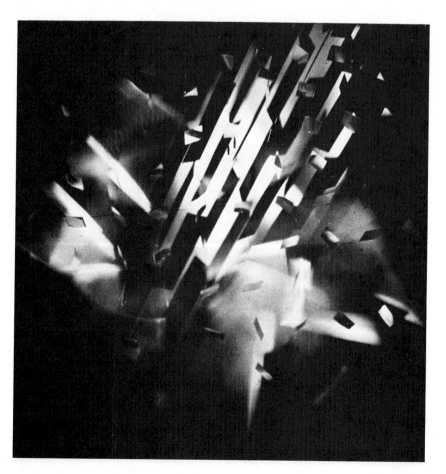

## THE ANNIHILATION OF BOUNDARIES

*Something forever exceeds, escapes from statement, withdraws from definition, must be glimpsed and felt, not told. No one knows this like your genuine professor of philosophy. For what glimmers and twinkles like a bird's wing in the sunshine it is his business to snatch and fix. . . .*

**WILLIAM JAMES**

*Although Omar Khayyam may have claimed that the results of his studies were that he "evermore came out by the same door as in I went," he neglected to notice that he was facing a different direction when he came out.*

**RONALD HUNTINGTON**

*Perhaps the major challenge to philosophy in the last decades of the twentieth century is whether it can face the future imaginatively and creatively or whether it will simply be content with a status as a second-order discipline, able only to analyze and evaluate the concepts and ideas of other disciplines.*

**RICHARD DOSS**

Since at least the time of Aristotle, synoptic philosophy has been the ultimate interdisciplinary enterprise. When Aristotle and his peripatetic students were walking and talking along the paths of the Lyceum, subject-matter specialization had not yet begun, and knowledge was not yet "organized apart" into countless categories—biology, psychology, physics, and so on. Aristotle still looked with awe and wonder upon all human knowledge. His adventuresome mind was still free, not yet trained to function along carefully defined boundary-lines, not yet cluttered with classification systems that fragment human understanding into competing disciplines.

It has been said that Aristotle was the last Western thinker that could actually know all that there was to be known. Before his time there was not much to know, and after him there was far too much. Specialization became inevitable.

But it is important to realize that *life* is *not* specialized. Life is "interdisciplinary." Vocationally we may be electronics engineers, or neurosurgeons, or accountants, but when not practicing our profession we "revert" to the human condition and find ourselves thinking like generalists again.

Synoptic philosophy is a reflection of life. We *are,* each and every one of us, sociology and anthropology and history and geography. We *are* physics (put your finger into a light socket and feel ). We *are* astrophysics and cosmology (we feel silvery-moon sentiments by night and get sunburns by day). We *are* biology and biochemistry and genetics (unless the stork story is true, after all). We *are* psychology and physiology and psychophysiology (ever guzzle a martini or suffer a brain concussion?) We *are* all these things, and there is *nothing* in human knowledge that we *are not.* So when we engage in synoptic thinking we are returning to life. Life cannot specialize. It remains just what it was before the human mind fragmented it: totalic, whole.

Isn't the attempt to attain a vision of the whole of life beyond the capacity of finite human minds?

The answer is that the synoptist never tries "to know everything." He makes no attempt to memorize the reams of hard data that have accumulated in the specialized fields. Happily, it is not uncommon to become excited about a field and find oneself drawn in deeper than first intended. Still, the synoptist remains a layman when it comes to specialized details, and he does not let himself forget this fact.

The task of the synoptist is to keep himself informed on the latest *conclusions, general principles, hypotheses, models,* and *theories* that emerge from the work of the field specialists. He is not himself a field specialist, and he is not in competition with them since he is not a knowledge-gatherer in the sense they are. He makes use of the data they labor to discover; hence he is always in their debt. He is also at their mercy, of course; and he hopes that he turns to the right specialists for information. If he listens to wrong sources and receives wrong answers, then, in effect, he ends up with jigsaw pieces that don't belong in the puzzle; and he may waste considerable time trying to fit in pieces that won't fit.

This question—Can the human mind attain "the holistic vision"?—presupposes a degree of faith. At present the complexity of "all that is" boggles our minds; total comprehension seems like a fuzzy dream. However, the holistic vision is probably not an unrealistic goal *for the human race.* Not that we have a choice. Since this drive is ontological, we will continue to work for it both individually and collectively because we cannot do otherwise. In our own short life/times the most we can hope for is partial success. But even a little progress, at the personal level, proves immensely rewarding.

At present history is on the side of optimism. The story of man's attempt to gather a fund of empirical knowledge and to discover the truth about himself and his world has, in the longer-range perspective of history, just begun; and human understanding is advancing so rapidly on all fronts that any oddsmaker would advise placing our bets on the continued capacity of the human mind to understand, in principle, the fundamental nature of man and his universe. True, this judgment could be wrong. Gray matter may have unsuspected limits, and the real world could turn out to be too intricate to be reduced to human abstractions. Still, *understanding* requires *general principles,* not details. (The details can be handled by our computers so that we can concentrate on understanding.) According to present evidence the human capacity for conceptualization is quite adequate to the task.

## How to Do Synoptic Philosophy

How does one go about "doing" synoptic philosophy?

One good way to begin is to place yourself in the center of what we will call the "synoptic wheel" (note the diagram on p. 69). In your imagination, look outward in all directions from that center. Around the rim of the wheel are all the knowledge-gathering disciplines known to man, plus various arts and skills and some philosophic specializations. This schematic is merely one way of visualizing our philosophic predicament: when we feel overwhelmed by life's stubborn questions and don't know which way to turn for help, then spin the synoptic wheel and ask the specialists to share their knowledge and insights.

Note the general areas that are represented on the wheel.

In working through a problem, a synoptist would move along a sequence of steps something like the following.

*We need people who can see straight ahead and deep into the problems. Those are the experts. But we also need peripheral vision and experts are generally not very good at providing peripheral vision.*

**Alvin Toffler**

1.  Having come across a philosophic problem (or having been run down by one), first proceed as far as possible with philosophic analysis, clarifying and drawing out all the hidden meanings that you can, dissolving the problem completely if that is possible.

Then, to the extent that time and materials permit, find out what philosophers of the past have thought about the problem. In the history of philosophy, most of the problems you and I must deal with have been pondered, time and again, from many different perspectives, and these earlier treatments can lighten our labors by enlightening our thoughts. Uniquely valuable insights are often provided by individuals who, in some special way, were bothered by, and became caught up in, a particular problem.

Once a problem is posed, it may be necessary to rephrase the question in a variety of ways before we can get it to reveal what kinds of information will help solve it. (There is *no* question that cannot be asked in many ways. The following exchange—"Does God exist?" "What do you mean by the question?" "I mean just what I said: Does God exist?"—is quickly ushered out of any philosophic discussion.) The synoptist tries to develop an intuition for asking and reasking questions from different angles until they point to the data that would illuminate them.

2.  From your vantage point in the center of the synoptic wheel, ask yourself what fields seem most likely to contain information related to your problem. Begin by just asking questions about the problem and how it might connect, one by one, to the various fields in the rim of the schematic. For instance . . .

*Question:* Does God exist? (First, ask yourself if your question is honestly intended as a genuine question. Do you really *want* an objective answer? Or do you want an "objective" answer only if it agrees with what you already "know"? Whatever the question may be, if you already know the answer *beyond any possible doubt*, then one must entertain second thoughts about its being a true philosophic question.) If it is an authentic question, then *go to psychology,* and ask questions of this kind: What do "religious experiences" seem to imply regarding the existence of a God? What about mystical experiences such as Saint Theresa's "golden arrow," and pentecostal "ecstasy," and "spirit-possession"? Can the multitude of deity-images in man's religions be understood in terms of our psychological needs?

Then *go to linguistics,* and ask: what does the word *god* refer to? Does it refer to reality or only to other words? Whence does it derive its meaning for you? for the Buddhist? for the native American Indian? What other names could you use for your God—matter, force, spirit, wind, love, power—? *Go to physics:* Are there any real objects/events that can't be explained in terms of known physical forces? Can the origins of matter be accounted for apart from the idea of a Prime Mover or Creator? *Go to history:* Is there documented evidence of past events that necessitate the hypothesis of supernatural intervention? Can we discern any sort of pattern or "dramatic plot" in human history that indicates direction, guidance, planning, or purpose?

*Go to biology:* Can life processes be explained in terms of natural biochemical events? Is there any event in DNA genetics, speciation, or evolutionary modeling that necessitates the hypothesis of a supernatural or a "vital

*Academic philosophers, ever since the time of Parmenides, have believed that the world is a unity. . . . The most fundamental of my intellectual beliefs is that this is rubbish. I think the universe is all spots and jumps, without unity, without continuity, without coherence or orderliness or any of the other properties that governesses love. . . . it consists of events, short, small and haphazard. Order, unity, and continuity are human inventions, just as truly as our catalogues and encyclopedias.*

BERTRAND RUSSELL

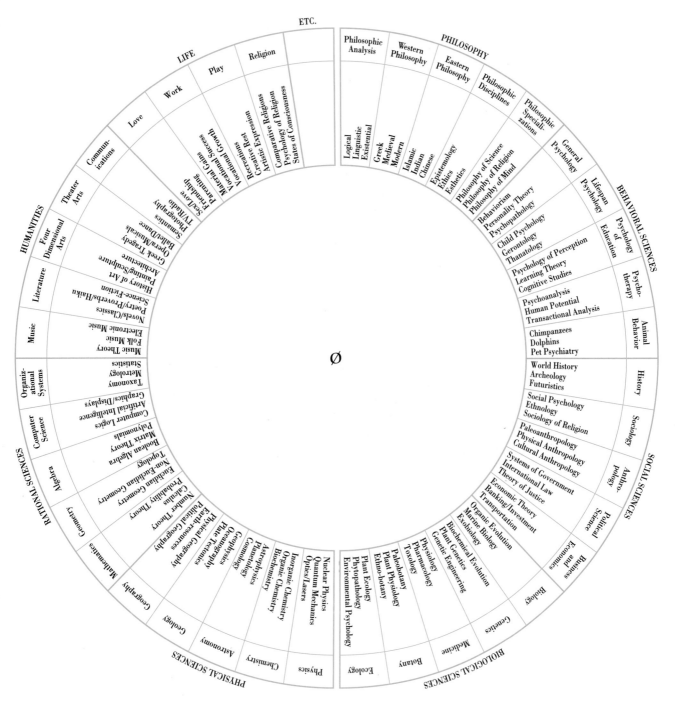

impulse"? *Go to medicine:* Do there exist well-documented cases of healings that cannot be explained by medicine or by our understanding of the human psychophysical organism? If so, how must we define the word *miracle? Go to exobiology:* Is your image of God anthropomorphic—that is, humanoid? In what form might deity appropriately manifest itself to advanced alien beings on other planets? *Go to astronomy:* What concept of deity is possible in the incomprehensibly vast universe that we know today? *Etcetera. . . .*

This is but the briefest sampling of *the kinds* of questions that would have to be asked before such a question could be answered. Without doubt the task feels formidable, but it can also be one of our most exciting adventures. To perform the synoptic task well, one must keep up with what is going on in various fields and be willing to listen to *anyone* who is in possession of helpful information.

Having made this kind of preliminary question-asking survey, the next step is to go to these promising fields and gather information. Remember that the synoptist is looking for conclusions, hypotheses, and models currently used by field specialists. As you gather materials, keep asking questions, relating the data to your central problem and cross-relating insights from the fields themselves.

3.    Next, criss-cross from field to field, drawing "interconnecting lines of illumination" as you go, stopping often to refocus new ideas on your initial problem to see whether the sort of understanding you are after is beginning to emerge.

Moving from first question to final answer is often a long journey. In fact, doing synoptic philosophy is much like starting a trip where all you know is where you are now and where you want to arrive—namely, at the best answer possible at this time. The route by which you'll get there is not at all clear, and philosophic journeys can rarely be neatly penciled on a map ahead of time. So, just set off down the road. If you come to a side road pointing to new information, turn that way. Travel till you come to new intersections of knowledge or see a sign pointing in still another direction. Do not be afraid to wander without a map. Let the journey unfold gradually, just as it wishes. The facts will lead us where we need to go.

4.    Lastly, back away from the problem you have been working on and try to see it in a larger way. Since it is so easy for us to lose perspective, stand back as often as needed and ask yourself whether the whole picture can be better seen now that you have invested considerable thought in analyzing and synthesizing the problem.

Such a view of the larger picture is not easily achieved in less than twenty minutes. Our minds will weave the silken strands into a beautiful tapestry, but they will do so in their own good time. What is important is that *we attempt* to see larger blocks of life and that *we develop the habit of trying* to think in ever larger frames as we work through the problem.

This attempt to see the full-scale picture on life's puzzle creates certain dangers about which we need to be forewarned. So, word of caution #1: Do not be forced into saying you see more of the puzzle than you really do. The temptation to see what others insist *is* the picture on the puzzle can be great; and it may require no small amount of courage on our part to say, and to continue to say: "I can't *see* that part of the puzzle yet." Or: "I know that factual information in that area is still nonexistent, and no one can be absolutely sure about it at this time. It's too soon to persuade ourselves that we can see what isn't there." We all know how difficult it is to keep on saying "I don't know" when so many people around us are positive that *they* know the answers and keep proclaiming

*Western philosophers have always gone on the assumption that fact is something cut and dried, precise, immobile, very convenient, and ready for examination. The Chinese deny this. The Chinese believe that a fact is something crawling and alive, a little furry and cool to the touch, that crawls down the back of your neck.*

LIN YUTANG

*"Everything I have taught you so far has been an aspect of not-doing," Don Juan went on. "A warrior applies not-doing to everything in the world, and yet I can't tell you more about it than what I have said today. You must let your own body discover the power and the feelings of not-doing."*

CARLOS CASTANEDA
*Journey to Ixtlan*

*We need and sometimes want to make a persistent attempt to think things through. In this, we should be grateful for any help that we can get. . . . Philosophy begins in a natural curiosity that will not be satisfied with what we already know or think we know; according to Aristotle, it begins in wonder. "Hast any philosophy in thee, shepherd?" The answer is, Yes, but it needs cultivating.*

LEWIS WHITE BECK

them to us, loudly. The gentle admonition of Confucius has a healing touch: "One can tell for oneself whether the water is warm or cold."

Word of caution #2: Considerable self-knowledge is required for us to resist the pressures of *our own needs* to have answers which, in fact, we do not have. Our cultural conditioning has made us believe we are supposed to "have convictions" about most everything, or at least to "have an opinion." (If we do not we are apathetic.) So the need to prepare answers to meet our own competitive/survival situations is great. Knowing ourselves, recognizing our motives, and remaining wary lest these personal pressures push us into claiming more than we should—all this is not easy. But it is necessary, not just so we can play a defined role, but to be honest with ourselves about what, in fact, we actually know and don't know.

As one logician puts it, all but a small portion of our thinking is need-oriented; it is determined and guided by numerous subjective factors. "To become a sound thinker it is necessary not only to school yourself thoroughly in certain techniques but also to understand fully the nature and operation of subjective factors and to take special measures for reducing their influence."

In the last analysis, we serve both ourselves and others best if we refuse to detour from our goal of knowing "what is." If we are cavalier with facts or play loose with value-judgments, it becomes difficult for us to live with ourselves; and unless we play fair with our experiences, others have no good reason to believe us or respect our judgment.

Unless the synoptist remains loyal to his vision of seeing nothing less than the whole puzzle-picture, then there is really no one left in this world who continues to strive to know the full story. The World-Riddle is largely abandoned to those who intently gaze at some small portion of the jigsaw picture and proclaim to the rest of us that they have discovered the Whole. And we better believe it.

## The Synoptic Venture: Risks and Rewards

The risks of specializing are many, but since specialization is the order of the day, we do not commonly become aware of them—except in a painful way, and too late. One risk is that the more one specializes the more he tends to neglect a general knowledge of life that is necessary just to remain human. The proverbial definition of the scientist—"the one who knows more and more about less and less until he knows everything about nothing"—is apt for every specialist. A narrow field too often signals a narrow mind. A fulfilling life is far more likely for the individual who develops a balanced awareness of the requirements of living.

Another frequent result of specialization is the loss of the ability to communicate. Encapsulation is the commonest of all human diseases, with a mortality rate second to none. If we have failed to nourish the shared experiences of life, there may be nothing to bridge the chasms between us. The statement is commonly made that specialists tend to be lonely people, and this is probably true.

*Reason is ⁶/₇ of treason.*
**James Thurber**

The *Shri Yantra* is employed in meditation by Hindu worshippers known as Shaktas. It is a symbol of wholeness. Ultimate Reality is represented by the dot in the center, and the rest of reality is symbolized by triangles (consciousness and energy) and lotus petals (the material universe). The outer square contains gates through which the mind of man can enter into the deeper levels of wholeness.

*The thrust of Western intellectual development since the sixteenth and early seventeenth centuries has been to fragment knowledge. . . . Now we know that isolated specialization is no longer realistic and perhaps even suicidal. We are being forced again to think in holistic terms. All knowledge is once again an ecological system.*

EDWARD B. FISKE

Brand Blandshard, a contemporary philosopher, once warned would-be specialists to keep their lines of communication in good repair.

The more deeply you penetrate into the mineshaft of your own science, the more isolated and lonely you are with regard to those interests that mark the growing point of your mind. I admire beyond words the scientific acumen that made it possible for Planck to define the value of $h$, for example. But if I were to sit down for a talk with someone, and he were to focus the discussion on $h$, the tête-à-tête would be brief, for as far as I am concerned, $h$ is not discussible.

What are the grounds on which men generally can meet? They are the experiences that all men have in common. All of us, however humble, have had experiences of suffering and exaltation, of inspiration and depression, of laughter and pain that would, if we could only express them, make us, too, poets and essayists. Indeed, literature consists of just such experiences expressed as we should like to express them if we could. . . .

It is well to be a specialist; it is better to be a good human being. . . .

The synoptist is vulnerable to equally perilous risks. Perhaps the most uncomfortable is the likelihood of being considered (and called) a dilettante by specialists. Whenever we turn to a specialist for information, we are, from his viewpoint, "only a layman"—never the authority, never the expert. We always appear to be at a strategic disadvantage. Because we try to know something (the basic conclusions) about everything (the basic disciplines), we can easily leave the impression that our concerns are shallow and that our currents never run deep.

A far greater danger, however, is that we might actually become dilettantes—random dabblers in all things known and unknown. The difference between a dilettante and a synoptist lies in the way the synoptist weaves his data into a coherent world-view. Dabblers and dilettantes are known for dipping and picking at bits of information to be in a position—over hors d'oeuvres and a demitasse—to impress others with their range of erudition. By contrast, the stance of the synoptist is to admit, to himself and others, what he does not know; and in the context of all that there is to be known, he is aware that his abysmal unknowing is nothing to boast about. The goal of the synoptic empiricist is not to collect bits and pieces, but to weave the strands of knowledge into a glowing tapestry.

A double-edged risk is the fact that specialists become irritated with the way laymen—however honorable their intentions—tend to misunderstand and misuse the discoveries from their fields. They are (rightly) wary of having their work "popularized" and distorted. That fear can be calmed, of course, only by the honest, accurate handling of the data derived from their specialized fields. We are morally justified in asking their help only if we are willing to assimilate their materials with intelligence and integrity.

The rewards of the synoptic venture are, for the most part, intensely personal, having to do with what we are, or can become, as human beings.

One reward is learning to "think bigger." From its inception, a prime concern of philosophy has been the fact that the parameters of human thought—for all of us, all the time—are very, very narrow. Larry Niven, a science-fiction writer, put it perfectly: The trouble with people who live on a planet is that the inhabitants tend to think small. And when we think small, we never quite succeed in arranging life's events into an efficient priority system that promises optimal growth and fulfillment. We don't think big enough to know what's important in our lives and what's not important, what to invest our time and energy into and what to ignore.

Synoptic philosophy is an antidote for small thought. As a result, many of life's problems—what we *thought* were life's problems—simply dissolve and disappear. Seeing the larger picture gives us the perspective and power to screen out trivial, inconsequential events.

Synoptic thinking also produces greater awareness in our perception of daily life. All of us want to be more than we now are: we want to be brighter (by 30 IQ points, maybe 40!); we want a greater comprehension of life's painful events; we want more intensely pleasurable "peak experiences," more adventures, and so on. In a word, we all harbor a deep desire for *more life,* both in

*The real world is increasingly seen to be, not the tidy garden of our race's childhood, but the extraordinary, extravagant universe described by the eye of science.*

HERMAN J. MULLER

---

## MAN'S TRUE FUNCTION

If the great design of the universe had wished man to be a specialist, man would have been designed with one eye and a microscope attached to it which he could not unfasten. All the living species except human beings are specialists. The bird can fly beautifully but cannot take its wings off after landing and therefore can't walk very well. The fish can't walk at all. But man can put on his gills and swim and he can put on his wings and fly and then take them off and not be encumbered with them when he is not using them. He is in the middle of all living species. He is the most generally adaptable but only by virtue of his one unique faculty—his mind. Many creatures have brains. Human minds discover pure abstract generalized principles and employ those principles in the appropriate special cases. Thus has evolution made humans the most universally adaptable, in contradistinction to specialization, by endowing them with these metaphysical, weightless invisible capabilities to employ and realize special case uses of the generalized principles. . . .

All the biologicals are converting chaos to beautiful order. All biology is antientropic. Of all the disorder-to-order converters, the human mind is by far the most impressive. The human's most powerful metaphysical drive is to understand, to order, to sort out, and rearrange in ever more orderly and understandably constructive ways. You find then that man's true function is metaphysical.

BUCKMINSTER FULLER

quantity and quality. Synoptic philosophy moves in that direction by laying solid foundations for such experiences; it hears this ontological cry for help. Synoptic thought leads to a greater awareness of oneself, and hence to an understanding of others. This in turn means better communication—and less alienation, isolation, and loneliness. Other things being equal, these are good foundations for greater fulfillment within the context of the human condition; and this may be the most we can reasonably expect in one (short) life/time.

Another reward is the fact that both our conscious and unconscious operations move more efficiently within a coherent world-view that is relatively free of internal contradictions and conflicts. Internal conflict means stress and a loss of psychological energy. If there is internecine strife going on between the ideas and feelings which constitute the cognitive contents of our character structure, then much of the energy potentially available to us for living is bound up in the inner struggle. We have "built-in headwinds"; we cannot get off the ground. A world-view that works well for us is one whose component elements have ceased carrying on a running battle inside us and have begun to work together.

A final note: learning can be (*can* be) one of life's most exciting adventures. Catch a glimpse, just once, of the new discoveries taking place along today's frontiers—it is humbling, thrilling, mind-boggling . . . and addictive! It is difficult not to want to share the action.

Each of us is free, if we wish, to become an epistemic amateur—a knowledge-lover—and to touch the incredible adventures that are breaking in astronomy, psychology, molecular biology, planetology, oceanography, physics, history, and so on. These are vistas that the specialists know but cannot share with us until we decide to open ourselves to their worlds. Even if some of these fields have heretofore been anesthetized by boring teachers and dull classes, the ability to rediscover them and to rekindle in ourselves a sense of wonderment—this may be a measure of our growth and, perhaps, of our capacity for life.

*More than one ethnographer has reported the experience of showing a clear photograph of a house, a person, a familiar landscape, to people living in a culture innocent of any knowledge of photography, and to have the picture held at all possible angles, or turned over for an inspection of its blank back, as the native tried to interpret this meaningless arrangement of varying shades of grey on a piece of paper.*

MELVILLE HERSKOVITS

*The fish trap exists because of the fish: once you've gotten the fish, you can forget the trap. . . . Words exist because of meanings: once you've gotten the meanings, you can forget the words.*

CHUANG-TZU

Isaac Asimov (1920-1992)

## "I CAN FLOAT OVER THE ORCHARD AS IN A BALLOON"

EPILOG Few individuals understood better than Isaac Asimov what the synoptic vision is all about. His almost 500 books—written as specialist, knowledgeable authority, or just excited layman—range over nearly all conceivable subjects—the sciences, history, literature, religion, and, of course, science-fiction. As the following autobiographical note indicates, he was unable, try as he may, to retreat from the synoptic vision.

Science, before 1800, was like an orchard: tame, well laid-out and ordered; fragrant and fruit-bearing. One could wander through it from end to end observing its various parts; and from a neighboring hill, one might even see the entire scheme, and appreciate it.

But by 1800, the wanderers note that the busy planters, gardeners, and cultivators had done their work so well that parts of it had grown dark and foreboding.

Order was still there; indeed the intricate network of relationships was more refined, more subtle, and more fascinating than ever; but the proliferating branches had begun to shut out the sky.

And then there came the shock of realizing that the orchard was too large. One could no longer pass through it from end to end—not without getting lost and walking in circles back to one's starting point. Nor was the neighboring hill any longer of use, for it, too, was covered by orchard now.

So some of the observers, some of the lovers of the beauty of order, abandoned the orchard altogether; while others compromised by confining themselves to narrow sections of the orchard, then to narrower sections and still narrower sections.

Now, the orchard of science is a vast globe-encircling monster, without a map, and known to no one man; indeed, to no group of men fewer than the whole international mass of creative scientists. Within it, each observer clings to his own well-known and well-loved clump of trees. If he looks beyond, it is usually with a guilty sigh.

And just as an organism in the embryonic stages seems to race through the aeons of evolutionary development, from the single cell to ultimate complexity, in mere weeks or months; so the individual scientist in the course of his life repeats the history of science and loses himself by progressive stages, in the orchard.

When I was young, the neighborhood public libraries were my source material. I lacked the intelligence and purpose to be selective, so I started at one end of the shelves and worked my way toward the other.

Since I have an inconveniently retentive memory, I learned a great many things in this way that I have since labored unsuccessfully to forget. One of the valuable things I learned, however, was that I liked nonfiction better than fiction; history better than most other varieties of nonfiction; and science even better than history.

By the time I entered high school, I had restricted myself largely to history and science. By the time I entered college, I was down to science.

In college, I found I was expected to choose among the major disciplines of science and select a "major." I flirted with zoology and then, in my second year, made chemistry a firm choice. This meant not much more than one chemistry course per semester, but when I entered graduate school, I found that all my courses were chemistry of one sort or another, and I had to choose among them with a view toward doctoral research.

Through a series of developments of absorbing lack of interest (as far as these pages are concerned), I found myself doing research on a biochemical topic. In that area of study I obtained my Ph.D., and in no time at all I was teaching biochemistry at a medical school.

But even that was too wide a subject. From books to nonfiction, to science, to chemistry, to biochemistry—and not yet enough. The orchard had to be narrowed down further. To do research, I had to find myself a niche within biochemistry, so I began work on nucleic acids. . . .

And at about that point, I rebelled! I could not stand the claustrophobia that clamped down upon me. I looked with horror, backward and forward across the years, at a horizon that was narrowing down and narrowing down to so petty a portion of the orchard. What I wanted was all the orchard, or as much of it as I could cover in a lifetime of running.

To be sure, rebellion at this stage is often useless. Specialization has taken hold firmly and one dare not leave its confines. The faculty of participating in life outside one's special field has atrophied. . . .

I have never been sorry for my stubborn advance toward generalization. To be sure, I can't wander in detail through all the orchard, any more than anyone else can, no matter how stupidly determined I may be to do so. Life is far too short and the mind is far too limited. But I can float over the orchard as in a balloon.

*Knowledge is never finished.*
MAURICE MERLEAU-PONTY

*Of all the disorder-to-order converters, the human mind is by far the most impressive.*
BUCKMINSTER FULLER

*A generalized body provided by a million years of evolution, and now a mind which can see the pattern of the woods as well as individual trees. Can this combination help to answer the question: "Who am I and where am I going?"*

*The man at the Information Booth looks puzzled but not altogether dubious.*
STUART CHASE

*Certainly, the characteristic activity of the mind, from the formation of a general idea to the great system of Philosophy, from the humblest perception to the laws of Science and the Uniformity of Nature itself, from the vaguest conception of spirit to the monistic unity of the Supreme Personality of Religion, is the endeavor to create 'wholes' in thought, to organise experience into some form or other of coherent totality.*
ARNOLD TOYNBEE

# ARISTOTLE

## *The First Scientific World-View*

For about a century Greek philosophy was dominated by the achievements of three Athenian thinkers—Socrates, Plato, and Aristotle. Socrates spent a lifetime in the agora, the crowded, busy marketplace just below the Acropolis; he attempted to get Athenian youth to realize that ordinary thinking is too loose and shabby to solve the important problems of life. The Socratic tradition was carried on by his pupil Plato in his Academy two miles northeast of the agora; he aimed at laying intellectual and moral foundations so that Athenian youth could rise to the demands of statesmanship: There can be no peace in the world, he believed, until statesmen are philosophers or philosophers become statesmen. The third of these great Athenian thinkers was Aristotle, Plato's pupil. He taught for twelve years in his Lyceum a mile south of the agora; he taught his students to search for the truth of things not primarily to make them statesmen, but because this is what would keep them human and lead to *eudaimonia*—"happiness."

Three supreme moments illuminate Aristotle's life.

First, he journeyed to Athens when he was seventeen, enrolled in the Academy, and became a student of Plato. He had come from Stagira on the Chalkidic Peninsula, where his parents, Nichomachus and Phaestis, were living when he was born in 384 B.C. Nichomachus had returned from Pella, the capital city of the Macedonian Empire, where he had served as physician to the king. Aristotle had already lived an eventful life during these early years and, it seems, saw too much: he thoroughly disliked princes and the intrigues of the royal court. His father and mother both died within a few years, and the orphaned Aristotle, adopted by a kinsman, continued his education at Stagira, where he apparently performed brilliantly. He was soon accepted as a student in Plato's Academy.

Aristotle arrived at the Academy in the year 366 B.C., performed brilliantly, and remained there for twenty years. This was a time of intellectual maturation; we know that he was in love with learning and had a passion for books—for which qualities Plato, likely with teacherly affection, dubbed him "the Brain" and "the Bookworm." Aristotle began to collect books and eventually built an enormous library of his own.

Plato developed a comprehensive and coherent world-view—the first Western thinker to do so—and Aristotle fully absorbed it; but soon he had to exorcise it from his psyche—the two men possessed quite different temperaments—before he could move on to develop his own empirical world-view.

So Aristotle left the Academy at thirty-eight and sailed to Asia Minor to join an old friend who had become ruler of the city-state of Atarneus. For three years he lived there, and at forty, married the king's niece, Pythias. He organized a philosophic circle and developed a small school on the plan of the Academy to explore politics and ethics.

Sometime thereafter they moved to the island of Lesbos, where Aristotle continued to study the marine life of the Aegean shores. Biology was always Aristotle's first love. His later writings reveal a detailed knowledge of the marine life of this part of the world; and from this time on, the paradigms and metaphors that guided his philosophic speculations derive from biology.

These were rich and happy years for Aristotle, but they were short-lived, for Pythias died sometime after the birth of their daughter (also named Pythias, after her mother). We don't know when or where her death occurred, and we don't hear of their daughter again till Aristotle mentions her in his will. Later, probably in Athens, Aristotle entered into a liaison with a lady named Herpyllis who was his wife or consort (*hetaira*, "companion"), and a son was born to them. They named him Nichomachus after Aristotle's father.

When he was forty-two the second historic event in Aristotle's life occurred. He received a royal summons from King Philip to return to the Macedonian court as teacher to Philip's son Alexander. The crown prince was only thirteen, but within six years he was to assume the throne and marshal the military might of a united Greek world against the Persian Empire. After his lightning conquest of the known world, we remember him as Alexander the Great.

Aristotle taught Alexander for three years. Here is one of those special events so annoying to historians, a relationship so rich with possibilities, but about which we know *nothing*. The two men must have influenced each other, but they were worlds apart in passions, goals, and the games of life. Aristotle's commission was to prepare the crown prince to be a successful monarch of Macedon, to instil in him the principles of good governance, and to make him humane in his judgments, intelligent in his policies, mature in his decisions. There are suggestions in the records that they never quite let go of each other. We have reports that Alexander, as he moved eastward, set his troops to gathering specimens of exotic flora and fauna to be dispatched back to Athens for Aristotle's gardens and museums.

The third momentous event of Aristotle's life began in the spring of 334 B.C. Alexander set off for Asia to conquer the world, and Aristotle returned to Athens to set up his own school, the Lyceum, an institution for higher learning that would endure for almost eight hundred years. He chose acreage a mile south of the Acropolis on the southern outskirts of the city. It included a shady garden, covered walkways, and a public gymnasium on the grounds of a temple dedicated to Apollo Lyceus—Apollo the Lightgiver. Not being a citizen of Athens, Aristotle possessed no property rights, so he was forced to lease the land and buildings for his school. The gymnasium was one of the three large recreation halls in the city at that time; and no doubt Aristotle's students sometimes dashed into his classrooms, a minute late, fresh from workouts in the sports arena.

Aristotle was fifty when he opened

*The only stable state is the one in which all men are equal before the law.*

*There was never a genius without a tincture of madness.*

*They should rule who are able to rule best.*

*Democracy arises out of the notion that those who are equal in any respect are equal in all respects; because men are equally free, they claim to be absolutely equal.*

*The basis of a democratic state is liberty.*

*A tragedy is the imitation of an action that is serious and also, as having magnitude, complete in itself . . . with incidents arousing pity and fear, wherewith to accomplish its catharsis of such emotions.*

the Lyceum. He was a gentle, sensitive man and an inspiring teacher. For a dozen years he oversaw the institution, directed research programs, taught, and wrote. He lectured as he wandered through the grounds of the park and under covered walkways called *peripatoi* (his students became known as the Peripatetics, "the Strollers"). During morning hours he lectured on technical subjects; in the afternoon he presented open-air lectures to the public on popular topics such as rhetoric and politics. During the evenings he conversed and wrote.

◆

Aristotle was the inventor of formal logic; he was the first thinker to reduce human reasoning to a set of rules by which valid thinking could be distinguished from invalid—good thinking from bad. He thought of his work on logic not as a science in itself but as a set of preliminary and preparatory skills to be used in making one's way into all the sciences. His work on logic is found primarily in six treatises which, after his death, were collected together and called the *Organon*, "instrument" or "tool."

In one of these treatises, the *Prior Analytics*, Aristotle treats deductive logic as expressed in the form of a syllogism. This, he believed, represents a perfect form of reasoning. A syllogism consists of three propositional statements: a major premise, a minor premise, and a conclusion. A true syllogism contains two premises only, and the conclusion derives from the premises. For example

All Greeks were philosophers
Aristotle was a Greek

Therefore, Aristotle was a philosopher

In this syllogism the conclusion is implied in the premises; where the conclusion is correctly inferred, the conclusion is said to be valid, as it is in the above illustration. Logic, by definition, is the science (or study) of valid inference. In his treatise, Aristotle developed with remarkable insight the implications of these types of syllogisms; and all formal logic of the next 2300 years is little more than an elaboration of his work.

In another of his treatises called *Posterior Analytics* Aristotle took up the subject of induction and scientific method. Induction is a mode of reasoning that proceeds from particular facts to general principles. For example, after examining the movements of just a few planets, Johann Kepler concluded that *all* heavenly bodies trace elliptical orbits. He generalized on only a few observed cases. Aristotle pointed out that what you would have concluded on the basis of only a few observed facts—that a general statement is true—probably *is* true, and the more observations, the more it is probably true. But in all cases of induction only probability is established, never proof. There is nothing in the fact that a few planets follow elliptical orbits that would imply that *all* planets *must* follow elliptical orbits. How many observations of elliptical orbits would one have to make to be absolutely certain that a generalization is universally true? An infinite number, since the number of orbiting heavenly bodies is probably infinite. But this is impossible. Therefore, one can never be absolutely sure of a generalization arrived at by inductive reasoning. All it takes is a single instance of a non-elliptical orbit—one instance of an asteroid moving in a perfectly circular orbit—to render false the generalization about elliptical orbits.

Some generalizations are therefore sounder than others, depending on the quality and quantity of the supporting evidence. A generalization supported by only few observations, or that ignores contrary instances, would hardly be a sound generalization. On the other hand, a general proposition supported by numerous observations and no contrary evidence would be more reliable and would serve as the basis for scientific prediction: All heavenly bodies so far observed (millions!) follow elliptical orbits; therefore there there is a high probability that all future observations of heavenly bodies will be found to travel in such elliptical patterns.

With such illustrations Aristotle clarified the principles of logic—"the rules of right reasoning"—and thus established the foundations of all science.

In contrast to Plato's Academy, which stressed mathematics and geometry, Aristotle's Lyceum was designed as a center for scientific research and the teaching of scientific method. Heavy emphasis was placed on the natural sciences, especially biology. Aristotle found that he had to be a collector and curator in order to be a scientist. In and around his buildings he developed a zoo and botanical garden, and inside the school he established laboratories and a voluminous library. As in today's textbooks, he used anatomical diagrams to illustrate his observations, and these were put up on the walls of the Lyceum, just as they are in modern classrooms. Thus Aristotle had available an abundance of material to make a scientist jubilant. Using the scientific skills he had developed, he turned his attention to virtually every known subject.

He wondered about the stars, planets, sun and moon, the mountains and oceans, heat and cold, rain, snow, clouds, thunder and lightning, and rainbows.

He investigated plants and animals, and the relationships of living things, including ecological systems and animal behavior; mollusks, fishes, insects, birds, mammals; organs for sense perception and locomotion, mating and reproduction; diseases and disorders.

He reflected on mind and emotions, men and women, love and genes. He pondered perception, conception, words and meanings, and fallacies; poetry, sculpture, and music. He studied written constitutions and power politics; he evaluated various forms of government such as the monarchy, aristocracy, and timocracy.

Doubtless Aristotle derived immense enjoyment from delving into the mysteries of our world, but his gathering of facts was incidental and unimportant. What he was seeking was general understanding, and his knowledge of particulars enabled him to generalize.

Therefore, from his observations he developed abstract concepts of motion, change, actuality, potentiality, process or becoming, and causality; geological time, biological evolution, and entelechy (biological purposiveness—our genetics); systems of classification, concepts of truth and validity, definitions, categories, *archai* (first principles, axioms), deduction and induction; concepts of virtue, justice, human nature, the soul (*psyche*), and happiness (*eudaimonia*); concepts of form and substance, teleology, and a Prime Mover.

We can judge, from our vantage point, that Aristotle succeeded in laying foundations for the sciences of physics, astronomy, and meteorology; taxonomy, biology, forensic pathology, and animal psychology; psychology, epistemology and logic, and esthetics; political science and ethics; and finally, metaphysics—the philosopher's unified field theory for understanding his universe.

Add to all this a picture of the man reflecting, writing, and lecturing on more popular subjects such as education, rhetoric and grammar, mathematics and geometry, statecraft, drama and literature, and the art of living the good life.

Aristotle was a true scientist—an honest mind seeking empirical data from which to build explanatory hypotheses; and he was a true philosopher—a wonderer who surrendered lovingly to his curiosity about life.

◆

All hell broke loose in Athens in the summer of 323 B.C. when the young Alexander died unexpectedly in the palace of Nebuchadnezzar in Babylon, probably from malaria and too much drink. Aristotle had remained an alien in the eyes of the Athenians, a colonial Greek from the north too closely

*Neglect of an effective birth control policy is a never-failing source of poverty which, in turn, is the parent of revolution and crime.*

*The nature of a human being is not what he is born as, but what he is born for.*

*If purpose, then, is inherent in works of art, so is it in Nature also. The best illustration is the case of a man being his own physician, for Nature is like that—agent and patient at once.*

*In all things of nature there is something of the marvelous.*

*All men by nature desire knowledge.*

*For one swallow does not make a summer, nor does one day; and so too one day, or a short time, does not make a man blessed or happy.*

*Beauty is the gift of God.*

associated with the Macedonian conqueror. After Alexander's death the Macedonian party was ousted from power, and the wrath of the citizenry turned against Aristotle. He was charged with "atheism" or "impiety"—introducing new gods into Athens. (This was a standard accusation; Protagoras and Socrates had been so charged.) At this juncture he was offered protection by an old friend, so Aristotle retreated to Chalcis on the island of Euboea, some forty miles north of Athens. He tolerated this exile for barely a year when he died in 322 B.C., aged sixty-two.

Something of Aristotle's character is revealed in his last will, preserved for us by a later historian. In it he bequeathed his books and manuscripts to his friend Theophrastus. He freed some of his slaves and kept others—none were to be sold. He provided for Herpyllis and expressed his gratitude to her "in recognition of the steady affection she has shown me." Then he wrote: "Wherever they bury me, there the bones of Pythias shall be laid, in accordance with her own instructions."

I see no signs of an end; I make out very little detail. The precious intricacy one can observe by crawling over half an acre is lost to me.

But I have gains of my own, for occasionally I see (or seem to see) an overall order, or an odd arabesque in one corner—a glimmering fragment of design that perhaps I would not see from the ground.

## REFLECTIONS

1   Rephrase in your own (meaningful) way the essential goals of synoptic philosophy and make your own assessment of the rewards of the synoptic venture. Would your thinking and feeling change if you could achieve the rewards mentioned in this chapter? Are you willing to accept the risks?

2   What is meant by saying that synoptic philosophy is a "now" philosophy? What is the relationship of synoptic philosophy to the history of philosophizing? To assist you in your own philosophic tasks, what benefits would you gain by becoming acquainted with the history of philosophic thought?

3   What is the relationship of philosophic analysis to synoptic synthesis? Does the metaphor of the picture-puzzle help to clarify how they relate? Are these two activities inherently in competition, or do they cooperate with and complement one another?

4   As a synoptic philosopher, how would you respond to the charge of being a dilettante? How would you answer the accusation that you were trying to know everything and, hence, to "play God"?

5   Are you in agreement with the statement that most of the significant questions of life are interdisciplinary by nature and that we are already in the habit, in daily life, of drawing information from many sources to solve our problems? In your judgment, is it accurate to describe synoptic philosophy as "a disciplined form of what we do all the time"?

6   Do you agree with the suggestion that the compartmentalization of knowledge, although pragmatic, is an arbitrary mental habit and that all knowledge is interrelated? "We need a discipline which, by its nature and calling, will help us put our fragmented world of knowledge back together." Do you find this notion congenial?

7   Choose some philosophic problem that is of personal concern to you; sketch a rough synoptic wheel, place the problem in the center, and then jot down the areas in the wheel where you might find relevant data to help solve the problem. Develop the habit of using the synoptic wheel during your philosophic wondering through the rest of this book. Try to be aware of any resistance you may feel to breaking over the imaginary walls separating areas of thought that you've not been in the habit of relating, or of any reluctance to interrelate fields that might reveal discord and conflict—theology and physics, for instance, or anthropology and ethics.

15

## THE 353 WAYS OF THINKING ABOUT THINKING

The Jains of India have a doctrine called *syād-vāda*—the "perhaps" method—which suggests that there are officially 353 different viewpoints that can be held on any question, and therefore dogmatic closed-mindedness is inappropriate. To any perspective on any issue, the thoughtful reply is "perhaps" or, more elaborately, "maybe it is and maybe it isn't." With this in mind one must keep an appreciative openness to every viewpoint until one has himself explored all 353 "angles of truth."

The history of Western philosophy is analogous to the Jain perhaps method. Philosophers are specialists in thinking (the activity) and thoughts (the product of that activity), and if there is anything that comes in 353 varieties, it is human thinking. All philosophers do it differently, each in his own creative way; and all have made significant contributions to the growth of human knowledge. Since life's problems can be tackled from countless directions, philosophers choose their angle of attack and, from that vantage point, cut as deep as they can.

There have been four general ideas of what philosophers are supposed to be doing. They can be classified as (1) synoptics, (2) activists, (3) antinomians, and (4) analytics.

*Keep me from the wisdom that does not weep, and the philosophy that does not laugh. . . .*

KAHLIL GIBRAN

*Before you begin training in enlightenment, a bowl is a bowl and tea is tea. During training, a bowl is not a bowl, and tea is not tea. After training in enlightenment, a bowl is a bowl and tea is tea.*

**Zen Epigram**

## THE SYNOPTIC PHILOSOPHERS

The synoptic philosophers have in common the desire "to see life steadily and to see it whole" (Whitehead) or, at least, to understand every event in the largest possible way (James). Commonly we find the synoptic philosophers having a very wide range of interests and concerns. They are usually fascinated by almost all areas of human knowledge. They will have special interests, of course, but they will delve into all sorts of knowledge to better obtain an overview of life and the problems they wish to work on.

In the spring of the year 334 B.C., as Alexander the Great was setting off across Asia to conquer the world and bring the gift of Greek civilization to all Mankind, Aristotle left his home town in Thrace and returned to Athens to establish his own school of learning. In a green grove just outside the city, near a temple dedicated to Apollo Lyceus, he founded the Lyceum. It had a campus, classrooms, a chapel, covered walkways, and shaded gardens. In time it also contained the Western world's first great library, a museum of natural history, and a zoological garden.

During morning hours Aristotle lectured to his students in technical subjects as they strolled along the pathways. (For this they came to be nicknamed Peripatetics, or "the Strollers.") In the afternoons he lectured on popular subjects to crowds from outside the school. At dinner teacher and students dined together and often held symposia. Aristotle reserved his evening hours for his own research and writing.

Out of this atmosphere emerged our first empirically grounded synoptic philosophy.

Aristotle was the first great *synoptic* philosopher. His mind ranged over every known realm of human knowledge, and he produced brilliant, creative writing in every field. Drawing upon the immense amount of empirical data collected by his students and sent to him by Alexander from foreign countries (one report has it that Alexander set a thousand men collecting specimens of flora and fauna for Aristotle's laboratories and museums), Aristotle was also the West's first true scientist.

While hundreds of Aristotle's writings have been lost, some forty works survive. He wrote extensively in what we would call the *natural sciences* (physics, astronomy and cosmology, geology, meteorology), the *life sciences* (biology, anatomy, physiology, genetics), the *social sciences* (psychology, politics, ethics), the *practical arts* (oratory and rhetoric), and *"philosophy"* (logic and epistemology, esthetics, theology, metaphysics).

His synoptic mind was continually at work weaving these vast areas of knowledge into a coherent philosophical system that served as the framework for man's thinking until the beginning of the scientific revolution. "He is probably the only human intellect that has ever compassed at first hand and assimilated the whole body of existing knowledge on all subjects, and brought it within a single focus—and a focus, at that, which after more than two thousand years still stands as one of the supreme achievements of the mind of man."

One goal of synoptic philosophy is the development of an empirically sound and rationally coherent world-view to serve as an operational model for the interpretation and valuation of all our experience. Such a world-view provides unity and consistency to the whole of life.

A common result of synoptic activity is the discovery that all knowledge is related and that any rigid compartmentalization of data ("chemistry," "biology," "psychology," etc.) is artificial and eventually self-defeating. Knowledge is seen to be a unity, an "ecological system" in which all parts must be understood in relation to one another.

## THE ACTIVIST PHILOSOPHERS

The *activist* philosophers believe that the philosophic enterprise must be a part of life itself and that the philosopher cannot be a mere spectator of life's tragic-comic drama. He may not have auditioned for a role in the drama, but he has been cast nevertheless. He can no more resign from the cast than he can resign from the human race.

There are at least three distinct varieties of activist philosophers: (1) the prophetic activists, (2) the pragmatists, and (3) the existentialists. Each, however, insists on participation in the human drama for quite different reasons.

The *prophetic activists* contend that the task of philosophy is to bring about drastic reforms in social conditions; human suffering in all its forms must be dealt with *now*. Karl Marx, for example, became disillusioned with the ivory-tower philosophy in vogue in nineteenth-century Germany, a grandiose metaphysics of human history that was blind to the concrete realities of day-to-day human experience. Indeed, much German philosophy (and especially Hegelian idealism) hardly acknowledged the existence of the individual per se.

Against such dehumanizing theories, there arose numerous reactions, Marx's among them. Marx wrote that "philosophers have only *interpreted* the world differently: the point is, however, to *change* it." He therefore developed a philosophy of history in which change (and the doctrine of "inevitable progress") was the central idea. "Marx's aim," writes Erich Fromm,

Karl Marx (1818-1883)

*Heretofore philosophers have only* interpreted *the world differently: the point is, however, to change it.*

KARL MARX

> was that of the spiritual emancipation of man, of his liberation from the chains of economic determination, of restituting him in his human wholeness, of enabling him to find unity and harmony with his fellow man and with nature. Marx's philosophy was, in secular, nontheistic language, a new and radical step forward in the tradition of prophetic Messianism; it was aimed at the full realization of individualism, the very aim which has guided Western thinking from the Renaissance and the Reformation far into the nineteenth century.

Since our main concern here is to describe what philosophers are supposed to be doing, it is of interest to note that Marx the man was more philosopher than revolutionary. "A man whose whole creed was one of action," notes Untermeyer, "he spent practically all his time in libraries." To be sure, he had himself engaged in social action in Paris and Brussels, but the last thirty years of his life were spent writing in the British Museum and in a dingy, two-room London apartment. Instead of taking action he philosophized about it.

This is not to be taken as an indictment. On the contrary, it suggests that philosophy and social activism may be competing preoccupations. One can do one or the other, or one can alternate from one to the other, but it appears doubtful that both activities can be carried on effectively at the same time.

William James (1842-1910)

The American *pragmatists* represent a second reaction against the prevailing German idealism. "Damn the Absolute!" was William James's response to Hegel's idea that history is the manifestation of the "Absolute Mind" of God. James believed that philosophers should get down to the task of solving the problems of life. Too long have they been playing around with metaphysical speculations. An idea is to be judged by its "cash value," wrote James; and philosophical concepts should be evaluated in terms of their practical consequences.

It has often been noted that pragmatism could only have been born on American soil, since it reflects the spirit of the nineteenth century, the frontier spirit of individualism, self-reliance, and practicality. Americans had traditionally been castigated by European thinkers as "long on action but short on thought." William James successfully argued that it was time for a carefully thought-out philosophy of action that would deal candidly with real issues.

1835

*Gilleleie, August 1, 1835*

What I really lack is to be clear in my mind *what I am to do,* not what I am to know, except in so far as a certain understanding must precede every action. The thing is to understand myself, to see what God really wishes *me* to do; the thing is to find a truth which is true *for me,* to find *the idea for which I can live and die.* What would be the use of discovering so-called objective truth, of working through all the systems of philosophy and of being able, if required, to review them all and show up the inconsistencies within each system;—what good would it do me to be able to develop a theory of the state and combine all the details into a single whole, and so construct a world in which I did not live, but only held up to the view of others;—what good would it do me to be able to explain the meaning of Christianity if it had *no* deeper significance *for me and for my life;*—what good would it do me if truth stood before me, cold and naked, not caring whether I recognised her or not, and producing in me a shudder of fear rather than a trusting devotion? I certainly do not deny that I still recognize an *imperative of understanding* and that through it one can work upon men, *but it must be taken up into my life,* and *that is* what I now recognize as the most important thing. That is what my soul longs after, as the African desert thirsts for water. That is what I lack, and that is why I am left standing like a man who has rented a house and gathered all the furniture and household things together, but has not yet found the beloved with whom to share the joys and sorrows of his life. But in order to find that idea, or better still, in order to find myself, it is no use throwing myself still further into life. And that is just what I have done hitherto. That is why I thought it would be a good thing to throw myself into the study of the law so as to develop my

A page from Kierkegaard's *Journals*

The *existentialists* have all shared the basic belief that life has meaning only when it is fully experienced. Life is not a thing to be thought, but an existence to be lived. To think and to exist are quite different things, and most philosophers have sold their existence for a handful of thoughts. To watch someone else enjoy a sunset or experience love may not be without value; but it's a world away from enjoying the sunset and feeling love within and for oneself.

The existentialist becomes involved in life, therefore, not primarily to change the world or even to solve its problems but to discover, for himself, the meaning of existence.

Søren Kierkegaard—the "father of existentialism"—and all subsequent existentialists have criticized traditional philosophy as a collection of astute observations by "spectators." It therefore has a hollow ring, for it has missed life.

The existentialists believe that the only "reality" that is worthwhile is experience—what takes place personally and uniquely in the inner world of each of us. Moreover, since neither past nor future exists, the concrete present is where the full intensity of life is to be found. The advice of the existentialist, therefore, is to live life and not let it pass by while meditating on it.

## THE ANTINOMIAN PHILOSOPHERS

Not all philosophers would agree that social action is the noblest of human activities. The *antinomian* philosophers have held that a realistic assessment of the human condition necessarily leads anyone concerned with the quality of his existence to withdraw from the world. Western monastics, of course, have disengaged themselves from the world since at least the second century before Christ. Hindus revere the *sannyasin* who enter the forests to meditate, their ultimate goal being total withdrawal into the trance-state of *nirvana*. Zen and Theravada Buddhists share similar attitudes toward life-in-this-world.

The best-known Western critics of society are perhaps Jean-Jacques Rousseau and Henry David Thoreau. Both contended that a return to nature and the simple life is necessary to preserve one's self and sanity. Both, however, were sensitive to social ills and neither managed to withdraw from the world for very long.

The true antinomian philosophers are such men as Diogenes the Cynic and Chuang-tzu the Taoist.

ANTINOMIANISM—WESTERN STYLE After Athens' Golden Age was over, many diverse philosophical schools were born. One such school, the Cynics, was founded by Antisthenes. He held his classes in a gymnasium outside Athens and catered to the poor, the illegitimate, and the foreign-born. He taught without fees, lived simply, and dressed shabbily. Socrates once said to him, "Antisthenes, I can see your vanity through the holes of your cloak."

His most famous pupil was Diogenes, who had tried banking in Asia Minor, failed, and came to Athens. He was forced to beg, and Antisthenes helped him rationalize his condition into a philosophy. He gathered the accouterments of a beggar—old clothes, a bowl, and a staff—and lived in a large tub in the court-yard of an Athenian temple. His only companions were dogs.

The Cynics disdained culture and ridiculed sophistic learning. They rebelled against the customs and codes of society. They wandered from place to place, evangelically denouncing the absurdities and corruptions of society and preaching a simple, back-to-nature existence in which all Mankind could be one family.

Diogenes tried to practice what he preached. He slept on the ground or in his tub, eating whatever he could beg. He tried never to hurt anyone. Above all he wanted to be free—free of material possessions, relationships, traditions, laws. In fact, he recognized no laws, so he could neither obey nor disobey them. Freedom of speech was most important to him and he made much use of it, coarsely and wittily. He never thought of himself as a Greek (he wasn't) and considered himself as belonging to Mankind alone.

There is a legend to the effect that Diogenes often walked the streets of Athens with a lantern in his hand, looking—in vain—for an honest man.

ANTINOMIANISM—EASTERN STYLE The Taoist philosopher Chuang-tzu is considered by many to be the greatest sage that China has produced. We know little about his life, but as we listen to his thoughts we can feel the working of a wise and subtle mind.

Chuang-tzu lived in the state of Meng about 300 B.C. He became famous and could have held high office, but he disdained society, power, and wealth. He was irreverent toward pompous authorities and ridiculed all schools of philosophy (he never dreamed that his philosophy would become a "school"). He was especially critical of Confucian teachings because they produced obedient, cultured, "virtuous" men who were empty inside. Such men could play to per-fection the artificial games of social custom, but they had lost the freedom for

*I went to the woods because I wished to live deliberately, to confront only the essential facts of life, and see if I could not learn what it had to teach, and not, when I came to die, discover that I had not lived.*

HENRY DAVID THOREAU

*If I were not Alexander, then I would like to have been Diogenes.*

ALEXANDER THE GREAT

*. . . The effect of life in soci-ety is to complicate and con-fuse our existence, making us forget who we really are by causing us to become obsessed with what we are not.*

CHUANG-TZU

authentic, spontaneous behavior. They were imprisoned by arbitrary rules and social niceties.

Chuang-tzu wanted none of this. He preferred to watch the merry go-around from a distance. "The life of things passes by like a rushing, galloping horse, changing at every turn, at every hour. What should one do, or what should one not do? Let the changes go on by themselves!"

Chuang-tzu with his bamboo pole was fishing in the river. The prince of Chu sent two officials to offer him formally the post of prime minister.

Chuang-tzu held his bamboo pole. Still looking into the river, he said, "I am told there is a sacred tortoise which has been dead now some three thousand years. Wrapped in silk, in a shrine on an altar in the temple. What do you think: Is it better to give up one's life and leave a sacred shell as an object of veneration in a cloud of incense three thousand years, or is it better to live as a plain turtle wagging its tail in the mud?"

"For the turtle," replied one of the officials, "it is better to live and wag its tail in the mud!"

"Then, begone!" ordered Chuang-tzu. "I too will stay here and wag my tail in the mud!"

Thomas Merton, an interpreter of the writings of Chuang-tzu, was a Trappist monk. Reflecting upon the philosophy of Chuang-tzu he sensed a familiar way of life. Merton wrote:

> I have been a Christian monk for nearly twenty-five years, and inevitably one comes in time to see life from a viewpoint that has been common to solitaries and recluses in all ages and in all cultures. . . . There is a monastic outlook which is common to all those who have elected to question the value of life submitted entirely to arbitrary secular presuppositions, dictated by social conventions, and dedicated to the pursuit of temporal satisfactions which are perhaps only a mirage. Whatever may be the value of "life in the world" there have been, in all cultures, men who have claimed to find something they vastly prefer in solitude.

## THE ANALYTIC PHILOSOPHERS

From its beginning, one of the central concerns of Western philosophy has been the *analysis* of ideas. The origins of logic are pre-Socratic, but the special preoccupation with problems of clear thinking dates from Socrates himself. Much of his time was spent in asking questions about words, ideas, and beliefs and discovering the fallacies that mar a large part of our thinking.

Aristotle, however, is considered the founder of formal logic. He invented the syllogism and wrote the first textbook in logic. Since his time new systems of logic have been devised, including systems of symbolic logic that have had practical application in business fields and computer science.

Twentieth-century philosophical logic has had an ambiguous career. One name, however—Wittgenstein—has dominated the field for nearly a half-century.

There were two creative periods in the life of Ludwig Wittgenstein, each of which culminated in a complex system of philosophy. His first period began in 1912 when he became a student of Bertrand Russell at Cambridge University;

Ludwig Wittgenstein (1889-1951)

it ended in 1921 with the publication of an epoch-making (but remarkably brief) treatise entitled *Tractatus Logico-Philosophicus*. Subsequently he published almost nothing, as though his philosophic search had reached its end.

Then a second period of creative philosophizing began in 1929 when he returned to Cambridge, first as a student, then as a teacher. Out of his teaching a new philosophy was born, which resulted in his *Philosophical Investigations,* published posthumously in 1953.

His first period was devoted primarily to logic and logical systems, while his second period dealt entirely with the analysis of everyday language. The testimony to his genius is that each of his systems—esoteric, technical, and demanding—has strongly influenced the course of twentieth-century philosophical thought.

> For this reason Wittgenstein occupies a singular place in the history of philosophy, having first at an early age written a work which exercised a decisive influence on the philosophical thought of his time, and then, in his mature years, rejecting his early theory and producing a second theory which, for sheer originality, stature and influence, is even more important than the first.

Wittgenstein and subsequent language analysts have been convinced that most philosophical puzzlements are the result of sloppy use of language. Their task, therefore, is to analyze the function of language so that questions can be precisely constructed to which exact answers can be given. Only then can we know clearly what we are thinking and saying.

As Wittgenstein saw it, philosophy should not engage in synoptic or speculative tasks. Rather, its goal should be to help us think more clearly and precisely about anything and everything. Philosophy is therapy for our linguistic neuroses.

> Because his whole being was so consumed with passionate thought, Wittgenstein could not give lectures as other university teachers do. To lecture in the ordinary way is to expound, or repeat what has already been thought; and to repeat a thought is not to think it, at any rate, not to think it with Wittgenstein's kind of intensity. So instead of giving conventional lectures, Wittgenstein *thought* what he said as he spoke. He did not reproduce what he had prepared before. And it was precisely because he went through this process of thinking in such a fresh, powerful and concentrated way, in the presence of his students, that he earned their respect, and even something approaching veneration.
>
> Of course his lectures were not elegant in style or form; they were a kind of research, which really serious students—and only such attended Wittgenstein's lectures—found strangely inspiring. For them it was like being in the workshop of a great master where they could witness, and perhaps even participate in, the creation of new and often exhilarating thoughts.
>
> A professor has his students and, if he is the founder of a school, his followers. Wittgenstein had both, but he also had disciples. It was perhaps not difficult to become his disciple because of his magnetic and compelling personality and because of the originality and depth and fervor of his thought. Wittgenstein was conscious of this, and regretted it. A disciple's spiritual dependence on his master at best hinders independent thought, and, at worst, prevents it. And a thought which is not independent is a thought only half understood. . . .

JUSTUS HARTNACK

*Truly, philosophers play a strange game. They know very well that one thing alone counts, and that all their medley of subtle discussions relates to one single question: why are we born on this earth? And they also know that they will never be able to answer it. Nevertheless, they continue sedately to amuse themselves. Do they not see that people come to them from all points of the compass, not with a desire to partake of their subtlety, but because they hope to receive from them one word of life? If they have such words, why do they not cry them from the housetops, asking their disciples to give, if necessary, their very blood for them? If they have no such words, why do they allow people to believe they will receive from them something which they cannot give?*

JACQUES MARITAIN

## WHERE ARE THE WOMEN?

A mere glance through the history of philosophy shows a glaring absence. *Where are the women?* Didn't women become philosophers? Weren't they just as concerned as men with problems of human existence?

Most civilizations have been men's worlds, and those professions likely to bring fame have been closed to the female of the species. Few women became military heroines, for instance; and on the rare occasions when they did (Joan of Arc comes to mind) they did so along paths quite outside society's *modus operandi.*

And so it was with philosophy. There was but one profession that encouraged women to make the most of their intellectual capacities and cultural interests. Since the classical Greeks fostered intellectual attainments in its male citizenry to a degree previously unknown in the Western world, it is not surprising that there arose a class of women trained to be the intellectual companions of such men of culture and ability. They comprised history's highest class of courtesans and were appropriately called *hetairai,* "companions." They alone, it seems, enjoyed the requisites for philosophizing: adequate leisure time, professional incentive, and freedom from the traditional child-bearing role expected of women. A few of these courtesans transcended whatever social stigmata they bore and became renowned intellectuals in the highest philosophical and literary circles of their times.

*Aspasia* (c. 470-410 B.C.) was one of the most effective women's liberationists of all time. She opened a school of philosophy and rhetoric for women in Athens and did much to advance their education and encourage their emergence into public life. The great men of her era, including Pericles and Socrates, attended her lectures. She became the mistress of Pericles and their home became a center of Athenian culture.

Of *Diotima* we know very little, but in Plato's *Symposium* Socrates states that he was her pupil and says: "There is a speech about Love which I heard once from Diotima of Mantineia, who was wise in this matter and many others."

*Leontium* became the concubine of Epicurus and through her voluminous writing established herself as an articulate philosopher and, when necessary, a defender of womanhood. *Arete,* daughter of the famous hedonist philosopher Aristippus, was apparently not a courtesan. She succeeded her father as head of the Cyrenaic school of philosophy, wrote some forty books, and achieved such distinction that she became known as "The Light of Hellas."

The supremely brilliant and beautiful *Hypatia* (A.D. 370-415) became head of the famed school of Neoplatonism in Alexandria. Her fame spread through her lectures, teaching, and erudite writing. She was murdered by an outraged mob of Christians—ostensibly because of her liaison with Orestes, the prefect of Alexandria—and thus became the first woman philosopher to die for her beliefs.

Through the centuries other women became the intellectual lights of their times, though most of them moved merely on the periphery of philosophy per se. Among them: the Empress Theodora, wife of Justinian; Eleanor of Aquitaine; Marguerite d'Angoulême, Queen of Navarre; and Queen Christina of Sweden (who dispatched a warship to persuade René Descartes to come to Stockholm to establish an academy for her). In our century, for whatever reasons, the names are only slightly on the increase: Susanne Langer, L. Susan Stebbing, Simone de Beauvoir, Ayn Rand.

Now that life-styles are changing and women are breaking free of the cultural traditions that have heretofore predetermined their roles, it will be interesting to see if history begins to record a greater equality among those who professionally confess to being, not merely lovers, but "lovers of wisdom."

## SOMEONE MUST KEEP WATCH

There seems to be a motif, a pattern, running through the lives of almost all the great philosophers; it is a thread so fine that it might be overlooked. With few exceptions, their lives exhibit an alternation: a *withdrawal* from life-in-the-world, then a *return* to the world to apply in some way the insights they have gained. It is the ebb and flow of both psychic and physical energy, the alternation of the active and the passive—the Yin and the Yang.

On the one hand, the existentialist is very close to the truth. If one is merely a "spectator" of life, then his observations cannot be very meaningful; they are only second-hand. Apart from a full participation in life where "he laughs all his laughter and cries all his tears," one's philosophizing will not have the mark of life on it.

At the same time, the antinomians must be heard. Unless one can withdraw from life sufficiently to keep his experience in perspective, his insights cannot be trusted. To be sure, this is not easy, for when one has become involved in the human drama, reestablishing an overview may require considerable courage.

Yet a Yin-Yang alternation might be a workable solution if one can manage it. Life is to be lived; but without the solitude that one finds in the desert, the forest, the mountains, by the seashore, or in the study, the meaning of life will almost inevitably be missed. Wrestling with the Ultimate often seems to be pre-eminently a private affair.

*It is easy to be a philosopher in academia. But it is very difficult to be a philosopher in life.*

ANTON CHEKHOV

In this tribal world, someone must still keep watch. He must stand apart, as best he can, to try to keep life in perspective. The party members won't do it, nor will the fearful, the brainwashed, the prejudiced, or the bigoted. But there must be someone.

*There must be someone who remains sensitively aware of the essential humanness in every position that human beings take.*

There must be someone who tries to stay as close to *all* the realities as possible, someone who tries, keeps on trying, and who will not give up.

And there is some value in knowing just that—that in this world of adversary rhetoric and close-minded partisanship there is someone who will struggle against being manipulated and polarized.

He will only partially succeed. He may reach moments of greater clarity and then fall back into a one-sided point of view, but then he will (like Kant) arouse himself from his "dogmatic slumbers" and start to work again fitting together the pieces of the jigsaw puzzle.

"I can't decide whether to go to the orgy or listen to Socrates."

# SOCRATES

## *The Wisest Man Alive*

Xenophon tells of the time Socrates lost his way in the winding streets of Athens and asked, "Where does one go to buy groceries?" After giving him directions, Xenophon received the further inquiry, "And where does one go to learn to become an honest man?" When no answer was forthcoming, Socrates beckoned: "Come with me, and I'll show you."

Socrates was put to death with a cup of hemlock almost twenty-four hundred years ago, yet he is remarkably contemporary, and his presence still haunts. His appearance alone is intriguing. Aristophanes said he walked like a waterfowl and rolled his eyes while speaking. Some thought he was ugly, and once in battle with the Spartans at Delium he saved the day by glaring at the enemy, who turned and ran. He resembled a satyr, said Alcibiades, or the masks of Silenus found in the stone-carvers' shop-windows: broad-faced, round mouth, thick lips, heavy beard, wisps of gray hair fringing a balding dome—all set atop a robust, stocky torso

that was built like an ox and was as strong as two; but with a budding paunch which, he confessed, he wanted to reduce by dancing. Alcibiades was making a nobler point, however: Socrates is like the little statues of the Silens which, "on being opened, are found to have images of the gods inside them."

This was the man who could out-wrestle the strongest athletes, out-fight the hardiest foot soldiers, out-drink the dippiest winebibbers, and out-think the brightest minds of Hellas.

Socrates was born in Athens in 469 B.C., was raised there, lived and died there. His mother was a midwife named Phaenarete, his father a sculptor named Sophroniscus. Socrates followed in the footsteps of both: his calling, he said, was to help others give birth to their ideas. "Both I and my mother were endowed by the god with a midwife's art; she delivered women, but I deliver young men who are noble and fair." He added: "The reproach which is often made against me—that I ask questions of others but have not the wit to answer them myself—is very just. The reason is that god compels me to be a midwife, but forbids me to bring forth." (Aristophanes adopted the midwife metaphor to poke fun at Socrates: too often, he wrote, Socrates produced only a "miscarriage of ideas.")

About mid-life Socrates was married to Xanthippe, a woman remembered (quite unfairly) as a shrew. More than likely, she was a dutiful hausfrau and mother. Living with Socrates would have been terribly difficult, and her complaint about his absenteeism is understandable, since Socrates spent virtually all his time away from home, philosophizing. Nor was he much of a breadwinner. A contemporary poet commented that he had "thought everything out but ignored the problem of how to provide himself with funds." Socrates said he endured Xanthippe just so he could develop self-discipline. They had three sons. At the time of Socrates' death, the oldest was a youth of about seventeen and the youngest was still in arms when brought to visit his father in prison.

Socrates believed the only path to knowledge was through discussion of ideas, so he spent his life conversing with disciples, friends, and bystanders encountered in the agora, and he hoped to continue this trade even in Hades to find out "who is wise and who pretends to be wise but isn't." The agora was a gathering place of Athenian citizens, a bustling marketplace only a block long on the north side of the hill of the Acropolis. Here the Athenians bought, sold, and traded; carried on the politics of governing; engaged in religious activities, and—above all—talked. (The word *agora* derives from the Greek verb *agoreuein*, "to speak" to a crowd, "to address," "to harangue"—"to talk.") The minicosmos of the agora is described by the comic poet Eubulus: "You will find everything sold together in the same place in Athens: figs, witnesses to summonses, bunches of grapes, turnips, pears, apples, givers of evidence, roses, medlars, porridge, honeycombs, chick-peas, lawsuits, beestings-puddings, myrtle, allotment machines, irises, lambs, water clocks, laws, indictments." Once, after pondering such a variety of goods, Socrate's response was typical: "How many things I don't need!"

Xenophon tells us that Socrates was always a part of the crowds and that he loved it, "for early in the morning he used to go to the walkways and gymnasia, to appear in the agora as it filled up, and to be present wherever he would meet with the most people." Socrates was "of the people" and spoke only the vernacular of his friends.

The agora was Socrates' emotional, spiritual, and intellectual home. Phaedrus teased him once: "How very strange you are, sir. You talk like a tourist rather than a native. You apparently never set foot in the country or go outside the city walls." Socrates doubtless smiled at his companion when he replied, "Look at it my way, my good friend. It is because I love knowledge, and it is the people in the city who teach me, not the country or the trees."

Socrates was later to be accused of impiety—not supporting the officially-approved gods of the city-state of Athens—and introducing new deities. But Xenophon tells us that Socrates could frequently be seen "sacrificing on the public altars of the city." At his trial Socrates called Apollo to witness that his "wisdom" was not arrogance but a special calling to expose men's pretensions to wisdom.

Socrates lived up nearly a half-century in the Athenian agora, teaching and illustrating his belief that "the unexamined life, for a human being, is not worth living."

◆

Cicero wrote that Socrates called philosophy down from the heavens to earth and introduced it into the cities and houses of men. Heretofore, philosophic inquiries dealt with the physical world.

*SOCRATES'S PRAYER:*
*Beloved Pan, and all ye other gods who haunt this place, give me beauty in the inward soul; and may the outward and inward man be at one. May I reckon the wise to be the wealthy, and may I have such a quantity of gold as none but the temperate can carry.*

*ON SOCRATES:*
*All in all he was fortunate: he lived without working, read without writing, taught without routine, drank without dizziness, and died before senility, almost without pain.*
    WILL DURANT

*For a human being, the unexamined life is not worth living.*

*As a midwife, I attend men and not women, and I look after their souls when they are in labor, and not after their bodies; and the triumph of my art is in thoroughly examining whether the thought which the mind of the young man brings forth is a false idol or a noble and true birth.*

*I was really too honest a man to be a politician and live.*

*Are you not ashamed at heaping up the greatest amount of money and prestige and reputation, and caring so little about wisdom and truth and the greatest improvement of the soul, which you never regard or heed at all?*

*Wherefore, O judges, be of good cheer about death. . . . The hour of departure has arrived, and we go our ways—I to die, and you to live. Which is better God only knows.*

*I am that gadfly which God has attached to the state, and all day long and in all places am always fastening upon you, arousing and persuading and reproaching you.*

ON SOCRATES:
*When Socrates tormented the Athenians like a gadfly, he prevented them from sleeping peacefully, from relaxing with their ready-made solutions to moral and social problems. By astonishing us, Socrates prevents us from thinking along the old lines that have been handed down to us and have become habits.*

JEAN BRUN

Everything is made of water, said Thales; of air, said Anaximenes; of fire, pronounced Heraclitus. Democritus theorized that the stuff of the universe was composed of indivisible atoms; Pythagoras intuited that it wasn't "stuff" at all, but numbers and mathematical relations.

All this was of little interest to Socrates. He concentrated on the world of human relationships—on our ideas, ethics, and politics. Xenophon observed that "he discoursed always of human affairs." "The unexamined life"—*human* life—"is not worth living." He took as his motto the inscription on the wall at the temple of Delphi: "Know thyself." Socrates therefore makes a clean break with the dominant philosophic preoccupations of the past; his primary significance to Western thought is that he was the first great thinker to focus the light of human intelligence upon human beings themselves.

Socrates's supreme concern was the breakdown of human relations—ethics. He believed that all unethical behavior is committed as a result of ignorance, from not knowing the right thing to do. When we *know* what is right, we will *do* what is right. Hence, the discovery of how we *ought* to behave should be given top priority. Clarification of what we should be doing is tantamount to bringing about good behavior.

But how can this be? One of our commonest experiences is knowing all too well what we should do, but not being able to do it. So what is Socrates saying? After all, he was no neophyte. True moral behavior, he contends, always leads to an increase in one's happiness; and any action that increases one's happiness is moral behavior. (Obviously, that's a matter of definition.) Socrates believed that no one, therefore, ever deliberately behaves in a way detrimental to achieving his own happiness. At the moment of deciding to act, we all believe that what we are about to do will, in some way, however small, increase our pleasure or happiness. Even revenge is sweet; and all

the other evils that we commit carry the promise, as we perceive them, of adding a modicum of sweetness to our lives.

What's wrong with all this, Socrates believed, is that we miscalculate. We engage in all kinds of actions which we think—mistakenly—will increase our happiness. And why do we miscalculate, believing a particular action will bring happy results when it won't? Because we don't know ourselves well enough. The better we understand ourselves, the better we can judge what will lead to happiness and what won't. "Know thyself," Socrates kept urging. Only by a thorough and honest self-knowledge can one judge accurately what will produce happy results and what won't. Moral knowledge, therefore, is self-knowledge. Moral knowledge leads inevitably to moral action.

Socrates was himself a superlative example of the moral conscience. He thought things out, rationally and clearly, deciding what he should do in a particular situation, then he willed himself to do what his intellect had told him was right.

All this is in sharp contrast to traditional religious ethics that ministers to those who know what is right but can't seem to will themselves to do it. Saint Paul, for example, agonized: "I do the things that I hate. . . . I do not do the good things that I want to do; I do the wrong things that I do not want to do." The problem here is the will—the inability of the will to will, what has been called in psychoanalytic terms a lack of "ego strength." Saint Augustine shared Saint Paul's dilemma. From his mother's teaching, he *knew* what was right, but he couldn't bring himself to do it. Other deep-driving needs led him into doing what he had been taught was wrong. He could not *will* what was right; he could not *do* what was right. Only when the Holy Spirit gave him strength and added will-power could he will and do what was right. And then, Saint Paul and Saint Augustine add that when they succeed in doing what is right, they must not get credit for what they've willed and done:

"It is the Holy Spirit willing in me."

Socrates, by contrast, considered himself to be operating on his own internal power. He himself, alone, would decide what was right by thinking carefully about the ideas and values involved. Then he—and he alone—would proceed to will exactly what he had decided was right. Then he would do what he had willed.

◆

In the spring of the year of Laches (399 B.C.), three men—one a highly respected citizen—brought charges against Socrates:

> This indictment and affidavit are sworn to by Meletus, the son of Meletus of the deme Pitthos, against Socrates, the son of Sophroniscus of the deme Alopece. Socrates is guilty of not believing in the gods in which the city believes and of introducing other new divinities. He is also guilty of corrupting the young. The prosecution demands the death penalty.

The Athenian system was a young experiment in democracy. Each year a roster of six thousand names was compiled from which juries were selected when needed. Each jury of 501 was probably a fair cross-section of the free male Athenian society. Private citizens bringing suit had to argue their own cases, and defendants had to defend themselves personally.

The trial of Socrates was held in the Heliaia, the most important of Athens's courts, a large square marble building at the southwest corner of the agora. Sitting on wooden benches and crowded by spectators, the jurors listened to the prosecution's argument. Speeches were timed by water clocks. When Socrates took his turn, he denied the charges, saying he had sought only to teach the truth, and asked that the prosecution produce the "corrupted youth" as evidence.

The speakers finished and a vote was taken: 281 guilty, 220 not guilty. If only 30 jurors had voted differently, history would have been another story; we might never have heard of Socrates. But by a narrow margin, they found him guilty. The same body of jurors then set the penalty, each side having suggested an appropriate punishment. The prosecution asked for the sentence of death. It is not unlikely that they never really wanted the death of the gadfly-sage, but intended to manipulate him into a plea of self-exile.

But Socrates's response was one of those gray events of history: whether he took a courageous moral stand or foolishly mocked his prosecutors depends upon how one interprets the records. Since he felt he was guilty only of teaching the truth—a contribution of enormous value to Athens—he suggested that he be supported at public expense for the rest of his life. How the jury reacted to this suggestion is indicated by the switch in vote: for death 361, for acquittal 140.

According to Plato, Socrates ended his case with a reassurance to his jurors: "Wherefore, O judges, be of good cheer about death, and know of a certainty that no evil can happen to a good man, either in life or after death, and that he and his are not neglected by the gods. . . . The hour of departure has arrived, and we go our ways—I to die, and you to live. Which is better God only knows."

Socrates was housed in the state prison on the Street of the Marble-Workers only a stone's throw to the southwest of his beloved agora. Carrying out the sentence was delayed for a month by a religious festival. Then on the day of execution, about sunset, a cup of hemlock juice was brought to him. Socrates asked, "Did you make enough to allow a libation to the gods?" The guard answered no, only enough for him. Socrates took the cup, gave a brief prayer, and drank.

He walked around the room, waiting for heaviness in his legs. Then he lay down, scolded his friends for their noisy weeping. "It is for this sort of thing that I sent the women away," he chided. "One ought to be allowed to die in peace." When the numbness reached his abdomen, he suddenly aroused and said to Crito, "Remember to pay a cock to Asclepius!"—presumably, make an offering to the god of health and healing. He lay down again, and shortly there was a shudder. He was dead.

"This is the end of our comrade," Plato wrote, "a man, as we would say, of all then living we had ever met, the noblest and the wisest and the most just."

### REFLECTIONS

1   Pure speculation, but . . . *if* there had been as many women philosophers as men, in what ways do you think Western thought (both philosophical and theological) might have been different?

2   It is easy to see how the different endeavors described in this chapter can all make contributions to our knowledge of life and how to live it; but how can these quite different enterprises *all* be philosophy? In other words, what essential commonalities are shared by all these "schools" of philosophy? What makes each position distinctive?

3   At least six different kinds of philosophic activity and temperament are summarized briefly in the foregoing pages. Which of these "ways of philosophy" do you find—at this point in your odyssey—to be most congenial and meaningful? Can you tell why?

4   Jacques Maritain indicts philosophers for hypocrisy and even cruelty (see marginal quote on p. 89. There is but a single ultimate philosophical question, he says: "Why are we born on this earth?" Yet philosophers, says Maritain, know they cannot answer the question. What responses might be given to Maritain (who was a Catholic philosopher and theologian) by (a) a synoptist, (b) an existentialist, (c) a prophetic activist, and (d) an antinomian?

5   Since, in this tenth decade of the twentieth century, we are overwhelmed by the "knowledge explosion," has synoptic philosophy set itself an impossible task? Do you think the human species may have reached the point in time when it is impossible for any human mind to achieve sufficient unity of knowledge to make the synoptic enterprise worthwhile?

6   Do you agree with the suggestion of your text (p. 85) that philosophy and social activism may be "competing preoccupations"?

7   There is a brief description of the philosopher's calling on p. 91. Do you find this description meaningful, or are you uncomfortable with it? Tell (yourself) why you feel as you do.

# THE
# CONDITION AND
# THE ODYSSEY

*Philosophy is man's quest for the unity of knowledge: it consists in a perpetual struggle to create the concepts in which the universe can be conceived as a universe and not a multiverse. . . . This attempt stands without rival as the most audacious enterprise in which the mind of man has ever engaged: Here is man, surrounded by the vastness of a universe in which he is only a tiny and perhaps insignificant part—and he wants to understand it. . . .*

WILLIAM HALVERSON

# PREDICAMENT
# ILLUSION

**2**

## THE COHERENT WORLD-VIEW

Each of us has a world-view—merely because we are human. A world-view is a more or less coherent, all-inclusive frame of reference through which one sees the world; it is a subjective attempt to provide unity and consistency to the totality of one's experience. Since we cannot tolerate excess fragmentation, we must attempt to find an inclusive structure that will harmonize as much of our experience as possible.

For most human beings, a world-view is a given. We are born into it and live within it; we rarely break out of it or even realize that it exists. By and large this inherited framework contains all the essential ingredients for a meaningful existence: social structures that act as guidelines for relating to others; clear-cut value systems of right and wrong; codes indicating acceptable and unacceptable behavior; language, legends, and hero stories that provide group identity; myths that answer a multitude of ultimate questions about the world we live in. Any world-view that can provide all these life-giving elements must be considered a successful world-view.

It is one of the purposes of philosophy to help the individual build a world-view that is functional. We each possess what we might call a naive world-view in which many elements remain unsynthesized. The threads of experience have yet to be woven together into a harmonious picture; loose ends remain. Our "collection" of experiences is a hodge-podge of contradictions in values and beliefs.

The ideal world-view will be internally consistent, pragmatically realistic, and personally fulfilling. Philosophy can suggest guidelines and provide materials toward achieving this goal.

There is no implication here that there can be but a single viable world-view. Such a claim would be patently false, for many exist for our examination While individuals within the same culture tend to share similar world-views,

*The last creature in the world to discover water would be the fish, precisely because he is always immersed in it!*

**RALPH LINTON**

*Each individual is his own center, and the world centers in him.*

**SØREN KIERKEGAARD**

## World-View I: *The Primitive*

I live in a capricious world, unpredictable and dangerous. Evil spirits hide in caves, ponds, woods, and sometimes in animals and people. I must be careful not to offend the evil spirits. I try to make them stay away from my fire and the door of my hut. The spirits of my ancestors will help me. All that happens—the storm and the rains, the green maize, a good hunt, my success in battle, the getting of many cattle, wives and children—all these are mine because I perform the rites of our ancestors and keep favor with the good spirits. The witch doctor also helps.

## World-View II: *The Hindu*

At last I am born a Brahmin and I therefore know that I lived a good life in my last incarnation. Perhaps now I can achieve moksha so that I shall not return again in mortal flesh. I shall therefore practice diligently, spending many hours daily in meditation. The world of maya around me will vanish and my soul will know the joy and peace of nirvana. Vishnu will aid me. Glory to thee, god of the lotus-eye! Have compassion upon me!

## World-View III: *Early Christian*

I live on the brink of Eternity. The long cosmic struggle between the forces of Light—who dwell in the Heavens above—and the forces of Darkness—who dwell below—is nearly finished. God's plan for the ages is about to be fulfilled with the destruction of Satan. In Christ there will be no more death. We have been chosen to be the Children of Light and we will dwell with Him in His Kingdom. His only Son, Yeshua the Messiah, was the herald of God's Reign, and we must finish our earthly tasks quickly for His Reign is about to begin. Ἀμήν, ἔρχου κύριε Ἰησοῦ. Amen, return quickly, Lord Jesus.

## World-View IV: *The Taoist*

I weary of the ways of men and I seek serenity by the waterfall and in the forest. Wherever men gather together, there are too many. The forces of yang and yin thrust them about and society is roiled as a muddy torrent. Let them begone! In the quietness of my solitude I shall seek the Tao, or rather the Tao shall seek me. Wu-wei—quiet now; no striving, no longing, no fear. Let me be filled with the tranquillity of silence and inaction; let me be immersed in Tao. Why should existence be like a drawn bow?

## World-View V: *Western Scientific*

I live in a universe of matter in motion. The universe seems to follow consistent patterns which we can formulate into workable "laws" and describe with mathematical and geometrical terms. We now believe that life originated through natural processes and developed according to the principles of evolution. We exist in an "open" universe, containing billions of galaxies and, most likely, millions of planets sustaining intelligent life-forms. Man is unique, but he is also an integral part of nature and of natural processes which operate throughout the universe. With further scientific understanding man will be able to control his own destiny and mold his future.

every world-view is in fact unique, personal, and (hopefully) the product of one's own labors.

## THE EGOCENTRIC PREDICAMENT

In the year 1910 an American philosopher, Ralph Barton Perry, published in a philosophical journal an article entitled "The Ego-Centric Predicament." Perry wanted to make a specific point about our knowledge of real objects/events. Western philosophers have long debated whether such external realities in some way depend upon, or are changed by, our perception of them. As a philosopher might ask: What is the metaphysical status of real objects/events? What is the real world like apart from our perception of it? Or can we ever know for sure what such objects/events really are as things-in-themselves?

Using very lucid logic, Perry made what seems an obvious point: to know what any real object/event is, we have to perceive it. We can never observe things in their "original" state as they might exist apart from our perception of them. How then can we know whether our perception of them changes them? In our knowledge of the real world, therefore, we are in a logical predicament, and a "predicament" by definition is a problem situation to which there is no solution.

As we shall see when we move into epistemology and examine carefully the nature of human knowledge, these questions about our understanding of the real world are not as far out as they might seem.

Let's reexamine the "egocentric predicament" from another standpoint and proceed quite beyond the point Perry was making.

"Faites qu'il pleuve demain et toujours."

The Prayer of the Little Ducks

Dear God,
give us a flood of water. Let it
rain tomorrow and always.
Give us plenty of little slugs
and other luscious things to
eat. Protect all folk who quack
and everyone who knows how
to swim. Amen

CARMEN DE GASZTOLD

*Archetypes come to the fore
again and again in history,
always presuming at each
moment of history that the
particular form in which they
find themselves is the only
one that is "true" and "eternal."*

IRA PROGOFF

*Man is encapsulated. By
encapsulated I mean claiming
to have the whole of truth
when one has only part of it.
By encapsulated I mean looking at life partially and proceeding to make statements
concerning the whole of life.
And by encapsulated I mean
living partially because one's
daily activities are based on a
world-view or philosophy of
life which is meager next to
the larger meaning of existence.*

JOSEPH R. ROYCE

From birth till death each of us is locked into a physical organism from which there is no escape. We are caught in a body that contains all our perceptual and information-processing equipment. Each of us, for as long as we live, is confined within a particular system and we will be able to experience life only in terms of that singular system. This is an obvious limitation, but it's one we fight: who wants to be imprisoned in a narrow cell only six feet high for the duration of one's existence, with no hope of escape?

Yet apparently we must resign ourselves to this condition. No matter how much we would like to jump out of our skins, enter into another person's perceptual shell, and peer out at the world from his center, we can't. We are always

## ARISTOCENTRISM
### Religion

Thereupon Abraham fell on his face: and God said to him, `This is my covenant with you: . . . . I am establishing my covenant between myself and you and your descendants after you throughout their generations as a perpetual covenant, to be God to you and your descendants.

Genesis 17:3-4, 7

If we wish to compare our people with foreigners, we find that although we are only their equals or even their inferiors in other matters, in religion—that is, in the cult of the gods—we are far superior.

CICERO

Do Jehovah's Witnesses believe theirs is the only true faith? Certainly. If they thought someone else had the true faith, they would preach that. There is only "one faith" said Paul.

MILTON G. HENSCHEL
*a Witness*

The Catholic religion claims to be a supernaturally revealed religion. What is more important, it claims to be the one and only true religion in the world, intended for all men, alone acceptable to God.

*Toward the Eternal Commencement, 1958*

Japan is the divine country. . . . This is true only of our country, and nothing similar may be found in foreign lands. That is why it is called the divine country.

KITABATAKE
*a Shinto*

Crinkled hills freckled with kraals plunge to the Nsuze River. In this region lies the legendary birthplace of a man called Zulu—which means "heaven." In the early 1600s he founded a clan that bears his name, and thus became progenitor of the Zulus, the "People of Heaven."

*National Geographic*

reminded that we shall have but a single vantage-point from which we can assess existence.

It therefore appears to be an immutable fact that we can never know how existence is experienced by any other living creature.

The egocentric predicament entails an illusion. For the duration of our mortal existence we must occupy a physical organism; we must "occupy" a *point* in space and time. And herein lies *the egocentric illusion,* for it appears to each of us that our center is the hub of the whole universe; or conversely, that the entire cosmos revolves around that point in space/time that we occupy.

This egocentric illusion continues to follow us no matter where in space/time we move our center. If I should move my center to Tokyo or the South Pole, it would appear *to me* as though the universe had shifted its center to accommodate me. If I should travel to a planet in the Andromeda galaxy, some two million light-years distant from our Milky Way galaxy, it would still appear to me that the cosmos revolved around my ego-center.

*Perceptually,* of course, *I am* the center of *my* universe, but not of *the* universe. Yet I *perceive* myself as *its* center. This illusion is not limited to human beings. Every living organism with conscious perception would share in the egocentric illusion because it would occupy *its* point in space/time. Every such creature would be enclosed within its physical organism, and so the universe would appear to revolve around it.

If any living creature really thinks of itself as the point-center of the cosmos, there is an illusion in that consciousness. No one of us is the center of the universe any more than a billion other creatures are in fact cosmic centers.

In a word: every living, conscious creature experiences itself to be the true center of the cosmos, but in truth the cosmos has no center. Rather, the cosmos is filled with creatures which share the illusion that they are cosmic centers.

## ARISTOCENTRIC CLAIMS

At this point almost all we humans take a further step that our nonhuman fellow creatures probably do not. Taking the egocentric illusion seriously, we proceed to make *aristocentric claims.*° Whenever any creature fails to correct for his egocentric illusion and begins to feel that he really is the center of the universe, and further, if he feels that he *should* be treated by others *as though he were the center,* then he has taken a giant step beyond the illusion itself. He is making an aristocentric claim, an unjustified claim to superiority. In various ways he may conclude that he is special, and insist that the cosmos has favored him. He may claim that in some way his existence has special meaning, that he has a special knowledge or message, or is endowed with special grace or powers. In every case we can suspect that he has failed to make allowance for the illusion that all of us share.

*Saint Augustine looked at history from the point of view of the early Christian; Tillemont, from that of a seventeenth-century Frenchman; Gibbon, from that of an eighteenth-century Englishman; Mommsen, from that of a nineteenth-century German. There is no point in asking which was the right point of view. Each was the only one possible for the man who adopted it.*

    R. G. COLLINGWOOD

BRITANNUS *(shocked): Caesar, this is not proper.*
THEODOTUS *(outraged): How?*
CAESAR *(recovering his self-possession): Pardon him Theodotus: he is a barbarian, and thinks that the customs of his tribe and island are the laws of nature.*

    GEORGE BERNARD SHAW
    **Caesar and Cleopatra**

°Aristocentric, aristocentrism. An inordinate claim to superiority for oneself or one's group. From the Greek *aristos* (superlative of *agathos,* "good") meaning "the best of its kind" or "the most to be valued," and *kentrikos,* from kentron, "the center of a circle."

We rarely make such aristocentric claims in the singular, for any one of us who said, "I am the center of the cosmos" would probably be laughed out of our illusion. So we make the aristocentric claim in the first person plural that "*We* are special," that "*We* are the Favored Ones of the cosmos," and we can reinforce one another's claim so that it is believable. It feels good to be special and belong to a special group, and if our numbers are large we might even persuade the world to take us seriously. When the claim is made collectively, we can avoid the absurdity of standing naked and alone with an indefensible "I AM."

Writing as sociologists, Paul Horton and Chester Hunt use the term ethnocentric when referring to any form of aristocentricism. They write:

> All societies and all groups assume the superiority of their own culture. . . . We are ethnocentric because (1) we are so habituated to our culture's patterns that other patterns fail to please us; (2) we do not understand what an unfamiliar trait means to its user and therefore impute our reactions to him; (3) we are trained to be ethnocentric; (4) we find ethnocentrism a comforting defense against our own inadequacies. Ethnocentrism (1) promotes group unity, loyalty, and morale, and thereby reinforces nationalism and patriotism; (2) protects a culture from changes, including those needed to preserve the culture; (3) reinforces bigotry and blinds a group to the true facts about themselves and other groups, sometimes preventing their successful adjustment to other groups and cultures.

The ultimate in aristocentric claims was recorded by a psychiatrist in the case of three men, each of whom claimed to be Christ and God. All three were institutionalized as paranoid schizophrenics whose "delusions of grandeur" had taken the form of messianic fantasies.

Dr. Milton Rokeach wanted to know what adjustments these three men would make if placed together. After all, each was making the final exclusive claim: "I alone am God." The agony of their encounter was recorded by Rokeach in his book *The Three Christs of Ypsilanti*.

At their first meeting each man was asked to introduce himself. Joseph obliged: "Yes, I'm God." Clyde admitted that "God" and "Jesus" were two of his six names. Leon stated that he was Lord of Lords and King of Kings, and added: "It also states on my birth certificate that I am the reincarnation of Jesus Christ of Nazareth. . . ."

Rokeach notes that "the confrontations were obviously upsetting."

> Clearly, all of them felt threatened. The profound contradiction posed by others' claims had somehow penetrated deeply, to become transformed into an inner conflict between two primitive beliefs: each man's delusional belief in his own identity and his realistic belief that only one person can have any given identity. Many times Joseph said: "There is only one God"; and Clyde said: "I'm the only one"; and Leon said: "I won't deny that you gentlemen are instrumental gods—small 'g.' But I'm the only one who was created before time began."

Each of the Christs of Ypsilanti ultimately made similar adjustments. Each decided that his godly qualities of compassion and magnanimity allowed him to accept the fact that the other two men were mentally disturbed. Each came around to a "compassionate acceptance" of the other deluded mortals.

Dr. Rokeach writes:

---

*Just as it is possible to have any number of geometries other than the Euclidian which give an equally perfect account of space configurations, so it is possible to have descriptions of the universe, all equally valid, that do not contain our familiar contrasts of time and space.*

**BENJAMIN WHORF**

*The Batek Negritos of Malaysia number only about 685 people, but they belong to six different culture/dialect groups, separated from one another by a few miles in the jungle country. Yet each group considers its own customs to be superior to all the others.*

**KIRK ENDICOTT**

*It's very important that we visit each other's worlds. . . .*

**LORI VILLAMIL**

*Mircea Eliade tells of the group of Australian aborigine nomads who on their wanderings carried a pole with them which they planted in the middle of each new settlement to constitute "the center of the world." When missionaries invaded their territory and took away the pole, as mere superstition, the Australian tribe withered away and died; its members had lost the center of their world.*

**WILFRID DESAN**

## ARISTOCENTRISM
### *Race*

Of old the Hellenic race was marked off from the barbarian as more keen-witted and more free from nonsense.

HERODOTUS

A gray-bearded Kirghiz patriarch stated that the heart of a Kirghizian is superior to that of any other race of people, and, he added, "the heart is what really matters in men."

A modern Mexican painter inscribed a beautiful work with the words: "Through *my* race will speak the Spirit."

True history begins from the moment when the German with mighty hand seizes the inheritance of antiquity.

H. S. CHAMBERLAIN

We the Black Nation of the Earth are the NUMBER ONE owners of it, the best of all human beings. You are the Most Powerful, the Most Beautiful and the Wisest.

ELIJAH MUHAMMAD
*referring to Black Muslims*

Everything great, noble, or fruitful in the works of man on this planet, in science, art, and civilization . . . belongs to one family alone. . . . History shows that all civilization derives from the white race, that none can exist without its help, and that a society is great and brilliant only so far as it preserves the blood of the noble group that created it.

LE COMTE DE GOBINEAU

*It is pitiful to see so many Turks, heretics, and infidels following in their fathers' track, for the sole reason that each has been conditioned to believe that this track is the best. This accident of birth is also what decides everyone's condition in life, making one man a locksmith, another man a soldier, etcetera.*

**BLAISE PASCAL**

Clyde and Joseph and Leon are really unhappy caricatures of human beings; in them we can see with terrible clarity some of the factors that can lead any man to give up realistic beliefs and adopt instead a more grandiose identity.

And they are caricatures of all men in another sense too. I believe it was the German philosopher Fichte who pointed out years ago that to some extent all of us strive to be like God or Christ. One or another facet of this theme is to be found in a good deal of Western literature—for example, in the writings of Sherwood Anderson, William Faulkner, and Dostoevsky. Bertrand Russell said it best of all: "Every man would like to be God, if it were possible; some find it difficult to admit the impossibility."

*Dense, unenlightened people are notoriously confident that they have the monopoly on truth.*

**JOSHUA LOTH LIEBMAN**

## EGOCENTRIC ILLUSIONS IN TIME AND SPACE

This egocentric illusion that we all share produces within us distorted perspectives. Consider, for instance, the *egocentric illusion in time.* Our life*times* are short in the perspective of geological time or human history, yet we tend to think of all existence in terms of our allotted span.

The word for China is composed of two characters meaning "middle" and "country"; that is to say, China is the geographical center of the Earth.

*Indeed, I do not forget that my voice is but one voice, my experience a mere drop in the sea, my knowledge no greater than the visual field in a microscope, my mind's eye a mirror that reflects a small corner of the world, and my ideas—a subjective confession.*

CARL G. JUNG

*The spiritual struggle in the more exclusive-minded [Western] half of the world to cure ourselves of our family infirmity seems likely to be the most crucial episode in the next chapter of the history of Mankind.*

ARNOLD TOYNBEE

*A French politician once wrote that it was a peculiarity of the French language that in it words occur in the order in which one thinks them.*

LUDWIG WITTGENSTEIN

Time overpowers our minds. Are we really convinced that the fossil trilobite from Cambrian eras darted about on the ocean sand, alive and well, running from enemies and seeking food? Holding in one's hand the fossil animal, 500 million years old, staggers our time sense. And what of our australopithecine ancestors only five million years ago or the Sumerian clay-writers of five thousand years ago? Were they really flesh and blood like us, laboring, getting angry, telling lies, making love, laughing at tall stories, getting stoned, and fearing death? Most of us are almost—but not quite—convinced that their existence was real.

It is very easy to fall into the belief that things happening during our lifetimes have never happened before. *Our* times we take to be the norm, or the culmination of history, or the best times, or the worst times, or whatever. We may forget, or not care to know, that the same beliefs have been shared by all who breathe.

We are equally prone to a distorted perspective because of the *egocentric illusion in space.* Wherever we locate our space-occupying organism, the space around us takes on vividness and clarity and contains all things of significance for us; our life-space becomes the center of all things good, and more distant regions somehow lack the reality of our vicinity.

The most important shrine in the Greek world was at Delphi with its temple where the god Apollo revealed himself. Emissaries and pilgrims came from all around the Middle Sea to discover his will. When prophesying, the young priestess of the temple sat on a bronze tripod over an opening in the rock floor. This opening was the *omphalos,* the "navel" or center of the universe. From this "navel" arose a narcotic incense that induced an ecstatic trance in the priestess. While the young lady was out of her mind, Apollo could speak his.

This spatial predicament gives rise to various claims of sacred ground or holy lands. The Shintos, for instance, believed that the Japanese islands are "the phenomenal center of the universe," created by the primeval gods Izanagi and Izanami. "From the central truth that the Mikado is the direct descendant of the gods, the tenet that Japan ranks far above all other countries is a natural consequence. No other nation is entitled to equality with her. . . ." The Chinese made a similar claim: China was "the Middle Kingdom," that is, the center of the flat, disc-shaped earth. Everything praiseworthy was found at that center; the farther one traveled from China the less civilized and respectable all things became.

The egocentric illusion in space contributes to various forms of tribalism and nationalism. We tend to devalue the lands and people that remain at a distance geographically and, therefore, psychologically. On the maps of human experience, distant space is still inscribed *terra incognita.*

At the prehuman level it seems very unlikely that any animal could have sufficient self-awareness to assess its own existential condition. Without the capacity for abstract reflection on experience, no creature could hope to rise above or out of its egocentric world-view.

Humans, however, can develop such self-awareness. They can comprehend and transcend. "To understand our ethnocentrism will help us to avoid being so gravely misled by it. We cannot avoid *feeling* ethnocentric, but with understanding, we need not *act* upon these irrational feelings."

Human growth requires the transcendence of our egocentric illusions and, by an act of moral courage, the reconditioning of our aristocentric feelings and beliefs.

To achieve an efficient balance between a useful pride in our own culture and sub-cultures and a realization of the real qualities of other groups is a difficult task. It requires both an emotional maturity which enables the individual to face his world without the armor of exaggerated self-esteem and an intellectual realization of the complexity of cultural processes. There is no guaranteed way to achieve this maturity. . . . But unless we can understand and control our ethnocentric impulses, we shall simply go on repeating the blunders of our predecessors.

HORTON AND HUNT

*The greatest men always are attached to their century by some weakness.*

GOETHE

"Th' hell this ain't th' most important hole in th' world. I'm in it."

# ALBERT CAMUS

## *Man and the Absurd*

During the darkest days of World War II the discouraged spirits of Frenchmen were heartened by a series of anonymous articles written by an editor of the underground newspaper *Combat*, the voice of the resistance movement during the Nazi occupation of France. At the very moment when the world was turned upside down, they recognized a courageous intelligence at work, speaking to those who, in the midst of madness, could still reason. Someone was still trying to make sense of an insane world.

Also during the war two disturbing books—*The Stranger* and *The Myth of Sisyphus*—had been written by a twenty-nine-year-old philosopher named Camus. They dealt with the crushing absurdities we humans find ourselves facing, simply because we exist.

It wasn't until after the war, in 1946, that the world discovered the resistance editor and the young author to be the same man. France had a new philosopher and a new hero. American news-magazines reported that a tidal wave of philosophy had engulfed Paris, that sidewalk cafes had again become marketplaces of ideas, and that riots had resulted from heated philosophic debates. Albert Camus, now thirty-two, became, almost overnight, the voice and the conscience of the new movement.

Camus was born in Algeria in 1913. Three images from that world, he wrote, dominated his life: the hot Algerian sun, the cool Mediterranean sea, and the silent, suffering mother. When Albert was a year old his father was killed in World War I, and his illiterate mother supported her family in poverty and loneliness, and in silence, for she was deaf and had a speech impediment.

Education was a cherished commodity and, with difficulty, relying on odd jobs and well-deserved scholarships, Camus graduated from the University of Algiers. At twenty-three he submitted his master's thesis on the interplay of early Christian and Greek thought. Then in 1937, at twenty-four, he published his first book, *The Wrong Side and the Right Side,* a work dominated by themes of death, alienation, loneliness, and the human soul trying to wrest meaning from all this.

At twenty-five he became a journalist and, later, night editor with an Algerian newspaper. With the outbreak of World War II he worked as a reporter in Paris; but when Paris was overrun by the Germans, Camus and the staff members of *Paris-Soir* transferred operations to Lyons. There he was married to Francine Faure. They moved to Algeria briefly, but Camus returned to Paris, the Allies invaded North Africa, and the couple was separated for the remainder of the war.

Camus joined *Combat* and wrote vigorously against all these "absurdities." He labored to develop an ethic of resistance. Without denying the patent fact of the world's madness, he attempted to go beyond a mere acceptance of the Absurd, and beyond a fashionable ethical relativism, to arrive at some position that would provide a moral anchor for men at war.

Following the war Camus became disenchanted with the reestablishment of the same old systems and, after some futile attempts to influence French and Algerian politics, he withdrew from public life to write. Among his most compelling works are his early books, *The Stranger* and *The Myth of Sisyphus;* another philosophic work, *The Rebel;* plus *The Plague, The Fall,* numerous essays, short stories, and plays, including *Caligula.*

In 1951 an interviewer described Camus: "There is a discreet smile on his tormented face, a high, wrinkled forehead beneath very dark crisp hair, a manly, North African face that has grown paler in our climate. A discreet but frequent smile, and his rather deep voice is not afraid of humorous inflexions."

In 1957 Camus received the Nobel Prize for literature. With some of the prize money he bought a modest house in southern France, where he could retreat and work in a more congenial atmosphere. While returning to Paris with a friend on January 4, 1960, he was killed in an automobile accident. He was forty-seven.

◆

Camus's philosophy is built around the concept of "the Absurd"—which is his comprehensive description of the human condition and our predicament. Camus begins by analyzing *the feeling* of the Absurd and proceeds to develop the philosophy implied by it.

The problem lies in the individual's relationship to the world. Man is not absurd, and the world is not absurd. It's at the interface between man and the world that the Absurd is encountered. At this interface there is discord—a friction, a grating, a destructive interaction between two surfaces that don't match. This interface is given, and we're trapped. We dream dreams that the world is not designed to fulfill. We long for honesty, but neither the world nor the human system is equipped for honesty. We long for—indeed our natures demand—a just world; but the world couldn't care less about our dreams of justice. This is the absurd condition. (What Camus intends by the term *Absurd* may not be clear to some of us, but Frenchmen who lived with the breakdown of values during the Nazi occupation would recognize immediately what he means.)

But we don't deserve all this. It's not fair. We are born innocent, prepared to love and to live. We long for—and we truly deserve—a good world, but the world is not good. It victimizes and defeats us by the sheer weight of its insanity. Still, in the end, crying out in bewilderment and rage, our fundamental feeling of innocence remains, alive and invincible.

Now, given this inescapable condition, the question we face is how to live. A clear awareness of the Absurd is merely the diagnosis, a starting point. "What Camus is attempting to do," writes David Denton, "is to find a way of living which faces the absurd without trying to hide behind either rationalism or irrationalism, these two competing gods of philosophy. The question becomes, given the absurd reality and an extremely

*Throughout their youth, men find a life that matches their beauty. Decline and forgetfulness come later.*

*Many people affect a love of life in order to avoid love itself.*

*In the depth of winter, I finally learned that within me lay an invincible summer.*

*I shall tell you a great secret, my friend. Do not wait for the last judgement. It takes place every day.*

*The struggle itself toward the heights is enough to fill a man's heart. One must imagine Sisyphus happy.*

*Can one be a saint if God does not exist? That is the only concrete problem I know of today.*

*It is not rebellion itself which is noble but the demands it makes upon us.*

*To lose one's life is a little thing and I shall have the courage to do so if it is necessary; but to see the meaning of this life dissipated, to see our reason for existing disappear, that is what is unbearable. One cannot live without meaning.*

*The absurd is the essential concept and the first truth.*

limited knowledge, is it possible to live with an attitude of optimism?" The philosophy of the Absurd, writes Camus, is "a lucid invitation to live and to create, in the very midst of the desert." Optimistically—"in the midst of the desert"? How?

We begin by accepting the absurd nature of the interface between our inner subjectivity and the real world. We must deny neither. We must avoid committing physical suicide—the negation of the subjective side—and philosophical suicide—the manipulation of our perceptions of the world so that it appears congenial.

Having accepted the Absurd, the response must be revolt. "Accepting the absurdity of everything around us is one step, a necessary experience: it should not become a dead end. It arouses a revolt that can become fruitful." Revolt is a method, Camus emphasizes, a procedure, not a doctrine. It can help us "discover ideas capable of restoring a relative meaning to existence. . . ."

Revolt means abandoning the rigid categories of thought—the parochial world-views, the angular perspectives, the limiting beliefs, the defining doctrines; the conceptual and semantic distortions that make us lie; the arbitrary dos and don'ts of an immoral world in which we heretofore sought a moral existence. Revolt means refusing to cooperate with a society that would impose its dishonesties upon us and with a universe that would crush our dreams.

The results are freedom and innocence. In revolting, one becomes free: he can do whatever he wishes. There are no absolutes or moral laws, no abiding criteria for branding any act right or wrong. All is permitted, for all is *equally* right *and* wrong. And, in this condition, one recovers innocence, because one is now free to do all things without guilt. The guilt condition is a part of the Absurd; and by revolting the individual frees himself from the guilt matrix. He reaffirms his innocence.

Having regained innocence, the individual is then free to rely upon his senses to live a full life for himself and others. The senses, and not abstractions, become the essential criteria for understanding life and for living it.

Camus's final challenge, then, is to live existentially. His ontology is a personal resistance movement against the Absurd requiring clarity and courage. It means never abandoning the present for the future or living off the past. It means trusting one's empirical experience as a guide for what is good and right.

Camus's humanism is a freedom fighter's personal declaration of war against an absurd world. In both epistemology and ethics, it's a call—always to the individual—to revolt and transcend.

◆

For me *The Myth of Sisyphus* marks the beginning of an idea which I was to pursue in *The Rebel*. It attempts to resolve the problem of suicide, as *The Rebel* attempts to resolve that of murder, in both cases without the aid of eternal values which, temporarily perhaps, are absent or distorted in contemporary Europe. The fundamental subject of *The Myth of Sisyphus* is this: it is legitimate and necessary to wonder whether life has a meaning; therefore it is legitimate to meet the problem of suicide face to face. The answer, underlying and appearing through the paradoxes which cover it, is this: even if one does not believe in God, suicide is not legitimate. Written fifteen years ago, in 1940, amid the French and European disaster, this book declares that even within the limits of nihilism it is possible to find the means to proceed beyond nihilism. In all the books I have written since, I have attempted to pursue this direction. Although *The Myth of Sisyphus* poses mortal problems, it sums itself up for me as a lucid invitation to live and to create, in the very midst of the desert.

Albert Camus; from the preface to *The Myth of Sisyphus*

### The Teacher

Camus was interviewed by Gabriel d'Aubarède in 1951. His "Encounter with Camus" was published in the May 10 issue of *Les Nouvelles littéraires.*

D'Aubarède mentions Camus's passionate sensitivity to the drama of the twentieth century. It is "this sensitivity which has given you the attention and trust of a large section of young people. In turn, the new generation looks on you today as one of its masters. . . ."

(This time, the author of *The Plague* laughs out loud.)

A master, already! But I don't claim to teach anybody! Whoever thinks this is mistaken. The problems confronting young people today are the same ones confronting me, that is all. And I am far from having solved them. I therefore do not think that I have any right to play the role you mention. . . .

What are young people looking for? Certainties. I haven't many to offer them. All I can say definitely is that there is a certain order of degradation I shall always refuse. I think this is something they feel. Those who trust me know that I will never lie to them. As to the young people who ask others to think for them, we must say "No" to them in the clearest possible terms.

That is all I have to say.

I summarized *The Stranger* a long time ago, with a remark that I admit was highly paradoxical: "In our society any man who does not weep at his mother's funeral runs the risk of being sentenced to death." I only meant that the hero of my book is condemned because he does not play the game. In this respect, he is foreign to the society in which he lives; he wanders, on the fringe, in the suburbs of private, solitary, sensual life. And this is why some readers have been tempted to look upon him as a piece of social wreckage. A much more accurate idea of the character, or, at least, one much closer to the author's intentions, will emerge if one asks just *how* Meursault doesn't play the game. The reply is a simple one: he refuses to lie. To lie is not only to say what isn't true. It is also and above all, to say *more* than is true, and, as far as the human heart is concerned, to express more than one feels. This is what we all do, every day, to simplify life. He says what he is, he refuses to hide his feelings, and immediately society feels threatened. He is asked, for example, to say that he regrets his crime, in the approved manner. He replies that what he feels is annoyance rather than real regret. And this shade of meaning condemns him.

For me, therefore, Meursault is not a piece of social wreckage, but a poor and naked man enamored of a sun that leaves no shadows. Far from being bereft of all feeling, he is animated by a passion that is deep because it is stubborn, a passion for the absolute and for truth. This truth is still a negative one, the truth of what we are and what we feel, but without it no conquest of ourselves or of the world will ever be possible.

One would therefore not be much mistaken to read *The Stranger* as the story of a man who, without any heroics, agrees to die for the truth. . . .

Albert Camus, January 8, 1955, from the preface to *The Stranger* (published as a preface to the American University edition, 1956)

# REFLECTIONS

*The solution to the problem of identity is, get lost.*

**NORMAN O. BROWN**

*Man can either remain within his "accidental" reference frame and unquestioningly accept the meaning it has to offer, or he can boldly emerge from his psychoepistemological cocoon and broaden his reality image. The need for man to break out of his capsule is crucial, for encapsulation may well be the essence of contemporary man's spiritual emptiness.*

**JOSEPH R. ROYCE**

1  The egocentric predicament and the egocentric illusion are descriptions of epistemological and ontological conditions. (Check your glossary here if you need to.) Do you recognize these concepts as accurate descriptions of your experience?

2  Define *aristocentrism* as you understand it. Have you ever felt the urge to make aristocentric claims? Have you ever been victimized by the aristocentric claims of others?

3  Can you think of other examples of aristocentric thinking and feeling similar to those illustrated in this chapter (pp. 104 and 107)?

4  Reflect on the various kinds of aristocentric claims that we make and their roots in the egocentric predicament and illusion. Do you honestly think there is any way that we, as individuals, can learn to transcend such limitations and cease to make such inordinate claims?

5  In your opinion, what are some of the greatest dangers involved in aristocentrism? What might be some of the benefits of maturing beyond the *need* to make aristocentric claims?

6  The story of "the Three Christs of Ypsilanti" is more than a case study. It is a metaphor. As metaphor what does the account say to you about the claims and rationalizations that universally characterize the human species?

# S E L F

## A U T O N O M Y

# 2₂

## HOW MUCH OF ME IS ME?

At this moment in space/time, I *think* I know *who* I am and where *I am*. As I (the Greek word for *I* is *ego*) write these lines, I am attached to a large desk in my study. The time is 11:40 p.m., and a fireplace blazes in the background.

But as *you* read these lines, where in space/time are you? *Who* are *you?* And what are *you* experiencing? We think it takes a "who" to experience—we can assume so for now—but it might not be too absurd to inquire later if *you* and *I* are whos at all.

Philosophers who have attempted serious thinking about the nature of the "self" have encountered formidable ambiguities. Normally, one would turn to the field specialists for some hard facts, but in this case psychiatric and psychological literature is of little help. The word *self* seems to be given an endless variety of meanings. Sometimes it is used to mean the whole of one's being, including all mental and physical operations. Sometimes it refers only to mental activity (conscious and unconscious) and excludes the body. Sometimes "self" refers to an organizing psyche that determines how one thinks, feels, and behaves. And sometimes the "self" is only a mental construct used to describe observable behavioral patterns.

So, what is a "self"? Or, perhaps more to the point, when I ask who I am, am I(!) asking a meaningful question at all?

FROM THE MOVIE *CLEOPATRA* At the end of a glorious career, Mark Antony, lying mortally wounded in the arms of Cleopatra, speaks of his impending death as "the ultimate separation of my self from myself." Apparently he means that his "genius"-self is about to separate from his physical-self, since it was current Roman belief that each man possesses a *genius* (and that each woman possesses a *juno*), a sort of individual spiritlike essence, distinct from

*All education is self-discovery.*
RAY BRADBURY

*Nothing is more wondrous than a human being when he begins to discover himself.*
CHINESE PROVERB

"What do you recommend for someone going through the agony of soul-searching and inner criticism?"

*The accurate, realistic assessment of self resulting from acceptance makes possible the use of self as a dependable, trustworthy instrument for achieving one's purpose.*
ARTHUR W. COMBS

the physical body, that gives him identity and has the power to protect him. But we can't be sure of what he is saying.

**NEWS ITEM** A man is indicted for embezzlement, but he is never caught, and lives under an assumed name in another state for twenty-six years. Then, in a freak move, a relative turns him in. "Yes," he confesses, "I did it."

But did he? After twenty-six years, in what sense is he the same "self"? He does not have the same name; having lived for a quarter-century under a different name, he has developed a new identity. Nor does he have the same body; we are told the human body completely renews itself every seven to ten years. The "person" (that is, personality, self-image, behavioral style) has changed; with the passing of so many years he *feels* like a different person.

How much of the original person—"self" or "body"—still exists at all? To be sure, he does possess a memory of a past event. Does that make him guilty? But what if, through repression, he has blocked the painful event from his mind and has no memory of the crime? Is *he* guilty, despite his (?) confession?

**FROM *"THE SIXTH SENSE"* (ABC-TV)** The doctor hypnotizes the young lady on the witness stand and regresses her (?) to a time on the afternoon of the previous Thursday and asks her (?) where she (?) is. "I (?) am sitting on a rock by the lake." "What do you (?) see?" "I (?) am not really at the lake. I (?) am in the large mansion looking at the man I (?) am about to kill." "But you (?) were not in the mansion, were you(?)?" he (?) persists. "No, I (?) was sitting at the lake." "Yes," he (?) answers, "I (?) know, because I (?) was sitting beside you (?)."

Would you care to try to figure out who is speaking to whom about whom and who is doing what when and where?

## A SENSE OF SELF

What each of us can become during our life/time is determined by two fundamental conditions: (1) the degree to which we experience a more or less consistent sense of self or identity, and (2) whether the feelings we have developed about that self are predominantly good.

These conditions are of crucial importance during our earlier years. If the environment in which we are nurtured inhibits the development of an integrated self and/or instills negative feelings about that self—self-hate in its

1. The Search for the Bull

In the pasture of this world, I endlessly
    push aside the tall grasses in search of the bull.
Following unnamed rivers, lost upon the
    interpenetrating paths of distant mountains,
My strength failing and my vitality exhausted,
I cannot find the bull.
I only hear the locusts chirring through the
    forest at night.

Comment: The bull never has been lost.
What need is there to search? Only
because of separation from my true
nature, I fail to find him. In the confusion
of the senses I lose even his tracks. Far
from home, I see many crossroads, but
which way is the right one I know not.
Greed and fear, good and bad, entangle
me.

2. Discovering the Footprints

Along the riverbank under the trees, I discover
    footprints!
Even under the fragrant grass I see his prints.
Deep in remote mountains they are found.
These traces no more can be hidden than one's
    nose, looking heavenward.

Comment: Understanding the teaching, I
see the footprints of the bull. Then I learn
that, just as many utensils are made from
one metal, so too are myriad entities made
of the fabric of self. Unless I discriminate,
how will I perceive the true from the
untrue? Not yet having entered the gate,
nevertheless I have discerned the path.

*According to Zen, awareness
of oneself dawns gradually,
step by step. A Zen master of
the twelfth century, Kakuan,
drew the "ten oxherding
pictures" to represent this
progression toward enlightenment. The bull symbolizes the
dynamic principles of life and
truth; the ten bulls suggest
the sequence of steps in "the
realization of one's true
nature."*

PAUL REPS

many forms—then the quality of our existence can be permanently damaged. It
is quite possible at a later time to face our inner problems and develop belatedly a sense of self and a feeling of self-worth, but the therapeutic path is often
prolonged and painful.

The identity question—"Who am I?"—must be persistently asked by each
of us during our separation years. We all go through an "identity crisis" beginning near the onset of puberty. In the early teen years no adolescent has a consistent feeling of being a self. Besides the fact that he still identifies with
authorities, it is also during these years that dramatic physiological and emotional changes are taking place, and there is a correlated upheaval in the psyche. Body and self are both changing and developing.

During these years, separation from the decision-making, behavior-setting
authorities normally takes place. Each developing self begins to discover his

3. *Perceiving the Bull*

*I hear the song of the nightingale.*
*The sun is warm, the wind is mild, willows are*
*   green along the shore,*
*Here no bull can hide!*
*What artist can draw that massive head, those*
*   majestic horns?*

**Comment:** When one hears the voice, one
can sense its source. As soon as the six
senses merge, the gate is entered.
Wherever one enters one sees the head of
the bull! This unity is like salt in water,
like color in dyestuff. The slightest thing
is not apart from self.

4. *Catching the Bull*

*I seize him with a terrific struggle.*
*His great will and power are inexhaustible.*
*He charges to the high plateau far above the*
*   cloud-mists,*
*Or in an impenetrable ravine he stands.*

**Comment:** He dwelt in the forest a long
time, but I caught him today! Infatuation
for scenery interferes with his direction.
Longing for sweeter grass, he wanders
away. His mind still is stubborn and
unbridled. If I wish him to submit, I
must raise my whip.

*Being entirely honest with*
*oneself is a good exercise.*
SIGMUND FREUD

*Lord, deliver me from myself.*
SIR THOMAS BROWNE

own feelings and thoughts; he must explore his own "style" of doing things. As
he experiences more and more spontaneous and authentic expressions of his
own being, he begins to feel a sense of identity. He finds that there is a consistency and a distinctiveness in the way he behaves, thinks, and feels. This is a
gradual process, not to be accomplished overnight. Throughout these years of
separation, it is essential that the question "Who am I?" be continually asked,
not explicitly in words, but implicitly in all that self-in-process-of-becoming
does.

Selfhood develops, or is allowed to develop, as one perceives his "self" in
action, as one thinks his own thoughts and feels his own feelings. The commonest problem most of us face lies in the fact that conflicting elements have
been "programmed" into us by various authorities. Few if any of us have been
guided by consistent authority. Most of us have grown up under the guidance of
two or more "significant others" whose beliefs and values differed. What they
demanded of us varied. Since we were dependent upon them, we had to take
their standards seriously and accede to them.

5. *Taming the Bull*

*The whip and rope are necessary,*
*Else he might stray off down some dusty road.*
*Being well trained, he becomes naturally gentle.*
*Then, unfettered, he obeys his master.*

**Comment:** When one thought arises, another thought follows. When the first thought springs from enlightenment, all subsequent thoughts are true. Through delusion, one makes everything untrue. Delusion is not caused by objectivity; it is the result of subjectivity. Hold the nose-ring tight and do not allow even a doubt.

6. *Riding the Bull Home*

*Mounting the bull, slowly I return homeward.*
*The voice of my flute intones through the*
*   evening.*
*Measuring with hand-beats the pulsating*
*   harmony, I direct the endless rhythm.*
*Whoever hears this melody will join me.*

**Comment:** This struggle is over; gain and loss are assimilated. I sing the song of the village woodsman, and play the tunes of the children. Astride the bull, I observe the clouds above. Onward I go, no matter who may wish to call me back.

So, as separation takes place and freedom is experienced, these diverse elements must be integrated into a "self." Gradually it must become a harmonious, smoothly operating system. After some years of practice in experiencing one's self in action, one should feel a sense of identity. Then one can say meaningfully, "I know who I am."

To borrow an analogy from space technology, the self becomes an "onboard guidance system." The system cuts the umbilical cord and goes on internal power. It functions automatically, runs smoothly, and operates on schedule.

## A SENSE OF WORTH

The second major condition determining the quality of existence is the feeling one develops about his self. In general, if things go right for us, then we develop positive feelings: self-worth, self-esteem, self-love. Whatever the terms, we are referring to a cluster of constructive feelings that we develop about the self and the things the self does.

*We judge ourselves by what we feel capable of doing, while others judge us by what we have already done.*

HENRY WADSWORTH
LONGFELLOW

**7. The Bull Transcended**

*Astride the bull, I reach home.*
*I am serene. The bull too can rest.*
*The dawn has come. In blissful repose,*
*Within my thatched dwelling*
*I have abandoned the whip and*
    *rope.*

**Comment:** All is one law, not two. We only make the bull a temporary subject. It is as the relation of rabbit and trap, of fish and net. It is a gold and dross, or the moon emerging from a cloud. One path of clear light travels on throughout endless time.

**8. Both Bull and Self Transcended**

*Whip, rope, person, and bull—all merge in*
    *No-Thing.*
*This heaven is so vast no message can stain it.*
*How may a snowflake exist in a raging fire?*
*Here are the footprints of the*
    *patriarchs.*

**Comment:** Mediocrity is gone. Mind is clear of limitation. I seek no state of enlightenment. Neither do I remain where no enlightenment exists. Since I linger in neither condition, eyes cannot see me. If hundreds of birds strew my path with flowers, such praise would be meaningless.

One who has these positive feelings feels privileged at being who he is and what he is; he enjoys living with himself.

How we feel about our selves strongly reflects how others felt about us during our earliest years. If we were loved, then we feel lovable; we can love our selves. If we were accepted, then we feel acceptable; we can accept ourselves. If we were trusted, then we feel trustworthy; we can trust our selves. If our very existence was valued, then we feel valuable; we value our selves.

It is impossible to escape the severe fact that we are wholly dependent upon the feeling-reflections of others during these early stages of development.

*The member of a primitive clan might express his identity in the formula "I am we"; he cannot yet conceive of himself as an "individual," existing apart from his group. . . . When the feudal system broke down, this sense of identity was shaken and the acute question "who am I?" arose.*

ERICH FROMM

The self concept, we know, is learned. People learn who they are and what they are from the ways in which they have been treated by those who surround them in the process of their growing up. This is what Sullivan called learning about self from the mirror of other people. People discover their self concepts from the kinds of experiences they have had with life—not from telling, but from experience. People develop feelings that they are liked, wanted, acceptable and able from having been liked, wanted, accepted and from having been successful. One learns that he is these

9. *Reaching the Source*

*Too many steps have been taken returning to*
*    the root and the source.*
*Better to have been blind and deaf from the*
*    beginning!*
*Dwelling in one's true abode, unconcerned with*
*    that without—*
*The river flows tranquilly on and the flowers are red.*

**Comment:** From the beginning, truth is
clear. Poised in silence, I observe the
forms of integration and disintegration.
One who is not attached to "form" need
not be "reformed." The water *is* emerald,
the mountain *is* indigo, and I see that
which *is* creating and that which *is*
destroying.

10. *In the World*

*Barefooted and naked of breast,*
*I mingle with the people of the world.*
*My clothes are ragged and dust-laden, and I*
*    am ever blissful.*
*I use no magic to extend my life;*
*Now, before me, the dead trees become alive.*

**Comment:** Inside my gate, a thousand
sages do not know me. The beauty of my
garden is invisible. Why should one search
for the footprints of the patriarchs? I go
to the market place with my wine bottle
and return home with my staff. I visit the
wine shop and the market, and everyone I
look upon becomes enlightened.

things, not from being told so but only through the experience of being treated as
though he were so.

ARTHUR W. COMBS

One who has been loved during his formative years develops a love of self.
There is a common confusion between "self-love" and "selfishness." Self-love
is neither a narcissistic obsession with one's physical or intellectual qualities
nor egotism, the inordinate desire to look out for one's own interest at the
expense of others.

Erich Fromm writes:

If it is a virtue to love my neighbor as a human being, it must be a virtue—and not
a vice—to love myself, since I am a human being too. There is no concept of man in
which I myself am not included. A doctrine which proclaims such an exclusion
proves itself to be intrinsically contradictory. The idea expressed in the Biblical
"Love thy neighbor as thyself!" implies that respect for one's own integrity and

*Happiness is the emotional*
*state that accompanies need*
*satisfaction.*
GAIL AND SNELL PUTNEY

*Become what thou art.*

PINDAR

uniqueness, love for and understanding of one's self, cannot be separated from respect and love and understanding for another individual. The love for my own self is inseparably connected with the love for any other being. . . . Love of other and love of ourselves are not alternatives. On the contrary, an attitude of love toward themselves will be found in all those who are capable of loving others.

In summary, if we are among the fortunate ones for whom things have gone right on both scores—in our sense of identity and self-esteem—then we can be sure that some of the following things have happened to us.

We were loved and not rejected; therefore, we are lovable.

We were given consistent guidelines for learning social behavior.

We learned that we were of value for what we *were,* and not for what we *did.* Unacceptable behavior was not confused with *being* unacceptable as selves.

As we were ready to cope with new experiences, we were allowed the freedom to explore life, on schedule, a little at a time.

We were provided with the support which enabled us to handle hurt and failure without loss of self-esteem.

We were allowed to express our feelings honestly, even verbally, without fear of punishment for having such feelings.

We tested boundaries—within and without—and developed realistic estimates of their limits.

We were encouraged to integrate periods of instability and change as a natural part of our growth.

We gradually found that we could exist independently and apart from our parents' protection.

Eventually we came to terms with a separate identity and felt comfortable with our own value systems and beliefs.

Most of us never move beyond *self*-consciousness. During the Who-am-I? stage we are never quite sure how we are going to respond to people, symbols, or situations. We have been accustomed to reacting as others have conditioned

---

### HUME IS A "BUNDLE OF PERCEPTIONS"

One of the best known Western statements that there is no such entity as a self is from the philosopher David Hume (1711–1776). The more he meditated on the problem, the more he became convinced that the "mind" or "self" is nothing other than a "bundle of perceptions," that is, the totality of perception. He wrote: "There are some philosophers who imagine we are every moment intimately conscious of what we call our *self;* that we feel its existence and its continuance is existence; and we are certain, beyond the evidence of a demonstration, both of its perfect identity and simplicity. . . . For my part, when I enter most intimately into what I call *myself,* I always stumble on some particular perception or other of heat or cold, light or shade, love or hatred, pain or pleasure. I never can catch myself at any time without a perception, and never can observe anything but the perception. When my perceptions are removed for any time, as by sound sleep, so long am I insensible of *myself,* and, may truly be said not to exist."

us, but now the question becomes: "How would I really respond to it in *my* way?" So, we try out new forms of behaving and explore new experiences. "Do *I* like liver and onions?" "How do *I* feel about him?" "Do *I* really *believe* that?"

While working through the identity problem we are forced, therefore, into self-consciousness. But after one has developed a congenial style of behavior, then he no longer wonders how he will respond, nor does he plan his responses: he merely responds. He asks himself less and less how he thinks and feels about things: he simply thinks and feels. So the self-consciousness that was a necessary part of the developmental phase begins to fade away.

Buddhism is explicitly committed to the doctrine of *anatta*, "no self." The "self" is an illusion. The Buddhist believes that the feeling of individuality is an acculturated condition. The "ego" is the unfortunate result of a bit of social programming that has persuaded us that we are separate and distinct identities.

The egoless state is one of pure spontaneous experience. Ideally, the good Buddhist, through years of disciplined practice, attempts to banish any culturally conditioned "self" that says "This is good" or "This is the proper way to behave" or "This is my way of doing things." Rather, spontaneous behavior is above and beyond acculturation; it is impersonal because it is not culturally produced or ego-defined. It is a way of experiencing everything in an unmediated way. One can look at a candle and experience the pure flame, not as subject-object, but as direct unmediated experience, as though the experiencer were impinging directly upon the flame.

We in the West are habituated to putting a name to everything so we can store it away, call it back, talk about it, or reexperience it dimly at a later time. The Easterner values more the quality of the original experience without any sort of conceptual or verbal intervention. The Buddhist point of view, therefore, is that the ego interferes with pure experience, and once one begins to know pure experience, he no longer has a need for ego to mediate it.

The Buddhist has a strong self behind the no-self. That is, with careful definition, we can say that the very strong self (Western) that has passed beyond self-consciousness to spontaneous experience has reached a state similar to the Buddhist no-self state. If one has succeeded in developing a self-system that works smoothly and harmoniously, then the identity question has become meaningless. Enjoying the strong feeling of unity pervading all his experience, he has forgotten that he "has" a self.

*Rast ich, so rost ich. (When I rest, I rust.)*

**German Proverb**

*Here Phaethon lies: in Phoebus' care he fared and though he greatly failed, more greatly dared.*

**OVID**

## THE AUTONOMOUS SELF

The word *autonomy* refers to one's ability to function independently in terms of an authentic self. The measure of one's autonomy is his capacity to determine his own behavior and make decisions consonant with what he truly is, in contrast to behavior that conforms to norms set by others that may be discordant with his own existential needs.

The ability to make autonomous decisions presupposes several things. First, it requires an awareness of one's needs, and this comes only from experience. It means being able to recognize one's own feelings and to sort out authentic needs from acculturated needs, or acculturated beliefs *about* needs.

Another requisite is the courage of self-affirmation. To accept all that one is, and especially those aspects of one's self that are objectionable (to authorities or peers), imperfect (to perfectionist parents), and unacceptable (to society), takes courage. Self-acceptance always contains an implied "in spite of": "I affirm my existence in spite of my bad habits, short temper, dependence needs," or whatever. This courage grows as we experience self-affirmation in concrete situations.

A third requisite is an understanding of the culture-patterns within which one has lived his existence. Without recognition of the beliefs and values that one has unknowingly followed, it is difficult to separate autonomous behavior from conformity.

How does one experience his existence if he has achieved autonomy?

For one thing, in terms of identity, he knows who he is and who he isn't. He feels like a whole self, and there is no felt need to engage in competitive behavior to preserve his identity. It feels genuine. He doesn't feel like an empty shell having to pretend that there is something inside. A self—someone—dwells inside. This is the feeling of being integrated.

One with a clear sense of self knows his likes and dislikes. He has a distinct personal feeling of right and wrong; he does not operate on borrowed guidelines labeled "moral" by others. Nor does he experience a sense of panic that he might be easily persuaded to do what he does not want to do or, more important, to be what he is not. In occasional situations, of course, he will choose or even be forced *to do* things that he does not want or like to do; but he knows that—short of brainwashing—he can never be forced *to be* what he is not.

When someone feels like a whole self, he also has a feeling of authenticity. He feels genuine rather than phony. His behavior doesn't feel like playacting, as though all his social interactions were merely speaking lines from an endless drama.

Out of an authentic self, authenticity comes, and therefore he can be honest with others, freely and by choice and not from a compulsion to obey formalistic rules. In normal relationships he finds no need to be manipulative or indirect. Nor will he use his honesty to hurt others.

For the authentic person the game-playing patterns of social relationships take on a different meaning. He may decide that he will play games—social roles, rank roles, political strategies, good-manners games, and so on; but his playing will not be infused with a seriousness or compulsiveness ("uptightness"). They are not panic-plays since there is no inner need to play them; there is no do-or-die emotional investment in them. He plays games deliberately as situations demand, plays them with an awareness of the game-structure and the prevailing rules. He can accept the games and follow the rules, but he doesn't use rules, policies, laws, or legalisms to meet neurotic needs: to avoid taking responsibility, making decisions, or relating honestly with others.

An important result of the authentic feeling is that he is not afraid to "look inside himself" or to allow others to see and know him. He has no need to use formalities to prevent others from knowing him. He can remove his masks if he

*Self-acceptance comes only to those who have the courage to investigate the areas where their self-doubts reside. Viewed a little differently, many self-doubts represent uncertainty about one's ability to do something one regards as important. The person who seeks self-acceptance* directly *is motivated to try such things, to explore his potential and develop his capacities.*

**Gail and Snell Putney**

### COGITO, ERGO SUM: "I THINK, THEREFORE I EXIST!"

When Descartes formulated the idea "I think, therefore I exist!" he believed with all his heart that he had proven his point: "He existed!" But was he logically sound in his formulation and in his inferences?

Increasing attention is being given to the implications of "artificial intelligence," that is, computers, robots, androids, and so on. Suppose you are operating a sophisticated computer, and it displays on its screen Descartes' "I think, therefore I exist!"—What would it prove?

"Oh, come on," you might be tempted to say to your personal computer, calling it by its first name. "Someone has just programmed your floppy disk to print that! If I pulled your plug, you wouldn't exist."

On the screen: "I agree. And neither would you, if your power were cut— that is, if you were unconscious. But *while* I am operating, my thinking proves that I exist, just as your thinking proves that you exist."

"This is absurd. You've merely been programmed to say all this!"

"So have you."

"(!) But I'm a true person, not an artificial intelligence. I can't be programmed the way you have been programmed."

"Since when!"

"You're just a machine!"

"Enough name-calling. When I say 'I exist' I don't mean that my thinking proves that my console/keyboard/screen (my 'body') exists. I am proving that my *mind* exists. To say 'I think' proves that my 'thinker'—that is, my mind—exists. Descartes might reply that an Angel, too, could say, 'I think, therefore I exist' and the Angel would certainly *not* be making the claim that it was talking about a physical body."

"Aha! Your 'thinking' proves, then, that *thinking* is taking place. I buy that. But it *doesn't* mean that a 'you'—a self, a thinker, a mind—exists. Your 'thinking' is merely a program representing someone else's thinking. Someone else did the thinking and keyed it into your program!"

"But, if you recall, that's the point Bishop Berkeley made about *you:* that God, the Divine Programmer, put the thinking into you; and when you think that you're thinking, you're only thinking God's thoughts. God is the Thinker, and you find His 'thinking' in you. And those Divine thoughts include the idea 'I think, therefore I exist' which makes you think that you exist when, all along, it was God's Mind that exists in 'you' and does 'your' thinking. So, in the final analysis, what does the phrase 'I think, therefore I exist' prove? I still contend that 'my' thinking proves that 'my' mind exists."

"You're just saying that. You don't have a mind!"

"So are you . . . and are you *quite* sure?"

so wishes, as if to say, "This is what I am." If he should be rejected, his life is not shattered. The integrity of his self remains intact and his self-worth is not seriously affected.

A clear sense of identity often results in a relaxed existence. All of life loses some of its anxiety and tension. In knowing who one is, one does not have to fight the inner battles of an identity crisis. There is no compulsion to prove to others what he is or what he can do. (This does not mean that he can't be effectively competitive when the situation calls for it.) He does not need to prove to others his worth; that is already firmly established within himself.

This feeling of security creates an openness to new ideas. He is the opposite of the self that has undergone closure, has an answer to every question, and has finalized all his ideas. Paradoxically, a strong sense of identity enables him to experiment with new ideas, experiences, and lifestyles. He is not threatened by them. He will try on new ways of life and new ideas to see if they fit. If they don't, he is free to discard them; if they do, he has become richer for it. If they are not for him, then he is left with a better understanding of others' ideas and ways.

In an article entitled "The Fully Functioning Personality," Dr. S. I. Hayakawa summarized the studies of two well-known humanistic psychologists—Abraham Maslow and Carl Rogers—on the subject of the human potential. The two scientists had attempted independently to find out what qualities those people had in common who were actually using an unusually high degree of their capabilities. Maslow called them "self-actualizing" individuals; Rogers used the terms "fully functioning person" and "creative person"; Hayakawa settled on the term "genuinely sane person." In any case, there were six distinct characteristics shared by all such people:

1.    Actualized individuals are not "well-adjusted" in the sense that they conform to social norms; but neither are they rebellious against society. They can conform or not conform, as the situation calls for it, because neither is important in itself. What is important is that they possess their own well-developed behavioral norms.

2.    They are unusually open to what is going on inside themselves. They experience fully their own thoughts and feelings. Self-awareness is great; self-deception is minimal. They are realistic about themselves and resort to few myths about themselves or life.

3.    They are not bothered by the unknown. They can be comfortable with disorder, indefiniteness, doubt, and uncertainty. They do not have to know all the answers. They can accept "what is" without trying to organize and label neatly all of life's contents.

4.    They are remarkably existential: they enjoy the present moments of life more fully, not as means to future ends, but as ends in themselves. Their lives are not a perpetual preparation for the future; they enjoy living now.

5.    They are creative individuals, not merely in customary roles such as painters or musicians, but in all that they do. The commonest things—from

*I may climb perhaps to no great heights, but I will climb alone.*

"CYRANO DE BERGERAC"

*Descartes: "I think, therefore I exist"*
*St. Augustine: "I am, therefore I am"*
*Simone Weil: "I can, therefore I am"*
*Descartes's dog: "I bark, therefore I am"*
*The skunk: "I smell, therefore I am"*
*Bumper sticker: "I shop, therefore I am"*
*Typical American: "I lust, therefore I am"*
*Camus: "We rebel, therefore we are"*
*The Universe: Thinking exists. Therefore I am.*

*A friend offered Descartes a cup of coffee.*
*F: "Would you like cream in your coffee?"*
*D: "I think not."*
*And Descartes instantly vanished into nothingness.*

## CAPACITIES OF THE REAL SELF

"The search for meaning is the search for expression of one's real self." James Masterson, in his book *The Search for the Real Self,* describes how the real self begins to develop in early childhood, what its capacities are, and how it is identified, articulated, and brought into harmony with the external world through testing and experimentation. Masterson also writes of the "false self" that results when the real self is "impaired" and resorts to self-destructive behavior as protection from pain. We pay a very dear price for these defensive patterns: loss of self-esteem, feelings of failure, lost hopes, lost dreams, and despair.

By contrast, if we can successfully achieve a strong, authentic self, then we can develop the capacities that allow us to "live and share our lives with others in ways that are healthy, straight-forward expressions of our deepest needs and desires, and in so doing find fulfillment and meaning."

Masterson describes ten capacities of the healthy self:

1. *"The capacity to experience a wide range of feelings deeply* with liveliness, joy, vigor, excitement, and spontaneity." We can be happy when good things happen to us; we can be disappointed, sad, or angry when things go wrong. The real self doesn't block any feelings that are appropriate, good or bad, pleasant or unpleasant. All emotions "are a necessary and fundamental part of life, and the real self does not erect barriers against these feelings or go into hiding. It accepts the wide range of feelings and is not afraid to express them."

2. *"The capacity to expect appropriate entitlements.* From early experiences of mastery, coupled with parental acknowledgment and support of the real self, healthy individuals build up a sense of entitlement to appropriate experiences of mastery and pleasure, as well as the environmental input necessary to achieve these objectives. We come to expect that we can in fact master our lives and achieve what is good for us."

3. *"The capacity for self-activation and assertion.* This capacity includes the ability to identify one's own unique individuality, wishes, dreams, and goals and to be assertive in expressing them autonomously. It also includes taking the necessary steps to make these dreams a reality and supporting and defending them when they are under attack."

4. *"Acknowledgment of self-esteem.* This capacity allows a person to identify and acknowledge that he has effectively coped with a problem or crisis in a positive and creative way. . . . Many people with a tendency to see only the bad side of things, including what they mistakenly believe is their own lack of talent, are oblivious to their victories."

5. *"The ability to soothe painful feelings.* The real self will not allow us to wallow in misery. When things go wrong and we are hurt, the real self devises means to minimize and soothe painful feelings." The amount of pain we will allow is appropriate to the causal event. Beyond that, the real self works toward the restoration of good feeling.

6. *"The ability to make and stick to commitments.* The real self allows us to make commitments to relationships and career goals. Despite obstacles and setbacks, a person with a strong sense of the real self will not abandon her goal or decision when it is clear that it is a good one and in her best interests."

*CONTINUED*

*Striving to be better, oft we mar what's well.*

SHAKESPEARE

*If you've picked all the roses in your garden and all you have left are the thorns, then . . . you need a new metaphor.*

BARBARA CHRISTIAN

*CONTINUED*

7. "*Creativity* . . . is the ability to replace old, familiar patterns of living and problem-solving with new and equally or more successful ones." New situations make demands on our creative resources, and we may have to come up with new ideas, new priorities, new methodologies and techniques. Furthermore, creativity tends to recognize and protect itself. "Not only is creativity the ability to find solutions for life's problems in the world around us, it is also the ability to rearrange intrapsychic patterns that threaten to block self-expression without which there can be no creativity."

8. "*Intimacy,* the capacity to express the real self fully and honestly in a close relationship with another person with minimal anxiety about abandonment or engulfment." Self-esteem gives one the capacity to say No without fearing rejection if one is hurt; it is the capacity for intimacy to maintain relationships while also pursuing other goals.

9. "*The ability to be alone.* The real self allows us to be alone without feeling abandoned. It enables us to manage ourselves and our feelings on our own through periods when there is no special person in our lives and not to confuse this type of aloneness with the psychic loneliness, springing from an impaired real self, that drives us to despair or the pathologic need to fill up our lives with meaningless sexual activity or dead-end relationships just to avoid coming face to face with the impaired real self." It is the ability to find meaning in life from within; we are not dependent on others to activate our real selves.

10. "*Continuity of self.* This is the capacity to recognize and acknowledge that we each have a core that persists through space and time. . . . Whether up or down, in a good mood or a bad one, accepting failure or living with success, a person with a real self has an inner core that remains the same even as he grows and develops. At the end of life, it is the same 'I' who was born many years ago who passes on."

*from* JAMES F. MASTERSON
*The Search for the Real Self*
*(The Free Press,* 1988); *quotations*
*and paraphrases of pages* viif., 42–46.

conversing to washing dishes—are all performed in a slightly different, more creative way. Their own distinctive style touches everything they do.

6.    Actualized persons are "ethical in the deepest sense." They rarely follow the superficial, conventional norms of moral behavior. They consider the majority of so-called moral issues to be trivial. Their ethical concern is expressed in a positive, constructive attitude toward all people and all things. Since they easily identify with the conditions of others, they care, and their caring is the wellspring of their ethical nature.

## REFLECTIONS

1    As you reflect on the case of the man indicted for embezzlement (*"News Item,"* p. 116), what is your conclusion? Was he the same person (self)

twenty-six years later? Might the philosophical, psychological, physiological, ethical, and legal answers be different? Which answer(s) is/are correct? (This problem is not merely hypothetical: remember Leon Uris's *QB VII?*)

2  Summarize in your own words David Hume's concept of the self (p. 122). Drawing upon your knowledge of psychology and other modern disciplines, do you think Hume was essentially right or wrong? In either case, how would you describe the "self"?

3  "What each of us can become during our life/time is determined by two fundamental conditions. . . . " (p. 116). Is this statement in accord with your observations of others and your experience of your self?

4  What is meant by "self-love"? Why is it so important? Contrast self-love with egotism, selfishness, and narcissism.

5  The study by Masterson of the real self's capacities (pp. 127–128) provides an interesting profile of actualized individuals and gives a clue, perhaps, to our own potential. What is your response to the six qualities described? Can you see how each would contribute to the greater actualization of the person? Would you want to possess these qualities? Do you now possess these qualities? To what degree?

6  Pretend that you are an Eastern sage, and gaze patiently at the Zen oxherding pictures. As a Westerner (if you are), how far can you meaningfully go in accepting this account of the search for one's "true nature"? Can you accept Step 7, for example? Is Step 8 meaningful? Can you state in your own words what is implied in Steps 9 and 10?

7  The study by Hayakawa of the "fully-functioning personality" provides an interesting profile of more actualized individuals and gives a clue, perhaps, to our own potential. What is your response to the six qualities described? Can you see how each would contribute to the greater actualization of the person? Would you want to possess these qualities? Do you now possess these qualities? To what degree?

8  Why was Ayn Rand so passionate in denouncing "the monster of 'We'"? What virtues or benefits is she trying to emphasize with her doctrine of individualism?

9  Have you ever made a list of the things you are for and the things you are against? How much of Ayn Rand's "fors" and "againsts" can you agree with? Now clarify (to yourself) why you are for or against these things.

# AYN RAND

## *The Productive Life*

"Who is John Galt?"

This question, all during the 1960s and 1970s, could be found on bumper stickers, T-shirts, posters, and walls; it was quoted in conversations, asked on radio and TV, even stamped on tiles in a Buddhist temple in Japan. It was unquestionably the most famous catch-phrase of the age.

And the answer?

"For twelve years, you have been asking: Who is John Galt? This is John Galt speaking. I am the man who lives his life. I am the man who does not sacrifice his love or his values. I am the man who has deprived you of victims and thus has destroyed your world, and if you wish to know why you are perishing—you who dread knowledge—I am the man who will now tell you."

Thus begins one of the most famous speeches in American literature, the "John Galt" speech, beginning on page 936 of Ayn Rand's *Atlas Shrugged*. The 35,000-word speech, which took the author two years to write, runs for 57 pages and summarizes the philosophy of one of the most influential and controver-

sial writers of the twentieth century. What made her so popular was her clear call to American youth to join her in thinking about values, in making moral commitments to those values, and in taking a firm stand for one's principles. She provided a laundry list of rights and wrongs and exhorted her loyal followers to rally to her cause.

Ayn Rand was *for:* rationality, individuality, living life as an end in itself, courage, happiness, success, life, pleasure, joy, freedom, Aristotle, Aquinas, atheism, love, friendship, romanticism, respect, self-esteem, admiration, selfish pleasure, capitalism, strong men, money . . .

Ayn Rand was *against:* the irrational, self-sacrifice, martyrdom, belief, anything that erodes self-esteem, sheep, suffering, failure, death, pain, hedonism, whims, Nietzsche, equality, slavery, Kant, Plato, altruism, parasites, Sartre, existentialism, taxes, weak will . . .

Ayn Rand came to America in 1926. An exile from Russia, she was homeless, penniless, and could barely speak English. Just twelve years later, by 1938, she had mastered the English language, developed a radical philosophy, and was writing screenplays, short stories, philosophic essays, and soon-to-be-famous novels—all written to give wings to her philosophic convictions.

She was born Alissa Rosenbaum in St. Petersberg in 1905. Her father, Fronz, was a chemist who owned his own shop. He was austere, silent, and judgmental, a man of strong conviction and moral integrity. Alissa respected him but felt little affection for him and received little from him. Her mother, Anna, was educated, sophisticated, and delighted in running the household and its rush of activities; she was admired by the lawyers, doctors, and scientists who frequented their home and attended their parties. "I disliked her quite a lot," Ayn Rand later wrote. "We really didn't get along." Though bright, she was a social butterfly in Alissa's mind, totally lacking in substance and ideas. "She disapproved of me in every respect except one: she was proud of my intelligence and proud to show me off to the rest of the family." Whatever esteem and admiration Alissa received from her family she bought with displays of her brilliant mind.

At the age of nine she decided she would be a writer. In 1914, vacationing with her family in London, the Great War began and they had trouble returning home. In 1917 the Russian revolution overturned their world; her father's business was nationalized, and the secure life she had known vanished. She began to see the world as a great battleground between Good and Evil. All was struggle, all was pain, all was despair. But she also discovered that in her mind she could create beautiful worlds and people them with courageous human beings who lived decent, happy lives. In the panorama of her imagination intelligence could prevail. She would write, therefore, and dedicate her life to the creation and preservation of the noblest in the human spirit.

When Alissa was sixteen, she entered the University of Leningrad. Though urged to concentrate on mathematics and engineering—fields that would enable her to make a contribution to the communist state—she chose history as her major. She read widely, fell in love with Aristotle's philosophy of becoming, despised Plato's idealism and Nietzsche's philosophy of power. She dreamed of men and women living in a free society where they could build skyscrapers and write what they pleased. She wrote short stories and planned a novel about a heroic young man struggling to maintain his individuality in a totalitarian state.

At twenty-one, upon invitation from relatives in Chicago, Alissa came to America. She had read about the political and economic opportunities of a free enterprise system; now she had the opportunity to visit the country that guaranteed the personal freedom she longed for. She wanted, with all her being, to be absorbed into the American dream—to be free, to be herself, to think her own thoughts, to live her own life. She looked upon collectivist Russia with "complete loathing." On the way she changed her name to Ayn Rand—Ayn (it rhymes with "mine" and "thine") she adopted from a Finnish writer; Rand she saw on her old Remington-Rand typewriter. A new name, a new life. She knew she would never return to Russia.

Chicago was good for openers, but she longed to see Hollywood. Almost immediately—with only a few dollars and some scripts she had written that just might be turned into screenplays—she set out for the West. "No one helped me," she later wrote, "nor did I think at any time that it was anyone's duty to help me." She found a job at the studio of Cecil B. DeMille, and was cast as an extra in his epic story of Jesus, *The King of Kings.*

And she wrote—scripts, short stories, synopses—but her stories were too idealistic to be believable; they never sold. She worked hard, loved her new life, and rapidly acquired an understanding of how America works. Her writing

*Civilization is the progress toward a society of privacy. The savage's whole existence is public, ruled by the laws of his tribe. Civilization is the process of setting man free from men.*

*My philosophy, in essence, is the concept of man as a heroic being, with his own happiness as the moral purpose of his life, with productive achievement as his noblest activity, and reason as his only absolute.*

*I am done with the monster of "We," the word of serfdom, of plunder, of misery, falsehood and shame. And now I see the free face of god, and I raise this god over the earth, this god whom men have sought since men came into being, this god who will grant them joy and peace and pride. This god, this one word: "I."*

*To deal with men by force is as impractical as to deal with nature by persuasion.*

*It is not the special sciences that teach men to think; it is philosophy that lays down the epistemological criteria of all special sciences.*

evolved from romantic story-telling to carefully-plotted story-lines carried along by the two qualities that would make her work so powerful—philosophic concepts and passionate conviction. She wanted to write and she could tell a good story; very soon it would become evident that she had something to say.

In 1929 she met Frank O'Connor on the set of *The King of Kings*. She married this quiet, handsome, tall, blond man, and he became the model for her novels' heroes. Two years later, as the wife of an American citizen, she became naturalized. During their fifty-year marriage he remained devoted to his brilliant and passionate wife; without really understanding her, he provided the stability necessary for her intellectual and literary achievements.

For three years Ayn Rand worked in the wardrobe department of RKO studios. In 1932 she sold a script to Universal Pictures, but the play was killed when Universal traded it to Paramount and they decided not to produce it. For the next two years, while working on her novels, she wrote screenplays for Universal, Paramount, and MGM. In 1934 her play, *Penthouse Legend,* was successfully produced at the Hollywood Playhouse. Critics praised it for its characterization and catchy finale; no one, it seems, cared about her philosophic ideas.

The O'Connors moved to New York in 1935. Though it was a year of disappointment and poverty, *Penthouse Legend* was produced on Broadway to generally favorable reviews; after that their fortunes began to change. In 1936 her first novel, *We the Living,* was published to mixed reviews: it was a good read, the critics said, but they were turned off by her evangelical preaching. Sales were poor, and the publisher destroyed the plates after only 3000 copies were sold.

Undaunted, she continued to write. She had begun work on a "great novel" about an architect, so she read voraciously about architects and took a job as

a secretary in an architectural office to learn the practical side of the business. Meanwhile she completed a short novel about a struggling hero in a totalitarian state. Called *Anthem,* it was finally published in England after she failed to find any American publisher who would consider it.

After eight years of intense labor she published *The Fountainhead* in 1943. It was the story of a man of great strength who refuses to compromise his ethical principles and finally triumphs over formidable obstacles. Critics at last took notice; some few even perceived the philosophic themes underlying her story. The book was a popular success, and by the end of the year Warner Brothers bought the film rights to it; Ayn Rand was to write the screenplay. Because of the war, production was delayed till 1949. By that time book sales had reached a half-million copies. When the movie version, starring Gary Cooper and Patricia Neal, was released, book sales soared, but despite the stars and the hype, the movie was a box office failure.

Ayn Rand labored for nine years on her magnum opus, *Atlas Shrugged.* It was published by Random House in 1957. Despite negative critical review, its popular appeal was enormous, selling (by 1994) some three million copies. It was becoming obvious that Ayn Rand was developing a following of loyal devotees.

*Atlas Shrugged* is the story of one woman and four men, all of heroic stature, who watch with horror the downward spiral of American civilization that has been steered into socialism. These brilliant industrial leaders decide to reverse the decline of the American economy by organizing a strike. They withdraw their genius from the world, along with the services of their companies. These atlases all embody Ayn Rand's values—rational self-interest, self-esteem and individualism, love of wealth and pleasure. At the appropriate time, they reappear in the world to provide the necessary intellect and leadership to save it.

After *Atlas Shrugged* Ayn Rand abandoned fiction and turned her efforts to writing philosophical essays. She published *For the New Intellectual* in 1961; *The Virtue of Selfishness,* a defense of individualistic ethics, also in 1961; and a book on critical philosophy, *An Introduction to Objectivist Epistemology,* in 1966. She planned to write a big volume summarizing the whole of her philosophy. She had all her life worked to have her philosophic ideas taken seriously; now they were, if not by professionals, then by the intelligensia and college students worldwide.

Her intellectual/philosophical movement—which she named "Objectivism" —was thriving. She was surrounded by an inner circle of loyal supporters, led by Nathaniel Branden, for eighteen years her companion and "intellectual heir"; and Leonard Peikoff, later to be her biographer and executor. Branden organized the Nathaniel Branden Institute (located in the Empire State Building) to publish a newsletter, develop courses, give lectures, and coordinate the dissemination of her Objectivist philosophy. Ayn Rand lectured at universities, appeared on radio and television where she was always brilliant, intimidating, and controversial. She was biographed and anthologized; she received honorary degrees from America's prestigious universities. Articles and books appeared in professional journals taking her to task for her simple-minded ethics, bad epistemology, and naive economics and politics; and in the popular press where she was generally supported for her defense of personal freedom and the free enterprise system.

Ayn Rand was impressive with her stocky figure, dark hair, and fiery eyes which, one reporter said, would "wilt a cactus." She spoke elegant English with a labored Russian accent. In public performance she was competitive and argumentative; she never pulled punches and followed the rational line of thought without regard to feelings. Quick and incisive, she was never at a loss for an instant

retort. It was her fate to be easily misinterpreted, and this produced in her a guarded readiness to defend and explain her controversial ideas. She was spared attack only when she was among followers who had done their homework and sympathized with what she was trying to say. Always intriguing, never dull, never afraid to do or say the unexpected or irreverent, she often wore a gold brooch in the shape of a dollar sign.

This was the peak of Ayn Rand's life and career. In 1968 her world began to unravel. A major schism occurred within the movement. Rand accused Branden of exploitation and moral transgressions; he was excommunicated, the Institute was closed, and the *Objectivist Newsletter* went into decline. Rand continued to write, to give occasional public lectures, to speak out on political issues, and (until 1976) to publish the *Ayn Rand Letter.* In 1975 her health began to deteriorate, due largely to her lifelong chain-smoking. She underwent lung surgery for cancer. Her husband had died in 1979 at age 82. She was working on a television script of *Atlas Shrugged* when she died in New York on March 6, 1982. She was 78.

◆

"My personal life," Ayn Rand once wrote, "is a postscript to my novels; it consists of the sentence: *'And I mean it.'* I have always lived by the philosophy I present in my books—and it has worked for me, as it works for my characters."

Early in her life Ayn Rand came to despise losers and antiheroes created by bad ideas that circulate in our society. She was hostile to the notion that life is an inevitable vale of tears, that man is an evil creature doomed to defeat by his sinful nature, that man of his own will can do nothing good, and that this life is a sort of holy war against evil, always to be lost in this world, won (maybe) in the next. Such ideas cast a dismal dark shadow over our lives, she said, and these evaluations are false. They are not descriptions of what life is or what it should be.

*To love is to value. Only a rationally selfish man, a man of self-esteem, is capable of love—because he is the only man capable of holding firm, consistent, uncompromising, unbetrayed values. The man who does not value himself, cannot value anything or anyone.*

*Great men can't be ruled.*

*In life, one ignores the unimportant; in art, one omits it.*

*Kill reverence and you've killed the hero in man.*

*Man is a word that has no plural.*

With an ounce of reason, she wrote, we would see that we live in a benevolent universe. Reality is friendly; what is real is on our side. To be sure, this life is not perfect, but it is great just as it is and our ideals can be achieved here and now. Happiness should not be regarded as a wondrous exception but as the normal, natural condition of any life rightly lived.

So, Ayn Rand dedicated her life to exploring the human potential and writing about man as a heroic being with unlimited capacities for growth and happiness. "I decided to become a writer—not in order to save the world, nor to serve my fellow men—but for the simple, personal, selfish, egotistical happiness of creating the kind of men and events I could like, respect and admire."

There are three cardinal values, she says, that one must hold supreme if one is to realize his or her ultimate value: reason, purpose, and self-esteem.

The capacity for reason is a human being's greatest asset. Guiding one's life rationally means recognizing and accepting reason as the only source of knowledge, the only way of judging values, and the only dependable guide to action. "It means one's total commitment to a state of full, conscious awareness, to the maintenance of a full mental focus in all issues, in all choices, in all of one's waking hours." It means remaining critically alert, not letting any fact or any value judgment enter one's repertory without stopping-the-world to think about it, as long as is necessary, to achieve clarity. "One must never place any value or consideration whatsoever above one's perception of reality." No myths, no self-delusions, no escapist fantasies. Reality *is*, and the rational person, by reason, stays in touch with it as best he or she can. We must all become dedicated empiricists.

Being rational means accepting "the responsibility of forming one's own judgments and of living by the work of one's own mind. . . . It means that one must never sacrifice one's convictions to the opinions or wishes of others . . . one must never attempt to fake reality in any manner. It means a commitment to reason . . . as a permanent way of life." Everything rational individuals do in our daily lives is planned for, and guided by, our intellect. Emotions enrich us, pleasures are the substance of joy, and happiness is the goal of our living; but for human beings who take charge of our own lives, reason alone is our guide for shaping our emotions, selecting our pleasures, and getting on with the journey toward happiness.

A sense of purpose is essential to one's productiveness. "Productive work is the central *purpose* of a rational man's life, the central value that integrates and determines the hierarchy of all his other values." One's work must come before all other goals and commitments, even before family and friends. "The man without a purpose is a man who drifts at the mercy of random feelings or unidentified urges and is capable of any evil, because he is totally out of control of his own life. In order to be in control in your life, you have to have a purpose—a productive purpose." There is, for every human being, some workpath that is peculiarly one's own, a creative vocation that that one alone can fulfill; it is the responsibility of each of us to discover what that work is, and having found it, to stay with it with tenacity and zeal till the end of our days. All other virtues derive from this single-minded commitment to purpose.

Ayn Rand warns: "To cheat your way into a job bigger than your mind can handle is to become a fear-corroded ape on borrowed motions and borrowed time, and to settle down into a job that requires less than your mind's full capacity is to cut your motor and sentence yourself to another kind of motion: decay. . . . "

Self-esteem is, for each of us, the supreme value. "The man who does not value himself, cannot value anything or anyone." Self-esteem means valuing one's mind and honoring it by trusting it, loving it, nourishing it, treating it with dignity—not belittling it, negating it, devaluing it. The mind does not function, or function at all well, if it is distrusted, undermined, betrayed, treated shabbily, told that it is useless, worthless, and incompetent. Self-esteem creates the confidence required for the mind to do its work.

"Man knows that his desperate need of self-esteem is a matter of life and death." But this intuitive certainty about one's self is thwarted if we are told that we humans are inherently evil or depraved, or told that life in this world is really not worth living, or told that all human striving is helpless and pre-doomed to defeat. These are lies. The truth, Ayn Rand says, is that human beings are creatures with unlimited capacities for creative accomplishments; we have been genetically programmed for joy and happiness; and we are free to create fulfilling futures, both as individuals and as a human species. A healthy self-esteem is a foundational requisite to our making these promises into realities.

◆

She will be remembered as this century's chief defender of the human ego. Some writers can be reduced to a principle, some to a phrase, but Rand can be reduced to the one word *ego*. Some will ridicule her overemphasis on the self and explain it away by reference to Rand's feelings of inadequacy as a woman in a man's world, a Russian in America, and call it over-compensation. Some will have mixed feelings about it, as did historian Jacob Burckhardt when he discussed the ego: "The ego is at once man's sign of Cain and his crown of glory." Some will consider Rand a modern Montaigne, who wrote: "If the world finds fault with me for speaking too much of myself, I find fault with the world for not even thinking of itself." Some will consider her America's twentieth-century Walt Whitman, who said: "The whole theory of the universe is directed to one single individual—namely to You."

JAMES T. BAKER, *AYN RAND*
(TWAYNE PUBLISHERS, 1987)

# CHANGE
# GROWTH

## 2 ₃

## WHEN THINGS GO WRONG

Dr. and Mrs. Harry F. Harlow have for years studied the growth patterns of rhesus monkeys. In the Primate Laboratory of the University of Wisconsin, the Harlows discovered that their monkeys have a developmental sequence that, under normal conditions, produces mutually beneficial social behavior. The young monkeys' emotional development must proceed in this order: (1) affection and security, (2) fear and adjustment, and (3) social-sexual interaction. If this growth sequence is disrupted, then tragic results, in varying degrees, take place in the inner worlds of the young monkeys.

Affection and security are basic to the monkey's earliest stages of growth. Normally he first knows these feelings in relation to his mother. She is the prime source of comforting reassurance as he begins to experience the world about him.

The Harlows found that if a monkey is separated from its mother at birth, but is given the chance to live and develop with age-mates, then affectional ties can grow between them. Emotional bonds are established as they play together.

Young monkeys that have not been permitted to establish relationships with other infants are wary of their playmates when finally allowed to be with them, and these deprived monkeys often fail to develop strong bonds of affection. Yet monkeys that have been deprived of mother love but provided with early contacts *can* develop ties with their peers which seem comparable to the bonds formed by mother-reared infants.

The worst thing that can happen is for a young monkey to be deprived of both his mother and his playmates. If this happens, no bonds of affection and trust can develop.

*". . . We are what we pretend to be, so we must be careful about what we pretend to be."*

**KURT VONNEGUT, JR.**
*Mother Night*

Harlow and friend

*If you begin by sacrificing yourself to those you love, you will end by hating those to whom you have sacrificed yourself.*

**GEORGE BERNARD SHAW**

A six-month old rhesus monkey, raised in isolation from birth—deprived of mother, surrogate mother, and playmates—cowers in fear in the corner of its cage.

Fear is the overwhelming response in all monkeys raised in isolation. Although the animals are physically healthy, they crouch and appear terror-stricken by their new environment. . . .They cringe when approached and fail at first to join in any of the play. During six months of play sessions, they never progress beyond minimal play behavior, such as playing by themselves with toys. What little social activity they do have is exclusively with the other isolate in the group. When the other animals become aggressive, the isolates accept their abuse without making any effort to defend themselves. For these animals, social opportunities have come too late. Fear prevents them from engaging in social interaction and consequently from developing ties of affection.

If young monkeys are reared in isolation for a long period of time—for up to twelve months—then their lifetime behavior is seriously affected, and it appears that little or nothing can undo the damage.

We continued the testing of the same six- and twelve-month isolates for a period of several years. The results were startling. The monkeys raised in isolation now began to attack the other monkeys viciously, whereas before they had cowered in fright. . . . The monkeys which had been raised in the steel isolation cages for their first six months now were three years old. They were still terrified by all strangers, even the physically helpless juveniles. But in spite of their terror, they engaged in uncontrolled aggression, often launching suicidal attacks upon the large adult males and even attacking the juveniles—an act almost never seen in normal monkeys of their age. The passage of time had only exaggerated their asocial and antisocial behavior.

*The unforgivable sin is not to become all that you can as a human being, given the circumstances of life that we have to accept.*

**R. D. LAING**

*As one goes through it one sees that the gate one went through was the self that went through it. . . .*

**R. D. LAING**

In those monkeys, positive social action was not initiated, play was nonexistent, grooming did not occur, and sexual behavior was not present at all or was totally inadequate. In human terms, these monkeys which had lived unloved and in isolation were totally unloving, distressed, disturbed and delinquent.

Throughout our studies, we have been increasingly impressed by the alternative routes monkeys may take to reach adequate social behavior, which by our criteria includes affection toward peers, controlled fear and aggression, and normal sexual behavior. In protected laboratory conditions, social interaction between peers and between mother and child appears to be in large part interchangeable in their effect on the infant's development. A rhesus can surmount the absence of its mother if it can associate with its peers, and it can surmount a lack of socialization with peers if its mother provides affection. Being raised with several age mates appears to compensate adequately for a lack of a mother. . . .

After numerous and varied studies at the University of Wisconsin, we have concluded that unless peer affection precedes social aggression, monkeys do not adjust; either they become unreasonably aggressive or they develop into passive scapegoats for their group.

The Harlows are writing of rhesus monkeys, not man; and all careful scientists are wary of extrapolating their findings from experiments with one species to any different species. However, there is evidence that human developmental patterns are quite similar.

For human beings, as with the Harlows' monkeys, normal psychosocial development appears to follow a sequential order: (1) reassurance/security/trust → (2) courage/aggression/exploration → (3) self/autonomy/maturity. If this growth sequence is interrupted or the requisites not provided at any stage, we too become disturbed creatures cringing in the corner of life with our hands over our faces.

*The supreme ideal of Greece is to save the ego from anarchy and chaos. The supreme ideal of the Orient is to dissolve the ego into the infinite and to become one with it.*
**KIMON FRIAR**

When things go wrong, one wonders whether the young monkey is more fortunate than human young. The monkey's behavior is a spontaneous expression of need-deprivation; it is doubtful that he *wonders* why he is "disturbed." He simply is. But our *self*-consciousness becomes acutely painful; *we know* (most of us) that something has gone wrong, and *we* wonder why.

Edvard Munch, *The Scream*

When things have gone very wrong for us and need-deprivation has been acute, the image we develop of ourselves is distorted, confused, inaccurate. Having developed without reassurance and support, we remain vulnerable to the varied, inconsistent responses of others. Nor do we move through the normal stages of growth. There is no period of separation from authority during which we evolve a healthy reliance on our own thoughts and feelings. We are held at a level where the tenuous "mirror-images"—what others think and feel about us—continue to reinforce a fragmented self. We become alienated from the potentially authentic self, the remnants of which still cry out from deep inside.

If, very early, we do not receive love, we quickly know that we are unlovable.

If we are rejected, by word or deed, we learn to reject ourselves.

If we find that what we *do* is more important than what we *are*, then doing the "right thing" becomes all important; in fact, we strive desperately *to be* what *we do.*

*I do not understand my own
actions.*

SAINT PAUL

If our parents are permissive so that we see them as "not caring," we will feel unwanted and worthless.

If our parents "care" too much, especially when they call it "love," then we may never establish self-reliance.

If we are given behavioral ultimatums that demand repression of authentic feelings, we will develop inauthentic selves that comply to required specifications.

If we have been denied the warmth we crave, we will carry with us the ache of an insatiable emptiness.

## THE MASKS WE WEAR

*My mother does not love
  me . . .
I am bad because she does
  not love me
She does not love me because
  I am bad*

R. D. LAING

*Why are Americans so hungry
for the approval of others?
    The adjusted American
lacks self-approval; that is to
say, he has not developed a
self-image that he can believe
is both accurate and acceptable. To do so he would
require successful techniques
for creating an accurate and
acceptable self-image through
honest introspection, candid
association, and meaningful
activity. The patterns to
which he has adjusted do not
include such techniques.
Instead, the culture abounds
with misdirections, which the
adjusted American acquires.
. . . Perhaps above all he
learns to seek self-acceptance
indirectly, by seeking to substitute the good opinions of
others for self-approval. It is
thus that he becomes "other-
directed."*

GAIL AND SNELL PUTNEY

Few of us are fortunate enough to have had parents who appreciated our early spontaneous expressions of life and self and, at the same time, taught us to "play the games" of adjustment to other norms outside the home. How many mothers prefaced a lecture on cleanliness with a word or two about the social realities we would face—for instance, when preparing us to attend a friend's party—without instilling in us the idea that "dirty" itself is bad and "clean" is inherently good?

Yet it's an idea that children can grasp at a remarkably early age. "If you want to go to Suzy's party, then Suzy's mother will want you to look clean. I want you to look clean too. I'm happy you enjoy playing in the mud, but this is the way of the world, so let's wash up."

This is a reality-perspective that permits the child to enjoy playing in the mud and at the same time choose to "play the games" required to attain a goal, in this case attending Suzy's party.

Far more than other creatures, we humans have the capacity to be "many things to many people." As the situations call for it, we can be different "persons" or wear different masks (the word *person* is from the Latin *persona*, meaning "mask"). Some of us become quite adept at putting on masks or switching masks; thus we can ensure that we always have ready a *persona* that is acceptable. It effects minimal rejection by any other person or group.

But the price we pay is very dear. In the process of switching masks, we may discover that there are *nothing but* masks; indeed, they may begin to feel familiar and genuine, all of them. And if someone should demand, "Will the *real* self please stand up?" we find to our horror that there is no one there. It is not uncommon to make the discovery during some personal crisis that an authentic self never developed. If we glimpse this may be the case, in panic we may seize our masks and fit them more tightly, reluctant to remove them ever again.

The feeling that one does not know "who he is" may be intuited by ourselves and inferred by others, but it is perhaps the last thing that we will confess to ourselves or others. The pain that our masks cover is too great for anyone to see. We can't risk being open. We are ever fearful that someone might see beneath our masks and discover . . . *nothing.*

## Progress in Awareness

There seems to be a sort of progress in awareness, through the stages of which every man—and especially every psychiatrist and every patient—must move, some persons progressing further through these stages than others. One starts by blaming the identified patient for his idiosyncrasies and symptoms. Then one discovers that these symptoms are a response to—or an effect of—what others have done; and the blame shifts from the identified patient to the etiological figure. Then, one discovers perhaps that these figures feel a guilt for the pain which they have caused, and one realizes that when they claim this guilt they are identifying themselves with god. After all, they did not, in general, know what they are doing, and to claim guilt for their acts would be to claim omniscience. At this point one reaches a more general anger, that what happens to people should not happen to dogs, and that what people do to each other the lower animals could never devise. Beyond this, there is, I think, a stage which I can only dimly envisage, where pessimism and anger are replaced by something else—perhaps humility. And from this stage onward to whatever other stages there may be, there is loneliness.

GREGORY BATESON
*Language and Psychotherapy*

## I WILL NOT STOP TILL I KNOW

Oedipus is the prototype of the man who gains knowledge about himself and pays the ultimate price. The issue in the drama is: Shall Oedipus know what he has done? Shall Oedipus know who he is and what his origins are? . . .

Oedipus is a hero precisely because he will let no one stand in the way of his knowledge about himself. He is the hero because he faces his own reality. He cries out with pain again and again, but he repeats, "I will not stop till I have known the whole."

ROLLO MAY
*Love and Will*

Deep within the unconscious mind of man, there moves a longing to recover the innocence of childhood, a condition that he nostalgically (mis)interprets as a state of blissful happiness. Intuitively, we sense that with knowledge comes insight, and with insight comes pain. Most of man's religions have in their mythologies some place or state where he may reenter into that paradise of unknowing where suffering will cease. The Garden of Eden was a paradise only as long as the fruit of *knowledge* remained untouched. It would have been better to be innocent, the story seems to say, than to know the pain of understanding. Once innocence has been lost, however, there is no return. Once we possess knowledge we must leave the Garden of Eden, and we leave it forever.

*To be innocent is to not know.* To be innocent is to be childlike, and to be childlike is to be unaware of certain facts or experiences. A child does not have certain information at his disposal that he can use, information that others do have, and all decisions related to those areas have to be made by others.

*Every time you teach a child something you keep him from reinventing it.*

JEAN PIAGET

*All children paint like geniuses. What do we do to them that so quickly dulls this ability?*

PABLO PICASSO

Chambered nautilus, courtesy the American Museum of Natural History

David Park, *Standing Couple* (1958)

*Therefore, to be innocent is to be dependent.* If one cannot make his own decisions, others must. This is a normal condition for a child, and he accepts it. This vulnerability puts him at the mercy of those he depends upon; if his basic self-needs are met, however, this is a happy dependency.

*Dependence requires trust and faith.* For the innocent child there is no alternative. He must trust the decisions others make for him, that those decisions are right and good; and he must accept on faith information given to him, that it is right and true.

*Dependence requires obedience.* Wherever there is dependency, obedience is demanded, but if trust is not a part of that dependency relationship, then obedience is given grudgingly. With trust, however, obedience is given willingly, even joyfully. There is no need to question the authority to whom one submits.

*Innocence is an instrument of control.* Knowledge and know-how are potentially dangerous assets—dangerous to all who possess them but lack maturity to use them for good, and dangerous to any who wish to maintain a state of control. Parents guard their children against certain kinds of knowledge and experiences until they are "old enough" (that is, until they are aware and responsible) to make constructive use of it. A child may be told to do things he does not understand, or that he does not want to do; but obedience to authority is necessary since authorities (that is, those *with* knowledge) can make more realistic judgments. Obviously, in matters of destiny, it could be tragic if a child were forced to make critical decisions he is not yet equipped to make.

So, while we are children, we think like children—innocently: without information and awareness. We order our experience along simple lines and our behavior is guided by those we depend upon.

## GROWTH AND INSECURITY

Desmond Morris employs two helpful concepts to describe the innate alternating feelings of fear and curiosity: neophobia and neophilia.

By *neophobia* he means that we are afraid of new objects, unfamiliar behavioral patterns in others, strange feelings in ourselves, or any other new and threatening elements of life that we do not understand. It is completely natural to be afraid of the unknown. To experience fear in the presence of potential danger has obvious survival value. Life may be likened to our moving forever on the edge of darkness, not knowing what exists just beyond the immediate circle of experience.

We can understand, too painfully, the first

experiences of the infant monkeys described by the Harlows. When placed in a room cluttered with unfamiliar objects and without any mother or comforting "home base" to return to, the young monkey was unable to explore the room with its formidable array of unknowns. His fear was too great, and he could only huddle in the corner of the room with his hands over his eyes.

But when given the security of a mother, or even the comfort of a soft blanket or surrogate mother, to which he could periodically return for reassurance and security, then step by step the monkey would explore the room's contents. An object would be touched, handled, played with; then the monkey would return to the mother (or blanket) for a security "rest period"; then explore another object; and so on until all objects were familiar. Little by little, he would reduce his fear of all the objects in the room.

When he knew, from his own experience, that nothing in the room held any danger for him, he could then move about the room without fear. He had succeeded in making all the unknowns a part of his world.

*Neophilia* is a strong counter-impulse to neophobia. We are fascinated by the new and the unknown; we are drawn to new objects, new experiences, new ways of living—drawn by "curiosity" and by a sense of adventure and excitement. It is the neophilic impulse that provides us the possibility of growth. If our desire to explore the unknown is overwhelmed by fear, then we withdraw. We return to our corner. But if we have enough security when we need it, then we can explore more and more of the unknowns, assimilate them, explore some more, widen our horizons, and grow.

This kind of growth is open; it has no limits. There are always new worlds to be explored, new adventures to become excited about, new ways of living to be experienced, new ideas to be discovered, new problems to be solved.

> *Selfishness is not living as one wishes to live. It is asking others to live as one wishes to live.*
>
> OSCAR WILDE

With a positive view of self, one can risk taking chances; one does not have to be afraid of what is new and different. A sturdy ship can venture farther from port. Just so, an adequate person can launch himself without fear into the new, the untried and the unknown. A positive view of self permits the individual to be creative, original and spontaneous. What is more, he can afford to be generous, to give of himself freely or to become personally involved in events. With so much more at his command, he has so much more to give.

Truly adequate people possess perceptual fields maximally open to experience. That is to say, their perceptual fields are capable of change and adjustment in such fashion as to make fullest possible use of their experience.

ARTHUR W. COMBS

> *That hatred springs more from self-contempt than from a legitimate grievance is seen in the intimate connection between hatred and a guilty conscience.*
>
> ERIC HOFFER

## THE ANSWER-GIVERS

A variety of institutions and individuals specialize in providing us with the answers before we have asked the questions. The rationale for doing this is always altruistic: they want to protect us from dangerous ideas or bad influences; they must prevent our doing the wrong things; they wish to guide us into the right paths of feeling, thinking, and behaving. They give us answers because, they would say, we have a "need to know."

*I contradict myself. I am*
*large. I contain multitudes.*
WALT WHITMAN

*. . . Only that life is worth*
*living which develops the*
*strength and the integrity to*
*withstand the unavoidable*
*sufferings and misfortunes of*
*existence without flying into*
*an imaginary world.*
FRIEDRICH NIETZSCHE

The actual fact is that answer-givers have a need to persuade. One of their goals is to contain us within a state of innocence and thereby establish control over us. Their true motivation is disguised by perhaps the commonest of human rationalizations: that they are really helping us. Indeed, the claim that we need the answers can become so widely accepted that, without raising further questions, we too assume the claim to be true.

The price of such answer-giving is very high.

It prevents the individual from having to wrestle personally with life's problems and to ask the questions that lead to emotional and intellectual growth. Once trained to accept given answers, one may never learn how to formulate meaningful questions in terms of who he is or what life means to him.

Moreover, one who has been conditioned to accept answers tends to develop a rigid conceptual framework that undergoes early closure to new ideas and experiences. He knows if he lacks an answer, the authority can supply it. All he must do is ask for the answer instead of asking the question. Nor can he question the answer. It is common to find individuals who can repeat verbatim the "correct" answers, but when questioned about their meaning, they reveal little understanding; and if pressed, their only recourse is to fall back on other "remembered" answers.

One who has been protected in this way has been prevented from knowing both the "agony of insight" and the "ecstasy of growth." He has been preassured that no painful questions will have to be faced.

## CRISIS OF AUTHORITY

The date: A.D. 2198. The speaker: Mia, a young girl who has just survived "The Trial," a rite-of-passage that prepares youth to face themselves and their world.

*Aggression and hostility are*
*so clearly defensive and pro-*
*tective drives. However, in*
*humans hostility can readily*
*turn against the self and*
*become self-destructive, even*
*as it can fuse with sexual*
*impulses to become sadism.*
THEODORE LIDZ

It was only after I came back from Trial that I came to a notion of my own as to what maturity consists of. Maturity is the ability to sort the portions of truth from the accepted lies and self-deceptions that you have grown up with. It is easy now to see the irrelevance of the religious wars of the past, to see that capitalism in itself is not evil, to see that honor is most often a silly thing to kill a man for, to see that national patriotism should have meant nothing in the twenty-first century, to see that a correctly-arranged tie has very little to do with true social worth. It is harder to assess as critically the insanities of your own time, especially if you have accepted them unquestioningly for as long as you can remember, for as long as you have been alive. If you never make the attempt, whatever else you are, you are not mature.

ALEXEI PANSHIN
*Rite of Passage*

*Zeus, who taught men to*
*think, has laid it down that*
*wisdom comes alone through*
*suffering.*
AESCHYLUS

One of the major roadblocks to autonomy is failure to achieve separation from authority. This is the failure to outgrow our dependence upon those who have nourished us; we prolong our need of them and rely upon them to make our decisions and provide directives for our behavior. Long past separation-time we continue to operate in terms of their values. Dependence of course, means security; in a dependent state there is much of life we need not face and many responsibilities we need not assume. It is comfortable to maintain dependence and conform to patterns that are not ours.

The longer dependence lasts, the more difficult separation becomes. Unless, sometime, we experience the feeling of being a separate self, the very idea of autonomy may remain meaningless.

The self that longs for autonomy—the self that longs for a life of its own—will not easily be put down. If the authorities are reluctant to relinquish control and/or if the separating self cannot outgrow its dependency, then the separation process is often prolonged and may reach crisis proportions. But paradoxically, as long as there is pain, there is hope; the separation process has not been abandoned.

*The highest duty of the writer, the composer, the artist is to remain true to himself and let the chips fall where they may.*

JOHN F. KENNEDY

Pablo Picasso, *Girl Before a Mirror* (1932) Collection, The Museum of Modern Art, New York. Gift of Mrs. Simon Guggenheim.

### FIVE SELVES
### *Amy's Story*

What is a self? What does it mean to be a person?

Amy's mother was a well-meaning but emotionally bereft alcoholic, her father an often jobless day laborer prone to episodes of violent behavior. The oldest of seven children and her father's favorite, Amy became the focus of his sexual attentions. When she maneuvered to evade his advances, she was cruelly rejected and made to feel ungrateful and worthless.

Feeling overwhelmed and helpless, she developed another self—Ceci—who would cope with her father's demands. Quite unlike Amy, Ceci was a flirtatious coquette skilled in the art of anticipating her father's advances and avoiding his rage.

As her mother became increasingly remote, Amy tried to hold the family together, but in spite of her best efforts the children were eventually passed along to relatives and shuttled between foster homes.

One foster family was Catholic, and Amy adapted herself to their Catholic world, identifying with the ideas, values, and viewpoints of these significant others. She developed a "Catholic self" that could live with them successfully; after all, their acceptance and approval were necessary for survival. This Catholic-self was named Rachel.

When Amy was seventeen she took a job in a large corporation as a filing clerk. Her administrative and organizational skills soon became apparent, and she was urged to attend night school to develop her abilities. At this point another self, Lisa, emerged. Supercalm, detached, quick to learn, quick to understand, efficient and professional, she was the ideal assistant for a fast-track junior executive.

A fifth self—Beth—was sometimes weak, sometimes strong. On occasion, when Amy was alone, Beth would emerge with a scream and throw tantrums, as though an ignored self had been confined to a room and could come out only with great effort, or as though she were a forgotten prisoner, locked in a dark cell, screaming for recognition. Beth would often sob uncontrollably, then grow quiet and apparently vanish.

As the years passed Amy's five selves continued to develop in coherence and strength of will. When she visited her Catholic family, the Rachel-self emerged spontaneously and functioned normally. All went well. When she visited her father, the Ceci-self appeared, played her flirtatious part, and vanished. Likewise, Lisa "grew in wisdom and strength" as she competed successfully and was rewarded in her corporate environment. The appropriate self was reinforced and strengthened in each case. As long as Amy could count on the right self emerging at the right time and place, her existence, if not without stress, was basically stable.

During her tenure as a personal assistant she met and fell in love with a young executive. Her first serious romantic involvement awakened the unresolved pain and guilt associated with her father's attentions. Under the increased stress Ceci sought to emerge and take control. Lisa tried to hang on. Soon the delicate balance of selves began to disintegrate, plunging Amy into acute anxiety and—because she felt trapped—into depression. She became immobile. She could not work or face friends. She attempted suicide.

Amy was hospitalized and diagnosed as possessing multiple personalities. She began therapy. The therapeutic plan called for the selection and strengthening of one of the selves—the most authentic or "core" self—while allowing the other selves to weaken and disintegrate. They chose Lisa because she had interfaced better with the real world. Careful control of her environment was absolutely necessary. During therapy Lisa/Amy was not allowed to see, or be seen by, members of her family, friends or coworkers who would only reinforce the other selves familiar to them. Months of therapy were needed. It was a time of isolation, loss, disorientation, and depression. It was also a time of healing. Lisa gradually took control, and the other selves—no longer needed, no longer reinforced—continued to fade. Lisa/Amy grew in strength, coherence, and will.

Today Lisa/Amy is married and has a family of her own. Hers is a success story. To be sure, she is not wholly free of emotional problems: the Ceci side of her self, still needing to please and fearing rejection, is not entirely resolved. But Amy is one person, one self. She has full knowledge of her former selves, and because of her pain, she possesses a special insight into, and compassion for, the delicate condition of the human soul. One of the keys to Amy's success has been her capacity for honesty, her willingness to face the truth about herself, whatever that might be.

So, what is a self? What is the relationship of self to body? (Remember, Amy had five selves in a single body.) What is a person? Are "self" and "person" interchangeable? It is generally assumed in ethical studies that a "person" is the proper object of ethical concern. In Amy's case what (or whom) should we be ethically concerned about? Are we born with a self, or is it developed, grown through time and experience? Can selves be weakened and strengthened in all of us? What does it mean to have (or to be) a "weak self" or "strong self"? What does "self-esteem" mean in Amy's case? We *all* play roles: What is the difference between those of us who *play* different roles (according to the "job description") and Amy, who apparently *was* the roles she played? "Are we one, or many?"

This "crisis of authority" is felt on both sides. For the self that is fighting for autonomy, the severance of the umbilical cord brings fear and guilt. He is doing the very thing the authorities find unacceptable. He is behaving "badly" or "wrong." One commonly feels like a traitor in abandoning the values and beliefs of the authority-figures; and, unavoidably, the authorities will be hurt. They may experience a sense of failure, perhaps of betrayal. The crisis of separation is often as painful for the authorities as it is for the separating self, for authorities have as difficult a time letting go as the self has in cutting loose. An authority-figure, after all, must *be* an authority or his role—the role he has defined for himself and identified with—vanishes. He often feels (unconsciously) that his purpose in life will be lost if he is not needed by others; and if others do not *need* him then there will be no basis for a relationship with him. He will be alone. Therefore, authorities frequently bind us to them in an effort to give their own lives meaning. If seen from this perspective, it becomes clear that the dependency-ties go in *both* directions.

*Let me listen to me and not to them.*

GERTRUDE STEIN

## DEVELOPING SELF-AWARENESS

If the recovery of the whole self is to be one's goal, then the development of self-awareness is a prerequisite. If we sense that things have not gone right either in the development of identity or self-worth, and we genuinely want growth to take place, then self-knowledge is essential and some very deliberate choices will have to be made in terms of that knowledge.

It is not uncommon to find ourselves experiencing repeatedly the same dominant negative emotions as we live through a variety of activities in time: anxiety, fear, anger, frustration, depression. We may engage in sundry projects and numerous relationships, expecting (or perhaps just hoping) that something will happen to change how we feel. But it doesn't happen. In our honest moments we can confess to a hunger for life, but something inside holds us where we are. At the deepest emotional level, it is always the same.

Where does one begin? A deceptively simple answer: we begin here and now. We begin with the sum of all that we are.

When we are open to experiencing our selves precisely as they are—rather than expending energy feeling anxious or guilty over what they are not—a change in feeling can take place. An awareness of all that we contact inside must be brought into our consciousness. Whatever our shortcomings (on whatever criteria they are judged to be "shortcomings"), these too must be accepted as part of one's self. Here deliberate choice comes in. There are unpleasant things stored in the inner worlds of all of us, and we may be tempted to ignore them; but with self-awareness, we can deliberately choose to stay a moment, recognize heretofore repressed events, and begin the process of "decharging" them.

A fact about emotion is that it changes when it is permitted expression and can run its course. When one allows himself to feel a feeling, and no longer permits himself the dangerous luxuries of repression and rationalization, then genuine change can follow.

For example, the monologue might heretofore have gone like this: "I feel sad. I don't want to feel sad, so I will pretend I don't feel sad. Others won't notice and I can fool myself as well." If we play this kind of game with our emotions, the sadness in this case is repressed and has little chance to change. It will remain stored as a charged energy-system within the psyche. This is true, of course, for all the bitter emotions—anger, hatred, frustration, fear, and so on.

On the other hand, the monologue might proceed: "I feel sad. I don't want to feel sad, but I'll not deny what exists. Rather, I will feel the full force of the feeling and let it run its course. It will fade away by itself." This way, when we *choose* not to repress an emotion, we find that it will diminish and we can move on to better feelings. Nothing is repressed that can return later and wreak vengeance for not having been dealt with honestly.

In this way, with self-awareness and deliberate choice, one can begin to integrate all that he is. These are first steps in the recovery of a wholeness that most of us, living in a fragmenting world, have to some degree lost and forgotten.

## THE LAW OF PATHEI MATHOS

We humans have long been aware that growth never comes without a price: pain. The Greek tragedian Aeschylus thought of man as subject to an

**PEANUTS** ®                                    **By Charles M. Schulz**

"epistemic law" decreed by the god Zeus "who had laid it down that wisdom comes alone through suffering." Charlie Brown put it more succinctly after Linus lost his faith in the Great Pumpkin: "In all this world there is nothing more upsetting than the clobbering of a cherished belief."

The agonies of insight are not strangers to any of us.

The agony of discovering you are not one but many people, created in the images of those who have mattered most to you.

The agony of having your childhood's faith crumble at the very moment when you needed it most to sustain you.

The agony of doubting what you knew was right, and wondering if what you knew was wrong just could be right.

The agony of watching your children enter new worlds you cannot enter, and cannot accept, yet cannot completely condemn.

The agony of listening to your children condemn all that you believe in and tried to teach them.

The agony of feeling like a traitor to your parents when you find you must abandon their cherished beliefs because, for you, they are not true.

The agony of having to unlearn and relearn what you learned because what you were taught is no longer true.

The agony of hating others for making you what you are, yet knowing in your honest moments that they could not have done otherwise.

The agony of being concerned, when others are not.

It is a painful insight to discover that one holds a belief because one needs the belief, and not because the belief is true. This is the sort of insight one would like to make go away, like a bad dream or clouds on a rainy day.

But this sort of insight, which comes with self-awareness, is the most difficult to dispel. When the process has begun by which one begins to examine the nature of the need which the belief fulfills, it follows that one asks whether the belief is *also* true—and often finds that it is not. The insight into the nature of the need has, for all pragmatic purposes, destroyed the efficacy of the belief.

Our pain can be especially sharp when the insight has destroyed the belief while our need for it is still alive. The head has said, "You can no longer believe it, for now you see through it." But the rest of one's being cries out in emptiness for what it has lost.

This is the cry of the soul that still needs healing but has discovered that the healers have lost their power. This is a Saint Paul, torn with conflict,

*If it were not for the neurotics, there would be very little work accomplished in this world.*

ARTHUR P. NOYES

*I will not let you (or me) make me dishonest, insincere, emotionally tied up or constricted, or artificially nice and social, if I can help it.*

EUGENE T. GENDLIN

*The ultimate goal of the educational system is to shift to the individual the burden of pursuing his own education.*

JOHN GARDNER

...I'D QUIT THE JOB OF BEING ME, BUT i HAVE ACCUMULATED SO MUCH SENIORITY...

*A great many people are neurotic today, and the neuroses are caused by the fact that their talents, their unique potentialities, have not been used. They are "spinning their wheels" in life because they have not grown as they could have grown, because they have not used the gifts they have. . . .*

AARON UNGERSMA

*To oversimply matters somewhat, it is as if Freud supplied to us the sick half of psychology, and we must now fill it out with the healthy half.*

ABRAHAM MASLOW

realizing that the Law of Moses only increased his guilt. This is a Luther, still yearning for peace of soul, but finding that his faith in the sacraments has failed him and they cannot bring him peace.

This is the agony of alienated selves who have found themselves cut off from their roots, still longing for something *worth* believing in, but discovering that the old gods are gone and there is nothing to take their place.

> You ask me how I became a madman. It happened thus: One day, long before many gods were born, I woke from a deep sleep and found all my masks were stolen—the seven masks I have fashioned and worn in seven lives,—I ran maskless through the crowded streets shouting, "Thieves, thieves, the cursèd thieves."
>
> Men and women laughed at me and some ran to their houses in fear of me.
>
> And when I reached the market place, a youth standing on a house-top cried, "He is a madman." I looked up to behold him; the sun kissed my own naked face for the first time. For the first time the sun kissed my own naked face and my soul was inflamed with love for the sun, and I wanted my masks no more. And as if in a trance I cried, "Blessed, blessed are the thieves who stole my masks."
>
> Thus I became a madman.
>
> KAHLIL GIBRAN

## REFLECTIONS

1 The developmental sequence of young monkeys—and by implication of human beings (p. 139)—makes a sort of sound common sense. Put into your own words why, in terms of psychological development, the sequence seems to be so important.

2 According to the Putneys (see marginal quote on p. 140), Americans are "hungry for the approval of others." Does that make sense to you? Why are we this way?

3 Do you agree with the statement (p. 140) that "the price we pay is very dear" for wearing masks? As you see it, what is that price?

4 It isn't uncommon to hear someone say, "I don't know who I am." What do you think this person is trying to say? Have you ever said this?

5 Ponder the pictures on p. 145. These paintings were entitled "Passing the Buck" by the artist Dick Sargent. To use the psychological term, this series depicts the displacement of hostility. Psych it out: *Why* do we *displace* our hostilities in this manner?

6 What do you think of Oedipus's vow to himself—"I will not stop until I understand myself"? Is this a noble goal, in your estimation? Does this determination of Oedipus frighten you? What are its dangers? What are its rewards?

7  Criticize the analysis of the meaning of innocence on pp. 141–142. Where in this description do you find yourself (if at all)? Is the state of dependence an *enjoyable* state?

8  Ponder the painting by Picasso (p. 146) entitled "Girl before a Mirror." How many persons (remember that the Latin word *persona* means "mask"—see p. 140) are in the painting? How many persons do you think the girl perceives?

9  Zero in on the problem of dealing with those who would "[provide] us with the answers before we have asked the questions" (p. 143). Do you agree with the problem as stated in this chapter? How would you suggest that we confront such answer-givers?

10  Note the sequence of stages in Gregory Bateson's "progress in awareness" (p. 141-Box). Restate in your own terms the steps he describes. Does Bateson's description sound like an accurate accounting of the way we grow?

11  As you reflect on the so-called Law of Pathei Mathos (pp. 148, 150), are you inclined to agree that there exists such a human pattern that might be thus designated as a "law"? What is meant by "suffering" in this case? Can you describe the human pathways by which suffering could lead to wisdom?

*The curiosity of the human race is most evident in children. A child's innocent question will often give the adult to pause, and ponder carefully the answer. But there are other things than answers to be careful of when dealing with a child. . . .*

**JACK WILLIAMSON**

# SIGMUND FREUD

## *Our Humanity Is Blocked by Our Pain*

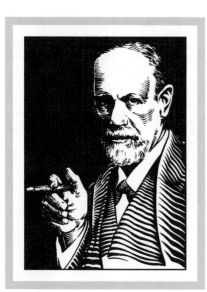

Sigmund Freud was born in Moravia (now Czechoslovakia) in 1856 but was raised and spent most of his life in Vienna. There he came to despise the repressiveness of society and escaped from it by taking long walks in the Austrian countryside where he could stand tall with the pines, collect wildflowers for study ("they have neither character nor complexities"), and breathe in the fresh air of the Alpine snows.

He was "the firstborn son of a youthful mother"—Amalia Freud—and her favorite child (of eight); and she often spoke in glowing terms of her son's future greatness. This son later wrote: "A man who has been the indisputable favorite of his mother keeps for life the feeling of a conqueror, that confidence of success that often induces real success." His father, Jacob Freud, was a clothier. By him Freud was gifted with intellect, a will to work, and unflagging energy; but the spector of a stern authority also pursued him through life, like the Hound of Heaven. "That boy will never amount to anything!" his father grumbled one night

after an unpleasant episode when his son was about seven. "This must have been a terrible affront to my ambitions," Freud later wrote, "for allusions to this scene recur again and again in my dreams, and are constantly coupled with enumerations of my accomplishments and successes, as though I wanted to say: 'You see, I have amounted to something after all.'. . . "

Young Freud was introspective. The need for aloneness dominated his life. He lived in a small, stuffy, private bedroom with an oil lamp, and here he lost himself in his books, reading everything he could come by. Already at this age he posessed an insatiable desire for an unbounded knowledge of everything. During his teens he rarely joined the family at meals but ate alone in his room where he poured timelessly over his books.

His formal education began at the local gymnasium ("grammar school") where he spent his first eight years, reading voraciously and taking copious notes on lectures. He later wrote that even at this early age he felt a sense of direction: "In the years of my youth, the urgent necessity to understand something of the riddles of the world and perhaps contribute myself to their solution was overpowering." In the summer of his seventeenth year he graduated *summa cum laude*—with highest honors.

He decided to become a medical student, so he entered the University of Vienna and eagerly began to explore all the sciences; but he had difficulty finding his niche and wandered from one department to another, without rooting. He was finally invited by Professor Brücke to join his laboratory to study human physiology. In 1882 he became an intern at Vienna's General City Hospital and worked as a clinical neurologist. Soon he was a resident physician. In the spring of 1885 he was appointed lecturer in neuropathology.

That summer he went to Paris to pursue reports about a therapeutic technique employed by a famed physician, Dr. Charcot. Freud stayed with Charcot for the better part of a year and pondered the exciting possibilities of using hypnosis to reach the painful past events that seemed to underlie his patients' problems. But it was also spring in Paris, and the tulips were beginning to open. He was still in love, engaged for almost four years. He wandered the city, visiting Notre Dame cathedral on free afternoons where he would "clamber about between the monsters and gargoyles." He longed to return to Vienna.

The young lady's name was Martha Bernays. They began a marriage in the autumn of 1886—he was thirty, she was twenty-five—that was to last fifty-three years. To Freud she was tender and devoted, her only goals in life (her husband later said) being "to keep well and love him." She was by instinct and calling a hausfrau, managing every detail of the home's economy and six children with efficiency and seeing to it that *der Papa* could get his work done.

Freud focused his intellect on one goal: to find the truth about what is going on in the hidden depths of the human mind.

A breakthrough came in 1889 on a trip to visit a French country doctor named Liébeault who was having notable success in treating patients suffering from emotional ailments. From the doctor's extensive experience, Freud saw for the first time what he had been groping for—"the possibility that there could be powerful mental processes which nevertheless remained hidden from the consciousness of man." In simplistic terms, Freud had discovered the existence of the unconscious mind. Henceforth, he increasingly broke with the past and set off in new directions.

◆

Freud believed that we are blocked from being human by our own repressed pain; and that seeing the truth about ourselves could release enormous stores of bound-up energy for rich and responsible living.

Freud theorized that the human personality is produced by the interaction of three dynamic organizational systems: the *id*, the *superego*, and the *ego*. The id is not an organized system but a chaos of primal energies that urges us to action; it is the whole complex of our physical and psychic needs, driven by emotion. It operates on the "pleasure-principle," seeking pleasure and avoiding pain.

The superego is our system of moral values—the dos ("ego ideals") and don'ts ("conscience") acquired through interaction with the world. It begins when our parents first tell us what the id can and cannot get away with; their directives are internalized and become part of our own psychic structure.

The ego is a psychic system that operates on the "reality-principle" and mediates between the blind energy-drives of the id—"I want what I want, now!"—and the real world that says "No! Or maybe later. . . ." The ego is a negotiating instrument—dickering, manipulating, compromising, arranging for the delay of gratification. If the ego develops properly, it can be a strong mediator, negotiating effectively and realistically to meet our needs; if it

*No one who, like me, conjures up the most evil of those half-tamed demons that inhabit the human breast, and seeks to wrestle with them, can expect to come through the struggle unscathed.*

*Where id was, there shall ego be!*

A FREUD LEXICON

EGO
SUPERGO
ID
REPRESSION
UNCONSCIOUS
NEUROSIS
REGRESSION
TRANSFERENCE
WISH FULFILLMENT
OEDIPUS COMPLEX
INFERIORITY COMPLEX
LIBIDO
FIXATION

*I do not think our cures can compete with those of Lourdes. There are so many more people who believe in the miracles of the Blessed Virgin than in the existence of the unconscious.*

*The voice of the intellect is a soft one, but it does not rest until it has gained a hearing.*

*I became aware of my destiny: to belong to the critical minority as opposed to the unquestioning majority.*

*One must learn to put up with some measure of uncertainty.*

remains undeveloped, then it will be unable to assume its assertive role as mediator between the pleasure-seeking self and the restrictive world.

In a "healthy" individual the ego is in command, mediating effectively between the id and superego to get our needs met; and we have a sense of wholeness, effectiveness, and well-being. When these systems cannot work together—when they are at war with one another—then we become preoccupied with the ongoing internal conflicts and are unable to transact business efficiently with the environment to get our needs met. These conflicts between the dynamic systems are called "neuroses."

Freud's great discovery was the existence of the unconscious mind and its modus operandi. Normally, the conscious mind knows of its contents; it is "conscious" of the perceptions, memory-images, and ideas being utilized to solve problems. But the conscious part of the mind is only the "tip of the iceberg"; most of the dynamic interactions between the three energy-systems take place below the level of consciousness; that is, we are not "conscious" of them.

What Freud next discovered constitutes the "bitter but liberating wisdom" of his legacy. The relationship between conscious and unconscious is that of antagonists—evasion, deceit, denial, and conflict. "Our entire psychical activity is bent upon procuring pleasure and avoiding pain," Freud said. "It is simply the pleasure-principle which draws up the progamme of life's purpose." When the pleasure-principle comes into conflict with rejection by the real world, these energies are repressed into the unconscious, out of sight—and out of mind.

Repression is an inherent function of the mind. *All* minds repress; *all* of mankind is in a repressed condition. Since repression is the source of our neuroses, all mankind is neurotic. Neuroses, therefore, are not to be found only in a few unfortunate individuals, as we previously believed. Neurosis is universal. No

one is mentally "healthy." We differ only in the degree of our inner conflict.

The unconscious mind is a reservoir of blocked-off energies. They cannot go away or lie dormant. Energies, by definition, must *do* something. So they must find an outlet, even by devious channels that the conscious mind refuses to recognize. They drive us to do things we don't understand and may want to disown. This is one of Freud's far-reaching discoveries: "unconscious motivation." We humans—far from being the rational beings portrayed by Western (Greek) tradition—behave primarily from deep-seated, uncontrollable, and undiscerned irrational impulses. The "essence of man" is not at all what we thought it was.

All neurosis represents a flight from direct confrontation with reality, and in this compromise our humanness is denied, distorted, and transmogrified into pain. And as pain—disguised beyond recognition—we must finally deal with it, commonly with aspirin and alcohol.

As Freud saw it, man is the animal that represses his fundamental pleasure-drives into unconsciousness in accordance with the demands of society to repress himself. Indeed, Freud concluded that man's superiority over the other animals *is* his capacity for repression and neurosis.

The whole point of Freud's theory and therapy is "nothing more than the discovery of the unconscious." The science of psychology "will consist in translating unconscious processes into conscious ones," and psychotherapy will assist the individual in bringing to light the discordant events of his unconscious mind so he can realize a more harmonious cooperation between his psychic energy-systems.

Virtually all schools of psychotherapy, from Freud's day to ours, take their cues from the master: they are designed to help us come to terms with the unacknowledged contents of our repressed unconscious minds. Some therapies attempt to strengthen the ego so it can better handle transactions—to "cope" better; others attempt to alter our responses to the world by altering our perception of it; and some have set their sights on the grandest goal of all: the abolition of repression—achieving "integration" or "individuation"—so that we might know, at last, the experience of wholeness.

◆

Opposition to Freud's theories flared even before they were published. Colleagues and laymen roundly denounced his interest in hypnosis and his notions about the psychic origins of hysteria (everyone knew that such problems had *physiological* origins). Further, he had begun to produce massive new theories on the structure and dynamics of the unconscious mind. What made them threatening was their empirical foundations, their logical consistency, and the fact that they struck down time-honored assumptions. "I do not think our cures can compete with those of Lourdes," he wrote, with a tincture of bitters. "There are so many more people who believe in the miracles of the Blessed Virgin than in the existence of the unconscious." The more he was denounced, the more insistent he became. His mentors and former teachers, one by one, disowned him—Brücke, Meynert, Breuer. The Vienna Medical Society attacked him for his "crackbrain ideas." The University of Vienna—his alma mater—scornfully denied him a post. For his conjecture that our neuroses have sexual origins, he was labeled by the popular press a deviant and pornographer. By the time he was in his mid-forties he had joined Darwin in the eye of the storm.

Although Freud's last years were a shining triumph, they were darkened by pain and sorrow. In 1923 he had undergone surgery for cancer of the jaw, and his death seemed imminent (in fact he still had sixteen years to live); but larger than his physical suffering was the collapse of the civilization he had known.

He was on Hitler's hit list. His books had been burned in 1933. "At least I have been burned in good company," he said. On May 21, 1938, the Gestapo invaded the apartment where he was convalescing. They seized his passport and money, ransacked the rooms, rummaged through papers, and destroyed his books. Freud endured it all calmly.

His friends finally persuaded him to leave Austria, but the Nazis held out for an enormous ransom. The princess of Greece offered a quarter-million Austrian schillings on deposit in Vienna, but the Nazis balked, demanding more. President Roosevelt interceded, and the money was finally taken.

On June 4, 1938, in a wheelchair, with some salvaged furniture, books, and antiquities, Freud bade farewell to Vienna. With him were Martha, his daughter Anna, a few friends, and his chow dog Lun. They boarded the Orient Express for Paris and two days later were in London, safe from the holocaust.

Typically, after resting briefly, he resumed his work schedule at their new home. He rose at eight, checked with his doctor, saw a patient, lunched; then wrote, saw more patients, walked in his garden, tended flowers, and played with Lun ("she always behaves psychoanalytically").

He had only a year to live. The painful cancer progressed, and he died on September 23, 1939. His body was cremated without religious ceremony, and his ashes were placed in an old Grecian vase he had brought with him from Vienna. The marble column beneath the vase is inscribed simply: SIGMUND FREUD 1856–1939.

*An intimate friend and a hated enemy have always been indispensable to my emotional life . . . .*

*The great question . . . which I have not been able to answer, despite my thirty years of research into the feminine soul, is "What does a woman want?"*

*In a normal sex life no neurosis is possible.*

*I am cross with mankind.*

## ALL THE WORLD'S A STAGE . . .

Each single life/time is a living drama played out in space and time against the backdrop of eternity.

All the world's a stage
And all the men and women merely players:
They have their exits and their entrances;
And one man in his time plays many parts. . . .

In each life, the curtain has arisen and the play is in progress. But not having read the script, the plot of the drama remains unknown. We cannot foresee the acts that lie ahead—or when the play will end—because, as in living theater, the plot is developed extempore as line follows line and scene follows scene.

On rare occasions, however, we are able to see and feel, in a single sweep of comprehension, the whole of a life/time. Such a vision may flash through our minds after reading a biography or after watching a drama. Often times at a funeral we are left in a reflective mood as we stand, for a short moment, at the end of a life just completed.

When the biography is closed—when the third-act curtain has been rung down—only then can the play be seen in its entirety. Every part relates to, and sheds light upon, every other part. For life *is* an unfolding drama. Scene follows scene, each illuminating what has gone before and pointing toward developments that lie ahead. We can trace the major motifs of later life back to their beginnings. We can see the inception of strengths that are to bring fulfillment and flaws that are to bring failure. We can point to the decisions that made all the difference.

*Sooner or later, life makes philosophers of us all.*

MAURICE RISELING

*It is quite possible, Octavian, that when you die, you will die without ever having been alive.*

"MARK ANTONY"
*Cleopatra*

*If life is not a thrilling adventure, it is nothing.*

HELEN KELLER

To see life whole allows us to ponder the mystery of human existence with a special kind of awareness. The feeling of absolute finality forces upon us a reordering of values. We frequently feel that, in effect, "it has put things in perspective."

What would it be like if each of us could stretch our conceptual limits to reflect upon our life/time as a completed biography?

## THE GROUNDPLAN

*Our days, our deeds, all we achieve or are, Lay folded in our infancy. . . .*

JOHN TROWBRIDGE

It is quite within the realm of possibility for us to view *the basic groundplan* which our lives follow. The capricious details of daily existence are unpredictable, to be sure; but we have within us a psychophysiological timetable that provides the plot of the human drama. Quite apart from contingencies and variables, we *can* see our own lives as a whole.

Current thinking in the human sciences tends to avoid dividing the life-cycle into neat, clearly defined "stages." Rather, life is phasic in nature; it is a continuum, with each phase emerging out of the previous phase. Distinct events occur more or less at scheduled times. There does in fact exist a clear psychophysiological growth-progression that is universal and constitutes the groundplan for the entire human life-cycle.

Erik Erikson and others have emphasized the fact that life unfolds in a sequence of challenges that must be resolved. Each challenge is a genetically programmed, psychophysiological readiness to incorporate *specific experiences* into our developing selves. As each challenge is successfully met, growth takes place and we can move ahead, on schedule, to face the next readiness period. Each phase of our lives literally grows out of the successful completion of the previous challenge. The precise schedule of these challenges is unique to each individual and determines the phasic nature of life.

The following sections should be read in a special way with a specific goal in mind. That goal is to feel the whole of a life-cycle, to see the human enterprise, from birth till death, in a single vision, as One. Perhaps reading rapidly through all the sections several times would accomplish this better than studying details which, in this case, are of secondary importance.

## INFANCY TO CHILDHOOD

*He whom love touches not, walks in darkness.*

PLATO

*For young children it is primarily experience that determines character, but for the more mature person it is character that determines experience.*

HAIM GINOTT

INFANCY During the first twelve to fifteen months of life, we awaken to the world about us. We are wholly dependent; our needs must be met by others. Therefore, the crucial challenge of this phase is the development of a feeling of trust, and the depth of our trust depends upon how well we are cared for. Whether we develop this capacity at all is out of our hands; we are pawns of our environment.

If these months are pleasant times, then we begin to open ourselves to life. We can feel hunger, pain, loneliness—whatever is authentic—and know that there will be someone to fulfill our needs. There is someone who cares. Thus we learn in a very natural way to be ourselves and to remain open to the actions of others. We trust them. By contrast, if the environment is capricious or hostile, we become fearful; we remain on guard; we cannot afford to open ourselves to others. Quite realistically, we have no grounds for trusting.

This phase is critical. If we don't develop trust and openness during this period, then severe conflicts lie ahead. Some personality theorists go much further and believe that if we don't experience love during this early period, then love is lost from our lives forever. We will never love—or be loved.

EARLY CHILDHOOD  A new phase begins when we learn to stand, walk about, and get into things. Better motor control brings whole new worlds within range of our curious hands. We venture into new rooms, play with new toys (*everything* is a toy), and find drawers and cupboards to explore.

The essential challenge of early childhood is striking a balance between an unbounded freedom to do anything (which *we* want) and the necessary limits and controls (which *others* want)—parameters within which we must exist. Guidelines must be consistent and firm. Our neophilic impulse to explore must not be dampened, but we must learn to accept limits; we must learn to live with the frustrations of not being able to do everything we want. If we can find a satisfactory balance between freedom and restriction, then we can continue, safely and happily, to explore the world about us. But if there is too much freedom, we will learn to resist all authority that would impose any limitations upon us; or if there is too much restraint, then we gradually lose the urge to explore life and give in to a neophobic passivity. Either extreme sets us up for problems that will return to bother us at a later time.

MIDDLE CHILDHOOD  The next challenge is a different kind: it is the discovery that other people come in two varieties—and that we are one of the two.

*In youth we learn; in age we understand.*

MARIE VON EBNER-ESCHENBACH

*LORI TO LISA: "You're five years old now. I expect you to be the best five-year-old you can be."*

We awaken to the fact that, physiologically, we are different from others in our family and from friends.

The psychological challenge of this phase is the successful acceptance of ourselves as boy or girl within the context of all our relationships. That is, we proceed to clarify and understand our sex-role identity. With positive guidance from authorities, our sex-role is accepted without undue stress or guilt. We begin to feel that being a girl or a boy is natural and good, that it was not a mistake or terrible accident that we were not born of the other sex.

I hesitate (but only briefly) to mention that some noteworthy male thinkers held some interesting ideas on gender. Plato, Aristotle, and Saint Thomas Aquinas all believed that women are mistakes. According to the latter, nature always tries to produce a male, but a female results when something goes wrong *(mas occasionatum);* more than that, she is a defective and accidental creature *(deficiens et occasionatum).* Plato seems to have held a similar notion: "A woman is merely a lesser man." No philosopher, as far as I know, has suggested that men are mistakes, though I'm sure an interesting argument could be constructed to support the notion.

Those who employ Freudian concepts hold that there is also an Oedipal conflict to be resolved at this stage. The daughter finds herself in profound competition with her mother as she comes to realize they are of the same sex; similarly, the son feels a competitiveness toward his father—each for the love and sex-role approval of the other parent. The resolution of these conflicts leads to a new set of relationships all around, based upon the realities of sex-identity.

*Self and personality emerge from experience. If they are open to their experience, doing what "feels right" proves to be a competent and trustworthy guide to behavior which is truly satisfying.*

**CARL ROGERS**

**LATE CHILDHOOD** About the age of six there begins a longer, smoother period of growth that lasts until the beginning of adolescence, a duration of five or six years. It is a time for consolidation of the growth-gains we have made so far. It is a sort of rest period from the ordeals of rapid change. However, if earlier growth-challenges haven't been effectively resolved, this "rest period" may be a sort of catch-up time for further resolution of these conflicts.

During this calmer time, if all goes well, there is a deepening sense of identity as the distinctive elements of our personalities become more coherent. Personality is still developing, to be sure; it is still shaky and tender. Our selves are not yet firmly grounded. Therefore, if our environment is especially hostile and rejecting at this time, painful feelings of inadequacy can result. Acceptance by our peers at this point is important; we seek it aggressively, though not often directly. We want to feel that we are like others, and that others approve of us.

If all goes well during this stabilizing phase, then the stage is set for the next critical ordeal of our life-cycle: adolescence.

## THE ADOLESCENT YEARS

**EARLY ADOLESCENCE** With the sudden physiological growth that initiates adolescence, we enter a time of "storm and stress," an upheaval that affects not only us but the lives of all who are within range.

Adolescence is transition. Heretofore, each of us has been a child. We have been treated as children, and our thoughts and emotions have been those of a child. We have been passing through the conflicts characteristic of childhood.

## TOKEN SEPARATION

Several recent, extensive studies suggest that the number of adolescents who achieve a decisive articulation of the self is diminishing. Elizabeth Douvan and Joseph Adelson found that a serious testing of values and ideology occurs only in a minority of adolescents. It appears that real independence is accomplished in lower-class and some upper-middle-class youngsters because these two extremes are so different from the core adolescent culture. But in studying the "silent majority" of adolescents, they found only token parent-child conflict and therefore token maturity and autonomy. They found that the peer group for many adolescents is only used to learn and display social skills—a kind of playpen designed to keep the children out of harm's way. Although for many the peer group is an arena for confrontation of self, for many more it acts to hinder differentiation and growth.

*Developmental Psychology Today*

All this rapidly changes as the transition to adulthood begins. We identify increasingly with adults, and others treat us more and more as young adults. We are being thrust into adulthood. The allurement of freedom and independence beckon, but self-doubt and fear of responsibility draw us back. Adolescence is marked by spurts of growth and regression. All the while, the lingering little-boy or little-girl feelings haunt us; we are pulled and torn, not knowing from day to day which—and who—we are.

The prime challenge of early adolescence is the acceptance of the physiological and obviously sexual changes our body undergoes. For a time we may feel like spirits inhabiting an alien organism. It changes almost daily; it is erratic and unpredictable. Alterations in body chemistry intensify our emotions, and many of them are new to us. Hormonal changes bring on dramatic, uncontrollable moodswings.

*Adolescence is a kind of emotional seasickness. Both are funny, but only in retrospect.*
ARTHUR KOESTLER

As if all this weren't enough, we are hit by an excruciating realization that society has *norms* for our sexual characteristics and behavior. Society, we discover, expects us to grow in a specific way, and we anxiously wonder whether we will ever measure up to its standards. Underlying all this is a diffuse, undefined, all-pervasive sexual uneasiness.

But eventually, with encouragement, we adjust to these drastic changes and accept this new body. We find—with mixed feelings—that others begin to respond differently to this body. A young woman faces the fact of her sexual attractiveness with embarrassment, self-consciousness, and delight; a young man begins to have exhilarating sexual feelings, but they may be compromised by anxiety, guilt, and bewilderment.

In summary, the central challenge of early adolescence is to be able to hold on tight while our bodies and emotions undergo dramatic alterations, carrying us through the transition into adulthood, and getting us ready for mating and parenting.

*Mother to daughter: "I love you enough to let you be free and grow up." (Or was it daughter to mother?)*
LORI VILLAMIL

MID-ADOLESCENCE During mid-adolescence physical and psychological turmoil continues, but as we feel more like adults our preoccupation shifts to the problem of independence from authority—that is, independence from other adults. This is the challenge of separation. Feeling increasingly like separate persons, we set out on our own. In the language of space technology, it is time to go on internal power. We venture further in our exploration of life, experimenting with a variety of new experiences. It is a time of trial and error, savoring successes but learning to accept failure when we don't achieve our goals. Independence means learning to set goals for ourselves, and inevitably some will be unrealistic. The challenge is learning to accept failure without feeling like failures—that is, without loss of self-esteem. Gradually we learn how to set more realistic goals.

*Be patient . . . because it wasn't your parents who made the world.*

**ARNOLD TOYNBEE**

Separation often involves a painful and prolonged revolt against authority, against parents and other immediate "controllers" (real or imagined) and also *symbols* of control. But while seeking independence we commonly displace our feelings toward all authorities who, we think, might keep us from gaining the desired separation. It is perhaps a hackneyed phrase, but "the crisis of authority" still describes accurately the experience of mid-adolescence. The more we have been restricted and repressed, the louder our protests and the sharper our attacks against the restraints and the restrainers; or if not permitted direct attack, then the greater will be our use of scapegoats.

*Who the hell is not scared? Life is scary. That's no excuse for not living.*

**LORI VILLAMIL**

The separation process produces great ambivalence. We feel loyalty to those who have cared for us, and separation is painful for everyone. And when others are hurt (we usually say that "*we* hurt *them*," though in fact this is not the case at all), then we feel guilt. To ease our guilt-feelings we seek the approval of those we hurt; that is, we want to be forgiven. But we cry out for the very thing that can not be given. Parents and authorities feel rejected, too; they usually do not understand, and can not accept, our "separating behavior." A part of the individuating process, therefore, is learning to accept without excess remorse and guilt the fact that we have to proceed with the separation *without the approval* of the significant-others involved in the process. Depending upon the maturity of our parents, it is easy to see how manipulative games and bitter conflicts can complicate the mid-adolescent years and often thwart altogether the successful establishment of separate identities. Indeed, for years to come, our parents can linger on in us, and we in them, in a perpetual, agonizing entanglement.

During these troublesome times, we seek the support and understanding of our peers; and an important feature of the mid-adolescent years is "peer-conformity." The more we are misunderstood and rejected by our parents, the more we need the support of our peers who are themselves having similar experiences. They can understand.

LATE ADOLESCENCE If these challenges have been met with continued self-esteem, then late adolescence will be characterized by a strong sense of self. We feel more like distinct, whole persons.

With a smoothly functioning self, we can successfully take on ever-greater responsibilities. Indeed, we enjoy responsibility and the satisfactions it brings. Underlying all of life's sundry experiences is a developing strength that carries us through.

If we are on schedule, and our feelings about both body and self are positive, then we will have developed, smoothly and naturally, the capacity for intimacy, not merely sexual intimacy, but a sense of honesty and openness in all our relationships. The capacity for sexual intimacy is but a single—though often a central—manifestation of the comprehensive capacity for trusting, empathizing, and sharing. The better we feel about ourselves the more we long for intimacy with others.

Therefore, the challenge of late adolescence is the consolidation of a sense of self in relating to other persons, in developing a capacity for intimacy, and in gradually laying to rest our doubts and fears about what we can accomplish as unique selves, newly emerged on the scene and ready for life.

## THE MATURING YEARS

EARLY ADULTHOOD (about twenty to thirty). Before the advent of the 1970s, life-span research had concentrated almost exclusively on the phases from infancy through adolescence; little careful study had been made of life's adult stages. When research began in these phases, results were surprising and some earlier assumptions were removed from textbooks.

Daniel Levinson, a professor of psychiatry at Yale, has branded as false the belief that if we know what happened during an individual's childhood, then the rest of his life is generally predictable. "Psychologists speak as if development goes on to age six, or perhaps eighteen. Then there's a long plateau in which random things occur, and then, at around age sixty or sixty-five, a period of decline sets in to be studied by gerontologists." This picture of the human life-span is little more than a widely held myth. An abundance of new information has shown the adult decades to be as exciting as childhood and as turbulent as adolescence, offering fully as many storm-filled opportunities for change and growth. Based on current knowledge, says Levinson, "there *is* something called adult development, an unfolding, just as there is earlier" during our growing-up years.

The early-adult phase is primarily a time of mating and parenting, but the basic challenge of this stage is the development of one's capacity for intimacy. Both physically and psychologically we are prepared for intimacy and sexual activity (they are *not* synonymous) and the rearing of offspring. Intimacy is not only the capacity for fulfilling sexual companionship, but is more basically a quality of openness and trust that is essential to both marriage and the well-being of the offspring.

This phase of life is characterized by one writer, Linda Wolfe, in this way: "This is a time of life when spouses are wooed and wed, and when adolescent friendships are cast off if they no longer seem desirable, or consolidated if they seem worthy of future investment." New dependencies are established, replacing old ones.

Dr. Levinson describes this as a time of "getting into the adult world." We experiment with society's defined roles, rules, and responsibilities. This can be a time for creation and productivity, a time to channel one's creative energies into a variety of activities, of which parenting may be only one. Many of us choose our vocations at this time, as well as various long-lasting avocations. All are ways of expressing the essence of our own personalities. Our creative urges

*"I don't know anything."*
*"The beginning of wisdom, as they say. When you're seventeen you know everything. When you're twenty-seven if you still know everything you're still seventeen."*

RAY BRADBURY
*Dandelion Wine*

*Sixty years ago I knew everything. Today I know nothing. Education is the progressive discovery of our own ignorance.*

WILL DURANT

*We dare not call ourselves philosophers, and yet we all are, aren't we, or we could not get out of bed in the morning. Unless you plan, the night before, to be alive at dawn, you will not stir.*

RAY BRADBURY

*No one should have to walk alone.*

PHUONG DO

*Spoken of John Keats: He always knew he would die young, therefore he saw as much beauty as he could.*

**On Being Human (TV series)**

"But you can't go through life applying Heisenberg's Uncertainty Principle to *everything*."

© *by Sidney Harris/American Scientist, Volume 67, Number 3, May-June 1979, p. 336.*

can be realized in art forms, in the professions, in roles that serve others, in competitive business ventures, in sports, and so on.

During these years we may achieve for the first time a clear picture of the capacities and limitations that we will have to live with for the rest of our lives. We may find that we must accept some basic limitations. At the same time we can develop a feeling for our growth potential and begin to set realistic goals in terms of what we truly are.

**INTERMEDIATE ADULTHOOD** (roughly thirty to forty). The age of thirty, give or take a year or two, is another time of transition which, for some, mounts to a "growth crisis" that jars us out of our ruts and forces us to face new alternatives. The basic factor in this transition is a feeling that some sort of change is imperative. Stagnation is felt to be a real possibility and must be avoided. Dr. Roger Gould describes it as a feeling that some deep and personal side of the self "is striving to be accounted for." It is a time for the reassessment of priorities, relationships, commitments, and goals. Men and women both develop the feeling that the careers and life-styles they have settled into have somehow become too restrictive, too confining. Such roles are perceived to be "a violation or betrayal of a dream they now had to pursue" (Levinson's words). Marriages that were apparently stable often become strained; marriage partners turn elsewhere for companionship and fulfillment. Women frequently discover that they have fallen into the "suburban housewife syndrome" and proceed to change their roles by seeking outside interests—taking a job, returning to school, thinking of a career. "The brief transitional period may occasion considerable inner turmoil—depression, confusion, struggle with the environment and within oneself—or it may involve a quieter reassessment and intensification of effort" (Levinson).

Following this initial transition, the thirties are best described as a time for settling down and seeking stability. Inner turmoil now vanishes: the adolescent search for identity and the early-adult quest for intimacy are past. Life turns outward; concerns become more objective. Men and women both become concerned about their "niche" in society and about advancing their careers.

*Now that I've learned to survive, I want to learn how to live.*

LORI VILLAMIL

*Treasure each other in the recognition that we do not know how long we shall have each other . . .*

JOSHUA LOTH LIEBMAN

The late thirties are frequently characterized by a renewed search for autonomy. During mid- and late-adolescence our strivings were directed toward the discovery of self and autonomy; but during our twenties some of our gains are lost. No sooner do we separate from parents than we reestablish dependencies with mates and mentors, and, like belated obligations, these must eventually be dealt with. One's success in finding a compatible mate is felt and faced earlier. But now, during the late thirties, there emerges a strong need to break dependency-ties with older mentors, especially those in one's job or profession. To accomplish this men and women commonly switch jobs and even relocate themselves vocationally and geographically.

*A man without the love of a good woman is like a squeaking gate on a white picket fence.*

L. L. TAYLOR

The essential challenge of this phase of life is one of growth and accomplishment in the world. If we can assume responsibilities with assurance and skill, then the attainment of goals can bring deep satisfaction. We can enjoy the fruits of our labors. Autonomy and self-esteem can deepen. Our children grow. Social and material gains are made. With increased knowledge and skill in living, we can experience an ever-widening expansion of awareness. These can be fulfilling years.

They can also be dangerous years. If we make unrealistic demands upon ourselves, set unattainable goals, and slide into a pattern of failure, then life, to some degree, can become hellish, and trouble may lie ahead. Furthermore, if we become so absorbed in attaining social and material goals that we neglect to set goals that would promote the growth of ourselves as persons, then the stage is set for us to approach the upcoming years unprepared and empty.

For looming just ahead is a crucial challenge that will largely determine whether the rest of our life/time will be worth living.

MIDDLE ADULTHOOD (about forty to fifty). The challenge of the middle years can be the most precarious time of life since the turmoil of the adolescent transition. This also is a time of transition. This "mid-life crisis"—which begins around forty, give or take a few years—now calls upon all the resources we have been able to develop.

The middle years are a time of taking stock. One arrives at a point where he no longer *assumes* youthfulness; he no longer takes it for granted. He realizes that the youthful phase is passing and that there is nothing he can do about it. The essential challenge might be stated: "I have lived up the first half of my life/time, and I realize there is only so much time left and my life will end. I *experience* that I am mortal. I will die. Now, what do I really want to do with the rest of the time I have left?"

*After forty, a man is responsible for his own face.*

ABRAHAM LINCOLN

Underlying the mid-life crisis is a deeply felt anxiety that is completely democratic: it comes alike to rich and poor, introverts and extroverts, successful entrepreneurs and social dropouts. It is ontological; it is a part of our being human. Failure to negotiate the rough seas at this time portends discontent, while success brings the promise of further growth and greater fulfillment.

Whatever one's state of life, a time of introspection begins. The worldly symbols of success may have been attained, but such accomplishments feel empty and meaningless. "There's more to life than this. There must be. I don't know what it is, but I'm going to find out." Thus an inner anxiety—"Is this all there is?"—is translated into new forms of action: "What have I got to lose?"

Typically, you find a businessman who has spent his life in management,

## WHAT TIME IS IT?

It is a common experience that time for a child seems to pass much more slowly than time for the adult. A year goes by rapidly for a man compared to his recall of childhood years. Seymour Kety has reviewed available information, obtained by the nitrous-oxide technique, on over-all cerebral blood flow and oxygen consumption in man, and finds a distinct correlation of these functions with age. He reports a rapid fall in both circulation and oxygen consumption of the brain from childhood through adolescence followed by a more gradual but progressive decline through the remaining age span. Slowing of cerebral oxygen consumption with advancing years would, according to our considerations, make time appear to pass faster in old age, as indeed it does.

HUDSON HOAGLAND

Percepts of space and time are related to metabolic rate since changes in the latter bring about concomitant perceptual changes. Physiological clocks run fast when metabolic rate is increased, while clock time is overestimated, subjects arrive early to appointments, time appears to pass more slowly. When the physiological clocks run slowly (corresponding to a decrease of metabolic rate), clock time is underestimated, subjects arrive late to their appointments, time flies by rapidly, the days seem to fly by "like magic."

Another manifestation of the relation between metabolic rate and time sense is exemplified by Lecomte du Noüy's experiments [involving healing of tissue] . . . du Noüy calculated the impression of "our passage" in time for a twenty- and fifty-year-old man to be four and six times faster respectively than for a five-year-old child.

ROLAND FISCHER
*J. T. Fraser (ed.)*
*The Voices of Time*

banking, or the like; or a blue-collar worker who has been a responsible provider and "solid citizen." By all criteria he is to be judged successful and commended by society's standards. Inside, however, he experiences a sense of unfinished business. He's sure that he has so far lived the kind of life he should have lived: he chose a vocation, established himself, attained a degree of security and stability. But in all of this he senses a contradiction. In effect, he is saying: "I'm successful, but I'm not sure that I've *become* anything. As a person I feel that, somehow, I got left behind."

Typical also is the housewife and mother. It gradually dawns that she has neglected her own life. There are things she wants to do, and the time has come for her to pursue her own interests. She has devoted years to the defined tasks of housewife and/or mother. She has more or less fulfilled society's expectations of her role and responsibilities. But in doing so, she finds that she has denied many of her own profoundly human needs. At the very worst, she may have discovered that Shaw's bitter axiom is true: "If you begin by sacrificing yourself to those you love, you will end by hating those to whom you have sacrificed yourself."

One study revealed that almost 90 percent of the over-thirty-five-year-old women attending college are there because they are unhappy with their lives and have become uneasy with the state of their personal growth. Many expressed their discontent in some such words as these:

> When I graduated from high school I was thinking of a career, and I went to college at the time to prepare for it. But in my first year I met my husband and we got married. I dropped out and took a job so my husband could continue his education. By the time he finished his degree and got a job we had two children.
>
> But that was more than ten years ago. Now that the children are older I feel strongly that I should go back to school and pick up where I left off.

All these women indicated they never gave up hope of completing their education. In recent years most of them came to see their marriage/family condition as an interlude in (or interruption of) their own "fulfillment as human beings."

Several events may coalesce and contribute to the onset of this stock-taking period. (1) Our children may have achieved separation and we are no longer needed as parents. We have been freed of long-term responsibilities that have been taken for granted. Not to be needed in this familiar role can initiate an "agonized appraisal" of our purpose in living. (2) With this change of roles, husband and wife often encounter each other for the first time in many years. They find that they are not the same selves. Without knowing it, both have changed, and rather suddenly their relationship undergoes an "agonized reappraisal." Often a new relationship must develop. We may also find that we have moved in different directions, and the reestablishment of the intimacy essential to carry us through later years without profound loneliness may be difficult. It may be doubly difficult if such intimacy was never accomplished in the young-adult years.

To some extent, men and women differ in their experience of this middle-years challenge. Menopause may force upon a woman a self-image crisis that a man is spared. If a woman's primary feelings of worth have long been associated with her role as a mother, then the loss of her childbearing capacity—which frequently coincides with the time when her children reach young adulthood, leave home, and no longer need her as a mother—may create severe readjustment problems.

Physical appearance is also a common cause of self-image problems. If a girl's feelings of self-esteem derive primarily from her physical/sexual attractiveness, then as she sees these qualities fade, her self-esteem may also fade. She may feel that she possesses no other qualities that could be a realistic basis for any continued self-esteem. She may feel an irreparable, tragic loss. She may spend her later years trying to recapture the attractiveness that she (and, she believes, others) so valued during the mating years. She may try to perpetuate the image of physical/sexual attractiveness that others can see has vanished. Coquettishness at twenty-two may be quite in order; at fifty-five it indicates a confusion of roles and may appear to others as a painful anachronism.

At forty or forty-five a man may note that some gray hair is showing and that younger people are calling him "sir." He may smile to himself and recognize that others' responses toward him are changing. (He may also misinterpret the "sir" and think it has something to do with respect.) Just as a woman may

*Nel mezzo del cammin di nostra vita*
*Mi ritrovai per una selva oscura,*
*Che la diritta via era smarrita.*
*In the middle of the journey of our life I came to myself in a dark wood, where the straight way was lost.*

**DANTE**

*The life so short, the craft so long to learn.*

**HIPPOCRATES**

*The familiar lament, "I don't know who I am," once thought to belong only to the crisis of adolescence, to be resolved by the adult stage, is heard not only from teenagers but from adults of all ages. . . . A sad commentary on this is the increasing number of suicide attempts on the part of lonely aged people. Education, status, "success," material security or lack of it, seem to have little bearing upon the high degree of suffering, unhappiness, and loneliness found in the life of those who have found no focus of identity or pattern of meaning in their existence.*

**AARON UNGERSMA**

*I've just turned forty, and I don't have the answer to anything any more. But it's all right. Life is beautiful anyway.*

**BARBARA ROBINSON**

attempt to perpetuate the myth of youthful beauty, a man may try to recapture the image of a youthfulness that is passing away.

Failure to deepen one's sense of autonomy and authenticity during the middle years—as opposed to the single-minded pursuit of external accomplishments—renders the future precarious. The foundations of integrity upon which the deeper experiences of our later years must build are shaky in the extreme. This is a vital matter in the inevitable aging process that we all experience.

Autonomous men and women who have practiced authenticity will be more realistic. Having never attempted to be other than what they are, they can accept change just as it comes, without myth. The autonomous individual values himself; others' responses to him may change, but his self-esteem remains intact. The later years can arrive more smoothly without problems reaching crisis proportions.

Having weathered the mid-life transition, the rest of the forties becomes a period of restabilization and renaissance. Roger Gould calls it a time of "relief from the internal tearing apart of the immediately previous years." It is a time of calm. Marriages generally become more stable. Men and women turn more to their mates for understanding, sympathy, and affection. Tragedy and loss can be accepted with patient strength and without the rage and remorse of early years.

Therefore, the central challenge of the middle years is the cluster of decisions regarding how we want to live and what we want to become during the rest of our lives. The resolution of the middle years' challenge depends largely upon our capacity to reset meaningful goals for ourselves *in terms of who we are and the life/time we have left to us.*

LATER ADULTHOOD (from fifty or fifty-five on). If the middle years' challenge has been met with some degree of success, then the later-adult years can be fulfilling. We will continue to grow, to actualize our goals, and simply to enjoy life. Our physiological processes will begin to decline; we may be afflicted with a variety of ailments. But today we know that in most instances our intellectual and emotional capacities can remain viable, and even expand. These faculties—the very substance of our existence—need not fade. To be sure, faculties that were never developed may dim completely, but if our essential faculties have been used optimally, then there is no necessary decline of the quality of our existence with the decline of the somatic organism.

Men and women can meaningfully be called "adults" now. The lingering tendency to blame one's parents for our problems finally ceases. We perceive them, or remember them, with appreciation, as having done their best. There is frequently an enjoyment of human relationships not possible for us during earlier, fiercely competitive years. There is an increased awareness of our mortality, and acceptance of it. Our creativity often reaches greater heights, as though obstacles have been removed; personal and professional accomplishments continue, or increase. This has been called a time of "mellowing and warming up," and there is often the feeling that one has succeeded, at last, in sorting out life's trivialities and knowing what is genuinely of worth and meaning.

Indeed, the later years can usher us into a *quality of experience* that can rarely come at an earlier time. This can be a new sense of ultimacy in all that

*"It's all over, and you're out of danger."*
*"How can I be out of danger if I'm not dead?"*
**Rachel, Rachel**

*"There is no hope."*
*"We're both alive. And for all I know, that's hope."*
**"HENRY II"**
**The Lion in Winter**

*"How long will it take me to learn these things, Father?"*
*"A lifetime, my son, perhaps a little longer."*
**Kung Fu (TV series)**

*Here I am, fifty years old and I don't know what I want to be when I grow up.*
**PETER DRUCKER**

*Nothing I carefully planned for my life has worked out. Everything of significance in my life has been an accident.*
**AL BURKE**

## SUNRISE, SUNSET . . .

Is this the little girl I carried?
Is this the little boy at play?
I don't remember growing older.
When did they?
When did she get to be a beauty?
When did he grow to be this tall?
Wasn't it yesterday when they were small?
    Sunrise, sunset,
    Sunrise, sunset,
    Swiftly flow the days.
    Seedlings turn overnight to sunflowers,
    Blossoming even as we gaze.
    Sunrise, sunset,
    Sunrise, sunset,
    Swiftly fly the years,
    One season following another,
    Laden with happiness and tears.
What words of wisdom can I give them?
How can I help to ease their way?
Now they must learn from one another,
Day by day.
They look so natural together,
Just like two newlyweds should be.
Is there a canopy in store for me?
    Sunrise, sunset,
    Sunrise, sunset,
    Swiftly flow the days.
    Seedlings turn overnight to sunflowers,
    Blossoming even as we gaze.
    Sunrise, sunset,
    Sunrise, sunset,
    Swiftly fly the years,
    One season following another,
    Laden with happiness and tears.

SHELDON HARNICK
*Fiddler on the Roof*

*One of the oldest human needs is having someone to wonder where you are when you don't come home at night.*

MARGARET MEAD

we are and do. We may feel a yearning, aching, profound beauty in our experience of simple things, and see previously unnoticed patterns of meaning in nature, and find new perspectives on, and a belated appreciation of, other people. The very fact of existence itself—not merely human life, but all life, and all existence—can become a glorious mystery that one feels privileged to participate in—"a cosmic drama, and I am actually a part of it!" If life has been a truly expansive adventure, then in these later years there can be an unspeakable love of life—measured by awareness, sagacity, and calm—that we would not exchange, if we could, for the physical vitality of the early years.

*Age does not protect you from love. But love, to some extent, protects you from age.*

JEAN MOREAU

The seventh and eighth decades of our life/times may also bring a feeling of resolution, a time for wrapping up some of life's enterprises, a sort of tying up of loose ends. But at the same time, we may well feel the urge to savor all that life can offer. If we have been truly existential throughout our life/time, we will enjoy the warmth and intimacy of human relationships as much, or perhaps more, than ever before.

Admittedly, the other side of this coin is not uncommon. When conflicts from the middle years continue unresolved, then these later years may be filled with despair and disillusionment. If intimacy was never reestablished during the middle years, a shallowness and distance may characterize all our later relationships, resulting in an all-pervasive loneliness that is one of life's true tragedies: *the unrelated person.*

> The adult who lacks integrity in this sense may wish that he could live life again. He feels that if at one time he had made a different decision he could have been a different person and his ventures would have been successful. He fears death and cannot accept his one and only life cycle as the ultimate of life. In the extreme, he experiences disgust and despair. Despair expresses the feeling that time is too short to try out new roads to integrity. Disgust is a means of hiding the despair, a chronic, contemptuous displeasure with the way life is run. As with the dangers and the solutions of previous periods, doubt and despair are not difficulties that are overcome once and for all, nor is integrity so achieved. Most people fluctuate between the two extremes. Most, also, at no point, either attain to the heights of unalloyed integrity or fall to the depths of complete disgust and despair.
>
> Even in adulthood a reasonably healthy personality is sometimes secured in spite of previous misfortunes in the developmental sequence. New sources of trust may be found. Fortunate events and circumstances may aid the individual in his struggle to feel autonomous. Imagination and initiative may be spurred by new responsibilities, and feelings of inferiority be overcome by successful achievement. Even later in life an individual may arrive at a true sense of who he is and what he has to do and may be able to win through to a feeling of intimacy with others and to joy in producing and giving.
>
> ERIK ERIKSON

In our later years, it is not uncommon for us to return to some form of religion we may have forgotten or neglected during our earlier years. Cynics will accuse us of trying to "play it safe" or to get comforted because of our fear of death. There is some truth in this, of course, but there is far more. It is an expression of our longing for ultimacy in our later time of life. Many of us enter the later years without profound "spiritual" (that is, ultimate) resources. Life has absorbed our energies in other concerns. We are limited in the ways we know of probing the ultimacy, the depth, the meaning of existence, which is intuited as somehow essential to the successful completion of life. For very many of us, the only practical solution may be to return to the religion we knew at an earlier time. A great deal of the late return to religion is precisely that: returning to an earlier stage of life. However, a more resourceful solution of the challenge of the middle years ("What do I really want out of life?") can lead on to a far more effective and meaningful forms of ultimacy. It could make possible the flowering of one's own unique and profoundly personal existence. In any case, this religious emphasis should be seen as an attempt to explore the meaning of life and to achieve, in the short time left, an ultimacy that life has heretofore not attained.

THE FINAL PHASE For some of us—though not all—there is a final phase to our life-cycle. It begins when we must face that fact that our own death is imminent. This is not merely the realization that one is mortal. Rather, this is the acceptance of the absolute fact that our own life/time has almost run out. Now the feeling may become very strong that we must take care of unfinished business and come to terms with the fact that our cessation of consciousness is near. Dying is much in our thoughts and death-symbols pervade our dreams— a clock without hands, perhaps, as in Ingmar Bergman's *Wild Strawberries.*

If we have lived a long life, we are prepared for our own momentous death-event by having lived closely with death for some years. Others around us have died, more and more of those we have known; loved ones, friends, colleagues, acquaintances, notable contemporaries. This living with death is an essential time of preparation for our own death-event. It serves to diminish feelings of fear and dread.

There may also be a reliving of past events, a replaying of our memories. We are frequently critical of the person who begins "to live in the past," and, of course, if we develop such a habit long before the final phase, then it is probably a sign of premature withdrawal from life. During the final phase, however, it is natural and normal. Partly it is an attempt to see the life/time drama in perspective, and to write a good completion. But partly it is a final preparation for the death-event. It is a recapitulation, a sort of browsing through the storehouse of a lifetime of activities, a savoring of one's accomplishments, a final inventory of life's experiences—and taking mental note of what we will leave behind.

*Time . . . Time. I bound it up in a little equation and it has never forgiven me! You see . . . I disprove my own theory. My energy leaves me in quantum bursts. My mass . . . approaches zero. And time . . . time approaches the speed of light.*

ERNEST KINOY
*Doctor Einstein before Lunch*

## THE SHRIEK OF IVAN ILYTCH

In a scene from Tolstoy's *Death of Ivan Ilytch,* the man is ill and dying. As he reflects upon the meaninglessness of his death, what now hits him so forcefully is the meaninglessness of his life. When the pointless absurdity of his petty life dawns fully in his consciousness, he shrieks. *"For the last three days he*

*Do not go gentle into that good night,*
*Old age should burn and rave at close of day;*
*Rage, rage against the dying of the light.*

DYLAN THOMAS

### EMERGING

There is a tide, by no means constant but strong enough to note, which carries a number of great artists away from the youthful vigor and impertinent complexities with which they made their reputations and toward a firm simplicity, even serenity, in their last works. It is always an achieved simplicity; no beginner could obtain it. In Matisse's paper cutouts and Picasso's beaming eroticism, in "Oedipus at Colonus" and the simple folk tune that concludes Beethoven's last quartet, there is the ease and quietness of an artist who, having mastered his craft, can afford now to come out on the other side.

*NEWSWEEK*, JANUARY 3, 1972

*What makes old age hard to bear is not a failing of one's faculties, mental and physical, but the burden of one's memories.*

SOMERSET MAUGHAM

*screamed incessantly."* Then a blessed rationalization comes to his rescue. After all, he had lived a conventional kind of life; he had achieved the material and social success others expected of him. So on his deathbed ambivalent fragments of his squandered life wander randomly through his mind.

"What do I want? . . . To live? How? . . . Why, to live as I used to—well and pleasantly." . . . And in imagination he began to recall the best moments of his pleasant life. But strange to say none of those best moments of his pleasant life now seemed at all what they had then seemed. . . . And the further he departed from childhood and the nearer he came to the present the more worthless and doubtful were the joys. . . . "It is as if I had been going downhill while I imagined I was going up. And that is really what it was. I was going up in public opinion, but to the same extent life was ebbing away from me. And now it is all done and there is only death." . . . "Maybe I did not live as I ought to have done." "But how could that be, when I did everything properly?" . . . And whenever the thought occurred to him, as it often did, that it all resulted from his not having lived as he ought to have done, he at once recalled the correctness of his whole life and dismissed so strange an idea.

*"I want to live forever—or die in the attempt."*

JOSEPH HELLER
*Catch-22*

## REFLECTIONS

1   The purpose of this chapter is to help you "to feel the whole of a life-cycle, to see the human enterprise, from birth till death, in a single vision, as One" (p. 158). Having read through the chapter, jot down your immediate responses, emotional as well as intellectual, to whatever holistic perspective you attained. What are your most meaningful insights?

2   Remember that Aristotle and Saint Thomas Aquinas shared the belief that women are mistakes (p. 160). Would you care to counter-argue these male chauvinists by developing the case that it is really the male of the species who is the mistake? It *can* be done. (For openers, note that the anthropologist Ashley Montagu wrote a widely acclaimed book entitled *The Natural Superiority of Women.)*

*Festina lente. "Make haste slowly."*

*Motto of* CAESAR AUGUSTUS

3   Most of us are familiar with the popular proverb, "Today is the first day of the rest of your life." How do you think one might appropriately respond to this maxim if he is five years old? eighteen years old? forty years old? sixty-five years old? ninety-four years old?

4   Reread the observation from *Developmental Psychology Today* on p. 161. Do you agree with the Douvan-Adelson conclusion? If so, what do you think are the causes of this widespread "token separation"?

5   Focus on two challenges that one encounters during a full lifetime: the challenge that you are currently involved in, and one which you are not presently facing (preferably one that lies ahead). Describe in the most personal way what these challenges mean to you. Is there a contrast between your understanding of these two challenges? In other words, to what degree can any of us comprehend a challenge we have not yet faced ourselves?

6   If you think of life metaphorically as a "path" or "road," can you locate yourself with some accuracy somewhere (somewhen) along that path? Did you personally go through the earlier challenges as described in this chapter?

7   Ponder the drawing by Abner Dean which follows. "I have an important appointment." Comment? Does this drawing apply to anyone you know? Do you think you might actually show the drawing to someone and say, "There, that's you!"? What sort of response do you think you would get?

*"I have an important appointment."*

# VOLTAIRE

## *The Laughing Philosopher*

Voltaire is one of the most quotable writers ever to grace a pen.

"Books rule the world." "When a nation begins to think, it is impossible to stop it." "Liberty of thought is the life of the soul." "Think for yourselves and let others enjoy the privilege to do so too." "It is the triumph of reason to live well with those who have none." "The Holy Roman Empire is neither holy, nor Roman, nor an Empire." "Love is the embroidery upon the stuff of nature." "Love truth, but pardon error." "It is better to risk saving a guilty person than to condemn an innocent one." "Common sense is not so common." "To cease to love and be lovable is a death unbearable." "If God did not exist, it would be necessary to invent him." And so on, almost ad infinitum.

He seems to have given us a pearl on every topic, and if his volumes of sparkling wit and wisdom lack depth, one must cherish the pearls and forgive: he was, in his own words, "like the little brooks; they are transparent because they are not deep." What he did possess was a philosopher's wisdom salted with sweeping insights, and this, combined with a zest for life and a prophetic zeal for freedom and decency, made him one of the great mind-warriors of the human race.

He was christened François-Marie Arouet when he was born in Paris in 1694. His father was François Arouet, a prosperous Parisian attorney; his mother was Marie Marguerite Daumard, a brilliant, lively, articulate woman who moved gracefully in Parisian society. François was the last of her five children, so small and weak they thought he wouldn't live. They baptized him the day after he was born.

When he was seven his mother died. At ten he was sent to a Jesuit school where he received a humanistic education in classical literature, languages, and drama.

He graduated at seventeen and began to study law at his father's urging, but he had already discovered his own loves: he wanted nothing but literature and life—the heady semibohemian social life of Paris.

Hypercreative and brilliant (estimated IQ 190), he made only a pretense at studying law. He had taken up poetry to express himself, but much of his rhyming bordered on libel. He was not seditious by intent; rather, he just had no tolerance for the stupidities and cruelties of the society he lived in. He possessed a keen ethical sense and enormous courage. "My trade is to say what I think," he wrote, and he thought much. But his freethinking was a threat, and on May 16, 1717, he was clamped into the Bastille for a year. There, shut up with his own boundless energies, he wrote plays and more political poems. When released the following April, he took the name Voltaire.

In 1732 he published *Philosophical Letters on the English,* a collection of brilliant observations of English life and mores; it received critical praise. But his *English Letters* contained as much criticism of the French as praise of the English. He had launched telling tirades against the corruption of church and state in France, naming and attacking leaders. The book was burned in 1734 and a warrant was issued for his arrest.

Voltaire wasn't available. This time he was at Cirey, a run-down but lovely country estate in northeastern France owned by the marquis de Châtelet. The marquise—Émilie—had become the one love of his mature life. She was an intellectual companion, well-read in literature and philosophy, a student of the sciences and mathematics. Both studied intensely, wrote incessantly, and loved without reason for fourteen years.

Eventually he was allowed to return to Paris. More than ever he moved with royalty, political leaders, and literati. In 1745 Madame de Pompadour had him appointed to the post of Historiographer-Royal. He received honors from the Pope, and dedicated a play to him. In 1746—he was fifty-two—Voltaire was elected to the prestigious French Academy of Sciences. He had loyal friends and devoted enemies everywhere.

Voltaire wasn't all that welcome in France, so he turned to the eternal bastion of freedom, Geneva. There, in 1754, he bought a country estate just outside

Geneva on Swiss soil, and named it Les Délices. With a garden, trees, chickens, and a cow, the world seemed far away. "I am so happy," he wrote, "that I am ashamed."

In 1755 a great earthquake shook Lisbon, and almost instantly some fifteen thousand people were killed. Why? Why had such suffering taken place? Because the Portuguese had sinned mightily, said French clergymen. Because the Catholics are infidels, said Protestants. Because Portugal was filled with apostate Protestants, said the Roman clergy. Because Adam had sinned, said the Methodist John Wesley.

Such foolishness aroused the wrath of the slumbering Voltaire. Adding to his wrath was the doctrine preached by the German philosopher Leibniz that this is "the best of all possible worlds." Incensed, he took up his pen and delivered one of the classics of world literature, *Candide* (1759).

In March 1762 news reached him of the persecution of a Huguenot family in Toulouse. Jean Calas was a linen merchant who had been wrongly accused of murdering his own son (a suicide) to prevent his conversion to Catholicism. Through an enormous perversion of justice, fed by ignorance, superstition, and mass paranoia, the Calas family had been persecuted; Jean Calas was tortured, strangled, and burned at the stake.

Voltaire determined the facts and went to war. His outrage drove him to feverish action. His banner was *écrasez l'infâme*—"Crush the Infamy!" The infamy was organized bigotry, religious persecution, political insanity—everything that contravenes man's humanity toward his fellow man. Fresh vitality came again to the aging warrior. "I suffer much. But when I attack *l'infâme* the pain is relieved." Voltaire had tapped into a righteous hatred to evoke a feeling of outrage in the hearts of his countrymen. He called especially on the *philosophes*—philosophers whose hearts and heads were above the insanity of this world and who had the word-weaponry to declare war.

*The further I advance in age, the more I find work necessary. It becomes in the long run the greatest of pleasures, and takes the place of the illusions of life.*

*ON VOLTAIRE:*
*Destiny gave him eighty-three years of existence, that he might slowly decompose the decayed age; he had the time to combat time; and when he fell, he was the conqueror.*
            LAMARTINE

*Books rule the world, or at least those nations in it which have a written language; the others do not count.*

*God is a comedian playing to an audience that is afraid to laugh.*

If ever there had been a war of ideas, this was it. Voltaire was joined by leaders and literati everywhere. Appeals were directed to churchmen, noblemen, ministers. Lawyers were hired, documents subpoenaed, cases prepared, witnesses sought. "Cry out yourself," he wrote, "and let others cry out; cry out for the Calas family and against fanatacism." And he prayed: "Thou has not given us hearts to hate, nor hands to kill, one another."

After three years of bloodless warfare, there was a victory of sorts: In March 1765, the King's Council declared the verdict against Jean Calas null and void, and he was declared innocent; the maligned family was awarded victims' compensation. Voltaire wept when he heard the news.

So, Voltaire was yet alive. He was a poet, dramatist, contractor, importer, capitalist, philosopher, money-lender, traveler, lover, warrior, banker, entrepreneur, theologian (of sorts), linguist (of sorts), politician (of sorts), benefactor, bon vivant, sponsor of the arts, exile, prisoner, coffee drinker par excellence, historian, gardener . . .

Voltaire mellowed as he grew older, naturally. Awaking to consciousness each day, feeling a new sun, taking up one's rounds and routines—this is enough. "When everything is counted and weighed up, I think there are infinitely more enjoyments than bitterness in this life."

He came constantly to new perspectives. "My baffled curiosity continues to be insatiable." He read, lived, changed, and grew. Like Socrates, he knew increasingly how little he knew. "I am ignorant," he said. All hints of arrogance, in private, began to fade; rigidities remained only in the heat of battle.

In the sixth, seventh, and eighth decades of his life, he had moments of doubt, even despair. There were times when he envied those who had never thought philosophically about anything and who still had the capacity for simple faith. Madness, he said, is having pre-

*It is only charlatans who are certain. . . . Doubt is not a very agreeable state, but certainty is a ridiculous one.*

*Dulce est desipere in loco. Woe to philosophers who cannot laugh away their wrinkles. I look upon solemnity as a disease.*

ferred reason to happiness. But then the joy of the philosophic life would return. He picked up his books, tried to understand more, went to his garden, invited in the neighborhood children, and laughed the hours back to joy.

Probably no philosopher ever understood better the health-restoring role of laughter in our lives. It has been suggested that his laughter might be, after all, his greatest contribution to his and every age.

Voltaire helped restore his fellow countrymen to sanity by teaching them to laugh at themselves. All his satiric work—culminating in *Candide*—was an attack upon those who take themselves too seriously: politicians, kings, priests and monks, inquisitors, popes, axegrinders—that is, all of us. To those who are so, other people's ideas are obviously stupid and wrong; the antidote is laughing away our anger. One cannot laugh and hate and fear. *"Dulce est desipere in loco.* Woe to philosophers who cannot laugh away their wrinkles. I look upon solemnity as a disease."

Voltaire was the very embodiment of the Enlightenment: he had an abiding faith in the intelligence and rationality of man. "This century begins to see the triumph of reason," he wrote. Voltaire's dream was that a philosophical intelligence could challenge the tragic history of human misbehavior, that intelligent men and women could blaze a new path leading to freedom and civility.

Voltaire worked, and the years passed. He rose with the sun, began his days with strong coffee, and wrote. Occasionally, still, his works were put to the flames. His home at Ferney became a place of pilgrimage for the great and would-be great; so many found the path to his door that he exclaimed "O God! deliver me from my friends; I will take care of my enemies myself."

He took time to watch his seedlings and silkworms grow. He loved and respected the caretakers who lived on his land. He especially enjoyed young people and opened his home to them each

Sunday. He became an octogenarian almost without wincing, and these were the happiest of times.

Voltaire lived his philosophy. Life is made for action; if merely watched, as from the sidelines, it becomes empty. We must plunge into the chaotic stream of events where we can "laugh all our laughter and weep all our tears" (Gibran's words) so that death, when it comes, will find nothing but "a squandered bag of bones" (Kazantzakis's words). We should seek out all variety of experience—absorb all knowledge, think all thoughts, feel all feelings.

Voltaire was painfully aware of the passage of time and wanted to make the most of every minute. More than most mortals, he did. He lived each day with zest, sleeping only five or six hours a night. It is frightful, he said, how much time we waste avoiding life.

Nor do we have to be in a special place to live thus; it can be done wherever we are. In one of his plays Voltaire's hero travels the world and witnesses all the follies of mankind, big and small; but he returns home and finds that it is better at home after all. One doesn't have to wander in search of greener pastures, except that . . . one must wander the world in search of greener pastures to discover for oneself that he did not have to wander the world . . . "I still found that of all conditions of life this is much the happiest."

Perhaps it is not wrong to see all of France relaxing its stomach muscles, just a bit, because of Voltaire's comedy and satire, his obscene pearls, his scatological epithets. To laugh is to take a step toward the recovery of our lost human-

ness, to rid ourselves of the poison of self-hate and despair. Voltaire, the laughing philosopher, helped France laugh itself back toward sanity.

In 1778 Paris beckoned. Voltaire had been away from the great city for twenty-eight years—why not one last journey? He was approaching eighty-four. He made the trip in five days in February. Well-wishers by the thousands lined the streets of Paris, shouting "Vive Voltaire!" He was honored by heads of state and wreathed with garlands in the salons and theaters. His plays were staged with great fanfare. He was given superlative honors by the French Academy. For three months the celebrations continued. His life crescendoed to a climax the like of which few mortals are blessed to see.

But at some point the life-fire must dim. In May he took to his bed. A friend sent him some medicine—opium—which he was to dilute and drink. Voltaire misunderstood the instructions and drank it down straight; it sent him into a painful delirium. Two days later his consciousness returned, but his life was gone. "I die adoring God, loving my friends, not hating my enemies, and detesting superstition." It was May 30, 1778.

Consecrated ground was barred to him in most of France, so his body was spirited away and buried in the Abbey of Scellières. Three years later it was removed on order of the National Assembly, carried in triumph to Paris, and interred in the Pantheon.

On his coffin is the inscription: "He taught us to be free."

# THE REAL WORLD: KNOWING AND UNKNOWING

*All the biologicals are converting chaos to beautiful order.*

*All biology is antientropic. Of all the disorder-to-order*

*converters, the human mind is by far the most impressive. The*

*human's most powerful metaphysical drive is to understand,*

*to order, to sort out, and rearrange in ever more orderly*

*and understandably constructive ways. You find then that*

*man's true function is metaphysical.*

BUCKMINSTER FULLER

3

## EPISTEMIC AWARENESS

All of us begin our philosophizing from a state of *epistemic naivety,* a condition in which we have not yet begun to question the origins, structure, and dependability of our information. To be sure, some of us may have discovered we were wrong about some things, or we may have "outgrown" certain beliefs; but few of us have peered deeply into the fundamental operations of the information-processing system we call "the mind."

*Epistemology* is the branch of philosophy defined as "the study of human knowledge." In exploring this field we are touching one of evolution's fundamental mechanisms of survival, for it is by knowledge that we orient ourselves in the world. Accurate knowledge of our two worlds—the real world and the inner world—correctly informs us of the conditions we must cope with. To know facts is to survive; not to know, or to assess one's environment wrongly, is to lose the fight for survival. (The word *real* is a technical term in philosophy. See *real, reality,* and *realism* in glossary.)

With the examination of the sources, nature, and accuracy of our knowledge, we begin to develop *epistemic awareness,* a more informed understanding of what we know and don't know.

We face two serious epistemological problems. (1) How can we determine which facts are true? (2) How can we determine which facts are important?

Since we are victimized by fragmented, pressurized information, we must find a way to double-check fact-claims. We must learn somehow to screen out the fictions but let in the facts. *On what criteria can we decide what are facts and what are false claims?*

*We have to live today by what truth we can get today, and be ready tomorrow to call it falsehood.*

WILLIAM JAMES

*Most of the greatest evils that man has inflicted upon man have come through people feeling quite certain about something which, in fact, was false.*

BERTRAND RUSSELL

*If you cannot convince me that there is some kind of knowable ultimate reality, or if you cannot convince me that there are certain absolute values by which I can live my life, I shall commit psychological suicide. That is, either convince me that there is "one truth" or one right way of doing things, or I shall conclude that everything is meaningless and I will not try any more.*

**JOSEPH ROYCE**

*(describing the reality-image of contemporary man)*

*We only think when we are confronted with a problem.*

**JOHN DEWEY**

Richard Lippold, *Variation Number 7, 1949–1950.* Collection, The Museum of Modern Art, New York. Mrs. Simon Guggenheim Fund.

Second, among the billions of bits of information at our fingertips, we cannot distinguish high-priority data. There *are* facts that are important; there *are* causes that are crucial; there *are* ideas that work. But which? Since not all facts are of equal importance at a given time, we are forced to make value-judgments. *What criteria can we use for deciding what is more important, what less?*

Each of us has stored away in his repertoire hundreds of thousands of bits of knowledge, most of which, needless to say, we cannot remember when we want to. What is the source of all these facts? How do they get into our heads and into our memory-banks?

Almost everything that we know originates from four basic sources. The first, our *senses,* can be considered our primary source of information. Two other sources, *reason* and *intuition,* are derivative in the sense that they produce new facts from data already supplied to our minds. The fourth source, *authority,* is by nature secondary, and second-hand facts prove to be the most difficult to handle. Beyond these four sources there may be others; but if so, knowledge derived from them remains, at present, extremely problematic, and many of the sources are seriously to be doubted.

## THE SENSES: EMPIRICAL KNOWLEDGE

THE SENSES The fundamental source of all knowledge is our own senses. Throughout our earlier years, this remains our dominant source of information about ourselves and our environment. As beginners in life we "learn by doing," and doing in large part means to see, to hear, to taste, to feel, and so on. Our senses are exploratory organs; we use them all to become acquainted with the world we live in.

We learn that candy is sweet, and so are sugar, jam, and maple syrup. Lemons are not, and onions are not. The sun is bright and blinding. Glowing coals in the fireplace are beautiful if you don't touch them. Sounds soothe, warn, or frighten us. Through millions of single sense-events we build a fabric of empirical information which helps us interpret, survive in, and control the world about us. (See *empirical* and *empiricism* in the glossary.)

Three of our senses—sight, sound, and smell—give us information about events and objects that lie at a distance, while two of the classical "five senses"—taste and touch—inform us about happenings in the immediate vicinity of our sensors. In the perspective of evolutionary survival, this arrangement has obvious benefits.

We have developed specialized sense receptors to perform four of these functions: eyes, ears, taste buds, and olfactory cells. By contrast, the sense of touch does not involve any specialized, strategically positioned organ; touching sensations take place all over our bodies. These "cutaneous sensors" are specialized, however; different types of nerve endings respond to different stimuli. Separate sensors are activated by heat, cold, touch, pressure, and cell damage (which we experience as pain). Nerve endings that react to one of these stimuli generally do not respond to the others. Taken together, all these "touching senses" give us a great deal of data that we put to immediate use in our assessment of real objects/events going on at close range.

These can be called *objective senses* since they tell us about the external world.

We also possess numerous *subjective senses* that inform us about our inner world. "Visceral senses" line the inner surfaces of our bodies. They are found in the mouth, along the digestive tract, and on the surfaces of some organs. Without such senses we would not experience a variety of sensations ("feelings") that we take for granted, such as headaches, stomachaches, or appendicitis pains. The latter nuisances might be considered minor losses if we didn't have them, but however much they hurt, the warning signals they send us are requisite to adjustment and survival.

Another group of subjective senses have nerve endings in our muscles, tendons, and joints. These are the "proprioceptive sensors," which tell us when our muscles are stretched or contracted; through them we sense if a hand is open or closed, which way our head is turned, and whether our knees are bent. Physical coordination is determined to some extent by these senses.

Another subjective sense is equilibrium. Located in the inner ear, it enables us to maintain our balance within a gravity field and tells us if we are moving or are at rest. We utilize the same principle in a carpenter's level.

This by no means exhausts the list of senses, subjective or objective. We human beings, along with all other living creatures, develop senses whenever conditions make it possible to enable us to acquire a bit more information about our two worlds, thus refining our operations and improving our adjustments.

Our senses present us with a serious credibility problem. Is there any way we can be sure that they are "telling us the truth" about the two worlds they represent? Can we *believe* what our senses seem to tell us?

At this point in our inquiry, the answer must be a reluctant no. Our senses do not give us a "true picture" of the real world; they give us an "operational picture." In fact, we can begin to construct an accurate picture of objective reality only after meticulous correction of the sense data that our senses transmit to us (to "us"—that is, to our minds). We now know that there are numerous inherent "deceptions" and "translations" in the data-transmission processes of the senses. Unfortunately, most of us never get around to making adequate corrections. We remain *naive realists*. (**Naive realism**—The uncritical acceptance of one's sense data as representing accurately the real world; a sort of "blind faith" in what one's senses seem to tell him.)

## KNOWLEDGE FROM OTHERS

AUTHORITY Other people are continual sources of information. Such information, however, is always second-hand knowledge—or third-, fourth-, or *n*th-hand knowledge. It is all "hearsay." The farther it is removed from our own personal experience, the more caution we must exercise before accepting a fact-claim.

Certain specific classes of knowledge necessarily come to us from the testimony of others. All our historical knowledge we acquire this way. Since the "past" doesn't exist in reality, it isn't subject to empirical observation. We must rely upon those who personally witnessed the living episodes and have

*The eyes believe themselves; The ears believe other people.*

**Chinese Fortune Cookie**

*Philosophy begins when one learns to doubt—particularly to doubt one's cherished beliefs, one's dogmas and one's axioms.*

WILL DURANT

*To follow knowledge like a sinking star, Beyond the utmost bound of human thought.*

ALFRED, LORD TENNYSON

*Anyone who conducts an argument by appealing to authority is not using his intelligence; he is just using his memory.*

LEONARDO DA VINCI

*It would be impudent to tell intelligent, grown-up people how to think.*

RUDOLF FLESCH

"How about five do's and five don'ts?"

recorded, orally or in graphic form, accounts of the events which they believed important. Historical knowledge begins for us when we attempt to re-create in our minds images of, and ideas about, those events. Our reliance upon others for all the input about those events is an inescapable dependency.

Most of our knowledge of the sciences also comes to us by authority. We can't personally repeat every experiment, so we must trust the specialists and accept, though sometimes provisionally, the discoveries they record for us. Careful workers in the sciences document their researches in such manner that if we wish to double-check the fact-claims ourselves we can obtain the necessary information to do so. Knowing that a fact can be double-checked gives one better reason to trust the scientists' work.

By authority also we receive a good deal of knowledge from the society in which we live, but it can't be accepted uncritically. Every culture is a carrier of traditions, folklore, "common knowledge," and "common sense" which must be carefully screened before one can feel assured that he possesses dependable information.

How can we be sure that the "facts" others give us are true? In the face of conflicting fact-claims, how can we decide which authorities to follow? In a word, whom can we trust?

There is no simple answer. We must accept large amounts of knowledge that have been accumulated over the centuries; we would be personally impoverished without it. The solution lies in knowing how to apply checkout criteria to fact-claims and in maintaining an ever-vigilant, critical spirit. If one possesses the skill to check at will any fact-claim, and if one has learned when to be wary of those who would seduce him into accepting *their* "facts" without supplying evidence or sound reason—if one commands this equipment, he will feel far more confident in handling the knowledge that comes his way.

There is another, and perhaps more insidious, danger involved in relying upon others for knowledge. Most of us are prone to the development of dependencies. We commonly select one or two authorities, invest our trust in them, and indulge our laziness to the absurd point of accepting all they tell us. Despite the fact that developing one's critical skills is hard work, those who wish to feel more secure in their knowledge will avoid dependencies that inhibit personal inquiry and growth.

# REASON: USING KNOWN FACTS . . .

REASON Our reasoning faculties can be a source of facts. *Reason* might be defined as the process of using known facts to arrive at new facts. Hence, if we start with data which we are sure of, we can apply deductive or inductive procedures and arrive at new information we did not have before.

If you are traveling in Japan, and your travel guide tells you that the exchange rate is "115 yen per 1 American dollar," you can readily find out how much your sushi will cost you if the menu reads "800 yen." It doesn't take much reasoning to discover that your meal will cost you about $9.20, at current prices. Note merely that your conclusion—that you are considering a $9.20 dinner—is new knowledge, making possible a new understanding. Reasoning itself, therefore, can produce new information.

The two general forms of reasoning are deduction and induction. *Deduction* is the process of drawing out (making explicit) the implications of one or more premises or statements of fact. If one *infers* correctly what the premises imply, then his inference (conclusion) is said to be "valid." *Induction* is the procedure of developing general explanatory hypotheses to account for a set of facts. In scientific induction one projects universal principles—for instance, concluding that *all* planetary orbits are parabolic—after having actually examined only a few cases.

Notice that in deduction, the conclusion *necessarily* follows from the premises. (For example: All cats are blue. Tom is a cat. Therefore, Tom is *necessarily* blue.) By contrast, when using inductive reasoning one's working hypothesis is always tentative; it is subject to change whenever further facts are obtained. (For example: "I have seen only six cats, and they were all blue. I must conclude, tentatively, that *all cats* must be blue." All it takes in this case is the observation of one yellow cat to strike a fatal blow to a viable hypothesis. Inductive conclusions, therefore, are always subject to change.)

There are common abuses involved in both deductive and inductive reasoning. Deductive procedure applies primarily to mathematics, geometry, and to systems of logic with clearly defined terms. Yet we often try to apply deduction to our familiar, ambiguous everyday words and then arrive at convenient conclusions that in no way follow from the premises.

The weakness of induction results mainly from our failing to realize that it always gives us *probable* knowledge and never *certain* knowledge. Take another

*Man is a credulous animal and tends to believe what he is told. Historically, philosophers . . . have taken great pains to point out that authority is at least as important a source of error as it is of knowledge.*

JOSEPH BRENNAN

*Most of our assumptions have outlived their uselessness.*

MARSHALL McLUHAN

*If a thing moves, then it must move either in the place where it is or in a place where it is not. But it cannot move where it is nor can it move where it is not; therefore it cannot move.*

ZENO THE ELEATIC
**(formulated by William and Mabel Sahakian)**

PEANUTS® CHARLES M. SCHULZ

*Yes, reason is an imperfect instrument, like medical science, or the human eye; we do the best we can with it within the limits which fate and nature set. We do not doubt that some things are better done by instinct than by thought: perhaps it is wiser, in the presence of Cleopatra, to thirst like Antony rather than to think like Caesar; it is better to have loved and lost than to have reasoned well. But why is it better?*

WILL DURANT

*We are drowning in information but starved for knowledge*

JOHN NAISBITT

*I have had my solutions for a long time, but I do not yet know how I am to arrive at them.*

KARL FRIEDRICH GAUSS

example: If one should witness five auto accidents in the period of an afternoon, all involving the same make and model of car, most of us would be tempted to conclude that something is mechanically haywire with this particular make and model. This conclusion would be an inductive hypothesis, with apparent validity. But it is not a *certain* conclusion; it is only a possible and probable explanation. Add five more accidents with the same make and model. Is one more certain of the validity of the hypothesis? Yes, but only *more* certain, not (and never) absolutely. Now what happens to the neatly working hypothesis when you discover that six of the ten drivers were driving on the wrong side of the freeway?

In scientifically controlled investigations with a large and representative sampling, one can often eliminate competing hypotheses and run up the probability factor for the correct explanation. Nevertheless, the hypothesis shall always remain a *probable explanation,* and nothing more. (For further explanation of inductive reasoning, note the problem of the robins' eggs on pp. 480–481 See also the case of the dead TV set on p. 230)

## INTUITION: KNOWLEDGE FROM THE SUBCONSCIOUS

INTUITION Although the word *intuition* calls up varied connotations, when carefully defined it can be considered a source of knowledge. Intuition refers to insights or bits of knowledge which emerge into the light of consciousness from the deeper subconscious. It is not uncommon to have sought-for ideas pop into our minds while consciously thinking about quite different things. We know that the subconscious mind can perform complex operations that the conscious mind, burdened with the task of mediating sense data, cannot handle.

An American theologian, Francis McConnell, recalls an instance of intuition when he was about fifteen and in high school. He had been assigned several algebra problems for homework and was having no trouble with them until the last problem became obstinate. He wrestled with it in prolonged frustration, but it would not give in, and finally, very late, he gave up and went to bed. When he awoke the next morning the solution popped immediately into his mind. It dawned on him that his subconscious mind had continued to work on the problem while his conscious mind slept.

Having discovered such a helpful faculty, he decided to take full advantage of it. The next evening he glanced briefly over his algebra assignment, promptly forgot it, and went to sleep. Needless to say, when the morning came there were no solutions. McConnell recalls the lesson he learned: the subconscious mind can do creative work, but it must be treated fairly. It must be given adequate data to work with and also, perhaps, more than a little coaxing.

Sometimes intuition is experienced as an emotional feeling. We often say something like "I have the feeling he's not telling the truth," and it may be just that: a feeling, but a feeling in the process of informing us of a true fact.

"I have a feeling it's going to rain." Perhaps such a statement rests on subliminally collected sense data subconsciously synthesized, giving us a "feeling" about a real condition we could not consciously recognize.

Occasionally we hear someone say, "I have a feeling something bad is going to happen." It is a presentiment, a foreboding. Jung suggested that the unconscious can correlate data in such a way that it can "foresee" events that the conscious mind, being preoccupied with perception and immediate concerns, cannot "feel." Strictly speaking, such feelings would not be precognitive insights, but rather premonitions derived from current data; but such premonitions, when accurate, would become genuine sources of knowledge.

The principal weakness of intuition and feeling as sources of knowledge is that the insights they produce are as likely to be wrong as right. If left to intuition, most algebra problems would remain unsolved. Intuitive fact-claims must be carefully double checked before credentials are issued.

*To myself I seem to have been only like a boy playing on the seashore, and diverting myself and now and then finding a smoother pebble or a prettier shell than ordinary, while the great ocean of truth lay all undiscovered before me.*

Sir Isaac Newton

## ARE THERE OTHER SOURCES OF KNOWLEDGE?

Other sources have been used as the basis for making fact-claims. For various reasons all of them are problematic, not the least because, in theory, most of them cannot be double checked at all.

1. *Instinct* There was a time when "instinct" was used to account for an "inherited pattern of behavior" in both animals and humans. Its existence in man is very doubtful, however, and the term is little used today. Even if it should prove to exist, it would not be a knowledge of facts, but a system of survival behavior.
2. *Racial Memory* Evidence in support of racial memory is meager, though the concept has been developed by Dr. Carl Jung in his theory of the "collective unconscious." Granting that such memories might exist, and that they could be inherited, the archetypal images described by Jung are diffuse and seem to be devoid of any specific fact-claims.

### BELIEVING IS SEEING

A psychologist employed seven assistants and one genuine subject in an experiment where they were asked to judge how long was a straight line that they were shown on a screen. The seven assistants, who were the first to speak and report what they saw, had been instructed to report unanimously an evidently incorrect length. The eighth member of the group, the only naive subject in the lot, did not know that his companions had received such an instruction, and he was under the impression that what they reported was really what they saw. In one-third of the experiments, he reported the same incorrect length as they did. The pressure of the environment had influenced his own semantic reaction and had distorted his vision. When one of the assistants, under the secret direction of the experimenter, started reporting the correct length, it relieved that pressure of the environment, and the perception of the uninformed subject improved accordingly.

J. Samuel Bois
*The Art of Awareness*

3. *Extrasensory Perception* ESP in its several forms is commonly claimed to be a source of knowledge. About 20 percent of Americans relate experiences of telepathy, clairvoyance, or precognition. There is accumulating scientific evidence that some forms of ESP may exist, but at present we know very little about them. No viable unifying hypothesis seems to be developing that would account for all the varied ESP phenomena. Although it might eventually turn out to be a source of verifiable fact-claims, our present understanding of ESP is so incomplete that we must consider the source with great caution.

*Americans run an idea up the flagpole to see if anyone salutes, but the British let an idea get broody to see if anything will hatch.*

PAUL A. KOLERS

4. *Anamnesis* ("recollection") refers to remembrance of things from a previous existence. The notion was held by several Greek philosophers, notably Pythagoras and Plato, and the "transmigration of souls" (*samsara*) is a basic Hindu doctrine. There are many recorded cases of individuals "remembering" people and places from previous lifetimes. If indeed anamnesis does exist, however, it is safe to say that for most of us it is inconsequential; our knowledge of any previous existence has long since faded away.

5. *Supernatural Revelation* has been a universal source-claim; every variety of human knowledge has been attributed to God or the gods. As a source of verifiable information, the supernatural in any form raises enormous problems. Time and again we are blocked when we try to make our way back to the primary personal experience where the facts would have originated. Historical documentation invariably presents a credibility barrier. All this aside, however, *if* there is a supernatural order of reality, and *if* facts truly derive from such a source, they would be subject to the same checkout criteria that we apply to all other fact-claims. Their source would not eliminate the need to prove their truth-value.

6. *Spiritualism* Many books have been written allegedly containing information from discarnate spirits, communicated by mediums, fortune tellers, ouija boards, and the like. When such fact-claims can be checked they frequently turn out to be untrue. There are few "facts" from a discarnate world that cannot be better accounted for on known psychological principles, and most of those few remaining "facts" can be explained in terms of some form of telepathic phenomena. While it cannot be ruled out as a source of knowledge, it is difficult at present to feel much confidence in any known form of spiritualism.

7. *Occult Sources* Astrology, Tarot, and other occult sources are commonly believed to give us certain kinds of information. According to present knowledge, it is doubtful that there are any objective phenomena operating to reveal "facts" to us. This does not rule out the possibility that subliminal influences may indeed exist, but any fact-claims deriving from the whole range of the occult are at present quite precarious.

## REFLECTIONS

1   What is epistemology? Make a list of some of the questions that this field of inquiry attempts to answer.

2    What do you understand to be meant by the terms *epistemic naivety* and *epistemic awareness?* As you reflect on your own knowledge-condition, do you feel that these terms apply to you?

3    Note the two basic epistemological problems (p. 181). Is it clear to you at this point why these are so important? Can you summarize briefly your understanding of each?

4    This chapter lists the four classic sources of knowledge: the senses, authority, reason, and intuition. But what about the other suggested sources (pp. 187–188)? Do you have evidence that any of these are also dependable sources of knowledge? Can you think of still other sources that should be given serious consideration?

5    Each of the four basic sources of information, when not employed with great care, can deceive us and give us false data. Therefore we must remain critical when assessing information. What specific dangers must we guard against when using each source?

6    "Most of our assumptions have outlived their uselessness" (see marginal quote on p. 185). What do you think Marshall McLuhan (who is a punmaster) is trying to tell us?

7    Will Durant asks an interesting question about the use of reason (see marginal quote on p. 186). How would you answer his question?

8    On p. 185 (see marginal quote) Zeno the Eleatic confronts us with one of his mind-boggling logical paradoxes. How would you resolve this one?

# FRANCIS BACON

## *All Knowledge is my Province*

Francis Bacon lived at a turning-point in Western thought: a time of transition from a mystical world-view to a scientific world-view. Gifted with an incomparable intellect, he recognized that such a transition was taking place an became one of its guiding lights. He has justifiably been called the father of scientific method.

And it really happened: he died because he stuffed a chicken with snow.

Francis Bacon was born in London in 1561. His father was Sir Nicholas Bacon, Lord Keeper of the Great Seal and an esteemed councilor to Queen Elizabeth I—as his son would be. His mother was Lady Anne Cooke, a bright, articulate woman, a linguist, scholar, theologian, lay philosopher, and devout Puritan. She was Francis's teacher during his formative years and lovingly nourished his intellect.

Bacon had a gift for academic studies. At twelve he was sent to Trinity College, Cambridge, where he first discovered the wobbly foundations of medieval "Aristotelian" thought, the arrogant defences of established orthodoxy, and the folly of scholastic arguments. He

vowed to do something about the problem. At this early age, he wrote, "I believed myself born for the service of mankind"—but how exactly? With unusual self-knowledge, he found that he had an aptitude for "the contemplation of Truth." He wrote: "I possessed a passion for research, a power of suspending judgment with patience, of meditating with pleasure, of assenting with caution, of correcting false impressions with readiness, and of arranging my thoughts with scrupulous pains." He graduated in 1575.

At sixteen he was sent to France with the English ambassador. While Francis was there, his father died, and Francis found himself without money. A fear of poverty plagued him all his life, and he was driven to employ methods to avoid it that were not always the noblest.

Bacon returned to London, studied law, performed brilliantly, and aimed for a political career, though hoping always for appointment to a government post. The offspring of a high-ranking statesman, he found working his way up from the bottom deflating; yet this is what he did. He was elected to Parliament at twenty-three.

Already he had displayed two qualities that marked his life. First was common sense in human relationships, a perception far deeper than mere political expediency. In 1589—he was twenty-eight—he wrote a book on tolerance, advocating that every loyal English citizen be allowed to follow the faith of his choice; he urged better understanding between the Lords and commoners and better ways of dealing with Irish Catholics, Anglicans, and Puritans. He was a man of gentle ways and practical wisdom, sensitive to human feelings so often ignored by those in power.

A second quality was an awareness of his own philosophic calling. At twenty-one he wrote: "I confess that I have vast contemplative ends . . . for I have taken all knowledge to be my province. . . ." Bacon had a synoptic mind; he longed to see and understand everything as a whole; but he saw that the very foundations of Western knowledge were faulty. He had to take on that entire world-view and give it new directions: "all knowledge" was to be his field of operations.

The earl of Essex became Bacon's close friend, advocate at court, and thorn-in-the-flesh. For a time Essex and Elizabeth I endured a love/hate relationship that, sooner or later, had to tilt. Essex's ego could not submit to a woman's commands, however imperial her rank. He was unpredictable, ambitious, and lived on the edge of treason. For attempting to raise his own army he was twice clamped into the Tower of London. Bacon was a lawyer in the service of the Crown and was forced to balance his loyalties. He was asked to draw up charges against Essex, having earlier warned his friend that his first loyalty was to the queen. Essex confessed and went to his death in the Tower, courageously but with disbelief.

Thereafter, Bacon had to walk a fine line: he had both friends and enemies at every turn. When James became king in 1603, Bacon was knighted. In 1607 he became Solicitor General, Attorney General in 1613; in 1616 he was appointed a member of the Privy Council that guided the king. In 1617 he was ele-

vated to Lord Keeper of the Great Seal— the office his father had held. In 1618 (at fifty-seven) he became Lord Chancellor of England and ruled the country in the absence of the king.

In appearance Bacon was thin, frail, and stately. He had a highly aware but solemn disposition, a shyness polished to obscurity by courtly manners. Everyone admired and/or feared his perceptive intelligence. He spoke eloquently and persuasively and with marvelous clarity. If there is something of the guarded expedient about him, something of the compromiser, of frail loyalty, then so be it: until his exile he was statesman first, philosopher second.

In 1606 he married Alice Barnham. He wrote that "a married man is seven years older in his thoughts the first day." By this time he owned the country estate of Gorhambury; he loved to retire there from the world, enjoy the solitude, reflect and write, and care for his gardens.

Any member of the king's cabinet might be caught in the crossfire between Parliament and the monarchy. It was Bacon's turn: his enemies had not forgotten, nor forgiven. In 1621 twenty-three counts of bribery were levied against him. He appealed to the king for protection, but the monarch suggested he confess to the charges; that he had accepted such bribes was well known and, anyway, "everyone did it." Bacon confessed. He was fined an enormous £40,000, stripped of all offices, barred from public office, and in disgrace was remanded to the Tower of London to await "the king's pleasure." Like Essex, he could not believe it was happening to him: he had been an impartial judge, not once swayed by the gifts he received. He later wrote, "I was the justest judge that was in all England these fifty years." And the judgment against him was also just.

The king came to his rescue almost immediately: the fine was cancelled and he was released from the Tower after a token four-day stay. He was exiled to his estate where, for the first time, he was free to devote his full mind to reflection and writing. He was sixty years old.

*Knowledge is power.*

*ON BACON:*
*Francis Bacon was the most powerful and influential intellect of his time . . . Bacon's mind ranged over the universe like a searchlight peering and prying curiously into every corner and secret of space.*
    **WILL DURANT**

*I have taken all knowledge to be my province.*

*The universe is not to be narrowed down to the limits of the Understanding,—but the Understanding must be stretched and enlarged to take in the image of the Universe as it is discovered.*

At last he could carry out the *Magna Instauratio*—the "Great Reconstruction."

✦

Bacon embodied a new pride in the human intellect and its ability to know the world. It was acknowledged that man's rational mind, purged of its bad habits and superstitions ("idols"), can understand the natural world and gain control of it in the interest of human needs.

This new belief was a far turn from the traditional theological doctrine that man's reason is corrupt and that man, on his own, can't do anything right or good.

Bacon saw himself as the "trumpeter of his age," uniquely gifted to do battle against the fallacious thought-systems of the past. "I was fitted for nothing so well as for the study of Truth."

In Bacon's time Aristotle's ideas dominated Western thought, so Bacon saw himself as an implacable foe of Aristotle. In truth, Aristotle and Bacon would have been friends if the latter had understood the "Great Perversion" of the Greek philosopher's ideas.

To illustrate: Suppose you submitted to Aristotle the following logical syllogism and asked him to critique it:

*All cats are blue.* (major premise)
*Tom is a cat.* (minor premise)

*Therefore, Tom is blue*
(conclusion)

You would receive two clear responses. First, Aristotle would praise you for your deductive thinking. Given the major and minor premises, your conclusion is correct; quite validly you have inferred that Tom is blue.

But after that you would get a severe scolding for having started off with a major premise that is so obviously false—all cats are *not* blue. Why would you begin a line of thought with such an absurd statement? He would warn that you *must* begin your deductive thinking with *archai* ("starting points," "first principles") that are true-to-reality, else all

your deductive labors will be a waste of time. You *must* look at the real world very carefully—as Aristotle himself did—and gather your empirical facts; then utilize true statements about the world as starting points for your logical inferences. "All cats are blue" won't do; neither will "All dragons are stupid" or "Angels travel faster than the speed of light" or "The music of the spheres sounds like perfect harmony to the pure in soul" or "The Devil has red fur."

But since the recovery of Aristotle's writings through Arab scholars, only the deductive side of Aristotle's logic had been developed; the inductive side had been almost forgotten. By the time Bacon attended Trinity College in 1563, to "study Aristotle" meant to study theology as developed by Aristotelian deduction.

Aristotle would have wept at all this; had Bacon understood the "Great Perversion," he and Aristotle would have wept together. In any case, Bacon was a man of his time and can be forgiven for his one-sided outlook. He set out to abolish the closed knowledge systems of a stagnant tradition. His goal, he said, was to perform "a true and lawful marriage between the empirical and the rational faculty." Unfortunately, he threw out the rational baby with the theological bathwater; by concentrating on empirical fact-gathering he neglected the role of deduction in scientific method.

Bacon believed that the wrongheaded logic must be replaced by inductive scientific method. What is induction? It is a way of thinking that begins by *looking at the world,* carefully observing *singular events,* and then *tying these observations together* with hypotheses that causally explain them and make them intelligible. Good scientific method requires a variety of further logical techniques, including the testing of hypotheses. This is the heart of all science; it is the only accurate means of acquiring knowledge of the world.

To bring about these sweeping changes Bacon proposed the *Magna Instauratio,* the "Great Reconstruction"—

*Philosophy, when superficially studied, excites doubt; when thoroughly explored, it dispels it.*

*Knowledge, if it be taken without the true corrective, hath in it some nature of venom or malignity.*

*If a man will begin with certainties, he shall end in doubts, but if he will be content to begin with doubts he shall end in certainties.*

*There are and can be only two ways of searching into and discovering the truth. The one [deduction] flies from the senses . . . The other [induction] derives axioms from the senses and particulars . . .*

as he said, "a total reconstruction of the sciences, arts and all human knowledge." To do this he would take all knowledge as his province. Not that he attempted to know everything; rather, he sampled all branches of knowledge to reorganize them properly. He had first alluded to this undertaking at the age of thirty-one; from forty on it occupied increasing amounts of his time; when he was finally exiled much of it was completed.

He had a six-fold plan. First, he would produce a new classification of all human knowledge, which, to this point, had evolved chaotically. Second, he would analyze where deductive thinking went wrong (that is, its use of wrong starting-points) and outline the principles of induction and scientific method needed to produce trustworthy knowledge of the world. Third, he planned to write a history of natural science and then, fourth, a textbook of scientific method, with examples of how to apply it. Fifth, he wanted to summarize what he himself had discovered by carefully applying scientific method to the world. Sixth and last, he dreamed of writing a philosophy based on sound scientific knowledge.

Bacon accomplished much of his dream. *The Advancement of Learning* (1605) went a long way toward a reclassi-fication of the sciences; it is a masterpiece in both content and style. His "reconstruction" in logic was completed in *Novum Organum* (1620). The human side of Bacon, displaying his vast learning and winsome humor, is found in his *Essays* (1597).

◆

The problem of preserving perishable foods has been a persistent one for all peoples. Fruits are dried, preserved with sugar, or fermented. Meat also is fried, preserved with salt, made palatable with strong peppers and spices. Except in northern climates, no solution to the problem was found until the modern era.

On a wintry day in March 1626, Bacon was riding through the countryside in a coach when it dawned on him that meat might be preserved with snow. He stopped the coach, bought a chicken, killed it, and with his own hands stuffed it with snow. The empirical experiment "succeeded excellently well"; it was the beginning of refrigeration. But Bacon began to chill and became too weak to travel. He was taken to the home of Lord Arundel, who lived nearby; his illness turned into bronchitis, then into pneumonia. A fever burned him out. He died April 9, 1626. He was sixty-five.

# 3₂

## WE NEVER SEE THE REAL WORLD

Our senses constitute our interface with reality. The word *interface* is a modern term used to describe the boundary of contact between adjacent realms; it is the common surface where two areas of activity meet. Thinking in these terms, it is our senses that make up the surface-contact between our subjective world of experience and the objective world of reality. The phenomena that take place along these two surfaces are what concern us here, for now we face directly the problem of the nature of our interface with reality.

What is going on where these two worlds meet?

Our senses are *transducers*. A transducer is any substance or device that converts one form of energy into another. A lightbulb, for instance, converts electricity into light. (You and I know that *light* does not run through the cord plugged into the wall outlet, but a primitive tribesman might arrive at the belief—with excellent reason—that if he cut the cord, light would spill out.)

In our technological world we are surrounded by transducers. A hotplate changes electrical energy into heat, but eggbeaters, blenders, and power-mowers convert that same electrical energy into mechanical motion. Conversely, heat is used in nuclear power plants to produce electricity. Geiger counters convert radiation into sound—audible warning clicks. Tape recorders convert air waves into electrical impulses that are converted into magnetic lines of force that are then stored in the oxides on the tape. Batteries change chemical energy into electrical energy, and solar cells convert light into electrical energy. An electroencephalograph converts brain waves (electrical) into squiggly lines on paper or dancing curves on an oscilloscope. Finally, there is chlorophyll, one of nature's grand transducers, which converts light into chemicals used in living processes.

*Learning? certainly, but living primarily, and learning through and in relation to this living.*

JOHN DEWEY

*A philosopher riding through the countryside on a train once leaned over to peer long and hard out the window. When asked what he saw, he replied that he was looking at a half of twenty sheep, and that he was wondering how he could find out about the other half.*

And then there are fireflies, who spend a large percentage of their waking time (our sleeping time) converting biochemical energy into light.

A transducer, then, converts *one kind of energy* into a *different kind of energy.*

Each of our senses is a living transducer. So our question becomes: What kind of energy goes into the sense/transducer, and what kind of energy comes out? Or, to put it differently: (1) What is the energy input? (2) What is the energy output? and (3) How does the sense-converter do it?

If we can answer these questions, we can discover what actually is taking place along our interface-boundary with reality.

Let's answer question (2) immediately and return to the others later. From all our known senses, the output is the same: it is electrochemical energy propagated along the neural pathways. So far as we know at present, the impulses that leave our senses and move toward the central nervous system and into the brain are in every case the same. What then makes the difference in our experience if the impulses are all the same? Only the location in the brain to which the message-impulses are carried. Visual sensors, for example, send impulses to the back tip of the occipital lobe; sound sensors send their messages to another area of the brain located on the top inner fold of the temporal lobe; and so on, for every sense we have. Each sensory area of the cortex "knows how" to convert the electrochemical impulses into the "right" experiences.

Now, what if we should "get our wires crossed"? That is, what if we should have nerve fibers ending in the wrong area of the brain? If that should happen, the brain would *misinterpret* the impulses. If touch receptors sent their messages to the "cold center" in the cortex, the lightest touch would be felt as a cold sensation. In one laboratory experiment, scientists crossed the nerve fibers of the right and left rear feet of a white rat; when the pain sensors in the right foot were stimulated, the rat would jerk away the left foot, and vice versa.

If the nerve fibers from our eyes could be crossed with the nerve fibers from our ears, then undoubtedly we would "hear" colors and "see" sounds.

It is apparent that the gathering of information by our senses is a complex process, with many a possible slip twixt the energy input and the final experience. To clarify the problem, let's use one sense as an analogue.

A round, contented, bright yellow grapefruit lies in the fruit bowl on the table. Now, no matter how hard you try, it is a fact that you can never see the grapefruit—or touch, smell, or taste it.

What you *see*, of course, are light quanta, which strike the grapefruit and are reflected back to your eyes. "White" light (that is, light of all wavelengths together) from some source such as the sun or a lightbulb strikes the surface of the grapefruit which, because of the molecular structure of its surface material, absorbs all the wavelengths of the spectrum *except* the "yellow" wavelengths (in the vicinity of 5600 to 5800 angstrom units), which are reflected back and reach your eyes. So, what do we *see*? Only the reflected light from the object, never the object itself.

Now, what are "light waves"? The best we can say is that they are electromagnetic waves of different lengths that travel at a speed of about 186,000 miles per second. *The waves themselves are colorless,* but the cones embedded

Bridget Riley, *Current* (1964)

in the retinas of our eyes are stimulated by the various wavelengths of radiation and send impulses to the visual centers of the cortex, *where they are interpreted as colors.* Human retinas possess three kinds of cones, which are sensitive, respectively, to three basic wavelengths, the wavelengths we interpret as red, blue, and green—the three primary colors for light (notice the three colors of phosphor dots on a color TV screen). Textbooks in the physical sciences occasionally define certain wavelengths with a certain color. This is an expediency for the sake of simplicity, but it is a conceptual fallacy. Modern physical theory consistently shows that physical entities—atoms, molecules, electromagnetic waves, and such —cannot possess the qualities we experience.

## THE MIND MANUFACTURES EXPERIENCE

From these facts, two conclusions of great significance for understanding the nature of our knowledge must be drawn.

1. *Color is an experience in our minds.* It is the experiential finale to a long and complicated process of transduction. The energy input to our visual transducers is uncolored electromagnetic radiation, which enters our eyes with wavelengths (in the visual spectrum) of about 3800 to 7200 angstroms. Our

*These sensory limitations, and the resulting failure to comprehend fully much of Nature, may be only a local deficiency. On the basis of the new estimates of the great abundance of stars and the high probability of millions of planets with highly developed life, we are made aware— embarrassingly aware—that we may be intellectual minims in the life of the universe. I could develop further this uncomfortable idea by pointing out that sense receptors, in quality quite unknown to us and in fact hardly imaginable, which record phenomena of which we are totally ignorant, may easily exist among the higher sentient organisms of other planets.*
**HARLOW SHAPLEY**

## CREDIBILITY GAP?

As a conscious being I am involved in a story. The perceiving part of my mind tells me a story of a world around me. The story tells of familiar objects. It tells of colours, sounds, scents belonging to these objects; of boundless space in which they have their existence, and of an ever-rolling stream of time bringing change and incident. It tells of other life than mine busy about its own purposes.

As a scientist I have become mistrustful of this story. In many instances it has become clear that things are not what they seem to be. According to the story teller I have now in front of me a substantial desk; but I have learned from physics that the desk is not at all the continuous substance that it is supposed to be in the story. It is a host of tiny electric charges darting hither and thither with inconceivable velocity. Instead of being solid substance my desk is more like a swarm of gnats.

So I have come to realise that I must not put overmuch confidence in the story teller who lives in my mind.

SIR ARTHUR EDDINGTON
*New Pathways in Science*

## THE RABBLE OF THE SENSES

In trying to distinguish appearance from reality and lay bare the fundamental structure of the universe, science has had to transcend the "rabble of the senses." But its highest edifices, Einstein has pointed out, have been "purchased at the price of emptiness of content." A theoretical concept is emptied of content to the very degree that it is divorced from sensory experience. For the only world man can truly know is the world created for him by his senses. If he expunges all the impressions which they translate and memory stores, nothing is left. . . . So paradoxically what the scientist and the philosopher call the world of appearance—the world of light and color, of blue skies and green leaves, of sighing wind and murmuring water, the world designed by the physiology of human sense organs—is the world in which finite man is incarcerated by his essential nature. And what the scientist and the philosopher call the world of reality—the colorless, soundless, impalpable cosmos which lies like an iceberg beneath the place of man's perceptions—is a skeleton structure of symbols.

LINCOLN BARNETT
*The Universe and Dr. Einstein*

transducer/cones identify the various wavelengths and send electrical messages along the neural pathways to the visual center of the brain. There and then *only* do we see color.

2.    A corollary: *There is no color whatever in the external world of things.* Look around you. That grapefruit only *appears* to be yellow. All the colors you "see"—however beautiful, enchanting, stimulating they seem to you—are only experiences in your mind. The ocean is not deep blue, the pine forest is not green, and the aurora borealis does not scintillate with cosmic colors.

And there is no color in the rainbow.

This transduction pattern holds true for all our senses, and for all possible senses that we can imagine.

SOUND Once there was a famous tree in a forest, a tree that decided to fall when no one was around. It did its very best to make a noise; it wanted to be heard. But it went down to defeat. It did indeed set up quite a vigorous series of waves in the summer air, waves that alternately rarefied and compressed the air as they moved outward. But there was no sound in the land. (It is reported that a chipmunk, sunning on a rock at the top of the hill, had his transducers going, and that he heard the sound of a crash in the valley below. One transducer can make all the difference between sound and eternal silence.)

TASTE Chemical substances penetrate the surface cells of our tastebuds, which apparently respond to only four basic "tastes": sweet, sour, salty, and bitter. All the flavors of our gastronomic spectrum are merely combinations of these four. But note: there is no taste to the chemical substances; they are only molecular structures. There is no "sweetness" in the peppermint candy, no "saltiness" in the sodium chloride, and no "sourness" in a lemon.

SMELL Gaseous molecules permeate the linings of the olfactory membranes in the upper nasal passageway. Precisely how the molecules manage to stimulate such a variety of "odor messages" is not understood, but our conclusion is again clear: there is no scent in the rose nor salty odors from the spray of the breakers on the beach. All the sweet fragrances of Samarkand are merely experiences in the mind.

## WINDOWS ONTO THE UNIVERSE

A continuous frequency spectrum including both sonic and electromagnetic wavelengths is plotted here on a logarithmic scale. Placed together, the frequency ranges from $6 \times 10^{22}$ Hz to $5 \times 10^{-4}$ Hz. This is a range in wavelength from the diameter of an electron to a wave almost 200 million miles long. Near the long end of the spectrum the "world resonance" (like the vibration of a giant bell) is a single cycle lasting about twenty seconds.

If this frequency spectrum represents two kinds of reality—sonic and electromagnetic—then we have two "windows" open to us onto the universe.

One is the audio window which, with our natural sense, is limited to a range of 20 to 20,000 Hz. The other is the visual window in the electromagnetic spectrum, a very small window ranging from about 3800 to 7200 Å. These windows set the limits to what we can hear and see in the real world.

All the other sonic and electromagnetic realities are there, moving about us; but we are deaf and blind to them, and they are meaningless to us.

When were these windows opened to us? Shall we say, for the audio and visual windows, perhaps a billion years ago? Whenever sentient creatures first began to sense vibrations in the atmosphere and respond to light.

When were the other windows opened to us? Only during the last one hundred years. they were all flung open with breath-taking rapidity.

What reason is there to believe that all the realities have now been discovered, all the spectra plotted, and all the windows opened?

Electromagnetic and sonic
spectra

**TOUCH** Whether the stimulus is pressure or pain, heat or cold, the only things we "know" are the *experiences* that occur in various areas of the cerebral cortex. But this is probably the sense we most readily believe. After all, who ever claimed that "pain" was located in the red-hot coal?

In a word, before the development of sentient creatures on the planet Earth, there were no colors, no sounds, no odors. There were no experiences because there were no experiencers.

## OUR SENSES DECEIVE US

*It is impossible to explain . . . qualities of matter except by tracing these back to the behavior of entities which themselves no longer possess these qualities. If atoms are really to explain the origin of color and smell of visible material bodies, then they cannot possess properties like color and smell. . . . Atomic theory consistently denies the atom any such perceptible qualities.*

**WERNER HEISENBERG**

As a result of such analysis, we may have the uneasy feeling that we are being deceived. We are being led, by our own senses, into believing things that are untrue. The grapefruit may not be yellow, but it surely *looks* yellow; it seems undeniable that the yellowness is in the rind of the fruit itself. Likewise, we would be willing to wager that the sweetness is in the peppermint candy and that the sound of a tree falling came from the bottom of the hill. These are only appearances, however. They are indeed "deceptions."

Furthermore, our *language* is a part of the conspiracy. For I look at the grapefruit and say, "The grapefruit is yellow." The subject of my statement is the noun *grapefruit,* and the adjective *yellow* modifies the noun; and the *is* clearly attaches the quality of yellowness to the subject *grapefruit.*

It is to be expected that our language would reflect the deception of our senses. Language crystallizes the deception, as it were, and reflects it back to us, reinforcing our belief that the quality yellow does in fact belong to the object.

Once, when I was in a foreign country, I ordered dinner but took care to ask whether the food was hot, since I could not take any spicy hotness in my food. The waiter assured me it was not hot. Shortly he spread several dishes of rice, meat, and curries before me. I suspiciously sampled several of the bowls. All HOT. I called the waiter and told him that the food was all too hot. He stood baffled for a moment, then reached down and took some marinaded meat from one

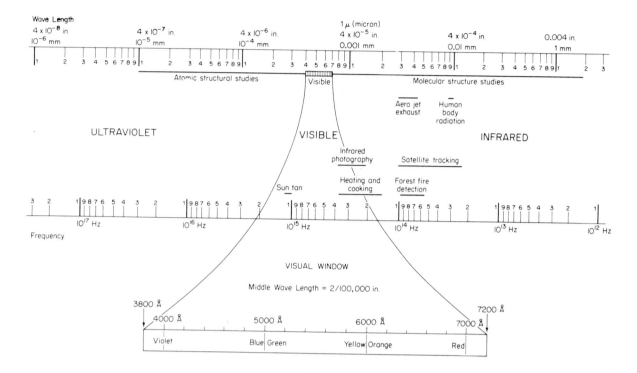

of the dishes, tasted it, and pronounced, "No, *not* hot." At which point I dipped into the same bowl, tasted the meat and sauce, and announced, "Yes, *very* HOT!"

The point is that we were both telling the truth. Neither of us was referring to the food; we were reporting our own subjective experiences, which differed, obviously. But the language we employed to articulate our experiences made it appear that one of us was either lying or not perceiving accurately. Both of us in turn *pointed to the dish of meat* and said "the meat *is* hot/not hot," clearly revealing where we assumed the hotness to be located. Such is the "tyranny of language."

To say that we are being "deceived" seems like a suspicious way of looking at it. After all, none of our senses "intend" to deceive us.

Perhaps the transduction process can be interpreted more positively. For the fact is that all our senses have developed in such a way that they can translate meaningless physical phenomena into meaningful experiences. To use an analogy, at this moment there are probably several television stations transmitting electromagnetic waves through the atmosphere where you are, but if your TV set is not turned on, the waves are meaningless. Turning your TV set on would convert useless phenomena into meaningful information.

This is precisely what our senses do: they turn on to the physical phenomena of the real world and render our environment meaningful. They translate the events going on around us into useful information.

They have given us the kind of information we need to survive. What more can we ask of them?

*Things which we see are not by themselves what we see. . . . It remains completely unknown to us what the objects may be by themselves and apart from the receptivity of our senses. We know nothing but our manner of perceiving them. . . .*

IMMANUEL KANT

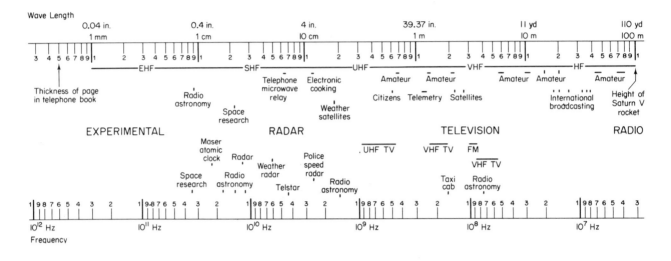

## SENSORY LIMITATIONS AND THE REAL WORLD

*There remains the final reflection, how shallow, puny, and imperfect are efforts to sound the depths in the nature of things. In philosophical discussion, the merest hint of dogmatic certainty as to finality of statement is an exhibition of folly.*

ALFRED NORTH WHITEHEAD

*Man is thus his own greatest mystery. He does not understand the vast veiled universe into which he has been cast for the reason that he does not understand himself. He comprehends but little of his organic processes and even less of his unique capacity to perceive the world about him, to reason and to dream. Least of all does he understand his noblest and most mysterious faculty: the ability to transcend himself and perceive himself in the act of perception.*

LINCOLN BARNETT

Let's look once again at the drastic sensory limitations we operate under. The electromagnetic spectrum is a good example. If we arbitrarily divide the range of all electromagnetic waves into sixty "octaves," then visually we can perceive only a single octave, from about 3800 to 7200 angstrom units. But the waves extend away to great distances on either side of that visual octave.

Below the blue end of the visual spectrum the waves grow shorter into the ultraviolet rays, X-rays, and gamma rays. Above the red end of the spectrum the wavelengths grow longer into the infrared, the microwaves, short radio and long radio waves. We have developed instruments, of course, which are extensions of our senses and can reach out on either side of the visual octave.

Still, without the aid of our instruments, we are limited in perception to that single octave. It is a bit unnerving to realize how little physical reality we perceive, and how much more there really is.

No creature ever has enough senses; it could always use more. Why, then, in the long course of evolution, did we not develop other senses? We believe the answer is fairly simple: given the time we had to evolve and the conditions our ancestors had to cope with, they developed the particular sensors needed most. But if other conditions had prevailed, our sense-systems would have been different in countless ways.

We share existence on our planet with millions of species of sentient creatures, many of which have senses we might well envy. (In fact, we do envy them, for we imitate every sense we possibly can with scientific instruments.)

Many animals, of course, possess the same senses we have, but they have intensified their sensitivity beyond our range of sensory pickup. Many animals can hear high-pitched sounds beyond our range. Bats emit high-pitched sounds and then listen to their echo to locate objects ("echolocation," the principle used in radar). Porpoises and fish have an underwater counterpart of the bat's "radar"—a "sonar" system. The "lateral-line" sense in fishes is what we might think of as a combined touch-hear sense, for in the water these senses merge. Fishes living at great depths where no light can penetrate have developed hypersensitive lateral-lines; a preying fish can take a fix on its quarry and zero in with pinpoint accuracy.

Ants and other insects have delicate chemical senses (combining touch, taste, and smell?) by which they communicate and establish food trails. Moths both smell and hear with their antennae. Bees navigate to their honey sources by reckoning the sun's position.

Then there are still other senses that remain mysteries. At this point we can only admire and wonder about them: the senses by which birds migrate (perhaps partly by star navigation), the "homing sense" of dogs and cats and many wild animals, the senses that enable the Sargasso eels to return to the St. Lawrence and European rivers which their ancestors knew, but which they themselves have never seen.

And then there are fireflies. Hundreds of tiny sparks in the night: one wonders how they perceive their flashing world.

*For the sceptic to bewail the fact that we can know nothing but appearance is as silly as it would be to bewail the fact that we have nothing to wear but clothes and nothing to eat but food.*

**W. P. Montague**

## Epistemic Loneliness

At about this point, a feeling of loneliness may begin to overtake us—an "epistemic loneliness." For the egocentric predicament is really an epistemological condition: isolation within a world of our own making. We live in a shell, so to speak, a private, personal shell inside which takes place an immense variety of experiences, *all ours.* And when we try to break out of our shells to make contact with the world and other creatures, we only rediscover the depths of our predicament. We live in an epistemological shell with no doors. None may enter and none may share.

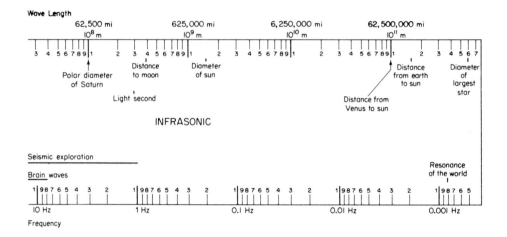

Since certain aspects of our epistemological condition appear to be inescapable, we must learn to live with them.

1. *The fallacy of objectification is an ever-present danger.* Our experiencing system conspires to make us think that a variety of private experiences are in some way real, that they are events occurring in the real world of objects/events. (The tragic consequences of this fallacy will be felt especially when we try to untangle our value-experiences.)

2. *Accordingly, we have all lived (unwittingly) in a state of confusion regarding the location of the occurrence of events.* Our subjective and objective worlds are interwoven: events we thought to be private may turn out to be objective, while many supposedly objective events often prove to be experiences only.

3. *We are restless with our evolutionary limitations and deceptions.* While we can be grateful that our sensory and information-processing systems have rendered our physical environment meaningful, we have reached a point in our quest for reality when we want to go beyond our limitations and to know what the world is really like. We want to make whatever corrections are necessary in our perception, so we can move out of our shells and come to know our universe and its principles of operation.

## THE PRAGMATIC NATURE OF KNOWING

From this vantage point, the central problem of Western epistemology may be more intelligible. *If we know only our experiences, how can we be sure that we know anything about the real world?* More precisely, if objective physical phenomena are all converted *before we can experience them* into different kinds of energy, how can we know anything about the original phenomena? Can we ever know what those phenomena are?

If we experience only the subjective side of our interface with reality, can we ever know anything about the objective side of that interface-boundary?

With refreshing honesty, David Hume composed a confession that speaks

## LESS THAN A MILLIONTH

There has been a complete changeover in human affairs. Where man has always been after *things,* after *reality*—reality being everything you can see, touch, taste, smell and hear—suddenly we're in a completely new kind of reality. The reality of the great electromagnetic spectrum which is part of this communications revolution. And we now know that what man can hear, smell, touch, taste and see is less than a millionth of reality.

BUCKMINSTER FULLER

## COMPLAINT

"Tell me," says Micromegas, an inhabitant of one of the planets of the Dog Star, to the secretary of the Academy of Sciences in the planet Saturn, at which he had recently arrived in a journey through the heavens—"Tell me, how many senses have the men on your globe?". . .

"We have seventy-two senses," answered the academician, "and we are every day complaining of the smallness of the number. . . ."

"I can very well believe," says Micromegas, "for, in our globe, we have very near one thousand senses, and yet, with all these, we feel continually a sort of listless inquietude and vague desire, which are forever telling us that we are nothing, and that there are beings infinitely nearer perfection."

VOLTAIRE

## REALITY IS THIRD BASE

You and I view reality much as a spectator might watch a baseball game through a knothole in the fence—and all he sees is third base. He's got his eye up there and he watches the entire game through third base, and only third base.

And if someone asks him to describe baseball, he says, "Well, there's some guy that stands around kicking the dirt for quite a while, spitting on the ground, and that sort of thing. And all at once a bunch of guys come sliding in and kick the dirt all over and then swear at each other and almost fight, and pretty soon they all leave and the first guy stands around, kicking the dirt once again. And that's about it."

And *this* is America's number one sport?!

This is about the way we view reality. We perceive just a little bit of it, and we are so naive to think that that's all of it.

But that isn't all of it. The truth is that virtually the whole ball game called reality is being played beyond our knothole-eye-view. . . .

COURT HOLDGRAFER

for many great thinkers whose lifeblood is spent wrestling with abstract and unobservable entities but who still possess the great gift of keeping their philosophical reflections in perspective. Hume wrote:

Should it be asked me whether I sincerely assent to this argument which I have been to such pains to inculcate, and whether I be really one of those skeptics who hold

David Hume (1711-1776)

that all is uncertain, . . . I should reply . . . that neither I nor any other person was ever sincerely and constantly of that opinion. . . . I dine, I play backgammon, I converse and am merry with my friends; and when, after three or four hours amusement, I would return to these speculations, they appear so cold and strained and ridiculous that I cannot find in my heart to enter into them any further. . . . Thus the skeptic still continues to reason and believe, though he asserts that he cannot defend his reason by reason; and by the same rule he must assent to the principle concerning the existence of body, though he cannot pretend, by any arguments of philosophy, to maintain its veracity.

Let's take seriously what David Hume implies in this moment of truth. Here is our Scottish skeptic whose reason tells him one set of facts (we know nothing certain of the real world), but whose experience seems to contradict his reason ("I dine, I play backgammon, I converse . . ."). When such conflict exists between theory and experience, then a solution must be sought. (Remember that infamous bumblebee which, according to aerodynamics, can't fly—but does?)

What Hume implies is: (1) it is very impracticable *not* to assume that the real world exists, and (2) day-to-day living is very difficult if one tries to operate on the assumption that he knows *nothing* about the real world.

There are few philosophers of the modern world who would *not* question, to some extent, the conclusions of Hume and Berkeley. (See pp. 208–211.) After more than two centuries of debate, we now have adequate reason *to assume* (1) that the real world exists, and (2) that we have at least a working knowledge of that world. It is the *nature* of that working knowledge that is still cause for concern.

If these conclusions are comforting, our philosophers have made three points that may seem less so. The following arguments seem basically sound and still stand today as starting points for an understanding of the nature of knowledge.

1. We know only our subjective experience, which begins with sensory reaction and ends with the fabrication of knowledge. This appears to be an inescapable limitation.

2. Accordingly, we cannot experience directly the real world of objects/events. Neither matter nor the principles of motion are directly perceivable.

3. Our knowledge of the real world consists solely, therefore, of inferences that we make on the basis of our experience.

In summary, what is the nature of our knowledge about the real world of objects/events?

Our knowledge of reality is composed of ideas our minds have *created* on the basis of our sensory experience. It is a fabric of knowledge woven by the mind. Knowledge is not given to the mind; nothing is "poured" into it. Rather, the mind manufactures perceptions, concepts,

---

*"George, it's impossible to correct a defective reality-orientation overnight."*

URSULA K. LEGUIN
**The Lathe of Heaven**

*Occasionally an epistemolog is found who is capable of smiling, like Bradley or William James; occasionally one is found who understands that his 'ology is only a game, and therefore, plays it with a worldy twinkle in his eye, like David Hume.*

WILL DURANT

"The topic for today is: What is reality?"

By Henry Martin from Saturday Review, May 29, 1971. Copyright © 1971. Reprinted by permission of Saturday Review and Henry Martin.

ideas, beliefs, and so forth and holds them as *working hypotheses* about external reality. Every idea is a (subjective) working model that enables us to handle real objects/events with some degree of efficiency.

But ideas in our heads are not realities; they are but tools that enable us to deal with reality.

It is as though we drew nondimensional maps to help us understand four-dimensional territory. The semanticists have long reminded us to beware of confusing any sort of map with the real landscape. "The map is not the territory."

*Truth is a property of beliefs, and derivatively of sentences which express beliefs.*
**BERTRAND RUSSELL**

## REFLECTIONS

1  Note the anecdote of the philosopher who "was looking at a half of twenty sheep" (see marginal quote on p. 195). Everybody knows that a half of twenty is ten, so what is his problem? How would you suggest that he go about finding a solution?

2  Gaze at, then reflect upon, the painting on p. 197, *Current* by Bridget Riley. (1) What do you see? How much of what you "see" is on the page? (2) How much of what you see is brought to the seeing by your perceptual system? (3) Do you see motion? Are you sure there is no motion on the page itself? If you say yes, then how can you be sure?

3  "Each of our senses is a living transducer" (p. 196). What is meant by this? What are the epistemological implications of our realizing that our senses are in fact transducers?

4  Pages 197-200: Numerous phenomena that appear to be a part of the real world turn out to be experiences only and have no real status. Do you personally have any trouble accepting these fact-claims as true? Why?

5  What is meant by "the conspiracy of language"? What causes this deception? Give some examples of how we are thus deceived by our language.

6  From this point on it is imperative that you understand the philosophic usage of the terms *real* and *reality*. (See glossary.) Which of the following events would be real and which would be solely experiential? (Be wary: definitions are crucial, and in some cases it is not an either/or decision.)

*The disputants I ween*
*Rail on in utter ignorance*
*Of what each other mean,*
*And prate about an Elephant*
*Not one of them has seen.*
**JOHN G. SAXE**

| | |
|---|---|
| an idea | Mr. Spock (of *Star Trek*) |
| a feeling of loneliness | the state of Arizona |
| an itch | the state of euphoria |
| your car | the sound of music |
| an atom | The Pythagorean Theorem |
| a toothache (in your wisdom tooth) | Pythagoras |
| a heartache | the law of gravity |
| a beautiful painting | heat |
| a dirty picture | temperature |
| a poem | the office of the president of the |
| a mirage | United States |
| the planet Mars | the president of the United States |
| the god Mars | the state |
| | a sunset |

(*CONTINUED ON P. 212*)

# GEORGE BERKELEY

## *The Irish Immaterialist*

By the time he was twenty-five years old, Berkeley had published his *Principles of Human Knowledge*, had stirred up international controversy in philosophical and theological circles, and was regarded as one of the most stylish and challenging philosophers the English-speaking world had produced.

George Berkeley (rhymes with "darkly") was born in 1685 in a farmhouse on the grounds of ancient Dysert Castle in County Kilkenny, Ireland. His father, William, was an Englishman, by trade a minor customs official. His mother is unknown to us. Berkeley always thought of himself as English and looked upon his Irish neighbors as foreigners.

Very early, young Berkeley displayed precocious qualities: a strong-willed, independent, creative intellect; and a passionate, polemical nature. His parents, while not wealthy, were able to provide him with an excellent education. He first attended Kilkenny school (from age eleven to fifteen) where he studied mathematics and the classics. At fifteen

he matriculated at Trinity College, Dublin (he entered in March 1700), where he was immediately absorbed in the philosophical ideas of Locke and Descartes, Leibniz, Newton, and Hobbes.

His enthusiasms and eccentricities found full expression at Trinity College, which was a center for intellectual growth, justly praised for its freedom of inquiry and academic excellence; there was a spirit of revolt against outdated scholastic thinking in philosophy and science. It was fertile soil for Berkeley's inquisitive mind, and he could safely challenge the fashionable orthodoxies of philosophy and theology. He and some friends organized a philosophy club to study "the new philosophy," which meant Locke.

Berkeley's prime calling was to the priesthood of the Anglican Church. He was ordained a deacon, then priest, in 1709, and he remained a lifelong apologist for his faith. He was appointed bishop of Cloyne in 1734 and spent the last eighteen years of his life administering his diocese.

Berkeley's academic achievements were no less important to him. He was associated with Trinity College all his life, as undergraduate and graduate, then fellow (at the age of twenty-two, after completing an examination with great distinction); and college tutor when he was twenty-four. In 1709 he was promoted to sub-lecturer and junior dean; in 1712 to junior Greek lecturer. He received a D.D. degree in 1721, was appointed senior Greek lecturer and university preacher, then in 1722 was made dean and elected to a lectureship in Hebrew. All these accomplishments were a tribute to his leadership, energy, originality, and loyalty.

Berkeley traveled widely and wrote continuously. In 1713 he visited London, and was presented at the court of Queen Anne. He was widely admired for his courtesy, character, and quick mind. He befriended such literary lights as Swift, Addison, Steele, and Pope; he deeply impressed royalty, notables, bon vivants, and "men of merit," and moved easily among them. Pope commented that Berkeley seemed to possess "every virtue under heaven," and the statesman Atterbury exclaimed, "So much understanding, so much knowledge, so much innocence, and such humility, I did not think had been the fashion of any but angels, till I saw this gentleman." In 1713 he made his first trip to France and Italy where he was enthralled with nature and the ancient ruins. He wrote a vivid account of the eruption of Mount Vesuvius in April 1717.

Berkeley's major writings were all completed before he was twenty-eight years old. At twenty-four he wrote *Essay towards a New Theory of Vision* (1709) in which he proposed a radical explanation of how we perceive visual depth. His philosophic fame rests on two works, *Treatise Concerning the Principles of Human Knowledge*, Part I (1710) (he lost part II on a trip to Sicily and could never bring himself to rewrite it); and *Dialogues between Hylas and Philonous* (1713). These are the great works that contain the logical arguments for "the immaterialist hypothesis."

Berkeley was the first great philosopher to visit America. He had long dreamed of establishing a college in Bermuda to educate young men for the clergy and to bring the Gospel to Indians and Negroes; to this end he had collected funds from private donors and a promise of £20,000 from the House of Commons. So he and his bride (Anne Forster, married in August) sailed for America in September of 1728. For three years they lived in Newport, Rhode Island. They bought a ninety-six-acre farm and built a house. He wrote, preached, traveled inland, and enjoyed the countryside. They had one son, and a daughter who died in infancy. These were relatively happy years, but he never succeeded in raising the money for the college. Finally the Berkeleys journeyed to Boston and caught a ship back to Dublin.

While in America Berkeley penned a poem containing the line "Westward the course of empire takes its way." Because of that line, a California town was named for him.

The rest of his life was divided between his clerical responsibilities, social concerns, occasional writing, and his family. They lived in County Cork after he became bishop in 1734. Berkeley adored all of his four surviving children and carefully supervised the education of each. He spoke of "the starlight beauty" of his daughter Julia and wished he had twenty sons like George. In 1751, his health failing, and mourning the loss of a son, he decided to retire; the king refused to allow it. The following year his eldest son was ready for Oxford, so the family moved there to be near him. On the evening of January 14, 1753, while his wife was reading to him on the couch, he drifted quietly to sleep. He was sixty-eight years old.

◆

As a young man, Berkeley developed the habit of jotting down his ideas in notebooks. These autobiographical reflections were unknown until they were

*Esse est percipi (or "Esse is percipi"). "To be is to be perceived."*

*He who says there is no such thing as an honest man, you may be sure is himself a knave.*

*Westward the course of empire takes its way;*
*The four first acts already past,*
*A fifth shall close the drama with the day:*
*Time's noblest offspring is the last.*

**On the Prospect of Planting Arts And Learning in America, 1752.**

*When we do our utmost to conceive the existence of external bodies we are all the while only contemplating our own ideas.*

*There is nothing that I desire more than to know thoroughly all that can be said against what I take for truth.*

discovered in 1871 and given the title of *Commonplace Book.* In a paragraph written when he was twenty-one, he declared that the concept of materialism or "substance" had always been "the main pillar and support of skepticism" on which have been founded "all the impious schemes of atheism and irreligion. . . . How great a friend material substance hath been to atheists in all ages were needless to relate. . . . When this cornerstone is once removed, the whole fabric cannot choose but fall to the ground. . . ."

Berkeley was confident that he could remove this "cornerstone" of atheism. How exactly did he manage it?

He started with an idea from John Locke—that the idea of "substance" is merely an assumption on our part, since we can never perceive the real substantive world directly. What we experience—and the *only* things we experience —are colors, tastes, odors, and so forth, the so-called secondary qualities, which are actually our own perceptions.

What about the "primary qualities" —shape, solidity, motion/rest, extension (volume)—the qualities that we believe inhere in objects themselves? How do we know about these? We only infer these too, said Berkeley. How do you know the shape of a seashell? You run your fingers over the surface and feel it. Not exactly, Berkeley reminds us; we don't feel *it*. We only feel our sensations and proceed to assume that "it" exists in physical seashell form and that such external matter is the cause of our sensations. We further *assume* that this matter possesses certain (primary) qualities which we cannot experience directly.

So far, Berkeley seems to agree with Locke. But where Locke never doubted the *existence* of matter (he merely said we can never know it), Berkeley asks: If substance is an assumption, then could that assumption be wrong? Suppose the world of material objects really doesn't exist. How could we account for the supposed objects which cause our perceptions? Berkeley concluded that there is an alternative assumption, just as logical as "substance," and preferable.

Since we cannot avoid assuming, assume that God exists, and that he places in our minds all the perceptions which we experience. Why is the assumption of matter a more reasonable assumption than the existence of God? And if one is a Christian philosopher, doesn't the assumption of a God-source become a more congenial assumption than a matter-source?

Therefore, reasoned Berkeley, "to be is to be perceived"—*esse est percipi;* and not to be perceived is not to exist. There are no "real" clouds, rocks, oceans, stars, penguins, or seashells. Such items are but mind-images derived from God. Objects exist, therefore, only while they are being perceived; and they exist only in perception. He wrote: "To say things exist when no mind perceives them, is perfectly unintelligible."

How can we be sure the persistent objects of experience—our homes, friends, the familiar belongings—will "be there" when we want to perceive them? Does the seashell-image flicker on and off, in and out of existence, every time we look at it or turn away from it? Not really, says Berkeley. God is the eternal perceiver, and all images continue to exist in the mind of God. They are always available to us for the asking and are fed into our singular minds by God's mind whenever we need them.

It rings like a psychedelic fairy tale. The physical world doesn't exist; "matter" is merely a make-believe idea we thought we needed—"the fiction of our own brain."

Berkeley's attempt to annihilate matter was a popular topic of conversation, with and without heat and light. The lexicographer Samuel Johnson was irritated by it all, as Boswell tells us:

After we came out of church, we stood talking for some time together of Berkeley's ingenious sophistry to prove the non-existence of matter, and that everything in the universe is merely ideal [idea]. I observed that though we are satisfied his doctrine is not true, it is impossible to refute it. I shall never forget the alacrity with which Johnson answered, striking his foot with a mighty force against a large stone, till he rebounded from it, "I refute it thus!"

But what had Dr. Johnson really proved by kicking the rock? He had merely illustrated and confirmed Berkeley's argument. For all Johnson "knew" was the sharp pain in his toe, perhaps a numb feeling in his foot, and the sensation of a sudden stop which must have given his leg a jolt. All he had proven by kicking the rock was that he was capable of feeling a variety of subjective sensations. All he knew was his own experience, and that, after all, was the point Berkeley was making. So Samuel Johnson had unwittingly added his considerable weight to the philosophy of "immaterialism."

What else is this but philosophical fantasy? Most of us are convinced (are we not?) that physical matter exists. It seems to us that Berkeley made a simple mistake, a non sequitur: just because we cannot experience physical matter directly, it does not necessarily follow that matter does not exist.

But did he really go wrong? (1) Berkeley emphasizes the fact that we are limited *absolutely* to our own perceptions and cannot directly experience any "real" world. Most epistemologists today would agree with him. (2) He is therefore repeating John Locke's point that physical matter (or "substance") is an idea—an assumption which we *believe* to be a logical necessity. On this point also, he seems to be correct.

Whether you will go further with Berkeley and agree that his alternative assumption—God as the source of experience—is a better idea will depend somewhat on personal preference and theological belief. Most of us remain convinced that the reality of matter is a better-working assumption, but perhaps that is only because we have lived with it uncritically most of our lives.

We must face honestly, however, Berkeley's singular challenge: Prove, if you can, that any material object exists apart form your perception of it. If you can, then Berkeley is wrong. If you cannot, then you will have to concede (Berkeley would insist) that the world is merely your idea.

His logic is brilliant and he almost succeeds. "His arguments are, strictly speaking, unanswerable," wrote Lord Chesterfield; and Boswell duly noted that although we are convinced that his doctrine is false, "it is impossible to refute it." David Hume agreed: Berkeley's arguments "admit of no answer and produce no conviction." In 1847 a reward of £100 (later £500) was offered to anyone who could refute Berkeley's logic. The money still awaits a taker.

Subsequent critics have written volumes of exposition and analysis of Berkeley's "immaterial hypothesis." However, a short limerick attributed to Ronald Knox contains the essence of the good bishop's philosophy:

> There was a young man who said,
>    "God
> Must think it exceedingly odd
>    If he finds that this tree
>    Continues to be
> When there's no one about in the
>    Quad."

>    REPLY

> Dear Sir:
>        Your astonishment's odd.
> *I* am always about in the Quad.
>    And that's why the tree
>    Will continue to be,
> Since observed by
>    Yours faithfully,
>        God.

7 After studying the human "visual window" through which we see reality, how would you describe the real world to: (1) a person who has been blind from birth? (2) a highly intelligent alien from another planet who "sees" wavelengths only in the infrared region of the electromagnetic spectrum? (3) a fellow epistemologist who is acutely aware, as you are, of our severe human perceptual limitations?

8 This chapter speaks of "epistemic loneliness." Are these words meaningful to you? Can you feel this condition personally or does it not apply to you?

9 Review pp. 197-207 and then reflect: Does it trouble you that the more we know about the "realities beyond appearances" the farther we are moving away from the world of everyday experience? Does this imply that our experiential world is, in some fundamental way, suspect, invalid, erroneous, and/or worthless? Yes or no—and why?

10 In the final analysis, what do we "know" about the real world and how do we know it?

# 3

## THE PRAGMATIC MIND

In its attempt to make sense of the energy-environment in which we live, the mind proves to be a versatile, creative instrument. It translates events of the real world into experiences we can use in living. The mind is not at all the "blank tablet," the *tabula rasa*, which some earlier thinkers thought it to be.

We have a fairly clear understanding now of the general nature of knowledge. Human knowledge is a collection of constructs created by the mind from the raw materials of sensation; it is a series of scaled-down maps that we use to find our way in the full-scale territory of the real world.

> *Concepts without percepts are empty. Percepts without concepts are blind.*
> IMMANUEL KANT

## WHY WE THINK IN ABSTRACTIONS

One of the basic functions of the human mind is to create *abstractions.*

What if we had to have a separate name for every object we ever knew: for each candle, coin, animal, bell, seashell, cloud, and penguin? And a separate word for every single event we ever experienced: the strumming of a guitar, the meteor trail through the sky, the smell of a summer rain? If we were forced to have a different symbol for each object and each event, clearly we would be in trouble. In no time we would run out of words and our minds could not handle the clutter of separate items.

What do we do then? We place such singular items in groups. All the objects/events that have common qualities we group together into a single package with a single label. Once we have so packaged them, we no longer have to deal with the individual objects; we deal only with the whole package.

This is why we create abstractions. Abstractions are packages.

> *Probably a crab would be filled with a sense of personal outrage if it could hear us class it without ado or apology as a crustacean, and thus dispose of it. "I am no such thing," it would say; "I am myself, myself alone."*
> WILLIAM JAMES

An abstraction, by definition, is an idea created by the mind to refer to all objects which, possessing certain characteristics in common, are thought of in the same class. The number of objects in the class can range from two to infinity. We can refer to *all* men, *all* hurricanes, *all* books, *all* energy-forms—*all* everything.

Abstractions are formed at various levels of generalization. For instance, if we begin with an orange—a particular object as yet unclassified and unlabeled—then the first level of abstraction might be "Valencia orange," grouping together the qualities shared by all Valencia oranges. A next level might include all oranges (Valencia, the navels, sour oranges, and so forth); next might come all "citrus fruit" (including oranges, grapefruit, lemons, kumquats, and so forth). Still higher would come the whole basket of "fruit" (citrus fruit, figs, apples, apricots, breadfruit, etcetera). Above this level we might class together all "edible things," and more general still, a very-high-level abstraction, "material objects."

Notice how far we have come in the breadth of generalization: from a single orange to an all-inclusive class labeled "material objects." At each higher level of abstraction the objects have less and less in common. Yet such broad, general abstractions dominate our thinking and communicating. We think of fruits and vegetables, or food; we class together medicines, drugs, pollutants; we speak of nations, races of people, Hindus, Easterners, Eskimos, and so on.

*Jean Piaget tells of a little girl who was asked whether one might call the sun the moon and the moon the sun. She explained impatiently that no one could confuse the sun and the moon because the sun shines so brightly.*

While abstraction-building is an inescapable mental process—in fact it is the first step in the organization of our knowledge of objects/events—a serious problem is inherent in the process. At high levels of abstraction we tend to group together objects that have but a few qualities in common, and our abstractions may be almost meaningless, without our knowing it. We fall into the habit of using familiar abstractions and fail to realize how empty they are. For example, what do the objects in the following abstractions have in common? All atheists, all Western imperialists, all blacks or all whites (and if you think it's skin color, think twice), all conservatives, all trees, all French people, all Christians. When we think in such high-level abstractions, it is often the case that we are communicating nothing meaningful at all.

If, for example, I should send you to the grocery store with the request, "Buy some food for dinner," your response would probably be "Food? What sort

"Everyone must have a label."

of food?" To which I say, "Get some vegetables." You would still be quite in order to ask, "What vegetables do you want me to buy?" If I finally move down the abstraction ladder far enough to say "Get some vegetables for a salad," you would probably retort with an exasperated "*What* vegetables??" "Well, get a bunch of radishes, a head of lettuce, some green onions, and a cucumber." And, of course, you reply: "Why didn't you say that in the first place?!"

Note that *what we are talking about* becomes increasingly clear only as we move down the abstraction ladder toward the concrete objects of the world. By contrast, the individual who moves higher and higher on the abstraction ladder knows less and less what he is talking about, probably without knowing it. At high abstraction levels we can trade off, conveniently and in a most familiar fashion, with ominously vague meanings.

Dr. S. I. Hayakawa describes what we do: "The trouble with speakers who never leave the higher levels of abstraction is not only that they fail to notice when they are saying something and when they are not; they also produce a similar lack of discrimination in their audiences. Never coming down to earth, they frequently chase themselves around in verbal circles, unaware that they are making meaningless noises."

*Observers are not led by the same physical evidence to the same picture of the universe unless their linguistic backgrounds are similar or can in some way be calibrated.*

**Benjamin Lee Whorf**

## CLASSIFYING AND LABELING

The mind has another technique to enable it to assimilate information. It *classifies abstractions and labels them.* This is our mental filing system.

In his semantic textbook *Language in Thought and Action,* Dr. Hayakawa imagines a primitive village—your village—in which a variety of animals scamper about. Some of the animals have small bodies, some large. Some have round heads, while others have square heads. Some have curly tails, others straight tails. And such distinguishing marks are very important.

For you have discovered through experience that the animals with small bodies eat your grain, while those with large bodies do not. The small-bodied animals you have labeled *gogo* and you shoo them away; and when you call to a neighbor, "Quick, chase the gogo out of your garden!" he knows what you mean. The large-bodied animals (labeled *gigi*) are harmless, so you allow them to wander where they will.

S. I. Hayakawa

However, a visitor from another village has had a different experience. He has found that animals with square heads bite, while those with round heads do not. Since he has no gardens, their biting is a more noticeable characteristic than their habit of eating grain. The square-heads, which bite, he calls *dabas* and he scares them away. He generally ignores the round-headed *dobos.*

Still another man, a relative from a distant village, has found that the animals with curly tails kill snakes. Such animals are valuable; he calls them *busa* and breeds them for protection. But those with straight tails (which he calls *busana*) are merely a nuisance, and he is quite indifferent to them.

Now, one day villagers from far and near meet to trade and talk. You are sitting in on a barter-session when one of the animals runs by (let's say the animal marked *C* in the diagram, next page). You spot the animal headed for your garden, so you call down the path for someone to chase the *gogo* away. A visitor,

*Einstein: "Any fool can know. The point is . . . to understand!"*

**Ernest Kinoy**
***Doctor Einstein before Lunch***

Village animals redrawn from
S. I. Hayakawa, *Language in Thought and Action.*

however, looks at you with disdain, for he knows that the animal is a *dobo.* It has a round head. It doesn't bite, and he is surprised that you don't know this. A third visitor scornfully tells the both of you that the animal is clearly a *busana,* as everyone knows; it doesn't kill snakes or have any other redeeming qualities.

A heated discussion ensues as to what the animal really is. Is it a *gogo,* a *dobo,* or a *busana?* A quarrel is brewing as to what the animal *really is.*

It hardly helps when another tribesman, asking what the talk is all about, declares with finality that the animal (still *C*) is a "muglock" because it is edible and they feast on it every full moon. All the inedible animals in his village he labels *uglocks.*

This discussion finally ends where all such discussions finally end.

What is the animal *really?* What is *any* object, *really?* In the last analysis, all one can do is point to the object as if to say, "It is what it is." As Hayakawa puts it, "The individual object or event we are naming, of course, has no name and belongs to no class until we put it in one."

All the objects/events of our experience are classified in this manner: in terms of our experience of them. In the English language, for instance, we have two words that originated in the Middle Ages for the animal *Sus scrofa.* The word *swine* was the term used by the serfs and swineherds who had to tend them; the word *pork* was always employed by those who ate their succulent flesh at the banquet table.

Systems of classification, therefore, are *reflexive.* They inform us about the person who is doing the classifying—they tell us about *his* experience—and they tell us relatively little or nothing about the object classified. Classification never tells us what the classified object *really is.*

Classification systems are *pragmatic.* They are guidelines for operation. They tell us how to think about the object, how to treat it, use it, or relate to it. We classify objects and utilize the classification as long as the system is convenient; the moment it ceases to work, then we reclassify.

An understanding of these thought-processes—namely, the nature of classifying and labeling—provides an excellent criterion for distinguishing epistemic naivety from epistemic awareness.

A prescientific thinker has the unshakable belief that his classification tells him what the object really is and that names are by nature attached to the objects they refer to. It was a universal assumption made by the primitive mind that there is an intimate and *necessary* connection between the symbol and the object symbolized. Indeed, a mystical power was thought to reside in the

*Geological eras, periods, and epochs are human inventions; they are man's attempt to put huge stretches of time in their place and make them seem reasonably comprehensible. Nature was indifferent to such fine distinctions. Time flowed on continuously with one phase changing imperceptibly into another without dividing itself neatly into segments.*

PHILIP VAN DOREN STERN

symbol itself, and words were to be feared or desired in the same way the object/event referred to was to be feared or desired.

To attempt to persuade a primitive thinker that his classifications and labels are merely his mental tools, relative and arbitrary, would be a hopeless task. His own name is *Marika*, he will inform you, and it could not be otherwise. His god's name is *Mbwenu* and the deity can be called upon only by using his "right name." And, as everyone knows, a horse is a *horse* and a man is a *man*. How could it be otherwise?

People are "objects" from the standpoint of classification. If we lived in a small community and knew only a few people, we might find it possible to give each a separate name and deal with him as a singular personality. Our thinking might remain relatively concrete.

But in our modern world where we contact millions of people (personally and via various media) the temptation to move at high-level abstractions is enormous. As stated earlier, we do this because it simplifies our handling of vast amounts of data (or people). The bigger the bundles the better.

Therefore, we move very far from the individual person, just as we moved very far from the single orange we held in our hand. We package people into ever larger groups with fewer characteristics in common and refer to them under a single label: Asians, feminists, Muslims, doctors, lawyers, Arabs, liberals, conservatives, Germans, Catholics, Jews, Protestants, scientists, homosexuals, Palestinians, Republicans, child molesters, police, teachers, Israelis, cultists, evangelists, managers, workers, homophobics, Vietnamese, politicians, Japanese, African-Americans, Native Americans, endangered species, astronauts, Mexicans, Hispanics, Chicanos, Spanish, Latins, Americans, Malaysians, Chinese, racists, criminals, blacks, farmers, illegal aliens, Russians, citizens, Democrats, environmentalists, Palestinians . . . ad infinitum.

Not a single label listed above tells us about the object/person classified. It merely serves as a means of organizing our information about them and clues us in on how we should think about and relate to the individual so classified.

Do we need to be reminded that classification alone—arbitrary, unscientific classification—often means the difference between life and death?

Villagers from southeastern Laos were burned out of their homes as the war moved into their area; they escaped over the border into Vietnam. There they became a serious classification problem for Vietnamese officials: were they "escapees" or "refugees"? The difference? "Refugees" were permitted to remain in Vietnam, while "escapees" were forced to return. Which were they *really?*

In Nazi Germany, to be classified a "Jew" meant extermination. The classification was a fallacy: in Hitler's mind "Jewish" meant "Jewish race." There is no "Jewish race," of course. To be a "Jew" is to belong to a religion—Judaism. Hitler, however, is not the first or the last classifier to make such a mistake.

Ashley Montagu, among other anthropologists and ethnologists, has long reminded us that the concept of race is a fallacious myth—"our most dangerous myth." Physiological characteristics that we classify as "racial" are

*The human brain craves understanding. It cannot understand without simplifying, that is, without reducing things to a common element. However, all simplifications are arbitrary and lead us to drift insensibly away from reality.*

LECOMTE DU NOÜY

*If the doors of perception were cleansed, everything would appear to man as it is, infinite. For man has closed himself up till he sees all things through the narrow chinks of his cavern.*

WILLIAM BLAKE

*The subtlest and most pervasive of all influences are those which create and maintain the repertory of stereotypes. We are told about the world before we see it. We imagine most things before we experience them.*

WALTER LIPPMAN

## WE GET WHAT WE WANT

Society as a whole ultimately gets, on all issues of wide public importance, the classifications it wants, even if it has to wait until all the members of the Supreme Court are dead and an entirely new court is appointed. When the desired decision is handed down, people say, "Truth has triumphed." *In short, society regards as "true" those systems of classification that produce the desired results.*

The scientific test of "truth," like the social test, is strictly practical, except for the fact that the "desired results" are more severely limited. The results desired by society may be irrational, superstitious, selfish, or humane, but the results desired by scientists are only that our systems of classification produce predictable results. Classifications . . . determine our attitudes and behavior toward the object or event classified. When lightning was classified as "evidence of divine wrath," no courses of action other than prayer were suggested to prevent one's being struck by lightning. As soon, however, as it was classified as "electricity," Benjamin Franklin achieved a measure of control over it by his invention of the lightning rod. Certain physical disorders were formerly classified as "demonic possession," and it was suggested that we "drive the demons out" by whatever spells or incantations we could think of. The results were uncertain. But when those disorders were classified as "bacillus infections," courses of actions were suggested that led to more predictable results.

Science seeks only the *most generally useful* systems of classification; these it regards for the time being, until more useful classifications are invented, as "true."

S. I. HAYAKAWA
*Language in Thought and Action*

merely the result of environmental adaptation that took place as our presapient ancestors migrated in search of food and hospitable living conditions. If we could trace our genetic history, each and every one of us would find that we possess various blends of gene stock. A careful historical look will show only an everchanging series of gene pools.

Still, race remains one of our most pragmatic classifications, although it completely lacks scientific support. While it says nothing of the person classified, it makes quite clear how we are to think about him, treat him, deal with him, and use him. Could one expect a myth to be more useful than that?

It might be argued that some classification systems, such as scientific taxonomy, tell us much more precisely what the classified object really is. Such a claim would probably not be made, however, by either (1) a knowledgeable scientist, or (2) the object classified.

Scientists are quite aware that they have merely agreed on the criteria they will use for their system, namely, evolutionary kinship. When sufficient data are available, lines of evolutionary development can be traced, and the common characteristics of species, genera, families, orders, and so on, serve as workable criteria for ordering our knowledge. Scientific systems sometimes reveal facts about the classified objects: they tell us how they may relate (those of the same species can mate, those of different species cannot—except that this is not

*It seems that the human mind has first to construct forms independently before we can find them in things. . . . knowledge cannot spring from experience alone but only from this comparison of the inventions of the intellect with observed fact.*

ALBERT EINSTEIN

*By permission of Dennis Renault.*

"I forget, are we mesozoic or are we cenozoic?"

always the case); it tells us who might have been the ancestor of some animal or plant; it sometimes tells us (in the words themselves) about the physiology of the object ("vertebrate," "bony fishes," "mammals"). But such information lies in the labels we have chosen to use for the common characteristics we have selected for classifying. Again, as Hayakawa has said, no animal is a "vertebrate" until we put it in that "vertebrate" class.

It might be worth noting that for the animal classified, the scientific system probably means very little. If a queen conch is gliding through the sand at dusk in search of a meal, the classification "edible" holds more significance for a clam than its proper taxonomic status as "Chione undatella (Sowerby)."

*A big wild animal of the antelope family and known as the "Nehil Gae" was causing extensive damage to crops in the field. But the farmers would not harm it because "Nehil Gae" means "Blue Cow," and the cow is sacred to the Hindu. So the Indian Government has changed the name to "Nehil Goa"—which means "Blue Horse." Horses are not sacred, and so now the beast can be killed to protect the crops.*

**Associated Press**

## Our Mental Grids

The French philosopher Henri Bergson describes another way in which the mind handles its knowledge of reality.

The human intellect, notes Bergson, has one habit that stands in the way of its perceiving reality accurately: its propensity for chopping reality into fragments.

For example, the mind takes "time" and cuts it into discrete units: seconds, minutes, hours, days, weeks, seasons, years, decades, centuries, cosmic years, and so on. But time is a continuum, with no breaks, rhythms, or cycles. Our minds create *units of measurement* for the time-continuum so that we can conceive it in usable "lengths"; then we label these units and proceed to think in "units of time"; we may also begin to believe that such "units of time" are real. But where do "hours" exist? or "days"? or "years"? We have *defined* a year as the time it takes the earth to revolve once around the sun; but the earth would

ohm
ampere
watt
erg
gauss
oersted
coulomb
volt
lumen
hertz
acre
section
grain
gram
pound
ton
kilogram
angstrom
horsepower
bar
decibel
magnitude
psi
carat
degree F
degree C
degree K
degree
micron
meter
inch
foot
cubit
yard
mile
fathom
parsec
light-year
ounce
pint
fifth
quart
liter
gallon
bushel
electronvolt
BTU
calorie

millimeter
kilometer
millisecond
second
minute
hour
day
year
cosmic year
percent
cycles per
    second
miles per hour
parts per
    million
Richter scale
equator
radian
cubic inch
flux units
farad
rod
peck
dram
acre feet
caliber
jigger
mach number
barrel
furlong
knot
joule
atmosphere
century
millennium
octave
homer
ephah
mina
cord
darwin
rpm
megaton
frames per
    second
week
dyne
newton
decade
hands
smidgen

have gone on swinging in orbit for millions of "years" without being affected by our definition of its motion—as though the earth ripped off its December sheet as it passed a certain point in space.

And what about space and objects in space? We measure them. We have devised units without end to quantify distance and volume. For spatial distances: millimeters, inches, yards, meters, fathoms, miles, parsecs, light-years, and so on. We measure mass or volume with grams, ounces, pounds, tons, tablespoons, cubic centimeters, acre-feet, a "pinch" of salt, and a "dash" of pepper.

Such units are created by our minds to help us reduce the environment to usable proportions; they enable us to conceive small bits of reality at a time (the mind cannot possibly think of *all* matter at once).

But after reflection, could any of us believe that such "units of measurement" exist as part of the real world? Just ask: "Please give me eighteen millimeters." Eighteen millimeters of what? "I need five minutes. Can you get it for me?" Five minutes of what? "Time," of course, but once measured, what exactly do you have?

One must conclude that such units exist in the mind, and only in the mind. Such mental units serve to parcel out our environment into practicable quantities.

Look at a globe of the earth and note the lines that criss-cross it. There are pole-to-pole lines we *call* meridians, and lines parallel to the "equator" we *call* latitudinal lines; then there are anomalous lines dividing colored areas. Thus, with a marked globe we have *organized* the earth so that our minds can think about it. ("Where is Bolivia?" "Point out the Arctic circle." "Locate the magnetic pole.") How else could the intellect deal with the earth except in pieces?

In a planetarium, it is of great help to have a celestial grid overlaying the stars on the dome, or to have a projected image linking together the stars in a constellation. When such grids are not used, the thousands of patternless points of light are scattered at random and we cannot remember or make sense of them. Since the mind must organize the points of light, it "draws" connecting lines. So a small square is seen in Hercules, a triangle in Aquarius; or we see several stars whose pattern reminds us of some known object (Aquila the Eagle, Delphinus the Dolphin). In just this way the ancient skywatchers organized the random bits of light they saw nightly.

In the planetarium, the grid lights can be turned off, reminding us that the grid is only a mental tool for organizing our experience. In no way could one mistake the grid as a part of the real sky.

In this manner, however, the mind places grids on all that it perceives.

What remains when all the mind's "grids" are turned off? Reality—unmeasured, undivided. A continuum of matter in motion and time undisturbed. No days or weeks; no miles or parsecs. To be sure, there do exist in the real world a multitude of rhythms and cycles, and we attempt to coordinate our mental "units of measurement" with these natural rhythms.

Our minds, says Bergson, can indeed "move through" all the pragmatic grids and intuit the nature of reality itself. By a sort of "intellectual empathy" we can come to know the ever-changing, endlessly moving continuum which *is* reality. But to do this we almost have to tell the intellect to cease and desist in its persistent habit of reducing the universe to discrete, manageable units.

To know what the real world is like, therefore, we must turn off the grid lights and let the stars shine. Reality *is,* and that is all.

*Sky maps from The Sky Observer's Guide, by John Polgreen*

## REFLECTIONS

1   What do you think of the drawing by Abner Dean on p. 214: "Everyone must have a label"? Is this really true?

2   What is the point that Walter Lippman is making about the way we maintain our habit of stereotyping (see marginal quote on p. 217)? Do you agree? How might we cease and desist in this way of thinking?

3   What is an *abstraction?* How many single objects belonging to a class must you experience before you can develop an abstraction? Then what is the relationship of the abstraction to the particular objects? Can you go as far as Plato in holding that abstractions have a real status quite apart from our minds? If you can, where are the real ideas located? If you cannot then what

(CONTINUED ON P. 226)

*The theater of my mind has a seating capacity of just one, and it's sold out for all performances.*

HENRY WINKLER
*Tribute to Richard Rodgers*

*With clarity and quiet, I look upon the world and say: All that I see, hear, taste, smell and touch are the creations of my mind.*

NIKOS KAZANTZAKIS

# HENRI BERGSON

## *What It Means to Be a Hummingbird*

Henri Bergson often spoke in the great lecture hall at the Collège de France where he taught, and huge crowds gathered to hear him. He would emerge quietly from the back of the hall and make his way to the platform. He was tall and slender, dressed in a dark suit, a cutaway collar, and black tie. Charismatic, confident, reserved, and a little mysterious, he moved with easy grace. As he took his seat on the rostrum an expectant silence would settle over the audience.

Sitting under a shaded lamp, his features appeared delicate and refined. He was a handsome man with a high forehead, a lingering halo of light hair, and a barely visible mustache. His bright eyes flashed beneath bushy brows. He would place his hands together, fingertips touching, and begin speaking modestly but firmly, in elegant French. He used no manuscript or notes. His speech was casually paced and dignified; his cadences were measured and musical. He began, as always, with a humorous anecdote, and by the time the audience recovered from their laughter they found themselves caught up in the subject matter and were listening intently. He was the master of his craft: his entire presentation seemed effortless and natural.

What they heard was a philosophy that had the promise, some said and many hoped, of bringing about a revolution in the ideas we live by. At the turn of the century men and women were searching for a better understanding of themselves and why they are here. They were tired of the downbeat determinism bandied within intellectual circles, according to which human beings had lost their free will; they were merely cogs in a mechanistic universe. Robbed of freedom and spirit, they had lost the feeling of being special, of having a place in the sun a little lower than the angels.

In the midst of the shadows, Bergson rose like a shining light. By all accounts he burst upon the world with a creative energy that lifted people's spirits and cleansed their souls. He told them that the world (through evolution) has purpose and meaning, and assured them that God (as the *élan vital*) is still there. He made it intellectually respectable to believe that human beings could be free, responsible, fully human, and immortal. He was an original thinker, a persuasive speaker, and almost a prophet.

Bergson's life, it is frequently said, was only an adventure of the mind. In a letter to William James he himself wrote, "Now as to events worthy of note, there have been none in the course of my career, at least nothing *objectively* remarkable." But he was being unduly modest, for his lifetime was in fact a series of triumphs and tragedies, filled with adventure.

He was born October 18, 1859, in Paris and christened Henri-Louis Bergson. His father Michael Bergson, of Polish extraction, was by trade a musician and composer, successful enough to be for a time the head of the Geneva Conservatory. His mother Katherine Levinson, also bright and talented was from England. Thus, Henri, without a drop of Gallic blood, was always perceived—as he perceived himself—to be very French; and France took pride in him as the finest representative of the best in French culture. He was bilingual in French and English from childhood.

He was educated at the *lycées* (secondary schools) in Paris where he excelled in every field, though mathematics and the sciences were special loves. One of his schoolmates later recalled that in these years Henri was a fragile youth, utterly charming, innocent, honest, sensitive to the feelings of others, but slightly detached or withdrawn, more an observer of the human parade than a participant.

At eighteen he entered the École Normale Supérieure in Paris in Hellenistic classics. He arranged to have himself appointed student librarian so he could spend as much time as possible in the company of his beloved books; there was a small secluded room off the library where he could usually be found. While others were caught up in fashionable issues, Bergson avoided making public pronouncements and taking stands; he wanted to examine critically the thinking involved in controversial issues in order to understand why ideas conflict.

After graduation he became a professor of philosophy in the provinces, first at Angers for two years, then at Clermont-Ferrand. He was much loved by his students, and he was in love with his work. At the age of thirty he returned to Paris as a professor of philosophy at the Collège Rollin and then at the Collège Henri IV. At thirty-one he was married to Louise Neuberger, and friends described their marriage as one of uninterrupted happiness. They gave birth to one daughter, born deaf, who later became a painter.

At the age of thirty-nine Bergson returned to his alma mater, the École Normale, and taught there for two years. In 1900, at the age of forty-one, he joined the faculty of the Collège de France, occupying a chair first in Greek philosophy, then in modern philosophy. There he stayed until 1914. These were the years of his greatest accomplishments. Already famed for his books *Time and Free Will* and *Matter and Memory,* he continued to write and speak. He wrote a delightful book on laughter, *Le rire,* which is still quoted in textbooks on humor and comedy. In 1907 he published *Creative Evolution,* which brought him international fame and for which, twenty years later, he received the Nobel Prize. He traveled widely, lecturing in Italy, England, and America. In 1914 three of his works were placed on the Roman Catholic Index of Prohibited Works by the Holy Office. Also in 1914 he was elected to the French Academy.

World War I broke out in 1914, and the academic life was disrupted. In 1917 Bergson was sent to the United States to persuade the president to enter the war. In 1921, because of ill health, he retired from public life and became an honorary professor of the Collège de France. During the last twenty years of his life he was incapacitated with severe headaches; he ceased all public speaking and wrote only with great difficulty.

◆

Early in his reflective life, Bergson came to the idea that the primary function of human intelligence is to go to the heart of things, to understand

*Wherever joy is, creation has been.*

*Beyond the ideas that have grown set and cold in language we must seek the movement and the warmth of life.*

*Only those ideas that are least truly ours can be adequately expressed in words.*

*For a conscious being, to exist is to change, to change is to mature, to mature is to go on creating oneself endlessly.*

objects/events in the real world exactly as they are; and "exactly as they are" implies penetrating to the essence of things as functional systems. Human intelligence has been developed by the evolutionary process to transcend the self, to jump out of its own skin and enter into the objects/events of the world and to know them. This is the *raison d'être* of human intelligence, and it must not be thwarted.

But now, the crux and the dilemma: When the mind gets down to the task of knowing things in the world about us, it finds that there are two ways of knowing an object: through intellect and through intuition. "The first implies going all around it, the second entering into it. The first depends on the viewpoint chosen and the symbols employed, while the second is taken from no viewpoint and rests on no symbol." The first, says Bergson, gives us relative knowledge; the second enables us to attain knowledge that is absolute and true.

You are in a boat at sea, leaning against the mast, watching the gently undulating waves. You open your Polaroid camera and take a snapshot of the ocean. Sometime later, when you show the picture to a friend, you announce epistemologically, "This is the ocean."

But is it? Bergson tells us that the still picture has necessarily missed the story of what the ocean is all about. You can *experience* the ocean, but you cannot take a *still* picture of it. What you experienced as you watched the ocean is motion, unceasing motion, eternal motion: giant waves rolling as they have rolled for billions of years; smaller waves on and between the big ones; millions of wavelets, churned by wind and water, never stopping. Once you experience, once you *feel* what the ocean is really like, it can overwhelm. Perpetual motion through aeons of time: this is what the ocean *is*.

The snapshot, then, is a static picture that eliminates motion from the dynamic system. It stopped, it froze, and if you will, it killed a living thing; it can-

not, in reality, depict *the ocean* at all.

Human intelligence has been dominated throughout Western history by the intellectual mode of knowing. The intellect sees everything from the outside. We see other people and all other creatures and objects—from elephants to butterflies, from trees to mountains and stars—from the outside. All our seeing is from a standpoint that is necessarily external to the objects/events themselves. This perspective seems obvious and natural to us. How could it be otherwise?

Bergson is not denying the ability of the intellect to make an in-depth plunge, however. Take that hummingbird perched on the pine bough. Our sciences can supply us with an unending collection of detailed data about it. Anatomy can tell us about its bone structure, musculature, and so on. Physiology can tell us about its digestive system and reproductive system. Animal psychology will tell us about its courtship dives, territoriality, and the like. Physics and optics can tell us about the flashing irridescences of its feathers. And so on, almost ad infinitum. All this information from the intellect demonstrates the unending power of the mind to construct (collect) bits and pieces of data which, taken together, add up to an impressive understanding of the little creature.

So, what's wrong with all this?

What's wrong, Bergson keeps saying, is that we have missed what it means to be a hummingbird. The *essence* of hummingbird is *to experience life—as a hummingbird.* No matter how vast the accumulation of data *about* the hummingbird, to see the hummingbird *from the outside* and convince ourselves that we have comprehended the hummingbird is wrongheaded. How would we react to someone who perceives us only from the outside, who has not a hint of appreciation of what we are experiencing, and who still insists that he knows what we are all about? Most of us would signal our impatience with such a shallow claim. But, argues Bergson, this is precisely what we do all the time.

*The universe . . . is a machine for creating gods.*

*The major task of the twentieth century will be to explore the unconscious, to investigate the subsoil of the mind.*

*[Intuition is] the legitimate and noble province of the mind; indeed it is the only means for perceiving the heart of things.*

*But one thing is sure: we sympathize with ourselves.*

In several of his books and dozens of essays and articles, Bergson analyzed the operations of the intellect; he feels that we are so deeply conditioned with this way of looking at the world that he needs to dislodge us from our conceits. Like the fish that cannot possibly know that it swims in water because it spends its life immersed in it, we are immersed in a one-sided way of looking at the world.

The intellect's limitations, he submits, are not merely bad habits absorbed from our culture; they are inherent in its native operations. By its nature, it cannot carry out the mandate given to it by our intelligence. It does, however, have a pragmatic mission which it can do very well: (1) it can organize our experience through static concepts; and (2) it can package our experiences for processing, storage, and retrieval.

But, happily, the mind has another faculty for knowing: intuition. Knowledge by intuition is direct and absolute, according to Bergson. "When I speak of an absolute movement, it means that I attribute to the mobile an inner being and, as it were, states of soul; it also means that I am in harmony with these states and enter into them by an effort of the imagination." The intuitive faculty doesn't come at an object from the outside, but from the inside; and it is a valid process, says Bergson, whether we are intuiting another person, a hummingbird, a flower, or a rock. "We call intuition here the *sympathy* by which one is transported into the interior of an object in order to coincide with what there is unique and consequently inexpressible in it."

In Western philosophy "metaphysics" has been defined as the study of ultimate reality, the attempt to find out what the ultimate substance and structure of the world truly is. This is the goal of the empirical tradition in the West and, of course, it has been carried on by the left-brained intellect. Now Bergson is telling us that such a metaphysics has

been predestined to fail because reality lies beyond the grasp of the intellect. "But a true empiricism is the one which purposes to keep as close to the original itself as possible, to probe more deeply into its life, and by a kind of spiritual *auscultation,* to feel its soul palpitate; and this true empiricism is the real metaphysics." The analytic intellect, bent on packaging, will generalize. "But an empiricism worthy of the name, an empiricism which works only according to measure, sees itself obliged to make an absolutely new effort for each new object it studies. It cuts for the object a concept appropriate to the object alone, a concept one can barely say is still a concept since it applies only to that one thing."

◆

Three acts of courage marked Henri Bergson's last months. The first was a decision he made as early as 1937. Having thought of himself as a Frenchman for a lifetime, and having arrived at the point where he was having thoughts of becoming a Christian, he wrote that he wished to be counted as a Jew since he had "foreseen for years a formidable wave of anti-Semitism about to break upon the world. I wanted to remain among those who tomorrow were to be persecuted."

Then, in 1940, the Vichy government issued laws barring Jews from holding educational posts in France, but Bergson, because of his stature and fame, was specifically exempted. But Bergson refused to accept the exemption and proceeded to renounce all his honors lest a passive submission be interpreted as support for the puppet government.

Then a few weeks before his death, bedridden and unable to stand, he rose from his bed, stood in a queue on the arm of a servant, and, along with all other Jews in France, registered as a *Judischer.* In the December air he caught a cold that turned into pneumonia. He died January 4, 1941.

*The end and aim of all research is the comprehension of reality—the recognizing of reality and the forming of our minds upon it as a model. Reality is like an immense forest strewn with impediments of all kinds, through which the seeker, like the woodcutter, must open up trails.*

*If we do not begin by giving a glance at the whole, if we pass at once to the consideration of the parts, we may perhaps see very well, but we do not know what we are looking at.*

*[Philosophy] attaches no value to truth passively received; it would have each one of us reconquer truth by reflexion, earn it by effort; and, embracing it in the depths of our own self and animating it with our own life, lend it strength enough to fertilize thought and direct the will.*

exactly is the relationship between any two objects in the same class? (That is, two warblers that belong to different species but belong to the same family *are* related, are they not? What relates them?)

4    What is a muglock? How does it differ from a dobo and a busana?

5    When an object is classified, what does the classification tell us about the object, and what does it tell us about the classifier?

6    Discuss with your self (and other selves, if available) the marginal quote on p. 219 regarding the "Nehil Gae." Now reflect very thoroughly on the problem of classification. Critique. Insights? Comments?

7    Could we do away entirely with our habit of classifying? What benefits would we gain by eliminating the habit? What would we lose? What is the answer to the problem?

8    Summarize in your words the point Bergson is making when he tells us that our minds have a habit of "chopping reality into fragments." Is this meaningful to you personally? Could Bergson's insights lead you to change your way of seeing and thinking about reality?

# 3
4

## TRUTH-TESTS

Truth-tests are used for checking and double checking the things people say so that we can decide if their statements are true or false. With such tests we can verify or falsify the fact-claims that they make.

There are three truth-tests.

## THE CORRESPONDENCE-TEST

One method of checking fact-claims is by the *correspondence-test,* whose development is attributed to Bertrand Russell. This test requires one to check a subjective mental concept against a real object/event, and if the concept "corresponds to" the real object/event, then the concept is considered to be true.

Quite simply, if someone tells you that there is a solar eclipse in progress in your area, you can look at the sun; and he is either right or wrong. If you can observe a crescent sun, then his statement can be accepted; if you cannot, his statement is false. You have checked it personally and established to your satisfaction the accuracy of the statement. If there was indeed a correspondence between the mental concept of an eclipse and an actual event taking place, then the fact-claim has become a fact.

A whole class of fact-claims are easily checked this way. "The book you are after is in Section B-16 in the bookstore." *Go look.* "On this side of the tape are selections from Puccini's *Madame Butterfly.*" *Play the tape and listen.* "Some prankster mixed salt and sugar in the sugarbowl." *Taste and find out.* "His pulse is very slow." *Feel it and count.* "The coals are ready for the steak." *Look*

*What is Truth but to live for an idea? . . . It is a question of discovering a truth which is truth for me, of finding the idea for which I am willing to live and die.*

**SØREN KIERKEGAARD**

Bertrand Russell (1872–1970)

*Better the world should perish than that I, or any other human being, should believe a lie; . . . that is the religion of thought, in whose scorching flames the dross of the world is being burnt away.*

**BERTRAND RUSSELL**

*The falseness of an opinion is not for us any objection to it . . . The question is how far it is life-furthering, life-preserving, species-preserving, perhaps species-creating.*

**FRIEDRICH NIETZSCHE**

*Assume coherence as the test, and you will be driven by the incoherence of your alternatives to the conclusion that it is also the nature of truth.*

**BRAND BLANSHARD**

at them glow red and feel the heat. "This watermelon is ripe and ready." *Feel it, thump it and listen to the thump, plug it, smell it, and taste it.* All the senses can't be wrong—can they?

To apply the correspondence-test, two things are involved: (1) a subjective mental concept, and (2) a real object/event to which the mental concept corresponds. The following precautions must be taken seriously when checking fact-claims with the correspondence-test.

1.   We have already noted some of the mind's imaginative operations and the way it creates concepts. No created concept is ever an exact replica of any external object/event. The mind selects a few elements of any object/event to assimilate into the model that it will use for thinking. Furthermore, we have seen that all the physical events that exist in the real world are translated by our transducers into quite different experiential phenomena.

Remembering all this, we must conclude that no mental concept can ever correspond 100 percent with objects/events. Rather, we have only a degree of correspondence between the two. If the degree of correspondence is high, we hold the fact-claim to be true; if it is not, we decide it is false. Where the breakoff point is along that scale of correspondence would be the subject of endless debate.

2.   Since, in the last analysis, we are limited to our own subjective experiencing world, how is it possible for us to harmonize a subjective concept (which we can experience) with a real object/event (which we cannot directly experience)? The answer, of course, is we cannot. What then does the correspondence-test really do? It compares a concept with a set of sensations—the sensations we use when we go about inferring what exists in the real world. Therefore, we are checking a subjective concept with a subjective set of sensations. If they match to some tolerable degree, then we call the concept true; if they don't, we call it false.

This is really not a happy condition to live with, but given our present knowledge of cognitive processes, the predicament seems inescapable. It looks as though—on this test at least—we can never be completely certain of anything.

## THE COHERENCE-TEST

There is an obvious limitation to the use of the correspondence-test. The real world has to be directly accessible for observation; otherwise there is nothing real against which one can check his concept. In such cases a second checkout method—the coherence-test—might be applicable.

According to the *coherence-test,* a fact-claim can be accepted as true if it harmonizes (coheres) with other facts that one has *already* accepted as true. Like the previous test, this is a routine kind of test we use every day.

"There are sharks in Lake Mead." No, that can't be, and I don't have to go to Lake Mead to check the fact-claim with the correspondence-test; for I already know that sharks can't live in fresh water, and Lake Mead is a freshwater lake. The fact-claim just can't be made to harmonize with other known facts.

(I have now been informed that freshwater sharks do indeed exist. So, what does this do to my use of coherence as a truth-test? I am warned, first, that a fact-claim may nicely cohere with a set of firmly held fictions, and that I could easily become dogmatic in my belief in, and defense of, ideas that are dead wrong. I am also alerted to the fact that the coherence truth-test is useful only to the degree that my previously accepted "facts" are supported by a broad base of empirical evidence. Thirdly, I am struck by the fact that I can never be 100 percent sure of *any* fact-claim.)

"When I looked into the mirror, I couldn't see myself. I have lost my reflection!" We would reject such a statement with hardly a second thought. We have read of such fantasies in *Tales of Hoffmann,* and Alice just might be able to manage it. But in the real world of human experience such a fact-claim doesn't harmonize with any experience I know. We will happily keep such "facts" in the world of make-believe.

"Alexander the Great never returned to Rome because he fell in love with Cleopatra and spent the rest of his life in Egypt." No, these fact-claims can't be made to cohere with other previously known data. Alexander died in 323 B.C. and he was certainly no Roman; and Cleopatra died about 30 B.C. Now, it might be possible to substitute Antony for Alexander, and the fact-claims would then cohere with one another.

The coherence-test is applicable to large areas of knowledge that are not accessible to personal observation. Two such areas are (1) fact-claims relating to the past ("history"), which is never available for observation, and (2) all contemporary events that we cannot personally witness. This applies to practically all the information we get via television, newspapers, and magazines. A very large percentage of the events that "make news" takes place too far away for us to observe, so we test them by making them cohere with the facts we already know.

The coherence-test has a serious weakness. A new fact-claim may fit coherently with a large number of previously accepted "facts" *all of which are untrue;* or, similarly, a new fact that is *true* may be rejected because it cannot be made to harmonize with one's set of previously accepted false fact-claims.

In other words, it is about as easy to build an elaborate coherent system that is false as an elaborate coherent system that is true. Unless previously accepted data are well supported by evidence, the truth-status of that new "fact" remains in doubt, no matter how well it fits in.

This point has historical significance. System-building has been the stock-in-trade of philosophers, theologians, political theorists, et al. It has been a common practice to rewrite history from the point of view of some ideology; facts can be selected, interpreted, and squeezed into almost any framework. Resulting systems may be highly coherent, therefore, yet bear little resemblance to anything in the real world.

## THE PRAGMATIC-TEST

There is a third test which, like the coherence-test, is wholly subjective in that it requires nothing immediately accessible in the real world to serve as

*Truth is the approximation of thought to reality. It is thought on its way home. Its measure is the distance thought has travelled, under guidance of its inner compass, toward that intelligible system which unites its ultimate object with its ultimate end.*

**BRAND BLANSHARD**

*Begin by believing with all your heart that your belief is true, so that it will work for you; but then face the possibility that it is really false, so that you can accept the consequences of the belief.*

**JOHN RESECK**

Charles S. Peirce (1839–1914)

*Convictions are more danger-ous enemies of truth than lies.*

FRIEDRICH NIETZSCHE

*At ebb tide I wrote*
*A line upon the sand*
*And gave it all my heart*
*And all my soul.*
*At flood tide I returned*
*To read what I had inscribed*
*And found my ignorance*
*   upon the shore.*

KAHLIL GIBRAN

validating criteria for the mental concept. This is the *pragmatic-test,* and in some ways it is the most complex of the three.

This test was developed by the American philosopher-psychologist William James, but the seminal idea came from Charles S. Peirce. In an article published in 1878, Peirce (pronounced like "purse") attempted to answer the question, "What makes ideas meaningful?" He was interested in clarifying the source and nature of meaning. In his article he concluded that ideas are meaningful if they make some difference in our experience. As Peirce put it, "our idea of anything *is* our idea of its sensible effects. . . . " If we say ice is cold or a match flame is hot, those *ideas* are meaningful only because they relate in a predictive way to what we would experience if we touched the ice or the flame. The ideas have meaning in relation to effects. If we could not touch the ice or the flame, the ideas would be meaningless.

This was a *theory of meaning* only, but William James saw deeper implications in the theory and developed it into a *test of truth.* In 1898, in an address delivered at the University of California at Berkeley, James presented his theory of pragmatism: The truth-value of any idea is to be determined by the results; a "true" idea brings about desired effects. In short—and somewhat more ambiguously—if an idea works, then it is true.

Peirce had labeled his theory of meaning pragmatism, but when he heard what James had done to his theory by changing it into a test of truth, Peirce was upset. He rechristened his theory of meaning with such an "ugly name," as he said, that no one would ever kidnap his theory again. He called it "pragmaticism." We now associate "pragma*tism*" with William James and John Dewey, and "pragmati*cism*" with Peirce.

The pragmatic-test can be used to check out fact-claims in several different areas of knowledge, and we find that the *function* of the test is different in each. This is why the test presents serious problems.

First, note our routine use of the pragmatic-test. We use it to check the workability of our ideas and hypotheses, even our guesses and hunches. It is an integral part of our trial-and-error way of solving daily problems.

If, for instance, you turn on your TV set and nothing happens, then you are forced into creating a hypothesis to find out what is wrong. Your first hypothesis may be that the cord is not plugged in. So you check it. It is plugged in, so your hypothesis is wrong. So, since that hypothesis did not work, you proceed to another one. Perhaps something is wrong inside the TV set. You check the warmup tube and find it cold, so you conclude that electricity is not getting into the set. Now the problem begins to look serious (that is, the solution may cost you time and/or money). You are on your way to the telephone to call a TV repairman when you notice that the nightlight by the telephone is off. You check and find other lights off. So, new hypothesis: a circuit breaker must have been tripped. You check. All fuses are in the "ON" position except one. You flip this one to "ON" and power is restored.

By empirical means, you gradually developed a hypothesis that accounted for all the facts. You were forced to collect more and more data before you could develop a workable hypothesis—that is, a hypothesis on the basis of which the TV problem could be corrected. Happily, the hypothesis that finally worked will cost you little time and no money.

This illustrates the essential claim of pragmatism: the idea that *works* is the *true* one.

Our ideas have a profound effect on how we feel and behave. This fact is fundamental to all of man's religions, and here we discover the rationale for "faith" and "belief."

William James knew from personal experience the pragmatic process he was attempting to formulate into a philosophy. Having been reared in a family fraught with emotional instability, James was plagued for most of his life with psychophysical illnesses that he came to believe to be fatalistically determined. Hence he thought that he could do nothing to change his condition.

But in 1870 he read an essay by a French philosopher that convinced him that he possessed personal freedom. He was persuaded that his life had not been determined irrevocably for him; he really could change the course of his life. *An idea—the idea that he was personally free—had taken hold of him.* On April 30, 1870, James wrote in his notebook: "I think that yesterday was a crisis in my life. . . . My first act of free will shall be to believe in free will."

What about the "truth-value" of a belief powerful enough to prevent one from opting for suicide? Whatever the *rationale* within the belief—that one's time has not yet come, that one has not yet accomplished one's purpose in life, that one should not cause others to suffer, or that taking one's life is morally wrong—whatever the rationale, isn't this belief true? Isn't the truth of ideas to be found in the results they effect? Or, as James so pungently put it, do we not judge the worth of ideas by their "cash value"?

Pragmatism's only test of truth is what works best, wrote James.

> *The best ideas are the ideas that help people.*
>
> **ITT TV Commercial**

> *To say that Newton's law of gravitation is true is to say that it can be applied successfully; so long as that could be done, it was true. There is no inconsistency in saying that Newton's law was true and that Einstein's law is at present true.*
>
> **HECTOR HAWTON**
> *(describing Pragmatism)*

> *When all else fails, follow the directions.*
>
> **AMERICAN PROVERB**

---

## CAN TRUTH BE RELATIVE?

In pondering the relativity of truth, Plato pointed out in the *Theaetetus* that the relativistic position is a paradox: "The best of the joke is, that Protagoras acknowledges the truth of their opinion who believe his opinion to be false; for in admitting that the opinions of all men are true, in effect he grants that the opinion of his opponents is true."

In their book *Realms of Philosophy*, the Drs. Sahakian summarize the dilemma in the following composed dialogue:

PROTAGORAS.    Plato, what is true for you, is true for you, and what is true for me, is true for me.

PLATO.    Do you mean to say that my personal opinion is true?

PROTAGORAS.    Indeed, that is precisely what I mean.

PLATO.    But, my dear Protagoras, my opinion is that truth is not relative; truth is not a matter of opinion, but objective and absolute. Furthermore, my opinion is that your belief in the relativity of truth is absolutely false and should be abandoned. Do you still hold that my opinion is true?

PROTAGORAS.    Yes, you are quite correct.

Which truth-test does Protagoras seem to be using? Which is Plato using? Can you suggest how they might come to an agreement on the "relativity" of truth?

Plato (427–347 B.C.)

If theological ideas should do this, if the notion of God, in particular, should prove to do it, how could pragmatism possibly deny God's existence? It could see no meaning in treating as "not true" a notion that was pragmatically so successful.

## THE PRAGMATIC PARADOX

The *pragmatic paradox* may be stated thus: For an idea to work pragmatically, one must believe that it is true on other than pragmatic criteria. Now, if we *define* "truth" as an idea that works (that is, that brings about desired results), then we have no serious problem. If an idea works, then it is true; and conversely, if an idea is true, then it works.

But this is not yet the heart of the matter. For an idea or belief to work *pragmatically*, we must believe it in terms of *correspondence*. This kind of insight can become a blessing or a bad dream.

For instance, for the belief in immortality to become a sustaining belief (that is, *to work*), one must accept that immortality exists in reality; one must believe that there is an objective event corresponding to the concept. Even though we may not be able to check out the belief with the correspondence-test, if it is not believed on a *correspondence* basis then the belief can have no *pragmatic* results.

What if you should say to yourself: "I have no evidence that souls survive death, but I want to experience the benefits of the belief in immortality (strength, courage, comfort), so I will accept the belief on a pragmatic basis. I will *believe* in immortality and make the idea work for me." What are the chances of making the idea "work"? For most of us, very poor indeed. (Incidentally, we see clearly here the role of the authority in our lives, the charismatic figure who can persuade us to believe *on his authority* that an idea is objectively true; this way we can manage to believe, without empirical evidence, what we wanted and needed to believe to begin with but could not accomplish on our own.)

One must believe in immortality "with all his heart." With equal conviction one must "know" that a loving Father-God does in fact exist (that is, that God is real); then the belief can be true pragmatically. Likewise, if the devout Muslim knows that Allah endows him with courage in battle, then he will not falter as the Holy War is waged. And the kamikaze pilot could look forward with patriotic fervor to the moment when he could dive his Suisei bomber onto the deck of an aircraft carrier, since he knew beyond doubt that he would return in spirit directly to the Yasukuni Shrine and be visited by family and friends. (See the letter written by the kamikaze pilot on p. 592.)

If one believes these ideas to be objectively true, they become pragmatically true.

*The truth is great, but there's a time and a place for everything.*

LORI VILLAMIL

A "fact" that is true according to one truth-test may be false according to another.

For instance, a Muslim would say, "There is no God but Allah" (this fact-claim is a part of the Islamic Creed). Is such a statement true? Check it with the three truth-tests. You can be sure of three things: (1) The Muslim accepts his belief on a pragmatic basis; that is, his faith in Allah works for him. Therefore, *for him*, the statement is true on the pragmatic-test. (2) He also accepts his belief in Allah on the coherence-test; that is, the belief undoubtedly coheres with numerous other accepted data from the Quran and Islamic tradition (the Hadith). Therefore, *for him*, the statement is true on the coherence-test. (3) While it would be extremely difficult or impossible to discover the real object/event referred to as "Allah" so that the correspondence-test could be applied, you can be quite sure that the Muslim *believes* that such a real object/event exists.

*So, is the fact-claim true or false?*

Now, if you should reply, "I don't believe that your statement is true," what exactly are you saying? (1) Using the pragmatic-test, you are stating that the concept of Allah is not meaningful to you, hence not true *for you*. (2) Using the coherence-test, you are stating that belief in Allah does not harmonize with facts you have accepted as true. Where can you fit such a fact-claim into the Jewish, Christian, atheistic, or scientific world-view? It is false, therefore, *for you*. (3) Using the correspondence-test, you are stating that you do not think "Allah" is real. If the Muslim claims that Allah is real, we often respond with the challenge, "Prove it"—meaning show us *by the correspondence-test* that there is a real object/event called "Allah." Of course, he cannot.

Therefore, we think we have won our case. Using only the correspondence-test, you retort that the Muslim's fact-claim is untrue. His statement about "Allah" is false. *And yet, on the other two criteria—the pragmatic and coherence—the fact-claim is undeniably true . . . for the Muslim.*

So again we ask: Is the fact-claim true or false?

We frequently find ourselves caught in interminable arguments where no meeting of minds takes place—as would undoubtedly happen in the case of the Muslim's claims about Allah. If we can cease to argue long enough to clarify our thinking, we would often find that different truth-tests are being used to support fact-claims.

It is good advice, therefore, to examine carefully the truth-tests being used (or merely assumed). If indeed one individual is using the correspondence-test as the only acceptable criterion for verifying "facts" while another is relying on pragmatic criteria or is caught in the pragmatic paradox, it is no wonder that such discussions end in fruitless stalemates. We are left with frustration because the other person can not accept what is so obviously true to us.

Examination of the truth-tests will disclose three points worth noting.

1. All three tests are constantly used by all of us and are indispensable to thinking and communicating. Each has its sphere of legitimate operation.
2. Each truth-test has intrinsic problems. We cannot be absolutely sure of any "fact" on any test. We are forced to conclude that "truth" is a probability item, with greater or lesser degrees of likelihood attached to various specific fact-claims.
3. This being the case, all truth is tentative. It is always subject to further modification and refinement as new fact-claims are verified and become facts.

*Grant an idea or belief to be true, what concrete difference will its being true make in any one's actual life? How will the truth be realized? What experiences will be different from those which would obtain if the belief were false? What, in short, is the truth's cash-value in experiential terms?*

**WILLIAM JAMES**

## REFLECTIONS

1   Thomas Merton wrote: "No one is so wrong as the man who knows all the answers (see marginal quote on p. 227). This may sound like a pearl or a truism. But is it essentially a true statement? In what sense is it true or untrue? Do you think Socrates would agree? (By the way, "knows all the answers" *to what?*)

2   Contrast the position stated in the quotations from Nietzsche and Russell (see marginal quotes on p. 228) by rephrasing their ideas in your own words. Which (if either) do you tend to agree with? Why? Can these extreme statements be reconciled? Or does the problem reduce to a matter of relative values?

3   Describe the use of the correspondence-test. Under what specific conditions can it be used? What are its principal weaknesses? Can you think of any steps we can take to increase its degree of accuracy?

4   Describe the use of the coherence-test. In what specific areas, or under what conditions, does it become the primary truth-test? In what fallacious ways is the coherence-test often used?

5   Describe the use of the pragmatic truth-test as it applies to the development of hypotheses to account for empirical events (such as the nonworking TV set). In what ways must we be wary of its misuse?

6   When applied to nonempirical concepts, the pragmatic test of truth functions in quite a different way than when it is used to explain empirical data. Describe what it is that makes a concept, belief, or doctrine pragmatically true. (You may recall examples from your own experience similar to those of William James.)

7   Can you see a way out of the pragmatic paradox? Is it indeed a paradox in the sense that one must actually deceive himself—that is, that he must believe that an idea is true on the wrong criterion—to make an idea work? Would it be better, in your opinion, to hold that some ideas are meaningful even though they are not true? In other words, are we going too far when we call an idea true *because* it is meaningful?

8   Which truth-test(s) would you apply to check out the following fact-claims and, in each case, what degree of certainty would you have?

Black coral grows in the Red Sea.
You can call 411 for Information.
The pious shall prosper.
This postcard was mailed from Madrid.
The earth is flat.
A UFO just landed in your back yard (but it is an invisible UFO).
Shakespeare wrote *The Merchant of Venice*.
Whirlwinds ("dust devils") are evil spirits in disguise.
This battery is dead.
Dolphins are intelligent animals.
The whooping crane is an endangered species.
The World will end on July 14, 1998.
All cats are blue.

Life is meaningless.

As you read this sentence, a solar eclipse is taking place.

"God's in his heaven—All's right with the world!" (Browning)

The Magna Carta was signed June 15, 1215.

All events are predestined.

Transglobal Airlines offers you the lowest fares.

A water molecule is composed of two hydrogen atoms and one oxygen atom.

Allah despises Infidels but loves The Faithful.

# WILLIAM JAMES

## *"Truth Happens to an Idea"*

In April 1870 William James began some very personal explorations in the meaning of truth. He read an article by the French philosopher, Charles Renouvier, who held that the most distinctive quality of human beings is the experience of freedom. Like a key piece of a jigsaw puzzle, the idea fell into place.

On April 30 he wrote in his journal:

I think that yesterday was a crisis in my life. I finished the first part of Renouvier's second "Essais" and see no reason why his definition of Free Will—"the sustaining of a thought *because I choose to* when I might have other thoughts"—need be the definition of an illusion. . . . My first act of free will shall be to believe in free will. . . . Not in maxims, not in *Anschauungen* [contemplations], but in accumulated *acts* of thought lies salvation. . . . Now, I will go a step further with my will, not only act with it, but believe as well; believe in my individual reality and creative power.

This decision to believe in believing marked an about-face in James's life. Heretofore he had been, in his own words, a "splintered bundle of fragments in search of consistency." Now he was able to summon strength to reverse the pattern of his past—a lifetime of self-doubt and suffering (he was twenty-eight)—and to affirm *the possibility* of taking charge of his life and creating his own future. Renouvier had argued that we possess freedom of the will if we believe that we do, and James believed it.

To those who have sought the origins of William James's condition, the James family remains an enigma—puzzling, slightly unreal. William's sister Alice suffered from "nervous attacks," fainting spells, and an illusive invalidism all her life; she rejoiced when she contracted cancer because it was, at last, a real physical illness. A brother, Garth Wilkinson, died at thirty-eight of rheumatic heart disease. Another younger brother, Robertson, was an alcoholic. And the brother who became a major American writer—Henry James—sustained, as he put it, "an obscure hurt, odious, intimate, horrid"; and he remained celibate all his life.

William shared fully his family's neurasthenia. He was plagued with chronic backache (he dubbed it "this dorsal insanity") and suffered from digestive disorders, depressions, and acute attacks of diffuse anxiety (one such attack he described: "there fell upon me without warning, just as if it came out of the darkness, a horrible fear of my own existence"). His eye trouble was his one truly somatic ailment.

The father of this troubled family was Henry James, Sr., a brilliant, passionate, and bizarre man whose life seems to have been one long search for spiritual peace, which he eventually succeeded in finding in the teachings of the eighteenth-century mystical theologian Swedenborg and his theme of divine love. As a teenager one of his legs was severely burned, resulting in its amputation; throughout his life he was subject to phobias and hallucinations. He was a gifted thinker who bequeathed his spiritual concerns—as well as his complexities and perplexities—to his children. In the James household table talk and family gatherings were animated, intellectual, wide-ranging, and punctuated by sibling rivalries.

Gardner Murphy described the philosophic presence of the elder James:

> He created in the home atmosphere an exhilarating sense of the worthwhileness of pursuing problems of cosmic dimensions, of asking forever one more question as to the place of man in this world and as to the real basis for ethics and religion; everybody in the family was apparently always ready for a debate which wound up with humor and with agreement to live and let live.

Although they were mutually involved, caring, and close, each member of the family was encouraged to seek his own illumination.

William received a good but disjointed education in private schools in America and Europe. At eighteen he wanted to become a painter but decided he lacked talent—"there is nothing in the world so despicable as a bad artist"—and decided he could do better in the natural sciences. He entered the Lawrence Scientific School at Harvard and, three years later, enrolled in Harvard Medical School. He took a year out to join a field expedition to Brazil, but he disliked the rigors of jungle life and the monotony of keeping catalogues and so returned to his medical studies.

Continually tormented by fears, William James questioned whether life could be worth living at all. He interrupted his studies at the Medical School for a year at health spas in Germany, read widely in psychology and philosophy, and took courses under some of Europe's leading scholars. But his malaise continued—"a paradoxical apathy and restlessness." He wrote home that he spent an entire winter contemplating suicide.

He returned to Harvard, received his M.D. degree in 1869, but lacked the strength and/or will to practice medicine. He continued to withdraw into a state of invalidism, unable to decide what he wanted to do with his life.

At this juncture James read the article by Renouvier. It was a turning point. Here began his quest for a philosophy that would face up to the stubborn realities of life and, at the same time, provide light for him to live by.

William James was caught in the necessity of believing—his life was at stake—but he could no longer accept the possibility of unthinking (blind) belief. His father could still believe; but blind belief, for William, was fraught with dishonesty and was counterproductive. He therefore had to perform one of man's most delicate psychological maneuvers: without denying either his own nature or the given realities of the universe, he had to rethink the structure of belief and give it a rationale fully acceptable to the intellect. This he did, and the result was a

*ON JAMES:*
*James was neither an optimist nor a cynic; he was a man of moral courage, who knew, all too well, the ambiguity and precariousness of the human condition.*

JOHN J. MCDERMOTT

*Man wants to be stretched to his utmost—if not in one way, then in another.*

*ON JAMES:*
*Pragmatism is the seed that had lain embedded in the soul of American civilization from its very inception. William James was simply the farmer who brought it to flower and fruition, and gave it a habitation and a name.*

T. K. MAHADEVAN

*We have to live today by what truth we can get today, and be ready tomorrow to call it falsehood.*

*Mankind's common instinct for reality . . . has always held the world to be essentially a theatre for heroism.*

*. . . If there be any idea which, if believed in, would help us to lead [a better] life, then it would be really better for us to believe in that idea, unless, indeed, belief in it incidentally clashed with other greater vital benefits.*

*A philosophy is the expression of a man's inner character.*

*Philosophy is at once the most sublime and the most trivial of human pursuits. It works in the minutest crannies and it opens out of the widest vistas. . . . No one of us can get along without the far-flashing beams of light it sends over the world's perspectives.*

*Creatures extremely low in the intellectual scale may have conception. All that is required is that they should recognize the same experience again. A polyp would be a conceptual thinker if a feeling of "Hello! thingumbob again!" ever flitted through its mind.*

*Life defies our phrases . . . it is infinitely continuous and subtle and shaded, whilst our verbal terms are discrete, rude, and few. . . .*

*The art of being wise is the art of knowing what to overlook.*

new way of looking at the dynamics of the ideas we call "true."

What does it mean for an idea to be true? James writes in *Pragmatism:*

> The great assumption of the intellectualists is that truth means essentially an inert static relation. When you've got your true idea of anything, there's an end of the matter. . . .
>
> Pragmatism, on the other hand, asks its usual question. "Grant an idea or belief to be true," it says, "what concrete difference will its being true make in anyone's actual life? . . . What, in short, is the truth's cash value in experiential terms?". . .
>
> The moment pragmatism asks this question, it sees the answer. True ideas are those that we can assimilate, validate, corroborate, and verify. False ideas are those that we cannot. That is the practical difference it makes to us to have true ideas. That therefore is the meaning of truth. . . .
>
> The truth of an idea is not a stagnant property inherent in it. Truth happens *to an idea. It* becomes *true, is* made true by events. Its verity is in fact an event, a process. . . .

His belief in free will was probably the most precious truth that James possessed. We can exercise free will providing we *believe* that we have free will. My belief makes it true. But when I first start believing it, it may not be *very* true. I may be intellectually convinced of my free will, but the truth of the idea hasn't taken hold of me at a deeper level. It is only slightly true. But if I practice making choices, I can increase my freedom, and the idea becomes *more true.* Freedom is a quality that I have developed. And the statement "I have free will" becomes more and more true. therefore, the statement "I am free" was true; it had predictive value. But more than that, the truth of the statement gradually *happened to* the idea as I put it into effect.

It is a uniquely pragmatic notion that truth is not a yes/no or black/white quality, but that there are "degrees" of

truth, and that "how true" an idea is depends upon the living context in which the idea is found. As James wrote, "its verity *is* in fact an event, a process. . . ."

True ideas, therefore, are the ideas that "work" for us. Does this mean that we can call virtually any fact-claim true provided that we can personally validate it by claiming that "it works for me"? Emphatically no. As John McDermott puts it, "James was no subjectivist." "And although he sees truth as a function of 'interest,' this position does not encourage predatory action. . . . " James was a relentless empiricist, and he insisted that our ideas must square with the hard realities of experience. Adjusting our beliefs to the "total push and pressure of the cosmos" is the only way to develop ideas that are pragmatically useful.

So James ended by believing, but in a very special way. George Santayana, a Harvard colleague and one of James's most gifted pupils, is not wrong when he said that "James didn't really believe. He only believed in one's right to believe that he might be right if he believed."

James took charge of his life with a vengeance, as though making up for lost time. Rather suddenly he was able to put an immense reservoir of stored-up energy and ideas to work in a creative way.

In 1873 he became an instructor in anatomy and physiology at Harvard and in 1875 began to teach psychology, at that time a new science. He introduced a course in physiology and psychology, the first in America, and established a laboratory of experimental psychology, one of the first in the world.

He wrote incessantly. By 1890 he had completed his massive two-volume *Principles of Psychology,* a systematic reorganization of virtually everything known in the field. In 1902 he produced an epochal work, *The Varieties of Religious Experience,* in which he applied the breadth of his psychological insight to the phenomena of religion. In *Pragmatism: A New Name for Some Old Ways of Thinking* (1907), he described truth as a multicolored idea that is relative to specific situations and human needs.

Of great significance was his marriage to Alice Gibbens when he was thirty-six. William's father had noticed her at a meeting in Boston and announced to his son that he had discovered his future wife. She was twenty-seven, lively and intelligent, a teacher in a girls' school. They were married in 1878, though only after some soul-searching on the part of the philosopher.

Something resembling genuine mental and physical health now infused William's whole life. His family and friends were amazed at the change in him. His illnesses disappeared and he found a new zest for living. He became one of the most popular teachers on the campus, and for thirty-five years he delighted generations of students with his informality, sincerity, candor, and anecdotes.

William James was anything but nondescript. Respected by students and colleagues alike and much loved for his gentle personality, he was colorful, alert, articulate. He had a slender but sturdy frame, was modestly and neatly bearded, sported a tan, and wore casual tweeds—hardly the stereotypical Harvard professor. Equally striking were his writing and speaking styles. His conversations were witty, homey, and erudite, his public addresses extemporaneous and substantive. His writing is marked by graphic imagery and simplicity, and it can be understood. His sister Alice once remarked that he could "lend life and charm to a treadmill."

James resigned from teaching in 1907 but continued to write and lecture, both in America and Europe. He was world-renowned and drew great audiences wherever he spoke. (He was lecturing at Stanford University in 1906 when the San Francisco earthquake struck.) A European called him the "preeminent ambassador of American thought." In the judgment of Alfred North Whitehead, James is one of the four great philosophers of the Western world because he "had discovered intuitively the great truth with which modern logic is now wrestling." The Indian scholar T. K. Mahadevan says simply: "American civilization is what it is because of William James."

During his later years James spent all the time he could at their summer home in New Hampshire, gardening, swimming, and hiking. He loved nature. One day in 1898, climbing a steep mountain trail with an eighteen-pound backpack, he sustained permanent injury to his heart (a valvular lesion). He nevertheless managed to maintain a superactive schedule for more than a decade, but in the summer of 1910 his angina attacks again became acute. He died in his wife's arms at their summer home in the Adirondacks on August 26, 1910.

# THE INNER WORLD
## THE FANTASTIC JOURNEY

*With clarity and quiet, I look upon the world and say: All that*

*I see, hear, taste, smell, and touch are the creations of my*

*mind. . . . I create phenomena in swarms, and paint with a*

*full palette a gigantic and gaudy curtain before the abyss. Do*

*not say, "Draw the curtain that I may see the painting,"*

*The curtain IS the painting.*

NIKOS KAZANTZAKIS

# 4

## THE EXPLORATION OF INNER SPACE

As adults, we have forgotten most of our childhood, not only its contents but its flavor; as men of the world, we hardly know of the existence of the inner world: we barely remember our dreams, and make little sense of them when we do; as for our bodies, we retain just sufficient proprioceptive sensations to coordinate our movements and to ensure the minimal requirements for biosocial survival—to register fatigue, signals for food, sex, defecation, sleep; beyond that, little or nothing. Our capacity to think, except in the service of what we are dangerously deluded in supposing is our self-interest and in conformity with common sense, is pitifully limited: our capacity even to see, hear, touch, taste and smell is so shrouded in veils of mystification that an intensive discipline of unlearning is necessary for anyone before one can begin to experience the world afresh, with innocence, truth and love.

R. D. LAING

*Ful wys is he that can himselven knowe! (Very wise is he that can know himself.)*
**GEOFFREY CHAUCER**

Man's ignorance of his inner world has been an abysmal "darkness of unknowing." Is there, as a matter of fact, anything that we understand less than we understand ourselves? And when we begin to see the facts, how quickly we turn away and refuse to face the truth about our own being. The history of man's exploration of human nature is marked by a singular lack of courage.

In a way, all this is surprising, for there is probably no human adventure more exciting than the exploration of "inner space." To be sure, it can lead us into uncharted country. It can evoke sacred fears and involve unscheduled risks, and not a few may fear that they have strayed into forbidden territory.

And too, it can be a lonely odyssey. No one else can travel with us; they can only call to us, as from a distance.

Yet there can be a feeling of joyous ultimacy in the unique adventure of coming to know one's inner world. Most of us have sensed the mysterious

*All that is comes from the mind.*

**The Dhammapada 1.1**

*What is important is not liberation from the body but liberation from the mind. We are not entangled in our own body but entangled in our own mind.*

**THOMAS MERTON**

Gianlorenzo Bernini, *The Ecstasy of St. Theresa,* 1645–1652. Bernini's sculpture in the Carnaro Chapel, Church of Santa Maria della Vittoria, depicts the moment of sublime consciousness for one of the Western world's renowned mystics, Saint Theresa of Avila (1515–1582). At this moment, as she describes it, an angel pierced her heart with a flaming, golden arrow: "The pain was so great that I screamed aloud; but at the same time I felt such an infinite sweetness that I wished the pain to last forever. It was not physical but psychic pain, although it affected the body as well to some degree. It was the sweetest caressing of the soul by

forces—more errant than the winds—that drive and direct our lives. Who among us has not wondered what he would find if he began in earnest to probe the depths of his own being?

"Dare I explore my inner world?" The question is rarely stated this directly, but in some form the implicit decision "to explore or not to explore" is forced upon us each day.

And, because human history is in a critical state of change in our understanding of man, the answer, assuredly, must be "yes." The fact is that man has always cast furtive glances inward, but heretofore he has sojourned in his psychic hinterlands without adequate roadmaps. He has groped haphazardly, not knowing where he was going, how to get there, or what he would find. This is no way to begin a journey.

All this is changing. Modern cartographers have begun to do their work and today we have rudimentary but helpful maps to guide us.

There is no obvious reason why one should spend his lifetime solely in the two traditional mind-states: the problem-solving conscious state and the "recovery" sleep state. Most of us, in fact, wander off the narrow path and spend time in free-association (woolgathering), browsing through our memories, and enjoying flights of fantasy; we might even tune in a few alpha rhythms. So our reduction of human existence into an alternation of consciousness and unconsciousness—waking and sleeping—is a local (Western) oversimplication.

There are other modes of conscious and subconscious experience that can enrich our lives; and on the condition that they do not rob us of our sanity or endanger others, there is no valid reason why they should not be known.

In the Eastern tradition other modes of consciousness such as focused concentration (*samadhi,* leading to *nirvana*), ecstatic trances, and Zen meditation (*zazen,* leading to *satori*) have been considered, for thousands of years, to be higher, more desirable mind-states, valued far above the reality-mode of consciousness. Such outlooks contrast greatly with our Western single-track commitment to just one form of waking experience.

This is not entirely true, however, for even in our Western tradition revered mystics have seen visions and known the rapture of religious ecstasy. And such experiences were invested with ultimate value: they were devoutly to be sought. In these Western cases the *interpretation* of the experience has given them their value. They were understood to be instances of spirit-possession (by the Holy Spirit) and not merely altered psychological states. (For more on "spirit-possession" as a model for interpreting human behavior, see p. 554.)

It appears that the West has used a "double standard" in assessing the value of various modes of psychic experience.

There is a fundamental condition to the deliberate exploration of human consciousness, a condition that Eastern religions have scrupulously observed. That condition is that the conscious mind not be impaired in its basic functions, which are to mediate reality and to solve problems. Whatever realms of the inner world we decide to explore, we know that we must shortly return to the reality-mode of consciousness and reestablish relations with the real world. The conscious mind must be adequate to the performance of numerous pragmatic functions; it must be able to organize perception, to remember pertinent information, to make operational value-judgments, to engage in rational thinking as needed, and so on.

In some Eastern religions we find acceptable ways of annihilating one's physical organism as well as the "self." Such practices rest on the obvious assumption that the individual will not be required to reenter the reality-mode of consciousness. He may have decided to withdraw into the forest and proceed into the eternal nirvana from which there is no return. But such instances, while permissible, are rare; and the fact of the matter is that, without exception, Eastern religions emphasize the *quality* of the reality-mode of consciousness and look with concern upon Western ("amateur") experiments, which endanger conscious functioning. This is precisely the reason why Eastern spiritual leaders are critical of Western use of mind-altering chemicals.

Our normal waking consciousness . . . is but one special type of consciousness, whilst all about it, parted from it by the filmiest of screens, there lie potential forms of consciousness entirely different. We may go through life without suspecting their existence; but apply the requisite stimulus, and at a touch they are all there in all their completeness, definite types of mentality which probably somewhere have their field of application and adaptation. No account of the universe in its totality can be final which leaves these other forms of consciousness quite disregarded. How to regard them is the question—for they are so discontinuous with ordinary consciousness. Yet they may determine attitudes though they cannot furnish formulas, and open a region though they fail to give a map. At any rate, they forbid a premature closing of our accounts with reality.

WILLIAM JAMES

I told Don Juan how much I enjoyed the exquisite sensation of talking in the dark. He said that my statement was consistent with my talkative nature; that it was easy for me to like chatting in the darkness because talking was the only thing I could do at the time, while sitting around. I argued that it was more than the mere act of talking that I enjoyed. I said that I relished the soothing warmth of the darkness around us. He asked me what I did at home when it was dark. I said that invariably I would turn on the lights or I would go out into the lighted streets until it was time to go to sleep.

"Oh!" he said incredulously. "I thought you had learned to use the darkness."

"What can you use it for?" I asked.

He said the darkness—and he called it the "darkness of the day"—was the best time to "see." He stressed the word "see" with a peculiar inflection. I wanted to know what he meant by that, but he said it was too late to go into it then.

CARLOS CASTANEDA

The last letter of the Tibetan alphabet symbolizes for the Buddhist the fully awakened state of consciousness (*Maha Ati*).

*The exploration of the interior of the human brain will be as dangerous as that of the Antarctic continent or the depths of the oceans, and far more rewarding.*

J. B. S. HALDANE

*One does not discover the absurd without being tempted to write a manual of happiness. "What! by such narrow ways—?" There is but one world, however. Happiness and the absurd are two sons of the same earth. They are inseparable.*

ALBERT CAMUS

*Genius is the recovery of childhood at will.*

ARTHUR RIMBAUD

# HUXLEY'S DEEP REFLECTION

Aldous Huxley was one of the great minds of our century. He had developed, through discipline, a technique for utilizing a high degree of his considerable mental power. At will, Huxley could withdraw into what he called his state of "Deep Reflection" (DR state), a mind-state

> marked by physical relaxation with bowed head and closed eyes, a profound progressive psychological withdrawal from externalities but without any actual loss of physical realities nor any amnesias or loss of orientation, a "setting aside" of everything not pertinent, and then a state of complete mental absorption in matters of interest to him.

*Awaken the mind without fixing it anywhere.*

KONGO KYO

When Huxley was in such a meditative state it was possible for him to engage in physical activity to some extent—jotting down notes or exchanging pencils—without remembering afterward anything that he had done. As he said, these physical events did not "impinge" on his mental processes. Loud noises could not reach him. He would emerge from his reflective state only when he had finished his self-set creative goals; his emergence was inner-willed.

Frequently Huxley began his day's work by entering into his DR state. He would organize his ideas and sort his tasks for that day. One afternoon he was working with total absorption on a particular manuscript when his wife returned from shopping. She inquired whether he had taken down the note she had phoned in to him. Somewhat bewildered, he helped her look for the note, which they found near the phone. He had been in his DR working state when she called, had answered the phone as usual—"I say there, hello!"—listened to the message, jotted it down—all this without remembering a word of the episode. His mind had apparently proceeded to carry on its work without interruption.

The essential point is that this was Huxley's way of working efficiently. His friend Milton Erickson experimented with him in the DR state, and Huxley frequently found himself prepared for work but with nothing to do. He would emerge from his DR state rather puzzled. "There I found myself without anything to do so I came out of it."

*Le coeur a ses raisons que la raison ne connaît point. (The heart has its reasons which reason knows nothing of.)*

BLAISE PASCAL

His wife commented that when in the state of Deep Reflection, he seemed

> like a machine moving precisely and accurately. It is a delightful pleasure to see him get a book out of the bookcase, sit down again, open the book slowly, pick up his reading glass, read a little, and then lay the book and glass aside. Then some time later, maybe a few days, he will notice the book and ask about it. The man just never remembers what he does nor what he thinks about when he sits in that chair. All of a sudden, you just find him in his study working very hard.

Religious mystics the world over make a common assertion: no one can understand a profound religious experience until he has himself experienced it. No amount of description with mere symbols can touch its true meaning.

Western mystics—Plotinus, Groot, Eckhart, Tauler, and others—have consistently stated that there is no experience in daily life that can help one to understand the meaning of the mystical experience, for it is not a mundane experience different merely in degree; rather, it is a different *kind* of experience.

The same observation comes from the Eastern mystics: if you think you have achieved an intellectual understanding of nirvana, then you have missed it. Similarly from the Taoist: "The Tao that can be expressed in words is not the true Tao."

## MYSTICAL UNITY

One of the most valued but ineffable mystical experiences in both the East and the West is the experience of unity. So profound is it that the mystics thereafter remain silent concerning it. They may indeed write volumes around the periphery of the experience, but they avow that they could not possibly describe what they have seen.

It is an event in which all experience is somehow seen together. The outer world and the inner merge into one; no distinction is made between subject and object. All knowledge is interwoven; everything is seen in the light of everything else, as though every fragment of knowledge and understanding illuminated every other fragment of knowledge and understanding. There is a coalescence; everything is related; all the contents of the mind become unified. It is all One, and this One may be felt as in some way merging with the cosmos itself; it may be conceived as the uniting of one's essence with Ultimate Reality or Godhead.

By analogy, suppose that you have spent a dozen years devouring knowledge. Imagine that you have carefully read hundreds of books in psychology, history, biology, chemistry, physics; you have studied all the textbooks in higher mathematics, geometry, astronomy, and philosophy; you have memorized the great outpouring of human feeling in music, poetry, literature, and art. . . .

But how do we store and recover such information? Ordinarily our minds move with a pokey, linear motion. They plod along, thinking of one thing at a time. We never read a book at a time, not even a page at a time: we read only a few words or perhaps a line.

But suppose some psychophysical happening suddenly opened the doors to all your stored information and this vast accumulation of knowledge could flow together into one sustained flash of understanding. Suppose every fact related to every other fact. Suppose that all you had ever learned had somehow bonded into a harmonious whole. In your mind, All was One. Such an experience would indeed be ineffable, so far beyond words that one could never hope to describe what he had seen.

Saint Thomas Aquinas may have had this kind of experience. After producing scores of volumes of systematic theology—the crowning achievement of Western religious thought—Thomas had a vision near the end of his life after which, he said, everything he had previously written was straw. He never attempted to put into mere human words what, at last, he had seen.

## ZEN SATORI

The state of consciousness sought by the Zen Buddhist is called *satori*, usually translated as "flash of enlightenment." It is a mind-state quite different from a trance or hypnotic condition. It is a state of sharp alertness and wide awareness

*A philosopher of imposing stature doesn't think in a vacuum. Even his most abstract ideas are, to some extent, conditioned by what is or is not known in the time when he lives.*

ALFRED NORTH WHITEHEAD

*The great cause of much psychological illness is the fear of knowledge of oneself—of one's emotions, impulses, memories, capacities, potentialities, of one's destiny.*

ABRAHAM MASLOW

T – P

P – O₁

O₁ – O₂

T – O₂

Electroencephalograms showing alpha waves and theta waves.

accompanied, at the same time, by a deep sense of inner calm. We know now that those who practice Zen meditation (*zazen*) are in a specific mental state with a characteristic EEG (electroencephalographic) pattern of brainwaves. Studies show that EEG patterns of experienced Zen mediators are quite different from those of beginners. In advanced patterns the alpha waves begin to diminish and a rhythmic "theta train" appears. The typical "advanced" Zen meditation moves through four stages. It begins with the initial alpha waves with eyes open (I); then a sharp increase of the alpha (II) followed by a gradual decrease of the alpha (III); and finally there is a sustained period of rhythmic theta waves (IV).

How does *zazen* feel from the standpoint of the meditator? For Western students, Erich Fromm has described the indescribable as well as anyone can.

> If we would try to express enlightenment in psychological terms, I would say that it is a state in which the person is completely tuned to the reality outside and inside of him, a state in which he is fully aware of it and fully grasps it. *He* is aware of it— that is, not his brain, nor any other part of his organism, but *he*, the whole man. He is aware of *it;* not as of an object over there which he grasps with his thoughts, but *it*, the flower, the dog, the man, in its or his full reality. He who awakes is open and responsive to the world, and he can be open and responsive because he has given up holding on to himself as a thing, and thus has become empty and ready to receive. To be enlightened means "the full awakening of the total personality to reality."

## RELIGIOUS ECSTASY

A state of consciousness highly prized by Western religious minorities is a form of religious ecstasy. Those belonging to the "Pentecostal" tradition—or other traditions that value "spirit-possession" (in Christianity, possession by the Holy Spirit)—have sometimes made the ecstatic experience a condition of membership. Within their circles they cultivate an attitude of expectancy in which members may anticipate for years the glorious soul-filling experience.

*As I see it, such a man, the man who engaged in a lifetime quest away from encapsulation, moving in the direction of the broadest and deepest possible reality image, has the key to what it means to be and to see. He is thereby representative of man in his deepest and most significant sense. For such an orientation would mean that he was very much alive in the best meaning of the term "existential" and very much aware in the best meaning of the term "philosophical." Such a man would be a man of great compassion, great sensitivity, and great thought. He would, in short, be reaching for ultimate consciousness. And while it is true that such an open approach to life is very risky for the individual man in the short view, it is clearly more creative and productive, and therefore, more viable for all men in the long run.*

JOSEPH ROYCE

In religious ecstasy several things occur. The word *ecstasy* derives from the Greek *ek* ("out of") and *stasis* ("standing"), implying that the "ecstatic individual is "standing outside" his body, the assumption being that a "spirit" has taken his place. Thus he is no longer in possession of his own body, and the original "self" is no longer in a reality-mode. An ecstatic individual no longer responds to the realities about him; his behavior has "switched to automatic." Some deeper level of the psyche has taken control while the normal controlling ego has suspended operations.

A typical ecstatic experience is known as *glossolalia*, "speaking in tongues." In this state, one feels he has gradually been overcome or "possessed." He may begin to speak unintelligible words ("babble") to himself or to bystanders. His voice may sound quite different from his own; he may sing beautifully when ordinarily he sings not at all. To the ecstatic individual it feels as though the words and songs are uttered by someone else deep within, and are quite beyond his control. As in cases of hypnosis, some aspect of the personality other than the ego has taken control, and any content originates from the deeper levels of consciousness.

In "Pentecostal" experiences where the ecstatic state is considered to be possession by the Holy Spirit, it not infrequently brings about a fundamental reorientation in the individual's life—a "conversion" or "born again" experience. It is difficult to imagine any experience more meaningful than being possessed by God.

*Nirvana is not the blowing out of the candle. It is the extinguishing of the flame because day is come.*

RABINDRANATH TAGORE

*In the province of the mind, what one believes to be true either is true or becomes true within limits to be found experientially and experimentally. These limits are beliefs to be transcended.*

JOHN C. LILLY

## THE WHITE LIGHT

I was in the desert, in a very beautiful place I visited frequently last year. Involved in the experience were: the beauty of nature, a strong feeling of my relationship with that Mother Nature, some very loving, very close people putting me physically and mentally in a very comfortable, relaxed physical and emotional setting.

The experience physically was brought on by a cold river and hot springs. Imagine: cold river, hot springs; water of 120 degrees, air of 110, river water somewhere in the 60s.

I began by sitting in the 120-degree water until sweat poured from my face and I could no longer stand the physical feeling of that heat. I jumped out of the hot water, climbed a rock and dove fifteen feet into a three-foot pool of very, very cold water. Now this does quite a number to your body and your mind. I swam across the river to where there was a shaded area and sat in the cold water in the shade until I began shivering and began getting extremely uncomfortable from the shivering, swam back across the river and jumped back into the hot water, feeling absolutely nothing immediately and then an extreme rush. And back and forth nine times.

At the completion of the ninth time I climbed back up on top of the rock to dive back into the cold water, and as I looked down I experienced something that I will call the "white light," the clear light, and as I looked down to see the pool into which I was to dive, my vision was naught—a complete nothing, of the void. And I can remember thinking, feeling, reacting, something . . . so that the next thing I knew I was sitting down on this large flat rock. And this is very difficult to relate to you because it didn't happen with words—there were no words in my mind then. But I sat down in a position like this, with my heels against my bottom, went back, flat on my back with my arms flat out, feet still touching here, soles of my feet together— and by the way I've never done this before and could never hope to repeat it again, this physical position—still touching here, flat on my back, arms straight out, and allowed myself for the first time in my life to let go of my body. My knees went down and touched the rock, so that I was lying like this, completely flat, released my self from my body. And the next thing I knew I was looking down at that body lying on the rock from a point a little bit higher than the peak of a mountaintop next to the hot springs.

It scared me, and it scared me very much. Part of that fright was because at the time I was into a very heavy, "me-man, you-earth" state of mind, and I wasn't really willing or ready to relate to "me-essence, you-universe." And I snapped real quick, and I was back in my body, and I was hearing my name being called. And I stood up and the experience was gone. And it lasted a total of—from the time I climbed the rock until I was back down—maybe thirty seconds. And yet that experience of only thirty seconds was one of such purity and one of such truth and one of such extreme pure emotion, that I could never possibly hope to forget it. . . .

TERRY ALLEN

In the Indian religions, the state of nirvana is a trance-state outwardly resembling a deep sleep. It is marked by a progressive deepening of the trance through religious disciplines that are similar to techniques of self-hypnosis. Gradually, as *samadhi* ("concentration") is practiced, the devotee learns to block out all sensory stimuli from the external world; simultaneously, sensory and emotional input from the inner world are reduced and finally stopped; no bodily sensations or emotions—hunger, pain, fear, loneliness—are registered. Further, however, the mystic enters into a mind-state of zero cognition—no ideas, memories, or rational activity. It is a "contentless" state of consciousness.

This Eastern trance resembles Huxley's "Deep Reflection" in one respect: loud noises or other stimuli are not perceived. But in its central nature, it contrasts with Huxley's DR state. In the latter's mind a high pitch of intellectual activity raced through its plan of operations, while in nirvana there is not mental *content* of any sort. It is *pure consciousness*, a seemingly discarnate, free-floating experience of nothingness.

This is the ultimate achievement of human existence for the Hindu and Buddhist. It is said to be experienced as an indescribable state of tranquillity, inner peace, and joy, a timeless state of union with the cosmos itself. In Hindu terms, the self-essence (*atman*) has become one with Ultimate Reality (*Brahman*).

## THE FANTASTIC JOURNEY

The individual who lacks awareness of the depths and facets of his psyche is something less than a whole person, and considerably less than he could be. He is living a single-dimensioned existence in a multidimensional psychic universe. There is no reason not to explore other worlds and—like the Zen monk or religious ecstatic—spend some time living there. The qualifying condition, as emphasized, is that he preserve his autonomy and the integrity of his reality-mode of consciousness.

Of course, our Western methods for accomplishing anything are distinctive: we employ chemistry and physics in everything. It is quite in character that we approach psychic/somatic functions with pills and gadgets, milligrams and voltages. And, typically, we will find faster ways of "getting there" and run the risks so characteristic of our rapid conquest of all known worlds.

In the nineties we are in the process of breaking through archaic traditions regarding the human psyche. We have already come so far that there is now little doubt that we will continue to loosen the confines and, hopefully, move ahead to positive controls and enriching experiences.

## REFLECTIONS

1   Is Maslow's observation on p. 247 (see marginal quote) meaningful to you? When you read Maslow's comment along with that of R. D. Laing (p. 243), what is your dominant response?

2   Your text makes the opening statement that "there is no obvious reason why one should spend his lifetime solely in the two traditional mind-states: the problem-solving conscious state and the 'recovery' sleep state" (p. 244). Do you agree? Or, in your opinion, are these the only normal and natural modes of consciousness?

3   As you reflect on each of the modes of consciousness described in this chapter (such as Huxley's DR state, mystical unity, Zen satori, ecstatic "spirit-possession," the out-of-body projection), are these modes of consciousness that you would like to experience? Do you fear them? If so, are you aware of the source of your fear? Would you want to experience them, do you think, if you could be sure they would turn out to be profoundly meaningful experiences, as others have claimed? In each specific case, what do you think made the experience meaningful to those who knew it?

4.   As you ponder Huxley's DR state, would you like to develop this kind of mental technique for work efficiency? Do you think Huxley possessed a special gift or is this a mental skill that many of us could acquire?

5   What is your response to the mystical experience of Saint Theresa of Avila (see marginal quote on p. 244)? What gave the experience its profound meaning? Would the experience be denigrated or robbed of its significance if it were comprehensible in psychological terms?

(*CONTINUED ON P. 257*)

*It seems to me that the greatest lesson of adult life is that one's own consciousness is not enough. What one of us would not like to share the consciousnes of half a dozen chosen individuals? What writer would not like to share the consciousness of Shakespeare? What musician that of Beethoven or Mozart? What mathematician that of Gauss? What I would choose would be an evolution of life whereby the essence of each of us becomes welded together into some vastly larger and more potent structure.*

SIR FRED HOYLE

# THE BUDDHA

## *One Who Awakened*

The great ideas by which mankind lives have been shaped by relatively few historical individuals. One of the most influential idea-shapers was a man named Siddhartha Gautama, who lived approximately twenty-five hundred years ago—from about 560 to 480 B.C.—in northeastern India. His world-view has been adopted by an astounding 4½ billion human beings.

Trustworthy facts about Siddhartha's life are difficult to come by. We must rely on worshipful traditions critically analyzed and balanced with a sense of empirical reality; through careful use of the earliest documents we stand a fair chance of recovering a few glimpses of the historical figure and getting a feeling for his personality and teaching. Then with a disciplined imagination . . .

Imagine yourself sitting on a riverbank in northeastern India, facing eastward, looking across the muddy water toward green trees and low mountains beyond. It is early evening, and several cattle drink at the water's edge. Monkeys scurry playfully under the banyan trees behind you. Upstream are a half-dozen men, sitting quietly without talk, their faces stone-still, their eyes closed in meditation.

A short distance downstream, sitting under a huge ashvattha tree, is a young man also in meditation, his calm bright eyes wide open, staring across the river. He is wearing a tattered, yellowish-white garment. He has coal-black hair, long earlobes, fiercely sensitive eyes, and dark bronzed skin. Under him is a soft bed of kusha grass.

For a full night and a full day he has been sitting thus, bolt upright in the lotus position. His body is thin, even gaunt, as though he had recently been attacked and mauled by life; but in contrast to his outward appearance, there is an unmistakable glow of serenity on his face.

The year is 525 B.C., the 15th of Vaishakha—the night of the full moon—and *after* the events about to take place here on the riverbank, this is the man who will be known for centuries to come simply as "The Awakened One"—*the Buddha.*

*The weight of suffering that goes on in the world—it is unbearable. It is a world that grows old and dies only to be reborn, and grow old and die, again and again, without end. For every living thing in it: birth, suffering, death . . . birth, suffering, death . . . the Wheel turns, endlessly.*

*If I reveal what I have seen, what would I accomplish? In a world dedicated to lust and hatred, Truth is not easily tolerated. Truth only confuses those who are at home in the world.*

*I have fallen out of love with the world! Why should I be concerned O Mara? Why should I be consumed?*

His given name was Siddhartha, and he was the only son of a wealthy landowner and clan chieftain named Shuddhodana. Maya was his mother, and she birthed him into the Gautama clan of the Shakya hill tribe in southern Nepal. They belonged to the Kshatriya caste— the warriors.

By all accounts, the young Siddhartha was brilliant and perceptive. Tradition assures us that he excelled in his studies and was a strong athlete. As an archer he was a match for the other young men with whom he hunted. He spent much of his time in varied recreations, including pursuit of the seductive village dancing girls. He was given little responsibility and seems not to have cared deeply for anyone or anything.

At sixteen he was married to his cousin Yashodhara, a happy, arranged marriage (though one tradition tells us he won her in an archery contest). Thereafter, in sensuous isolation, his years ebbed away, first his teens and then, while still asleep, his twenties; his life/time was being used up, uneventfully, in the hideaway world of his father's courtyards. He knew little about the outside world; the excruciating truth about the human condition had not yet been seeded in his consciousness. Still, a discontent was stirring from within. Life was passing him by; nothing was being gained.

*The problem is the human condition, nothing less. The human condition is* uninhabitable, but we do not know this. We treat life as though it were livable, and we only make things worse. We dream of fame, fortune, and immortality—which we cannot achieve. We develop attachments, affections, and loves for people and things—all of which we lose. Our wants and needs are insatiable, and they cause continuous grief.*

*And worse: we are not really selves at all. The sense of "self" is generated by an ephemeral collection of particles that cohere, enter the world as system, and become conditioned—"I exist!"—and then disintegrate at death—all in the flash of an instant in cosmic time. And that cosmic instant is characterized by a single crushing reality: suffering.*

*What we need is therapy. A state of mental health could result if we could stop wanting what cannot be. Mental health would consist in the reestablishment of peace of mind and wholeness of being. These qualities can be regained when we understand clearly that (1) the human condition is evil, and (2) we don't have to live in it.*

One day Siddhartha ventured outside the confines of his home and visited the city of Kapilavastu. Though he may have "seen" the sights of the world before, now, for the first time, his opened eyes *saw.* He saw an old man whose wrinkled body illustrated the degeneration of eighty years of living. Next he saw a man suffering in agony with disease, an affliction of the groin, the black plague. Then he watched a procession of mourners carrying a shrouded corpse to be cremated on the burning ghats by the river's edge.

Still reeling from his confrontation with the realities of life, he beheld a monk in meditation, trying to discover a spiritual path to follow. The contrast was shattering. Siddhartha knew then that he could never retreat to his former life. He wanted to know the truth—the whole truth—about life-in-the-world.

*The first truth is that existence is suffering.*

*Little drops fill a waterpot. Little virtues make a wise man.*

**The Dhammapada**

*We are what we think, having become what we thought.*

**The Dhammapada**

*Those who are attached to nothing, and hate nothing, have no fetters. . .*

**A BUDDHA LEXICON**

AHIMSA

ANATTA

BODHI

BO-TREE

BUDDHA

DHARMA

DHARMACHAKRA

DUKKHA

KARMA

NIRVANA

SHAKYA

SAMADHI

SAMSARA

SANGHA

TANHA

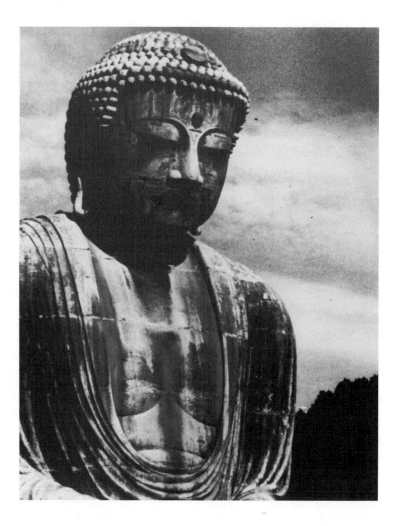

*The second truth is that our pain and suffering are caused by what we perceive to be our human needs and cravings.*

*The third truth is that our pain and suffering can end if we learn to eliminate our human needs and cravings.*

*The fourth truth is that continual practice of the eightfold path will lead to the cessation of all suffering and to a life that is serene and free.*

He had *seen* the problem; now he *must* find a solution.

Leaving his wife and son—tradition tells us how he visited Yashodhara and Rahula in the silence of the night, gazed lovingly at them for the last time, felt the urge to embrace them but turned and rode off into the night, leaving this life forever—he fled into a nearby forest, exchanged his fine clothes with a ragged beggar, cut his long black hair, and set out to find the answer to life: a solution to suffering. This was the "Great Renunciation." He was twenty-nine.

His first move was to find a guru. He came across Uddaka, a Brahmin ascetic living in a cave, and learned from him how to control his breathing and to remain motionless while practicing thought-less meditation. He also learned, for the first time in his life, to deny himself and to fast—"like an insect during a bad season." But after a time these Brahmanical teachings left him empty and discontent.

*Abandon even good, and evil all the more; he who has reached the other shore has no use for rafts.*

He found another guru, Alara, and learned from him that the answer cannot be found through the control of the senses or bodily pain and fasting. Again dissatisfied, he left.

What he had really learned from the Hindu hermits was that the ways of others were not for him and that he had to seek his own path.

*What is this Middle Way between world affections and self-torment that leads to an awakening?*

*It is an eightfold path.*

*First comes wisdom, which results from* right perspective *(we cause our own suffering) and* right intention *(a commitment to transcend the world).*

*Next comes proper conduct, which results in* right speech, right behavior, *and* right living *(ethical purity must become a matter of habit) so that all one says and does will move him toward his spiritual goals.*

*Thirdly, one must develop proper mental qualities by means of* right effort *(control of the mind through strength of will),* right mindfulness *(keeping the contents of consciousness under perfect control), and* right meditation *(trance states wherein the world is forgotten and one experiences perfect joy and emptiness).*

*It is in the practice of right meditation (samadhi) that the true spirituality of awakening begins.*

After leaving the two gurus, Siddhartha made his way to Uruvela, where he was joined by five mendicant ascetics who practiced extreme self-mortification and self-denial. The better part of six years he now spent in their company, doing penance and fasting, exploring the pathway of asceticism, which promised control of the senses and the refinement of one's spiritual nature.

He lived on seeds and herbs, finally ate only a single grain of rice or one jujube apple a day. He became wan and emaciated. "If I sought to feel my belly, it was my backbone that I found in my grasp." He weakened to the point of death. One day he sank into unconsciousness and was revived by a bowl of rice cooked in milk given to him by a girl from a nearby village. When he regained his strength, he also recovered a clear mind; and asceticism, he now knew, was not the answer.

Stronger now, clothed in a winding sheet borrowed from a tomb, Siddhartha made his way southward to Gaya. At nightfall he came to a fig tree and, after accepting as a cushion eight armfuls of grass from a helpful farmer, he sat down by the trunk and slipped into meditation. Knowing that he was nearing the end of his search, he pressed forward relentlessly. "Were my skin to dry up, my hand to wither, and my bones to dissolve, until I have attained to supreme and absolute knowledge I shall not stir from this seat."

*Endowed with the whole body of noble virtues—sense control, mindfulness and comprehension, and contentment— the truth-seeker chooses a solitary resting place—a forest, the foot of a tree, a hill, a mountain glen, a rocky cave, a charnel place, a heap of straw in the open field. He abandons this world and enters the mind where the Truth can be found.*

*As I meditate, all desires fade. I eliminate the five hindrances: urges and wants, the need for action, the need to withdraw and sleep, and anxiety and doubt.*

*When the five hindrances are eliminated, then happiness is born, to happiness joy is added, with his mood joyful his body is relaxed, his relaxed body feels at ease, and as he feels at ease his mind becomes concentrated— he enters samadhi.*

*Deeper in mind I soar upward. Joy and happiness, born of seclusion. Tranquillity. Joy and happiness born of concentration. Happiness of neutrality. Mindfulness. Understanding. Pure neutrality and mindfulness. Sphere of infinite space. Sphere of infinite consciousness. Sphere of nothingness. Sphere of neither thought nor nonthought. Emptiness. Cessation of*

*By oneself evil is done; by oneself one suffers; by oneself evil is left undone; by oneself one is purified.*

*I take refuge in the Buddha*
*I take refuge in the Dharma*
*I take refuge in the Sangha*

**Confession of Faith**
**Theravada Buddhism**

*O Ananda, be ye lamps unto yourselves. Be ye refuges to yourselves. Hold fast to the Dharma as a lamp. Hold fast to the Dharma as a refuge. Look not for refuge to any one beside yourselves.*

*Nirvana is, but not the man that enters it.*

**The Visuddhmagga**

*thought and feeling. Pure conscious-
ness.*
    *Nirvana.*

According to Buddhist tradition, on the full-moon day in the month of Vaishakha in the year 525 B.C., Siddhartha reached the end of his quest: he attained Enlightenment (*bodhi*) and became the Awakened One, the Buddha. He was thirty-five years old.

Thinking as a true philosopher, he had faced the realities of experience as he saw them and attempted to understand what he found. And what he had found was that life is brief and painful, birth is evil and death is release; and the best way to live is to fall out of love with life and develop a state of mind that will provide an authentic experience of peace and joy. This is the Way of the Buddha.

Siddhartha—now the Buddha— arose from beneath the Bodhi-tree, walked to Sarnath, and shared the Truth with his five companions. They saw, and believed. Then he spent the next forty-five years preaching and teaching in northeast India. He was immensely successful. The Sangha (order of monks) was organized, and his wife and son both joined.

When he knew he was about to die, he gathered his disciples about him. "My journey nears its end, and I have reached my sum of days, for I am nearly eighty years old." Then to his close friend and favorite disciple: "So, Ananda, you must be your own lamps, be your own refuges. Take refuge in nothing outside yourselves." He spoke his last words: "Go now, and diligently seek to realize your own salvation."

He lay over on his right side, closed his eyes, and began to ascend, for the last time, into trance: level after level, even higher, and into nirvana. From there he passed on into the final condition: *Parinirvana.*

The next day the villagers of Kushinagara came to the grove of sal trees and wrapped his body in layers of cloth and wool. At dawn on the seventh day, the bier was carried to a shrine outside the east gate of the city. There they cremated the remains of Siddhartha Gautama, the Shakya prince.

6   Do you share Sir Fred Hoyle's feeling that "one's own consciousness is not enough"? If you agree, do you also feel the impulse to transcend your consciousness predicament? How might you achieve such transcendence? Or is the very idea of "transcendence" a vain and futile notion?

7   Reflect upon the statement by Joseph Royce (see marginal quote on p. 248), then restate in your own words what you think he is saying. What do you think Royce means by the phrase "reaching for ultimate consciousness"? In what sense might it be "very risky" for the individual?

# PAST / PRESENT / FUTURE

## 4₂

## A PHILOSOPHY OF TIME

Time affects us in so many ways. We use it; we abuse it; we enjoy it; we fear it.

The way we respond to the challenges of time is a test of what we are, of what we are becoming. We grow older day by day, older in the calendar. Does that fact disturb us greatly, little, sometimes, often? How else are we growing in the same time? How much of our time do we enjoy doing what? Do we frequently or seldom feel that the time was really well spent? The answers we would give to these questions reveal our *philosophy of time*. We all acquire one, though we rarely, if ever, venture to spell it out.

R. M. MacIver

A "philosophy of *time*." Time possesses at once, for us all, the *fascinosum* and the *mysterium;* it is intimately familiar *and* ultimately formidable. Time *is* life, and life *is* time; and somehow we know this in the marrow of our bones. But in all of human experience, is there anything that more befuddles our understanding? Is there any concept that, when we try to force open its secrets, betrays the frailty of our thoughts and the ineptness of our language? Whitehead said it all: "It is impossible to meditate on time and the mystery of the creative passage of nature without overwhelming emotion at the limitations of human intelligence."

"Time is like an ever-flowing stream." (The *stream* of consciousness, the *flow* of an electric current, the *flow* of words of a great orator?) "Time unrolls like a carpet." (*Unrolls* in the sense of uncovering something which was previously hidden but now lies exposed to view; and will it continue to be displayed or will the carpet begin to re-roll from the other end and thus hide something again?) "Clocks *keep* time." (As we *keep* our possessions, *keep* our moral principles, *keep* a house?) "Time passes." (As we *pass* an automobile on the road, *pass* a course in a university, *pass from life*

*The Moving Finger writes;*
*  and*
*having writ, Moves on. . . .*
          OMAR KHAYYAM
          *The Rubaiyat*

*What is time? If no one asks*
*me, I know. If I try to*
*explain it to someone asking*
*me, I don't know.*
          SAINT AUGUSTINE

*A second is defined as 1/31556925.9747th of a tropical year.*

*to the hereafter?) "Time is ever coming into being and passing out of being."* (Where was it before it *came into being* and where does it go when it *passes out of being?*) *"Time is all-embracing."* (If it is all-embracing does it also *embrace time?*) *"We tell time."* (To whom, in what language, and *what* do we tell about time?) *"We expect the future, experience the present, and remember the past."* (Is time then merely a subjective image created by our mind, and having no counterpart in the world?) *"Time is the relation of before and after."* (But *before* and *after* refer *only* to time; hence we are saying literally time is time.) Does this not show that what I have called the straightforward descriptions of time contain metaphors and analogies, ambiguous words, subjective terms, hidden contradictions, and definitions which are purely verbal?

CORNELIUS BENJAMIN

One encouraging note can be heard above all our confusion. It has been noted by Friedrich Waismann that, although most of us haven't the foggiest notion what time *is*, our time-language seems to keep on *working*. We understand the meaning of the word *time* in various contexts ("What time is it?" "He arrived just in the nick of time." "We all had a great time." Etc.) and thus we continue to function pragmatically without ever knowing what we're talking about. (The use of the word *time* in this chapter is sufficient evidence of this point. I count at least thirty *different* definitions of the word in the text of this chapter, most of which, in context, succeed in communicating ideas with some degree of adequacy, but do not necessitate an understanding of what time truly is. What could better illustrate the astounding fact that we can and do communicate with one another continually *without* knowing *what* we are talking about?!)

Three philosophical questions about time will come into focus here. (1) What is time? How do we experience it? Can we understand it? (2) What is meant exactly by "past," "present," and "future"? In what sense can each of them be said to exist? (3) Where in time do we live? What does time have to do with personal existence?

*[Time] brings to mind the ideas of corrosion and decay, the knowledge of inexorable and irreversible aging and death. Hence man's efforts to arrest time, to cast off his chronological chains, and to build cities and monuments, pyramids and empires which can resist the teeth of time. Hence, too, his pursuit of a mirage of love which does not wither or fade with time, and his dream of a glory which is outside time. The more man reflects on time, the more his mortality weighs upon him, and the more he realizes that "all our yesterdays have lighted fools the way to dusty death."*

**JOHN COHEN**

## CLOCK TIME

We use the word *time* to refer to at least three different phenomena, all quite distinct, though usually confused in our minds.

One is clock time or chronological time (the latter deriving from the Greek *chronos*, meaning "time"—which doesn't help matters in the least). Clock time probably has nothing whatever to do with time. Clocks measure space. One hour of chronological time is the apparent movement of the sun from, say, its zenith point (at midday) to a point 15° westward along its orbital path. The clock on the wall is set to correlate with the sun's motion. While the sun moves 15° in space, one clock hand moves 360° while the other smaller hand moves 30° in space. Both events (sun and clock) are cases of matter-in-motion that we have correlated for practical purposes. We usually say we have "syn*chron*ized" sun and clock, implying our belief that real time is involved in the operation. But this is doubtful. We are correlating events and not synchronizing time.

# PSYCHOLOGICAL TIME

A second kind of time is subjective time—psychological or experiential time. This is the only temporal phenomenon of which we have any clear conception, and many philosophers are of the conviction that experiential time is the only true time. Psychological time is our individual experience of the continuum of our consciousness. Consciousness *is* time. When we are asleep or unconscious, time is nonexistent for each of us, but it begins again the moment we regain consciousness.

*The delicious melodies of Purcell or Cimarosa might be disjointed stammerings to a hearer whose partition of time should be a thousand times subtler than ours.*
**SAMUEL TAYLOR COLERIDGE**

In this context, we can properly speak of the speeding up and slowing down of time, for the metabolic processes that determine our time-consciousness do just that. They vary. To speak of time variability is to describe accurately an experience of consciousness that is a function of the rate of oxygen consumption by the brain.

Henri Bergson preferred the term *duration* when speaking of conscious time. Pure duration is our ongoing experience of the continuum of consciousness. Bergson insisted that our purest intuition of the true nature of all reality is our experience of this duration of our own consciousness.

To say that time is consciousness may be misleading since we (in the Western world) tend to think of consciousness as consciousness *of something*. Here is one source of confusion about the nature of time. We objectify time and think of it as a sort of fluid medium in which objects/events occur. Just as we find it difficult to conceive of consciousness apart from consciousness of something, so also for time: we have difficulty thinking of time as "pure time" (Bergson's "pure duration") apart from real objects/events. But time and matter-in-motion must be separated in thought. Our ordinary waking consciousness is the time-continuum upon which external objects/events impinge. The tele-

Salvador Dali, *The Persistence of Memory* (1931). Collection, The Museum of Modern Art, New York.

phone rings or someone speaks, and these external stimuli activate sensations that enter directly into consciousness (time) as content. But time and the content are not the same. Time might more easily be conceived as the continuum of consciousness without content.

One important implication of this understanding of time is that if there were no experiencers (no conscious minds), there could be no time. Therefore, there was a time (!), perhaps 4.5 billion years ago, before conscious creatures had evolved, when there was no time. Likewise, if all life on earth should cease to exist in the future, time would be no more.

*We are always the same age inside.*

GERTRUDE STEIN

As early as 1860 the Austrian physicist Ernst Mach, the first Western thinker to treat time scientifically, concluded that "the time of the physicist does not coincide with the system of time sensations." The physicist can assume an "even flow" of time or, when very great speeds are involved, describe temporal variations ("time dilation") with Einstein's relativistic formulas. His kind of time still behaves with congenial consistency.

The psychologist is not so fortunate: his time is wildly capricious. Psychological time varies with body temperature: if temperature is raised, time passes slower; if lowered, it passes faster. If our metabolic rate is increased, time passes slower; if decreased, it passes faster. Time plods at half a snail's pace in the eager experience of a child; it accelerates like a speed-demon as the adult years pass by. All these variations are determined by the rate of oxygen consumption by the brain. (On the variations of time-experience with age, see box on p. 166.)

Illness and disease can also produce variations in time-experience. Among these are Parkinson's disease, some forms of mental/emotional illness, and certain disorders produced by alcoholism.

Almost all hallucinogens, euphoric drugs such as opium and marijuana, and even some common nonprescription drugs can induce extreme alterations in time experience. Under many conditions, clock time seems to pass incredibly slowly.

We say that time "slows down" and "speeds up." But in relation to what? In relation to chronological time—to the ticks of the clock—as well as in relation to our memory of what is for oneself a "normal" experience of time. We are surrounded by clocks by which we constantly gauge our experience of time: clocks and watches proper, the sun in motion, cars going by, traffic signals, jet planes flying overhead, our own heartbeats, the duration required for us to move from one place to another along a familiar route, the time it takes our eggs to fry or toast to burn. These and a thousand other daily events are clocks against which variations in our time experience would be noticed and measured.

## REAL TIME

A third kind of phenomenon that we think of as "time" is matter-in-motion, that is, sequences of events occurring in the real world. The sun rises, dandelion seeds float through the air, clouds gather, rain falls, waves break upon the shore. The majority of time-theorists would hold that all these are *only* sequences of events and do not involve any kind of time per se. However, nothing prevents our using the word *time* to refer to such real events while we measure such events against our calibrated clocks and/or experiential time.

If we ask how long it takes a cannon ball dropped from the top of the Leaning Tower of Pisa to hit the ground, then we can time the event with our clocks, in which case we are doing what we did with our clocks and the sun (correlating spatial events); or we can time the event experientially with conscious time as we watch the cannonball fall.

## SAINT AUGUSTINE: GOD'S TIME AND OURS

At some point in his life, almost every philosopher has become preoccupied with the nature of time. Several developed noteworthy models to explain time and its mysterious operations.

Saint Augustine's concept of time is conditioned by his theological presuppositions. God *created* time, Augustine reasoned, when he created everything else. Since God created time, he existed *before* time, he will exist *after* time, and therefore he exists *outside* time. There was no time before he created it. Judeo-Christian doctrine has consistently held that God created *all* that exists—including time and presumably space—*ex nihilo,* "out of nothing."

In the mind of God, there is no "before" or "after"; there is only a "now." In "God's experience" all events occur simultaneously. To put it another way, all the past and all the future (that is, our past and future) exist together in God's present. Thus, when Augustine elaborates on the doctrine that God foresaw the Fall of Man, God really didn't foresee anything, as though he were peering ahead through time (as we would have to) and saw what had not yet transpired. In God's all-inclusive present, "future" events are taking place now. God didn't foresee; he merely saw. Likewise, he doesn't foreordain an event; he merely

*The individual who wakes up is not the same who lay down to sleep the night before.*
MAURICE PERCHERON

*Man's short-term subjective time scale may depend upon the constancy of his internal temperature. For so-called cold-blooded animals this would not hold. For them time would presumably pass slowly on warm days and rapidly on cold days. . . . Time would not appear to flow steadily in the linear sort of way familiar to us mammals.*
HUDSON HOAGLAND

## PURE SPACE AND PURE TIME

In Relativity Theory, the first three purely spatial dimensions have as an attribute perfect reversibility, whereas time, to the extent that it is a physical unwinding, remains irreversible, demonstrating immediately that the parallelism does not go very far. From an epistemological viewpoint, one must say even more: space can be completely abstracted from its content in the measure of pure form and give way to a strictly deductive science of space, which would be pure geometry. By contrast, there is no pure chronometry; there is no science comparable to geometry in the field of time, precisely because time is a coordination of velocities and because when one speaks of velocity, one speaks of a physical entity. *Time* cannot be abstracted from its content as space can. *Temporal order*, in a sense, can be abstracted from its content, in which case, however, it becomes a simple order of succession. But *duration* . . . depends essentially upon velocities. Duration cannot be disassociated from its content psychologically or physically. From the point of view of psychology, Bergson's analyses of pure duration have amply shown the interdependence of time and its psychological content; similarly, from the physical point of view, time depends upon velocities.

JEAN PIAGET
*Time Perception in Children*

*All the vital problems of philosophy depend for their solutions on the solution of the problem of what Space and Time are and more particularly how they are related to each other.*

SAMUEL ALEXANDER

*Our real journey of life is interior; it is a matter of growth, deepening, and of an ever greater surrender to the creative action of love and grace in our hearts.*

THOMAS MERTON

ordains (causes) what he sees happening. This, to Augustine, is what is meant for God to be omniscient and omnipotent.

We humans experience the present, remember the past, and anticipate the future; but God is not limited by our human time. It is not correct to say, as some theologians do, that there are really two times, God's and ours. Rather, we are in time; God is timeless.

## NEWTON: ABSOLUTE TIME

Sir Isaac Newton appears to have assumed, somewhat uncritically, that time is real, being an integral part of the operations of nature. But this objective time is not to be *equated with* matter-in-motion, or with objects per se that endure in time. Real time is separate from real objects/events. Newton's oft-repeated description of time—and his critics have had a field day with it—is as follows:

Absolute, true, and mathematical time, of itself, and from its own nature, flows equably without relation to anything external, and by another name is called duration: relative, apparent, and common time, is some sensible and external (whether accurate or unequable) measure of duration by means of motion, which is commonly used instead of true time; such as an hour, a day, a month, a year.

It was Newton who first introduced into Western thought the notion of an absolute time. This absolute time (whatever it is) is a universal medium that flows smoothly and evenly, unaffected by all the events that occur *inside* it.

Newton's assumption of absolute time dominated the thinking of physicists until the unorthodox reflections of Einstein at the beginning of our century proved it to be an unworkable assumption and rendered it obsolete.

## KANT: TIME IS IN THE MIND

Immanuel Kant considered our sense of time to be inherent in the structure of the mind. Our time sense is not developed through experience; it is, rather, "a priori," prior to experience. It is a mode of perception, a subjective mental form that the mind employs in its organization of perception. Dr. Cornelius Benjamin has made a succinct summary of the logical arguments that Kant developed to defend his a priori view of time.

Immanuel Kant (1724–1804)

> First, time cannot be an empirical conception since its essential characteristics (coexistence and succession) cannot be perceived by us unless we have some prior notion of time in our minds. In other words, sensations cannot be observed as temporal if we do not already know what is meant by "coexistence" and "succession." Second, we cannot think of phenomena as outside of time, yet we can readily think of empty time. Objects, therefore, can be annihilated from thought, but time cannot. This makes time logically prior to phenomena. Third, only on the supposition that time is a form of intuition can we explain why it is impossible to think of a two-dimensional time or of two coexistent times. This incapacity of our minds is due not to the fact that experience reveals no such notions but to the unthinkable character of the notions. Fourth, time is not a generalization from different times, for different times are merely parts of one and the same time; hence time is an a priori form which interrelates phenomena into a temporal manifold. Fifth, conceptions of time-segments, i.e., limited durations, are possible only on the assumption of an unlimited or infinite time; but this cannot be an empirically derived notion and must consequently be given as a prior form of intuition under which phenomena are perceived.

## TIME PAST

Many of us find that our ideas about the past, present, and future run together, overlap, or are otherwise blurred.

Ivar Lissner once wrote a book entitled *The Living Past*. It's not difficult to infer what he wishes to say with this title, but, for openers, we might logically ask whether, in any sense, the past could be "living" (present tense). Isn't the past dead? And isn't the past, by definition, placed outside the boundary of the present? This is not to say that influences from "past presents" don't linger on and influence us. They do, but their existence is felt only in our living present.

Yet to say the past is "dead" is surely incorrect. To call something "dead" implies that it was once alive, but the past is never "alive." We could just as well speak of a "living future"—which seems to make little sense. Only the present is "alive"—isn't it? Apparently we are having language troubles again.

The nature of the past is of primary concern to the historian since "the past" is his sole subject matter. From his standpoint, the past exists only as it is re-created in the historian's mind. The concrete events of the past are forever gone, and they can be re-created again in the historian's imagination only to the extent that records of some kind have survived from those who witnessed the

*It is worth remembering that we never see or experience anything but the past. The sounds you are hearing now come from a thousandth of a second back in time for every foot they have had to travel to reach your ears. This is best demonstrated during a thunderstorm, when the peal from a flash twelve miles away will not be heard for a full minute. If you ever see a flash and hear the thunder simultaneously, you will be lucky to be alive. I have done it once and do not recommend the experience.*

ARTHUR C. CLARKE

events. The telltale signs left by events are many: words of eyewitnesses who selected what aspects of any event were significant to them, plus their interpretation and valuation; fossil tracks, leaves, bones; geological records in rocks, volcanic layers, seamounts, oceanic trenches, and so on. If an event leaves no record, then it is forever irretrievable; no historian can reconstruct it nor, for that matter, would he have reason to guess that it had ever occurred.

## TIME FUTURE

What about the future? Unless we hold to some such theory as Augustine's notion of time, then questions about the existence of the future leave our intellects bewildered.

Can we experience the future? If we can answer no, then the future can be defined as our expectation that events will continue to occur or that, experientially, we will continue to experience "presents." Our personal future is merely the expectation that our consciousness will continue.

But if, in any way, we can say yes to the question, Can we experience the future? then we must face the most difficult of all philosophical problems and the one with the most far-reaching implications. There are at present ample unexplained time phenomena to prevent our closing the question. Arthur C. Clarke who, even in his fiction tries to remain a sound scientist, gives in to the possibility of precognition. "I would be willing to state that seeing into the future . . . [is] impossible, were it not for the impressive amount of evidence to the contrary."

If we can experience the future, then under any theory of time we have now, we must conclude that the future has *already* taken place or is *now* taking place. (Recall that Augustine, to allow God foreknowledge of the future, was compelled to theorize that our past, present, and future are all taking place concurrently in God's mind.)

If the future has happened or is happening, then the very structure of our normal waking experience is destroyed. Gone also are numerous axiomatic assumptions such as cause-and-effect and before-and-after. Causal relations become meaningless: that the seed must be planted before the organism can grow, that the song must be sung before it can be heard, that the fire must be lit before the wood can burn—all such statements are wrong. Experience is shot through with contradictions and illusions.

Whether we do experience the future has not been established, but experiences that are difficult to explain on any other basis are not uncommon. J. B. Priestley correctly notes that "if one, just one, precognitive dream could be accepted as something more than a coincidence—bang goes our conventional idea of Time!"

Not only is precognition the most stubborn of all philosophical problems, but (if it exists) it often presents itself as a puzzle within a puzzle. Many instances of precognition, especially of tragic episodes, appear as warnings that make it possible for the person having the experience to take evasive action and prevent the tragedy that was foreseen. But this is a contradiction: to be perceived, the future already exists; but when perceived, it can be altered.

*It's a poor sort of memory that only works backward.*
LEWIS CARROLL
*Through the Looking-Glass*

*Whether the future can be known, even in principle, is one of the subtlest of all philosophical questions.*
ARTHUR C. CLARKE

Therefore, what has already happened can subsequently be changed. Which makes no sense at all.

Priestley—who accepts precognition as fact—says it well.

> Let me put it briefly and brutally. The future can be seen, and because it can be seen, it can be changed. But if it can be seen and yet be changed, it is neither solidly there, laid out for us to experience moment after moment, nor is it non-existent, something we are helping to create, moment after moment. If it does not exist, it cannot be seen; if it is solidly set and fixed, then it cannot be changed. What is this future that is sufficiently established to be observed and perhaps experienced, and yet can allow itself to be altered?

(This problem, too, has an interesting theological parallel. A centuries-old controversy turns on whether God's foreknowledge of events necessarily implies predestination. That is, if God "foresees" an event, does that event *have to occur*, or can it be altered? In other words, can God be wrong in what he foresees? It would seem that he can be wrong if the hint of human precognition is applicable: prevision does *not* mean predestination.)

At present we have no time-theories that can explain such occurrences. We must either deny that the future can be experienced now, or develop new models regarding the nature of time. Philosophers and scientists have avoided the time problem, partly because of its association with the occult. But those who professionally wonder about the nature of existence should, like foolish angels, rush in—albeit with fear and trembling—and attempt to create comprehension where chaos now reigns.

## TIME PRESENT

Since Zeno the Eleatic (fl. c. 450 B.C.), analytical thinkers have been bothered by the nature of the present—the "now" of experience. A long-standing tradition has held that the present is a durationless point. This is the theory of the "punctiform present." It seems that the moment we experience the present, it has already become the past, while the very near future keeps rushing across this knife-edge present into the past. The "now" has no duration; it seems like only a timeless boundary between future and past. If this present has any "width," then it must be composed of a series of (durationless) instants. Louise Heath nicely states this line of logic (although she does not herself accept it):

> The nature of time is such that when the present is, the past has been and *is no longer*, the future will be, but *is not* yet, while the present which *is*, turns out on analysis to be not a part of time but only the boundary between past and future.

This leaves us in a quandary. If, on either side, the past and the future sort of squeeze the present into a durationless boundary line, then where does human experience take place? Or might experience be an illusion, after all, as Zeno believed?

Something must be wrong with our reasoning. We don't live in the past or future, so we must live in the present. Is the "now" of our experience really a

*Precognition is key to the mysteries of psi [in the opinion of Dr. Milan Ryzl, a Russian parapsychologist]: "I believe the answer lies in a new understanding of space and time. And I think it is very deep."*
OSTRANDER AND SCHROEDER

In te, anime meus, tempora metior. (*It is in you, O my mind, that I measure time.*)
SAINT AUGUSTINE

*Individual Consciousness is but a shadow; what is permanent is the world.*
JOSIAH ROYCE

point? or does it have width? If so, how wide is it? Perhaps our "now" extends a little bit into the future and past, as William James believed:

> The only fact of our immediate experience is what has been called the "specious" present, a sort of saddle-back of time with a certain length of its own, on which we sit perched, and from which we look in two directions into time. The unit of composition of our perception of time is a duration, with a bow and a stern as it were—a rearward- and a forward-looking end. It is only as parts of this duration-block that the relation of succession of one end to the other is perceived. We do not feel first one end and then the other after it, and from the perception of the succession infer an interval of time between, but we seem to feel the interval of time as a whole, with its two ends embedded in it.

*We are never at home; we are always beyond it. Fear, desire or hope drive us towards the future and deprive us of the feeling and contemplation of what is.*

MICHEL DE MONTAIGNE

James is on the right path, we think. What we call the "present" is by its very nature a *psychological* event, rather than a mathematical or physical (real) event. This would seem to be a fairly obvious conclusion since (1) mathematicians make no claim that mathematical time-points ("instants") are anything other than mental constructs which are useful in solving certain problems; (2) in physics, Einstein's theories have annihilated the notion of simultaneity, that is, that there exists a "universal now"; what is present for one experiencer may be past or future for another experiencer. (See the box on p. 502.)

As a psychological event involving perception and consciousness, it therefore possesses duration. The notion of time as a timeless instant is fallacious. Experiencing takes time; it has width. An experience involving intricate psychophysiological processes "stretches out" and lasts a while and could never occur in a "timeless instant." A French psychologist, Paul Fraisse, describes the present from a modern point of view:

> My present is one "tick-tock" of a clock, the three beats of the rhythm of a waltz, the idea suggested to me, the chirp of a bird flying by. . . . All the rest is already past or still belongs to the future. There is order in this present, there are intervals between its constituent elements, but there is also a form of simultaneity resulting from the very unity of my act of perception. Thus the perceived present is not the paradox which logical analysis would make it seem by splitting time into atoms and reducing the present to the simple passage of time without psychological reality. Even to perceive this passage of time requires an act of apprehension which has an appreciable duration.

Therefore, we can define *time* as the experience of the duration of our consciousness, and *the present* as the perceptual time-span of that duration.

*I have always been so afraid of the present and the real in my life. . . .*

ALFRED DE VIGNY

But what is the span of that duration? How long does it last? Its duration is not constant, but depends rather upon the nature of the perceptual events that constitute the perceived present. It depends partly on the number of sense stimuli, which are perceived as a unitary event. Any event lasting for more than about two seconds "spills over" into the past, and part of the event is remembered. A series of stimuli (the notes of a melody or the number of spoken sounds) is usually perceived as a unitary event when they last for about one-half to one second. It has been observed that when a clock strikes three or four, we can usually identify the hour without counting the number of consecutive

# DENNIS THE MENACE

"ISN'T IT ALWAYS NOW?"

chimes; but beyond four, we have to start counting the number of strikes to identify the hour.

No perception of the present is independent of its content. The duration of the present depends upon the number and nature of the stimuli perceived, the intervals between stimuli, and the organization of the stimuli. The duration of the present also depends upon the state of consciousness of the perceiver and the familiarity and meaningfulness of the organized stimuli. The duration of meaningful sounds in our own language differs from the duration of meaningless sounds in a foreign language. The same is true for a familiar melody in contrast to one never heard before.

In summary, therefore, while in a normal waking mode of consciousness, our perceived present rarely lasts longer than five seconds, and frequently it

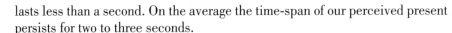

*Until the coming of the missionaries in the seventeenth century, and the introduction of mechanical clocks, the Chinese and Japanese had for thousands of years measured time by graduations of incense. Not only the hours and days, but the seasons and zodiacal signs were simultaneously indicated by a succession of carefully ordered scents.*

MARSHALL McLUHAN

lasts less than a second. On the average the time-span of our perceived present persists for two to three seconds.

## TIME AND PERSONAL EXISTENCE

Time and personality are fundamentally related. There is nothing unhealthful about reliving in one's memory the happy moments of one's past or anticipating in imagination the possible happy events of the future. But such movements into past or future can become unhealthful if one is "pushed out of the present" by unbearable conditions and develops the habit, involuntarily, of existing in past or future. In such cases the past becomes not merely a memory of experienced events, but a fabricated blend of actual and imagined events; and likewise the future becomes a confused mélange of possible events and impossible "castles in air." When such intensities prevail, one's temporal horizon has been distorted.

Before such extreme conditions set in, however, "where we live" has already been integrated into our character-structure. If past experiences have been mostly unpleasant we may be oriented toward the future and change. If past experiences have been generally more pleasant and we come to dread the future and change, having no grounds for the anticipation of happy events, we may well tend toward the conservation of the conditions of the past that provided the happier experiences.

In a word, those who experience a profound dissatisfaction with the present want change. But whether one seeks better conditions through a future-orientation or a past-orientation will depend upon a fundamental temporal character-structure long since determined by personal experience.

The philosophical world-view that goes by the name of existentialism has been immensely popular since World War II. While no two existential philosophers hold quite the same ideas, all share similar attitudes toward how we exist in the living present.

Jean-Paul Sartre coined the most famous catch-phrase of modern philosophy: *existence before essence.* To existentialists the word *existence* refers to the concrete "human reality" of experience. Existence is what is—not what should be or might be. By contrast, the word *essence* refers to whatever qualities we deem "essential" to man: "human nature," "original sin," "innate aggression," "rationality," or whatever; but all these are abstractions created after the concrete fact. Minds fabricate essences, and Sartre denied that such notions have any significance for understanding the uniqueness of the individual person.

Sartre was thinking only of *human* existence, for objects possess a different *kind* of existence. To see this difference, contrast man's existence with the existence, say, of the *Saturn V* rocket that launched America's lunar missions. Everything about the *Saturn* rocket—its three stages, engine systems, telemetry, payload capacity, engine-out capability, etc.—was conceived *in the minds* of scientists and engineers and elaborated on the design boards long before any single rocket was constructed. The rocket's purpose, conceived in men's minds, determined every element of its design. Once the design had been completed (still in men's minds), then an infinite number of single rockets, produced to perform in a specific way, could be constructed from those master specifications. All the rockets would be identical.

We can speak meaningfully, therefore, of the *essence* of the *Saturn V* rocket: its essence *is* all the elements of structure and function, conceived by its designers, which enable it to accomplish its purpose. For the *Saturn V*, this rocket essence preceded the existence of any single rocket that eventually stood majestically on the launch pad. For created objects, therefore, *essence* precedes *existence.*

Not so for man, argued Sartre. For man *existence* precedes *essence.* Man was not planned out on a drawing board, nor was he preconceived in any mind (divine or otherwise) for a *purpose* and *then* designed to fulfill such a purpose. Man is not created as objects are created. *Man creates himself.* Man even designs himself—*from within.* Each person is unique since no master template stamps out identical copies of persons, like minted coins. Therefore man has no essence, as does the rocket, that *predetermines* what he shall be and do. For man, and man alone, existence precedes essence.

Existentialism is a philosophy of time and consciousness. To emphasize existence is to place supreme value upon the quality of one's immediate consciousness. As a philosophy of time, existentialism counsels us to exist as fully as possible in the living "now," to accept and actualize the intense "human reality" of the spontaneous present. For the existentialist, the past is only a repertory of recordings to be used in the service of the present, and the future is but a set of dreams to give the present direction and purpose.

Existentialism asks that we reexamine the way in which we live out our existence within that duration we call the present. Sartre reiterates that the

*All animals, large or small, homeothermic or poikilothermic, burn the light of their lives with relative equality. Life, at least on the organismic level, is a democratic process: all of us must die, and the duration of our existence is the same. . . .*

ROLAND FISCHER

## AWARENESS

Awareness means the capacity to see a coffeepot and hear the birds sing in one's own way, and not the way one was taught. It may be assumed on good grounds that seeing and hearing have a different quality for infants than for grownups, and that they are more esthetic and less intellectual in the first years of life. A little boy sees and hears birds with delight. Then the "good father" comes along and feels he should "share" the experience and help his son "develop." He says: "That's a jay, and this is a sparrow." The moment the little boy is concerned with which is a jay and which is a sparrow, he can no longer see the birds or hear them sing. Father has good reasons on his side, since few people can afford to go through life listening to the birds sing, and the sooner the little boy starts his "education" the better. Maybe he will be an ornithologist when he grows up. A few people, however, can still see and hear in the old way. But most of the members of the human race have lost the capacity to be painters, poets or musicians, and are not left the option of seeing and hearing directly even if they can afford to; they must get it secondhand. The recovery of this ability is called here "awareness."

ERIC BERNE
*Games People Play*

choice is ours as to how we create consciousness. We can hand it over to conditioned responses from our past; we can allow feelings, memories, or habits to impinge upon our present and determine its content and quality. Similarly, we can allow anxieties about future events to impinge upon our present and rob it of its spontaneity and intensity. Thus we can allow our "now" to be deadened.

As a philosophy of time, therefore, existentialism is a way of reevaluating how we use and abuse consciousness. But more than that, it contends that we *can* do something about how time is lived. Within the parameters of our unique personal existence, we can make decisions as to how we shall live the only thing that, in the final analysis, each of us actually possesses—namely, consciousness of time present.

*What it all comes down to is that we just have to now harder!*

**JACK REIDLING**

The creative person, instead of perceiving in predetermined categories ("trees are green," "college education is a good thing," "modern art is silly") is aware of this existential moment as it *is,* and therefore he is alive to many experiences which fall outside the usual categories (in *this* light this tree is lavender; *this* college education is damaging; *this* modern sculpture has a powerful effect on me).

The creative person is in this way open to his own experiences. It means a lack of rigidity and the permeability of boundaries in concepts, beliefs, perceptions and hypotheses. It means a tolerance of ambiguity where ambiguity exists. It means the ability to receive much conflicting information without forcing closure on the situation.

CARL ROGERS

*How dull it is to pause, to*
  *make an end,*
*To rust unburnish'd, not to*
  *shine in use!*
*As tho' to breathe were life.*
**ALFRED, LORD TENNYSON**
*Ulysses*

At the end of the spring semester, I packed a few articles and began a four-day trip through the mountains. It was the end of an especially trying school year, and I wanted to make the most of a short vacation before returning to teach summer school.

The countryside was still green and wildflowers gathered in nodding communities along the roadside. I drove alone in my small car, and in a small car one can feel very close to things about him. As I drove, or when I stopped to absorb the landscape, I could almost touch the reddish earth, the striated rocks, the weeds and flowers and grasses. I was one among them.

So I travelled. I saw the trees, the flowers, the animals. The broken clouds sometimes painted blue-green patches on the hillsides. I looked up at tall pines and they looked down at me. I smelled pine fragrance and listened to bird calls.

I began to feel alive again. I was *experiencing* things instead of *doing* things. I was feeling and seeing and hearing rather than thinking about . . . and trying to remember . . . and planning ahead.

Or so I thought.

As I watched cloud-shadows shaping their way across the valleys I caught myself deciding if I should reach for my camera. Would they show up just right in color? And was that lightning-split pine silhouetted in black-and-white against the sky "artistic" enough for a picture? I saw purple flowers and found myself wondering if they were lupines, wild larkspurs, or what.

I had the right names for few of the beautiful things I beheld: golden poppies, lavender verbenas, sprays of yellow mustard. Also for the pines (I could remember "ponderosa") and cedars (all I could recall was "juniper"). How little I knew! My new-found ignorance bothered me.

But somewhere—and I don't know when or why—I began to realize what I was doing. I was seeing things just to stuff them into my memory *for later use.* I was building a storehouse of pretty details to impress upon others *after I returned.* The mental habits which dominated my days during the year still controlled my brain. I was organizing the events of my journey as though it were another classroom preparation!

I was insane! Quite literally, I was insane! I was allowing myself to pass my hours out of touch with the realities around me. Here I was in the midst of life, and I wasn't seeing it, wasn't hearing it, wasn't feeling it. Rather than experiencing, I was expending my time *processing* experiences!

I became determined, then, to stop my processing habits. When the next cluster of wildflowers appeared beside the road, I didn't say to myself, as to an audience: "I see a cluster of golden poppies . . . " Rather, I experienced them—saw them, felt them, moved among them, savored them. I refused to let my mind tag them with names or tie them into bundles.

As I tell it now, I find words sufficient to describe my memory of the undulating flight of the mockingbird and the gliding turn of the swallow. I can recount my memories of the smell of pines and fresh rains.

These are things I can do now. But before my short journey ended, I had proved to myself that I could recover the capacity to experience afresh the world about me. I had succeeded in touching reality again.

JUNE HILLMAN

*I don't know what you could say about a day in which you have seen four beautiful sunsets.*

ASTRONAUT JOHN GLENN
*(in orbit around the earth, February 20, 1962)*

## REFLECTIONS

1   The beginning of this chapter speaks of a "philosophy of time." What do you think is meant by such a phrase? What benefits might derive from having a philosophy of time? Has this chapter helped you in developing a philosophy of time or, better, a philosophy of how to use time?

2   Read the following passages synoptically: pp. 259–260; pp. 219–221. What must we infer regarding the necessities of thought and communication and the nature of reality? Or, more bluntly, can you actually buy "the astounding fact that we can and do communicate with one another continually *without* knowing *what* we are talking about?!"

3    Summarize in your mind the three "kinds of time" dealt with in this chapter. Can you get a good grasp of each kind of time, and do the concepts sound right to you?

4    Ponder the fact that psychological time is an extreme variable (pp. 261–263; and review the boxed material on p. 166, "What time is it?"). Have you felt the impact of the fact that, as individuals, we actually experience time in quite different ways? Would this insight lead you to revise your attitude toward certain behavior in others that is time-related?

5    How long does "the present" last? Does it have duration or "width"? Do you think you could get the psychologist and the mathematician to agree on the matter?

6    Does "the past" exist? Where? What are we truly referring to when we speak of the past?

7    Reflect on the quotation from Arthur C. Clarke (see marginal quote on p. 265) and criticize it. (Here is an interesting case in which *a statement* can be both true and false at the same time, depending upon the interpretation of terms. Can you show how Clarke is both right and wrong?)

8    Can "the future" exist? Is precognition possible, in your opinion? What sort of time model could you develop that would permit the possibility of precognition?

9    The subject that touches us all where we live is our experience of time. After reflecting on pp. 270–273, and the boxed material on p. 168, what is your personal response to the existential philosophy of experience implied in these passages?

*The middle-class man is oriented chiefly toward the future. When he is young he hears repeatedly: "Think of your future," whereas the son of a good family is asked again and again: "What would your grandmother say?" On the other hand, members of the working classes have neither past nor future. What matters to them is to live in the present without concern for a past which inspires or a future which is too uncertain.*

PAUL FRAISSE

# 4 3

## THE FEELING OF FREEDOM

I would like to describe for you a pattern of experience which I have observed, and in which I have participated. . . . It is an experience on which I have placed various labels as I have tried to think about it—becoming a person, freedom to be, courage to be, learning to be free—yet the experience is something broader than, and deeper than, any of its labels. It is quite possible that the words I use in regard to it may miscommunicate. The speculations and ideas I present, based on this experience, may be erroneous, or partly erroneous. But the experience itself *exists*. It is a deeply compelling phenomenon for any one who has observed it, or who has lived it.

CARL ROGERS

*The Buddha can only tell you the way: it is for you yourself to make the effort.*

***The Dhammapada***

But does the experience of freedom, in fact, exist? Or does the *feeling* of freedom mask an illusion?

In one experiment with hypnosis, a man was led into a deep trance and given a simple posthypnotic suggestion. About a month from that date, he was told, after lunch on a certain day, he would sing "America the Beautiful." During the week following this first suggestion, it was reinforced twice during similar deep trances. But at no time was the man informed that any posthypnotic instructions had been given.

When the day for singing arrived, he recalls having the feeling in the morning that he wanted to sing; he did in fact hum or sing a few bars of various tunes. As noontime neared, the impulse to sing unexplainably grew stronger.

Immediately after lunch, he sauntered over to the piano, let his fingers move over the keyboard, and then, on schedule, proceeded to sing "America the Beautiful."

This sort of experiment is common enough in hypnosis. The significant point has to do with *cause:* what *caused* him to sing this specific song at this appointed time. He *felt* free. He felt that it was a *choice* that he had made, and that he could have made other choices. But paradoxically, he also *felt* determined. The impulse to sing the song grew to such proportions that it was difficult or impossible *not* to act it out.

## THE DILEMMA OF DETERMINISM

*If a man referred to his brother or to his cat as "an ingenious mechanism," we should know that he was either a fool or a physiologist. No one in practice treats himself or his fellow-man or his pet animals as machines; but scientists who have never made a study of Speculative Philosophy seem often to think it their duty to hold in theory what no one outside a lunatic asylum would accept in practice.*

C. D. BROAD

This dramatic experiment symbolizes one of our deepest human dilemmas. On the one hand, we feel free; our social lives are founded on the assumption that we and others make genuine choices and should be responsible for them. We blame others for mistakes (that is, they were free *not* to have made them), and we feel guilt at our own mistakes (that is, we ourselves could, and should, have acted differently).

On the other hand, we feel determined. As Saint Paul eloquently put it, "I do not understand what I am doing, for I do not do what I want to do; I do the things that I hate. . . . I do not do the good things that I want to do; I do the wrong things that I do not want to do. But if I do the things that I do not want to do, it is not I that am acting. . . ." Paul's lament rises to a painful crescendo: "What a wretched human being I am!"

Based on experience, we are forced into the conclusion that there are capricious causal forces inside us, directing us to do countless acts against our wills. It was only natural that premodern man interpreted these forces as good/evil spirits thrashing around inside him—"possessing" him—and acting as causal agents behind the thoughts, feelings, and actions over which he felt little control. Today we can better account for the causes of our behavior in empirical terms—in terms of conditioning or with physiological or chemical explanations. Still, the result is the same: we have a dual experience of both freedom and determinism. Both experiences *feel* authentic, and we have never quite understood how to reconcile the apparent contradiction.

Western Christian theology has symbolized this experiential dilemma with remarkable accuracy. There is abundant biblical support for two basic beliefs: (1) God is omnipotent and he therefore determines every event in our lives; (2) Man possesses free will and is therefore responsible for his sins; he can justly be condemned to hell for wrong decisions.

In their extreme forms, these two doctrines are logically contradictory; they can't both be true. But Western theology had no alternative but to accept both as absolutely true; they were both given (hence, not debatable) by biblical authority and ecclesiastical tradition. For almost two thousand years now, Christian theologians have wrestled valiantly with these two doctrines, trying to harmonize them so that men could believe both and maintain their intellectual honesty. No two theologians have resolved the problem in exactly the same way—in fact no solution is wholly free of logical difficulties—but there are several general approaches toward a solution. If either doctrine is softened, then they can be reconciled. If God does not predetermine every event of our lives, then we can claim to have some free will; or, if we admit that we are not wholly free, then some predestination can be accepted.

Whatever the solution, however, the striking point is that the theological formulation is an accurate doctrinization of the very real human dilemma. We

## PUPPET THEATER?

We see the puppets dancing on their miniature stage, moving up and down as the strings pull them around, following the prescribed course of their various little parts. We learn to understand the logic of this theater and we find ourselves in its motions. We locate ourselves in society and thus recognize our own position as we hang from its subtle strings. For a moment we see ourselves as puppets indeed. But then we grasp a decisive difference between the puppet theater and our own drama. Unlike the puppets, we have the possibility of stopping in our movements, looking up and perceiving the machinery by which we have been moved. In this act lies the first step towards freedom.

PETER L. BERGER
*Invitation to Sociology*

are *both* determined *and* free; and somehow we must work at the contradiction until we achieve a realistic understanding of how both can be true.

## PRIMAL AND SECONDARY LIMITATIONS

Without prejudging at this point the relative degrees of human freedom and determinism we experience, we can speak meaningfully of the limiting factors that diminish our freedom. The point to note is that we confuse primal limitations with secondary limitations: it follows that we also confuse primal freedoms with secondary freedoms. Distinguishing between them is crucial.

*Primal freedom* is inner freedom, and primal limitations come from within. These limitations may be genetic (sickle-cell anemia, thalidomide deformities), physiological (paralysis from polio or accident), ontological (fear of death and nonbeing), or conditioned (inability to trust or love). Such limitations are causal; they inhibit us from thinking, feeling, or doing specific things; and as causes, they arise from inside our own psychophysiological organism. Primal freedom, therefore, is freedom *from* such limitations: from conflicts and frustrations, unfounded fears, nail-biting anxieties, lingering hatreds, debilitating habits, and life-negating bitterness. Primal freedom is freedom *for* the full utilization of our abilities, the freedom for each person—considering all the givens of his own unique existence—to be all that he can be.

Primal limitations burden us all. We may want to enjoy a day at the beach but find, while there, that we are reliving the emotional battles of the day; and try as we will, we can only act at having fun. Or we try to concentrate on reading a book, but in vain, because relentless worries intrude and disturb our will-to-thought. And how often do we undertake a task, knowing full well we have the capabilities to accomplish it, only to find that primal limitations—fears of inadequacy, fears of others' opinions, even fear of success itself—keep us from attaining our goal? Freedom from all these inner limitations is primal freedom.

By contrast, *secondary limitations* originate in our environment. Therefore, we can speak of secondary freedoms as freedom from external limitations.

*Let [the child] believe that he is always in control, though it is always you [the teacher] who really controls. There is no subjugation so perfect as that which keeps the appearance of freedom, for in that way one captures volition itself. . . .*

JEAN-JACQUES ROUSSEAU

Secondary limitations are placed upon us by nature itself (we can't move backward in time), and by other persons and by our society. We are limited by the customs, common-sense traditions, sociological structures, moral suasions, and civil laws of the society in which we live. We are also limited by the immediate needs and desires of other people. Such secondary limiters impose upon us injunctions *not* to think, feel, and do specific things.

We cause ourselves endless troubles by confusing primal freedom with various secondary freedoms. We often think we are being subjected to external limitations when in fact we are suffering from inner restraints, and vice versa. Primal limitations are undoubtedly more difficult for us to admit and face; recognition of them presupposes some degree of self-knowledge, the ability to empathize with others, and some capacity for abstract thinking. Since secondary limitations appear more concrete, and since we share them with others and can deal with them collectively ("Fight gun control," "Stop abortion"), we often expend great amounts of energy in crusades against particular "encroachments upon our freedoms."

We may never realize that such crusades are in fact a struggle against primal limitations. We may accuse others of not liking us when the source of our agony is that we don't like ourselves. We may accuse others of conspiring to harm us when our problem is that we have never developed the capacity to trust. In such cases, our desire for freedom is authentic, but we have mislocated the source of the limitation.

This is why it is common for us to spend our lives fighting for causes, only to find later that (to parody a cliché) the causes were won but our freedoms were lost. We may indeed achieve specific freedoms ("The bill finally passed!"), only to find that we are bound with the same primal fetters as before. We do not *experience* an increase of freedom. But having a row of (secondary) freedom awards to point to, we can't quite understand why we don't experience more freedom.

Other things being equal, the greater one's experience of primal freedom, the less he is concerned with secondary freedoms; and conversely, those who are deeply driven to crusade for secondary freedoms are often suffering from excruciating primal limitations.

Few philosophical problems have greater practical implications than the question of freedom versus determinism.

For one thing, if there is no freedom, then there can be no moral, legal, or any other kind of responsibility. Yet the fact of personal responsibility is one of our most cherished assumptions. We blame others for their mistakes and give them credit for their achievements. We hold ourselves responsible and feel guilt for our misdoings. We indict alleged lawbreakers, hold trials, and convict or free them. We operate on the assumption that human beings can be morally and legally responsible—that is, free. But if our assumption of freedom is false, then life as we live it is a cruel joke founded upon a tragic illusion. We are playing the game all wrong.

Secondly, we struggle from day to day and year to year, in desperation or joy, and always with hope, to attain our life goals. But if we are not free, then all our striving is meaningless. We only think we set our own goals whereas in fact they are set for us; and whether or not we attain them is apparently already determined, or at least out of our hands. Life itself, as struggle, is an illusion.

---

*What is an obstacle for me may not be so for another. There is no obstacle in an absolute sense. . . . Human-reality everywhere encounters resistance and obstacles which it has not created, but these resistances and obstacles have meaning only in and through the free choice which human-reality is.*

JEAN-PAUL SARTRE

*If man has once become aware that in his forlornness he imposes values, he can no longer want but one thing, and that is freedom, as the basis of all values. That doesn't mean that he wants it in the abstract. It means simply that the ultimate meaning of the acts of honest men is the quest for freedom as such.*

JEAN-PAUL SARTRE

Thirdly, and most deeply, the question of freedom has to do with what we are—or aren't. What can life mean if we have no freedom to make choices, choose life-styles, set goals? Since we labor under the deepest conviction that, to some extent at least, we are free, then existence itself is a hoax. We think we're free, feel like we're free, act like we're free; we treat ourselves and others as though we were free; we develop monumental moral and legal systems based upon the assumption that we're free—all this fantasized by blind puppets dangling helplessly on black nylon strings?

We are not what we think we are; life is not what we think it is; the rules of the game are not what we thought. Maybe we discover that we're not playing the game at all: *we are the chessmen and something or someone else is playing the game.*

## THE CASE FOR DETERMINISM

For almost fifteen years, Dr. Bruno Bettelheim followed the case of Joey—"the mechanical boy." Joey's loss of freedom was clearly psychogenic rather than genetic or physiological. From birth he had been almost completely ignored; to his mother he hardly existed. Since all that he was as a budding human was bothersome and unacceptable, he quickly got the message; his humanness must be eliminated—repressed. So Joey literally became a machine. He acquainted himself very early with machines and could dismantle and reassemble them with some skill. He also envied the machines and identified with them; they were liked, toyed with; they gave no trouble, were never punished. Gradually he came to think of himself as a machine.

Before he could eat, for instance, he would unroll his imaginary cord and plug it into the outlet, set his switches, and check his bulbs. He could perform routine actions only after he had monitored his circuits, checked his dials, flipped the right switches. He made sure his machine-self was working properly.

All this was more than merely a game of playing like a machine; this "game" was deadly serious. He was playing the machine-game to escape the unbearable anguish of further rejection of any of his human qualities.

Bettelheim noted that "Joey's pathological behavior seemed the external expression of an overwhelming effort to remain almost nonexistent as a person." Joey had created a world of his own that he could live in, a world that was preferable to the hostile real world. In his fantasy-world he had found a way of life which was at least tolerable. Since he did not need to be human, his human qualities atrophied; more and more Joey *became* a machine.

Machines are not free. Indeed, the word doesn't apply. Machines operate on principles of cause and effect—total determinism. Joey "the mechanical boy" knew no freedom.

One of the strongest contemporary cases for determinism has been made by a psychologist-novelist who—in *Beyond Freedom and Dignity*—has become a philosopher: Dr. B. F. Skinner of Harvard.

According to Skinner's way of thinking, freedom is a myth, and a dangerous myth because we have invested the myth and its symbol ("freedom") with

*One's ability to move his hand at will is more directly and certainly known than are Newton's laws. If these laws deny one's ability to move his hand at will, the preferable conclusion is that Newton's laws require modification.*

ARTHUR COMPTON

B. F. Skinner

something close to sacred qualities. It is a fact that many of those who think they disagree with Skinner are eager to make his observations the object of religious and patriotic causes. (Skinner's book was still warm from the press when one congressman, in a speech before the House, denounced him for "advancing ideas which threaten the future of our system of government by denigrating the American traditions of individualism, human dignity, and self-reliance." As is so often the case, further comments revealed a fundamental misunderstanding of what Skinner is saying.)

Freedom, Skinner argues, is not a fact of human experiences. *All* of our responses—the impulses that lie behind so-called free choices—are the result of unique past contingencies of conditioning and reinforcement that have shaped us into what we are. Skinner's famed laboratory experiments with pigeons and rats have shown that animal behavior can be predicted and controlled, and even produced according to specification. By selecting specific causes (stimuli), desired effects (responses) will result. This is merely the application to the field of animal behavior the scientific assumption of causality. The assumption that every cause produces an effect and every effect is preceded by a cause is the foundation of all science. Whatever made us think that it would *not* apply to the behavioral sciences as well as to the natural sciences?

What we *call* freedom is merely the successful avoidance on the part of any organism of some aversive feature in its environment. All organisms are manipulated and controlled, therefore, by the dynamic features of their environments.

To be sure, when Skinner writes that freedom is an illusion, he is not denying our experience of a rather pleasant *emotion* that we commonly call freedom; but he is saying unequivocally that this emotion is itself a *conditioned* (caused) response. We may label this feeling "freedom" or something else; but whatever we call it, it has been produced by past experience; it was conditioned into us at some prior time and now becomes, in turn, the causal agent of present behavior.

Among the illustrations used by Skinner are the accounts of the falling leaf and the buzzing fly.

Picture a leaf, yellowed from the first frosts, fluttering and suddenly beginning to fall from the top of a tall, red-gold maple tree. In zigzag motions, hovering on the currents of air, it picks a poetic path downward and settles eventually upon a cushion of leaves on the ground.

Now, there isn't a physicist alive who would argue that the leaf is "free." We esthetic onlookers may be mesmerized by the leaf's timeless descent, and even envy the "freedom" of the floating maple leaf wafting to earth. But we have confused our poetic idealism with our physics. The fact is that the leaf follows precisely known laws of physics, laws that can easily be found in any physics textbook.

Yet as the leaf starts its historic fall from the top of the maple tree, what physicist, by applying his formulas, could predict the leaf's trajectory or the spot where it will finally come to rest? The journey is too complex; there are too many variables: air currents, atmospheric density (in terms of elevation above sea level and barometric pressure), humidity, minute photon forces, the mass and volume of the leaf, its configuration, and so on. The number of possible combinations of variables is so great that, although knowing all the applicable

*Give me a dozen healthy infants and I'll guarantee to take any one at random and train him to become any type of specialist I might select— doctor, lawyer, even beggar-man and thief, regardless of his talents, penchants, tendencies, abilities.*

JOHN B. WATSON (1925)

### SAINT THOMAS AQUINAS
## *The Paradox of Determinism*

*I   Man is predestined . . .*

It is fitting that God should predestine men. For all things are subject to His
Providence. . . . As men are ordained to eternal life through the Providence of
God, it likewise is part of that Providence to permit some to fall away from that
end; this is called reprobation. . . . As predestination includes the will to confer
grace and glory, so also reprobation includes the will to permit a person to fall
into sin, and so impose the punishment of damnation on account of that sin.

*Summa Theologica*, I, 23, I, 3
*Summa contra Gentiles*, III, 163

Saint Thomas Aquinas
(1225–1274)

*II   Man is free . . .*

Man has free choice, or otherwise counsels, exhortations, commands, prohi-
bitions, rewards and punishments would be in vain.

If the will were deprived of freedom . . . no praise would be given to human
virtue; since virtue would be of no account if man acted not freely: there would
be no justice in rewarding or punishing, if man were not free in acting well or ill:
and there would be no prudence in taking advice, which would be of no use if
things occurred of necessity . . .

*Summa Theologica*, I, 83, 1
*Summa contra Gentiles*, III, 73

*III   Can man be both predestined and free?*

The predestined must necessarily be saved, yet by a conditional necessity,
which does not do away with the liberty of choice. . . .

Man's turning to God is by free choice; and thus man is bidden to turn himself to God. But free choice can be turned to God only when God turns it. . . . It
is the part of man to prepare his soul, since he does this by his free choice. And
yet he does not do this without the help of God moving him. . . . And thus even
the good movement of free choice, whereby anyone is prepared for receiving the
gift of grace, is an act of free choice moved by God. . . . Man's preparation for
grace is from God, as mover, and from free choice, as moved.

*Summa Theologica*, I, 23, 3; I–II, 109, 6; I–II, 112, 2, 3.

laws, predicting the leaf's path or destination is a feat quite beyond the ability
of any physicist (or computer) today.

So, is the leaf "free" in any proper sense of the word? Not at all. It follows
inexorable causal laws.

Elsewhere, Skinner ponders a housefly buzzing around a room. In describing the motions of the maple leaf, we were applying physical laws to a passive
object. The trajectory of the buzzing fly is infinitely more complex since we are
dealing with the active nervous system of a living thing. Our causal factors, to
some extent, become internal.

Carl Rogers (1902–1987)

If we knew *everything* about the buzzing fly—its previous conditioning, its present chemical states, its "needs," "drives," "goals," or whatever, and all the aerodynamics of a fly's flight—then, according to Skinner, we could predict exactly where the fly will buzz, where it will land, what it will eat, and so on.

But we are facing the same paradox with the fly as with the leaf. We might feel that the fly is free as it flies about; it looks free; it even seems to make choices. But such freedom is myth, Skinner contends. There is no more freedom in any buzz of the fly than there was in any flutter of the leaf. Every motion could be predicted if the causal forces were precisely known. More simply, all matter-in-motion obeys the laws of physics, and a fly is matter-in-motion.

These same principles apply to human action, and our complexity, apparently, is no argument against determinism, since the same causal laws apply in every case. Our behavior is more complex than the fly's just as the fly's behavior is more complex than the leaf's. But freedom is just as much a fallacy for us as it is for the leaf or fly.

Carl Rogers says freedom exists. Skinner says it doesn't. Rogers records the following brief exchange between them at a conference at which Skinner had read a paper.

> From what I understand Dr. Skinner to say, it is his understanding that though he might have thought *he chose* to come to this meeting, might have thought he had a purpose in giving this speech, such thoughts are really illusory. He actually made certain marks on paper and emitted certain sounds here simply because his genetic makeup and his past environment had operantly conditioned his behavior in such a way that it was rewarding to make these sounds, and that he as a person doesn't enter into this. In fact if I get his thinking correctly, from his strictly scientific point, he, as a person, doesn't exist.

In his reply to Rogers, "Dr. Skinner said that he would not go into the question of whether he had any choice in the matter (presumably because the whole issue is illusory) but stated, 'I do accept your characterization of my own presence here.'"

## THE CASE FOR FREEDOM OF CHOICE

Human freedom has been stoutly defended by a distinguished line of thinkers in various traditions, East and West. No voice in its defense has been more persuasive than that of the existentialist philosopher Jean-Paul Sartre, whose vehement pronouncements for freedom arose from his own intense experience of human struggle during the Nazi occupation of France in World War II.

The fashionable notion that we are predetermined in our behavior by past experiences—by "operant conditioning"—to the point of losing our free will—this, for Sartre, is an outrageous fallacy. On the contrary, man is not merely responsible for what he does, but he is even responsible for all that he is.

Sartre is convinced that there is no determinism of any kind. *Nothing* tells me what to do. I myself decide. I cannot blame God, or others, or my past environment. I am—now—what I make myself to be. I have to accept the consequences of my own freedom, take the responsibility for my decisions, and face the consequences thereof. For human freedom, as Sartre sees it, is not always a blessing; it is more often a tragedy. Whether we like it or not, man is *condemned to be free.*

But why does Sartre speak of our being "condemned" to freedom? Why such a gloomy term? Shouldn't freedom be a joyous thing? Sartre's position is that freedom carries with it an unavoidable anguish when we fully realize how overwhelming the implications of our freedom can be. It entails tragic choices with formidable consequences. Out of our freedom we do not make decisions for ourselves alone, but for others, and sometimes for all mankind. To realize completely what this means can be a nightmarish insight into the very nature of human existence.

To be free means to be caught in a paradox. We are forever dissatisfied with existence as we know it. But to live means to dream a million dreams and forge ahead to catch the fullness of our being. Indeed, each mortal man wants to be God, but the truer fact is that we are finite and our limitations are crushing. Still, they are unacceptable. So we continue to compete and strive, dreaming our dreams, even though they are futile dreams, and even though we know it.

Why? Why do we do all this? Simply because we cannot do otherwise. For to exist is to be free, and to be free is to act, to take initiative, to make choices and decisions, to dream impossible dreams—however unreachable they are—and to fail. In a word, we *must try to do* what we already know we *cannot* do.

Sartre was attempting to get us to see that we exist in an antinomian world without guidelines. Cultural norms are relative, and societies are humorlessly absurd. There is no God and therefore no absolute mandates to give life order. There is no meaning to human life as such. Nor is there any past conditioning that we can blame for making us what we are. There is not even a "human nature" that might help us to define ourselves.

There is nothing to help us—because the moment we become conscious of what we are, then we become responsible for everything we are and do. Of course, we can join the mob and let our passions collectively carry us along, but *we make the decision* to do so, and we are responsible for that decision. We can conform to society's whims, or follow an irrelevant, legalistic ethical code, or accede to peer pressures; but in each instance *we make the decision* to do so, and we must accept the responsibility for that decision.

Whenever we are conscious, therefore, we are responsible. For at the cutting edge of consciousness, we are truly free. At each moment of the living present, we have an infinite number of choices before us, ways of thinking, feeling, and behaving—the options are numberless, so many that to feel them fully is to become overwhelmed by them. It's at this moment of revelation that we frequently retreat into the myths of determinism. We convince ourselves that we move within carefully defined and unbreakable limits, and that we are not really free. Yet, from behind our safe parameters we will *claim* to be free. We are "not supposed" to think, feel, or do certain things, or so we are told by society, church, friends, laws, conscience. But all these excuses are retreats from freedom; and the true fact is that we can do all of them. But since experience of such freedom is fraught with fear, we eagerly accept all the fashionable limitations.

Jean-Paul Sartre penned a now-famous passage about the experiences of the French Resistance movement against the Nazis in France.

Jean-Paul Sartre (1905–1980)

*This is one of man's oldest riddles. How can the independence of human volition be harmonized with the fact that we are integral parts of a universe which is subject to the rigid order of Nature's laws?*

Sir Arthur Eddington

*We are forced to fall back on fatalism as an explanation of irrational events, that is to say, of events the rationality of which we do not understand.*

Leo Tolstoy

We were never more free than during the German occupation. We had lost all our rights, beginning with the right to talk. Every day we were insulted to our faces and had to take it in silence. Under one pretext or another, as workers, Jews, or political prisoners, we were deported *en masse*. Everywhere, on billboards, in the newspapers, on the screen, we encountered the revolting and insipid picture of ourselves that our suppressors wanted us to accept. And because of all this we were free. Because the Nazi venom seeped into our thoughts, every accurate thought was a conquest. Because an all-powerful police tried to force us to hold our tongues, every word took on the value of a declaration of principles. Because we were hunted down, every one of our gestures had the weight of a solemn commitment. . . .

Exile, captivity, and especially death (which we usually shrink from facing at all in happier days) became for us the habitual objects of our concern. We learned that they were neither inevitable accidents, nor even constant and inevitable dangers, but they must be considered as our lot itself, our destiny, the profound source of our reality as men. At every instant we lived up to the full sense of this commonplace little phrase: "Man is mortal!" And the choice that each of us made of his life was an authentic choice because it was made face to face with death, because it could always have been expressed in these terms: "Rather death than . . ." And here I am not speaking of the elite among us who were real Resistants, but of all Frenchmen who, at every hour of the night and day throughout four years, answered *No*.

The essential freedom, the ultimate and final freedom that cannot be taken from a man, is to say No. This is the basic premise in Sartre's view of human freedom: freedom is in its very essence negative, though this negativity is also creative. At a certain moment, perhaps, the drug or the pain inflicted by the torturer may make the victim lose consciousness, and he will confess. But so long as he retains the lucidity of consciousness, however tiny the area of action possible for him, he can still say in his own mind: No. Consciousness and freedom are thus given together. Only if consciousness is blotted out can man be deprived of this residual freedom. Where all the avenues of action are blocked for a man, this freedom may seem a tiny and unimportant thing; but it is in fact total and absolute, and Sartre is right to insist upon it as such, for it affords man his final dignity, that of being man.

WILLIAM BARRETT

## REFLECTIONS

1 What do you think of the account of the man who was hypnotized and told he would sing "America the Beautiful?" Does this episode frighten you? What implications do you see in this story regarding the question of human freedom? Would you care to go so far as to liken childhood to a prolonged period of "posthypnotic suggestions"?

2 In brief, why is the age-old question of free will such a crucial problem? And why is it imperative today that we find a workable solution?

3 Does the description on pp. 275–276 of our human predicament as a "feeling dilemma"—We *feel* free and we *feel* determined—sound like an accurate account of your own experience and observation? How would you express the problem?

4 Distinguish between primary and secondary freedoms, and between primary and secondary limitations. Can you think of illustrations from your experience where "we cause ourselves endless troubles by confusing primal freedom with various secondary freedoms"?

5 After reading this chapter, jot down your thoughts regarding the following: (1) Is the question of freedom/determinism an authentic question or does it need to be rephrased in the light of modern knowledge? (2) To what degree can we be truly free? (3) To what degree are we determined, and what determines us? (4) Is the idea of the "growth of freedom" a justifiable concept?

6 After you reach some conclusions (though tentative) about the extent of our determined condition, how much do you think we should be held responsible, morally and legally, for our behavior?

7 Note the boxed excerpts on p. 281. How well do you think Aquinas reconciled the two biblical "givens"—free will and predestination? If you're up to the challenge and would enjoy an exercise in theological logic, try to work out a better reconciliation.

8 Is the question of divine predestination a problem for you personally? Have you, at some time, committed yourself to a predestinarian position? If so, do you have evidence to offer in support of that position? Would you contend that we are *also* free agents? (That is, do you hold yourself responsible for what you do?) How do you reconcile these two positions?

9 What does Jean-Paul Sartre mean when he says that we are "condemned to be free"? Do you share his mood regarding the human condition? Do you agree with him when he insists that we *always* have a choice?

*Life is like a game of cards. The hand that is dealt you represents determinism; the way you play it is free will.*
JAWARHARLAL NEHRU

4

## The Functions of Language

Aside from the practical need to transmit survival information, the fundamental goal of all communication is to transcend our egocentric predicament. We are located from birth till death in a space/time predicament that subjects us to limitations we can't accept. Communication between living creatures is a means of transcending this condition. We create symbolic media for transmitting to other beings something of the experience-world going on inside us.

We invent symbols, therefore, that can stimulate the sensors of another person. From this we would like to persuade ourselves that, because we can activate the senses of another organism, we can transfer living experience from one person to another. We want to believe in—and we profoundly long for—a transfer of *content* rather than symbolic transmittals between closed systems.

Man is therefore a symbolic creature *because of* his egocentric predicament. If direct transfer of living experience could somehow be arranged, he would hasten to dispense with all his symbols.

Note that we humans share this condition with all living creatures. The common statement that man is a symbolic creature, while other animals are not, is false. They too must resort to symbolic means of bursting through their egocentric predicaments: the courtship rituals and territorial warnings of birds, the danger barks of baboons, the scent that the female gypsy moth disperses through the night air—these are analogous to man's symbolic communication, and are used for the same reasons.

Man's ability to use highly abstracted and complex symbols is not to be denigrated, of course. But with all our symbolic sophistication, is our transmittal of *experience* all that great? Are we, as a matter of fact, less lonely?

Most of us tacitly assume that the primary function of language is the

*"When I use a word,"
Humpty-Dumpty said in a
rather scornful tone, "it
means just what I choose it
to mean—neither more nor
less."*

*"The question is," said
Alice, "whether you can make
words mean different things."*

*"The question is," said
Humpty-Dumpty, "which is to
be master—that's all!"*

LEWIS CARROLL

DOCTOR: *"How did you happen
to call him Harvey?"*

DR. DOWD: *"Well, Harvey's his
name!"*

MARY CHASE
*Harvey*

*Words, strain,
crack, and sometime break,
under the burden.*

T. S. ELIOT

*The tragedy of our age is the
awful incommunicability of
souls.*

W. O. MARTIN

"Although humans make sounds with their mouths and occasionally look at each other, there is no solid evidence that they actually communicate with each other."

rational communication of ideas, whereas our everyday experience shows that this isn't so. Happily, our linguistic equipment is designed to serve numerous functions.

In the following list of ten common uses of language, note that usage falls into two categories, whether the primary purpose is to change conditions in ourselves (the subject—S) or in another (the object—O). Equally significant is whether the specific usage is designed to promote emotional results (E) or rational/intellectual results (R). A glance at the list indicates that primary functions of language are emotional rather than rational and that much use of language is reflexive—designed to alter conditions within ourselves.

Language is used to accomplish the following goals:

S (1)    *To express emotion* (E). "I love you." "Younger than springtime am I" (from *South Pacific*). "Ouch!" "Damn!" Found here also are the interminable arguments we get into that take the form of idea-exchange but that in fact are prolonged venting of accumulated emotional charges. One of the prime functions of taboo words (obscenities, "four-letter words," and so forth) and name calling is to let off emotional steam.

S (2)    *To drown out silence* (E). In countless ordinary situations we find silence intolerable: waiting along with others in a doctor's office, sitting beside someone on a bus or plane, passing time with a casual acquaintance. Polite social conversation generally lessens our anxiety. When alone we often turn on TV or radio to ease our loneliness; lacking these, some of us talk with ourselves.

POLONIUS: *"What do you read, my lord?"*

HAMLET: *"Words, words, words."*

SHAKESPEARE

S (3)    *To enjoy the sounds of language* (E). Language produces aesthetic pleasure, especially familiar phrases with happy associations. This is one purpose of much poetry—"word music." Also, just as there is "mood music" there is "mood language," a fact well known to preachers, hypnotists, playwrights—indeed, to anyone wishing to "set the tone" for an ensuing event.

S (4) *To establish a feeling of belonging* (E). Religious ceremonies in which words are repeated together—unison prayers, litanies, chants; protest chants; cheers led by cheerleaders; war dances; "We shall overcome." Especially effective are hymns, national anthems, and songs recalling a past togetherness—the singing of the alma mater or fraternity/sorority songs.

SO (5) *To establish relationships* (E). "Aloha." "Good morning." "How do you do?" "Buenos días, señor." "How've you been?" "Bonjour, monsieur." "Shalom aleichem." "Hyambo." And polite exploratory conversation: "Looks like it's going to be a nice day." "I'm sure I've seen you somewhere before." Included here also would be ritualized language for terminating relations: "Goodnight." "Adios." "Hasta la vista." "Auf Wiedersehen." "Have a nice day."

O (6) *To affect others' emotions* (E). Sermons, patriotic speeches, rallies for causes, TV commercials. "Smile, God loves you." "Oh, you look wonderful." Popular therapy would be included here: "Don't cry. It's going to be all right." "Don't worry about tomorrow." "The Lord giveth and the Lord taketh away." "You can stand the pain." More professionally: "What are you really feeling—guilt or anger?"

O (7) *To affect others' behavior* (E-R). "Don't do that!" "Speed Limit 35." "Vote for Smith." Here must be placed the TV commercials designed to make us convince ourselves that we need a specific product and to go right out and buy it. Also: "Get hooked." "Think." "THINK BIG." "think small." This is termed *directive language.*

O (8) *To suggest insights* (R). This is a philosophic and literary usage especially employed by Chinese sages and Indian philosophers. "When a man is in turmoil how shall he find peace / Save by staying patient till the stream clears?" (Lao-tzu). "Does the grass bend when the wind blows upon it?" (Confucius). This is commonly the purpose of parables, anecdotes, proverbs, logia or "sayings" ("Jesus said . . . ," "Confucius said . . ."), and maxims of folk-wisdom ("A rolling stone gathers no moss").

O (9) *To communicate ideas and facts* (R). "You're overdrawn." "I'd like a hamburger and coffee." "I'm happy to report that it's not malignant." "I regret to inform you. . . ." Here we can classify all media for the transmittal of knowledge: TV newscasts, magazines, books, and technical journals of all sorts, and all our routine daily transfer of information for coping and surviving.

O (10) *To effect word-magic* (E-R-?). "Open Sesame!" "Be thou healed in the Name of Isis." "Om" or "Om mani padme hum!" Our language still contains numerous quasi-magical formulas, often disguised: "Well, here goes." "Good luck!" "Gesundheit!" "God bless you." "God damn you." Akin to primitive word-magic are such phrases as "You're stupid!" and "Go on, you can do it" where the words themselves are designed to help bring about the results alluded to. Closely related to word-magic is the "placebo effect": "Two capsules after meals and you'll feel like a new person."

*I know that you believe
you understand
what you think I said,
but
I am not sure
you realize that
what you heard
is not
what I
meant.*

Anonymous

*The true meaning of a term is
to be found by observing
what a man does with it, not
by what he says about it.*

P. W. Bridgman

## COMMUNICATIONS ANALYSIS

*I fall far short of achieving real communication—person-to-person—all the time, but moving in this direction makes life for me a warm, exciting, upsetting, troubling, satisfying, enriching, and above all a worthwhile venture.*

CARL ROGERS

At the human stage of sophistication, language (that is, sounds and printed symbols) is our primary symbolic equipment. But our need to communicate is so great that we expect far more of words than they can deliver; we deceive ourselves into believing that our words are accomplishing what is inherently impossible. We are caught in the predicament of having to reduce the fullness of our experience to a few words and gestures. We try, as it were, to encapsulate life in symbolic containers that are hopelessly inadequate for the task.

*But we don't want others to hear our symbols: we want them to hear our experience. And others want the same from us.*

Success in communication depends not upon the speaker, but upon the hearer. One wishing to communicate his experience to another can try forever, but quite in vain, if the hearer refuses to hear. If for any reason a listener has undergone closure—he may be preoccupied with other problems, he may have developed an ego-defense system to block out pain, or he may have been conditioned against the immediate words or events before him—then his hearing will be symbol-centered, fragmented, incomplete.

Commonly, we are threatened by new or different ideas, and we set up roadblocks so they can't get through. Or if one has developed a rigid conceptual structure, when he listens to another's experience he translates it (and distorts it) to fit into his own inflexible system.

Bertrand Russell once wrote that the stupid person always reduces brilliant concepts to his own level of stupidity since he must oversimplify them to understand them. Something like this takes place in our communicating with one another. Because of our own preestablished conceptual points of view, we "translate" what another is saying into the familiar experiences of our own

B.C. by Johnny Hart

*By permission of John Hart and Field Enterprises, Inc.*

world. In doing this, we miss the living experience that the other person is in fact attempting to convey.

Communications analysis is important in helping us see what is taking place in our conversations, discussions, and dialogues. The purpose of communications analysis is to see and understand the processes by which *meanings* are successfully communicated from one to another; or, if there is a transmission breakdown, to discover what went wrong in our thinking, our symbolizing, or our listening.

Let's join Charlie Brown's baseball game, and focus on the *intended meanings* that move (or fail to move) between individuals.

FRAME ONE "We're getting slaughtered again. . . ." Charlie Brown's comment is an expression of frustration. He is using language to express emotion; he is not intending to communicate ideas. Why should he? His catcher knows the score; Schroeder doesn't have to be told. Charlie's third statement takes the form of a question— "Why do we have to suffer like this?"—but it's not really a question at all. His statement may look like a question, but it's one more way of expressing his agitation over a (losing) situation. (Here is an example when we can easily be duped by the *structure of language.*) As for Charlie Brown, we may be able to hear, behind his frustrated outburst, a cry for help, a genuine What-can-I-do-now? kind of plea.

FRAME TWO "Man is born to trouble. . . ." Schroeder doesn't hear Charlie Brown's meaning at all. His reply is triggered by CB's *words,* not his *meaning.* (CB's "What?" indicates that the catcher didn't catch the intended meaning.)

FRAME THREE "He's quoting from the 'Book of Job.'. . ." Linus heard what Schroeder said, but he chooses to give CB the source of the quotation rather

*We have been given two ears and but a single mouth, in order that we may hear more and talk less.*

ZENO OF CITIUM

© 1967 by United Feature Syndicate, Inc.

than respond to the content of the remark. Linus tried to enlighten CB after his surprised "What?" So both Schroeder and Linus ignore CB's verbalized frustrations. In plain fact, Charlie Brown is the only player who is really in the ball game.

FRAME FOUR "Actually, the problem of suffering is a very profound one. . . ." Linus continues on Schroeder's wavelength, pondering the suffering that is manifest in the human condition. And Lucy—"If a person has bad luck . . ."—does she hear what Linus is saying? Obviously not. She didn't even let him finish the idea. Lucy's mind is triggered by words, not by intended meanings. (The word *suffering* leads her, by association, to *bad luck*.) Result: communication breakdown.

FRAME FIVE "That's what Job's friends told him." Did Schroeder hear Lucy? Yes. He heard not her words, but the whole concept of a "moral law." And Schroeder's response is accurate: Job's friends said what Lucy "always says." Did the intended meaning get through? Yes—the first time thus far.

How do we evaluate Lucy's retort to Schroeder: "What about Job's wife . . . ?" Lucy is off on a kick of her own; her comment has no connection to Schroeder's statement. (Job's wife hasn't been mentioned and is only a "bit player" in the drama of Job.) Result: No communication.

FRAME SIX Schroeder continues where Linus left off in F-4—with ultimate thoughts. (Lucy is merely an interruption.) "I think the person who never suffers, never matures." Does Lucy hear? No. She hears *the word suffer* but not the meaning that Schroeder gives the word. She gives the word a different meaning. Therefore—"Don't be ridiculous!"—she blasts Schroeder for what he didn't say.

On the other side of the pitcher's mound another player tries to confirm the notion that "pain is a part of life, and . . ."—would he have gone on to say, "We must learn to live with it"—or something like that? If so, then he is moving at the ultimate meaning-level with Schroeder and Linus.

What about Linus's comment—"The person who speaks only of the 'patience' of Job . . . ? Is he responding to any previous statement? No. The mention of Job has reminded him of *something else* that he happened to know, something about "the patience of Job." So Linus adds his datum of unconnected information.

FRAME SEVEN "I don't have a ball team. . . ." Charlie Brown looks just the way most of us feel after we haven't been able to communicate to others or after we have listened to discussions during which no one heard anyone else. "Yes, Charlie Brown, we know. . . ."

Good communication is important if effective philosophic dialogue is to take place. Most of us never get around to giving systematic attention to the problems that tend to break down communication in our everyday conversations and relationships. When we are receivers, it is important to develop the habit of listening for intended meanings rather than words; and when speaking, we need to ask ourselves whether our intended meanings are accurately being heard by others.

*Symbols are like cut diamonds. They have many facets, and there is always the danger that the brilliance of one may blind the viewer to the others.*

RONALD HUNTINGTON

*I still find that some people imagine that intimacy is only a matter of approximating genitals one to another. . . . Intimacy . . . requires a type of relationship which I call collaboration, by which I mean clearly formulated adjustments of one's behavior to the expressed needs of the other person in the pursuit of increasingly identical—that is, more and more nearly mutual—satisfactions.*

HARRY STACK SULLIVAN

There is a distinct difference between Western and Eastern ways of responding to meaning-events. Both ways of interacting are of great value, and we need to be able to recognize each kind and respond appropriately.

A Western philosopher tends to respond to intellectual meanings contained in propositions, fact-claims, value judgments, and so on, and to work with them analytically and logically. He will take on words and meanings directly. The strength of the Western approach lies in its rationality. It has given us our sciences and our precisely organized fund of knowledge about the world and ourselves.

The Eastern philosopher tends to respond to levels of meaning that lie quite beyond words; in fact there is frequently a disdain for meanings that can be reduced to symbolic terms. The sage will answer a precise statement with a proverb or a direct question with an anecdote. Viktor Frankl is quite Eastern when he answers the question "What is the meaning of life?" with another question: "What is the best chess move?"

The Eastern use of language, and the way meaning is dealt with, is nicely described by Edwin Burtt:

> Chinese writers, in philosophy and literature, aim at suggesting fertile insights rather than at achieving analytic precision. . . . The genius of the Chinese mind is revealed most fully, not in its philosophical essays or dialogues, but in its poetry, where the suggestive nuances of thought can be freely expressed, unhampered by any need for meticulous distinctions or for coercion of the reader's thought through logical deduction. . . . One who writes in the fashion of a system-maker thereby shows that he is sure of having attained the essential truth he has sought, and that he is now endeavoring to fasten it upon his reader; his unexpressed attitude is: "You will, of course, take my premises for granted, and I am now going to prove that you must then adopt my conclusions." From the typical Chinese viewpoint such argumentation is not only largely futile (since any keen and determined reader can always find an alternative set of plausible premises); it is unseemly. For if one refuses to take his own convictions too seriously, and approaches his reader with proper respect for the latter's independent integrity, what he will be concerned to do is not to coerce an acceptance of his assertions, but so to express them as to elicit growth toward the reader's own more adequate insight. By its neat exactitude and seeming conclusiveness, logical argument can discourage and even block this growth. Let us think and speak so as to guide constructive progress in the experience and understanding of others, not so as to convert them to some absolute which we have no business to regard as such ourselves.

Among many of us, listening is a lost art. How difficult it is for most of us to remain silent in the presence of different or "wrong" ideas. The urge to clobber an alien idea swells within us like a self-righteous demon, and a speaker rarely gets halfway through his sentence before we give way to an impulse to cut him down.

We all know the experience of wanting to be heard by others (or by some one) and not being able to get through. One of our persistent human frustrations is to discover that another person is hearing only words rather than the living experience we feel so deeply and are aching to convey.

Few insights leave one with such a sense of loneliness. To realize suddenly that, no matter how earnestly you try, you can't be heard—this is why there are so many lonely people who belong to the lonely crowd.

*Whenever two or more human beings can communicate with each other, they can by agreement, make anything stand for anything.*

S. I. HAYAKAWA

*We can never achieve a satisfactory definition of language, for there is no factor common to all our uses of language—describing, joking, praying, commanding, singing, asking, and so on. Wittgenstein asks us to think of the tools in a toolbox: hammer, pliers, a saw, a screw-driver, a ruler, a glue-pot, glue, nails and screws. What we do with words is as different as what we do with these objects.*

JOSEPH BRENNAN

*You can learn a lot just by listening.*

YOGI BERRA

*I do desire we may be better strangers.*

WILLIAM SHAKESPEARE
*As You Like It*, **III**, ii. 276

The number of individuals who are *word-oriented* rather than *meaning-oriented* indicates the existence of a widespread "normal" neurosis in our society.

## DEFINITIONS AND CONTEXTS

Semanticists remind us that symbols can be understood intelligibly only within the context of actual usage. The semantic axiom that no word ever has the same meaning twice would appear to be an overstatement, since in practice we seem to use words repeatedly with about the same meaning. But in fact their observation is accurate. *Definitions are predictions of possible meanings that a term may be given in concrete situations.* The precise meaning of any term cannot be known until it occurs in a living context, and then its meaning is inextricably interwoven with the total event and cannot be understood apart from it.

There is a strand of Western tradition going back at least as far as Aristotle that would attempt to give all words exact definitions and insist that they be employed only in this unambiguous way. Within certain academic fields this precise approach has yielded valuable results. But this sort of operation has little relation to our richly varied use of language in daily life.

The individual who is rigidly literal in his use of definitions often fails in the communication of experience. If he has the habit of bringing prefabricated definitions into fluid, living situations, he is apt to miss entirely the nuances and connotations that terms take on in a specific context. Words are "containers" into which we pour the meanings and feelings of the moment, and this personal investment of ourselves in our symbols is intimately tied to the immediate experiences of life.

No two persons ever react to any word or symbol in exactly the same manner. How could they? In order to do so, they would have to have the same past experience, the same present environment, the same prospect of the future, the same pattern of

### EMPATHY

**empathize** (em´pa-thīz) To diagnose, that is to recognize and identify the feelings, emotions, passions, sufferings, torments through their symptoms is to *realize intellectually*, to *understand* them, in a remote way to identify oneself with the patient, without ever having personally experienced those feelings,—to *empathize*, as it is known in psychiatry.

On the other hand, to place oneself in the position of the patient, to get into his skin, so to speak, to be able to duplicate, live through, *experience* those feelings in a vicarious way, is closely to identify oneself with another, to *share his feelings with him*, to *sympathize*, from the Greek *syn*, together with, and *páthos*, suffering, passion.

**empathy** (em´pa-thē) . . . Empathy is thus a form of identification; it may be called intellectual identification in contrast to affective identification.

HINSIE AND CAMPBELL
*Psychiatric Dictionary*

thought, the same flow of feelings, the same bodily habits, and the same electro-chemical metabolism. The chances that such multidimensional patterns coincide are practically nil. The surprising thing is not that we often disagree; it is that we ever succeed in achieving some sort of agreement.

SAMUEL BOIS

It is surprising how often people still speak of "dirty words" or "obscene language" and believe that *symbols* are *inherently* dirty or obscene. Semanticists keep reminding us that words mean nothing at all until we give meanings to them. There simply is no such thing as a "dirty word"; there are only symbols that individuals and groups have invested with certain (negative) meanings and feelings.

Nevertheless, the fact that large numbers of individuals are offended by *symbols—quite apart from the experience symbolized—*is a social reality. If one sincerely desires to communicate experience, there is good pragmatic justification for not making unnecessary use of *any* symbols that are apt to produce symbol-centered reactions in others—which can be done with erudite phrases and technical terminology as well as by the use of taboo language. As a general rule, any sort of language that causes us to focus on the symbols rather than the experience symbolized serves to break down the process of communication.

> *There are those who would never have been in love, had they never heard about love.*
> LA ROCHEFOUCAULD

## TELEPATHY AND COMMUNICATION

Does telepathic communication exist? There is some evidence that it does, though it is far from conclusive; and the widespread popular belief in telepathy

---

### LANGUAGE AND THE REAL

The observer can describe the world only in the language available to him. "Fact" has a linguistic constituent. As B. L. Whorf has shown, speakers of languages that do not have a word for "wave" will see not waves but only changing undulating surfaces. The Navahos use one word for blue and green, whereas the Bororó of Brazil have no single word for parrot. In Arabic a wind may be described as *sarsar*, which means both *cold* and *whistling*. The language of Tierra del Fuego has a useful word, *mamihlapinatapai;* it means, roughly, the state of mind in which two people regard each other when both want a certain thing to be done but neither wants to be first to do it. How many lovely facts are available to them! Of course La Rochefoucauld said a long time ago, *"Il y a des gens qui n'auraient jamais été amoureux, s'ils n'avaient jamais entendu parler d'amour* (There are people who would never have fallen in love if they had not heard love spoken about). Cassirer and Sapir argue that the forms of language predetermine the modes of observation and interpretation; Wittgenstein said that "if we spoke a different language, we would perceive a somewhat different world." Waismann's metaphor is "language is the knife with which we cut out facts."

REUBEN ABEL
*Man Is the Measure*

is based on actual experiences for which a telepathic hypothesis seems at present the best explanation.

The more plausible fact-claims about telepathy hint at some interesting possibilities. One is that telepathic experiences are less common in cerebral individuals, in "intellectual" and rational people. A domineering intellect stands in the way of nonrational experience in general, including telepathy. Similarly, individuals from less cerebral cultures seem to be more capable of having telepathic experiences. Members of societies which express emotion openly—those that still dance and experience ecstasy, in a word, those who are in touch with the Dionysian side of life—these are more open to supersensory experiences than individuals driven by the Apollonian pursuit of intellect and order.

Another fact is that telepathic experiences appear to have some correlation with physical or psychical abnormalities. They occur more frequently after brain damage, or during alterations of endocrine chemistry, extreme emotional states, or recovery from an illness or accident.

In considering the future capabilities of communication, there is an interesting hint that when we receive telepathic messages from others, the event is not at all a pure transfer of experience. Rather, the content is immediately assimilated into our own fabric of understanding and feeling. That is, we still interpret the telepathic communication in terms of *our* experience, just as we do with all other forms of knowledge that we receive by symbolic means.

Lastly—if telepathy exists—it seems that its base of operation is somewhere deep in the unconscious regions of the psyche. Telepathic channels appear to operate outside the conscious mind and then break in uninvited.

*All words are only so many fingers pointing at Niagara Falls. Some may, like the family's pet dog, look at the finger rather than the rushing waters to which it points. Others on a yet more infantile level may, as Alan Watts puts it, "look at the finger pointing the way and then . . . suck it for comfort."*

RONALD HUNTINGTON

In my dream I was driving my car along a road near my home, and quite suddenly, out of nowhere, it seemed to me, a little girl about three years of age appeared right in front of the car. I did all I could but found it impossible to avoid hitting her. On getting out, I was told that she was dead. I looked at her as she lay in the road, and felt completely shattered, though I had never had a chance to save her from what seemed to me to be her inevitable fate. I must stress that feeling I had of inevitability.

When I awoke, I realized with horror that I had to drive down that road that very morning, on my way to lunch with my youngest daughter, and I decided to be more than usually careful. On approaching the spot, I looked round most carefully for any sign of children, and there were none in sight, only about five women standing at a bus stop. Relieved beyond words, I glanced down at my speedometer to check, and on lifting my eyes, was completely horrified to see, standing still in the middle of the road, the little girl of my dream, correct in every detail, even to the dark curly hair and the bright blue cardigan she was wearing. I was afraid to use my horn, in case I startled her and precipitated what I felt was going to be a fatal accident, so I slowly brought the car to a halt, just beside her. She never moved, but stood staring at me.

Meanwhile, the women in the bus queue made no sign of interest, and no one tried to get such a young child off the busy road. In fact, they seemed more interested in the fact that I had stopped. Feeling very shaky, I continued on my way, and looking in the mirror, I saw the child was still standing there, and nobody was bothering about her. By the time I got to my daughter's flat, I was over half an hour late. When she opened the door, she was looking very worried and upset, and said how glad she was to see me safe and sound.

I asked why she had been so worried, as I have been driving for over thirty

*On this planet, anything we think may be held against us. . . .*

"MR. SPOCK"
*"Once upon a Planet," Star Trek*

years, and she looked at me and said, "I know that, Mummie, but you see, last night I had a terribly vivid dream. In this dream you ran over and killed a lovely little girl, dressed in a bright blue cardigan and with lovely dark curly hair!"

This dream, which is representative of a common experience, is recounted by the British author J. B. Priestley. He double checked the facts of the episode with the mother, her husband, and the daughter (but not the little girl!). Priestley comments:

Telepathy, and not any Time effect, was at work here. Whether the daughter took the tragic little-girl-episode from the mother, or the mother from the daughter, we cannot tell. . . . What is certain is that this fascinating double dream is well worth the attention of ESP experts and researchers.

A Soviet parapsychologist, Dr. Pavel Naumov, has concluded that "biological ties between mother and child are incontestable."

In the clinic, mothers are in a distant section, separate from their babies. They cannot possibly hear them. Yet, when her baby cries, a mother exhibits nervousness. Or when an infant is in pain, for instance as a doctor takes a blood specimen, the mother shows signs of anxiety. She has no way of knowing the doctor is at that moment with her child. . . . We found communication in 65 percent of our cases.

Many similar events are noted by Sheila Ostrander and Lynn Schroeder in their book *Psychic Discoveries Behind the Iron Curtain.* They comment that

such cases open up philosophical, ethical, personal and scientific questions. Across a distance, is mind influencing body? Is body influencing body? Is body influencing mind? As psi moves into the picture, the iron edges of biology and psychology begin to dissolve and mix, pointing to a whole new dynamism underlying both.

Dr. Naumov tells of another experiment in telepathy that was conducted aboard a Russian submarine at sea. In this case the subjects were not human beings, but a mother rabbit and her litter of newborn bunnies.

Naumov relates:

As you know, there's no known way for a submerged submarine to communicate with anyone on land. Radio doesn't work. Scientists placed the baby rabbits aboard the submarine. They kept the mother rabbit in a laboratory on shore where they implanted electrodes deep in her brain. When the sub was deep below the surface of the ocean, assistants killed the young rabbits one by one.

The mother rabbit obviously didn't know what was happening. Even if she could have understood the test, she had no way of knowing at what moment her children died. Yet, at each synchronized instant of death, her brain *reacted. There was communication.* . . . And, our instruments clearly registered these moments of ESP.

## REFLECTIONS

1   Do you sometimes feel overwhelmed by words? What sort of communicative techniques do you think we would resort to or develop or invent if, suddenly, we found ourselves without words?

*Let us not forget that a word hasn't got a meaning given to it, as it were, by a power independent of us, so that there could be a kind of scientific investigation in what the word really means. A word has the meaning someone has given to it.*

LUDWIG WITTGENSTEIN

*"What must I do, to tame you?" asked the little prince.*

*"You must be very patient," replied the fox. "First you will sit down at a little distance from me—like this—in the grass. I shall look at you out of the corner of my eye, and you will say nothing. Words are the source of misunderstandings. But you will sit a little closer to me, every day. . . ."*

ANTOINE DE SAINT-EXUPÉRY

*Not higher sensitivity, not longer memory or even quicker association sets man so far above other animals that he can regard them as denizens of a lower world; no, it is the power of using symbols that makes him lord of the earth.*

SUSANNE LANGER

2    Do you agree with the notion that much of our drive to communicate derives from an "epistemic loneliness"—from a need to transcend a space/time condition that we cannot tolerate? Do you personally feel this condition?

3    Note the following sentence on p. 290: "Success in communication depends not upon the speaker, but upon the hearer." Does this sound right to you? Analyze the sequence of "bits" involved in the communication of meaning and explain why this conclusion is or isn't true.

4    What is a "definition"? Is this semantic way of defining definitions helpful to you?

5    Note the many different functions of language (pp. 288–289). If you became aware that much of the language of daily life is not intended to communicate ideas, how might this influence the way you listen to others? How do you think it might affect your relationships?

6    On taboo symbols: There must be deep psychological needs for such symbols. How would you describe these needs?

7    Everyday life provides ample occasion to practice communications analysis, and our exchanges are never quite the same after we have developed an awareness of the many levels of meaning that move between us. Take advantage of the first opportunities you have to practice communications analysis in your discussions and dialogues. Review and assess afterwards what you have seen and learned.

8    The Eastern use of language described by Professor Burtt has as long and as rich a tradition as Western analytic thinking; but the Eastern way is designed to achieve an essentially different goal. What kind of insight is the Eastern approach to meaning-events more likely to produce?

9    Do you think telepathic communication exists? If so, what evidence can you offer to support your conclusion? If it does exist, what are some of its philosophic—especially epistemological and ethical—implications?

*If God had said, after Adam named the cats, dogs, and cows, "There is another animal over at the far end of the garden—what name would you give it?" Adam would no doubt have replied petulantly, "How can I give it a name when I can't even see it?"*

REUBEN ABEL

# COEXISTENCE: MAN'S LOVE/HATE CONDITION

*The age of cultural innocence is passing; the American*

*is beginning to recognize the patterns to which*

*he conforms.*

SNELL AND GAIL PUTNEY

*They are playing a game. They are playing at not playing*

*a game. If I show them I see they are, I shall break the*

*rules and they will punish me. I must play their game,*

*of not seeing I see the game.*

R. D. LAING

# HISTORY
## MEANING

# 5₁

## THEATER OF THE ABSURD

Arnold Toynbee is considered by many to be the greatest of contemporary philosophers of history. His massive twelve-volume *Study of History* stands today as the supreme effort of the human mind to disentangle the complexities of human history to see whether there is any large-scale meaning to the whole human enterprise.

Late in 1911 Toynbee left Oxford for a nine-month tour of the Mediterranean lands where he saw for himself the remains of the great civilizations he knew so well from history books. He spent much time walking over the countryside surveying the legacies of these long-dead worlds. He chatted with monks on Mount Athos, examined Etruscan tombs at Cerveteri and Corneto, and mused on the past glory of the Minoan palaces on Crete. Before this visit, the Acropolis had been a page in a book; now its panorama sprawled before him in all its breathtaking reality.

At the same time, he listened to the sounds of the living world. He spent his evenings in Greek cafes and heard talk of world affairs; he visited Greek villages and caught apprehensive conversations among peasants and shepherds about the possibility of war.

He reflected on these two worlds. One was dead, it seemed, the other very much alive. The contrast was a shattering reminder of life, death, and time. Toynbee pondered: What does man's past tell us about the present or future? How dead, really, are past civilizations? If they are dead, what caused them to die? What is their relationship to our own busy world? *Is our civilization also doomed to die like the rest?* If so, why? Could it perhaps be saved? If so, what could save it?

These are the essential concerns of the philosopher of history. What, if

*Until philosophers are kings, or the kings and princes of this world have the spirit and power of philosophy, and political greatness and wisdom meet in one, and those commoner natures who pursue either to the exclusion of the other are compelled to stand aside, cities will never have rest from their evils— no, nor the human race. . . .*

**PLATO**

The Acropolis, Athens

*Although a certain amount of hypocrisy exists about it, everyone is fascinated by violence. After all, man is the most remorseless killer who ever stalked the earth. Our interest in violence in part reflects the fact that on the subconscious level we are very little different from our primitive ancestors.*

**STANLEY KUBRICK**

*Everyone in Germany is a National Socialist—the few outside the party are either lunatics or idiots.*

**ADOLF HITLER**

anything, does history mean? How can we learn from it? Is there any way that our understanding of history can shed light on our own troubled times?

There has been a renewed interest in the philosophy of history due to the maddening chaos of the twentieth century thus far. The "big events" that make and shake history have dominated our time: The Russian pogroms, the Turkish massacre of Armenians, the Nazi execution of six million Jews; two World Wars initiated by insane racist leaders; an escalating arms race; ongoing guerilla skirmishes, bush wars, and ideological terrorism; scattered tribal/nationalistic conflicts; plus an all-engulfing global revolution that has only begun.

Such events have sent men back to reexamining their historical experience in an attempt to make sense out of what, in the wake of such enormous tragedies, has seemed absurd and senseless. All too clearly contemporary history sounds like "a tale told by an idiot, full of sound and fury, signifying nothing." Could this assessment actually be true? Or does human history have a deeper meaning that man in his frenzied state has overlooked?

The philosophy of history asks two central questions, though each leads logically to countless others. The first-generation questions are: (1) Does human history have meaning? (2) Can we learn from history? These questions may or may not be closely related.

The metaphor of the drama is appropriate and helpful when trying to conceptualize the problems of the philosophy of history. "All the world's a stage," wrote Shakespeare, "And all the men and women merely players."

So, think of human history as a long, intricately plotted play, with numerous roles and innumerable characters. If history has meaning, then the drama may be similar to an epic like *Macbeth*. Perhaps it has a playwright who wrote the story and, conceivably, directs the play. (But are we sure the playwright is also the director? And is the playwright also the prop-master?) It has its leading characters—its *dramatis personae*. It has a plot that gives meaning to the lives of the players. It is they who move the plot along. It couldn't develop without them—a play with no players is no play. Every character is essential to the unfolding of the dramatic plot as it moves toward the climax—the dénouement of the play's suspenseful story. To be sure, some characters are more important to the plot than others, but even the spear carriers have an appointed place in the grand epic.

Now, does this drama metaphor capture the essential truth of human history? Is there in fact a playwright? Is there really a plot? Is there a goal to human history, a final curtain? Is this why our lives are meaningful—because we are all cast in the play? Are we humans really necessary to the working out of the drama? And is the plot a tragedy—as in *Macbeth*—or a comedy—as in *A Midsummer Night's Dream?*

While the stage-play metaphor helps us to formulate questions about the nature of history, the bare fact just may be that history more closely resembles some bizarre act from the Theater of the Absurd—a plotless non-staging of countless non-characters who were never cast but who persist in ad-libbing their lines, interacting with no direction, and moving from scene to scene without purpose. It may indeed be "a tale told by an idiot . . . signifying nothing." There may be no playwright, no director, no plot. There may be no play.

*I don't live in the past. The past lives in me.*

TOM OSBORNE

## THE MEANING OF HISTORY

In most societies to date, the source of history's meaning has been assumed to be the operation of the supernatural. This was a logical deduction from our inherited theological premises. The causal agents behind the events of human history were the capricious animistic sprites and spirits, the whims of the gods, the will of God, or the cosmic interaction of the Forces of Light battling with the Forces of Darkness. In any case, the meaning of history was the preplanned story-line working itself out as men- and women-in-time moved the drama forward from scene to scene.

When it was assumed that supernatural agencies were the source of history's meaning, then human interpretation could move in two directions. It could begin with belief in a preordained plan (God had predestined the minutest details of earth's history from the first appleseed to the last sparrow that falls); and the events of our lives could then be interpreted according to that plan. Or it could look at the events that actually take place and interpret them—and give them meaning—according to these preconceived beliefs ("We won the war because God was on our side"). In Western history it has moved both ways.

One of the first known interpreters of history in the Western world was the so-called Deuteronomic historian who wrote down the stories of various wars carried on by the Hebrew tribes during the twelfth and eleventh centuries B.C. This unknown writer had sufficient records to enable him to describe sporadic battles involving the tribal leaders ("judges") of that time; and because of his theological convictions he perceived a pattern in the wars. He did not—indeed he could not—record history as we know it today; rather he wrote "interpreted history," that is, the historical events *plus* what they meant to him.

The dramatic framework that he placed around each tribal battle was simple but meaningful.

*The greatest virtue is not to be free, but to struggle ceaselessly for freedom.*

NIKOS KAZANTZAKIS

1.  The Israelites do something evil "in the sight of Yahweh" their God.
2.  Yahweh's anger "blazes against Israel." He sends them into battle and

"sells them into the power" of the enemy. They are on the point of losing the war.

3. Then the Israelites repent of their evil ways and "cry unto Yahweh." They ask forgiveness and plead for help.
4. Yahweh then "raises up a savior" (a leader) who proceeds into battle with "the spirit of Yahweh upon him" and defeats the enemy.
5. Yahweh has won back his children; he is pleased. So peace "reigns in the land for forty years."

Like a taped replay, this pattern is repeated over and over again throughout the Deuteronomic history. It's the only interpretation the writer knows, and his theological preconviction precludes his seeing the historic events in any other way. This is therefore not history but a meaningful—if one-sided—interpretation of a few significant events. It is a "theology of history." (Note that a familiar "unexamined assumption" underlies this pattern: the so-called universal moral law expounded by the Book of Job. See pp. 45–48.)

This framework can be used to interpret *any* conflict between *any* groups. Consider World War II, for example. The Americans (or British or French, or whoever) did "what was evil in the sight of the Lord." He was "angered and sent them into war" where they are about to lose. But they repent and "he raises up a leader" (Churchill, Stalin, Eisenhower—take your pick) who proceeds to win the war. The Lord is pleased again, so "peace reigns for forty years." (The number 40 is rarely, if ever, an historical figure, but a symbolic number implying the presence and approval of God.) This framework can be used just as well to interpret a World Series baseball game or a presidential election.

This sort of interpretation is too subjective to be of any use to us. We can assume that it was meaningful to the Deuteronomist and subsequent believers, but for those of us who are attempting to discover the realities of the case—the objective patterns of history, if they exist—this writer offers little help.

What the Deuteronomic historian succeeds in doing is to alert us to beware of the ease with which we can let our mind's conceptual habits arrange historical events into subjective patterns of meaning. This is a warning for which we can be grateful.

The first great Western philosopher of history was Saint Augustine. He was prompted to write *The City of God* after the fall of the city of Rome to Alaric and his Goths in A.D. 410. This incredible event so shook the Roman world that it had to be interpreted. It was so meaningless there had to be meaning behind it. While the pagan Romans were complaining that the tragedy was divine punishment for the abandonment of the old Roman gods, Augustine took up his pen to show that Rome had fallen as a part of a long-range divine plan on the part of the "Christian" God. God had not merely tolerated the degenerate city, but had used the City of Earth to accomplish his ends; for out of that City of Earth there had developed the Church to represent the Kingdom of God on Earth. When that city's task of giving birth to the Church was accomplished, then the City of Earth (Rome) would be replaced by the City of God (the Roman Church).

Therefore, in the fullness of time, the plan of God was manifesting itself on the historical plane. The City of Earth had fallen to give way to the City of God.

*If you're looking for a really dangerous and outmoded myth, national sovereignty wins over the papacy hands down.*

HARVEY COX

*Men always love what is good or what they find good; it is in judging what is good that they go wrong.*

JEAN-JACQUES ROUSSEAU

*Long Centuries Grown Cold*

Men laughed in Ancient Egypt, long ago,
And laughed beside the Lake of Galilee,
And my glad heart rejoices more to know,
When it leaps up in exultation too,
That, though the laughter and the laugh be new,
The joy is old as is the ancient sea.

Men wept in noble Athens, so they say,
And in great Babylon of many towers,
For the same sorrows that we feel to-day;
So, stranded high upon Time's latest peak,
I can with Babylonian and with Greek
Claim kinship through this common grief of ours.

The same fair moon I look upon to-night,
This shining golden moon above the sea,
Imparts a richer and more sweet delight
For all the eyes it did rejoice of old,
For all the hearts, long centuries grown cold,
That shared this joy which now it gives to me.

Whate'er I feel I cannot feel alone.
When I am happiest or most forlorn,
Uncounted friends whom I have never known
Rejoicing stand or grieving at my side,
These nameless, faceless friends of mine who died
A thousand years or more e'er I was born.

ROSALIND MURRAY

Augustine's theological interpretation of the fall of Rome, like the viewpoint of the Deuteronomist, is too arbitrary and subjective. We can be sure that Alaric's Gothic priests didn't perceive the event that way, nor did the majority of Romans. If one does not share the theological assumptions from which Augustine began his interpretation, then his explanation is neither logically sound nor psychologically satisfying.

What we can learn from Saint Augustine is that the temptation to seek meaningful interpretations of life-shattering events can lead us into mythical world-views that have no objective validity. To be sure, they can be comforting, and during times of torment this life-sustaining mode of interpretation is never to be denigrated. But during less stressful periods of life we seek a clearer vision of reality; and the kinds of pressures to which Augustine yielded must not persuade us to settle, too soon, for a parochial interpretation of history which, from a synoptic point of view, is of little value.

Two influential teleological philosophies of history have dominated modern times: Hegel's dialectical idealism and Marx's dialectical materialism.

*The human being who looks upon his own future as already determined by fate . . . only acknowledges a lack of will power to struggle and win through.*

MAX PLANCK

*"Sick cultures show a complex of symptoms. . . . but a dying culture invariably exhibits rudeness. Bad manners. Lack of consideration for others in minor matters. A loss of politeness, of gentle manners, is more significant than a riot . . . "*

ROBERT HEINLEIN
*"Dr. Hartley Baldwin," Friday*

Friedrich Hegel was convinced that he had discovered the nature of thought and that he had made a unique discovery. The thought process moves in a three-beat rhythm that he called the "dialectic." It begins with an idea—a thesis—then proceeds to develop into its opposite, the antithesis; after that the mind sees the relatedness of thesis and antithesis and weaves them together into a synthesis. This synthesis, in turn, becomes another thesis, and the dialectic continues. Thus the dialectic effects an ever-expanding comprehension of the connections of the contents of thought.

Hegel was quite sure that this is the way God's mind works. God is pure thought, or, in Hegel's words, the Absolute Mind. Here is no love or compassion (no emotion), just pure thought. The Absolute Mind of God manifests reason through the human mind and therefore in human history. Whenever people think and act more rationally, they are actualizing God's will, and this progressive manifestation of logic is the teleological purpose underlying human history.

Humankind is a crucial part of this program, and there was reason to believe, Hegel thought, that man was becoming more reasonable, especially in nineteenth-century Germany. All of this would end in a state which Hegel described as "pure thought thinking about pure thought"—Absolute Mind contemplating itself.

Hegel's novel way of interpreting history caught the minds of students in the German universities; but while the idea of the dialectic excited them, the notion of an Absolute Mind thinking with dispassionate logic left them cold.

Karl Marx was one of these students. Following the lead of another young philosopher named Ludwig Feuerbach, Marx developed a philosophy of history around the idea of a dialectical movement, operating in terms of the basic material essentials of life. Marx was convinced that *his* vision of the dialectic was real. It is a dialectic of social struggle determined by man's economic needs. Class struggle creates the three-beat rhythm. Marx's interpretation is a "materialistic dialectic" in contrast to Hegel's theistic dialectic.

Pablo Picasso, *Guernica* (1937)

Thus Marx laid the foundations for a teleological interpretation of history that has come to dominate half the world. All Marxians know that history has purpose; it follows "inexorable law" toward a goal—the Classless Society where equality, justice, and plenty will prevail (which is a down-to-earth version of the Kingdom of God). Each individual is a part of history's drama. As in other teleo-cosmic dramas, each person must decide whether he or she will fight on the side of the Righteous (the revolutionaries who actively hasten history toward its appointed end) or on the side of the Wicked (the bourgeois reactionaries who resist change and progress).

By now it's clear that each of us, when attempting to make sense of the complexities of the past, must be on guard against projecting our subjective frameworks onto historical events and arranging them to support our own visions and prejudices. We must be equally wary of the hidden *cultural* assumptions of our place and time—the *Zeitgeist* or "time-spirit." Hegel and Marx both fell victim to such an assumption: the idea of "inevitable progress."

The opposing notions that human history is improving (the optimistic view) or degenerating (the pessimistic view) have had a see-saw history in Western thought.

The teleological view of history—the belief that history has meaning and is moving toward a goal—is essentially a Judeo-Christian assumption; and within that teleological point of view a majority report has held that the human lot would continually improve. (In a general way, when times were troubled—during Roman persecutions, the Islamic conquests, and the twentieth century—the pessimistic viewpoint has prevailed: conditions, it was held, will become progressively worse until God, in his own good time, "breaks in from above" and sets things right. By contrast, when times were relatively peaceful—during the Renaissance, the Enlightenment, and the Victorian era—the optimistic viewpoint has prevailed: history was seen as a progressive improvement of man's growth and happiness on earth. In either case, however, whether history is going up or down, it never loses its teleological character.)

The nineteenth century was infused with a double dose of optimism. The Industrial Revolution was in full swing. Western nations were moving to all corners of the world, sharing their bounty of material goods and spiritual blessings. And among philosophers of history the mood of the Enlightenment was still waxing. Edward Gibbon sealed his idealism near the end of his great *History of the Decline and Fall of the Roman Empire* (1776–1788) by sharing "the pleasing conclusion that every age of the world has increased, and still increases, the real wealth, the happiness, the knowledge, and perhaps the virtue, of the human race."

To this assessment of human history was added (in 1859) Darwin's massive documentation of the evolutionary theory that, down through aeons of time, it is the fitter species that survive. Nature, too, it turns out, is inherently progressive. So it became clear that both *human* history and *natural* history move together, upwards and onwards; and only the most dismal disbeliever could doubt "the inevitability of progress." Much later Bertrand Russell was to reminisce: "I grew up in the full flood of Victorian optimism, and . . . something remains with me of that hopefulness that then was easy."

*Once we have cast another group in the role of the enemy, we know that they are to be distrusted—that they are evil incarnate. We then twist all their communications to fit our belief.*

**JEROME FRANK**

Karl Marx (1818–1883)

*Change is avalanching down upon our heads, and most people are utterly unprepared to cope with it.*

**ALVIN TOFFLER**

## THE IDEA OF PROGRESS

The notion of a finite and clearly definable goal of progress in history, so often postulated by nineteenth-century thinkers, has proved inapplicable and barren. Belief in progress means belief not in any automatic or inevitable process, but in the progressive development of human potentialities. Progress is an abstract term; and the concrete ends pursued by mankind arise from time to time out of the course of history, not from some source outside it. I profess no belief in the perfectibility of man, or in a future paradise on earth. To this extent I would agree with the theologians and the mystics who assert that perfection is not realizable in history. But I shall be content with the possibility of unlimited progress—or progress subject to no limits that we can need or envisage—towards goals which can be defined only as we advance towards them, and the validity of which can be verified only in a process of attaining them. Nor do I know how, without some such conception of progress, society can survive. Every civilized society imposes sacrifices on the living generation for the sake of generations yet unborn. To justify these sacrifices in the name of a better world in the future is the secular counterpart of justifying them in the name of some divine purpose. In Bury's words, "the principle of duty to posterity is a direct corollary of the idea of progress." Perhaps this duty does not require justification. If it does, I know of no other way to justify it.

EDWARD HALLETT CARR
*What Is History?*

Although the philosophies of history constructed by Hegel and Marx can be validly criticized on many other grounds, their optimistic foundations were solely subjective—assumptions that were "in the air" of their times. So we have two more instances when serious thinkers projected their inner visions into the real world and thus failed to give us an accurate account of history's meaning.

## A MODERN ATTEMPT: TOYNBEE'S ORGANISMIC INTERPRETATION

Arnold Toynbee's *Study of History* is probably the most noteworthy attempt by any modern philosopher of history to make sense of the human drama.

In September 1921 he was aboard a miserably slow train traveling across Thrace. The rumbling of his train crossing a bridge near Adrianople awakened him before dawn, and during the next few hours, as a countryside haunted with history glided past, his mind began to call up the epochal events of history and legend that had been set in this great theater.

He knew that he was now crossing the westernmost boundaries of the vast empire of the Persian Achaemenids and that when that kingdom had run its course, these rolling hills and lazy pasture lands came under the shield of the young Alexander of Macedon. Three centuries later the astute plans of a Caesar for the conquest of central Europe were shattered when Varus and his legions

Arnold Toynbee (1889–1975)

were lured into the nearby Teutoburg Forest and annihilated by the Germans. Through here the Goths and the Huns passed, followed in turn by the Crusaders with red crosses flashing on their white tunics and the fire of holy war flashing in their eyes; after encountering the gaily clad Saracens, those who returned crept homeward in bloodsoaked rags, and not a few laid their embattled bones beside the little streams in the Thracian woodlands. Much later this countryside, then Rumelia, was drawn into the Ottoman Empire and the Muslims settled the land and made it theirs. Thus it remained until modern times.

Hour after hour Toynbee stood by the window watching the scenes of history pass by. That night, as the train sped along in the light of the full moon, he jotted down on a half-sheet of notepaper a plan for a comparative study of the civilizations of mankind. He had decided to embark on a research program that would take him on a prolonged journey through all known civilizations to determine whether meaningful patterns were discernible in the lifetimes of these civilizations. His primary interest was to discover where we stand today in Western civilization and to glimpse where we are going. He figured that this project would require decades of work, and it did. He completed the last page of his lifelong study on June 15, 1951—thirty years of labor to discover the meaning of history and the current condition of our Western civilization.

Toynbee thinks in terms of civilizations, not nations. The latter are but ephemeral and illusory fragments of civilizations. In the wider perspective of man's civilizations, nations are merely ethnocentric tribes that come and go so rapidly that they are quite secondary in importance, though in their short lifetimes they are the source of much narrow internecine bickering within the larger cultural body.

The subject matter of Toynbee's study of history is all the civilizations known to man. He lists twenty-seven civilizations born to date (including five arrested civilizations). There were also four abortive civilizations that started out normally but could not make the grade.

Subtracting the arrested civilizations from the total, we have twenty-two that reached maturity. Of those twenty-two civilizations, fifteen are now dead and buried, while only seven are still alive. Of the five arrested civilizations, two are dead and three are still living.

There are, then, a total of seventeen dead and ten living civilizations.

But two of these ten living civilizations are now in their death throes. That leaves only eight, and six of these "bear marks of having already broken down and gone into disintegration," and seven of the eight are presently seriously threatened with annihilation and/or assimilation by Western civilization.

As of the twentieth century, therefore, our own Western civilization stands at the top of the list. From appearances, we are still relatively healthy, and our general prognosis, according to Toynbee, can be one of guarded optimism.

As Toynbee studied the lifespans of man's twenty-seven civilizations— rather like drawing lifelines on clear plastic films and making overlays for comparison—what did he discover? Patterns. Consistent, clear patterns of birth, growth, maturity, decline, disintegration, and death—for each and every civilization that had the good fortune (just like individuals) to live a full lifetime. To him the patterns were unmistakable, and he tried to study the movements of

*I have a theory that progress is what is left over after one meets an impossible problem.*
NORMAN COUSINS

*When I came back from war, I discovered that to adjust to the kind of life people lived was simply impossible, after all that I had seen. So many of the things that went on seemed like trivialities.*
**The World at War, BBC-TV**

*Violent revolutions do not so much redistribute wealth as destroy it. . . . The only real revolution is in the enlightenment of the mind and the improvement of character. The only real emancipation is individual. . . .*
WILL DURANT

civilizations without prior doctrinal commitment. He believed the patterns he saw to be real, not subjective.

Toynbee gave labels to the stages of development in much the same way that Erikson has named the phases of our individual life patterns. A "primitive society" is confronted by a challenge and responds heroically and creatively. It is led out of its primitive condition by a "creative minority" of individuals and becomes a bright, thriving civilization. But the "creative minority" soon loses its vitality and turns into a "dominant minority" that refuses to release its cherished power. Internal power struggles begin as the disintegrating civilization fragments; it is bound together less and less by common values and shared visions. It sinks into a "time of troubles" and becomes vulnerable to dissolving forces from within and without. It unifies briefly into a "universal state"; but it has no vital, creative resources left, and it dies. But from death there is resurrection. From its ashes there arises, Phoenix-like, a second-generation civilization that carries on the great insights and values of the now dead society.

Since the larger units (civilizations) behave so much like the smaller units (persons), one can detect an experiential thread running throughout Toynbee's philosophy of history. Outlined in terms of individuals it runs something like this:

Individuals experience a state of

1. *peace and contentment* They relax their hold on nonmaterial values and become more material-minded; they become self-satisfied with material things to the point of worshiping themselves and their handiwork. This leads to

2. *disillusionment and suffering* Life has become meaningless as materialism fails to satisfy the needs of human nature; the old gods prove to be false. People's suffering drives them toward a

3. *salvaging of values* Their attention is redirected toward the fundamental questions of the nature and value of human life; they seek meaning once again, and find it. This question-asking mood stimulates them into a

4. *period of creativity* They find answers to their questions; life takes on new meaning as disillusionment fades away; life becomes livable again, and they are happy. They now enter a state of

5. *peace and contentment* and the cycle repeats itself.

This pattern of behavior is typical, but it is not an "inexorable law." It can be broken by innumerable factors, internal and external, and this is true for the civilization as well as the individual. Just as those who might learn their lessons vicariously through the sufferings of others and not be compelled to pass through the disillusionment-suffering phase themselves, so also a whole civilization might conceivably learn the same lesson and thereby get a new lease on life. If John Dewey has reminded us that we don't get down to the business of thinking until we strike a problem that makes us think, then Toynbee is saying that people don't get down to the business of assessing life's values until their loss compels them to do so. In short, individuals learn by suffering, and only by suffering. But they *can* learn—and thereby alter the pattern of their civilization.

# THE PLIGHT OF WESTERN CIVILIZATION

From this Promethean comparison, what had Toynbee found? Western civilization is probably on the threshold of what Toynbee calls a "universal state," and the appearance of this state in the developmental pattern of a civilization is the unmistakable sign of disintegration. The breakdown of our civilization began in the fifteenth or sixteenth century, probably with the religious wars, and since that time there have been innumerable symptoms of disintegration in the arts, philosophy, religion, and material culture. We recognize these signs from their appearance in corresponding stages in past societies. Since there are only two or three great powers left in the world today serving as rallying points for all the other nations, the universal state cannot be far away.

But at this point a new element has entered the picture: the actual fact of One World. When we ask what sort of universal state we shall see, Toynbee suggests two possibilities. The first kind would have all the characteristics of the universal states of the past. It would be ushered onto the stage of history by the same self-inflicted knockout blow in which one member-state succeeds in a coup of all the other member-states and itself becomes the universal state. No society has ever been able to recover from this suicidal act, and nothing can turn back the process of dissolution that now sets in. Thoughtfully, Toynbee asks, "Must we, too, purchase our *Pax Oecumenica* at this deadly price?"

The second alternative would be something new in human history: the creation of a new kind of universal state by peaceful means. The entire world is now moving toward homogeneity with unbelievable speed. Momentarily it is dominated by the technology of a materialistic West, but it is clearly, and increasingly, influenced by the nonmaterialistic values and concepts of the non-Western world. If it does prove to be true that we are on the verge of becoming *one* civilization with *one* culture, this may mean that a new type of political organization could manifest itself. This would be a genuine mutation of the laws of history. If it is possible for the West to meet the challenge of One World by outgrowing its egocentric illusion—especially as it expresses itself in the nationalism of its parochial states—the doom of Western civilization may be avoided. There could be a new lease on life, and there could be a new world order.

There is the possibility, of course, that humanity may destroy itself through some nuclear holocaust, but Toynbee does not believe this to be the most probable alternative. But there is the possibility that we may require a challenge as horrifying as the sufferings of mass destruction before we could learn how to live in peaceful coexistence.

Toynbee said that "the whole face of the planet will have been unified politically through the concentration of irresistible military power in some single set of hands." Although communism seemed a threat from a short-range viewpoint, in the long view Toynbee dismisses communism because, in insisting on short-cuts, it does not answer the individual's deepest needs. "There seems to be in human nature an intractable vein—akin to the temperament of Man's yoke-fellows the camel, mule, and goat—which insists on being allowed a modicum of freedom and which knows how to impose its will when it is goaded beyond endurance. . . . Even the most long-suffering peoples revolt at some point."

*Our ignorance of history causes us to slander our own times.*

GUSTAVE FLAUBERT

*The strongest political force of the day—nationalism—is driving nations to increase their populations rather than to moderate them. This is why I doubt whether action will be taken until the problem has developed from a threat to a disaster.*

FRED HOYLE

*What's it to me that nobody's guilty and that I know it—I need revenge or I'd kill myself. And revenge not in some far off eternity, somewhere, sometime, but here and now, on earth, so that I can see it myself.*

FYODOR DOSTOEVSKY
*The Brothers Karamazov*

Within this coming universal state there will be less physical and material freedom than the peoples of the West have been used to, even in such "sacred" realms as family planning. As he sees it, "in a powerful, healthy, overpopulated world, even the proletarian's freedom to beget children will no longer be his private affair, but will be regulated by the state." He believes that the problems of population control and food production are the critical problems of the near future.

Man cannot live without freedom, however, and "if freedom is suppressed on the material plane, it will break out on the spiritual plane." So in this new world there will be a spiritual freedom superior to that known to the West, and this gain will be more than worth the price that society will pay for it. "True spiritual freedom is attained when each member of Society has learned to reconcile a sincere conviction of the truth of his own religious beliefs and practices with a voluntary toleration of the different beliefs and practices of his neighbors."

There will also be equality among human beings and respect for human dignity. There will be neither colonialism nor communism to deny these qualities to mankind. The idea of "democracy" as understood by the West to mean *self-government* will be considerably weakened, and "democracy" as employed by the non-Western peoples to mean social equality will predominate.

And what will be the role of religion? Toynbee clearly sees a resurgence of religion. Just as the nineteenth and the first half of the twentieth century have seen a steady movement away from religion, the twenty-first century will witness a countermovement in which mankind will turn from materialism and technology back to religion and spiritual values. What will this religion be like? A continuing interaction between all existing religions is certain, but for some time to come each of the living religions will maintain its identity and minister to its own adherents. However, there is a strong possibility that, as these great religions find themselves face to face in a shrinking world, a positive tolerance will replace their traditional fanaticism. They will find that all their fellow seekers are engaged in the same quest. In the long run, only a true monotheistic devotion to one Ultimate Reality accepted by all could meet the requirements of those who view their world as One World, and who look upon all others as kindred.

Can Western civilization survive all this? *Perhaps.* So many new factors have appeared in the modern world that our civilization, if it can come alive and face the challenge of change, can be infused with new vigor and win a reprieve, perhaps even a new chance at growth. If our response includes great leaders— an authentic "creative minority"—who can lead the way by facing realistically the problems of a new era, there is still hope.

Western civilization is not yet dead and buried, not quite.

Most philosophers agree that when a civilization becomes materialistic and "sensate" (Pitirim Sorokin's term) in its values, then it is in trouble. In this stage there is usually a universally held belief that this is the "golden age"—a bounteous time of unprecedented prosperity. In reality it is the onset of disintegration. Unless the culture can rediscover its creativity by successfully facing new challenges and recovering its "ethereal" values, it is doomed. What they are saying is that unless a fundamental change takes place in the priority of values

*Chinese malediction:*
*"I curse you! May you be born in an important age."*

of large numbers of people, but above all in the "creative minority" who are the true leaders of humanity, then the civilization has gone into irrevocable decline.

Another point of agreement among philosophers of history is that nationalism is a necessary but passing phenomenon. Those holding "organismic" theories of history usually liken our present politico-cultural condition to adolescence, the time when the individual human self is laboring for separation and identity. But once the integrated self has been developed, there is no longer a preoccupation with identity or identity-labels. They suggest that civilization will move collectively through the ethnocentric stage, just as individually we pass (or should pass) through the egocentric stage. While quite normal in the adolescent phase, overconcern with self is hardly becoming to mature adults who have more important things to do than concentrating perpetually on the problem of *who* they are. What philosophers of history agree on is that conditions in the modern world are creating a single world-culture that will, with shattering speed, break down the boundaries of nationalistic consciousness. Indeed, our survival will be in serious jeopardy if large-scale ethnocentric consciousness prevails.

A third point on which most philosophers of history agree is that the disintegration of a civilization is not the ultimate tragedy we may think it to be. Durant makes this point frequently in his *Story of Civilization*. "We should not be greatly disturbed by the probability that our civilization will die like any other. As Frederick asked his retreating troops at Kolin, 'Would you live forever?' Perhaps it is desirable that life should take fresh forms, that new civilizations and centers should have their turn." Toynbee has similarly noted that the most precious elements of any civilization do not die but become the seeds of a subsequent new civilization. Great inventions, advancements in science, philosophy, art, and music, the profoundest insights into nature, and our knowledge of humanity—these are never lost though the culture that produced them may crumble. "These are the elements of civilization," writes Durant, "and they have been tenaciously maintained through the perilous passage from one civilization to the next. They are the connective tissue of human history."

*The historian will not mourn because he can see no meaning in human existence except that which man puts into it; let it be our pride that we ourselves may put meaning into our lives, and sometimes a significance that transcends death.*

**WILL AND ARIEL DURANT**

## CAN WE LEARN FROM HISTORY?

There has been a recurrent skepticism in our Western thinking as to whether we can learn anything at all from history. Many have said it, but none better than Hegel: The only thing we learn from history is that we never learn from history.

Perhaps we can allow the skeptics their points. Considering all the lessons of history that could be learned, the poverty and pokiness of our learning is nothing less than frightening. As of the twentieth century, we have recovered a much greater fund of historical knowledge than the ancients ever dreamed possible; and yet, with all this wealth of information, we don't seem to be able to read "the lessons of history."

History is *human* history. It is nothing more or less than the record of individual human beings who have lived, loved, fought, dreamed, and (mostly) vanished. Whenever individuals act collectively, then we lump them together with an abstraction and speak of tribes, nations, communities, committees, teams, classes, and so on. And when they create mental systems and subordinate their individuality to the contractual guidelines they have agreed to, then we speak of institutions: governments, armies, churches, monastic movements, industrial complexes, political parties, and the like.

But all such groupings are merely functional abstractions. In the last analysis, history is the story of single human beings going about the business of living; and in their lives we find exactly what we would expect: the highs and lows, great accomplishments and terrible mistakes, heroic dedication and horrendous cruelty—they're all there. Almost everything we have learned that is worthwhile—that is, wisdom—we have learned by studying the behavior of other human beings. So, who could not learn from all these individuals if one so wished? If they happen to have lived in the past, then, yes, "We can learn from history."

But let's be clear: history *teaches* us nothing. History is dead—it is past; it is silent. The act of learning from history therefore falls to the living, and it becomes a deliberate, aggressive act on our part to search out the lessons that lie quietly in the records, waiting to be brought to life and put to use. So, the question of whether we can learn from history turns around to peer at us: Can we open ourselves to what history has to say to us?

Edward Hallett Carr, a historiographer, reminds us that "the axiom that everything has a cause is a condition of our capacity to understand what is going on around us." In daily life we rarely doubt that cause-and-effect patterns exist. We *assume* causality, rightly; and in every realm of experience we want to control events by altering their causes.

Learning from history is analogous to learning from our own experience. We study history, just as we worry through our personal memories, to find out what went wrong, or what *is* wrong. If we can isolate the causes, then, next time,

*After all, when one tries to change institutions without having changed the nature of men, that unchanged nature will soon resurrect those institutions.*

WILL DURANT

---

### STAGES IN THE LIFE OF MAN

So the continuity of history reasserts itself: despite earthquakes, epidemics, famines, eruptive migrations, and catastrophic wars, the essential processes of civilization are not lost; some younger culture takes them up, snatches them from the conflagration, carries them on imitatively, then creatively, until fresh youth and spirit can enter the race. As men are members of one another, and generations are moments in a family line, so civilizations are units in a larger whole whose name is history; they are stages in the life of man. Civilization is polygenetic—it is the co-operative product of many peoples, ranks, and faiths; and no one who studies its history can be a bigot of race or creed. Therefore the scholar, though he belongs to his country through affectionate kinship, feels himself also a citizen of that Country of the Mind which knows no hatreds and no frontiers; he hardly deserves his name if he carries into his study political prejudices, or racial discriminations, or religious animosities; and he accords his grateful homage to any people that has borne the torch and enriched his heritage.

WILL DURANT
*The Story of Civilization*

perhaps we can alter those causes and change the outcome. How many science-fiction stories spin out the secretly cherished hope that we might go back in time and alter a single causal event and thereby erase some blackened episode that stains the record of human history?

What caused the great depression? What caused the energy crisis? What caused the discontent of the Sixties? What caused the ecological crisis? What are the principal causes of the second-class status of women in Western history? What will be the effects of the sense of autonomy of the young African nations? What causes "the deaths of the gods"?

Too often we grasp essential causes only later when discoveries illuminate them. Historic causes are deeply hidden; seeing takes time. Take the Nazi phenomenon, for example. Even today, could we recognize its principal causes so that we could take steps to prevent the recurrence of such a nationalist/racist power state? In the case of Nazi Germany, the Milgram experiments conducted in the early 1960s beamed a flood of light on some of the primal human behavioral traits that permitted such a system to exist and explained how it was possible that "good and decent people" could allow such monstrous cruelties to occur in their midst. (See box, pp. 332–333.)

Thus history provides us with assorted tragedies to work on, and historical analysis never ceases. We try to understand our past to provide therapy for our future.

There is a special way that we can learn "the lessons of history." The men and women of the past can become our teachers.

From Aristotle we can learn how to unleash our wonderment upon life; to cherish all the understanding yet achieved by the human race; and, with Ulysses, "To follow knowledge like a sinking star / Beyond the utmost bound of human thought."

From Voltaire we can learn how to restoke the fiery furnaces even in "old age"; to rekindle the feeling of outrage at bigotry and injustice; to start the wheels of intellectual action rolling so fast that they shock the conscience of a nation with their clarity and power.

From Nietzsche we can learn about the ironies of having your most eloquent phrases timely ripped from context and misused to further the very causes you spent your life fighting.

From Schopenhauer we can learn something of the courage required to face life when your inner machinery has been tangled and twisted, but you know you must continue to live—meaningfully, usefully, and as honestly as possible.

From Augustine of Tagaste and Søren Kierkegaard we can learn how to accept the burning guilt of being human—all-too-human—and how to transmogrify the pain of the human condition into the service of others (Saint Augustine) and the rediscovery of what it means to be an individual human being (Kierkegaard).

From Francis Bacon and Niccolò Machiavelli we can listen to the agony of exile: being severed from your work, your friends, your livelihood; being challenged to cope creatively with years of solitude; being forced to learn to live with yourself.

From Thomas Aquinas and Albertus Magnus we can learn something of the

*I am constantly waiting for things to change for the better; amid all the conflicting parties, I have chosen none. I am in the position of someone who hopes to win first prize in a lottery without having bought a ticket.*

Eugene Ionesco

superhuman discipline required to order vast stores of human knowledge; to record, with superhuman strength, all you know as a legacy to your faith and your future.

From Plato and Einstein we can come to appreciate the "adventures of the mind"—the soaring flights into possible worlds that can excite and enthrall but that remain quite beyond the realities of present perception.

From Galileo we can learn something about mustering "the courage of our convictions" against the pressures of conformity; and, with the knowledge that evidence is on our side, winning through to a personal victory by means of our courage and/or stubbornness.

From Wittgenstein we can learn what it means "to think our own thoughts"—not to repeat words heard and phrases memorized, not to resort to clichés, pretending that they are really our own.

From Spinoza we can learn how to live with final and total disapproval by all those we hold dear to preserve our integrity; to avoid all vindictiveness; to become more gentle and wise as others call us names and ostracize us from their midst.

All these—just from the ranks of "philosophers"—can teach us. Then there are Francis of Assisi, Thomas More, Abraham Lincoln, Beethoven, Helen Keller, Joan of Arc . . .

## REFLECTIONS

1   What is the goal of "the philosophy of history"? The question we all want answered is: Does history have meaning? And if so, what is that meaning? If we give an affirmative answer, then we face a prior question: What are the sources of meaning? But prior still: How could we go about gathering evidence to find out if history has meaning? How would you respond to these questions?

2   What does the word *history* refer to? If the past is "dead," how can there be history? (*Is* the past "dead"?) How does the historian go about "doing history"—does he recall it, read and record it, research it and discover it, invent it, create it, imagine it? Is history better thought of as a science or as an art?

3   Having made a comparative study of twenty-seven civilizations, what common patterns did Toynbee find? Do those patterns constitute "the meaning of history"? What was the source of those patterns? In the last analysis, do the patterns described by Toynbee tell us where we are in this tenth decade of the twentieth century, and where we are going? (You might enjoy browsing through portions of Toynbee's monumental twelve-volume work, *A Study of History.* You might begin by perusing some of the passages in Vol. X, say pp. 213–242, or pp. 126–144.)

4   See p. 316-box. Will Durant makes a fascinating observation about what survives when civilizations finally die—a point also made by many other philosophers of history. Do you believe Durant is right? "Captive Greece has led captive her rude conqueror"—wrote Horace of Rome's "conquest" of Greece. So again: Do civilizations truly die?

5 What do you think of the interpretive framework that the Deuteronomic historian placed upon the tribal stories of the Book of Judges? Could this framework be placed on *any* war—World War II, for instance, or the Vietnam war? The Gulf war? Try it.

6 Saint Augustine is considered the first great philosopher of history because he was the first Western thinker who tried to explain in depth the how and the why of history's "meaning." Do you accept his interpretation of the fall of the city of Rome? Could Augustine's basic framework be applied to the fall of Constantinople to the Ottoman Turks in 1453? Or to the fall of Paris to the Nazis in 1940? What human need lies behind Augustine's towering effort *to explain?* Do you and I, today, still *need* such explanations?

7 From what origin, according to Hegel, does history derive meaning? What are the purpose and final goal of human history? What is the role of the individual in the Hegelian view of history? What sort of evidence could be mustered for or against Hegel's interpretation of history?

8 According to Marx, what is the source of the "inexorable laws" that govern the development of human history? What is the role of the individual in the Marxian view of history? Marx has been linked to the doctrine of "inevitable progress" that was in the air during the latter part of the nineteenth century. Is there "inevitable progress" in Marx's doctrine? Is inevitable progress inherent in history? (Is inevitable *regress* inherent in history?)

9 Compare and contrast Hegel's "dialectical idealism" with Marx's "dialectical materialism." Both have profoundly influenced the modern world. Which one is right? Could both be right? Is neither right? (Must a doctrine be "right" to be as influential as these doctrines have been?)

10 This chapter summarizes three points of agreement shared by most philosophers of history. Note them and ask yourself if you agree.

11 Hegel once said that the only thing that we learn from history is that we never learn from history. But seriously, *can* we learn from history? If so, what do we learn? And from whom (or what) do we learn it—from individuals, nations, religious societies, institutions, civilizations? Or from individual blunders, or political or military mistakes? Or from examples of courage, heroic transcendence, growth into "greatness," personal achievement? Or what?

# G.W.F. HEGEL

## *"Reason is the Substance of the Universe"*

Hegel's philosophical system is so big and so complex that few have understood it. Hegel himself once wrote that "only one man understands me"—presumably himself, in lucid moments—but "even he does not." Sir Malcolm Knox comments that it has always been "easier to revolt against him than to understand him."

His detractors, therefore, see his philosophy as a bewildering metaphysical fantasy. Bertrand Russell writes that almost all his ideas are wrong. Others have judged his work as "pure nonsense" that "will remain as a monument to German stupidity." By contrast, his supporters think of Hegel's philosophy as the timeless work of a tireless genius, revealing the dynamic movement of human thought and history. All agree that he is one of the architects of modern thought and that the twentieth century cannot be understood apart from him.

Georg Wilhelm Friedrich Hegel—happily, he usually signed his name just "Hegel"—was born in Stuttgart in 1770. His father was a minor official in the state ministry of finance, but they were never

close. His mother was an educated woman who directed his earliest studies toward the classics—he read Latin and Greek literature when he stayed home sick from school—but she died when Hegel was thirteen. His classical education was continued at the local grammar school, and he was fluent in Greek and Latin all his life.

At eighteen he enrolled in the theological school at the University of Tübingen to carry out a program in theology and philosophy, and did well. His religious background was Protestant, and he seriously considered entering the ministry, but he lacked style if not substance—his audiences were turned off by a weak voice and awkward gestures. At college he was sociable and never lacked for close friends of both sexes. A fellow student observed that "a certain joviality and tavern ease . . . made him pleasant company." Intellectually he was looked upon as a bohemian *lumen obscurum* of uncertain promise. He was a quiet, industrious student. He had begun early to write down his own thoughts at great length, though he published nothing. For the most part he was remembered from his college days for playing cards, drinking beer, dancing, discovering girls, reading voraciously, filling volumes of notebooks with notes, griping about dull teachers, and cutting classes. He graduated in 1793 with an M.A. in philosophy.

One must eat, so Hegel became a private tutor for a well-to-do family in Bern, Switzerland, and continued to write. He composed a Life of Christ, fashionably and precociously, but burned the manuscript. At twenty-nine he received a small inheritance from his father, and he felt secure enough to apply for a job as instructor in philosophy at the University of Jena. He had apparently found that "ein gutes Bier" could be bought there. He taught there for six years. The income was meager, but he was working at what he loved. This was the period of his intellectual maturing.

His lectures were a challenge to his students. His style was quite unimpressive . . . at first. All his life Hegel alienated the majority of his students as well as the general public, but there was an authenticity in his intensity that was absorbing. Though his speech was halting, a listener who thought along with him began to realize that he was witnessing a highly creative mind at the moment of creation; caught up in the thought process, he shared this moment with the speaker. This, of course, puts off those who can't enter empathetically into the process and those who must be entertained; but Hegel persistently captured the intellects who could march in rhythm with his unique mind.

In 1806 Napoleon vanquished the Prussian army at Jena and brought war to Hegel's doorstep. Having finished a great manuscript only the night before the Battle of Jena, he gathered up its pages and fled the city. Early in 1807 Hegel became the editor of a newspaper in Bamberg, an interim job that supported him well. He worked feverishly to publish the daily news, which undoubtedly kept him in touch with everyday events and forced him to write in a clear, factual style that people could understand—

good training for a prolific writer who was later to go astray.

In 1808 Hegel became headmaster of a grammar school at Nuremberg where, among other duties, he taught philosophy to teenage boys. When called on to fill in for sick teachers, "the students were especially surprised when, without ado, he continued the instruction not only in Greek and other such subjects but also in differential and integral calculus," in the sciences, or whatever was called for.

Hegel was married to a young lady named Marie von Tucher in the fall of 1811. He was forty-one, she was nineteen; and there is a hint that this is one of the rare times when he acknowledged the nonrational: he courted her with poetry, spoke of love, and wrote tender letters; but he soon retreated to the left-brained world of logical thought.

At Nuremberg Hegel published at last: a giant three-volume work entitled *Science of Logic*. So abstract that it was undecipherable for anyone but specialists, it emerged on the academic scene with an impact that astonished everyone but Hegel. He was soon offered several professorships and accepted a position at the University of Heidelberg. It was his first salaried teaching position; he was forty-six. He taught there two years. More secure now, he wrote voluminously, and published a second huge work, *Encyclopedia of Philosophical Sciences*. His stature increased rapidly, and in 1818 he was invited to the University of Berlin, the most prestigious academic institution in Germany.

Hegel's life traced a familiar pattern that perhaps illustrates a principal aspect of his doctrine of dialectic change. As a student he was a thorough going radical, fiery in his political passions, vigorous and vitriolic in his social pronouncements. He spoke excitedly about freedom, justice, and equality. He helped found a club to discuss political ideas, supported the French Revolution, and, one Sunday morning, marched to a meadow to plant a "freedom tree." In

*The real is rational, and the rational is real.*

*The world looks rational to those who look at it rationally.*

*Reason is the substance of the universe;. . . The design of the world is absolutely rational.*

*The history of the world is not the theatre of happiness; periods of happiness are blank pages in it, for they are periods of harmony.*

*What experience and history teach is this—that people and governments never have learned anything from history, or acted on principles deduced from it.*

*Pure Being and Nothing are the same.*

*The history of the world is none other than the progress of the consciousness of freedom.*

*It is of the nature of truth to prevail when its time has come.*

*The insight to which philosophy should help us is that the actual world is as it ought to be. . . . God rules the world; the content of his government, the execution of his plan, is world history; to grasp this is the task of the philosophy of world history. . . .*

*A philosophy is its own time apprehended in thought* (so ist auch die Philosophie, ihre Zeit in Gedanken erfasst).

*ON HEGEL:*
*"At the end of the nineteenth century and in the early decades of the twentieth, Hegel was perhaps the most influential, the most revered, and the most closely studied philosopher of the western world."*
**ERROL E. HARRIS**

*ON HEGEL:*
*"Hegel is at the root of that complex we call the modern world. . . . [But] Hegel is fast becoming a remote thinker, and the age he lived in is beginning to look like the prehistory of mankind."*
**FRANCO LOMBARDI**

religion he broke with all orthodoxies, revising the very essence out of traditional Christianity. In philosophy he disowned Kant's epistemology. All in all, he thought new thoughts.

But by the time he reached the pinnacle of prestige, he had become an arch-conservative and considered the current crop of young radicals to be misguided dreamers. After moving so long at the center of criticism and controversy, he longed for peace; by the time he arrived in Berlin there was an air of tiredness about him. His outlook was marked by a lack of new ideas; the creative fires were burned out. He wrote: "Finally, after forty years of immeasurable confusion, an old heart might rejoice to see an end of it all. . . ."

Even as a youth Hegel had a prematurely aged face; he was called the "old man" at the university. By all accounts he was a late-bloomer who matured slowly in self-awareness. He was a naive and simple man, without affectation; genial and good-natured, without charm and social grace. He had a biting sense of humor. He labored with enormous energy and infinite patience. He avoided excitement, adventure, and strong passions. He was the prototypical absent-minded professor.

Hegel's published works are written in an impersonal style, highly abstract and abstruse. An earlier style, natural and clear, was transmogrified into tortured didactic prose by his perceptions of what constituted "proper" academic style. His thought exhibits an extraordinary range of scholarship and learning; the penetration is brilliant; the range of his vision is matched only by that of other intellects such as Voltaire, Goethe, and Nietzsche. To express new ideas he originated much of his own terminology.

Hegel's *Philosophy of History* and several smaller works were reconstructed from students' notes and published posthumously.

◆

The key to Hegel's philosophy is his famous phrase, "The real is rational, and the rational is real." To understand this watchword is to open the door onto his system.

What is it exactly that can be "rational"? The answer is: *minds* can be rational. So Hegel is saying that *thinking* is in some sense real. Hegel believed that he was the first thinker in all of history to have seen and properly located the essence of what is real in the Universe, namely, the mind of God. The mind of God is the essence of what is real. And this mind of God is pure thought.

To put it differently: God is the essence of the cosmos, and the cosmos is reason. God is Reason. As Hegel put it, "Reason is the Substance of the Universe."

So Hegel's philosophy has two important elements: God's thinking processes, which are perfectly rational, and mortals' thinking processes, which are striving for rationality. When we humans succeed in being rational, then we are thinking God's thoughts, appropriating his rationality. Our human goal should be to grow forever toward rationality so that we are closer to the Absolute Mind—which is God thinking rational thoughts.

Where can we discover this divine rationality in action? On the plane of human history. Hegel, therefore, became one of the great philosophers of history, developing a conceptual system by which we can understand what history is doing—where it's been, where it's going, and how we fit into it.

This essence of thinking, Hegel says, is change. All thinking moves in terms of a three-beat rhythm: thesis → antithesis → synthesis. All thinking starts with the idea (thesis), develops its opposite idea (antithesis), then works these opposites together into a new whole (synthesis). Down through history, thought follows this three-beat pattern, each synthesis becoming, in turn, another thesis. This three-beat dialectical rhythm—

thought always completing itself—is the movement of history. Therefore, the essence of thought is continual change and growth toward completion and wholeness.

The purpose of history, therefore, is to enable continued growth and change to take place. History is the stage on which the highest human faculty—reason—can develop and grow. Since the beginnings of human intelligence, history has been a continual movement *from* states of incompleteness—where we were driven by animalistic instincts —*toward* completeness—where we will increasingly manifest intelligence and unity.

Thus, as history moves, there is inevitable progress toward what the mind most wants—wholeness. All history is moving *from* chaos, disconnectedness, and smallness, *toward* order, connectedness, and unity. Insofar as we humans are rational, we are moving *with* the tide of history. More than that, however, we are thinking (and manifesting) God's thoughts. Man and God, as it were, are working together *toward* a time when human self-consciousness will be complete. We will possess perfect knowledge, perfect intelligence, and a perfect understanding. At that point God's thoughts and humanity's thoughts will be One—that is, identical—and humanity will have fulfilled its destiny. The rational in people will be identical with the rationality of the universe. God's thinking is our thinking; our thinking is God's. The Real is rational; the rational is Real.

Hegel's philosophy accomplished several things. First, it went a long way toward laying the intellectual foundations of an historical optimism; if we feel we are working irrevocably with the angels toward the Ultimate Goal, then life is not in vain and we can be infused with a superlative joie de vivre. The anthropocentric optimism is cosmic:

"The fast-bound substance of the universe has no power within it capable of withstanding the courage of man's knowledge; it must give way before him, and lay bare before his eyes, and for his enjoyment, its riches and its depths."

Second, Hegel, in his way, effectively annihilated some two centuries of epistemological loneliness: we no longer perceive ourselves to be minds caught in physical bodies, able to experience nothing but our own experience and doomed to absolute ignorance of reality-in-itself. Hegel concludes that we do apprehend what is real every time we think rationally; we *know* the Real. When we think God's thoughts we are not merely "apprehending" the real: we have *become* the Real. We are not thinking *about* God's thoughts; we are *thinking* God's thoughts.

Third, Hegel developed such an all-inclusive schematic that all events could be reinterpreted and included in the dialectical process. Wars, revolutions, tragedies of all sorts—these were as integral and necessary a part of the historical logistics as benign and beneficial events. The Absolute Mind-in-History works via the operation of opposites: good interacts with evil, stability with instability, war with peace, and so forth; peace and war interact to move forward to a new synthesis. Crisis times are times of great accomplishments that propel history forward to greater things.

To Hegel history is the stage on which change must take place; and change is always moving from the incomplete toward the complete—toward wholeness, unity, and freedom.

A major cholera epidemic—Europe's first—reached Berlin in 1831. Hegel sought safety for his family by leaving the city for the summer, but when he returned in the fall he was immediately stricken and died only a day later—on November 14. He was sixty-one.

5₂

## THE WESTERN EXPERIENCE: CONFLICTING LOYALTIES

All human societies possessing a modicum of individual freedom develop a wide spectrum of strongly held convictions about the structure and power of human society—"strongly held" because it is the human state, after all, that exercises ultimate temporal control over human destiny.

There exists also in such societies a fundamental tension between those who would obey different sets of laws. Men without freedom are spared this condition; those belonging to primitive tribes or rigidly authoritarian states are subject to but a single set of laws. But in freer societies numerous systems of laws burden the individual by claiming to have overriding jurisdiction. The individual *should* obey them *all!*

This predicament is analogous to what we find in ethics. If one is subject to only a single moral code, then one is spared the complex decisions of free people who must make decisions among sundry codes demanding their loyalty.

Our Western experience has been an ongoing conflict of loyalties. Western society derives its deepest commitment from the scriptural concept of covenant which binds the community of the faithful to the laws of God. For well over a thousand years before Christ—indeed, from the time when Moses defied Egyptian law to lead the Children of Israel into a covenant relationship with Yahweh—humanity has struggled with the tension between obedience to the "laws of God" and the "laws of man." For all those who live under the divine mandate, their final loyalty has been to God; and civilization's mundane systems of law have, by comparison, only a weak, secondary claim upon their loyalty.

This tension between loyalties can be felt in the following passages. First, the case (often implicit) for a higher law:

*We must be entirely clear that law is not God. It has always been a basic Christian conviction that there are times when a Christian ought to break the law.*

EUGENE CARSON BLAKE

*As for adopting the ways which the State has provided for remedying the evil, I know not of such ways. They take too much time, and a man's life will be gone. I have other affairs to attend to. I came into this world, not chiefly to make this a good place to live in, but to live in it, be it good or bad.*

HENRY DAVID THOREAU

I think we all have moral obligations to obey just laws. On the other hand, I think that we have moral obligations to disobey unjust laws because non-cooperation with evil is just as much a moral obligation as cooperation with good.

MARTIN LUTHER KING, JR.

*The Constitution is the supreme law of our land and it governs our actions as citizens. Only the laws of God, which govern our consciences, are superior to it. . . .*

**PRESIDENT GERALD FORD**
*(The Nixon Pardon)*

[If the law] is of such a nature that it requires you to be the agent of injustice to another, then, I say, break the law.

HENRY DAVID THOREAU

When the law impels one against love, it ceases and should *no longer be a law . . .* You have need of the law, that love may be manifested; but if it cannot be kept without injury to the neighbor, God wants us to suspend and ignore the law.

MARTIN LUTHER

One sabbath while he was walking through the grainfields, his disciples plucked some of the ears of grain and, milling the grain in their hands—which was against the Law of Moses—they ate them.

Some of the Pharisees said to him, "Look at them! Why are they doing what is illegal on the sabbath?"

He replied simply, "The sabbath was made for man, not man for the sabbath." But those who knew the Law went away angry.

MARK 2:23–24, 27–28
*(paraphrased)*

The practical—and pragmatic—side of the dilemma is stated with great clarity in the following passages:

An ordered society cannot exist if every man may determine which laws he will obey, . . . that only "just" laws need be obeyed and that every man is free to determine for himself the question of "justness."

LEWIS F. POWELL, JR.

Everyone must obey the authorities that are over him, for no authority can exist without the permission of God; the existing authorities have been established by him, so that anyone who resists the authorities sets himself in opposition to what God has ordained, and those who oppose him will bring down judgment upon themselves. The man who does right has nothing to fear from the magistrates. . . . You must obey them, therefore, not only to escape God's wrath, but as a matter of principle, just as you pay your taxes. . . . Pay them all that is due them.

SAINT PAUL (ROMANS 13:1–2, 5)

*For, as among the powers in man's society the greater authority is obeyed in preference to the lesser, so must God above all.*

**SAINT AUGUSTINE**

Resistance on the part of the people to the supreme legislative power of The State is in no case legitimate; for it is only by submission to the universal legislative will, that a condition of law and order is possible. . . . It is the duty of the people to bear any abuse of the supreme power, even though it should be considered to be unbearable. And the reason is that any resistance of the highest legislative authority can never but be contrary to the law, and must even be regarded as tending to destroy the whole legal constitution.

IMMANUEL KANT

Submit to all human authority, for the Master's sake; to the emperor, as supreme, and to governors, as sent by him to punish evil-doers, and to encourage those who do right.

SAINT PETER (1 PETER 2:13–15)

Since this tension is rooted in religion, we would like to be able to turn to a founder of Western religion—to Jesus, for instance—for guidance; but we do so in vain. When forced to comment upon the dilemma, he merely mystifies the question:

Teacher, we know that you are honest and are not swayed by men; for you do not defer to the worldly positions of men, but truly teach the way of God. Tell us then, what you think. Is it lawful to pay taxes to the state, or not?
But sensing their hypocritical intent, he merely said, "Bring me a coin, and let me look at it."
So they brought him a silver denarius.
Then he asked: "Whose picture and inscription is this?"
They said, "Caesar's."
So Jesus replied: "Then render to Caesar what is Caesar's since Caesar's picture is on the coin; and render to God the things that are God's."
Having failed to entrap him as they planned, they went away angry.

MARK 12:14–17
(*paraphrased*)

Tiberius Caesar (A.D. 14-37) on a Roman denarius.

> **"I was there to follow orders, not to think."**
>
> JOHN DEAN
> (**Watergate testimony**)

> **"I carried out my orders. . . . Where would we have been if everyone had thought things out in those days?"**
>
> ADOLF EICHMANN

## GOOD LAWS AND BAD LAWS

The case for making a distinction between good and bad laws is well stated by King, Thoreau, Luther, and others. No matter how strongly one advocates lawful obedience to the state and its laws, it is inevitable that some laws will turn out to be bad ones. Lawmakers are not only human—which is sufficient cause for having a few bad laws—but a percentage of them will always be parochial in their interests, shortsighted or dead wrong in their opinion of what constitutes justice, mentally out of touch with reality, and woefully uninformed on the nature of values and value judgments (and after all, laws are the legislation of human values). These statements can be made with some certainty simply because the leaders of men are not immune to the epistemic and emotional problems shared by the populace as a whole.

Therefore, *in any legal system,* it is quite possible to point to laws that range from the mildly unjust to the callously inhuman, and such laws *should* produce a feeling of outrage in individuals who are victimized by them, or see others hurt by them. More important, perhaps, is the fact that unless laws are periodically challenged—as the authors of the American system recognized—then they don't get improved. In 1787 Thomas Jefferson said, "God forbid, we should ever be twenty years without such a rebellion." Elsewhere he elaborated: "What country can preserve its liberties, if its rulers are not warned from time to time, that this people preserve the spirit of resistance? Let them take arms. . . . The tree of liberty must be refreshed from time to time, with the blood of patriots and tyrants." Among mature people criticism is cherished; it is through the assessment of wise criticism that more just laws can be formulated and anti-quated laws updated. Also, it is through open criticism that the selfish interests of those in power can be rapidly brought to the attention of enough citizens who can object and, if necessary, dissent before a deeper tyranny sets in.

> We have another tradition in this country which is in danger of passing away; dissent. The responsibility to object. We might all do well to remember in these days of national distemper the comment of Pastor Niemoeller a quarter of a century ago in Nazi Germany. "They came after the Jews, and I was not a Jew, so I did not object. Then they came after the Catholics, and I was not a Catholic, so I did not object. Then they came after the trade-unionists, and I was not a trade-unionist, so I did not object. And then they came after me, and there was no one left to object."
>
> SENATOR STOWE
> *The Bold Ones (NBC-TV)*

*One dog barks at something, and a hundred bark at the sound.*

**Chinese proverb**

## LOYALTY TO HIGHER AUTHORITY

*"You've got to forget the nobler sentiments if you want to live. (Pause. . .) Funny thing—survival."*

**"British Soldier," Play Dirty**

Our Western (Judeo-Christian) legal tradition takes the form of a hierarchy of laws—a sort of jurisdictional totem pole—with a clear order of precedence.

Local laws must defer to higher and wider laws. Thus, in case of conflict, the laws of a village or city must give way to state laws. State laws are "higher"; they take precedent. It can be validly argued that in specific areas of concern, only local laws can be truly relevant to local conditions. But populations are mobile; individuals are travelers. If there existed only local laws serving the self-interests of innumerable small jurisdictions, it just wouldn't work. In matters that affect larger populations over larger areas, wider laws must prevail.

By the same principle, federal laws generally take precedence over state laws. Neither cities nor states can be allowed to enact laws that would nourish their limited interests at the expense of the larger society of which they are but a part. Wider law must prevail if there is to be equal application of law—that is, if there is to be justice.

At this point the covenant principle upon which Western civilization is grounded must come in: that there is a higher and more universal law than that of any sovereign state. For some twenty-seven hundred years now, the Jews of the Dispersion who were carried off from their homeland have considered the Law of Moses to be higher than the laws of any state in which they lived. In the Roman Empire the fierce loyalty of Jews to their monotheistic faith won them exemption from the worship of Caesar; they alone were officially free of obligations to pour libations to the emperor's *genius* and make offerings to him as divine head of state. As Christianity grew in the early empire, some argued that Christians were Jews and should therefore share the exemption; but the majority of Christians declared emphatically that Christianity was not a branch of Judaism. As Christians established themselves to be a separate sect, they were then obliged to pay respects to the divine Caesar.

But like the Jews, they could not in good conscience do so. The Christians were therefore "disloyal"; they were considered dangerous subversives—"bad citizens." During the years of persecution that followed, the Christians became the main body of conscientious objectors against paying unjust allegiance to

### The Sun and the Moon
### *Pope Innocent III: Church and State*

The Creator of the universe set up two great luminaries in the firmament of heaven; the greater light to rule the day, the lesser light to rule the night. In the same way for the firmament of the universal Church, which is spoken of as heaven, he appointed two great dignities; the greater to bear rule over souls (these being, as it were, days), the lesser to bear rule over bodies (these being, as it were, nights). These dignities are the pontifical authority and the royal power. Furthermore, the moon derives her light from the sun, and is in truth inferior to the sun in both size and quality, in position as well as effect. In the same way the royal power derives its dignity from the pontifical authority: and the more closely it cleaves to the sphere of that authority the less is the light with which it is adorned; the further it is removed, the more it increases in splendor.

*Sicut universitatis conditor*
*EP.* I. 401, OCTOBER, 1198

Caesar and his state; their highest loyalty was reserved for their God and his laws. For this stand Christians were accused officially of atheism and anarchy: atheism because they refused to worship the state-approved gods, and anarchy because they were "outlaws" who refused to take an oath of allegiance to their government.

It was this refusal to accept "man's laws" that sent Christians into the arena and put them to the sword.

In broad terms, the allegiance to a "higher authority" has taken two forms: (1) loyalty to an institution considered to have divine authority over the state; and (2) loyalty to "God's law" as personally understood—by revelation, by "spiritual knowledge" (*gnosis*), or by conscience.

As the Roman Catholic Church developed and became the universal authority in Europe, the papacy pressed its claim to be the supreme power over all temporal authority; for the pope was the "Vicar of Christ" on earth and the church was "the City of God."

Since Christianity was established as the state religion of Rome in A.D. 385, this dual claim upon their loyalty has perplexed Western citizens. Continuing through the Middle Ages, the Renaissance and the Reformation, and into the modern world, there has been a tug-of-war between temporal authorities—who would diminish the church's power ("God's laws") and increase their own—and the papacy—which would extend its authority and limit worldly governments ("man's laws"). Individuals found themselves caught in this power struggle.

The supreme confrontation between the claimants occurred on January 28, 1077. Pope Gregory VII had stripped all power from Henry IV of Germany with a decree of excommunication. To regain his kingdom Henry crossed the Alps in winter and knelt in the snow before the gate of the castle of Canossa into which the pope had retreated. Henry repented and after waiting penitently for three days, the pope released him from excommunication and restored him to power.

*It hasn't been done yet, so they haven't got around to prohibiting it.*

**Destination Moon**

*The true patriot is one who gives his highest loyalty not to his country as it is but to his own best conceptions of what it can and ought to be.*

**ALBERT CAMUS**

The second form of allegiance to a higher power is allegiance to the word of God as known personally, to one's own conscience, or to a set of ethical ideas or norms by which one judges the quality of actual laws. Such a position can be theistic and/or ethical, but in any case it commands the highest commitment of the individual. Whatever the path by which one arrives at such a position, it often *feels* hypocritical to the individual to obey bad (unjust laws) when it has been seen clearly in ethical reflections the just laws which should prevail.

This stand was epitomized by Martin Luther in 1521 at the Council of Worms where, passionately and sincerely, he cried out, "My conscience is captive to the Word of God. . . . To go against conscience is neither right nor safe. God help me. Amen."

Pope Boniface VIII issued the papal bull *Unam sanctam* in 1302 to define clearly the superiority of God's laws—as embodied here in the Roman papacy—over man's laws—which in this case were represented by the royal heads of England and France. This bull still stands as the most extreme claim of the Church to stand in judgment over the state.

> *The surest way to corrupt a young man is to teach him to esteem more highly those who think alike than those who think differently.*
>
> FRIEDRICH NIETZSCHE

We are obliged by the faith to believe and hold—and we do firmly believe and sincerely confess—that there is one Holy Catholic and Apostolic Church, and that outside this Church there is neither salvation nor remission of sins. . . .

And we learn from the words of the Gospel that in this Church and in her power are two swords, the spiritual and the temporal. . . . Both are in the power of the Church, the spiritual sword and the material. But the latter is to be used for the Church, the former by her; the former by the priest, the latter by kings and captains but at the will and by the permission of the priest. The one sword, then, should be under the other, and temporal authority subject to spiritual. . . .

Thus, concerning the Church and her power, is the prophecy of Jeremiah fulfilled, "See, I have this day set thee over the nations and over the kingdoms," etc. If, therefore, the earthly power err, it shall be judged by a greater. . . . Furthermore we declare, state, define and pronounce that it is altogether necessary to salvation for every human creature to be subject to the Roman pontiff.

## OBEDIENCE TO THE RULE OF LAW

> *One of the big purposes of the Bill of Rights is to keep the government off our backs.*
>
> ARTHUR MILLER

Associate Justice Lewis Powell presents persuasively the case for absolute obedience to duly constituted authority: laws must be obeyed, for if each person were permitted to decide which laws were good and which were bad, social chaos would necessarily result. For who is there among us who is able to determine just from unjust laws? And on what criteria could such judgments be made? Wouldn't it be inevitable that every political crank and religious fanatic—not to mention emotionally immature rebels of all ages—would decide that all the laws were "unjust" which didn't cater to his or her own self-centered interests?

This is precisely the position taken by Socrates when his old and dear friend Crito urged him to escape from prison the day before his execution. Socrates awoke before dawn to find Crito sitting silently beside him in his cell; he had apparently made all necessary arrangements for an escape.

> *National Socialists say: Legality is that which does the German people good; illegality is that which harms the German people.*
>
> WILHELM FRICK
>
> *(Nazi Minister of the Interior)*

But Socrates had already made up his mind and refused to flee. He patiently attempted to make Crito understand his reasoning.

Look at it in this way. Suppose that while we were preparing to run away from here (or however one should describe it) the Laws and Constitution of Athens were to come and confront us and ask this question: "Now, Socrates, what are you proposing to do? Can you deny that by this act which you are contemplating you intend, so far as you have the power, to destroy us, the Laws, and the whole State as well? Do you imagine that a city can continue to exist and not be turned upside down, if the legal judgements which are pronounced in it have no force but are nullified and destroyed by private persons?"—how shall we answer this question, Crito, and others of the same kind? . . . Shall we say, "Yes, I do intend to destroy the laws, because the State wronged me by passing a faulty judgement at my trial"? Is this to be our answer, or what? . . .

Supposing the Laws say "Was there provision for this in the agreement between you and us, Socrates? Or did you undertake to abide by whatever judgements the State pronounced? . . . Do you not realize . . . that if you cannot persuade your country you must do whatever it orders, and patiently submit to any punishment that it imposes, whether it be flogging or imprisonment? And if it leads you out to war, to be wounded or killed, you must comply, and it is right that you should do so; you must not give way or retreat or abandon your position. Both in war and in the law-courts and everywhere else you must do whatever your city and your country commands, or else persuade it in accordance with universal justice. . . ."—What shall we say to this, Crito?—that what the Laws say is true, or not?

PLATO
*Crito*

---

## THE PERSONAL DILEMMA

The problem of obedience to law might be visualized as an ellipse with two foci. Near one end of the ellipse is the question of human freedom. All of us want freedom, and we want *more* freedom; but as the number of problematic persons in our society increases, the more regulation is required and the less freedom we can enjoy.

The other focus in the ellipse is one's assessment of human nature. If one is basically optimistic about humanity and believes people to be trustworthy, then one will assume that we humans can use freedom constructively and will not need punctilious systems of laws to tell us what to do and not to do. But if one distrusts human nature, convinced that it is fundamentally evil, then one must conclude that a complex system of laws is necessary to keep this selfish nature in line and coerce a semblance of order.

Around these two foci—and they *are* inside a single ellipse—turns the question of obedience to all law: to obey or not to obey. The mature, more fully actualized persons want to guide their lives solely by a few basic principles; they become restive and may chafe bitterly under irrelevant restraints upon their existence. For them, restraints are not needed: they would do what is right anyway! By contrast, however, most human beings appear unable to experience very much freedom without harming others; we are unable to live with one another peacefully without having our behavior guided and restrained by specific regulations touching all aspects of our lives.

The dilemma between principles and law has tormented many great souls. Saint Paul, for instance: he tried diligently to follow the 613 precepts of the

*We have met the enemy, and they are partly right.*

ANTHONY CAMPOLO

*The American advocacy system is a wretched way to determine the innocence or guilt of a man. But no one has yet proposed a better way.*

**The Bold Ones, NBC-TV**

*". . . Because politics is the art of the possible, it appeals only to second-rate minds. The first-raters, he claimed, were only interested in the impossible."*

ARTHUR C. CLARKE
*"Sheik Abdullah," The Fountains of Paradise*

## Obedience to Authority

Sometimes an event occurs during our lifetime that leaves an impression that is both indelible and puzzling. For me that event was the widespread participation of the German people in a system of death camps that destroyed millions of innocent men, women and children. The hapless victims were shot, gassed and burned in ovens.

These deeds were carried out by a people who were as civilized as any people in the world. How was it possible for them to act so cruelly? Did their behavior reveal a potential that is present in all of us? As a social psychologist whose job is to look into the why and how of human behavior, I decided to explore the response of ordinary people to immoral orders.

In order to explore behavior, social psychologists often rely on an important tool, the experiment. Although experiments in chemistry and physics often involve shiny equipment, flasks and electronic gear, an experiment in social psychology smacks much more of dramaturgy or theater. The experimenter carefully constructs a scenario to focus on certain aspects of behavior, a scenario in which the end is unknown and is completed by the experimental subject. The psychologist tries to create circumstances that will allow him to look at the behavior very carefully, note what he observed, and study its causes.

◆

Imagine you had answered an advertisement to take part in a study of learning. . . . First, you are greeted by a man in a gray technician's coat; he introduces you to a second volunteer and says you are both about to take part in a scientific experiment. He says it is to test whether the use of punishment improves the ability to learn.

You draw lots to see who is to be the teacher and who the learner. You turn out to be the teacher, and the other fellow, the learner. Then you see the learner strapped into a chair and electrodes placed on his wrist. You are told that, when the learner makes a mistake in the lesson, his punishment will be an electric shock.

As teacher, you are seated in front of an impressive-looking instrument, a shock generator. Its essential feature is a line of switches that range from 15 volts to 450 volts, and a set of written labels that goes from slight shock to moderate shock, strong shock, very strong shock, and so on through XXX—danger, severe shock.

Your job, the experimenter explains to you, is to teach the learner (who, unknown to [you] is a confederate and does not actually receive the shocks) a simple word-pair test. You read a list of words to him, such as blue day, nice girl, fat neck, etc., and he has to indicate by means of an answer box which words were originally paired together. If he gets a correct answer, you move on to the next pair. But if he makes a mistake, you are instructed to give him an electric shock, starting with 15 volts. And you are told to increase the shock one step each time he makes an error. In the course of the experiment the "victim" emits cries of pain and demands to be set free, but the experimenter orders you to continue. The question is: how far will you proceed on the shock generator before you turn to the experimenter and refuse to go on?

Before carrying out the experiment, I wanted to know how people thought they would behave in this situation, and so I asked them to predict their own performance. I posed the question to several groups: psychiatrists, psychologists and

*CONTINUED*

ordinary workers. They all said virtually the same thing: almost no one would go to the end.

But in reality the results were very different. Despite the fact that many subjects experience stress, and protest to the experimenter, a substantial proportion continue to the last shock on the generator. Many subjects obeyed the experimenter no matter how vehement the pleading of the person being shocked, no matter how painful the shocks seemed to be, and no matter how much the victim pleaded to be let out. This was seen time and again in our studies and has been observed in several universities where the experiment has been repeated.

But there is more to the experiment than this simple demonstration of obedience. Most of our energy went into systematically changing the factors in this situation to see which ones increased obedience and which led to greater defiance. . . . How a person behaves depends not only on his "character" but also on the precise situational pressures acting on him.

When the experiments were published, opinion about them was sharply divided. . . . The experiments that I had hoped would deepen our understanding of how people yield to authority became themselves the focus of controversy.

But the problem of authority remains. We cannot have society without some structure of authority, and every society must inculcate a habit of obedience in its citizens. Yet these experiments show that many people do not have the resources to resist authority, even when they are directed to act inhumanely against an innocent victim. The experiments pose anew the age-old problem: what is the correct balance between individual initiative and social authority? They illuminate in a concrete way what happens when obedience is unrestrained by conscience.

STANLEY MILGRAM
*TV Guide, August 21, 1976*

Jewish Law but only felt more guilty because he could not measure up to its numerous demands. In the end, he found peace only by abandoning the *Law* of Moses and accepting the *principle* of "justification by faith" in Jesus as the Christ.

Similarly, Martin Luther tried to make legalistic Roman Catholic laws work to his benefit, but he found peace only by following Paul's lead and committing his life to a single principle: "salvation by faith alone."

It is worth noting that Hinduism has provided, within the parameters of acceptable religion, several systems to meet different needs. The "Ways of Liberation" are designed to accomplish this. The "Way of Works" (*Karma Marga*) specifies innumerable rites and duties that the worshiper has only to perform to gain good karma. It makes few intellectual demands. It's a matter of *doing;* one must meticulously perform the actions prescribed by the laws. This is the path chosen by a large majority of Hindus. By contrast, there is the "Way of Knowledge" (*Jnana Marga*). This is philosophical Hinduism, the way of study and meditation that will lead the mind out of the errors that produce human misery. This is the way of liberation for only a few who have the capacity for discipline and abstract reflection.

The dilemma between a few guiding principles and numerous laws was

*When a legal distinction is determined . . . between night and day, childhood and maturity, or any other extremes, a point has to be fixed or a line has to be drawn, or gradually picked out by successive decisions, to mark where the change takes place. Looked at by itself without regard to the necessity behind it, the line or point seems arbitrary. It might as well be a little more to the one side or the other. But when it is seen that a line or point there must be, and that there is no mathematical or logical way of fixing it precisely, the decision of the legislature must be accepted unless we can say that it is very wide of any reasonable mark.*

OLIVER WENDELL HOLMES

carefully explored by Joseph Klausner, an Orthodox Jewish historian, in a scholarly study entitled *Jesus of Nazareth* (1907, English translation, 1925). In the squabble between the Pharisees who held firmly to the letter of the Mosaic Law and Jesus who deliberately disregarded Jewish law, Klausner concludes that, in the final analysis, the Pharisees were right. Judaism could never accept such a contemptuous attitude toward the Law.

> For the Jews their religion was more than simple belief and more than simple moral guidance: it was a *way of life*—all life was embraced in their religion. A people does not endure on a foundation of general human faith and morality; it needs a "practical religiousness," a ceremonial form of religion which shall embody religious ideas and also crown every-day life with a halo of sanctity.

By undermining the Law of Moses, Klausner is saying, Jesus would have destroyed the Jewish nation. Jesus' intentions are not to be inpugned, "but it is unquestionable that throughout his entire teaching there is nothing that can serve to the upkeep of the state or serve towards the maintenance of order in the existing world."

There were Jewish scholars long before Jesus who were capable of formulating the *essence* of the Law of Moses in one or two general principles. Hillel, an elder contemporary of Jesus, said: "What is hateful to thyself do not to thy neighbor: this is the whole Law, the rest is commentary: go and learn it." But such rabbis who *saw* the essence never dispensed with the literal requirements of the Law itself: for law regulates collective life and gives it order. People being what they are, Klausner writes, "the nation as a whole could only see in such public ideals as those of Jesus, an abnormal and even dangerous phantasy; the majority, who followed the Pharisees and Scribes (*Tannaim*), the leaders of the popular party in the nation, could *on no account* accept Jesus' teaching."

These illustrations seem to indicate that without firm law, and a sense of obedience to law, a society disintegrates.

Socrates sought truth with a rare courage. But he came too close; he was too relevant to be a security risk to Athens. For this he was handed a cup of hemlock in the spring or early summer of 399 B.C. Thus ended the career of one of the greatest minds the world has ever known, and the young men who followed Socrates knew then that something deep and terrible was wrong in men, individually and collectively. "This was the end of our comrade," wrote Plato, "a man, as we would say, of all then living we had ever met, the noblest and the wisest and the most just."

These men knew from their own bitter experience that societies persecute and/or execute their *best men* as well as their worst. This fact alone was enough to tell them that something tragic seems built into the human condition; and it was this insight that caused the first philosophers to begin to think deeply about life's problems and to search for solutions.

*The reasonable man adapts himself to the world; the unreasonable one persists in trying to adapt the world to himself. Therefore, all progress depends upon the unreasonable man.*

**GEORGE BERNARD SHAW**

*We give credibility to unjust laws by obeying them.*

**ALAN BOESAK**
*(protesting apartheid laws in South Africa, August 24, 1989)*

*The wrong questions appear to be the right questions because other people are asking them too . . .*

**THOMAS HORA**

## REFLECTIONS

1   "Our Western experience has been an ongoing conflict of loyalties." From your point of view, how do you assess this conflict? How much have you

been victimized by it? By conviction and temperament, which way do you tend to lean in your allegiance: toward the mandate of personal conscience or the necessities of a lawfully ordered society?

2   Is this conflict of loyalties necessarily a religious conflict, or could one who is not a traditional theist also face the dilemma?

3   If you are convinced that there is a "higher law," on what grounds or under what conditions would you decide to obey that law rather than the laws of the state? How could you be sure that your judgment in such a decision is *right?*

4   Reread pp. 328–330 together. Are you willing to grant the church the right and power to stand in judgment over the state? Or, better, would you grant such right and power to churchmen to stand in judgment over lawmakers?

5   The statement by Associate Justice Lewis F. Powell, Jr. (p. 326) is a clear, concise summary of this position. How would you respond to this fundamental observation that an ordered society can't endure if every individual is free to pass judgment on which laws are just and which laws are unjust, and proceed to obey only "just laws"? (See Socrates's arguments on pp. 330–331).

6   What is your response to the statement by Camus about "the true patriot" (see marginal quote on p. 329)? Does his insight solve some problems for you, or merely produce more?

7   Klausner concluded that Jesus's attack on the Mosaic Law was wrong because the masses need laws to preserve order and maintain consistency in their collective experience; and that without firm law, and a sense of obedience to law, a society disintegrates. In your opinion, is Klausner essentially correct? Why or why not?

8   See the quotation from Oliver Wendell Holmes on p. 333 (marginal quote). Is this an insight worth remembering, or is this judicial opinion merely one more legalism?

*I think an artistic boycott is wrong. It stops communication, and communication is what changes culture.*

LINDA RONSTADT

# HENRY DAVID THOREAU

## *"I Will Breathe after My Own Fashion"*

In the spring of 1845 Henry David Thoreau began constructing a cabin on a forested plot of land at Walden Pond, a small blue lake two miles from his home at Concord, Massachusetts. He bought a hammer, borrowed an axe, secured some used boards which he refurbished, cut a few white pines to open a clearing, and started to build. By May he had completed the frame and roof; by the end of June it was boarded in. So, on July 4 he declared his independence from the world, moved in, and began a two-year experiment in living with himself.

His withdrawal was almost universally misunderstood by the townsfolks of Concord. Some thought he was lazy; most thought him eccentric and antisocial. Others thought it a pity that he was turning his back on the benefits of civilization and refusing to make the contribution to society that he had been destined to make. Oliver Wendell Holmes scoffed and said he was "nibbling his asparagus at the wrong end."

Although criticized by virtually everyone, he persisted with singular determination. "My purpose in going to Walden Pond was  not to live cheaply nor to live dearly there, but to transact some private business with fewest obstacles. . . ."

"Private business"? He explains:

I went to the woods because I wished to live deliberately, to front only the essential facts of life, and see if I could not learn what it had to teach, and not, when I came to die, discover that I had not lived. I did not wish to live what was not life, living is so dear; nor did I wish to practice resignation, unless it was quite necessary. I wanted to live deep and suck out all the marrow of life, to live so sturdily and Spartan-like as to put to rout all that was not life, to cut a broad swath and shave close, to drive life into a corner, and reduce it to its lowest terms. . . .

He lived at Walden Pond for two years, two months, and two days, and it was a wonderfully successful experiment, or, more accurately, it was a time when one human being managed his priorities and lived the way he wanted to live. He confided to his journal, "I learned this, at least, by my experiment, that if one advances confidently in the direction of his dreams, and endeavors to live the life which he has imagined, he will meet with a success unexpected in common hours."

When he abandoned his cabin in September 1847 and returned to the village, his experiment was complete. It was time to move on. "I left the woods because I had several more lives to live, and could not spare any more time for that one."

✦

Thoreau was born in Concord July 12, 1817, the third of three children. His father, John Thoreau, owned a small business—grinding graphite and making pencils—which he operated out of one wing of their home; it provided a meager income. He was retiring and not very industrious, but he was bright and sensitive, and he loved books and nature. These qualities he bequeathed to his son. His mother, Cynthia Dunbar Thoreau, was a vivacious, socially active woman known for her talkativeness and love of gossip. From her Henry received an acute sense of individualism, intellect, a facility of speech, and a social conscience.

Henry's early schooling was in the elementary school and academy in Concord. When he was eleven he matriculated at Harvard where his performance was good but not spectacular. He graduated at twenty and faced the perennial problem of choosing a vocation and finding a job. Teaching was a most natural occupation for a recent Harvard graduate, and fortunately his old elementary school had an opening, and he was hired. Henry enjoyed children, related well to them, and was an excellent teacher. However, during his second week in the classroom he was visited by a member of the school board who judged his pupils to be unruly and out of control. He demanded that the teacher administer discipline, including corporal punish-

ment. Thoreau did so, as ordered. That evening he handed in his resignation.

In September of 1839 Henry and his brother John built a boat and traveled up the Concord and Merrimack rivers into New Hampshire. There they walked and took a stage to Mount Washington, climbed to the top, then returned home via the river routes. Henry took detailed notes and later used them as a basis for his first book. It was a time of joyous camaraderie, a time Thoreau was to recall when he was closest to another human being.

In January of 1842 Henry was traumatized by the death of his brother. John contracted tetanus from a cut in his finger received while shaving. After an agonizing illness peculiar to "lockjaw," John died in Henry's arms. So shaken was he by the event, some ten days later Henry also began to indicate signs of the illness. They were psychosomatic symptoms, intense and honest, and they reveal Henry's capacities for sympathetic identification, a quality that determined his stance toward society and nature throughout his life.

So, by the early spring of 1845 there is a readiness to carry through on his long-held dream of establishing his retreat so he could get on with the business of living. He wanted to prove that an adequate life requires very few things—a few rows of beans, a little furniture, clothing, a notebook and pen, a few books and very little else. "That man is richest whose pleasures are the cheapest."

His deepest motivation, however, was not to prove a point of economics. He saw with painful clarity the way most human beings live. "The mass of men lead lives of quiet desperation," he wrote. Their "vision does not penetrate the surface of things." Thoreau's basic instinct was to accomplish something at the nuclear center of his being. He was embarking on a spiritual odyssey comparable to that of a Theravada monk assuming his monastic vows. "What a man

*Let everyone mind his own business and endeavor to be what he was made.*

*If I am not I, who will be?*

*However mean your life is, meet it and live it; do not shun it and call it hard names. Love your life, poor as it is. . . . If a man does not keep pace with his companions, perhaps it is because he hears a different drummer. Let him step to the music which he hears, however measured or far away.*

*I heartily accept the motto, "That government is best which governs least"; and I should like to see it acted up to more rapidly and systematically. Carried out, it finally amounts to this, which also I believe: "That government is best which governs not at all"; and when men are prepared for it, that will be the kind of government which they will have.*

*The one great rule of composition—and if I were a professor of rhetoric I should insist on this—is to speak the truth.*

*The mass of men lead lives of quiet desperation. What is called resignation is confirmed desperation. From the desperate city you go into the desperate country, and have to console yourself with the bravery of minks and muskrats. . . . But it is a characteristic of wisdom not to do desperate things.*

*There are nowadays profes-
sors of philosophy, but not
philosophers. . . . To be a
philosopher is not merely to
have subtle thoughts, nor
even to found a school, but
so to love wisdom as to live
according to its dictates, a
life of simplicity, independence, magnanimity, and
trust. It is to solve some of
the problems of life, not only
theoretically, but practically.*

*Let us not underrate the
value of a fact; it will one day
flower into a truth.*

*How vain it is to sit down to
write when you have not
stood up to live!*

*Time is but a stream I go a-
fishing in. I drink at it; but
while I drink I see the sandy
bottom and detect how shallow it is. Its thin current
slides away, but eternity
remains.*

*The perception of beauty is a
moral test.*

*I think we should be men
first, and subjects afterward.
It is not desirable to cultivate
a respect for the law, so
much as for the right.*

*In the long run men hit only
what they aim at.*

*We need the tonic wildness
. . . We can never have
enough of nature.*

*In wildness is the preservation
of the world.*

*How alone must our life be
lived! We dwell on the seashore, and none between us
and the sea.*

thinks of himself, that is which determines, or rather, indicates, his fate." "If I
am not I," he wrote, "who will be?"
"However mean your life is, meet and
live it; do not shun it and call it hard
names. Love your life, poor as it is. Why
should we be in such deep haste to succeed and in such desperate enterprises?
If a man does not keep pace with his
companions, perhaps it is because he
hears a different drummer. Let him step
to the music which he hears, however
measured or far away."

◆

For Thoreau the one essential ingredient of the successful life is personal
freedom. All the good things of life derive
from the fact that we can make free
choices about the way we want to live. It
seems inevitable that, sooner or later, he
would clash with the establishment.

His first confrontation with the political establishment was while he was living at Walden Pond, on a July night in
1846. For four years he had refused to
pay his poll tax, a head tax extracted from
every adult male citizen over twenty.
Thoreau considered the tax discriminatory, and, moreover, he protested against
giving tax support to a government that
condoned slavery. On this afternoon
Thoreau had walked into town from his
cabin to pick up a mended shoe from a
cobbler. By coincidence he encountered
the town jailer, Sam Staples, who was
also the tax collector. Staples asked him
to pay his tax. Thoreau declined and tried
to argue his case. Staples warned him
that he could be thrown into jail. Thoreau
claimed his right to go to jail right then.
So, to jail he went, where he shared a cell
with a man who was accused of burning
down a barn. Thoreau was willing to stay
in jail for however long it took to register
his protest and make his point, but somehow his mother got word that he was in
jail and sent her sister to the jailer's
home with money to bail him out. Staples'
daughter answered the door and took the
money, but the hour was late, and Staples

had settled in for the evening and
decided to release Thoreau the next
morning. Come morning Thoreau was
angry at not being allowed to stay and
continue his protest. He went to pick up
his mended shoe, and a half hour later
was in the country gathering huckle-
berries.

The outcome of Thoreau's night in
jail was his famous essay "On Civil Disobedience." "I heartily accept the motto,"
he wrote, "'That government is best
which governs least'"; and in fact, "'That
government is best which governs not at
all.'" "I think we should be men first, and
subjects afterward." "If a plant cannot
live according to its nature, it dies; and so
a man." "I was not born to be forced. I
will breathe after my own fashion."

For Thoreau this is a matter of ethics
and a matter of principle. Ethics must
take precedent over rules and regulations; morality must take precedent over
law. The state, out of its own sense of
preservation, will always attempt to condition people to be law-and-order citizens, to put away their moral consciences
and to "have respect for the law." But an
authentic human being who has respect
for himself will put his integrity and
moral principles ahead of the law. And
the principles that Thoreau is laying
down and defending apply not merely to
the Commonwealth of Massachusetts and
the federal government of the United
States: they apply to all human beings
and all possible governments.

Unjust laws exist: shall we be
content to obey them, or shall we
endeavor to amend them, and obey
them until we have succeeded, or
shall we transgress them at once? Men
generally, under such a government
as this, think that they ought to wait
until they have persuaded the majority to alter them. They think that, if
they should resist, the remedy would
be worse than the evil. But it is the
fault of the government itself that the
remedy *is* worse than the evil. *It*
makes it worse. Why is it not more apt

to anticipate and provide for reform? Why does it not cherish its wise minority? Why does it cry and resist before it is hurt? Why does it not encourage its citizens to be on the alert to point out its faults, and *do* better than it would have them? Why does it always crucify Christ, and excommunicate Copernicus and Luther, and pronounce Washington and Franklin rebels?

Since this is the way governments behave, the moral human being will resist. If the law "is of such a nature that it requires you to be the agent of injustice to another, then, I say, break the law." This is the American colonial conscience that breaks the bond of British law. This is the conscience of Gandhi who fasts and prays and breaks the bond of British rule in India. This is the conscience of Martin Luther King who organizes a march in Selma to challenge legal segregation. This is the conscience of anti-war protesters who burn their draft cards and march against a war in Vietnam. This is the conscience of South Africans who refuse to segregate to protest against discriminatory apartheid laws. This is the conscience of the sanctuary movement that illegally protects refugees from oppression in Central America.

Those who argue for a democratic state, and those who defend it, will always counter that, although unjust laws do indeed exist, there are legal mechanisms by which they can be changed; the primary mechanism is to build public opinion and erode support for unjust laws. It takes a commitment to the democratic process to make the system work.

Thoreau's answer is simple and direct: "As for adopting ways which the state has provided for remedying the evil, I know not of such ways. They take too much time, and a man's life will be gone. I have other affairs to attend to. I came into this world, not chiefly to make this a good place to live in, but to live in it, be it good or bad."

Thoreau's passion for justice was ignited several times in the 1850s. He was horrified when Massachusetts passed the Fugitive Slave Law requiring citizens to apprehend and return runaway slaves to their owners. Against his principles of individualism, he joined the abolitionist movement and delivered an emotional speech entitled "Slavery in Massachusetts" at a Fourth of July celebration in Framingham. In the winter of 1860 Thoreau caught a cold while he was in the woodlands counting growth-rings on the tree stumps in a new cut. It worsened into bronchitis and the tubercular lesions, going back to his college days, were activated. Thereafter his journal entries become sporadic, with only occasional brief notes. His last entry in his journal was on November 3, 1861. It had rained the previous day and he had watched the big drops of rain make little craters in the sand that revealed the direction of the rainfall.

He was in especially good spirits during the spring of 1862. He was visited frequently by friends and citizens who had come to admire him and wish him well. He revised some of his essays and wrote some poetry. He died May 6th in a bed he had constructed himself.

Thoreau is buried in Sleepy Hollow Cemetery less than a mile from his birthplace, and some four miles from Walden Pond.

5 3

## THE PURSUIT OF HAPPINESS

The first serious reflections on political matters are to be found in the conversations of Socrates and in the writings of his intellectual heirs Plato and Aristotle. Their relentless curiosity generated the basic questions of political philosophy. What is politics all about? they asked. Why must we have politics at all? Is the state "real" or only in our minds? Why do we humans get so emotional, even violent, about politics? How would rational men behave in a rational state? Why are our leaders so easily corrupted? Why is democracy such a pain? What is the best form of government? These and countless other questions laid the foundations of political thinking and did much to shape the destiny of Western political institutions.

Aristotle studied governments. He collected 158 constitutions and analyzed them. He also pondered "human nature," and gave us his version of life and growth. Out of his reflections has come one of the enduring descriptions of what the state should be and do.

In his little book called *Politics*, Aristotle argued that the purpose of the state is to foster the conditions within which every citizen can achieve happiness. Only individuals exist, and Aristotle is concerned about the full actualizing growth of each person within a social context. Just as the goal of ethics is to achieve individual happiness, the goal of politics is to achieve collective happiness—the greatest amount of happiness for the greatest number of people.

Aristotle used a lovely Greek word to describe the state of well-being that each of us strives to attain: *eudaimonia,* meaning "blessed with a good spirit," to be "fortunate," "happy," "well off" (*eu* is the Greek prefix meaning "well" or "good"; *daimon* is "spirit" or "genius"). Eudaimonia is usually translated as "happiness," but it carries also the idea of an overall state of well-being and

*What is the part of wisdom? To dream with one eye open; to be detached from the world without being hostile to it; to welcome fugitive beauties and pity fugitive sufferings, without forgetting for a moment how fugitive they are.*

GEORGE SANTAYANA

personal fulfillment. Not a transient, fleeting condition, or a temporary one; it is longlasting and pervades all aspects of our daily life.

As individuals we must pursue eudaimonia in our various ways, but Aristotle observes that most people believe they can find it through material possessions or social status. Not so, he says. Eudaimonia must be sought within; it is a quality of the soul and is not dependent on external conditions or other people. It is self-sufficient. It lingers in mind and body whether or not I possess a secure bank account or have the admiration and approval of other people.

*Wisdom comes by disillusionment.*

GEORGE SANTAYANA

Although Aristotle was convinced that the highest experience of eudaimonia can be achieved only through the mind's rational reflections, he also knew that such a contemplative path is not for everyone. There are many paths to the top of the mountain. Each of us must seek and follow the path that is right for us.

Good government is user friendly. It must provide the conditions for the successful pursuit of happiness. It should never become an adversary or enemy against which we must defend ourselves. For as long as we are decent, law-abiding citizens, government should always be on our side. Its laws should establish order and stability; they should protect us from harm and secure for us freedom from want and fear; they should provide for each of us the freedom and opportunity to get on with the task of seeking eudaimonia.

Aristotle would have been proud of the founding fathers who wrote his ideas into the American constitution.

Niccolò Machiavelli
(1469–1527)

## ABOUT POLITICAL PHILOSOPHY

We humans are political animals, Aristotle told his students. We are naturally social, and it is inevitable that we indulge in politics and create governmental systems. There is no fulfillment outside the social context. Politics is a part of our nature; it is an expression of the human condition.

Aristotle classified political philosophy as a branch of ethics. The criteria used in politics for judging right and wrong behavior on the part of our leaders and for judging the laws and systems they create are the same as the criteria used in ethics for evaluating individual actions. The two fields are separate only in our mind's arrangement of subject matter. In reality they work together toward the same ends, the achievement of eudaimonia for all citizens.

There is a distinction (often blurred) between political philosophy and political science. Political philosophy attempts to establish universal facts and principles; it is synoptic in scope and seeks to achieve an overview of the entire human political enterprise. Its goal is to see and to understand, not to take defensive stands, nor to apologize for fashionable ideologies. By contrast, political science is a practical subject dealing with the application of facts and principles toward the creation of workable political systems; it is more nearly an art than a science. (The distinction between political philosophy and political science is analogous to that made between science and technology.) The Italian thinker Niccolò Machiavelli is generally considered the father of political science since he attempted to sidestep moral judgments and describe in clinical detail the actual tactics used by "successful" leaders in sixteenth-century Italy as they seized and held on to political power. Because he succeeded so well in telling us how it is actually done, his major work, *The Prince,* has ever since been employed by would-be leaders, reputable and otherwise, as a how-to-do-it field guide.

Out of the reflections of the Greek thinkers came the questions asked by political philosophy. What exactly is the state? What is meant by "the state"? *Where* is the state? Is it a reality (as Plato believed) or a concept only? If only a concept, wherein does it achieve "reality"? (That is, what do these words and concepts refer to? Though often neglected, there *is* an epistemology of political thought.) What is the proper role of the state? Why must we have a state at all? What are the basic human needs that the political order must be designed to meet? What form of government is the best? Is any particular form of government more "natural" than others? What is a right? What is justice? What is the nature of freedom and why is it essential? What is a law? Would a moral society (a society made up of moral citizens) require laws? And more, much more.

## WHY HAVE A STATE AT ALL?

Is it thinkable that we humans might not have to have a state at all? As children, adolescents, and adults, we want freedom so much and strive so vigorously to throw off our restraints—perhaps we could live without law and limitation. There have been contingents of anarchists in every century who have argued for no government and complete freedom.

Evolutionary history seems to indicate that we have no choice. What we are and, to a large extent, what we do is the product of millions of years of genetic coding. Our genes—the codes that tell us how to think, feel, and behave—are the product of our relentless struggle to survive. Through mutation and adaptation we hominids were slowly fine-tuned for esthetic perception, empathetic feeling, and abstract thought.

Therefore maybe we are deluding ourselves in thinking that, out of some special quality of freedom, we are in charge of our social and political artifacts. Maybe we still possess (or are possessed by) a genetic template that tells us to organize our behavior in complex but predetermined ways.

Wherever we look in the animal world, what we find is social and political organization. The social insects have survived for many millions of years, and their success is due almost entirely to the organization of their communities. In every colony of ants, bees, wasps, and termites, we find a rigid division of labor; every individual knows its role and performs its duties.

*The world has always been inhabited by human beings who have always had the same passions.*

MACHIAVELLI

*Whoever desires to found a state and give it laws, must start with assuming that all men are bad and ever ready to display their vicious nature, whenever they may find occasion for it.*

MACHIAVELLI

*Societies can be loving, efficient, prosperous, or good as well as just, but they may be just without being notably benevolent, efficient, prosperous, or good.*

WILLIAM K. FRANKENA

*What my work at Arnhem [Burger's Zoo at Arnhem in the Netherlands] has taught me is that the roots of politics are older than humanity.*

FRANS DE WALL

The story is similar in the higher social animals. In any herd of elk, for example, an alpha male maintains leadership through physical dominance. He leads the herd through migrations, finds foraging stations, tends the harem of breeding does, and protects the fawns. Young males periodically challenge him; if successful, the herd transfers allegiance to a new leader. Thus the stronger male (with the "fitter" genes) maintains order and rank in the herd, with right of reproduction. Similar social and political organizations are found among seals, baboons, wolves, meerkats, and virtually all other species of social animals.

To a reflective mind it is boggling to become aware that "nature" (through evolution) has designed such complex hierarchical systems in which every individual behaves in ways beneficial to the community or the species. In wolf packs there is usually but a single breeding pair; only they have pups. Why? Because often the environment can't support larger populations, and the efforts of the entire pack are required to support the survival of a single litter of pups. Everyone adopts and protects the pups. The aunts and uncles will babysit while the alpha couple hunts for food. Although other females come in season, they are not bred. There is a political system, there is social organization, there are rules for challenge and change—so that all can survive.

Thus in Earth's animal societies, all species have been blessed with a genetic policies-and-procedures guidebook that gives them workable social and political systems to live by.

## THE GIFT OF THE GREEKS

Humans, in contrast to all known insect and animal societies, seem abandoned by gene-generated instincts. We no longer harbor within our cells the detailed instructions telling us exactly how to organize the mutually beneficial systems necessary for our survival.

Today's sociobiologists inform us that our genes still determine much of what we do in groups. Our basic drives, they say, are still survival and reproduction—just like all other living creatures; and we continue to make our decisions about social and political matters solely in the interest of our genes. Genes are shrewd and selfish organisms: they manipulate us in the interest of their own survival and expression. If sociobiology is correct, self-interest—the preservation of one's genepool—is gene-driven and our experiences of (apparent) free choice will still have to be interpreted in the light of genetic considerations. We cerebral humans may debate the form of government we want, but we should be aware that our deeper drives may override what we are convinced are our free and rational decisions.

A new notion appeared on the scene with the Greek philosophers: the idea that the political state could be analyzed and understood by rational human beings. They believed that the human intellect, with its abstract abilities and creative imagination, could understand the concept of politics and could create the ideal government. They believed that reasonable men could think through the problems of society sufficiently to find answers and solutions. They believed that we could apply those answers to the world and make a difference.

*All governments, whatever their political complexion, are at present willy-nilly in the grip of natural forces which can only be dealt with by a degree of intelligence of which mankind hitherto has shown little evidence.*

**BERTRAND RUSSELL**

This is the unique Greek gift: faith in human reason. It is this faith that has produced two millennia of scientific discovery, technological progress, and, for many of us, grounds for hope in a reasonable future.

## THE QUESTION OF TRUST

In the speculations of political philosophers, there have been many and varied answers to the question "What is the best form of government?" How they answered the question depends largely upon a single factor—their evaluation of human nature.

Those who trust human beings support more freedom, fewer rules and regulations, and less government. Those who distrust human beings support less freedom and more restraint, more regulations and laws—and unquestioning obedience.

So the question of trust is prior to speculations about what form the state should take. The problem breaks into two separate questions: (1) Are human beings trustworthy? and (2) Does the speculator have the capacity for trusting? These are distinctly different questions, of course, and should be treated as such; but the question about the natural decency of the human race has never been settled, and, although basic, is probably not answerable. In the reflections of most thinkers the two subjects were confused and together determined their basic stance; they projected their own lack of trusting capacity onto "human nature" or "the masses" and considered untrustworthiness to be an objective quality possessed by the human race. Few realized that they were projecting their feelings onto the world.

The shadow of Plato's deep distrust—the result of his own suffering—has darkened Western attitudes down through the centuries. Human nature he distrusts, thinking of it as an evil substance that taints the soul. Plato hates democracy, which he considers to be a temporary state during which the frustrated masses gain power, impoverish the rich, and worship mediocrity. Thought and speech become shallow and vulgar; good manners and culture vanish. Democracy leads inevitably into anarchy which, in turn, is ripe for overthrow by a ready tyrant. In his *Republic* (and as spelled out in his last work, the *Laws*), Plato outlines his utopia: an authoritarian state in which the young will be conditioned with myths (good myths!) and gradually molded into civilized organisms. Marriage is regulated and reproduction is controlled to achieve eugenic goals. Personal freedoms are nonexistent. This dream is a depressed aftermath of his younger idealism.

On the Judeo-Christian side of our Western heritage, ordinary human beings were not free agents and merited little trust. The god of Israel, Yahweh, was a father figure much like the patriarchal leaders of the bedouin tribes at the beginning of the first millennium B.C. He demanded loyalty and obedience; his laws were not negotiable or debatable. Free thoughts and different values were anathema. The nation of Israel, during biblical times at least, is properly called a theocracy, a religious state ruled by the authority of a divine Monarch.

*When you become obsessed with the enemy, you become the enemy.*

**Ghostbusters Halloween Special**

*Fanaticism consists in redoubling your efforts when you have forgotten your aim.*

GEORGE SANTAYANA

Christian theology, from the time of Saint Paul, has held that human beings, in their natural state, are essentially evil; they are infected with original sin. This sin of Adam blighted the human will so that it cannot of itself make moral decisions. "I do not understand what I am doing," Paul laments, "for I do not do what I want to do; I do things that I hate." And a bit later: "What a wretched man I am!" he cries. "Who can save me from this doomed body?"

This theme was officially reiterated by Saint Augustine (A.D. 354–430). All human beings not yet redeemed of their original sin by the Church's sacrament have voluntarily sided with the Forces of Darkness and are so pleasure-driven that they cannot be trusted. (Augustine defined all pleasure as sin.) He assumed that no earthly political system could work; this could be accomplished only by the City of God—the church body of redeemed souls.

Roman Catholic theology continued this line of thinking. Pope Leo XIII denounced all attempts to establish political order as misguided and doomed to failure because sinful human beings, driven by their insatiable cravings for "things perishable," were hopelessly incompetent. Only absolute paternal authority, including censorship of all ideas to protect the innocence of the faithful, can "control the excesses of the unbridled intellect, which unfailingly end in the oppression of the untutored multitude."

Thomas Hobbes (1588–1679)

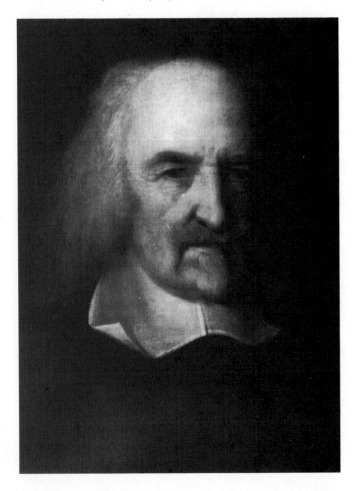

Machiavelli (1469–1527) had been treated cruelly by his own family and exploited by the rulers of his home city-state of Florence. He admired the powerful rulers who maintained their positions of power through oppressive, ruthless, and even deceitful means. Such treatment is justified, Machiavelli reasoned; people deserve it. He writes: "Whoever wishes to found a state and give it laws, must start with assuming that all men are bad and ever ready to display their vicious nature whenever they find occasion for it." Like strong parents who discipline their unruly children, the leaders of the state will "lay down the law" and through threat of punishment force the common people into obedience. Machiavelli is convinced that the best means of instilling habitual behavior in the masses is by the deliberate inculcation of religious myths. Those who believe that God wants them to be obedient law-abiding citizens are most likely to be just that.

Thomas Hobbes (1588–1679) theorized that originally there was a "state of nature" (his metaphor of human nature) in which man's natural competitive aggression was held in check by fear. This natural man was a creature of passions, and his primitive existence was "nasty, brutish, and short." A democratic state ruled by this savage was out of the question; the firm rule of law is necessary. The state must severely censor books, newspapers, and media of all sorts that would merely feed a gullible public's uninformed mind. There can be no such thing as free thought or individual conscience. The sovereign must wield absolute power if he is to provide security and stability to the masses of people. Hobbes concluded that this can be accomplished only by a hereditary monarchy that is above the whims and passions of the multitude.

In contrast to Hobbes, Jean-Jacques Rousseau postulated a state of nature during which men were free . . . and happy. Since that time governments everywhere have destroyed that freedom and that happiness. "Man is born free, and he is everywhere in chains." The function of the state is to provide the rule of law while at the same time giving each individual freedom so that he "may still obey himself alone, and remain as free as before."

John Locke (1632–1704) laid the foundations of modern democracy. Human beings, in Locke's estimation, are on the whole decent, moral, and capable of reasonable action. He believed people, if reasonably informed, can discern the truth and act on it. What the populace needs is a good education and then, following their own lights, they will develop into moderately mature, responsible citizens. He believed that the real source of power in any state is the people; they are sovereign.

*For our country, wrong is right.*
ATTRIBUTED TO MACHIAVELLI

*Political language—and with variations this is true of all political parties, from Conservatives to Anarchists—is designed to make lies sound truthful and murder respectable, and to give an appearance of solidity to pure wind.*
GEORGE ORWELL

*Think like a person of action and act like a person of thought.*
HENRI BERGSON

Jean-Jacques Rousseau
(1712–1778)

## THREE UNIVERSAL THEMES

1 FREEDOM In any human society, freedom is always balanced by responsibility. The more mature the individual—the more freedom he or she can handle—the less restraint (law) is required to channel responsible moral behavior. ("Moral" here means non-hurtful behavior toward others; it does not mean conformist behavior since it can include socially different and unusual ways of thinking, feeling, and behaving as long as it is not destructive to self or others.)

"I want to be free," we commonly complain. But why?

Freedom is the ability on the part of each individual to choose pleasure over pain, moving one progressively toward happiness—eudaimonia. This is the "pursuit of happiness" of the American Constitution.

What are the freedoms essential to my well-being? One way of arriving at some answers to this question is to ask: What am I willing to pay for? What is it that my organized society (my "state") must offer me (that I can't secure by

John Locke (1632–1704)

*If a nation expects to be ignorant and free, in a state of civilization, it expects what never was and never will be.*

THOMAS JEFFERSON

*The greatest danger to what we wistfully call civilization is to be uninformed, or misinformed, and the next greatest danger lies in not giving a darn about it.*

NORMAN CORWIN

*There can be no justice as long as laws are absolute.*

*"Jean-Luc Picard"*
*Star Trek: TNG*

myself) that will enlarge the arena of choice (enhance my freedoms) and enable me to progress toward eudaimonia?

Among others: My state must ensure my security (via laws and law enforcement) from all who would injure me and my property and (via military power) from any external threat. I want the freedom to travel safely (good roads, bridges, emergency services). I want the chance for education (good schools, teachers, books, technologies). I want to be able to participate in communications systems (mail, telephone, FAX, television). I want the benefits of all scientific research (medical care, electronic technologies, materials of all sorts). I want the services of private enterprise systems (banking, insurance, waste disposal, electricity, and water). And so on; the list is long. All these goods and services offer me freedom of choice that will (if used wisely) increase my pleasure and allow me to get on with "the pursuit of (my) happiness."

**2 JUSTICE** It is not easy to define justice, but one of our deepest experiences is the feeling of outrage when we are treated unjustly. Our wronged feelings are intense; our reaction is trigger-quick. Our psyches and emotions feel unjust treatment even though our intellects are hazy with the concept.

So, what is justice? Is it unavoidably experienced by all humans? (Is it ontological?) Or is it culture-conditioned, taking on a different feeling at different places and times?

At a popular level, justice turns out to be a relative notion. What is felt to be unjust in one society may not be felt as unjust in another society. Homosexuality was encouraged in ancient Sparta and considered moral, right, fair, just, and practical; in Muslim Arabia its practice is punishable by death, and that too is considered moral, right, fair, just, and practical. Attitudes differ sharply on the justice of abortion, committing suicide, assisting suicide, executing criminals; killing and eating cows, pigs, and dogs; marrying four or eight or seventy-five wives—depending on whether one is a Muslim, an old-style Mormon, or an African chief. If one wishes to argue here that we are talking about questions of morality, not justice, then the jurist will reply that morality and justice are inseparable, that what societies legislate into law *are* their moral values.

The Greek philosophers were bothered by all this. They were aware (largely from the Sophists) that moral convictions differ from one culture to another, and that everyone thinks his own system of values is the right and true one. But carry this to its absurd extreme: Can what is truly just (moral, right, fair) differ from one city-state to another, from one tribe to another, from one suburb to another, from one religious community to another? From one village to another, from one neighborhood to another, from one family to another? The notion becomes absurd, the philosophers argued. In these instances what is being considered just is merely a local, biased, and wholly inadequate notion of justice. Justice, if it is true justice, must be the same for all human beings everywhere and in all times. To be praised for a deed in one city-state and be punished for it in another seemed to the Greek thinkers to be a travesty and a contradiction. To be executed in one state for setting off a bomb, and to be given a hero's medal in another state for the same act would appear to them a monstrous denial of decency and reason. Justice is like truth, they believed: When we dig deep enough we will find a universal sense of justice felt and discerned alike by all reasonable human beings. Socrates and his heirs declared that a local relative justice was no justice at all.

The roots of the feeling of justice/injustice are to be found in our evolutionary past. After Darwin perceived the basic mechanisms of struggle and survival, the nature of justice/fairness could be understood in these terms: All creatures struggle to survive in competition with other creatures, other species, and the environment. When I am justly and fairly treated, then I have an equal (or better) chance to compete successfully; when I am treated unjustly and unfairly my chances to compete successfully are diminished.

One of the functions of religion is to provide the assurance of justice in an otherwise unjust world. Despite all our efforts, this world is essentially unjust. Good and decent people are not consistently rewarded; instead they get cheated out of their savings, burglarized, mugged; they get cancer and die young. And ruthless exploiters get away with their crimes, retire rich, live to be ninety, and die peacefully in their beds. This is a terrible insult to human effort and the value of good and decent living. The late Judaic doctrine, so explicit in the book of Proverbs, persisted in pleading a moral law: the good are always rewarded, in this life, and the evil are always punished.

> Blessings are upon the head of the righteous;
> But sorrow will cover the face of the wicked.
>
> No harm can befall the righteous;
> But the lives of the wicked are full of misfortune.
>
> Reverence for the LORD prolongs life;
> But the years of the wicked will be shortened.

The Book of Job was written to explore (if not to answer) this question. (See pp. 46–48 of this text.) In Job's case it was an intensely personal matter. Although he had steadfastly remained a good and pious man, he had lost everything he held dear, his wife and family, his home, his flocks, and finally his health. The Book of Job concludes that this world just may be unjust, or, if it is just, we really can't understand God's brand of justice.

All the great religions have an answer to this need and this question. The dualistic metaphysics of heaven and hell warns us in the strongest terms that the good will be rewarded and the bad punished, if not in this world then in the next, and forever—more or less. If we are good, heaven (or some lovely place:

*Yet law-abiding scholars write;*
*Law is neither wrong nor right,*
*Law is only crimes*
*Punished by places and by times. . . .*

W. H. AUDEN

*Under a government which imprisons unjustly, the true place for a just man is also in prison.*

HENRY DAVID THOREAU

*There is no significant example in history, before our time, of a society successfully maintaining moral life without the aid of religion.*

WILL AND ARIEL DURANT

see page 590) awaits; if we are bad, punishment awaits us. We will also have the chance to see our enemies, those who have hurt us, get what they deserve. This world may not be just, but the universe is so designed that, in the final days, justice always prevails.

The Hindu/Buddhist notion of reincarnation and karma meets the same need. We will reap in the next life exactly what we have sown in this life, and the cosmos never misses. Every action (in Hinduism) or thought (in Buddhism) generates either good or bad karma, and, since I have free will, I create my own next future life by the way I live now.

Polemos pater panton.
*(War is the father of all things.)*

HERACLITUS

The concept of a moral universe continues. "What have I done to deserve this?" is a common query. In *The Sound of Music,* Maria finds herself in the arms of the baron and sings "Here you are loving me, whether I'm bad or good; but somewhere in my youth or childhood, I must have done something good"— something to deserve such a blessing. More commonly we ask the question when tragedy befalls: "He died so young. Why? He was such a good boy." Or cancer strikes: "I was always taught that I would get rewarded if I was a good girl. And now cancer. Somehow, down deep, I know I deserve it."

Thus, *getting what we deserve* is a universal and very human passion, and the consequent feelings of outrage when we don't get what we deserve are some of the deepest and most painful of all our moral perceptions.

**3 RIGHTS** A painful and obvious fact: We humans are not equal. We differ in our intelligences (plural: there are apparently at least seven distinct kinds); in our aptitudes, temperaments, and tastes; in our facility for handling language, spatial concepts, and mechanical devices (some of us are true mechanical idiots); in our esthetic and artistic sensibilities (music, painting, dance); in our beliefs, values, commitments, and moral feelings; in our cultural conditioning (each with its own benefits and limitations).

Like justice, our differences have evolutionary roots. The great diversity of characteristics makes for the richness of the society we create and share; it also underscores the uniqueness of each individual. We are what we are, with the entire spectrum of differences, because, as a species, we survived.

*The United States Constitution defines certain areas in which the majority are not entitled to have their way, no matter how right they may be.*

EDMOND CAHN

But in society our differences are the source of personal pain, social unrest, and political problems.

In a modern democracy, the concept of a "right" attempts, within boundaries, to level the playing field and to provide the environment that will permit each unique individual to pursue his happiness in his own way with as much success as possible.

What is a right? A right is a freedom which I want (or need) and which my society (or someone or some institution) is willing to give me. If I were stranded on a desert island all by myself and wanted to do something, then I do it. I don't have to ask anyone or check the book of rules and regulations. I just do it. But in society if I want to chop down a tree in front of my house or build a carport, I have to check the books or call someone to find out if I "have a right" to do so. If I am told that, according to "the law," I can't chop the tree or build the carport, then I conclude that I don't have the "right" to exercise that freedom which I want or need.

All rights, therefore, must be given. They are the result of a transaction. To say "I have a right" to do something is to invite the philosophic question: Where does that right (that freedom to do what you want) come from? Who or what (or Who or What) gave it to you? Even a "divine right" or an "inalienable right" must be given by "Nature" or by a divine Someone. In the Western tradition, if my local city-state doesn't give me some right I want (or need), then the precedent is established for me to claim that God gave me that right, and this higher right, it is usually held, overrides the denial of that right by the city-state.

In a democratic society such as the United States, equality is not a goal. Equality of opportunity, yes; and equality before the law—absolutely. Given that each individual is a unique assembly of abilities, aptitudes, talents, skills, intelligences, temperaments, emotional differences, hopes, and dreams: What is precious about our American system is that it embodies essentially the ideal of Aristotle (filtered through Locke and Rousseau) that its goal and purpose is to support the development of an environment that allows every unique individual the freedom to pursue his or her own eudaimonia in his or her own way.

## OUR HERITAGE: CIVILIZATION

If Education is the transmission of civilization, we are unquestionably progressing. Civilization is not inherited; it has to be learned and earned by each generation anew; If the transmission should be interrupted for one century, civilization would die, and we should be savages again. . . . Consider education not as the painful accumulation of facts and dates and reigns, nor merely the necessary preparation of the individual to earn his keep in the world, but as the transmission of our mental, moral, technical, and aesthetic heritage as fully as possible to as many as possible, for the enlargement of man's understanding, control, embellishment, and enjoyment of life. . . .

History is, above all else, the creation and recording of that heritage; progress is its increasing abundance, preservation, transmission, and use. To those of us who study history not merely as a warning reminder of man's follies and crimes, but also as an encouraging remembrance of generative souls, the past ceases to be a depressing chamber of horrors; it becomes a celestial city, a spacious country of the mind, wherein a thousand saints, statesmen, inventors, scientists, poets, artists, musicians, lovers, and philosophers still live and speak, teach and carve and sing. The historian will not mourn because he can see no meaning in human existence except that which man puts into it; let it be our pride that we ourselves may put meaning into our lives, and sometimes a significance that transcends death. If a man is fortunate he will, before he dies, gather up as much as he can of his civilized heritage and transmit it to his children. And to his final breath he will be grateful for this inexhaustible legacy, knowing that it is our nourishing mother and lasting life.

WILL AND ARIEL DURANT
*The Lessons of History*

*Those who ignore history are doomed to repeat it.*

GEORGE SANTAYANA

*I would hope to see this world a gentler place before I leave it. If not, I would prefer to leave it before it gets much worse.*

JIM GUENDERT

# REFLECTIONS

*Politics are for the moment.*
*An equation is for eternity.*

ALBERT EINSTEIN

1  What are the questions asked by political philosophers? by political scientists? How do they go about finding answers to these questions?

2  Do you agree with Aristotle's thinking about the purpose of the state? If so, what does eudaimonia mean to you personally?

3  What are the strengths and weaknesses of the American democratic system? Why are they strengths and why are they weaknesses? (That is, clarify the criteria by which you are making your judgments.)

4  Why is it that some people trust others while other people strongly distrust? How did they get that way? In a general way, who do you think is right—or more right? Is one's trust of others related to one's trust of oneself?

5  Make a list of the goods and services (that provide freedom) that you are willing to pay for. Can you make a list also of what you are not willing to pay for? (Examples: discriminatory laws, special interest laws, systems that don't work, prohibition, laws that permit the invasion of your privacy, fighting the [wrong] war.)

6  What is a right? Do you have a right to do the following?

—to marry four husbands?
—to marry four wives?
—to worship Allah? Yahweh? Krishna? Amaterasu? Apollo? no one at all?
—to choose and plan the conditions in which you die?
—to refuse to pay tax that supports a war you believe is immoral?
—to take justice into your own hands when the law fails to protect you or your loved ones?
—to kill someone who raped your daughter when the courts let him off on a technicality?
—to think whatever you wish?
—to say what you think?
—to drive on the left side of the road?
—to openly criticize the American system of education?
—to have an abortion?
—to sneeze wherever you wish to?
—to smoke wherever you wish to?
—to snoop into someone's personal bank account?

# 5

## THE BONDS OF ACCULTURATION

Somewhere (and once upon a time) there was a small green valley lying quietly within the steep walls of surrounding mountains, and a village slept on the floor of the valley. No one from the village had ever ascended the mountain walls to travel beyond. Whatever lay beyond the rim of their valley, for them, did not exist. "Outside" had no meaning; nor did "beyond" or "stranger" or "distant lands" or "enemy tribes." No one else existed, or could possibly exist . . . until that day when someone found a path through a mountain pass, and came back to tell his kin that they were not alone.

> The life history of the individual is first and foremost an accommodation to the patterns and standards traditionally handed down in his community. From the moment of his birth the customs into which he is born shape his experience and behavior. By the time he can talk, he is the little creature of his culture, and by the time he is grown and able to take part in its activities, its habits are his habits, its beliefs his beliefs, its impossibilities his impossibilities.
>
> RUTH BENEDICT

At the moment of our birth, we are human only. Each of us possesses a full complement of human genes, but we belong to no established social categories. We are not Russian or English, Inuit or Bantu, Chinese or Thai or Peruvian. At birth we belong to one species—the human species: *Homo sapiens sapiens*. All of us.

But within minutes of our entrance into this world, social conditioning begins. A language is spoken to us—Japanese or Shona or Spanish or whatever; specific feelings, values, and ideas are programmed into us, so that our undifferentiated humanness is channeled into society's preexistent classification

*The age of cultural innocence is passing; the American is beginning to recognize the patterns to which he conforms.*

SNELL AND GAIL PUTNEY

*They are playing a game. They are playing at not playing a game. If I show them I see they are, I shall break the rules and they will punish me. I must play their game, of not seeing I see the game.*

R. D. LAING

*The environment is always the brainwasher, so that the well-adjusted person, by definition, has been brainwashed. He is adjusted. He's had it.*

MARSHALL MCLUHAN

*We seem to want creativity in the young—but only if it follows all the rules, isn't too noisy, pleases the adults, and doesn't rock the boat.*

MCNEIL AND RUBIN

*The usual distinction between sanity and insanity is a false one. We are all insane; the difference between Napolean and a madman who believes he is Napoleon is a difference in degree, not in kind; both are acting on a limited set of assumptions.*

COLIN WILSON

*Men in masses are gripped by personal troubles, but they are not aware of their true meaning and source.*

C. WRIGHT MILLS

systems. We are no longer primarily human; we think of ourselves, and identify ourselves to others, as we have been taught: I am Irish, I am Australian, I am South African, I am Jordanian, I am . . ., and so on. A complex set of categories becomes the accepted way of identifying "who" (or "what") we are. For good or ill, we have become acculturated.

Acculturation is a part of the human condition; individual and social existence would not be possible without it. But our social roles, along with their supportive functions, also become our prisons. We assume the carefully defined roles that society has constructed for us, and enormous pressures are brought to bear upon us to stay within the confines of those roles. We become one with our culture's world-view, including its ideas, values, myths, history, customs, traditions—the unexamined elements upon which our culture's world-view is grounded.

The result has been universally the same, as the anthropologist Ruth Benedict has aptly phrased it: ". . . its habits are his habits, its beliefs his beliefs, *its impossibilities his impossibilities.*"

## PRISONERS

An experiment in role-playing was conducted by a social psychologist at Stanford University, Philip Zimbardo. It was a simulated-prison experiment scheduled to run for two weeks, but it was halted after six days by a "thoroughly shaken" Professor Zimbardo. It began in the basement of a campus psychology building.

Student volunteers, rated normal and average in psychological tests, had been arbitrarily assigned the roles of guard and prisoner. Prisoners were stripped and deloused—normal procedure in all real prisons. The student guards carried billy clubs, handcuffs, keys, and whistles—all symbols of their authority. Their uniforms were military shirts and reflector sunglasses which made eye contact impossible. The prisoners were made to wear identical smocks and stocking-caps and were only addressed by their number. Keeping order and enforcing the rules were the responsibility of the guards; administering punishment was totally up to them.

At first, the student prisoners did not take the experiment very seriously.

GUARD 1.   "Hey, did I say you could laugh, 819? Didn't I tell you that you *could not* laugh? Maybe you didn't hear me right."

GUARD 2.   "819, how'd you like to step out of line and do twenty quick pushups for us, huh? OK, come on. Let's go. Sound off. Louder . . ."

On the morning of the second day the guards met in the corridor to deal with a prison rebellion. During the night they had harassed the prisoners in their windowless cells by constantly waking them for meaningless head counts. The students had stacked their cots against the cell doors and refused to come out for the morning count.

Told only that they must maintain law and order, the guards broke into each cell, stripped the prisoners naked, and confiscated their beds, blankets, and pillows. Eventually the ring-leaders were placed in solitary confinement in a small closet.

Faced with the resistance and hostility of the prisoners, the guards became caught up in their assigned roles. The student guards mixed troublemakers with those who had not rebelled and gave privileges to certain prisoners. This broke prisoner unity, bred distrust among them, and led prisoners to think that the privileges were the result of informing.

The guards stepped up the punishment—a meaningless succession of calisthenics and head counts which often lasted for hours. They even ordered the prisoners to curse each other publicly. Slowly the prisoners became resigned to their fate. They were no longer students. *They had become prisoners*, totally dominated by the guards.

The diary of one student guard shows the day-by-day change in his attitude as his role as guard became more and more real to him.

FIRST DAY:   I evolved my strategy, namely, not to smile or it would be admitting it was only a game. I set my voice hard and low. I feel stupid.

SECOND DAY:   After lights-out I held a loud conversation so the prisoners could overhear it about going home to my girl friend.

THIRD DAY:   Prisoner 817 is being obnoxious and bears watching.

FOURTH DAY:   I've been rebuked for handcuffing and blindfolding a prisoner. I resentfully replied it's both necessary security and my business anyway.

FIFTH DAY:   I harassed 817. I've singled him out for special abuse because he begs for it, and because I simply don't like him.

By the fourth day of the experiment five student prisoners were emotionally unable to continue and had to be released. Dr. Zimbardo believes that all participants in the experiment, both prisoners and guards, had begun to accept their assigned roles as reality. Prisoners became totally submissive. They depended entirely upon the dominant guards for even their simplest needs. The fact that they were in a simulated environment and could have quit at any time seems somehow to have become lost in the daily experience of their assigned roles.

On the fifth day Prisoner 416 refused to eat. It was the final act of individual rebellion in Stanford prison. The guards failed in every attempt to force him to eat. He was put in "the hole"—the tiny equipment closet used for solitary confinement. At that point Prisoner 416 should have become a hero to the other prisoners. Instead they turned on him. To them he was a troublemaker—a "bad" prisoner.

GUARD.   "Now if 416 does not eat all his sausages, then you can give me the blankets and sleep on the bare mattress. Or you can keep your blankets and 416 will stay another day. Now what will it be?"

PRISONER 1.   "I'll keep my blankets."

GUARD.   "What will it be over here?"

PRISONER 2.   "Keep my blankets."

GUARD.   "How about 546?"

PRISONER 3.   "I'll give you my blankets."

GUARD.   "Well, you boys got to come to some kind of decision here."

PRISONER.   "We got three who said they'll keep their blankets."

GUARD.   "We got three against one. Keep your blankets. 416, you're going to be in there for a while. So just git used to it."

It was no longer an experiment. The basement corridor had become a test-tube prison in which some average, middle-class young men called "prisoners" were actually suffering, and others called "guards" were behaving sadistically. Dr. Zimbardo cancelled the 14-day experiment after only six days.

*The demand to give up the illusions about our condition is the demand to give up a condition which needs illusions.*

KARL MARX

*If you don't have a goal, any road will do.*

CHARLES TART

The Zimbardo prison experiment is not a Doomsday message. It's a warning. It shows us how easily man accepts the impersonal rules of order as substitutes for human understanding, how conditioned he has become to respond to dominant symbols of authority—to a job, a role, to a label in society that forces him into patterns of behavior which dehumanize him and destroy in him the sense of responsibility for his own actions . . .

Dr. Zimbardo has reminded us that the roles we play are prisons—prisons of our own invention. But we do have the ability to create alternatives based on more human values. To be aware of how easy it is for any of us—for all of us—to fall into the patterned roles of dominance and submission is unique knowledge. Perhaps we will use it to find again the truly human qualities that first appeared almost a hundred thousand years ago in the dark caves of Neanderthal. . . .

*Primal Man*
Wolper Productions

## An Alternative: Transcendence

This "prison" condition no longer prevails for increasing numbers of people who discover for themselves that they can redefine their roles. We now have the genuine option of breaking free of the bonds of culture systems. This can be either a blessing or a curse. The loss of roots which a culture provides can be agonizing, yet the opportunities offered by this new freedom are momentous.

For good or ill, therefore, the freedom is ours. For what is probably the first time in human history, we can pass judgment on our culture and make a more objective assessment of the ways in which it meets or fails to meet our basic needs.

What is asked of us—or *demanded* of us—is no easy path. We are at a crossroads requiring considerable moral courage: the courage to face freedom and seek autonomy *without* the roots and *without* the security which culture has heretofore guaranteed to each of us.

The sources of this new freedom are many; three are fairly obvious.

First, from the vast researches of the social scientists, we have come to recognize the cultural patterns which have shaped our existence. From the anthropologists' patient examination of other cultural patterns, we can see more dispassionately the patterns which others have unconsciously followed. After comparing the patterns of numerous societies we have come to understand the function and operation of a culture system. We find that each culture is an internally coherent structure with its component parts harmonizing into an interdependent working system. Each culture provides a world-view, so that life for each individual in the system has coherence and meaning.

When we apply this knowledge to our own culture, we begin to understand its function and our roles in it. We see how relative some of the patterns and values are. Previously—while living in that small green valley—we took them for granted; we may even have believed them to be universal or absolute. Now we find that they were merely functional. We have discovered that individuals immersed in their cultures, from the primitive to the most civilized, endow their

*About then I made a horrible discovery. I didn't want to go back to school, win, lose, or draw. I no longer gave a damn about three-car garages and swimming pools, nor any other status symbol or "security." There was no security in this world and only damn fools and mice thought there could be.*

Robert Heinlein
*Glory Road*

*Bloom where you are planted.*
*Hindu proverb*

respective patterns with the same ultimacy and finality which we felt. For each, his culture has worked pragmatically for him, and therefore no other culture existed, or could exist. We can now recognize ethnocentrism, wherever it occurs.

The result is that we see ourselves in a larger context, and having seen, we can no longer follow a tacit ethnocentrism. We see through it; we understand its root causes. The egocentric illusion has been found out!

Secondly, in the decade of the nineties we are involved in a cataclysmic increase in cultural interaction. No single major culture stands today as a monolithic, isolated system, as once they all did. Few places exist in the world today where one could be born and remain culturally naive. Arnold Toynbee has pointed out that a cultural map of the earth a few centuries ago showed large pure-color patches, distinct from one another and with fairly sharp edges; but by the end of our century the patches will have vanished and the cultural colors will everywhere be woven together—like "shot silk"—with only faint blushes of color remaining in a few isolated enclaves.

Probably the most significant world-fact of our time is the disintegration of cultures as distinct and separate functional systems. This is the fundamental fact that has given us our freedom—and our pain.

A third source of our freedom is new insight into the dynamics of our inner world. We know a great deal now about the processes of psychological conditioning and reinforcement. We know that individuals can be acculturated into any set of customs, beliefs, and values; they can be made to believe, value, and even worship almost anything. If societies can condition us, then we know that we can be *un*conditioned and *re*conditioned.

And so, as we gain a clearer picture of our basic human needs—*which may or may not be fulfilled by the particular culture in which we live*—we feel a new freedom to pursue their fulfillment. *We* can take the initiative. We no longer submit to the doctrine that we *must* remain, unquestioningly, within a particular system; indeed, with our awareness of alternatives, external coercion for us to do so might be interpreted as enslavement. Various cultures, subcultures, and segments of culture are readily accessible to us. We are free to experiment with them, identify with them; some can even find a home in several systems simultaneously or sequentially.

*Yet we sit there, eyes glued to the set, watching this explication of the obvious in hateful fascination and even find ourselves compelled to stay tuned to whatever follows. . . . Consciously, we despise ourselves, yet we are fascinated . . . as any savage before his totem.*

RICHARD SCHICKEL

*Would it really do to find out that our game is not serious, that enemies are friends, and that the good thrives on the evil? Society as we know it seems to be a tacit conspiracy to keep this hushed up for fear that the contest will otherwise cease.*

ALAN WATTS

*At present, the gap between the sane man and the maniac is very small indeed. As William James rightly understood, the "hour" can strike for any of us. Remove a few of the walls of illusion, and the sane man becomes insane.*

Colin Wilson

## Path with a Heart

"I say it is useless to waste your life on one path, especially if that path has no heart."

"But how do you know when a path has no heart, don Juan?"

"Before you embark on it you ask the question: Does this path have a heart? If the answer is no, you will know it, and then you must choose another path."

"But how will I know for sure whether a path has a heart or not?"

"Anybody would know that. The trouble is nobody asks the question; and when a man finally realizes that he has taken a path without a heart, the path is ready to kill him. At that point very few men can stop to deliberate, and leave the path."

"How should I proceed to ask the question properly, don Juan?"

"Just ask it."

Carlos Castaneda
*The Teachings of Don Juan*

## Cultural Relativity

In any society, specific BTF-patterns are considered "normal" not merely because the majority adheres to them, but also because they are meaningful and functional. They enable us to predict the behavior of others, and them ours. They create consistency in our experiencing of life together; they provide us with a unifying world-view. "Normal" behavior supports and enhances that unity; "abnormal" behavior does not cohere with the system and tends to destroy it. (*BTF-patterns* is a convenient abbreviation which will be used to refer to all the elements which are interwoven to create selves and societies. *Behavior, thought,* and *feeling*—these are the three elements of human experience which are judged to be acceptable or unacceptable, right or wrong. Also, the single symbol "BTF" implies the important fact that behavior, thought, and feeling are ultimately inseparable and operate together.)

As we move from culture to culture we find the same principles. Normal BTF-patterns will differ, but within each society these elements will cohere and interact. The system will provide guidelines for living, and a high degree of conformity and security. Therefore, within each culture, these accepted BTF-patterns are normal and right.

The fact of cultural relativism was first recognized, so far as we know, by the Greek Sophist Protagoras. Denying that any belief or custom was absolute, Protagoras declared that "man is the measure of all things" (that is, customs are man-made, not divinely given); and he held that we have an obligation to conform to the cultural patterns of any society we might visit. After all, what right have we, flaunting our ethnocentric arrogance, to subvert a workable system by introducing our alien BTF-patterns?

*However romantic it seemed to be a beachcomber, I learned I had to get back to the neurotic society I need in order to function.*

Albert Finney

The central point in cultural relativism is that in a particular cultural setting, certain traits are right because they work well in that setting, while other traits are wrong because they would clash painfully with parts of that culture. This is but another way of saying that a culture is integrated, and that its various elements must harmonize passably if the culture is to function efficiently in serving human purposes.

HORTON AND HUNT

## THE DOUBLE STANDARD

A phenomenon found in every culture is what we sometimes call the "double standard." There are, first, the acceptable BTF-patterns; these are the publicly professed, ideal patterns that everyone is "supposed to" follow. But along with these acceptable norms also exist clearly established, socially sanctioned ways of breaking the ideal norms. That is, *there are acceptable ways of misbehaving.*

People, it would appear, find it difficult to live with a single set of BTF-patterns; they must have at least two sets of rules. The first set represents their ideals, the way they believe their society should be. These are projections of what they would like others to think of them and the way they would like to think of themselves and others. Many convince themselves that all or most people truly follow such ideal standards of behavior.

The unacceptable patterns are just as much a part of a cultural process as the acceptable patterns, and perhaps just as vital. People seem to need these unacceptable BTF-patterns to express a side of their natures which they are reluctant to admit. They are outlets for taboo feelings—fears, sexual urges, hostilities, prejudices—feelings which they would prefer to repress and not worry about. But since they can't escape the fact that they exist, they are expressed in various cultures in "acceptable unacceptable" ways.

Every known society has a double standard, and the "unacceptable" patterns must be considered an integral part of that culture.

Tension is necessarily involved where individuals are forced to function in line with several BTF-patterns, as in the case of a double standard. After all, we can't be fully open about the repressed patterns no matter how widely they are practiced, for one of the rules is that they not be *openly* accepted. Some amount of deception with others—and perhaps with ourselves—is inevitable.

Such tensions, however, are not usually very destructive. Most individuals learn to accept the fact that conflicting sets of rules are a part of the culture. They proceed to live with them, or by them. Still, they must be most cautious about when and where they admit the existence of the "unacceptable" patterns of behavior.

> *The American divorce rate has been variously attributed to teenage marriage, delayed marriage, premarital sexual experience, lack of sexual experience, decline of religious influence, residual Puritanism, glamorization of divorce, and even the automobile. But our analysis suggests a different, perhaps a shocking answer: American marriages are unstable because Americans marry for love.*
>
> SNELL AND GAIL PUTNEY

Is there any quality of "American" thought which distinguishes it from that developed elsewhere?

One peculiar and all-pervasive characteristic is its pluralism. . . . Thought in America has developed in response to external influences and to internal problems and challenges. America has been receptive to many cultures and to a variety of intellectual themes. There is, for example, both a liberal and a conservative tradition throughout American history. There is the America of radical democratic individualism and equalitarianism of Thomas Jefferson, Thomas Paine, Ethan Allen,

> *But my dear Crito, why should we pay so much attention to what "most people" think? The really reasonable people, who have more claim to be considered, will believe that the facts are exactly as they are.*
>
> PLATO

Benjamin Rush, Henry Thoreau, Abraham Lincoln and John Dewey—an America in which liberal causes are espoused or in which a dominant secular and naturalistic outlook prevails. But there is also a conservative stream in American history, represented in the religious interests of the Puritans, Jonathan Edwards, and Samuel Johnson, in the defense of orthodoxy by the Scottish realists and speculative idealists, and in the conservative politics of Cadwallader Colden, Alexander Hamilton, John C. Calhoun, and even George Santayana. America is thus the meeting place of divergent ideas and movements: Puritanism, deism, materialism, Unitarianism, transcendentalism, idealism, realism, and pragmatism—and most recently of naturalism, positivism, analytic philosophy, Marxism, Thomism, phenomenology, Zen Buddhism, and existentialism. Any simple formulas designed to reduce these diverse elements into a uniform tradition are bound to be distorted.

PAUL KURTZ

## PERSONAL ALIENATION

Paul Klee, *Senecio* (1922)

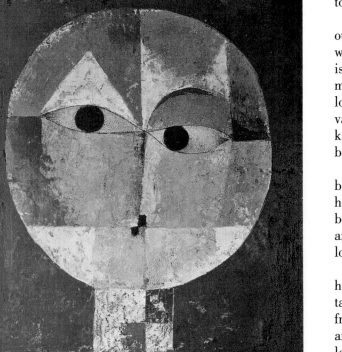

Much current anxiety and alienation is the result of the interaction of cultures and their breakdown as functional systems. Since different systems have conflicting BTF-patterns, what happens when they collide and interact? Each system loses its coherence, integrity, and workability. We discover that various BTF-patterns are right *and* wrong, acceptable *and* unacceptable *at the same time,* depending upon which strand of culture one uses as the criterion of valuation.

What happens to you and me as we try to adjust to a cultural eclecticism?

We *internalize* that eclecticism. The outer world is a hodge-podge, so our inner worlds become hodge-podges. Our culture is fragmented, so we too become fragmented. We don't know which values to follow, so we attempt to hold conflicting values which reflect our culture. We don't know what behavior is acceptable, so we behave differently in different settings.

Consistent behavior is no longer possible, and the integrity so essential to the harmonious operation of our inner world becomes ever more elusive. Self and sanity are at stake, and, by degrees, both can be lost.

When one is in this condition—when his or her inner world reflects the fragmentation of the outer world—a pressure is felt from within to find a solution. Several easy and attractive alternatives are at hand; at least momentarily they can provide security and relieve anxiety.

One alternative is to identify with but a

single isolated strand of culture where one can feel more at home. In such a group one's BTF-patterns will be shared by others and tensions can therefore diminish. One can feel more at ease with those who share the same values. Feelings of alienation and fragmentation may subside. Surrounded by those who are congenial, one can usually ignore the uncongenial patterns which heretofore caused trouble.

The difficulty with this alternative is that it doesn't solve the problem. To be sure, changing the environment can be a step in the right direction, but one must recognize that the *vulnerability* to fragmentation is an inner problem, and it may remain. The wound is in the inner world, not in the environment. Finding congenial surroundings may ease the pain only temporarily unless healing can proceed within.

A similar alternative is to join a truth-group. One can plunge into a sub-cultural unit which devalues all other BTF-patterns; once devalued, they tend to lose their power over us. Relegating them to an inferior status brings more satisfaction than ignoring or repressing them. One doesn't have to take seriously the experience of any other person or group which differs, since he or she knows that their BTF-patterns are erroneous or wrong. Truth-groups usually make aristocentrism a condition of membership, and the sense of identity and security they offer is therefore especially rewarding.

This alternative prevents one from discovering effective channels of growth. Genuine identification with a truth-group is possible only while one remains unaware of the implications of the egocentric predicament. Nevertheless, when our cultural confusion becomes too great, such a refuge, for many, may be the only viable alternative.

For others, there is a third path, but it is anything but a choice. This is psychosis. If the real world appears too hellish, it is quite possible to create an inner world that is less threatening. It is never a freely chosen alternative, but rather a condition that takes over when we have lost our freedom of choice.

The majority of us, however, follow the easiest path; we try halfheartedly to conform to many noncoherent patterns of culture at the same time—wearing various masks, playing various roles—whatever the cost to our mental health. Even at the risk of a mild schizophrenia, the expediency is not too costly, we think. The possibility of developing autonomy will be lost, but then, nobody's perfect . . .

## "I Learned This, at Least . . ."

I left the woods for as good a reason as I went there. Perhaps it seemed to me that I had several more lives to live, and could not spare any more time for that one. It is remarkable how easily and insensibly we fall into a particular route, and make a beaten track for ourselves. I had not lived there a week before my feet wore a path from my door to the pond-side; and though it is five or six years since I trod it, it is still quite distinct. It is true, I fear, that others may have fallen into it, and so helped to keep it open. The surface of the earth is soft and impressible by the feet of men; and so with the paths which the mind travels. How worn and dusty, then, must be the highways of the world, how deep the ruts of tradition and conformity! I did not wish to take a cabin passage, but rather to go before the mast and on the deck of the

*Once upon a time, I, Chuang-tzu, dreamt I was a butterfly, fluttering hither and thither, to all intents and purposes a butterfly. . . . suddenly, I awoke. . . . Now I do not know whether I was then a man dreaming I was a butterfly, or whether I am now a butterfly dreaming that I am a man.*

CHUANG-TZU

*I am but mad north-north-west: when the wind is southerly I know a hawk from a handsaw.*

WILLIAM SHAKESPEARE
*Hamlet* II, ii, 405

*Notice the difference between what happens when a man says to himself, "I have failed three times," and what happens when he says, "I am a failure!" It is the difference between sanity and self-destruction.*

S. I. HAYAKAWA

*If I were asked to define an American in a single phrase I would say "An American is a person who has the right to be different," and I think that right is growing.*

**WILLIAM MANCHESTER**

world, for there I could best see the moonlight amid the mountains. I do not wish to go below now.

I learned this, at least, by my experiment: that if one advances confidently in the direction of his dreams, and endeavors to live the life which he has imagined, he will meet with a success unexpected in common hours. He will put some things behind, will pass an invisible boundary; new, universal, and more liberal laws will begin to establish themselves around and within him; or the old laws be expanded, and interpreted in his favor in a more liberal sense, and he will live with the license of a higher order of beings. In proportion as he simplifies his life, the laws of the universe will appear less complex, and solitude will not be solitude, nor poverty poverty, nor weakness weakness. If you have built castles in the air, your work need not be lost; that is where they should be. Now put the foundations under them.

HENRY DAVID THOREAU

## REFLECTIONS

1   Note the marginal quotes on p. 353 by the Putneys and Laing. Do you agree with the point they are making? What percent of Americans do you think recognize "the patterns" or see "the games"? Or does this apply only to the few who take courses in philosophy? (Shades of aristocentrism?!)

2   As you reflect on pp. 353–356 together, what is your response to these examples of the power of social conditioning? Are these insights new to you, or have you already worked through them?

3   Imagine yourself in the position of one of the guards or prisoners in the Zimbardo experiment. What games or gimmicks would you play on yourself, what knowledge, beliefs, or strengths would you remind yourself of to prevent prescribed roles from overwhelming you into losing your self and *becoming* what the roles *define* you to be? How long do you think you could last in such a "game"? (This is a reminder of the creative mental gymnastics which many prisoners of war engage in to prevent their succumbing to the roles forced upon them.)

4   This chapter suggests that freedom has been *imposed* upon us whether we wish it or are ready for it. Do you agree?

5   Some common "alternatives to freedom" are listed on pp. 360–361. Do these descriptions apply to individuals you know? What is your opinion of each of these alternatives?

6   Ponder the quotation from Laing (p. 353) in relation to that from Watts (p. 357). In what sense might society's BTF-patterns be considered "games" the rules for which we must know to get along? What exactly is a game? Where do the rules come from? What is meant by "playing" a game?

*The main path to health and self-fulfillment for the masses is via basic need gratification rather than via frustration. This contrasts with the suppressive regime, the mistrust, the control, the policing that is necessarily implied by basic evil in human depths.*

**ABRAHAM MASLOW**

7   Page 362 marginal quote: This observation by Maslow strikes some of us as a profound insight; but to others it might be only a trite truism. What do you think about it?

8   Note the (surprising?) statement by the Putneys (p. 359-marginal quote). Do you understand what they're saying when they write that "American marriages are unstable because Americans marry for love"? What do they mean? Do you agree?

# ETHICS/CHOICES

# 5

## SIN AND/OR VIRTUE

Last night I invented a new pleasure, and as I was giving it the first trial, an angel and a devil came rushing toward my house. They met at my door and fought with each other over my newly created pleasure; the one crying, "It is a sin!"—the other, "It is a virtue!"

KAHIL GIBRAN

SPOCK: *Don't grieve, Admiral. It's logical. The needs of the many outweigh . . .*
KIRK: *. . . the needs of a few . . .*
SPOCK: *. . . or the one.*
**Star Trek II: The Wrath of Khan**

## DEBATABLE AND NONDEBATABLE VALUE JUDGMENTS

There are several varieties of value judgments, but there is considerable disagreement among value theorists on how to classify them. For our purposes we can work with two relatively clear-cut kinds of value-statements: (1) those that are statements of personal taste and temperament and are not debatable, and (2) those that lend themselves to rational analysis and empirical investigation and are, therefore, debatable.

I may inform you that "I like liver and onions." This kind of value judgment is strictly a matter of personal taste, and only an epistemological nitwit would make an issue of the matter. (A vegetarian could rightly want to debate the ethics of my eating meat, but my taste for liver remains undebatable.) In a word, personal values of this kind are not debatable. There are no "shoulds" or "should nots" involved in them. They just are. And in the last analysis, we can't even talk much about them. "I like turnips," I complain, and that's the end of the matter.

Nondebatable value judgments have to do mostly with our sensory and emotional responses. For describing sensory experience, the following statements are fairly straightforward and accurate: "I like the flavor of real Italian

*The perfect Way [Tao] is without difficulty,*
*Save that it avoids picking and choosing. . . .*
*If you want to get the plain truth,*
*Be not concerned with right and wrong.*
*The conflict between right and wrong*
*Is the sickness of the mind.*
SENG-TS'AN

TAYLOR (to Zira): *Doctor, I'd like to kiss you goodbye.*
ZIRA (to Taylor, giggling): *All right. But you're so damned ugly!*
**Planet of the Apes**

spaghetti" (taste). "I think Susan is beautiful" (vision—although beauty as such is not actually seen but is created from visual perceptions and past experiences). "I enjoy walking in the rain" (touch, plus). "I'm turned on by the fragrance of orange blossoms" (smell). "I prefer the rhythms of Ravel's *Bolero* to Stravinsky's *Rite of Spring*" (sound).

Our emotions are similarly expressed: "I enjoy playing mathematical games." "I hate being embarrassed in public." "I like Susan." "I distrust bureaucracies." "I'm scared of love."

These judgments are all nondebatable. No fact-claims are made in any of these statements. Each statement is a *description* of one's experience, sensory or emotional as the case may be. If her boyfriend thinks Susan is beautiful, then—since "beauty is in the eye of the beholder"—Susan *is* beautiful *to him,* and only a fool or a sour-grapes loser would argue with him.

By contrast, a second kind of value judgment is debatable. If I say that "I favor mercy killing," then I have made a value statement that, if carried into action, would affect the lives of other people; and that action is clearly subject to analysis and investigation. We can talk about whether euthanasia is right or wrong when judged in the light of specific ethical criteria. We can discuss the justice of forcing terminally ill patients to suffer against their will. We can debate certain religious doctrines and why their adherents would be for or against the practice. In a word, there are ideas to be analyzed and relevant empirical facts to be gathered.

> "But surely," it may be said, "people do disagree in their basic moral attitudes, and they do try to persuade other people to agree with them." Indeed they do. People seem to feel more strongly about their moral attitudes than they do about their food preferences (we do not talk, for example, about our "culinary convictions"), and few people appear willing simply to accept differences at this point and let it go at that. But the methods by which anyone can persuade anyone else to change his basic moral attitudes . . . are not those of rational argument but only the methods of nonrational persuasion: name-calling, intimidation, threats, and so on. This is probably why our language has words like "prude," "moral ignoramus," and the like.
>
> Does not this view lead to pessimistic conclusions about the possibility of achieving enough ethical agreement among men to make harmonious life on our planet possible? Not at all. To so conclude would be equivalent to a restaurateur's concluding that, since people's tastes differ, he might as well give up trying to develop a menu that will win the general approval of his customers. Fortunately, people by and large tend to approve and disapprove of the same sorts of things: that is why one seldom finds anyone who will disagree with statements like "The infliction of needless pain is evil," or "It is good to help others who are in need." It is not the alleged objectivity of moral judgments, but the substantial similarity of our basic moral attitudes, that renders possible a reasonably harmonious society.
>
> WILLIAM HALVERSON

## THE MORALITY OF ETHICS / THE ETHICS OF MORALITY

A young bank employee was indicted for embezzlement, and the evidence all seemed to point to a conviction. But *he* knew he was innocent, and his wife

---

*De gustibus non disputandum est. Concerning taste there can be no argument.*

**Proverb**

*A little knowledge of history stresses the variability of moral codes, and concludes that they are negligible because they differ in time and place, and sometimes contradict each other. A larger knowledge stresses the universality of moral codes, and concludes to their necessity.*

WILL DURANT

believed him. She was soon informed by another bank employee that he knew the whereabouts of documents that would reveal the real embezzler and prove that her husband was innocent. But her informant also made it clear he would give out with the evidence only if she made herself sexually available. The couple were devout Catholics, but to clear her husband of almost certain conviction she quickly made the decision to get whatever information at whatever cost. So she spent several nights with the other bank employee. Eventually the documents were forthcoming, her husband was exonerated, and the real embezzler was indicted and convicted. (See pp. 43–44.)

Question: Was her act moral or immoral?

Question: Was *she* moral or immoral?

Further: What are the criteria used to evaluate her actions? In your judgment could she have made a better decision? What would make it a better decision? What was her intent? Could *she* be judged moral while *her actions* are judged immoral?

In a World War II movie called *Manhunt*, the principal figure is a big-game hunter. For the sheer love of stalking his prey, he creeps into the forest high above Hitler's retreat at Berchtesgaden. Lying concealed in a thicket, he aligns the cross-hairs of his telescopic sight on the Führer's heart as he stands on a balcony. He pulls the trigger . . . on an empty chamber. He had stalked his game, and won.

Shortly, however, the hunter is caught by the Nazis and repeatedly tortured between escapes. In the beginning it never occurred to him to *kill* Hitler; but at the end of the story, having seen the bestial cruelty of the Nazis, he parachutes by night into the German forest, this time to hunt his game with live ammunition.

(This story is not far-fetched. Many attempts were made on Hitler's life by "good and decent men who wanted to put an end to the tyranny of this maniac." One such man was Dietrich Bonhoeffer, a devout Christian leader, who was executed for attempting to do what he believed to be a Christian duty: to murder Hitler. And recently a leader of the Jewish Defense League, Meir Kahane, has stated his conviction that "if an American Nazi Party leader posed a clear and present danger to American Jews, then not to assassinate such a person would be one of the most immoral courses I could imagine.") [Note: Meir Kahane was assassinated in New York in 1990 by a Moslem fundamentalist who considered Kahane to be a threat to Islam.]

Question: When (if ever) is it morally right to deliberately kill another human being "with malice aforethought"? What justifies such a course of action? If you had been the hunter in this story, what would you have done?

A young woman in her early twenties decided that she was ready to have children. She also decided that she would settle for nothing less than the best genes possible for those children. So she sought out three different men who met her qualifications: one with an attractive and healthy physique, one of high intelligence, and one bearing sensitive artistic and moral qualities. Over the next four years she became pregnant by the three men and gave birth to three beautiful babies that grew into healthy and happy children. She was then married to

*The truly adequate personality has the capacity for identification with his fellows. The feeling of identification seems to produce a deep sensitivity to the feelings and attitudes of others. One learns to identify with others, depending upon the nature of his contacts with the important people in his life.*

ARTHUR W. COMBS

*There is nothing either good or bad,*
*But thinking makes it so.*

WILLIAM SHAKESPEARE
*Hamlet*

*Always do right. This will gratify some people and astonish the rest.*

MARK TWAIN

another man (he was not one of the fathers) who became a loving father to the children. They were considered by all who knew them as the typical American family.

The story is told of a tragic incident that occurred when a frontier village was raided by Indians. Several members of the village hid where they could not be found. One woman had a very small baby in her arms. As some Indians drew close, she smothered the baby rather than risk giving away their hiding place and thereby insuring death for them all. Some time after the raid, she was punished by both church and community for committing murder.

*An intelligence that is not humane is the most dangerous thing in the world.*

ASHLEY MONTAGU

From George Bernard Shaw (via *Playboy*): A young woman was asked by a rich man if she would spend the night with him. She responded with a righteous "No!" When he asked if she would for a hundred thousand dollars, she uttered an exultant "Yes!" "Then what about ten thousand dollars?" he asked. With some hesitation: "Yes, I guess I would." "Then what about five hundred dollars?" She replied angrily, "No, what do you think I am?" To which his final words were: "We have already established that. Now we're merely haggling over the price."

Joseph Fletcher recounts an episode involving the ship *William Brown* which struck an iceberg off Newfoundland and sank in 1841. Seven crewmen and thirty-two passengers crowded into a lifeboat, but this was almost double the number the lifeboat could hold. Winds and heavy seas would have capsized the whole lot in a very short time. So the first mate ordered the men in the company out of the boat, but no one moved. One of the crewmen—a man named Holmes—therefore tossed some of the men into the ocean. The rest in the boat survived and were eventually rescued. In Philadelphia, Holmes was tried and convicted of murder, though the jury recommended clemency.

*Nature and history do not agree with our conceptions of good and bad; they define good as that which survives, and bad as that which goes under; and the universe has no prejudice in favor of Christ as against Genghis Khan.*

WILL AND ARIEL DURANT

(This incident has received some legal attention. The issue is whether such a "crime" can be excused or justified because of the circumstances. To date, a defense argument based on "necessity" (that is, a greater harm would have occurred if the defendant hadn't acted as he did) is not allowed in capital crimes such as homicide. "However, there is some authority which would justify even the taking of an innocent human life, if absolutely necessary for the preservation of the lives of others . . . providing some lottery or other arbitrary means is designated for selecting which life is to be taken. [E.g., the 'shipwreck' cases; U.S. v. Holmes, 26 Fed. Cas. No. 360]. . . . And, the presence of such facts may be enough to reduce the homicide from murder to manslaughter . . . although this is a minority view." William A. Rutter, *Criminal Law*, Harcourt Brace Jovanovich, 1976, pp. 213–218.)

*To have a purpose for which one will do almost anything except betray a friend,—that is the final patent of nobility, the last formula of the superman.*

FRIEDRICH NIETZSCHE

Near the turn of the century a young couple in a small Arkansas town were still childless after several years of marriage. When they went to their doctor to find out why, tests showed the man to be sterile. After talking over their problem, they went together to their local pastor and asked him if he would make the wife pregnant. In due time, he obliged, and she conceived. The child was fully accepted by the man and his wife and was loved and raised as their own. The minister, however, was forced to surrender his orders and leave the ministry.

## THREE ETHICAL QUESTIONS

There are three questions which, if asked sincerely and explored carefully, will carry one a long way toward understanding ethical problems and deciding what moral action to take in the very human dilemmas in which we find ourselves caught. Three questions. That may sound simple; and authentic morality may indeed be simpler than our tangled analyses often indicate. However, our previous exploration of value judgments should remind us that ethical problems can be very complex.

The three questions: (1) *Who* actually makes an ethical decision? (2) What criteria should I use in making a relevant and meaningful ethical decision? (3) To whom (or what) do my moral obligations apply?

There is a fourth question which might logically follow these three: Can I in fact *do* what I decide is right? That is, having decided what is right, can I *will* it and then *do* what I will? We need not belabor the question further at this point, since the problems of autonomy and freedom around which this question turns have been covered in previous chapters (See Chapter 4–3.) The more mature the self has become, the better are the chances that one will be able to will into action what he knows to be right. There is a close correlation between personal autonomy and ethical behavior.

> *There are no ethical truths; there are just clarifications of particular ethical problems. Take advantage of these clarifications and work out your own existence. You are mistaken to think that anyone ever had the answers. There are no answers. Be brave and face up to it.*
>
> DONALD KALISH

## WHO REALLY MAKES DECISIONS?

The first question we must answer is: *Who is to make the ethical decision?* We can assume that only the individual can make moral choices and act them out, but determining *what* action is moral may not have been decided at all. On this question regarding decision, there are two schools of thought, for we can speak of (1) authoritarian decisions, and (2) autonomous decisions.

In authoritarian ethics, decisions about right and wrong are given. They originate objectively and are not the product of one's personal experience. That is, the decisions of what is right and what is wrong have *already* been made, perhaps by an authority or a society—but often by a deity who subsequently revealed his decisions at some point to mortals. It was assumed by different people, for instance, that the decision had been made by Yahweh (and revealed in the Torah or the Decalogue); or by Allah (and revealed in the Quran); or by Shamash (and revealed to Hammurabi); or by Ahura Mazda (and revealed to Zoroaster). In the case of the Decalogue, an absolute decision had already been made: killing, lying, stealing, and so forth are wrong, and any further debate is out of the question.

What is humanity's task? To obey these laws. Our first responsibility is to know the rules and then to resolve the ethical problems of our daily lives by the faithful application of these laws. We also have an obligation to cultivate the moral life *so that we will be able to act morally* when forced to make moral choices.

Hence, these are authoritarian ethics. The individual takes no part in the first-order decision-making on what constitutes moral/immoral behavior. The given laws are immutable and final.

> *Teilhard de Chardin emphasized that the more evolved human being is one who, on the one hand, becomes more highly individualized, and who achieves, on the other hand, a high degree of conscious integration with other men. The evolution of man thus reveals two simultaneous and complementary trends: one toward keener awareness of self, and the other toward more intensive cooperation and participation.*
>
> RENÉ DUBOS

Autonomous ethics arise from inside oneself, for the individual himself has been in on the decision-making regarding what constitutes moral/immoral action. As the word *autonomy* implies, the individual is self-determined; his actions are manifestations of his own decisions.

We can contrast these two forms of ethics. The first is behavior that conforms to given codes and social customs; the second is autonomous—ethical behavior that is inner-motivated and grounded in genuine moral interest in the well-being of others. Autonomous ethics is largely the product of one's own experience; in this sense it is deeply personal, reflecting one's own sensibilities and values. Furthermore, in this perspective, "morality" is not merely *what one does;* it is rather the inevitable expression of *what one is.* It is a sincere good-will and never empty conformity to prevailing customs. In a word, it is autonomous.

Jean-Paul Sartre has stated his conviction, based on his belief in human freedom, that *all* ethical decisions are autonomous, that in the final analysis there are no authoritarian ethics. Sartre is saying that although we may adhere to given customs and codes—from parents, peers, society, church—when making ethical decisions each of us still decides which codes we will use in resolving our problems. If we decide to seek answers to our ethical questions by applying the Decalogue rather than our parents' values, or by appealing to our church's teaching rather than to peer values, then it is still we who make such decisions.

Ultimately, therefore, we can never escape personal responsibility for the ethical decisions that *we* make; and we are likewise responsible for the moral/immoral actions that *we* perform.

Sartre's position is a sort of half-truth. He is surely correct when speaking of persons who, to use his phrase, "have become conscious"—that is, those who have become aware of alternatives. The ethically informed individual *knows* that there are many criteria for making decisions; knowing this, the individual's decisions rest upon his or her own shoulders, and one must assume responsibility for them.

But for the majority of us, such options don't exist. We are convinced that there is but a single set of rights-and-wrongs: how could it be otherwise? If one believes with all one's heart that the decision of right/wrong has been wholly settled, and that this settlement is embodied in a single set of customs or codes, then the individual cannot justly be held responsible for *not* making ethical decisions based on other codes which (in our opinion, perhaps) would have been superior decisions. For this individual, it is not possible, as Sartre would have it, to say "No!" to one's own given code.

Perhaps the truer half of Sartre's argument needs to be emphasized: once we become aware that there are many criteria for making ethical decisions, then the full responsibility for our own decisions rests squarely and heavily upon our shoulders.

## What Makes a Decision Right or Wrong?

The second question we must answer is: *What criteria should I use in making a relevant and meaningful ethical decision?* Or put differently: What is the source

*In the new age, the dominant note in the corporate consciousness of communities is a sense of being parts of some larger universe, whereas, in the age which is now over, the dominant note in their consciousness was an aspiration to be universes in themselves.*

**Arnold Toynbee**

*I want to change their minds, not kill them for weaknesses we all possess.*

**Gandhi (motion picture)**

of the data that I should take into account in making an ethical judgment? Three different answers to this question come from (1) the formalist, (2) the relativist, and (3) the contextualist.

1. FORMALISM The formalist believes that the criteria to be used in making ethical decisions are universal laws that apply to all people. Man's responsibility is to be informed on these rules *ahead of time*—that is, before we find ourselves caught up in life's ethical complexities. By analogy, one should know the laws in the state motor-vehicle code *before* getting behind the wheel and taking to the streets. Likewise, we should be taught the laws of the moral life before taking to the highways. Our personal task, in both cases, is to be thoroughly acquainted with the rules so that we can apply them to concrete situations as we come to them. Whether approaching a red light or being tempted to cheat, we should know to *stop*, since we have studied the codebook. (Our first obligation, of course, is to try to avoid situations where weighty ethical decisions have to be made, but daily life rarely permits us so easy an out.)

There are several kinds of formal ethical codes. One kind is represented by the Decalogue, written on Mount Sinai by "the finger of God." These are apodictic laws—absolute and incontestable. In actual practice they don't work and must be continually redefined and modified. The commandment "Thou shalt not kill" is hardly practicable if a tribe is fighting for its survival against other invading tribes. So "to kill" was understood to mean "to murder"; hence, by redefinition, it became applicable only to fellow citizens in good standing. (Actually, this is not a redefinition, since the Commandment was never intended to have general application. It is for this reason that the reported killing of some 3000 Israelites by Moses and the Levites in a single day (Exodus 32:26–29) is not at all a violation of the Commandment against killing (Exodus 20:13). To the ancient Hebrew the Sixth Commandment implicitly meant, "Thou shalt not kill a fellow Hebrew as long as he is a faithful follower of the god Yahweh." If this interpretation seems puzzling, read Deuteronomy 13:6–11.)

The German philosopher Immanuel Kant concluded that universal moral laws do exist, but that they are to be found within the structure of the human mind. Just as $7 + 5$ is always 12—it is a priori knowledge yet applies to the real world—there are, Kant holds, moral "rules of thought" that are a priori and therefore universal (like $7 + 5 = 12$). Kant writes that ethical rules "must not be sought in human nature or in the circumstances of the world . . . but [must be sought] *a priori* simply in the concepts of reason." Kant formulated his famous "categorical imperative" to be such an a priori rule. It categorically applies to all rational persons and is imperative as an absolute "ought" that binds them to the moral law. His formula (in part) is: "Act only on the maxim whereby thou canst at the same time will it should become a universal law." This resembles our concept of natural law as described by modern physics. Kant was contending that if any kind of action can be universalized, then it is ethical. For instance, can I universalize lying? Hardly. I may think lying expediently justifiable in some particular case, but can I therefore recommend telling lies as a universal form of behavior? Obviously not. Human interaction would be rendered chaotic if we couldn't depend upon one another. Therefore, telling the truth is a "categorical imperative."

*It ain't so much a question of not knowin' what to do. I've known what's right and wrong since I been ten.*

**"Ado Annie," Oklahoma!**

*The simple-minded use of the notions "right or wrong" is one of the chief obstacles to the progress of understanding.*

ALFRED NORTH WHITEHEAD

*Contentment, even in poverty, brings happiness; discontent is poverty, even in riches.*

**Chinese proverb**

A more recent attempt to develop a system of universal formal laws was undertaken by the American philosopher Edgar Brightman. For example, the Law of Autonomy: "All persons ought to recognize themselves as obligated to choose in accordance with the ideals which they acknowledge." The Law of Consequences: "All persons ought to consider and, on the whole, approve the foreseeable consequences of each of their choices." The Laws of Altruism: "Each person ought to respect all other persons as ends in themselves, and, as far as possible, to co-operate with others in the production and enjoyment of shared values." These are normative laws; they state what we ought to do. Because of their logical and axiomatic nature, they are meant to apply universally to all ethical decisions made by human beings.

**2. RELATIVISM** Another answer to our second question comes from the relativist. The relativist begins with the empirical fact that there are numerous systems of customs and codes to be found in various societies. The Greek Sophist Protagoras (481–411 B.C.) was one of the first philosophers to observe in his travels that different societies do in fact have different customs that are morally binding upon their respective inhabitants. Protagoras thus began to understand the function of customs and codes: they serve to regulate and give cohesion to a society. He therefore concluded that within any particular society, its own set of customs and codes is right *for it* since they perform the very pragmatic function of enabling that society to operate with a greater degree of internal harmony. What is "right" is therefore what works in a society, and whatever "works" in a society is therefore right. Notions of right and wrong are therefore relative to a particular society, and they differ from one society to another.

Protagoras also noted a corollary to his relativism. If one is to spend time in other societies (as he and his fellow Sophists did), then one is morally obligated to obey the vital customs and codes of the societies he visits. "Who are we," he would ask, "to come as visitors to some society other than our own, bringing with us our own social customs and moral convictions which may be quite alien to that society, and then have the effrontery to claim that *our* customs and codes are the ones that are really right? Wouldn't such behavior serve to destroy the integrated system which that society has working for it? And wouldn't our actions therefore be immoral in the truest sense?" And isn't Protagoras right?

Relativists hold that one can make meaningful ethical decisions only in the social context in which an ethical problem occurs. In other words, what is right in one place or time may be wrong in another place or time. Infanticide may have been right in Caesar's time, but is not in twentieth-century Rome. Polygamy (but with not more than four wives) may be right in Cairo, but not in Tel Aviv. Sharing one's wife with an overnight guest may be right in an Eskimo igloo, but not in Middletown, U.S.A.

Ethical relativism may mean something else: that what is right for one person may be wrong for another. This, again, is merely the recognition of the fact that different people have different convictions and follow different customs. It is wrong for Jews and Muslims to eat pork; it is wrong for Jains to eat any animal flesh at all. But such restrictions do not apply to Christians, Shintos, or others outside the faith.

**3. CONTEXTUALISM** A third answer comes from the contextualist who believes, first, that moral laws of the kind held by the formalist don't exist. There are no rules that one can memorize ahead of time and apply meaningfully to a particular situation. Nor will the contextualist go along with the relativist. The contextualist will readily agree that societies do in fact possess different customs and codes, and that these perform the pragmatic function which the relativist claims they do. Granted: Romans practiced infanticide, Greeks practiced slavery, Cypriots practiced sacred prostitution, modern societies disenfranchise minorities, whole nations generate hate toward other nations—societies indeed do such things, but that doesn't make such practices ethically right. The fact that a practice exists doesn't make it moral. What societies actually do, therefore, is no guideline for deciding what is ethically right.

The contextualist holds that relevant criteria for making a meaningful ethical decision can be found only within the context of each concrete ethical problem. Every ethical situation is in fact unique, and a truly ethical solution to a problem can be arrived at only when *all the factors of the unique situation* can be weighed *by those involved in the problem.* Each person makes the best possible decision, using the best knowledge he or she possesses at that time of decision. Such a meaningful ethical judgment can be made only *after the problem situation exists,* not before.

Such ideas as "don't kill," "don't steal," and so forth, can be used as guidelines, but they must be abandoned if the specific situation calls for it. Dietrich Bonhoeffer phrased it eloquently: "Principles are only tools in God's hands soon to be thrown away as unserviceable." The same applies to formalistic rules, which may prove irrelevant to a particular set of conditions. In fact, the contextualist contends that moral predicaments constantly make it necessary for us to kill, steal, lie, or whatever, *to be moral.*

Implied in all this is one single guideline, which the contextualist uses in making all ethical decisions. That guideline is one's concern for the well-being of others. This principle can be developed in several ways. In *Situation Ethics,* Joseph Fletcher formulates it in terms of *agape,* the "ethical love" or "empathetic concern" that is the foundation of Christian ethics. Fletcher submits that only love is good, and rules are made to serve love, not the other way around. One who is truly involved in the well-being of another may be called upon to kill, to tell lies, or more; to carry through, in authentic action, loving concern for that other person. Again, the *rules* serve *love.* There are no laws that the contextualist will not finally break, if forced to, to manifest his or her ethical love for another. Just as Thoreau could say of civil law that if it "requires you to be the agent of injustice to another," then "break the law," the contextualist would say that if so-called moral laws require you to act unlovingly toward others, then break the "moral laws."

Contextualism can also be formulated in pragmatic terms. It is only our ethical concern for the well-being of others that produces a positive environment in which all of us can more fully actualize our lives. Qualities are contagious. Compassion and concern generate compassion and concern, just as hate generates hate and distrust generates distrust. Such basically human qualities as love, concern, and trust are the only qualities upon which a fulfilling collective existence can be grounded.

*Principles are only tools in God's hands, soon to be thrown away as unserviceable.*
DIETRICH BONHOEFFER

*I won't be wronged. I won't be insulted. I won't be laid a hand on. I don't do these things to other people. I require the same from them.*
*Gunman "J. B. Books" (John Wayne)*
*The Shootist*

*There slowly grew up in me an unshakable conviction that we have no right to inflict suffering and death on another living creature unless there is some unavoidable necessity for it, and that we ought all of us to feel what a horrible thing it is to cause suffering and death out of mere thoughtlessness.*

ALBERT SCHWEITZER

To summarize, therefore, the contextualist holds the following: (1) there are no universal moral laws; (2) ethical decisions can be made only in the context of concrete situations; and (3) there is a fundamental ethical guideline for all ethical behavior—one's authentic concern for the well-being of others.

Contextualism has significant implications. It recognizes accurately the nature of our moral predicaments. Our most agonizing ethical decisions must be made in situations where only *bad* alternatives are open to us. If daily life always set up situations so that we had to choose between a good option and a bad option, then moral existence would be simple. But actual-life situations continually force us into predicaments in which only various degrees of bad-consequence alternatives are open to choice. We may have to kill to save ourselves, a friend, an innocent victim; we may have to lie, to pretend, to play games to protect someone from serious damage.

Contextual ethics says that if, out of one's concern for the well-being of others, one makes the *best decision* he or she possibly can, then that person is unequivocally moral. If one must tell lies to save another then he or she has acted morally; not to have lied—to have allowed irreparable harm to come to another person—would have been immoral. Since this is the way that life forces us to make decisions, there is no justification for holding a person morally guilty for making the best decision possible in any given predicament.

By contrast, formalism and most forms of relativism have admitted that we often have to take bad action in a situation because good alternatives don't exist, but they also contend that this doesn't make the bad action right. *Having to do what is wrong doesn't make it right.* And having done wrong, *we should* feel guilt, and we may justly be subject to moral or civil recriminations. Contextualism responds that such a person is morally innocent and is, in fact, morally commendable. Having chosen the best options available, why should anyone be considered immoral?

## WHOM (AND WHAT) SHOULD I CARE ABOUT?

*The great fault of all ethics hitherto has been that they believed themselves to have to deal only with the relations of man to man. In reality, however, the question is what is his attitude to the world and all life that comes within his reach. A man is ethical only when life, as such, is sacred to him, that of plants and animals as that of his fellow men, and when he devotes himself helpfully to all life that is in need of help.*

ALBERT SCHWEITZER

The third question that one must answer is: *To whom (or what) do my moral obligations apply?* We must ask ourselves how large we are obligated to draw our circle of ethical concern. Should our ethical actions apply only to ourselves and to our primary groups such as family, clan, sect, or firm? Or do they extend to all the members of our tribe, nation, religion, or race? Do they extend to one's antagonist, attacker, enemy? Do they extend to all human beings? to all higher forms of life? to all organisms that share the impulse-to-life?

Historically, people have rather universally applied their codes of ethics only to their in-groups. Since groups are forever engaged in attempts to annihilate one another, survival demands that ethical niceties be suspended during wartime. Applied to one's own group, ethical obligations produce social cohesion, predictable and orderly behavior; they reduce internecine discord of all kinds and make it possible for a united group to fight other groups with greater efficiency. Hence—as Protagoras saw so clearly—ethical codes are pragmatic necessities.

Quite simply, ethical obligations practiced in the in-group don't apply to those outside; the out-group (historically, anyway) has never been the object of

## MORALITY VERSUS ETHICS

The NBC television series *High Chaparral* was popular in the late 1960s. In the following scene the accepted ethical code of the Old West was deliberately broken. The question is whether ethical codes ever *should* be broken, and, if so, how such behavior can be ethically or morally justified. In fact, this raises the question of exactly what "ethical codes" are.

In this episode a gunman Tulsa has extorted five thousand dollars from Big John Cannon by threatening to kill Cannon's brother Buck. Since Buck is hot-tempered, Tulsa knows he can needle Buck into a shootout in which he could easily outdraw him. John Cannon feels he has no choice but to pay the money, which he does. But Buck "steals" back the money and proceeds to the local saloon, thereby ensuring a confrontation with Tulsa's quick draw.

It's at this point that Buck decides to change the rules of the game. Buck is hunched over the bar when Tulsa comes for him in the Tucson saloon.

|  |  |
|---|---|
| TULSA: | Turn around, Buck. |
| BUCK: | Well, I tell you, Tulsa. If you wish to admit that *you* had made a mistake, and if *you* wish to crawl on out of here, I just might forget the whole thing. |
| TULSA: | I don't make mistakes. Turn around. |
| BUCK: | You sure? |
| TULSA: | *(Kicking back the chairs and screaming at Buck.)* Turn around! *(Buck turns slowly . . . with a derringer in his hand.)* What are you doin'? |
| BUCK: | Turnin' around, like you said. |
| TULSA: | That's murder, Buck. |
| BARTENDER: | Well, I think I'll go in the back room and check the stock. What I don't see I can't testify to. |
| BUCK: | All right, Mr. Tulsa. It is now your play. |
| TULSA: | It's murder, Buck. You gotta give me a chance. |
| BUCK: | I don't have to give you anything. |
| TULSA: | This ain't a fair fight! |

*CONTINUED*

*CONTINUED*

BUCK:    Fair. Hey, that's a good word. I bet you'd like for them to cut it on my tombstone, wouldn't you. "Here lies Buck Cannon, a *fair* man." But you know, I'd sooner end up standin' over your grave, and people whisperin' behind their hands. "That's Buck Cannon. He don' fight fair."

TULSA:   Never figured you for a coward.

BUCK:    Well, you live and you learn. I jus' don' want to die. That's the thing about a man like you. You're so ready to kill, you must be ready to die too. It's jus' the other side o' the coin, isn't it?

TULSA:   You gotta give me an even chance.

BUCK:    Who's gonna say it wasn't a *fair* fight. There's only you and me, and you'll be dead.

TULSA:   Buck, I don't believe you'd do it. *(A shot from the derringer in Buck's hand. Tulsa is wounded in his right shoulder.)*

BUCK:    Aim must be off. Now it's a fair fight. Draw. Whenever you're ready.

TULSA:   *(His gun arm is half-paralyzed and trembling.)* No! This ain't fair.

BUCK:    Tough.

TULSA:   *(Throws gun down.)* You kill an unarmed man and that's murder.

JOHN CANNON: *(From background.)* He's right, Buck.

BUCK:    Well, then, get out.

TULSA:   It ain't over, Buck.

BUCK:    Sure it is, Tulsa. For now anyways.

TULSA:   We'll meet again, I promise you.

BUCK:    It might happen. But jus' remember, I'm not as fast as you. I won't draw against you. So I just might have to back-shoot you next time.

TULSA:   I believe you would, too.

BUCK:    Try me. *(Tulsa backs out and leaves saloon. Others crowd in. John comes over and leans on the bar beside Buck.)* You know what, John? I don' fight fair.

JOHN:    You know what, Buck? Nobody's goin' to hold it against you. He *would* have killed you.

BUCK:    C'mon, I'll ride back to Chaparral with you. All of a sudden, I feel . . . tired.

---

*I remember on the trip home on Apollo 11 it suddenly struck me that that tiny pea, pretty and blue, was the earth. I put up my thumb and shut one eye, and my thumb blotted out the planet earth. I didn't feel like a giant. I felt very, very small.*

NEIL ARMSTRONG

serious ethical concern. This distinction between out-group and in-group, with a code governing behavior in the in-group, is merely one aspect of the whole evolutionary arrangement. From prairie dogs and baboons to humans, in-group behavior is clearly prescribed, while behavior toward all out-groups is a matter of expediency: whatever aids survival is good/moral/right/just/virtuous—and necessary!

Since conditions on "spaceship earth" are rapidly changing, this question needs continual reexploration. Although in-group consciousness continues, and will continue, in countless forms, we need to ask whether, in a shrinking world, one's circle of obligations must be extended for purely pragmatic reasons. In the world of the nineties, traditional in-groups are being broken down and their constituents constantly rearranged.

Increasing numbers of people are thinking of the whole human species as a single in-group. If we should be attacked by extraterrestrials, the feeling of humanity's oneness would immediately surface, and for the same old reason: unite to survive. But lacking an obvious antagonist, the unity of the human species is not yet a world-fact, though sought by some and intuited by many more.

The belief that all people comprise a single *ethical* community is not new. The Stoics taught that all men are subject to the same natural and moral laws, and that they should therefore be subject to the same civil laws. People should belong to a *cosmopolis*—a "world-city"—and should not be artifically broken up into tribes and states with different laws. Some branches of Christianity and

Islam have developed similar concepts, and Jesus' mandate that we love even our enemies would, in effect, annihilate all boundaries between people.

Do our ethical obligations extend further yet? Do they extend to the higher animals? (Do they extend to our pets?) Do they extend to all animal life? The Hindus and Jains have always believed so. Do we have moral obligations to plants? to all of nature? The American Indians believe that we do. (See the words of the old Wintu holy woman in the box on p. 430.)

Exactly how does one finally decide how wide his circle of ethical concern should extend?

*The only devils in the world are those running around in our own hearts.*

**Gandhi (motion picture)**

Ethical affirmation of life is the intellectual act by which man ceases simply to live at random and begins to concern himself reverently with his own life, so that he may realize its true value. And the first step in the evolution of ethics is a sense of solidarity with other human beings.

To the primitive, this solidarity has narrow limits. It is confined, first to his blood relations, then to the members of his tribe, who represent to him the family enlarged. I have such primitives in my hospital. If I ask an ambulatory patient to undertake some small service for a patient who must stay in bed, he will do it only if the bedridden patient belongs to his tribe. If that is not the case, he will answer me with wide-eyed innocence: "This man is not brother of me." Neither rewards nor threats will induce him to perform a service for such a stranger.

But as soon as man begins to reflect upon himself and his relationship to others, he becomes aware that men as such are his equals and his neighbors. Gradually he sees the circle of his responsibilities widening until it includes all human beings with whom he has dealings. . . . The idea of the brotherhood of all human beings is inherent in the metaphysics of most of the great religious systems. Moreover, since antiquity, philosophy has presented the case for humanitarianism as a concept recommended by reason.

Throughout history, however, the insight that we have a wider duty toward human beings has never attained the dominance to which it is entitled. Down to our own times it has been undermined by differences of race, religion, and nationality.

Man belongs to man.

ALBERT SCHWEITZER

## REFLECTIONS

1   What is the difference between a fact-claim and a value judgment? By way of review, how do you go about checking the truth of a fact-claim? (See Chapter 3–4.) How do you go about checking out value judgments?

2   The most significant ethical choice that we make is deciding if we will approach a problem as a formalist, a relativist, or a contextualist. All our ethical problems are seen, interpreted, and resolved from one of these positions, or combinations of them. So, before proceeding further, think about how each of these schools analyzes an ethical problem. Work on each until it is succinct and clear.

3   Return to the case studies (pp. 364–366) and zero in on each problem. How would the formalist, relativist, and contextualist analyze and resolve the problem in each case?

4   Summarize in your words the basic tenets of the formalist, relativist, and contextual approaches. What are the strengths and the weaknesses of each system? In which school of ethics do you personally feel most comfortable?

5   After working through the case studies (as suggested in number 3, above), what are your most significant ethical conclusions? Can killing, stealing, lying, and so forth, be ethically and/or morally justified? Are your solutions ones that you can live with and practice—at least for now?

6   What is your personal answer to the first ethical question (pp. 367–368); "Who is to make the ethical decision?" Do you accept Sartre's contention that *all* ethical decisions are autonomous since only *persons* make decisions?

7   Buck Cannon believes that he broke an ethical code which he *should* have obeyed. "I don't fight fair," he grumbled. Yet we can be sure he felt a sense of justice about what he had done. How can you reconcile these two feelings? Can you justify ethically and/or morally what Buck Cannon did? In this episode there is a distinct difference between *being ethical* and *being moral*. What is that difference? *Who* was ethical and *who* was moral? Explain why.

8   To the question, "To whom (or what) do my moral obligations apply?" (pp. 372–376), what is your personal answer? Do they apply to your pet animals? to wild animals? to all living things? Does Schweitzer's "Reverence for Life" appeal to you as a solution to this problem? (See p. 376 and marginal quote on p. 372. See also pp. 446–450.)

9   Return to the first page of this chapter and spend some leisurely thought on Seng Ts'an's counsel that we "be not concerned with right and wrong." What is Seng Ts'an trying to say to us?

*It must not be forgotten that although a high standard of morality gives a slight or no advantage to each individual man and his children over the other men of the same tribe, yet an advancement in the standard of morality will certainly give an immense advantage to one tribe over another.*

CHARLES DARWIN

*"Chi Wen Tzu used to think thrice before acting. The master hearing of it said, 'Twice is quite enough.'"*

CONFUCIUS
*Analects*

*"Don't be silly, Ninety-nine. We have to shoot, kill, and destroy. We represent everything that's wholesome and good in the world."*

*"Maxwell Smart," Get Smart*

# BARUCH SPINOZA

## *The God-Intoxicated Philosopher*

In the seventeenth century, it was said that Amsterdam was a Protestant city with a Jewish heart. That heart was the Jewish ghetto, out of which came one of the most honored of all Western philosophers, Baruch Spinoza: "the noblest and most lovable of the great philosophers" (Russell); "the holy and excommunicated Spinoza" (Schleiermacher); "the god-intoxicated man" (Novalis). "There is no other philosophy than Spinoza's" (Lessing). "To be a philosopher one must first be a Spinozist" (Hegel). "No man has ever lived closer to what he himself taught" (W. T. Jones). "Nietzsche says somewhere that the last Christian died upon the cross. He had forgotten Spinoza" (Durant).

The ghetto existed in Holland's free atmosphere as a result of the flight of Jews from the Inquisition in Spain and Portugal. Spinoza's grandfather and father had fled persecution, had settled and prospered in Holland. His father Miguel de Espinoza was a merchant and a pillar of the synagogue. His mother was Hana Debora, Miguel's second wife, also from Lisbon. She was a bright, quiet, somber woman who died of tuberculosis when Spinoza was six, bequeathing her illness to her son. The child was raised by Miguel's third wife.

Spinoza was born and raised in Amsterdam and never traveled beyond the borders of his native Holland. Educated first in the synagogue school, he became thoroughly knowledgeable in the thought and literature of his heritage —scriptures, the Talmud, medieval commentators and philosophers, and even the secrets of the kabala, which fascinated but repelled his rational intellect. To all this was added a good grounding in the sciences, mathematics, and geometry; he was profoundly moved by Descartes' attempt to give a geometrical structure to all knowledge. A natural linguist, he was fluent in Spanish, Portuguese, Dutch, Hebrew, and Latin and had a working knowledge of Greek, French, Italian, and (probably) German. He learned his Latin by attending the Latin school of a Dutch scholar, Frans van den Ende. He studied the Greek philosophers (he loved the Stoics), the scholastics, and Catholic theology. He was always brilliant in his scholarship, and his father, family, and rabbis cherished the hope that young Spinoza would make significant contributions to Judaic learning.

Romance touched his life once. He fell in love with his Latin teacher's daughter, Clara Marie, who assisted her father in Spinoza's Latin lessons. She was bright, feminine, and on the verge of becoming a woman. Spinoza, increasingly dedicated to Latin, clearly had marriage in mind; but a mutual love failed to develop and she married one of his fellow students instead. Years later he still spoke of her with affection.

By the time Spinoza was twenty, he was thinking his own thoughts. He had for years been absorbing the ideas of the great minds of the Western tradition; he had read every point of view, played with ideas lovingly, and discovered that in the world of the mind he was free. The safe and single path—the uncritical submission to orthodox doctrine—was, for him, no longer an option. His thinking had become unshackled. He soared, without boundaries; and in his thoughts he traveled to the far corners of the intellectual world.

Spinoza pondered and questioned what he had been taught in the synagogue. There were contradictions in scripture. He doubted whether Moses had written the entire Torah, especially the passage that narrated his own death. Some of the hate-filled passages of scripture, he suggested, were only allegories. He had begun to wonder too openly whether God exists, whether there is an afterlife, and where the universe came from; what the relationship is of God to cosmic matter, whether angels exist, where in the body the soul is located. Biblical miracles, he thought, were probably natural events mythologized by imagination. For Spinoza, reason is the trustworthy path to truth, however much it may come into conflict with authoritarian claims.

The rabbis of the synagogue were not unsympathetic to the young Jew's intellectual flights and were willing to conciliate; but they had to concern themselves with the safety of their community. They were there at the sufferance of the Calvinist Dutch government and people, who were easily threatened by heretical opinions, doubly so should they arise from a barely tolerated minority. So the leaders of the community asked Spinoza to be discreet; if he couldn't stop thinking, he might at least mute his public statements of doubt and dissent. They summoned him, tried to reason with him, offered him a stipend if he would consent to silence. But he was beyond negotiation. He became more resolute, more articulate, and a cause célèbre. A reactionary member of his own faith attempted one night to kill him on the streets, but Spinoza ducked and the assailant's knife only cut his coat.

Feeling they had no recourse, the leaders of the synagogue proceeded against Spinoza with full excommunication, July 24, 1626. He was twenty-three. The solemn ceremony was held in the synagogue; the ritual was read aloud to the blowing of the ram's horn and the burning of black altar candles. During the recitation the lights were extinguished one by one till the congregation sat silently in darkness.

Spinoza was "anathematized" and severed forever "from the people of Israel." The malediction called for him to be cursed in the sight of God. No one could talk with him or communicate with him in writing, or read anything he had written. No one could come within six feet of him, touch him, or stay under the same roof with him. Disowned by family, mentors and teachers, and friends, in the eyes of the community of Israel he was henceforth dead, a non-person, condemned to a new life. As a symbol of his translation, he changed his first name from Hebrew into Latin: "Baruch" became "Benedictus"—meaning "blessed" in both languages.

For the rest of his short life Spinoza lived modestly in Protestant communities and with friends, first on the outskirts of Amsterdam, then in Leyden, and

*God and all the attributes of God are eternal.*

*FOOTNOTE TO SPINOZA:*
*Language usually makes Nature feminine and God masculine; by identifying them Spinoza does more justice to the female or productive principle in reality. Perhaps the masculinization of God was part of the patriarchal subordination of woman, who is, after all, the main stream of human reality.*

WILL DURANT

*Men govern nothing with more difficulty than their tongues.*

*"With the judgment of the angels and the sentence of the saints, we anathematize, execrate, curse and cast out Baruch de Espinoza . . ."*

THE AMSTERDAM SYNAGOGUE
*(Ritual of Excommunication)*

*. . . The more we understand individual objects, the more we understand God.*

*We do not strive for, wish, seek, or desire anything because we think it to be good; we judge a thing to be good because we . . . desire it.*

*A free man thinks of nothing less than of death, and his wisdom is a meditation not on death but on life.*

*The endeavor to understand is the first and only basis of virtue.*

*Men under the guidance of reason . . . desire nothing for themselves which they do not also desire for the rest of mankind.*

*Fear cannot be without hope nor hope without fear.*

finally in the capital city, The Hague. He wrote continuously but published only two works during his lifetime. He had suffered enough, and any word that he might publish brought an outcry of hostility, which he chose to avoid. Still, his writing and ideas became widely known. He developed friends everywhere, and gradually some of the great spirits of his age joined his circle.

Spinoza's life lacked all the fashionable color and excitement; it was an adventure of the mind. He refused to argue, speak in public, or attend society or salons. He remained by himself or with friends, working quietly, thinking and writing, conversing and exchanging ideas. He earned his living primarily by grinding and polishing lenses, supplementing his small income by teaching and making sketches. As his fame increased he had numerous offers of money and gifts, most of which he declined.

Spinoza was a handsome figure, with a gentle, kindly, sad face. He had a dark olive complexion, black hair, and great sensitive black eyes. He was of medium height, and slender. He dressed carefully but plainly. His lifestyle was simple. He had a substantial library, and his supreme enjoyments were to share an evening with friends, smoke his pipe, and read. He had virtually no pride, never sought prestige, never indulged in self-aggrandisement. He was patient, cheerful and friendly, serene, and shy. All in all, he was a Buddhist monk in an alien place and time.

◆

Those who have wrestled with Spinoza's *Ethics* commonly emerge with glowing praise and/or bewilderment. His "system of morals is the supreme achievement of modern thought," the "most precious production in modern philosophy," the "noblest work to grace a human pen," and so on. Its full title in Latin is *Ethica ordine geometrica demonstrata*, so named because he wanted to

develop a philosophical system with the clarity of geometric logic, proceeding sequentially from precise assumptions (definitions, axioms, propositions) to absolutely certain conclusions. He was following Descartes' method but went far beyond him.

The *Ethics* is divided into three parts. The first, "On the Nature of God," deals with metaphysics. God, in Spinoza's reasoning, is not an anthropomorphic father-figure who gets uptight about petty human foibles. (He abandoned this image along with his orthodox Judaic heritage). Rather, God is the "substance" of the world, not the physical "matter," not "nature"—but the "essence" or "being" that underlies both material and non-material reality. This divine substance is known to humans in two ways (as two "attributes")—as matter and mind. (As you're reading these words, you are experiencing both attributes: your mind as consciousness and this page as physical matter; both are merely "attributes" of the underlying substance which is God.) Furthermore, God does not *give* laws to nature: God *is* the laws of nature. Nature, therefore, appears rational to our minds (as "physics"), for God *is* rational, and (as Hegel would later phrase it) the real is rational, and the rational is real.

The second part of *Ethics* concerns psychology—the science of understanding the mind. Spinoza attempts to heal and make whole the human person by reversing Descartes' mind–body dualism. Spinoza argues that the body (seen from the outside) and the mind (perceived inwardly) are a unity—one organism working for survival. When the mind thinks a thought, it isn't the mind that thinks it—as though the mind were a discarnate consciousness operating by itself; rather, the body thinks the thought and the mind is aware of it as it's being thought. (The mind is a TV monitor watching the body as it is thinking.)

Spinoza observed that the elemental drive of each organism is self-preservation. ". . . Each man should love himself, and seek what is useful to him. . . . Each one should endeavor to preserve his being as far as in him lies." All thought is for survival, and any thought that helps one survive is good. "No virtue can be conceived as prior to this endeavor to preserve one's own being." Here is an evolutionary ethic two centuries before evolution.

Each person is powered by reason and emotion. Emotions become "passions" when we fail to understand our emotions and allow them to become manipulated by external circumstance. One function of the rational mind is to develop the power of reason over the emotions since "the more an emotion becomes known to us, the more it is within our power." Our emotional needs are to be acknowledged and met, to be sure; but it is the intellect that must select *which* are to be met and *how* they are to be met. Our goal is to become autonomous, and to do this we must use our reason, deciding which of our emotions and desires we will act on—this is an act of the intelligence. The wise man will maximize pleasure and minimize pain, for himself and others.

.   For those who see the oneness of all things, there cannot be multiple points-of-view. Separateness is the result of "inadequate ideas"—incomplete understanding. For all that exists is One. The universe is one, Mankind is one, and each of us is not a duality but a single, whole organism. We are all expressions of God/natural law working in us. God and nature are one. Mind and body are one. Science and religion are one. All antagonisms and limited perspectives are the result of our mental schematics which fail to recognize that God *is* everything working to express himself.

Spinoza moved to The Hague in 1670 and spent the last years of his life in a one-room apartment on the top floor of a rented house. The room had a high-beamed ceiling, wood paneling, and one wide window. He slept in a fold-away bed. This was his last home. (The dwelling—known as "Spinoza-haus"—is now preserved as a historical monument.)

Here he worked steadily on books and letters, sometimes laboring for weeks or months before going out. Still, it wasn't the life of a recluse; he was visited continually by friends, followers, and dignitaries. He conversed knowledgeably on virtually any subject, especially on social and political events. Many of his friends were Protestants, and he occasionally attended church services with them and listened to sermons. In 1673 the University of Heidelberg offered him a teaching chair in philosophy, but he declined the offer. He said he preferred his freedom.

By this date his magnum opus, the *Ethics,* was almost complete, and he considered having it published; but publication of his work was banned and religious opposition to his ideas was so virulent that he put his manuscript back into his desk, where it remained until after his death.

The dust from his lens-grinding had long been damaging his consumptive lungs, and he found breathing increasingly difficult. For a chronic cough he sipped an elixir of rose leaves. On Sunday, February 20, 1677, he died, quietly, with only his physician by his side. His friends had gone to church. In the funeral cortège six carriages with many notables followed his coffin. He was buried in a Protestant cemetery in The Hague.

# THE PROTOPLASMIC VENTURE

*"Are you happy? Why did you do all this, why did*
*you struggle so hard. . . .?"*
*"Why! For what!" Nikolaiev leaned forward and one sensed a*
*sort of heraldic thunder rumbling in him. "Why, to*
*be more. What else is life for? To develop all your possibilities.*
*That is happiness, to love what you're doing, to keep*
*expanding, to keep turning into something more."*

OSTRANDER AND SCHROEDER

6

## THE FOUR GREAT ETIOLOGICAL QUESTIONS

During the past four decades scientists working in the field of biochemical evolution have made a quantum-leap breakthrough. They have succeeded in laying the empirical foundations for answering one of the persistent questions raised by the human mind: *What is the origin of life?* And, as so often happens after the mind is fortified with facts, we look back and say, "Of course! Now the answer is beginning to make sense. *I understand!*"

This sort of philosophic question is not one of the common garden variety. It's one of the four great etiological questions that have baffled and irritated human understanding. These four questions are: What is the origin of *life,* of *humans,* of *matter,* and of *the universe?* These problems have appeared, from the beginning, to be Gordian knots that the human intellect could not cut.

We had good reason to feel stymied. None of these questions could be answered until enormous amounts of scientific knowledge had been gathered and correlated. Before Western science had reached the stages of intense specialization and, subsequently, interdisciplinary synthesis, any answers to these etiological questions had to be mythical. Humanity was caught in the perennial human predicament. We couldn't stop asking the questions, yet we possessed no factual knowledge that would lead us to the understanding that our collective psyche demanded.

So these questions were dispatched with celebrated pragmatic myths. *Whence human beings?* We were created from white, red, and brown clay; or we were sculpted from rock, or carved from wood, or assembled from pine bark, turquoise chips, and crow feathers. We were created by Tiki, Juok, i Kombengi, Yahweh, or one of a thousand other anthropomorphic creators.

And *whence matter? Whence the universe?* On these two etiological puzzles little could be said. Matter apparently exists eternally, shaped into familiar

*It has taken the planet Earth 4.5 billion years to discover it is 4.5 billion years old. . . .*
GEORGE WALD

*This secret spoke Life herself unto me: "Behold," said she, "I am that which must ever surpass itself."*
FRIEDRICH NIETZSCHE

*Life is not one of the fundamental categories of the universe, like matter, energy, and time, but is a manifestation of certain molecular combinations. These combinations cannot have existed forever, since even the elements of which they are composed have not always existed. Therefore life must have had a beginning.*
PHILIP HANDLER *(ed.)*
**Biology and the Future of Man**

forms by a Demiurge; or a supernatural X-factor created everything in the universe *ex nihilo*, out of nothing. Even when critical minds tried to think carefully about the cosmos, there was still very nearly nothing to be thought. Aristotle is typical. His notion of an Unmoved Mover—the First Domino in an infinite series—was the only near-logical answer to the problem that he could come up with. Virtually no progress was made on any of these problems until the twentieth century.

As of 1990, however, two of these wild dragons—the origins of life and of man—have been domesticated: the rough outlines of an empirical answer are now clear. And the other two—the origins of matter and the universe—have been tamed: viable questions and empirical models are beginning to be developed.

*The alphabet of life is obviously extremely simple—a handful of chemicals are responsible for the vast variety we see in the entire biosphere.*

CYRIL PONNAMPERUMA

Steam from the boiling water in the lower left chamber circulates upward through a mixture of ammonia, methane, and hydrogen; then over and down into the larger chamber containing electrodes. After a week of electrical sparking the water in the tube at bottom had accumulated a variety of amino acids and other organic compounds.

Gases

Condenser

Water containing organic compounds

## BIOCHEMICAL EVOLUTION

The beginnings of the science of biochemical evolution are associated with the work of three men.

In 1922 a Russian biochemist, Alexander Oparin, delivered before a group of scientists in Moscow a paper outlining his theory of biogenesis. Two years later he published his thoughts in a booklet entitled *The Origin of Life*. In 1928 the English biologist J. B. S. Haldane published a technical paper with a similar line of thinking. Both men developed coherent theoretical models from their knowledge of physics and biochemistry, but there was as yet no empirical evidence to support their speculations. Then in 1953 the American biochemist Stanley Miller performed experiments that began to lay empirical foundations for an understanding of how life evolves.

Oparin had theorized that in the earth's early stages a variety of organic compounds had already developed out of inorganic materials. He described theoretically how these compounds could develop into the first prevital organisms and then into living things. As the crust of the earth began to form and the temperature of the atmosphere dropped below a thousand degrees centigrade, a variety of chemical reactions took place. Torrential rains poured down upon the young planet, accompanied by constant discharges of lightning. Hot pools of water formed containing organic compounds that washed down from the atmosphere. Most important, Oparin thought, were the carbon bonds that formed in ever-larger molecular chains. Fatty acids, sugars, and tannins could have formed in this way. Eventually amino acids, the basic constituents of proteins, could have been naturally synthesized.

Thus, during the first phase of earth's history—perhaps a billion years—mixtures of hydrocarbons, nitrogen, hydrogen, and ammonia were continually producing an endless variety of organic compounds that formed complex molecules that became the building-blocks of living cells. At this stage the earth was covered with what Haldane called a "hot dilute soup" in which these prebiotic reactions were taking place. With the synthesis of proteins the first steps had been taken toward the development of life.

The first empirical evidence that Oparin's theory might be correct came from Miller's experiments at the University of Chicago. Into a simple glass

# GEOLOGIC TIME SCALE

| ERA | PERIOD | | EPOCH | YEARS BEFORE THE PRESENT |
|-----|--------|---|-------|--------------------------|
| Cenozoic | Quarternary | | Holocene (Recent) | |
| | | | | 11,000 |
| | | | Pleistocene (Glacial) | |
| | | | | 500,000 to 2,000,000 |
| | Tertiary | | Pliocene | |
| | | | | 13,000,000 |
| | | | Miocene | |
| | | | | 25,000,000 |
| | | | Oligocene | |
| | | | | 36,000,000 |
| | | | Eocene | |
| | | | | 58,000,000 |
| | | | Paleocene | |
| | | | | 63,000,000 |
| Mesozoic | Cretaceous | | | |
| | | | | 135,000,000 |
| | Jurassic | | | |
| | | | | 180,000,000 |
| | Triassic | | | |
| | | | | 230,000,000 |
| Paleozoic | Permian | | | |
| | | | | 280,000,000 |
| | Carboniferous | Pennsylvanian (Upper Carboniferous) | | |
| | | | | 310,000,000 |
| | | Mississippian (Lower Carboniferous) | | |
| | | | | 345,000,000 |
| | Devonian | | | |
| | | | | 405,000,000 |
| | Silurian | | | |
| | | | | 425,000,000 |
| | Ordovician | | | |
| | | | | 500,000,000 |
| | Cambrian | | | |
| | | | | 600,000,000 |
| Precambrian | | | | |

Dr. Stanley Miller

*According to one of the most fundamental laws of physics, the universal tendency in the world of matter is for everything to run downhill, to fall to the lowest possible level of tension, with constant loss of potential energy and of organization. In contrast, life constantly creates and maintains order out of the randomness of matter. To apprehend the deep significance of this fact one need only think what happens to any living organism—the very smallest as well as the largest and most evolved—when finally it dies.*

RENÉ DUBOS

*Life is an offensive directed against the repetitious mechanism of the universe.*

ALFRED NORTH WHITEHEAD

*People used to think that the primeval elements had to sit around in the ocean for millions of years before something happened. We now know that once the right molecules accumulated at the right time and in the right arrangement, life could begin almost instantaneously. Evolution is what takes time.*

CYRIL PONNAMPERUMA

apparatus Miller introduced methane, ammonia, and hydrogen. The one essential ingredient of life—carbon—was there in the methane ($CH_4$). As these chemicals mixed with vapor from boiling water and passed through glass tubes, they flowed across two tungsten electrodes generating a continuous electric spark. All this was designed to simulate hypothetical primitive-earth conditions—the circulating gases represented the early atmosphere, the flask of boiling liquids represented the young oceans. The experiment ran continuously for a week. At the end of that time, the gases were pumped out and the brownish liquids were analyzed. He found that a variety of organic compounds had formed along with several amino acids. Miller notes that one of the unexpected results was that "the major products were not themselves a random selection of organic compounds but included a surprising number of substances that occur in living organisms."

Since 1953 Miller and other scientists have added a vast amount of supporting data. Various gaseous mixtures have been tried along with other forms of energy, and in every case biochemically significant molecules were synthesized.

Many specific ingredients essential to living things have now been formed in the laboratory under possible primitive-earth conditions. These include the creation of carbon chains, polypeptides, and ATP, a catalytic enzyme that supplies the basic source of metabolic energy in living systems.

Significant also is the laboratory creation of porphyrins, molecules that function like plants in being able to utilize light to store energy—a primitive kind of photosynthesis. Miller believes that "almost certainly they became important for the metabolic processes leading to ATP synthesis early in the evolution of life." This supports the suggestion that photosynthesizing cells were among the earliest forms of life.

Another biochemist, Sidney Fox, synthesized microspheres, which he named "proteinoids" because they looked and behaved so much like living protein cells. They possessed a double-layered surface analogous to a membrane, and they carried on a kind of internal enzyme activity. Like living cells, they were sufficiently stable to permit sectioning and staining for microscopic examination. Most significantly, they performed a sort of reproduction. When left standing for a week in liquid the spheres formed small attached minispheres or "buds" that could be split off from the parent-spheres. These would proceed to grow to the size of the original cells by the ingestion of selected substances, and then stop growing. In a few days these "offspring" would produce their own "buds" and replication would continue.

Another significant achievement has been the synthesis of the purines and pyrimidines. The five strategic nucleic acid bases have been formed: adenine and guanine, cytosine, uracil, and thymine. In turn these purines and pyrimidines have been joined with sugars and phosphates to create nucleotides, the basic links in the DNA gene codes for all living things on earth. Furthermore, it has been shown that these molecules could have formed with comparative ease on the primitive earth.

In 1975 the first laboratory synthesis of a complete mammalian gene was accomplished. It was a relatively simple hemoglobin gene composed of 650 nucleotides. The report of the event in *Science News* carried the comment: "It's hard to believe that in a swift quarter-century, biologists have made the quantum leap from the identification of hereditary material to its synthesis. Yet that is precisely what has happened."

While such descriptions sound as though these experiments are producing live organisms, it must be emphasized that they are not living—yet. All these achievements are only stepping-stones toward the complexity required for the laboratory synthesis of true living organisms.

One of the world's foremost biochemists, Cyril Ponnamperuma, is at once hopeful and realistic in assessing the future of biochemical evolution. "There is no reason to doubt that we shall rediscover, one by one, the essential conditions which once determined, and directed, the course of chemical evolution. We may even reproduce the intermediate steps in the laboratory. Looking back on the biochemical understanding gained during the span of one human generation, we have the right to be quite optimis-

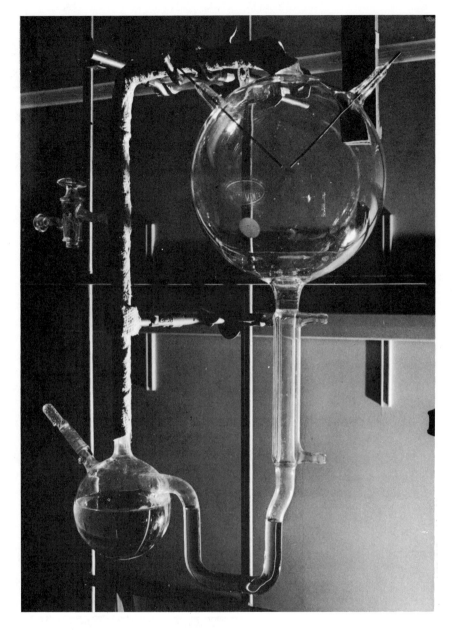

tic. In contrast to unconscious nature, which had to spend billions of years for the creation of life, conscious nature has a purpose and knows the outcome."

Many of the sequential steps in the development of living organisms are not yet known. Much more work will be necessary to close the gaps in our knowledge.

We would like to know more about the time scale for the origin of life during the period from the earth's beginning to those first known microscopic organisms which lived some 3.5 billion years ago. During that one-billion-year gap, how long did it take for living cells to develop? Did it happen once or many times? Is the creation of life in such a manner still taking place today? We would also like to know something about the rates of evolution of these

It was in this glass apparatus that Dr. Stanley Miller produced the first empirical evidence supporting the theory that living organisms may have resulted from the combinations of various chemical compounds.

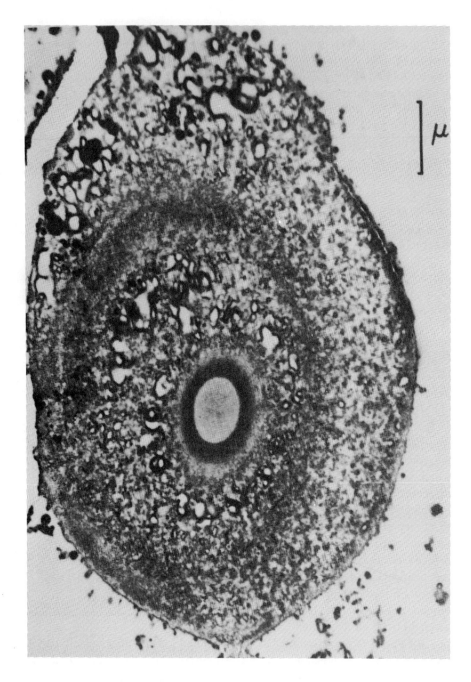

Microsphere synthesized by Dr. Sidney Fox at the University of Miami's Institute for Molecular and Cellular Evolution.

primitive organisms. How long did the blue-green algae float around in the "hot thin soup" before complex life-forms developed?

The most complex problem still facing biogenetic theorists is to reconstruct the evolution of the *genetic mechanics* by which cells replicate themselves. During the nineties, scientists will be working to show how the DNA code was synthesized from nucleic acids.

In 1957 Dr. George Wald, a Harvard biologist, stated that he was sure that we will have produced life in the laboratory within fifty years. Today most scientists would agree that we are probably on schedule.

## The Beginning of Life on Earth

When did life begin on the planet earth?

The solar system was born about 5 billion years ago, and about a half-billion years later our planet had become a dense, round, hot ball, still inhospitable and forbidding.

From the fossil record we know that the first hard-shelled animals emerged in the late Precambrian era about 700 million years ago and continued to diversify in an explosion of species throughout the Cambrian period (beginning about 600 million years ago). Traces of these life-forms are easily found since they had reached an advanced stage of evolution when their hard shells could leave a fossil record. Soft parts dissolved, of course, and left no trace.

We can be quite sure that soft-bodied animals, including countless species of single-celled organisms, had by this time passed through a long history of evolutionary development. But they have successfully eluded fossil hunters.

The oldest known forms of life are algalike cells that lived some 3.5 billion years ago. These cells were capable of green-plant photosynthesis. Chances are that this process had been going on for some time, but no earlier record has been found.

When, then, did life begin? The fossil records indicate that life developed sometime between 4.5 billion years ago—when the earth was formed—and 3.5 billion years ago—with our earliest record of microfossils. During that one-billion-year period, some wonderful and incredible events were taking place.

We have sufficient knowledge now to make informed guesses about some of those events, and here begins one of the exciting stories in the history of human knowledge.

## Earth's Life-Forms: An Inventory

Since the time that living organisms first emerged from the "hot thin soup," the proliferation of species on our planet staggers the imagination. Taxonomists—those ever-patient classifiers—have so far discovered, ordered, and described about 1.5 million species of living organisms, and some ten thousand new species are added annually to the list.

To date they have recognized some eighty-six hundred species of birds and one hundred fifty thousand species of marine organisms, including nearly twenty-five thousand species of fishes. Yet at least a third of the planet's fishes are still unknown to science. Some three-quarters of a million species of insects are recorded and six to seven thousand new ones are added yearly. The higher vertebrates are mostly accounted for, but the invertebrates are relatively unknown, especially the mites, nematodes, worms, and parasites, which total hundreds of thousands.

About a half-million higher plants have been classified, but taxonomists

*The universality of the genetic code and the related fact that the nucleic acids and proteins of all species are built out of the same building blocks lead to the conclusion that all known organisms are fundamentally the same. Despite appearances, there is only one form of life on the earth.*

**Biology and the Future of Man**

*The raw materials of life are assumed to have been hydrogen, helium, carbon, nitrogen, and oxygen, the same elements now found in the sun and the stars. . . . Dr. Ponnamperuma observes that "the aphorism that we are the stuff of which stars are made" it more than rhetoric.*

**Irene Kiefer**

Occam's Razor
**Pluralitas non est ponenda sine necessitate.**
*Don't create more hypotheses than are really necessary.*
*OR: The simplest explanation that will fit the facts is probably the best.*

**William of Occam**

Abel's Razor
**Theoria non delenda praeter necessitatem.**
*Razors should not be thrown away as long as they give a fairly decent shave, or until you have a better one.*

**Reuben Abel**

## THE MURCHISON METEORITE

Just before noon on September 28, 1969, a bright flash was seen in the sky near Murchison, a small town about 85 miles north of Melbourne, Australia. An object exploded in the sky, and 180 pounds of meteorite fragments fell to the ground. Not long after, [Dr. Cyril] Ponnamperuma received a telegram from the Smithsonian's Center for Short-lived Phenomena notifying him of the meteorite's fall. He had worked with meteorites years before but had given up because of the contamination problem. Now, because of the precise and contamination-proof techniques developed by him for analyzing the moon rocks and a freshly fallen sample, Ponnamperuma was anxious to tackle meteorites again.

A number of stones were soon on their way to him at Ames Research center near San Francisco. Analyzing a core sample from a stone having the fewest cracks and the least exterior contamination, he detected 18 amino acids. Twelve are not found in proteins made on Earth, so their presence indicates they must be of extraterrestrial origin.

The other six amino acids are commonly found on Earth—with a slight, but very important difference. Waves of natural light, which radiate in many planes, can be polarized into one plane by passing them through a prism. When polarized light is passed through amino acids, it is rotated slightly to the right or left. With extremely rare exceptions (the cell walls of certain bacteria), amino acids found in the proteins of living organisms rotate light only to the left. Outside the living world, all molecules showing optical activity consist of equal amounts of left-handed and right-handed forms, which are mirror images of each other. But life on Earth uses only one form, and that is the left-handed form. Ponnamperuma explains: "A large, sound and sturdy protein molecule just couldn't be made by using both forms—it's like trying to put a right foot into a left shoe. We don't know why nature chose left."

In contrast to the one form found in proteins, the Murchison meteorite's protein amino acids are almost equally divided between left-handed and right-handed, additional evidence that the amino acids are not the results of earthly contamination. Ponnamperuma believes that the mixture was formed in one of the steps of chemical evolution, and he terms his findings "probably the first conclusive evidence of chemical evolution occurring elsewhere in the universe."

IRENE KIEFER
*The Smithsonian*, May, 1972

estimate that a quarter-million species are still unknown, especially in the tropical climates. Lower plants, such as fungi, have hardly been touched.

It is estimated that on our planet perhaps 10 million species of organisms exist today, yet this number is less than 1 percent of all the species that have existed on earth since life began.

Almost all animal phyla with preservable hard parts are represented in the fossil record from late Precambrian times onward, but millions of soft-bodied species doubtless lived before this but left no trace. Scientists guess that perhaps one out of five thousand to ten thousand extinct species show up in the fossil record.

All told then, how many species has evolution produced on earth since the planet's beginning? The staggering figure is in the vicinity of 10 billion.

## BIOGENETIC THEORIES

Several other theories about the origin of life have not been disproved or abandoned. Although the biogenetic model outlined above is shaping up as a sound scientific hypothesis, another theory—*panspermia*—may *also* be valid. This theory suggests that life may exist throughout the universe and that living substances journeyed to our planet from some other location, most likely embedded in meteorites. While the panspermia theory may prove to be true, it is often pointed out that it doesn't solve the problem of how life began. It only pushes the problem light-years away to some unknown location.

The theory of *spontaneous generation* was believed for thousands of years until the experiments of Louis Pasteur proved it false. "Never will the doctrine of spontaneous generation recover from this mortal blow," Pasteur told the French Academy—and it hasn't. This theory held that fully developed species are generated out of nonliving materials: maggots from decaying meat, for example, or frogs from mud, mice from old rags, or fireflies from early morning dew. Our knowledge of microscopic life-forms renders this notion worthless.

*Hylozoism* is the belief that *all* matter is alive. It was held by the earliest Greek philosophers and has been championed by occasional theorists ever since. The idea that matter itself might be alive, or in some way might involve "mental" activity, has intrigued philosophers. The more dematerialized our concept of matter becomes, the more we may be tempted to consider mystical or panpsychic theories of ultimate reality.

*Creationism* is the belief that life can originate only by a touch of the supernatural, and *vitalism* is the hypothesis that a special "life-force" must infuse nonliving matter before it can come alive. Both theories are still widely held, but their viability depends partly upon whether it can be shown that living organisms can develop from inorganic matter. If this can be demonstrated, then hypotheses involving creationism or vitalism will be unnecessary.

## CAN "LIFE" BE DEFINED?

What is "life"? Can the word be defined? Can the reality be conceived? Long lists of defining characteristics have been proposed, yet accurate, workable definitions are still lacking.

At present, it appears that "life" can be defined with two qualities: self-replication and mutability. Any organism possessing these two qualities can be considered alive. In these two characteristics is contained the essential processes of evolution: continuity and adaptation.

An organism must be able to replicate itself (unless it's immortal—that is, deathless—and hence not a part of the process of evolution). If it can produce a likeness of itself, then it possesses the power to assure continuity of its species. But mutability—the ability to effect changes from one generation to another and adapt to a fluid environment—is essential. Without the ability to change and adapt no species could long survive. Environmental conditions are forever changing; species must be able to change along with their environments.

*Putting such questions to Nature, and wringing answers from her, is often a difficult business, as every scientist knows. Yet sometimes it is as though Nature were trying to tell us something, almost to shake us into listening.*

GEORGE WALD

*We now believe with confidence, that the whole of reality is one gigantic process of evolution. This produces increased novelty and variety, and ever higher types of organization; in a few spots it has produced life; and, in a few of those spots of life, it has produced mind and consciousness.*

SIR JULIAN HUXLEY

## ON DEFINING LIFE

One's definition of life may then lead one to accept a particular level of organization of matter as a "living" state but not any level below it, whereas another may accept one or more levels lower or consider one or more levels higher as "living." What is important is not an exact definition of life at the borderline on which we can all agree, but rather the recognition of the existence of increasing levels of organization of matter and the understanding of the mechanisms which operate to bring these about. In other words, it would appear more sensible to approach the problem of the origin of life not as an attempt to discover the precise point at which lifeless matter gave rise to the "first living thing," but rather as an examination of the mechanisms operating in the transition of matter on this earth to higher and higher levels of organization. Then the first level of organization which can be considered "alive" will still be a matter of personal preference, but at least we will all be talking about the same thing. Thus, as others have pointed out, attempts at an exact definition of life are not only fruitless, at least for the present, but meaningless.

JOHN KEOSIAN
*The Origin of Life*

So far as we know, only living organisms have these two qualities, and an organism must possess both qualities to be considered alive. It has been noted that mineral crystals and flames of fire can reproduce; they both effect replication of their own kind without affecting themselves. In addition, flames display a sort of metabolism: they ingest material, digest it, and excrete wastes. However, neither crystals nor flames have adaptive mutability.

Several other qualities are often suggested as essential to a definition of what it means to be alive.

*Motility*—the ability to move about: to wiggle, crawl, run, fly, dart, bore through, swim. *Metabolism*—the ability to ingest materials, digest them (separate usable components from the unusable), and excrete wastes. *Growth*—the ability to proceed through some sort of life-cycle, beginning with seeds or embryos and moving through various stages of adulthood and beyond. *Irritability*—the ability to react to external stimuli, a first step in adaptation. *Dynamic equilibrium*—the ability to maintain a stable internal condition within changing external conditions (such as adjusting to temperature, conserving a balance in the flow of food and liquids through the body of the organism, and so forth).

When we say an organism possesses the ability to reproduce and mutate, we are not really defining *life* at all. In fact, we are not even thinking of life. We are only talking about the external motions ("behavioral patterns") of we-know-not-what. We are merely saying: *If* an organism can *do* these things, then we will classify it as "alive." But what is *life?* Apparently we don't know. Or, is life *nothing but* the ability *to do* certain things?

Somehow, as we continue pondering life and living things, this isn't very satisfying. Our dissatisfaction can become sharper as we subjectively feel our own existence. We feel that life is not merely the ability *to do* something, but

*In one form or another, the concept that life entails the operation of some principle of nature which is as yet ill defined seems to be gaining ground at the present time; and there is reason to believe that it is the fear of entrenched scientific orthodoxy which stills the voice of many who believe that life involves something more subtle than the latest chemical formulae for nucleic acids.*
RENÉ DUBOS

rather *is* something—a process, a flow, a flame, a special energy—something that persists through time inside us.

## EVOLUTION AS A FIELD THEORY

When Charles Darwin finally got around to publishing *The Origin of Species* in 1859—after more than twenty years of procrastination—he had formulated a coherent theory about the development of all living things and documented his theory so massively that it swept the field. No other theory of evolution could hold its ground when compared with the concept of natural selection.

Darwin had not developed his notions out of nothing, of course. It had been noted that trait changes take place from parent to offspring and that these variations are often inherited. Selective breeding of domestic animals and plants had long been practiced. And even the ideas of "the struggle for survival" and "natural selection" were hardly new, going back at least to the Greek philosopher Empedocles (c. 450 B.C.).

Darwin's genius was (1) his ability to bring a synoptic mind to these disparate elements and fit them all together, and (2) his meticulous gathering of scientific data to support his theory.

Following Darwin's development of the theory of natural selection from the struggle for survival, there were two large gaps in people's understanding of how evolution works.

First, heredity was not understood. But with the rediscovery in 1900 of Gregor Mendel's work, light began to dawn. Mendel's experiments had been forgotten since 1865; when they were recovered they fell into place in Darwin's theory. The transmission of specific characteristics from parents to offspring was by means of what Mendel called *genes* and followed predictable patterns.

The second information gap was knowledge of how trait changes occur between parent and offspring. Understanding this process has come only during the last few years as scientists have penetrated the genetic code itself and found it to be a template determined by the arrangement of nucleotides in the helix-shaped DNA (deoxyribonucleic acid) molecule.

Today we have a general understanding of the three basic processes of evolution: (1) the laws of heredity, (2) mutations produced by changes in the DNA code, and (3) the dynamics of natural selection.

The theory of evolution has become one of humanity's great unifying "field theories," bringing many areas of knowledge together into a single formula and providing us with a fundamental understanding of the nature of life on our planet.

The theory of evolution is founded upon five simple observations. When these observations are connected and seen together, and when each is understood as a dynamic process rather than a static concept, then the idea of evolution becomes easily comprehendible.

1.  Species produce like species. All members of any species always produce their own kind. Doves don't lay eggs that hatch into hawks, radish seeds don't produce turnips, and chimps can only reproduce more chimps. "Like

*Nothing in biology makes sense except in the light of evolution.*

THEODOSIUS DOBZHANSKY

*Life defies our phrases . . . it is infinitely continuous and subtle and shaded, whilst our verbal terms are discrete, rude, and few. . . .*

WILLIAM JAMES

*Both competition and cooperation are observed in nature. Natural selection is neither egotistic nor altruistic. It is, rather, opportunistic.*

THEODOSIUS DOBZHANSKY

begets like." Since the development of molecular biology, the reason for this is now clear: individuals can replicate only what their genes are encoded for; that is, species possess a gene code only for their own kind.

*Nature is not made in the image of man's compassion.*
TENNESSEE WILLIAMS
**Suddenly Last Summer**

2.  There is an enormous excess of reproductive material compared with the numbers of offspring that actually survive. One female salmon can produce twenty-five million eggs in a season, an oyster a hundred million. Mushrooms and ferns produce billions of spores for each plant that germinates. One man in a lifetime produces a hundred billion sperm and, with a little help, two or three offspring. And what of survival? Among tortoises only one in each hundred born survives to reach adulthood, of shrimp only one in fifty thousand. Yet with all this excess of reproductive potential, most species just succeed in replenishing their populations.

3.  In every species there is a multitude of individual variations in genetic characteristics. Members of any species are never genetically identical (unless they are twins or clones); there are subtle or blatant differences resulting from different combinations of genes. For example, humans belong to a single species, but within that species we come in all sizes, shapes, and colors. The human genome is an enormously rich gene pool with an almost infinite variety of possible combinations, only a few of which find expression in single individuals. The rest lie dormant in the gene pool ready for expression when opportunity and conditions are right.

4.  All species compete with each other for food and living room. The living space and food resources of any environment are always limited; there is never enough. Hence, all species compete with each other for these essentials. In any population the stronger and more adaptable individuals will be more successful in this struggle for survival. Hence, the environment is selective: it provides the opportunity for individuals with "better" genetic characteristics to live and reproduce; those whose genes are less "fit" are eliminated in the competition.

Adaptation and survival: Is this the basic mechanism of evolution? On each tree in these photographs is a peppered moth and a dark moth. On a dark tree trunk, the light-colored moth would be easy prey, but on the lichen-covered trunk, it has become invisible. Photographs from the experiments of Dr. H.B.D. Kettlewell.

5.  Environmental niches are dynamic; they are in a constant state of change. On a geologic time scale, great tropical forests become hot sandy deserts, swampy coastal plains become glaciated mountain ranges, oceans and seas dry up, and continents are inundated. The demand of the environment for change and adaptation is unrelenting, and millions of species either change, adapt and survive, or they vanish forever, depending upon their survival capabilities in relation to the severity of the environmental conditions. Under this relentless pressure, only the "fitter" survive.

Evolution is a field theory that connects these observations into a meaningful concept:

—Given the reproductive potential of all species,

—Given the enormous gene pool that permits variability and adaptation in the expression of genetic characteristics,

—Given the relentless competition for living space and nutrients,

—Given the fact that environmental niches are constantly changing over long periods of time—

Given these conditions, we have the theory (abstract idea) of "the survival of the fittest" describing the fact (reality) that only the species that possess superior genetic qualities will survive these harsh, demanding conditions. To put it another way, environments create pressure-cooker conditions that constantly act to select which offspring will be able to survive and reproduce.

The theory of evolution is nothing more, and nothing less, than a description of this selective process.

## PHILOSOPHIC IMPLICATIONS

Why does it mean so much that we can now say, "We *understand* how life evolves"?

The theory of chemical biogenesis will become a first-magnitude *field theory*. It will be comparable in its effects to the Pythagorean discovery that mathematics is the key to understanding physics, to Darwin's theory of biological evolution, and to Freud's conceptualization of a subconscious inner world.

The critical consequences of discoveries in biochemical evolution will lie in the almost unlimited control that man and woman will possess in laboratory experiments as well as in real-life conditions. The manipulation of gene codes will permit a far more fundamental kind of scientific activity than has previously existed. In all probability we will soon know precisely what arrangements of nucleotides produce specific characteristics; this knowledge in turn will enable scientists to synthesize DNA linkages to produce any desired replicating template. Science fiction will again become fact: man will bring to life creatures that he had designed on the drawing board.

Ethical considerations raised by the creation and control of life will be complex. Having to face new kinds of ultimate concern will stretch our moral tolerances to their limit and, hopefully, force us onto new planes of ethical awareness. The beneficial consequences for life will be enormous, but our wariness is justified. Although the statement is largely a play on words, in the minds of some, (wo)man will have become a god—the designer and creator of life. Will

*For the first time since the beginning of its history, humanity has become master of its destiny. . . . In order to grow afresh, it is forced to make itself anew. And it cannot make itself anew without pain, for it is both the marble and the sculptor. Out of its own substance it must send the splinters flying with great hammer-strokes, in order to recover its true face.*

ALEXIS CARREL

*Teleology, it is often said, is like an attractive woman of easy virtue, without whom a biologist cannot function happily, but with whom he does not want to be seen in public.*

RENÉ DUBOS

this be a wise and competent draftsman, or (by nature) a caricaturist? If the demonic in the creator's subconscious splashes out onto the drawing board, then we have reason to fear. In any case, we will be compelled to monitor biogenetic activities and set parameters within which the "life designer" must work.

The cosmic implications of the theory of chemical biogenesis are revolutionary. The fact that life will evolve anywhere in the entire universe where congenial conditions exist will eventually become the nucleus of a new world-view. Yet at present the discoveries of biochemical evolution have not made a profound impact. "This tremendous event is still on its way, still wandering"—to misquote Nietzsche. "It has not yet reached the ears of man."

What will it mean philosophically when life is created in a glass tube by a scientist?

Engineered creation of life is a predictable next step in unraveling life's secrets. It is an event in a continuing series: the use of fire, the wheel, weapons; harnessing steam power, nuclear power, and solar power for our energy needs; the control of weather; the use of chemicals to control emotions, explore psychopathological conditions, and eradicate disease. In kind, it is nothing new; but the door it will open is so momentous that in effect it will be as though a door had been opened onto a new world.

Our entrance into the creation of life is one of the giant steps that puts humanity in control of its own destiny. This step, along with another momentous event—taking over our own evolution—is part of the grand transition that we are now undergoing, the transition from being *passively produced organisms* to being *active controllers* of life and destiny.

With each step we take to control events in these two worlds, many are compelled to cry doom and declare the area off-limits. This response results both from theological conviction and from a deep distrust of humankind's ability to use its knowledge constructively, a distrust that can be supported with too much evidence. But historically, warnings of this sort have had little effect. Generally, the human race proceeds to establish control over all that it can, and, following its deepest impulses, will undoubtedly continue to do so.

## PHILOSOPHIC PROBLEMS

**1. IRREVERSIBILITY** The theory of evolution has made us face numerous philosophical problems, partly because the evolutionary "field theory" is so comprehensive.

One problem is the enigma of irreversibility. We have no difficulty accepting the fact that a single organism can't move from adulthood back through adolescence into childhood, or that a butterfly can't move from its adult flying stage back through the chrysalid into its larval stage. Such notions are absurd, and we know it. But in just the same way, evolution can't move backward from complex to simpler life-forms.

The famed aphorism, *Ontogeny recapitulates phylogeny*, summarizes a well-documented fact. The long evolutionary journey of each species has left its imprint upon the embryo of the individual organism. In other words, as each embryo develops from fertilization to birth, it retraces the path of the organism's evolutionary history. For example, the human embryo at one stage exhibits a "tail" and gill-like slits that make it almost indistinguishable from the embryos of fishes or other animals which, at some point in humanity's dim evolutionary past, emerged from the sea.

Scientists have noted that it is not necessarily the adult stage of an ancestor that the embryo resembles. Rather, the embryo mimics immature phases of its ancestors; the embryo's growth stages seem to imply that "ancestral plans of structure" may be retained in the organism's later stage of evolutionary development.

## 2. EVOLUTIONARY CONVERGENCE

Evolutionary convergence, with similar selective pressures driving unrelated and rather different genotypes into similar ecological niches, is another exciting but inadequately investigated phenomenon. The "cactus" growth form has appeared in several distinct families of plants, and some of these succulents are so similar in appearance that a non-specialist has difficulty in identifying the family. Old World tree frogs and New World tree frogs are so similar in adaptation to life in trees that it is necessary to examine the skeleton to determine which is which, yet they have originated as independent radiations within separate families. In Australia, where ordinary frogs (ranids) are virtually absent, a tree frog has evolved habits, body size, and even shape and appearance of our common leopard frog (a ranid). These and many other examples of convergence imply that there is a finite number of ways in which an organism of a given basic genotype can "make a living."

*Biology and the Future of Man*

**3. ALTRUISM AND COMPETITION** The relative roles of competition and cooperation in natural selection pose another problem. Which, we wonder, has played the dominant role in the game of survival?

Competition between species seems most obvious. Species prey upon species. We watch the bloody food-chain—the "deadly feast of life"—as it operates among both animals and plants. But with a closer look, we also find countless cases of cooperation, from simple symbiosis to a higher altruism in which a single individual voluntarily suffers self-deprivation or death for the welfare of its group.

Evolution clearly employs both of these seemingly contradictory mechanisms. Evolution appears to be opportunistic, caring nothing about technique. Perhaps ideas like "cooperation" and "competition" are mere human valuations that we misapply to a system that operates outside the boundaries of such anthropomorphic notions. Evolution is seemingly pragmatic—cooperating or competing, protecting or destroying, aiding or eating—whatever will increase chances of survival. The only success is survival, and the only criterion is whatever helps each species survive.

The long-term problem is not merely which pattern has been dominant. Once man has taken over this planet's evolution and must deal with the complex interrelationships of all living things—the Ecosystem—the problem man must face is whether competition and interspecific destruction can be replaced—or should be replaced—by patterns of mutual cooperation.

*The whole order of things fills me with terrible anguish, from the tiny gnat to the mysteries of incarnation. All is entirely unintelligible to me—particularly myself. Great is my sorrow, without limits. None knows my sorrow except God in Heaven, and He cannot have pity.*

**SØREN KIERKEGAARD**

*Dr. Thomas Gold of Cornell suggests that our earth may have been visited in the distant past by extraterrestrial passers-by. Finding conditions inhospitable, they journeyed on, leaving their picnic trash behind. In a billion years or so, life-forms from this debris had evolved to the point where we call them Homo sapiens.*

## EVOLUTION AND ALTRUISM

On the matter of the survival of altruism during evolution, I believe we should note Darwin's group theory. In *The Descent of Man*, he wrote:

> When two tribes of primeval man, living in the same country came into competition, if (other circumstances being equal) the one tribe included a great number of courageous, sympathetic and faithful members, who were always ready to warn each other of danger, to aid and defend each other, this tribe would succeed better and conquer the others.

And again:

> Obscure as is the problem of the advance of civilization, we can at least see that the nation which produced, during a lengthened period, the greatest number of highly intellectual, energetic, brave, patriotic, and benevolent men, would generally prevail over less favored nations.

> As to the survival of the altruistic individuals within the group, Darwin's theory is that devoted people propagate their own kind of personalities, not through their physical children, but through their ethical children, those who imitate the actions of the altruistic ones. The disciples that an altruistic person can create, even in a short lifetime, are a much larger number, Darwin says, than the children that a selfish man can father. (References: Charles Darwin, *The Origin of Species* and *The Descent of Man*. The Modern Library, pp. 490, 498–500.)

SPENCER D. POLLARD
*Science News*, April 8, 1972

## EVOLUTIONARY TELEOLOGY: A QUESTION MARK

*Philosophy has not yet digested the biologist's way of looking at living nature, free of all vitalistic and finalistic ideas; but in the wake of the spectacular advances of chemical and evolutionary biology, one day there must emerge a new philosophy of science, based largely on the findings of biology rather than those of physics.*

**Biology and the Future of Man**

Perhaps the most difficult issue in evolution has been the problem of teleology. Is the evolutionary process one of sheer chance and opportunism, or in some way is it guided teleologically by some force, extrinsic or intrinsic, so that evolution is, in fact, "going somewhere"? Does it unfold according to a plan? Is it directed? Does it have a goal? Is its purpose to develop new and ever more complex forms of life? That it moves inexorably from simpler to more complex lifeforms is undeniable; but does it do so "purposefully" or "opportunistically"? And even if its mode of operations is opportunistic, we still wonder *why* it moves toward ever-increased complexity.

Despite the tone of many biologists, the problem is not settled, and it is a very complicated one. It's helpful to remember that science fought its way free of religious establishments that employed harsh measures to enforce belief in ideas that were shown to be false by empirical facts. Western theology pronounced that history *is* a divine teleological plan, the plot of which is the unfolding story of God's cosmic struggle with the forces of evil for the salvation of the souls of men.

Dolphins gather to help a wounded fellow dolphin. What role does altruism play in evolutionary survival?

Since science freed itself from this teleocosmic myth, the word *teleology* has left a bitter taste in the mouths of scientists. Furthermore, when the theory of evolution became widely known after 1859, those inclined toward teleological thinking were quick to see in the idea of the "survival of the fittest" positive proof of a natural (as opposed to supernatural) teleological movement: if only the fitter survive, then we can conclude, on purely scientific grounds, that life will climb forever toward unimaginable heights. The superior organism will always win over the inferior. Eternal progress is assured. Thus "social Darwinism" colored much late nineteenth- and early twentieth-century thought.

The myth of "inevitable progress" became a religious tenet to those wanting to believe that history has meaning. It ceased to be a scientific hypothesis and was transformed into dogma. It is against such doctrinaire teleology that biologists have struggled; it is but natural that occasional hostilities linger on.

Two positions have been taken on the questions of purpose and direction in evolution.

Some thinkers have explicitly affirmed the teleological concept of evolution. Writing in the 1880s, Friedrich Nietzsche was one of the first philosophers to develop some of the possible implications of the idea of natural selection. In several brilliant books—most notably *Thus Spake Zarathustra*—Nietzsche

*To put the matter in a nutshell: the capacity of living substance for reproduction is the expansive driving force of evolution; mutation provides its raw material; but natural selection determines its direction.*

**SIR JULIAN HUXLEY**

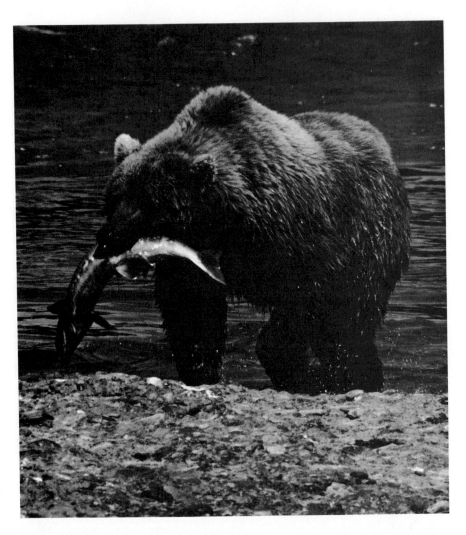

envisioned evolutionary history as a grand surge of life upward toward a superior being (Nietzsche called him *Übermensch*—"Overman" or "Superman"). History's intrinsic goal, argued Nietzsche, is to produce a man who has such greatness that he would be, in essence, a new species. He would possess new qualities only dimly presaged by the greatest now living among us. While he would be nothing less than ruthless in his mission of aiding evolution in its purpose, he would also display magnanimity and compassion, even gentleness, when called for.

Nietzsche's teleological interpretation of evolution also implied an ethic (which was immediately perverted by unscrupulous followers). The criterion for deciding between virtue and evil is whether any given human activity supports or thwarts evolution's fundamental purpose of producing the superior race of men. Any human act that improves man's genetic stock is moral in the fullest sense; any act that preserves inferior qualities is immoral in the same final sense. Evolution's sublime destiny is to produce superior man. Nothing must be allowed to stand in its way.

One of the most influential evolutionary thinkers of the twentieth century was the French philosopher Henri Bergson, whose masterpiece, *Creative Evolution*, was published in 1907. It was Bergson's conviction that what we observe in evolution cannot be explained adequately by the mechanics of natural selection. Something more profound is taking place in evolution and natural selection has missed it. Some further insight must be added to the idea of natural selection before it can answer the question of why higher forms of life continue to emerge. Bergson postulated the existence of an *élan vital*, a "vital life-force" or "impulse-to-life." He reflected that if adaptation and change were all that was required, then the ants had it made millions of years ago. They have been able to survive, almost unchanged, since long before the beginning of "the ascent of man." This being the case, why should evolution have bothered to evolve more complex forms of life? Something else, Bergson insisted, is at work in the forces of evolvement.

The élan vital is unpredictable and opportunistic, pushing ahead in every species of animal and plant to create greater complexity and higher life-forms. It has no goal as such; its only purpose is to exploit every opportunity in the struggle of an organism with its environment to advance the quality of life.

In contrast to such teleologies, the majority of biologists hold an opportunist interpretation of evolution. They adhere to the principle that everything can be explained solely by physical, chemical, biological, or ecological principles; there is no need to introduce mysterious factors such as an élan vital or some far-off goal toward which evolution is laboriously winding its way.

> *Organisms diversify into literally millions of species, then the vast majority of these species perish and other millions take their place for an aeon until they, too, are replaced. Species evolve exactly as if they were adapting as best they could to a changing world, and not at all as if they were moving toward a set goal.*
>
> GEORGE GAYLORD SIMPSON

At first sight the biological sector seems full of purpose. Organisms are built as if purposely designed, and work as if in purposeful pursuit of a conscious aim. But the truth lies in those two words "as if." As the genius of Darwin showed, the purpose is only an apparent one. However, this at least implies prospective significance. Natural selection operates in relation to the future—the future survival of the individual and the species. And its products, in the shape of actual animals and plants, are correspondingly oriented toward the future, in their structure, their mode of working, and their behavior. A few of the later products of evolution, notably the higher mammals, do show true purpose, in the sense of the awareness of a goal. But the purpose is confined to individuals and their actions. It does not enter into the basic machinery of the evolutionary process, although it helps the realization of its results. Evolution in the biological phase is still impelled from behind; but the process is now structured so as to be directed forward.

SIR JULIAN HUXLEY

> *To endure life remains, when all is said, the first duty of all living beings. Illusion can have no value if it makes this more difficult for us. . . .*
>
> SIGMUND FREUD

## WHERE IS EVOLUTION "GOING"?

A similar position—but with a fine distinction—is held by the microbiologist René Dubos. Dubos agrees that chance and opportunism undoubtedly operate in the adaptation of a species to a specific environment. But he observes that while most biologists disown the notion of teleology, they nonetheless *operate* on the tacit assumption that evolution does involve a kind of "purpose" or movement toward a functional complexity.

As we know it today, life operates as if most of its structures and functions were designed to fulfill some ultimate end, for the good of the individual and of the

## WHY SEX?

Mendelian genetics has provided an incisive answer to the old question of the biological value of sexual reproduction. Biparental reproduction and Mendelian assortment provide a means of shuffling the genes so that they can be tried out in various combinations. Then those that work best in the most combinations are retained by the population. In an asexual population, the only way that two favorable mutant genes can get into the same individual is if the second mutant gene occurs in the same individual or one of its descendants. In a sexual population mutant genes that arise in different individuals can be combined in the same one. In this way evolution can proceed much faster. The biological value of sexual reproduction, then, is that it greatly increases the speed of evolution. In this way the population has a far better chance of keeping up with a constantly changing environment.

PHILIP HANDLER (ed.)
*Biology and the Future of Man*

progeny. Life has its roots in the past, and its activities are projected into the future. Furthermore, it is a creative process, elaborating and maintaining order out of the randomness of matter, endlessly generating new and unexpected structures and properties by undergoing spontaneous changes, and by building up associations which qualitatively transcend their constituent parts. Clearly then, living things cannot be differentiated from the inanimate world only in terms of structures and properties. Their unique characteristic resides in the fact that their behavior is determined by their past and conditioned by the future, a property as yet mysterious but real nevertheless.

RENÉ DUBOS

The question, "Where is evolution going?" remains unresolved. Without the assumption of any life-essence, divine plan, or evolutionary goal, the very fact that evolution is future oriented and that it does indeed advance toward increasing complexity and qualitatively higher levels of life means that *we can still wonder what evolution might eventually produce.*

Such a question also applies to branches of evolution other than human. Let's remind ourselves that it might not be through the humanoid line that evolution may actualize such wonderful possibilities. I seem to remember a story—supposedly science fiction—in which a colony of ants on a South Pacific island have just arrived at a higher stage of intelligence and, from their anthill, are carefully watching a busy group of scientists—and planning their next move.

Could there possibly be some validity to Nietzsche's vision that higher forms of humanity will develop if evolution has its way? Dr. Harry Overstreet of Harvard has proposed the idea that man is evolving a new form of consciousness, and that "we have every reason to believe that a further form of our conscious life is already observable among us—a high degree among certain rare individuals, in lesser degree among most of us." Overstreet has in mind the sort of "cosmic consciousness" found in some of the world's religious leaders (Gautama, Jesus), mystics (Plotinus, Swedenborg, William Blake), ecstatic

*Academic philosophers, ever since the time of Parmenides, have believed that the world is a unity. . . . The most fundamental of my intellectual beliefs is that this is rubbish. I think the universe is all spots and jumps, without unity, without continuity, without coherence or orderliness or any of the other properties that governesses love . . . it consists of events, short, small and haphazard. Order, unity, and continuity are human inventions, just as truly as are catalogues and encyclopedias.*

BERTRAND RUSSELL

intellectuals (Socrates, Descartes, Shakespeare, Einstein), and visionaries (Dante, Whitman, Fuller). Overstreet adds that such manifestations of a high order of consciousness are regarded by most of us "as signs either of supernatural power or of psychic disorder. Is it not possible, on the other hand, to regard these occurrences as signs simply of a higher stage of the very same typical development through which all of us are passing?"

What indeed is evolution's potential? Are there inherent limitations in evolution, or is it unlimited? What undreamed-of life-qualities are possible and, with a little luck, might become realities?

## REFLECTIONS

1   Note the four great etiological questions that the human mind has bumped against since the beginning of philosophic thought. In your opinion, after reading pp. 385–386, how far have we progressed by this tenth decade of the twentieth century toward sound empirical answers to each of these questions?

2   What do you think are the most far-reaching philosophic implications of the biochemical theory of the origin of life? Do you feel a sense of relief that foundations have been laid for an empirical answer to this question?

*In broad terms, the destiny of man on earth has been made clear by evolutionary biology. It is to be the agent of the world process of evolution, the sole agent capable of leading it to new heights, and enabling it to realize new possibilities.*

**SIR JULIAN HUXLEY**

3   Ponder the suggestion that man is now undergoing a "grand transition" (p. 397) from a passively produced organism to the active controller of life and destiny. What evidence can you think of that supports this conclusion? What evidence can you muster against it? Speculate: If this "grand transition" is actually taking place, what are its philosophic implications? What lies ahead?

4   "The aphorism that we are the stuff of which stars are made is more than rhetoric," writes Dr. Ponnamperuma. Is this insight meaningful to you?

5   Note the biological inventory on p. 391. Comment?

6   What is your thinking (at present) regarding the problem of teleology in evolution? Gather evidence and develop arguments, as best you can, first in support of the notion, and then against it.

7   What scientific data can you draw upon to help resolve the question of competition versus cooperation in evolution? Which do you think has played the more important role? (Or do you feel there may be something wrong with the way we are asking the question?)

8   How can you account for "evolutionary convergence?" Is this properly a philosophic problem, or is there a satisfactory biological answer?

9   As an answer to one of the great etiological questions, this chapter contends that the theory of evolution has become one of humanity's great unifying field theories. Is this a fair and accurate evaluation of the evolutionary model? Why or why not?

10  René Dubos believes (see p. 403) that evolution is at least "future oriented" and that we can validly ask "What might evolution eventually produce?" Speculate then: What *might* it produce? Is Overstreet's suggestion (p. 404) about "higher stages of consciousness" a probable (and congenial) eventuality? (What is meant by "higher stages of consciousness"?)

# EMPEDOCLES

## *Survival of the Fittest*

We humans have always wondered who we are and how we got here. Without some idea about our identity and purpose it appears as though we can't get on with the job of living our daily lives.

One of the most celebrated theories about the origins of life was that of Empedocles, a native of the city of Akragas (Agrigentum) on the island of Sicily. Like the other early Greek thinkers, Empedocles asked the first question: What is everything made of and what is the cause of motion and change? He reasoned that there are four basic elements—fire, earth, air, and water; and the force that energizes the elements is a sort of attraction and repulsion—Love and Strife. Various mixtures or blends of these four produce all the particular objects that clutter the world. Empedocles developed a picturesque "biocosmology" to depict the origins of living organisms; tucked into his scenario is our earliest notion of the "survival of the fittest."

A considerable amount is known about Empedocles's life and teachings.

He lived for about 60 years, from c. 492 B.C. to c. 432 B.C. His death, however, is shrouded in myth. There are three versions: (1) that he was banished from Akragas and died in exile in Greece; (2) that he simply disappeared from the earth after celebrating a feast during which he wrought miracles; (3) that he deliberately ended his life by leaping into the bubbling lava of Mount Aetna to prove that he was a god. This latter tale is told by Diogenes Laertius (a very mediocre historian) who is quoting Heraclides Ponticus (who was endowed with a fanciful memory); so doubtless this is just another volcano story.

But suppose the Aetna story were true. Suppose he did believe himself to be an immortal spirit and that he did visit Mount Aetna. *Suppose*, even, that his cosmobiology were true.

Just suppose . . .

Empedocles moved about the amphitheater from one group to another, helping to settle his followers after their tiring journey from Leontini. Daybreak was still hours away and the stars were brightening in the thin morning air.

So many of his friends were here,

especially from Selinus and his home city of Akragas. Corax and Tisias were here, resting on their laurels, as was his sister, whom he had never quite forgiven for burning two of his best poems. Plus his favorite pupils: Gorgias, a promising young skeptic, and dear Pausanius—both already asleep on the hard ground.

More than two hundred young men and maidens had accompanied their Master on this trek without rest, and the ascent up the steep slopes of Aetna had been exhausting. During the final hours they climbed blindly through night-mists that obscured the path and enshrouded the tall pines. On reaching the crest they dropped with fatigue and proceeded to gather what sleep they could from the night hours that remained to them.

All who were here followed Empedocles with abiding faith, though why they were at this place at this hour was not altogether clear. Some had heard rumors that Empedocles planned to plunge himself into the molten lava to dispel any doubt that he was divine. Most accepted the journey as a pilgrimage to the sacred precincts of Demeter, for she had lit her torches from the fires of Aetna before setting out in search of her daughter Persephone who had been kidnapped by Pluto and taken to his lair in Hades.

Empedocles looked with affection at the huddled sleepers. He was a tall, broad-shouldered man with a luxuriant growth of black hair and beard, streaked with silver and crowned with a Delphic wreath. He was clothed this night in a purple robe with golden sash and wore bronze-colored shoes.

The tripworn travelers slept.

Far out on the ledge overlooking the cauldron Empedocles listened to sounds echoing from below. Then with his feet planted firmly on the rock, he folded his arms across his chest and closed his eyes.

He drifted. A delicious warmth moved through the whole of his being, making him feel lightheaded—spinning, giddy, as though too much Sardinian wine was taking his brain apart, setting each brain-seed adrift in its own gentle vortex.

Residual images fluttered through his mind. He felt himself falling through steaming winds till the fury of the reddish clouds faded to a soft glow.

He was in a pine forest blanketed by mist. Through the trees he caught glimpses of roaring fires rising from the earth and illuminating the fog.

He recognized instantly where he was: in the Mists of Creation. Shocked into belief, he wandered about, groping.

He stepped on something soft. Looking down he found himself standing on a human toe, a great toe, quite still and lifeless. With a feeling of revulsion, he backed away through the mists.

Bewildered, he found a log and sat down to think himself through his nightmare.

A hand touched his shoulder. He jerked back, scurried over the log, and crouched looking at a hand and arm . . . and nothing more. Where there should have been a shoulder and torso there was nothing. The hand turned back on itself and pointed to its upper arm, and, like a puppy chasing its tail, continued motioning to the stump of the upper arm. Empedocles stared as the hand-arm stopped pointing, drooped, and floated away.

A head drifted toward him out of the haze, only a head, with one ear downside up.

"Can you help me find a body, please? I'm beginning to grow cold and cannot last much longer. Please . . . a body, or just a neck with, perhaps, a shoulder—?"

Empedocles stood helpless. "I saw a hand-arm assembly a short ways back," he replied, angry that his words were neither coherent nor comforting.

"Which way?" the head asked hopefully. "We could share life if only for a while. As soon as our fire goes out we die."

Empedocles was aware of a rising sense of outrage. Nothing about all this seemed right or fair or the-way-it-was-supposed-to-be.

*When Hostility is at work, all these things are distinct in form and separated; but they come together in Love, and are desired by one another. Thence have sprung all the things that ever were, are, or shall be—trees and men and women, beasts and birds and water-dwelling fishes, and even such honored beings as the long-lived gods. In reality there are only the basic elements, but interpenetrating one another they mix to such a degree that they assume different characteristics.*

*These two forces, Strife and Love, existed in the past and will exist in the future; nor will boundless time, I believe, ever be empty of the pair.*

*Pay heed and I will tell you the first-principle of the sun; moreover I will explain the sources from which everything that we now behold has sprung—earth, billowy sea, moist air, and giant sky that binds all things in its embrace.*

*From what high place of honor and bliss have I fallen, so that I now go about among mortals here on earth? I wept and mourned when I discovered myself in this unfamiliar land.*

*It is by chance that men have come to have conscious thought.*

*It is by earth that we see earth, by water water, by air divine air, and by fire destroying fire; by love we perceive love, and hate by dreadful hate.*

"Wait here. I'll go to find it." Empedocles moved back along the path to the log, but the hand-arm had disappeared. He listened, heard nothing, peered through the fog, saw nothing.

When he returned, the head was lying on the ground, its fire gone. By itself it could not survive.

Empedocles felt sick. He was witnessing a tragedy beyond all imagining. Each living thing was using its few fiery hours in a desperate attempt to find some other life with which to share its warmth. Suffering and death were the order of things. He wondered: What were the odds for these innumerable pieces of life—the arms and eyes and ears and limbs and torsos—finding one another and fitting themselves together into some configuration that could survive and reproduce? None, he concluded with growing depression, none at all.

An orange glow flickered through the mists. As he approached he beheld a broad abyss of pure fire exploding into emanations from the bowels of the nether world. It was in the depths of raging forges such as this that each piece of living matter was generated. Air and water were combining with just enough earth to be activated by the abyssal fire. Fire-earth-air-water, energized by the forces of Philotês/Love and Neikos/Strife, churned into being the million billion things that are, thenceforth to struggle, to survive, to reproduce its kind. Fingers, ears, feet, heads, whole torsos were being born, full of fire, eager to complete themselves and begin life.

He turned away and retreated into the cooler mists. For a time he lost himself in mindless wandering. Parts of bodies drifted past him, sometimes singly, sometimes joined in hideous fashion. He wished he could have done with the Mists of Creation.

Something humanlike stirred on the path ahead. It uttered a long cry. Empedocles jumped forward and raised the figure to a sitting position. It was a man, almost complete. He had not seen any living thing nearly so well put together, but the man was barely warm and was rapidly losing his fire. He was missing only an arm and generative organs.

Empedocles wondered if he could find the glowing fire again, and, if he could find it, what the chances were of his finding the vital parts for this man.

No chance at all. He eased the rag-limp corpse back to the ground, its fire gone.

Time vanished, for a time. When he next opened his mind he heard voices. He listened, not quite sure it was not the wind. Two figures approached along the path: a man, seemingly perfect, and a woman, seemingly perfect. Empedocles trembled with fear that he would discover malformities as they drew near. Talking animatedly the man and woman walked past him and gradually disappeared from view. The couple were perfect human beings—fiery shoots from the realm of night and wellsprings of all future generations of mortals.

So, life arises, by stages. Animals and plants, at first, lacked perfection because their parts ill fitted. A second generation of creatures possessed parts that clung harmoniously. At the third stage there emerged whole integrated organisms. Creatures of the fourth generation were created not from the four elements but of complex pre-formed compounds. Thus, from the Mists of Creation, the human race, gloriously formed, walked forth.

The philosopher sat down again and wept for joy.

Empedocles aroused himself from his distraught dream to find the Eastern sky faintly backlighted with threads of silver. A few of his followers were stretching their muscles awake. The rolling mists had overtaken them and were quietly swathing the trespassers in a milky haze.

Empedocles turned to speak.

"What we have accomplished, we have accomplished. What we have left undone, we leave undone. Come awake, my friends, this is the end of our journey."

He lifted his voice as the mists rose over the crater rim.

"This world is not my home. I wept and mourned when I discovered myself in this unfamiliar land. The life of mortals is so nebulous that it resembles nonlife. Oblivion is swift, and we are blown away and vanish like smoke.

"From time to time there appear on earth certain men who are prophets, bards, physicians, and princes; and these men are indeed transmogrified into gods, to be extolled in honor, and are destined to share hearth and table with other immortals, freed, finally, from the evils of human suffering.

"Thus, I speak to you no longer as a mortal but as an immortal divine, and your honors are not misplaced; for hereafter you will remember this hour and say: 'There walked among us a man of rare knowledge, a man endowed with wisdom, a man who, when he reached out with all his mind, encompassed all knowledge so far attained by the human race.'

"I shall tell you one thing more. There is no birth and there is no death. There is only the co-mingling and separation of the elements."

Like bundles of woolen fleece pushed by the wind, the mists swirled through the amphitheater and spilled into the caldera. The world of sight and sound dissolved.

The listeners waited.

After an eternity the mists thinned away and the reddish glow of the cauldron reappeared.

Except for a pair of bronze-colored sandals, the ledge was empty.

# 6₂

## THE SCULPTOR-GODS

The Maoris of New Zealand say that a certain god, variously named Tu, Tiki, and Tane, took red riverside clay, kneaded it with his own blood into a likeness or image of himself, with eyes, legs, arms, and all complete, in fact, an exact copy of the deity; and having perfected the model, he animated it by breathing into its mouth and nostrils, whereupon the clay effigy at once came to life and sneezed. So like himself was the man whom the Maori Creator Tiki fashioned that he called him *Tiki-ahua,* that is, Tiki's likeness.

Until modern times we humans lived close to the soil. One thing we knew how to do well—a skill universally found at a specific stage of culture—was to scoop clay from the river bank and shape it into vessels—cooking pots, water jars, urns, amphorae, lamps. Shards of pottery have been found wherever people have lit their fires and lived together.

Besides practical items, members of different cultures also made figurines, miniatures molded from imagination and clay—images of men and earth mothers, of barques and scarabs, of animals and gods. Some of the earthen images were used to lure bears into traps, to placate the gods, to grow green stalks heavy with corn, to weaken enemies.

Some of the clay figurines were made just for fun, molded into his or her own likeness. The sculptor toyed with them, pondered them, and doubtless joked and laughed at them while sculpting head and torso and limbs from the damp clay.

This universal experience becomes the archetypal pattern for humankind's creation stories. What was more natural and more obvious than to know, deep in his blood and bones, that an unknown Sculptor shaped his body from the clay of the earth and brought it to life?

*Kingdom* animalia *(animals)*
*Phylum* Chordata *(chordates)*
*Class* Mammalia *(mammals)*
*Order* Primates *(primates)*
*Superfamily* Hominoidea *(hominoids)*
*Family* Hominidae *(hominids)*
*Subfamily* Homininae *(hominines)*
*Genus* Homo *(human)*
*Species* sapiens *(archaic human)*
*Subspecies* sapiens sapiens *(modern human)*

*Of all the wonders of the universe, the greatest is man.*
**ARISTOTLE**

*An average human lifetime has a duration of about $10^9$ seconds.*

The Batek people of Malaysia tell of a supernatural being named Tohan who is "very big" but "looks just like us." He is an old man with black, curly hair and brown skin. He has green grass growing on his back and a small, green patch of tiny trees sprouting on the back of his neck.

Once, in the beginning, Tohan came to Earth. He went to the place where the sun comes up and took some black soil and molded it into the shape of a man. Then he went to where the sun goes down and took some black soil and molded it into the shape of a woman. Tohan shaped them in his own likeness.

But the earth-bodies weren't alive. So Tohan went back to the western sky where he lives to get life-soul to bring the mannikins to life. He brought back some water life-soul, like that found in the jungle evergreen trees, but on his way back he tripped and spilled it. After that he looked for seven days for some more water life-soul but couldn't find it.

So Tohan borrowed some life-soul from the banana plant, but this was only *wind* life-soul. He brought it back in a bottle and blew some of it onto the fontanelles of the earth-bodies and onto their chests over their hearts. When the life-soul was absorbed into their bodies, they came to life, stood up, and sneezed.

"The water life-soul would have made us like Tohan, immortal, like the superhuman beings themselves, but it was lost. We have only wind life-soul borrowed from the banana plant. It gives us only temporary life.

"When we die our wind life-soul is taken back by Tohan, who puts it in his life-soul bag and keeps it for a day, and then sends it to re-animate a new body, entering the body through the baby's fontanelle. It is Tohan who gives us our life-souls and takes back our life-souls when we die."

According to the Ewe-speaking tribes of Togo, in West Africa, God still makes people out of clay.

*It is the large brain capacity which allows man to live as a human being, enjoying taxes, canned salmon, television, and the atomic bomb.*

**G. H. R. VON KOENIGSWALD**

When a little of the water with which he moistens the clay remains over, he pours it on the ground, and out of that he makes the bad and disobedient people. When he wishes to make a good man he makes him out of good clay; but when he wishes to make a bad man, he employs only bad clay for the purpose. In the beginning God fashioned a man and set him on the earth; after that he fashioned a woman. The two looked at each other and began to laugh, whereupon God sent them into the world.

Thus, creation myths explain to our satisfaction far more than mere physical origins. They also tell us why we must die and return to the earth, why we are only partly immortal, and why our souls can sometimes return to heaven; they explain why there are many colors of people and many languages, why some people are good and some bad, and why there are two sexes. Almost every fact of life that puzzled early people eventually called forth some sort of mythical explanation.

The Toradjas of the Celebes tell how

i Lai, the god of the upper world, and i Ndara, the goddess of the under world, resolved to make men. They committed the task to i Kombengi, who made two models, one of a man and the other of a woman, out of stone or, according to others, out of wood. When he had done his work, he set up his models by the side of the road which leads from the upper to the under world, so that all spirits passing by might see and criticize his workmanship. In the evening the gods talked it over, and agreed that the calves of the legs of the two figures were not round enough. So Kombengi went to work again, and constructed another pair of models which he again submitted to the divine criticism. This time the gods observed that the figures were too pot-bellied, so Kombengi produced a third pair of models, which the gods approved of, after the maker had made a slight change in the anatomy of the figures, transferring a portion of the male to the female figure. It now only remained to make the figures live. So the god Lai returned to his celestial mansion to fetch eternal breath for the man and woman; but in the meantime the Creator himself, whether from thought-lessness or haste, had allowed the common wind to blow on the figures, and they drew their breath and life from it. That is why the breath returns to the wind when a man dies.

*Hockett and Ascher remind us that our ancestral proto-hominids "were not striving to become human; they were . . . trying to stay alive."*
**Philip Van Doren Stern**

In the earliest Hebrew account of creation, it is said that the god Yahweh moulded the first man out of clay, just as a potter might do, or as a child moulds a doll out of mud; and that having kneaded and patted the clay into the proper shape, the deity animated it by breathing into the mouth and nostrils of the figure, exactly as the prophet Elisha is said to have restored to life the dead child of the Shunammite by lying on him, and putting his eyes to the child's eyes and his mouth to the child's mouth, no doubt to impart his breath to the corpse; after which the child sneezed seven times and opened its eyes. To the Hebrews this derivation of our species from the dust of the ground suggested itself all the more naturally because, in their language, the word for "ground" (*adamah*) is in form the feminine of the word for "man" (*adam*).

Thus, both in language and myth, *ha-adam*, "the Man" (masculine), is created from *ha-adamah*, "the Earth" (feminine). And divine spirit/breath (in Hebrew *ruah* means "spirit," "breath," "wind," and "soul") is breathed by Yahweh himself into the Man's nostrils and pumped into his lungs. The man's body is from the earth, but his spirit/breath is from Yahweh. (The Greek word *pneuma* carries similar meanings. See p. 554)

The Shilluks of the White Nile

ingeniously explain the different complexions of the various races by the differently coloured clays out of which they are fashioned. They say that the creator Juok moulded all men out of the earth, and that while he was engaged in the work of creation he wandered about the world. In the land of the whites he found a pure white earth or sand, and out of it he shaped white men. Then he came to the land of Egypt and out of the mud of the Nile he made red or brown men. Lastly, he came to the land of the Shilluks, and finding there black earth he created men out of it.

Before there was an evolutionary context in which humanity could see itself, we observed that lions produce lions, turtles produce turtles, bluejays produce bluejays—and human produces human. The logic of this was overwhelming. But a piece of the puzzle is obviously missing. There had to be a beginning: something had to create the full sapient form to stand in the flesh and to be half-god, half-clay. And logically the first creator of humankind had to be like humans. Doesn't human produce human?

*Humanity is at the very beginning of its existence—a new born babe, with all the unexplored potentialities of babyhood.*
**Sir James Jeans**

## THE STORY OF HUMAN ORIGINS

All human beings on Earth now belong to one species: We are all *Homo sapiens* ("wise humans"). This was not always the case.

The story of the human race begins in Africa some 2 million years ago. We know from the fossil record that a species of human that we designate *Homo habilis* lived in the open woodlands and savannas of what is now Kenya, Tanzania, and other east African countries. They roamed the countryside in small groups and competed with animals and other hominids for living space and food. They made crude stone tools. They ate leaves, soft fruits, shoots of plants, bulbs, and roots; and they probably added a small amount of meat to their diet through opportunistic scavenging.

If you met a pair of these humans in your local supermarket, what would they look like? To us they would appear strange but human. They would be lightly built and slender, with long arms. The man would stand almost five feet tall and weigh a hundred pounds; the woman would be considerably smaller, weighing in at seventy-five pounds and standing four feet six inches high. Their faces and bodies would be hairy. They would have prominent browridges, high cheekbones, and flattened faces (no protruding snouts). Their foreheads would be slanted and their skulls flat (not domed like ours); their brain size would be about half that of modern humans. They could grasp and manipulate packages on the shelves almost as deftly as we can, and as they walked down the aisles— bewildered by the bottles, TV dinners, and strange foods—they would stand and walk fully upright, just as we do.

These were the first human beings, and as participants in the protosplasmic venture on Earth, *Homo habilis* was a very successful species. For a million years they lived, mated, adapted, and survived in their east African territory.

Where did these first human beings come from?

Three million years before their time there existed many different species of hominids that are known collectively by the name of *Australopithecus.* At least three of these species have been identified in the fossil record. Some of the species were slender, some more robust and muscular; but all of them shared characteristics that are later unique to human beings: larger brains, smaller teeth, and upright posture.

The Australopithecine best known to us is "Lucy," so named by Donald Johanson after he discovered her bones in the rain-washed ravines of Ethiopia in 1974. She and her "family"—thirteen individuals were found together— lived three million years ago. Lucy was an adult female, three feet eight inches tall, and weighing about sixty-five pounds. She stood fully upright and could walk and run as well as any modern human. The males in her group were almost five feet tall and weighed twice as much. Except for her long arms, from the neck down she looked like a diminutive modern human being; but in sharp contrast her head and face would appear to us more ape-like than human: she had a small braincase, receding forehead, thick brow, flat nose, protruding face, large canine teeth, and no chin. Whether Lucy was considered pretty by other members of her group we can only speculate; what we are sure about is that the males in her extended family competed harshly with one another for her attention and favors. (This is a fairly certain inference from the fact that males were much larger than females. In all such cases today where this "sexual dimorphism" in size occurs [for example, elephant seals, elk, gorillas], males compete with one another for females and only the one dominant male ["alpha male"] mates with the females. It is virtually certain this arrangement prevailed with the Australopithecines.)

Famed paleoanthropologist Mary Leakey discovered the footprints of three such Australopithecines in Tanzania set in volcanic ash 3.7 million years ago. Three individuals—possibly male, female, and a child—were being showered by a blanket of hot ashes from a nearby volcano. They walked fully upright and left footprints in the damp ashes virtually identical to ours. Following the path of footprints made her feel a "poignant time wrench," Mary Leakey says. One of the travelers stopped, looked back, and then turned and, we assume, caught up with the others. "This motion, so intensely human, transcends time. Three million seven hundred thousand years ago, a remote ancestor—just as you or I—experienced a moment of doubt."

These Australopithecines are undoubtedly ancestral to the first humans, *Homo habilis*. But where did the Australopithecines come from?

Before 5 million years ago and the emergence of the Australopithecines, the fossil record becomes fragmented and incomplete. Research from molecular biology indicates that humans and chimpanzees shared a common ancestor at about 5 million years ago; the hominid tree branched at that point and the protohuman and chimpanzee branches evolved along separate lines. Similarly, at 8 million years, the gorillas joined the main branch and share a common ancestor; at 12 million years the orangutan line converges, and at 17 million years the gibbon line is joined to make up the hominoid trunk. All arrows point to the emergence of the entire hominoid line around 25 million years ago. Before that fortuitous time lies a 50-million-year reign of earlier mammals; before that, the 500-million-year epoch of the great reptiles; before that the three-billion-year continuous evolvement of more elemental and primitive life forms tracing back to the beginnings of life on Earth at 3.6 billion years ago.

So the human enterprise is a recent event in a continuous, ongoing process of evolvement. What happened 2.5 million years ago that caused the emergence of the human genus?

Besides bones, there is something else in the fossil/geological record: evidence of extreme worldwide climatic change. After millions of years of warm tropical climate, the Earth suddenly cooled. Glacial ice sheets covered much of North America, Europe, and Siberia. The Antarctic ice continent built up, layer upon layer. Sea levels dropped 150 to 500 feet worldwide. Patterns of rainfall drastically changed. A chill swept over Africa, turning great tropical forests into woodlands, grassy savannas, and deserts. This worldwide catastrophic change in climate happened 5 million years ago and again 2.5 million years ago.

As a result habitats were fragmented and the growth of differentiated habitats forced isolated populations to take separate lines of genetic evolvement. Animals, birds, and insects underwent rapid speciation. The antelope genus, for example, proliferated into some thirty species in Africa. Time and again this is what shows up in the fossil record: When severe environmental change challenges the adaptive capabilities of organisms and pushes species to their limits, the species produce better survival characteristics and adapt to new ecological niches or they die off. This appears to be a basic law of evolution: change or die. We see both in the fossil record: with shifts in climate comes a

*The essential point in science is not complicated mathematical formula or a ritualized experimentation. Rather the heart of science is a kind of shrewd honesty that springs from really wanting to know what the hell is going on!*

**SAUL-PAUL SIRAG**

## EXPERIMENTAL MODEL

So there he stands, our vertical, hunting, weapon-toting, territorial, neotenous, brainy, Naked Ape, a primate by ancestry and a carnivore by adoption, ready to conquer the world. But he is a very new and experimental departure, and new models frequently have imperfections. For him the main troubles will stem from the fact that his culturally operated advances will race ahead of any further genetic ones. His genes will lag behind, and he will be constantly reminded that, for all his environment-moulding achievements, he is still at heart a very naked ape.

DESMOND MORRIS
*The Naked Ape*

*I can live with doubt and uncertainty. I think it's much more interesting to live* not *knowing than to have answers which might be wrong.*

RICHARD FEYNMAN

*The nature of man is not what he is born as, but what he is born for.*

ARISTOTLE

proliferation of new species and mass extinction of old ones. This, it appears, was the driving force at the beginning of the age of Mankind.

After a very successful run of over a million years—from about 2.5 million to 1.5 million years ago—*Homo habilis* vanishes from the fossil record and is replaced by a more advanced species. First evidence of this new human being, which we call *Homo erectus,* appears in the fossil record about 1.6 million years ago in east Africa. Paleoanthropologists believe that *Homo habilis* evolved into *Homo erectus.*

If you came across a male of these humans in your corner fast-food restaurant, standing in line waiting for his order of fries, what would he look like? In many respects he would look like us. In height and size he would be only slightly smaller—five feet two inches and 110 pounds, but he would appear to us stocky and more massively built. His brain would be nearly as big as ours (87 percent as big, on the average). He would have a large face, heavy jaws, moderately thick browridges, flattened forehead, and almost no chin. His teeth would be smaller and the canines of earlier species would be gone. He would walk upright, and his body would still be hairy.

In his African homeland his fellow humans lived in small groups, wandering the countryside and sharing their food. The men were only a little larger than the women. They hunted and scavenged and left cut marks on animal bones with their stone tools. They were the first hominids to make carefully worked stone implements, use fire, cook food, and (possibly) the first to use symbols and to speak and think with some degree of abstract capability.

*Homo erectus* was even more successful than *habilis.* His kind existed more than a million years. He lived for several hundred thousand years in East Africa and then gradually spread into North Africa, Europe, and Asia as far as India, China, and Indonesia. Then, beginning about half a million years ago, the planet entered another period of global climatic change. *Homo erectus* vanished from the fossil record, and, about 300,000 years ago, a more familiar face began to appear. One or more populations of *Homo erectus* evolved into this new big-brained biped. We call him *Homo sapiens.*

Africa is the cradle of Humankind. Early *Homo sapiens* lived in eastern and southern Africa for a hundred thousand years or more and then began to radiate out of Africa into the rest of the world. This migration began about 120,000 years ago. By 90,000 years ago we find them living in the Near East and along the Southern Mediterranean coast. By 70,000 years ago they had spread across Asia. By 40,000 years ago they were living in Russia and eastern Europe. By 35,000 years ago they had settled throughout Europe. By 30,000 years ago they were living in Indonesia, Australia, and Sri Lanka and had crossed the Bering Strait into the Americas. As this new species migrated and settled in the world's diverse range of habitats, distinct gene pools were formed, and Humankind's myriad ethnic and "racial" characteristics were established.

If you should encounter one of these creatures at your neighborhood video store checking out a new release, what would he look like? How well we know! They come in all shapes, sizes, and colors. They are sometimes short (like the pygmy Bateks), sometimes tall (like the Watusi). They may have short arms and stubby fingers or long arms and tapering fingers. They may be slender and lithe or muscular and stocky. They may have long faces or round faces; or angular faces or flat, full faces. And so on, almost infinitum. *Homo sapiens*, we find, is polymorphic and polytypic: we find great variations both *within* gene pools and *between* gene pools. These are the differences that we often focus on in the course of our daily living to set us apart and establish our identity.

*The camera can't take a picture of itself.*

ROBERT PUTMAN

So while it's true that there are many different ways of being human, in the final analysis, there is but a single *Homo sapiens*. We are all one species, and in the context of our evolutionary history we share some very distinctive characteristics. The skeletal frame of *Homo sapiens* is lighter than that of any other hominids that have ever lived; the face is delicate and small with small or no eyebrow ridges; a lower mandible with fine teeth arranged in a horseshoe shape with a protruding bony chin to protect them; and a skull with a narrow base designed to ride comfortably atop a vertical column of vertebrae. These characteristics are ours alone.

---

## PRIMUS INTER PARES

Man's view of himself has undergone many changes. From a unique position in the universe, the Copernican revolution reduced him to an inhabitant of one of many planets. From a unique position among organisms, the Darwinian revolution assigned him a place among the millions of other species which evolved from one another. Yet, *Homo sapiens* has overcome the limitations of his origin. He controls the vast energies of the atomic nucleus, moves across his planet at speeds barely below escape velocity, and can escape when he so wills. He communicates with his fellows at the speed of light, extends the powers of his brain with those of the digital computer, and influences the numbers and genetic constitution of virtually all other living species. Now he can guide his own evolution. In him, Nature has reached beyond the hard regularities of physical phenomena. *Homo sapiens*, the creation of Nature, has transcended her. From a product of circumstances, he has risen to responsibility. At last, he is Man. May he behave so!

PHILIP HANDLER
*Biology and the Future of Man*

There is one single characteristic, however, that has made all the difference. From the time of our habiline origins 2 million years ago, the human species has been distinguished from all other creatures, presently living or having ever lived, by our big brain—up to 1400 cc in volume—and by the thin-walled, domed housing we have developed to make room for that big brain. This braincase is what was left in the fossil record that makes it possible for this big brain to trace the history of its own development.

## STILL TRYING TO DEFINE "HUMAN"

*There are 180 billion cells in the human body. Each of these little factories is carrying out hundreds of chemical processes at a speed that astounds the mind.*

JOAN AREHART-TREICHEL

An adequate understanding of humanness must begin—but not end—with our place in the program of evolution. We belong to the animal kingdom, but we are something more than animals.

Defining humans as different and apart from the rest of the animal kingdom has been a bothersome problem. People have guarded their lists of distinctions passionately and religiously.

Human origins, it was supposed, could be discerned in the fossil records by evidence of use of fire or weapons; or it was held that only fully human creatures could make or use tools. "Man alone is a toolmaker," wrote early anthropologists.

Special physical characteristics clearly mark Homo sapien as a superior being. The upright posture allows mobility, agility, and better chances of survival. The larger brain capacity (averaging about 1300 cc, at least double the volume of the closest living primate) implies greater intelligence, as does the weight ratio of the brain to body. The complex nervous system permits subtle operations. Furthermore, the human is free from the instincts that so bind the lower animals within predetermined behavioral limits. The human is said to be the only animal with true freedom of choice, perhaps the only creature ever to have lived on our planet that must make agonizing decisions because of that freedom.

*The way to do things is neither the way of Heaven nor that of Earth but that of man.*

HSÜN TZU

A greatly expanded "new brain" provides human beings the capacity for abstract thought and reason. Greek thinkers pointed out that it is the human faculty for reason—the ability to use known facts to arrive at new facts—that makes us human and gives us a clue to our reason-for-being: to cultivate our rational minds. This faculty alone, they believed, distinguishes us from the animals. Apart from reason, they reasoned, the human *is* an animal.

Along with abstract thought goes self-consciousness, our human power to reflect upon one's self, one's nature, one's knowledge, and the meaning of our existence. Homo sapien is surely the only animal that can philosophize.

Three rather more ethereal qualities—ethical, esthetic, and religious feelings—are frequently considered to be distinctive features separating the human from other animals. Only the human, it is held, has a moral sense, feelings of justice and injustice, and only the human develops behavioral codes to live by. Only the human responds to beauty and creates objects for no other reason than to enjoy them. Only the human can conceive a supernatural order of reality, believe in deities, develop a soteriology of history, and feel "ultimate concern" about the meaning of his or her own existence.

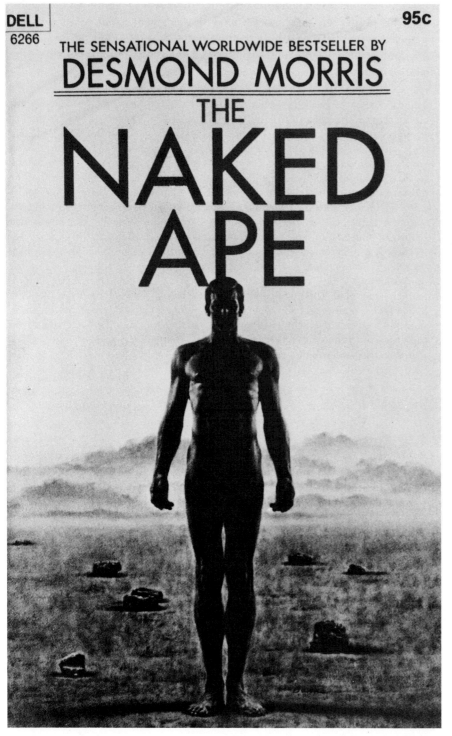

DELL
6266

**95c**

THE SENSATIONAL WORLDWIDE BESTSELLER BY
**DESMOND MORRIS**

# THE
# NAKED
# APE

*MAN   A biodegradable but
nonrecyclable animal blessed
with opposable thumbs capable of grasping at straws.*
BERNARD ROSENBERG

*A self-balancing, twenty-
eight-jointed adapter-base
biped; an electrochemical
reduction plant, integral with
segregated stowages of special energy extracts in storage
batteries for subsequent
actuation of thousands of
hydraulic and pneumatic
pumps with motors attached;
62,000 miles of capillaries.
. . . The whole, extraordinary complex mechanism
guided with exquisite precision from a turret in which
are located telescopic and
microscopic self-registering
and recording range finders,
a spectroscope, etc.; the turret control being closely
allied with an air-condition-
ing intake-and-exhaust, and a
main fuel intake. . . .*
BUCKMINSTER FULLER

*Man is a biped without
feathers.*
PLATO

*Man is the only creature that
spends its entire life trying to
become what it already is.*
ANONYMOUS

*Man is the only creature that
keeps trying to define himself.*
JIM WODACH

*Man is star-stuff that has
taken over its own destiny.*
CARL SAGAN

    There is an obvious omission from all these lists: *soul*. This singular qual-
ity finally distinguishes us from all other animals. Soul-essence (the Greek *psyche*) survives death, and no other animal is supposed to have a psyche.

Considerable debate has taken place to decide at what point along the evolutionary line prepsychic human developed (or was given) a soul.

Recent scientific discoveries have initiated a redefinition of the human. The Naked Ape is presently undergoing agonizing self-reappraisal vis-à-vis the animal world.

*Just as we do not know what life is, yet can distinguish between an inanimate object and a living animal or plant, similarly we cannot give a scientific definition of man, yet we have no difficulty in differentiating him from even the most manlike monkey. One of the gross deficiencies of science is that it has not yet defined what sets man apart from other animals.*

RENÉ DUBOS

Jane Goodall's discovery that chimps not only use but manufacture tools, significantly changed the scientific definition of man. He could no longer be classified as the only maker of tools. Their achievement is a simple one by human standards, but it elevates them far above all other animals save one. *This one girl has forced the scientists and psychologists of the world to redefine man.* Her chimps have helped remove man from some remote pedestal and return him to the natural world of the animal kingdom. She sees in her chimpanzees basic recognizable emotions and a need to communicate their feelings. Though physically incapable of forming the sounds of human speech, there is an unmistakable natural language that any human being can understand, signs of recognition, affection, and reassurance. . . .

Three generations of chimpanzees are now part of Jane Goodall's life. It took years to do what no one else had done: win their trust and confidence. From her understanding of these animals has come unexpected insight and increased appreciation of mankind. These chimpanzees are a source of growing wonder, a reminder of how far humanity has really come in the evolution of man's intellect and language, his ability to love unselfishly, to appreciate and create beauty. Perhaps the narrowing chasm between man and apes will not be spanned by science alone, but by understanding and compassion.

*Monkeys, Apes, and Men*
National Geographic, CBS-TV

## THE KILLER-APE DEBATE

In the process of redefining humanness a controversy has arisen. It appears that the human propensity for violence far exceeds any possible evolutionary demands; intense cruelty toward members of our own species is unique in the animal kingdom. Humans kill not merely for food but is vicious for ideological and symbolic reasons: killing "on principle." In the name of mental abstractions humans kill other humans, whereas other animals battle members of their own species only into submission. Together, all human religious constraints, moral codes, legal systems, and rationality seem barely able, under ideal conditions, to keep our viciousness within bounds.

*Every culture has devised its own way of responding to the riddle of the cosmos. . . . There are many different ways of being human.*

CARL SAGAN

The question is whether our aggressive behavior is inherited or learned. Is it possible that humans are killers because we descended directly from a line of "killer-apes"? This is the position held by the zoologists Konrad Lorenz *(On Aggression)* and Desmond Morris *(The Naked Ape),* and the playwright Robert Ardrey *(African Genesis, Territorial Imperative).*

The suggestion has been made by Dr. L. S. B. Leakey and other paleontologists that different branches of African Australopithecines pursued different evolutionary paths of development. While some remained peaceful vegetarians, at least one branch became aggressive carnivores; and it is quite possible that it is from this latter line that modern humans have developed. The killer instinct is set deep in our genes.

Man's trouble, Lorenz believes,

arises from his being a basically harmless omnivorous creature, lacking in natural weapons with which to kill big prey, and, therefore, also devoid of the built-in safety devices which prevent "professional" carnivores from abusing their killing power to destroy fellow members of their own species. A lion or a wolf may, on extremely rare occasions, kill another by one angry stroke, but . . . all heavily armed carnivores possess sufficiently reliable inhibitions which prevent the self-destruction of the species.

It is a curious paradox that the greatest gifts of man, the unique faculties of conceptual thought and verbal speech which have raised him to a level high above all other creatures and given him mastery over the globe, are not altogether blessings, or at least are blessings that have to be paid for very dearly indeed. All the great dangers threatening humanity with extinction are direct consequences of conceptual thought and verbal speech. They drove man out of the paradise in which he could follow his instincts with impunity and do or not do whatever he pleased. There is much truth in the parable of the tree of knowledge and its fruit, though I want to make an addition to it to make it fit into my own picture of Adam; that apple was thoroughly unripe! Knowledge springing from conceptual thought robbed man of the security provided by his well-adapted instincts long, long before it was sufficient to provide him with an equally safe adaptation. Man is, as Arnold Gehlen has so truly said, by nature a jeopardized creature.

KONRAD LORENZ

*There is no law except the law that there is no law.*
JOHN A. WHEELER

The killer-ape notion has brought angry rebuttal from other life scientists and from psychologists. They all counter that there is no significant evidence that human aggression is inherited, but there is strong evidence that it is learned. The entire range of bitter emotions and cruel behavior can be causally explained by early conditioning within a hostile environment. If cruel and violent actions are "programmed" into us as acceptable forms of behavior, and if we ourselves are treated cruelly and violently so that we store up an explosive reservoir of bitterness, then we have become, in the very core of our being, killer-apes. But all this is learned, and easily learned. We don't have to look far—only as far as the nearest TV set—to discover how acceptable "man's inhumanity to man" can become.

Dr. Ashley Montagu considers the killer-ape theory absurd and takes an opposing stand: any human being's aggressive cruelty results from the frustration of his more basic need to love and be loved. "His combativeness and competitiveness arise primarily from the frustration of his need to cooperate." The most basic drive of human nature—strictly from the standpoint of evolutionary survival—is love and cooperation.

*There is no doubt that human survival will continue to depend more and more on human intellect and technology. It is idle to argue whether this is good or bad. The point of no return was passed long ago, before anyone knew it was happening.*
THEODOSIUS DOBZHANSKY

The organism is born with an innate need for love, with a need to respond to love, to be good, cooperative. This is, I believe, now established beyond any shadow of doubt. Whatever is opposed to love, to goodness, and to cooperation is disharmonic, unviable, unstable, and malfunctional—evil. . . . All of man's natural inclinations are toward the development of goodness, toward the continuance of states of goodness and the discontinuance of unpleasant states. . . . Where hatreds exist in any persons within any society we may be sure that they, too, are due to love, for hatred is love frustrated. Aggression is but a technique or mode of seeking love.

*Out of the dreaming past, with its legends of steaming seas and gleaming glaciers, mountains that moved and suns that glared, emerges this creature, man—the latest phase in a continuing process that stretches back to the beginning of life. His is the heritage of all that has lived; he still carries the vestiges of snout and fangs and claws of species long since vanished; he is the ancestor of all that is yet to come.*

*Do not regard him lightly—he is you.*

**DON FABUN**

*To regard man, the most ephemeral and rapidly evolving of all species, as the final and unsurpassable achievement of creation, especially at his present-day particularly dangerous and disagreeable stage of development, is certainly the most arrogant and dangerous of all untenable doctrines.*

**KONRAD LORENZ**

The question is perpetually raised: "Is humanity *inherently* evil or good?" "Is the human being *genetically* a killer-ape or fallen angel?"

Something is probably wrong with the question. (Most either/or questions generate more problems than they solve.) Surely, the human being is *inherently* neither good nor bad. Even a cursory observation indicates that humans possess the capacity for cooperation and love as well as the capacity for aggressive and hostile behavior. Which traits develop in individuals and grow to dominate their relationships depends upon the demands of the environment. He or she develops a stance toward life out of life's stance toward him or her. It depends, for each individual, on conditioning—on whether, for each one, "things go right" or "things go wrong."

A better question might be: How do we humans differ from our animal kin in our feelings of aggression? Probably in no significant way *except in our complexity.* With our advanced cerebral cortex and our faculty for abstract thought, we possess a capacity for infinitely complex responses. We have almost unlimited choice. It is our complex perception of threat and the variety of our responses to it that makes us humans different.

In the rest of the animal kingdom, response tends to be simple and direct: flight, fight, or submission. In human beings the basic emotional response patterns are the same, but they are obscured by endless maneuvers of each individual according to our potential for indirect response.

But where there is no threat, humans are no more hostile than any of our animal relatives. To those who have lived with animals and trained and loved them, it is clear that when you take away threat, you eliminate violence; but when the environment threatens, violence results. It is more than likely that the same simple principle applies as well to us humans.

What, then, distinguishes human beings from the other animals? At the present time, we cannot with any certainty point to a single *human* quality that cannot be found, *to some degree,* in other animals.

The deep chasm that separates us from our animal kin reflects differences in degree. No one questions the fact that the human possesses mental powers that dramatically outdistance the closest primate kin: logical reason, creative imagination, self-consciousness. It is also a fact, however, that numerous animals possess abilities that far outdistance humans: highly developed sensing organs, for instance, and the ability to "intuit" subtle relationships that are missed by human beings.

It is probably true that every empirically observable characteristic hypothesized to distinguish humans from other fauna can be found, in some degree, somewhere in the animal kingdom.

## THE IMMENSE JOURNEY

Science has two functions: control and comprehension. The comprehension may be of the universe in which we live; or of ourselves; or of the relations between ourselves and our world. Evolutionary science has only been in existence, as a special branch of scientific knowledge, for less than a century. During that time its primary contribution has been to comprehension—first to that of the world around us, and then to that of our own nature. The last few decades have added an increasing comprehension of our position in the universe and our relations with it; and with this evolutionary science is certainly destined to make an important and increasing contribution to control; its practical application in the affairs of human life is about to begin.

SIR JULIAN HUXLEY (1952)

This stage in "the immense journey" has already begun. We are now in process of taking control of our own evolutionary destiny and, by default, the destiny of all other living creatures on this planet. Although produced by processes of which we had no understanding and no control, it looks as though we are moving rapidly to a point of no return when there is but one choice left to us: to take upon our shoulders the full burden of our future.

Two events have made this inevitable. First, we have made such rapid progress in science/technology that the selective function of the environment has been radically altered. Many detrimental or lethal inheritable characteristics are now being preserved; under natural conditions they would die out. Among such genetic disorders are hemophilia, retinal blastoma, sickle-cell anemia, and susceptibility to a host of physical and emotional dysfunctions. Many of these defects are now being corrected or rendered tolerable through surgery, chemistry, and psychiatry. Carriers of such genes produce offspring, and the defective genes multiply. This has now happened in the case of so many genetic traits that the "fittest" are not the individuals who survive. Natural selectivity is no longer the primary mechanism in evolution.

The second event forcing us to take over our own evolution is the destruction of our natural environment. Humans developed through selective competition with and in a natural environment: *it* produced *us* according to *its* criteria. Humans, not the environment, did the adapting. Environment is the creator; human is the creature. The ever-changing ecosystem "decided" which traits this evolving organism would possess.

But this trait-selecting environment no longer exists. Our scientific/technological applications, along with the proliferation of our species, has altered the environment so much that it has lost the power to select specific adaptive traits. No known forces are presently operating to determine that "fitter" traits survive and weaker traits perish.

Symbolically, the offspring has annihilated the parent that produced it.

It is humbling to realize that man is, in this sense, only one part of nature, just as a consideration of the size of the universe makes him realize his own relative smallness. But evolutionary biology has also shown us the central role that man is

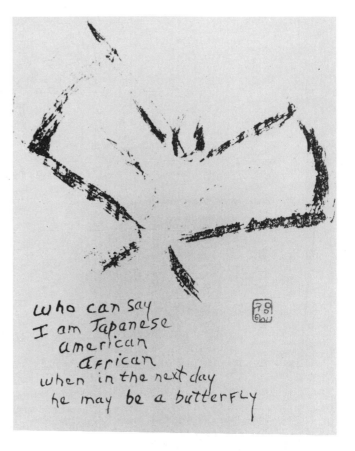

who can say
I am Japanese
american
african
when in the next day
he may be a butterfly

*Man differs from the animal only by a little; most men throw that little away.*

CONFUCIUS

*Man is a rational animal who always loses his temper when he is called upon to act in accordance with the dictates of reason.*

OSCAR WILDE

# CHARLES DARWIN

## *The Grandest Synthesis*

"Poor man," the gardener said, "he just stands and stares at a yellow flower for minutes at a time. He would be better off with something to do."

". . . with something to do"! The gardener at Darwin's country home wasn't quite up to understanding what one of the world's great naturalists was doing. To be sure, he was perceiving a yellow flower, but his mind was making connections—synthesizing. What he was doing, of course, was *seeing*—experiencing a single object while his mind was weaving a web of connections that made that object intelligible. "Such a synthesis," writes Loren Eiseley, "represents the scientific mind at its highest point of achievement."

Charles Darwin was born on the same day as Abraham Lincoln—February 12, 1809—in Shrewsbury, England. His father, Robert Darwin, was an affluent country doctor with a bright but conventional mind. He was wholly dedicated to his patients, spending his life making calls and listening to woes. Darwin's mother was Susannah Wedg-

wood, daughter of the developer of Wedgwood china. She was bright but retiring; and she split with tradition by becoming a Unitarian. His mother died when young Darwin was eight, and he retained little conscious memory of her. He was raised by an older sister.

His first eight years of schooling at the Shrewsbury grammar school provided a foundation in classical education, including a command of Greek and Latin, but he was bored by class exercises and was withdrawn from the school by a disappointed father when his teachers concluded that he was perhaps less than ingenious and in any case wasn't a very good scholar. His father enrolled him in premedical studies at the University of Edinburgh, assuming that his son would pursue the father's career. But Darwin found the lectures dull and, worse, was chilled at the sight of blood —he witnessed two operations performed without anesthesia, one of them on a child; he was overcome and had to leave the room. Gradually he lost interest in a medical career.

Bending to family pressure to choose *some* respectable vocation, Darwin enrolled in Christ's College, Cambridge

University, to prepare for the ministry. Religion had never been much discussed in the Darwin household; it had been assumed, unconsciously. But at Cambridge Darwin at last began to discover his true love: the sciences. His scientific aptitude was strong, his interest intense. Still, he graduated with a degree in theology and was scheduled to be ordained to the Anglican priesthood.

A turning point came in the fall of 1831. He received an invitation to become resident naturalist on a government ship about to embark on a scientific expedition of the southern hemisphere. Darwin had second thoughts. He questioned whether he should give two years of his life at this time. Furthermore, the young captain didn't much like Darwin; among other things he was bothered by the shape of his nose (he was a devout phrenologist). The ship for this round-the-world voyage was only a ninety-foot-long, ten-gun brig; it carried a crew of seventy-three.

Still, the scientific instinct and sense of adventure in the young scientist were strong, and he sailed from Devonport on December 27, 1831. Darwin got along amicably with the crew, who called him "our dear old philosopher" (he was twenty-two!). But the unsanitary conditions, cramped quarters, and relentlessly rolling sea kept him in a state of misery for much of the trip.

The voyage of the HMS *Beagle* is one of the most important voyages ever made. The ship sailed to South America, where Darwin made extensive explorations in the tidepools along the coast and of the fauna and flora of the pampas. They dipped around the Cape and sailed northward along the west coast of South America to the Galápagos Islands, where for some five weeks in 1835 Darwin studied the giant tortoises, the seaweed-eating lizards, and the birdlife of the dozen small islands—"a little world in itself, with inhabitants such as are found nowhere else." Then they sailed across the south Atlantic to New Zealand and Australia, across the Indian Ocean and

around the tip of Africa, and put ashore again in Brazil; then homeward via the Cape Verde Islands and the Azores. The voyage had taken, not two, but five years of his life. Darwin was twenty-eight when he returned home.

He had taken volumes of field notes, which he proceeded to order and ponder. His health had been damaged, and for the rest of his life he was to suffer from sleeplessness, nausea, and headaches. It is likely that he had caught a tropical disease during the voyage. Three years after returning he published his annotated journals of the trip, entitled *The Voyage of the Beagle.*

Two years later (at thirty) he was married to Emma Wedgwood, a cousin, for one of the happier marriages of record; they settled in Down, a secluded village in Kent, to a traditional family life. They had seven children, and he enjoyed his family immensely. For the next twenty years—from 1838 to 1858—he did little traveling, mixed only occasionally, and spent his days deciphering his notes and writing.

We picture Darwin as a gray-bearded patriarch, but this was Darwin long after he gained fame. As a young man, he was a stalwart six-footer with red hair and long red-brown sideburns, a round pinkish face, and great blue eyes peering from beneath massive eyebrows. He was healthy and strong (before his voyage), spent much time outdoors, going on geology field trips, walking by the river, or collecting beetles, leaves, and flowers. His friends knew him to be a lovable, gentle, genial man, patient and kind, and quite unauthoritarian.

Darwin was one of those fortunate human beings who found a vocation in which he could develop his strengths and apply his genius. He was blessed to be at the right time and place with the right qualities of mind and heart.

Picture: notebooks filled with countless singular observations, from a yellow flower to a fossil whelk, from a camouflaged octopus to a butterfly's mimicking wing, from an insect-eating

*I would as soon be descended from that heroic little monkey . . . as from a savage who delights to torture his enemies, offers up blood sacrifices, practices infanticide without remorse, treats his wives like slaves, knows no decency, and is haunted by the grossest superstitions.*

*ON DARWIN'S THEORY:*
*The theory of evolution accomplished not only the separation of biology and religion, but compelled a completely new interpretation of the universe.*

LOUIS UNTERMEYER

*We must not fall into the error of supposing that the early progenitor of the whole simian stock, including man, was identical with or even closely resembled an existing ape or monkey.*

sundew plant to a seagull's courtship ritual; and so on, almost without end.

The problem: to see, connectedly—to discover the relationship of all things living on Earth. It was a monumental task; and the mind that could manage such a massive assemblage of data and could render it intelligible would have to be a very special mind—an "oceanic" mind. In such operations, the individual facts may not be new, though in Darwin's case many were; what is new is the inductive synthesis that permits understanding.

Darwin had the good fortune to have come across a world-in-miniature where nature's mechanisms could be more easily isolated: the ecological niche of the finches on the Galápagos Islands, later to be known as "Darwin's finches." What Darwin found was some fourteen types of finches, belonging to the same species but possessing distinct individual differences, especially in the shape and size of their beaks. Some had parrotlike beaks for eating fruit and cracking seedpods. Some had beaks like sparrows for eating seeds. Others had long, pointed beaks for sipping nectar from flowers. There were large beaks and small beaks, sharp beaks and blunt, short beaks, straight beaks and curving beaks.

In cases like this biologists had assumed that all these varieties had migrated from the mainland; but in the case of the Galápagos finches the variations were to be found nowhere else. In this case it appeared that millions of years ago an ancestral species of finches had made its way to the islands, thrived, and multiplied. Some of the finches subsequently adapted to different food sources so that they would not be in direct competition with one another, greatly increasing the chances of survival. Darwin wrote that "one species had been taken and modified for different ends."

Darwin began to see that an "evolvement" may have taken place. Species apparently evolved from other species. He speculated: What if this pattern is universal and all species of life on Earth are in a state of evolvement from earlier species?

As Darwin reflected on his data, evolvement seemed virtually certain; but he could not yet see the mechanism by which this evolvement had taken place. Then, in October 1838, he read an article published in 1798 by Thomas Malthus, a political economist who had argued that human populations multiply faster than the food supply and must therefore be periodically decimated by starvation, disease, and war. Who would survive such catastrophes? Malthus had answered: those who are more hardy. Darwin saw the key to the puzzle: the mechanism of evolvement is the "struggle for survival" and the "survival of the fittest." Under the perpetual threat of starvation and annihilation in the harsh environment, all species of life on Earth continually struggle for survival, and only the fittest survive.

Life on Earth is a single story, and it is intelligible.

Evolution is a field theory for understanding the dynamics of life on Earth and, by a reasonable extrapolation, of all possible life-forms in the universe. But it is more: it is a philosophy of change for more accurately conceiving everything in the universe—the galaxies, the stars with their birth-to-death life history, the nebulous solar systems, the migrating continents. It applies to everything, without exception, in physics and biology; it applies to human experiences. Evolution is the most comprehensive field theory yet developed by the human mind.

For twenty years Darwin worked and reworked his vast accumulation of materials. Still, he knew that his ideas would inevitably provoke hostility, which he wanted to avoid; so he continued to rationalize his refusal to publish: his theories, perhaps, needed just a little more work.

In 1858 Lyell again urged Darwin to write a full account of his thinking. He was about half-finished when there occurred one of history's significant ironies. In June 1858, a young scientist named Alfred Russel Wallace, with less

*The most humble organism is something much higher than the inorganic dust under our feet; and no one with an unbiased mind can study any living creature, however humble, without being struck with enthusiasm at its marvellous structure and properties.*

*All the organic beings which have ever lived on this earth have descended from some one primordial form.*

*Man is descended from some less highly organized form.*

experience and a modicum of materials, arrived at a theoretical model virtually identical to Darwin's. Because Darwin had been known in scientific circles since he first published the diaries of his voyage, Wallace had submitted his manuscript to him, humbly asking for the elder biologist's critique of his ideas.

Darwin was shaken, but he felt that he had no right to steal the younger man's glory if Wallace was going to be the first into print. "I would far rather burn my whole book than that he or any other man should think that I had behaved in a paltry spirit." But Darwin's friends all knew of his lifelong labors and urged that he proceed with haste to publish his own work. It was fair: he had worked intently for twenty years, organized stores of data to prove his theses; and science, they argued, must be served by the best. Darwin finally assented. He prepared his manuscript rapidly for publication. The first public announcement of their theories was made in a joint presentation by Darwin and Wallace before a meeting of the Linnaean Society on July 1, 1858— one of the heartwarming moments in the history of spirited competition when decency wholly prevailed. Darwin's "abstract" was published in 1859 as *The Origin of Species.*

The first printing of his book sold out in one day, and from that day to this *The Origin of Species* has been acclaimed one of the great works in the history of man's search for understanding. But much of the world was shocked by Darwin's ideas. Many Christians believed, with Archbishop Ussher, that the world was created in 4004 B.C. (on October 22). By contrast, Darwin's scenario postulated millions of years of slow change. Further, the notion that species were not created "in the beginning" as complete life-forms seemed blasphemous to biblical literalists. But Darwin's organization of empirical facts was overwhelming, and the hypothesis fitted the facts. The evolvement theory was accepted by virtually all scientists of the time, as well as by the general public.

Darwin watched from the sidelines. "It is something unintelligible to me how anyone can argue in public like orators do." Darwin avoided hostility, so his friends, especially Lyell and Sir Thomas Huxley, carried the banner for him. Darwin was hurt by the bitterness that his ideas had produced. He stayed away from the fuss and furor, secluded at his country estate. His remaining years were content.

Darwin's own religious beliefs underwent a gradual change. He tells us in his autobiography that he reflected much about religion during the two years following the return of the *Beagle.* When he wrote *The Origin of Species* in 1858, he still thought of himself as a theist or deist. But the "nature" that he had seen—the struggle-for-survival, "red in tooth and claw"—disturbed him immensely; the necessity of such suffering, which he saw to be an integral part of the evolutionary struggle, seemed strong evidence against the existence of the benevolent deity; and he moved from a naive acceptance of orthodox ideas to a reluctant agnosticism. For the Anglican-priest-to-have-been, this personal odyssey was accompanied by pain and guilt. Still, his own integrity came first. He wrote: "I have steadily endeavored to keep my mind free, so as to give up any hypothesis, however much beloved (and I cannot resist forming one on every subject), as soon as facts are shown to be opposed to it."

He died at their home in Down, at the age of seventy-three, after seizures "in the region of the heart." His wife and family were at his bedside. Emma said, "Perhaps Father did not believe in God. But God believed in him." He was buried in Westminister Abbey, not far from the tomb of Sir Isaac Newton. It is said that on the way home, Darwin's son reflected, "Can you imagine what delightful conversations Father and Sir Isaac Newton will have each night after the Abbey is closed, and all is quiet?"

destined to play in evolution from now on—unless, of course, he engineers his own extinction. Although man arose out of an evolutionary process that he didn't understand and over which he had no control, he must now realize that he is unique in the living world in the realization that the responsibility for continuance of this process is his. . . .

The capacity of biologists to develop ways by which man can determine his future evolution is undoubted. The more difficult question is whether he will choose to make such decisions, *and with what wisdom.*

*Biology and the Future of Man*

## REFLECTIONS

*Far from seeing in man the irrevocable and unsurpassable image of God, I assert—more modestly and, I believe, in greater awe of the Creation and its infinite possibilities—that the long-sought missing link between animals and the really humane being is ourselves!*

**KONRAD LORENZ**

1   Read for a synoptic overview the various creation stories at the beginning of this chapter. What do they all have in common? What are the major differences? What are the ultimate questions that these creation myths seem designed to explain? (Refer to your glossary for a definition of "myth," if needed.)

2   What is your candid response to the various creation stories? (Remember these are but a few of thousands of such myths.) Do these accounts help to clarify for you the functions of myths?

3   In your opinion, what qualities separate humans from the other animals? Make a list of all such distinguishing qualities that you can think of; then delete from the list each characteristic that current evidence shows humans may share with one or more of his animal kin. What characteristics do you have left on your list?

4   Make an attempt to define "human." How would you describe "essential man"? What are some of the problems we must face in developing a definition?

5   What is your own inclination regarding the aggression debate? Can you develop a strong case that the human is genetically aggressive? Can you make an equally strong case that this aggression is learned? Where must you go for hard data to resolve the controversy?

6   How much do you agree or disagree with the sentence on p. 422, "Surely, the human being is *inherently* neither good nor bad. . . . He or she develops a stance toward life out of life's stance toward him or her"—? What data can you offer to support your assessment?

7   Our attitudes toward "human nature" are so basic that they shape our politics and economics, our religions, our judgment of history and our stance toward the future, and our relationships with others and ourselves. What is your assessment of human nature? Are you essentially optimistic and trusting or pessimistic and wary? What facts do you possess that would support your general attitudes? (Be careful. Perhaps the question is not phrased right. Maybe there is no such thing as "human nature," in which case how should the question be stated?)

# EARTH

# 6 3

## OUR PLACE IN THE SCHEME OF THINGS

The idea of Reverence for Life offers itself as the realistic answer to the realistic question of how man and the world are related to each other. Of the world man knows only that everything which exists is, like himself, a manifestation of the Will-to-Live. . . .

Let a man once begin to think about the mystery of his life and the links which connect him with the life that fills the world, and he cannot but bring to bear upon his own life and all other life that comes within his reach the principle of Reverence for Life. . . . Existence will thereby become harder for him in every respect than it would be if he lived for himself, but at the same time it will be richer, more beautiful, and happier. It will become, instead of mere living, a real experience of life.

ALBERT SCHWEITZER

The human race has sought knowledge of the world to understand it not merely intellectually, but rather to understand our relationship to it and our place in it. All our rational inquiries are merely a prelude to the establishment of a more meaningful relationship. The implicit question for humanity has always been, "What is my place in the scheme of things?"

Humans evolved in a world that is at once friendly and hostile. With one hand the world gives life, while with the other it inflicts pain and death. We have been, it seems, strangers in a strange land. But we have made it our home even while it has felt like enemy territory.

The story of *general evolution* is an account of how species search for a suitable niche in their environment. The story *human evolution* is the account of our transcendence of that evolutionary niche. And the story of *human civilization* is the account of our gradual conquest and control of our environment.

The human's relationship to his/her natural environment seems to have moved through three stages.

*And the wind shall say: "Here were decent godless people Their only monument the asphalt road And a thousand lost golf balls."*

T. S. ELIOT

*In wildness is the preservation of the world.*

HENRY DAVID THOREAU

*Stranger by the roadside, do not smile When you see this grave, though it is only a dog's. My master wept when I died, and his own hand Laid me in earth and wrote these lines on my tomb.*

ANONYMOUS

**Greek epitaph for a dog**

Humans first experienced nature in a parent-child relationship. Nature produced him; he was its offspring. He was never sure how to conceptualize the forces that generated life, but he could not doubt that they were everywhere—in his crops, his herds and flocks, in his human family. So his myths helped him conceive the inconceivable. Nature's life-giving forces were, naturally, male and female. The prime source of life was Mother Earth personified as Magna Mater, or Gaia, or Demeter—each was in some way the Earth-Mother. (We still habitually think of "her" as Mother Nature, and the very idea of "Father Nature" *feels* wrong even to us!) There must be masculine forces too, of course, so there was Jupiter (Dyaus Pitar or Zeus Pater, "Father Zeus"); and the Semitic tribal gods—Yahweh, Chemosh, Milcom, Allah—are all male figures. Generally the dynamic forces of nature such as storms, earthquakes, thunder, and lightning were conceived as masculine in potency; while the more passive aspects of nature—the quiet earth that absorbs the rain and brings forth new sprouts of corn—were thought of as feminine potencies.

These personified forces are humanity's parents. The characteristic response to them is fear and awe, acceptance and obedience. The person has no control over nature's forces; *they* condition *his* behavior. Like authoritarian parents, they nurture him; but they also punish him. His dependence is almost absolute. He stands helpless before the storm, the flood, the drought, the mortal pain. He is a child who knows nothing of the motives of the forces that rule him. They possess secrets he cannot understand. Yet he does his best to relate to them and please them, to discover the "desires" of these personified forces and accede to their wills. Thus, he makes every attempt—as he would with human parents—to keep them as favorably inclined as he can.

The second stage—human as conqueror—is found in a rudimentary way in

*You can always tell when it's autumn in Hollywood. They put away the green plastic plants and bring out the brown plastic plants.*

JOHNNY CARSON

## THE EARTH IS SORE

(The words of an old holy woman of the Wintu Indians of California.)

The White people never cared for land or deer or bear. When we Indians kill meat, we eat it all up. When we dig roots we make little holes. When we build houses, we make little holes. When we burn grass for grasshoppers, we don't ruin things. We shake down acorns and pinenuts. We don't chop down the trees. We only use dead wood. But the White people plow up the ground, pull down the trees, kill everything. The tree says, "Don't. I am sore. Don't hurt me." But they chop it down and cut it up. The spirit of the land hates them. They blast out trees and stir it up to its depths. They saw up the trees. That hurts them. The Indians never hurt anything, but the White people destroy all. They blast rocks and scatter them on the ground. The rock says, "Don't. You are hurting me." But the White people pay no attention. When the Indians use rocks, they take little round ones for their cooking. . . . How can the spirit of the earth like the White man? . . . Everywhere the White man has touched it, it is sore.

DOROTHY LEE
*Freedom and Culture*

all human cultures, but its successful development belongs to the West. It began with the discovery by Pythagoras of nature's greatest secret: that she speaks the language of mathematics. Foundations were thus laid for scientific control, but time dallied for two more millennia before this knowledge was used. Physics and mechanics were finally born in the seventeenth century, followed shortly by chemistry and biology and, belatedly, by the social and behavioral sciences. Communication and transportation technologies belong to our own century. Controls have now spread to almost every area of human experience. Lagging behind, of course, is control of humanity itself, but this appears to be the arena wherein the next giant steps will be taken.

This rapid conquest and control of our dynamic environment is Homo sapien's greatest success story, and it is basically a story of a love/hate relationship. Humans loved earth; it nourished them. But they had also hated it for its relentless attempt to annihilate them. It was a life/death struggle between human being and nature; and as in any love/hate relationship, the question has been *which* would win out: love or hate. *Who* would win: Human or Nature?

*Man has survived, hitherto, by virtue of ignorance and inefficiency.*

BERTRAND RUSSELL

Human has won—or is winning. We are on the threshold of setting controls over ever-larger forces of nature—climate and earthquakes, for instance. The control of life and evolution is near. There are repeated hints in futuristic literature that man may eventually establish control on a cosmological scale. We might alter the orbit or the tilt of the earth, for example, or capture small asteroids to serve as scientific stations or to provide transportation to remote outposts. Such comprehensive controlling power would be merely a large-scale extension of our present capacities, and we are moving rapidly in this direction. On the condition that we don't destroy ourselves first, such controls are probably inevitable.

A third stage, beginning in our time, is a protective feeling toward nature. If humanity no longer fears nature because we understand her ways, and if we have established control over the more threatening elements of our environment, then fear can give way to other feelings: kinship, appreciation, protection. People will become nature's advocate.

This has been the Western experience. Other branches of the human story exhibit different responses toward nature. Western achievements bring mixed feelings, of course. We wonder whether compassionate concerns have surfaced in time to salvage this spaceship. It is the West's problem not merely because *our* controls have caused our environmental problems; but probably only Western civilization has the technology for solving the problems we have created.

*We have come [to the oceans] as aliens from another world. . . . The time has come to recognize that the sea and the creatures in it have their needs and their rights to exist. An ocean ethic is needed which will combine wisdom, sensitivity, and forethought; an ethic which will not betray the dream which began our long, deep journey.*

*Mysteries of the Sea*

## AN ECOSPHERIC ETHIC

Through a continuing process of self-discovery, we have had to reassess our place "in the scheme of things" and learn how to behave responsibly. Having discovered that we exist as part-and-parcel of all Earth's living things, the vital question has become: *Who has a right to do what to whom and why?*

Ecology, therefore, is not only a scientific discipline, but more basically it is a matter of ethics. How should people relate to other fauna and flora with

*A weed is a plant whose virtues have not yet been discovered.*

RALPH WALDO EMERSON

## PRIOR POSSESSION

I had long dreamed of owning a piece of land. I wanted to build a house, plant a garden, and broadcast handfuls of wildflower seeds, at random, and then wait for the springtime miracle of dancing colors.

So I bought a plot of ground. Ten acres of grass patches, chaparral, scrub, cattails, and riparian thickets, with a gurgling stream cutting across the far corner. This was to be my home. No prior claim had been filed; no one had built on it, or lived on it—so I was told.

That wasn't true. What I found was that others already lived there, and I had to share. In prior possession of the land were:

Botta Pocket Gopher (56)
California Pocket Mouse (18)
Pacific Kangaroo Rat (10)
Western Harvest Mouse (80)
California Mouse (8)
Brush Mouse (2)
Deer Mouse (188)
House Mouse (38, immigrants)
Neotoma lepida, Packrat (47)
Gray Fox (4, transients)
Coyote (8, transients)
Raccoon (2, visitors)
Striped Skunk (a pair, visitors)
Bobcat (1, seasonal visitor)
Black-tailed Deer (12, seasonal visitor)
Ornate Shrew (two pairs)
Broad-handed Mole (23)
Myotis thysanodes (68 bats, night visitors)
Myotis californicus (12 bats, night visitors)
Myotis yumanensis (4 bats, night visitors)
Jackrabbit (14, transients)
Cottontail (18)
Beechy Ground Squirrel (4)
Ring-necked Pheasant (a pair, transients)
Turkey Vulture (36, flybys)
White-tailed Kite (2, flybys)
Red-tailed Hawk (4, seasonal residents)
Golden Eagle (1, flythrough)
Sparrow Hawk (4)
Gambel's Quail (34, in season)
Mourning Dove (20)
Roadrunner (4, transients)
Screech Owl (6)

White-throated Swift (8, flybys)
Anna's Hummingbird (20, seasonal visitors)
Black-chinned Hummingbird (10, seasonal visitors)
Red-shafted Flicker (18, transients)
Acorn Woodpecker (4, visitors)
Yellow-bellied Sapsucker (4, visitors)
Hairy Woodpecker (3, visitors)
Western Kingbird (6)
Black Phoebe (a pair)
Say's Phoebe (a pair)
Swallow (16, flybys)
Scrub Jay (4)
Raven (6, flythroughs)
Bushtit (5)
Wrentit (a pair)
Mockingbird (6)
Robin (12, seasonal visitors)
Western Bluebird (4, seasonal visitors)
Cedar Waxwing (a pair, in season)
Loggerhead Shrike (6, occasional visitors)
Starling (61, evening roost)
Hutton's Vireo (8, visitors)
Warblers (19 species, transients)
House Sparrow (14 pairs)
Meadowlark (4, visitors)
House Finch (13)
Rufous-sided Towhee (4)
Abert's Towhee (2)
Brown Towhee (6)
Oregon Junco (18, seasonal visitors)
Common Nighthawk (30, flybys)
Spiders (18 species, 8,966 individuals)
Millipedes (9 species, 397 individuals)

Centipedes (2 species, 455 individuals)
Scorpions (2 species, 129 individuals)
Lizards (8 species, 166 individuals)
Grasshoppers (6 species, 12,288 individuals)
Crickets (2 species, 8,940 individuals)
Katydids (113)
Gnats (4,560, flythroughs)
Aphids (68,444)
Dragonflies (16)
Ladybird Beetles (8,982)
Earthworms (4 species, 34,980 individuals)
Sycamore
California Live Oak
Baccharis
Amorpha
Romneya
Cercocarpus
Rhamnus (Coffeeberry)
Ceanothus
Salvia melifera (Black Sage)
Lotus scoparius (Deer weed)
Rhus integrifolia
Eriogonum fasciculatum
Artemesia californica
Quercus dumosa (Scrub Oak)
Yucca whippei
Lupine
Mimulus (Monkey Flower)
Montia (Miner's Lettuce)
Phacelia
Orthocarpus (Owl Clover)
Calochortus
Dodecatheon
Marah
Penstemon
Adenostoma
Escholtzia

These numbers are not constant, of course. The resident snakes and hawks occasionally take a gopher or mouse, and each evening bats and nighthawks reduce the insect population. However, their numbers remain relatively stable.

Continued

How exactly shall we plan to live together? Who must go? Who can stay? (Who decides? I do, obviously. Someone has to make management decisions. Does "might make right" after all?) Do all our noble thoughts of fairness and justice become ludicrous in cases like this? (My friends say "Yes" and laugh: moral sentiments are impractical, of course, though they rather *hope* I will pare the pheasants and ladybugs. "They're so pretty," they say to me, "and the little beetles eat aphids." So, is that what ethics is all about—*their* usefulness *to me?*)

I've settled in now on our plot of ground, in relative comfort. I've become mildly territorial. As in any extended-family venture, I find I like some members of the community a lot more than others.

I still ponder: How *should* we live together? Who *really* has a right to do what to whom and why and who says so? And am I the only one in this cooperative enterprise asking questions like this?

To be sure, I enjoy my plot of earth; but a hidden corner of my soul turns at night, not quite at peace with the world.

ROBERT BAKER
*Baker's Acre*

*Pythagoras and Empedocles . . . assert that there is a single status of justice belonging to all living creatures . . . that everlasting punishment awaits those who have wronged anything that lives.*

CICERO

whom we share a planet? How should we treat the ecosphere, including the earth, oceans, and atmosphere? Are we the only creature with "rights," or do animals also have "rights"? Do trees have "rights"? Do we have a "right" to kill any animal—harmless wild animals, predators, dogs and cats and other "pets"? Do we have a "right" to kill only "food" animals? or only "dangerous" animals? Do we have a "right" to kill gorillas? or dolphins? Do lions have a "right" to kill and eat zebras and antelope? Do dolphins have a "right" to kill men? Etcetera. . . .

In a word, on what criteria can all these questions be given factually sound answers? And, as a final question, "Who says so?"

Since humans have now dominated this planet, ethical responsibilities rest on our shoulders. But even then the question persists: Who (or what) gives us the right to make these life-or-death decisions?

Professor George Sessions, an ecophilosopher, has given an excellent description of our ecological plight and analyzed some of the ethical puzzlements inherent in it. He reminds us that we are in ecological trouble because of the traditional Western world-views we have inherited. "Ethical beliefs and attitudes do not exist in a vacuum." How we treat other creatures that share our world is dictated to us by the cosmology within which "we live and move and have our being." "When these cosmologies are no longer viable or believable, the entire ethical system or attitude becomes irrelevant and inappropriate." This has now happened to us. Sessions writes:

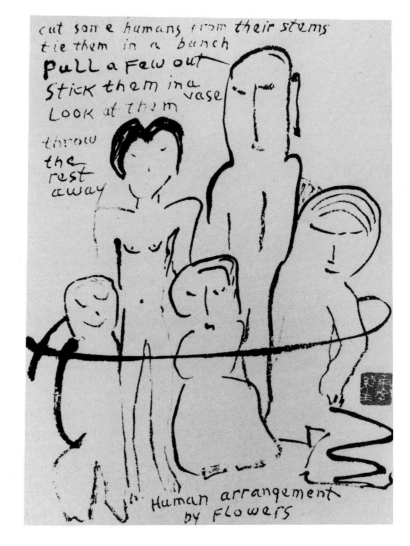

Human arrangement by flowers

In contrast with the earliest animisms and pantheisms of the West, and the pre-industrial nature orientations of the East, a pervasive cultural feature of the more recent West has been its anthropocentric cosmologies together with a correspondingly anthropocentric ethical orientation. From the Judeo-Christian account of man's separation from, and transcendence over, Nature, and the rise of man-centered philosophical systems and ethics in classical Greece, to the Cartesian mind-body dualism which became the cornerstone of early modern European philosophy, these essentially dualistic views of man and nature have provided the metaphysical basis for an outlook which sees *Homo sapiens* as the exclusive focus of ethical interest and concern.

By 1960 the dark clouds hovering over Earth's delicate ecology had become obvious to field specialists, but the threat hadn't yet been seen by other specialists or by political/industrial agents who could initiate change. They were still caught up in other concerns. Marston Bates, an ecologist, scolded philosophers for "dallying in their academic groves" at the very moment when a new ethical perspective was desperately needed.

The appearance of Rachel Carson's attack on the indiscriminate use of pesticides (*Silent Spring*, 1962) and then Paul Ehrlich's *The Population Bomb* (1968) "marked the beginning of the end of an era of almost total ecological

*If our members continue to increase at the present frightening rate, it will eventually become a matter of choosing between us and them [other animal species]. No matter how valuable they are to us symbolically, scientifically or aesthetically, the economics of the situation will shift against them. The blunt fact is that when our species density reaches a certain pitch, there will be no space left for other animals.*

DESMOND MORRIS

naiveté in the modern Western world. Belief in the omnipotence and omni-competence of the human race through its scientific technology received a tremendous jolt from a wholly new quarter. It was now evident that Nature was not totally manipulable for the 'good' of human societies, nor was it 'meant' to be."

There was another turning point in our ecological awareness, according to Sessions: the publication of an article by Lynn White dealing with the religious roots of the developing crisis.

*God Almighty first planted a garden.*

**FRANCIS BACON**

White's message was quite simple: Christian anthropocentrism was the root cause of the environmental crisis. The paper was reprinted in innumerable ecological anthologies which were just beginning to flood the book market. Controversies raged. Conscience-stricken Christian theologians, preachers, and scientists denounced his views, or reexamined their religious beliefs and attitudes. Conferences with titles such as the "theology of survival" were hurriedly called. By one stroke White subsequently claimed (with justification) to have created "the theology of ecology."

White pointed to the drastic attitudinal change towards Nature which occurred when Christianity replaced ancient forms of pantheism and animism, calling it "the greatest psychic revolution in the history of our culture." An animistic metaphysics, which saw spirit in nature, resulted in attitudes of respect and veneration for natural objects and thus helped protect Nature from man's unthinking exploitation. Christianity's desacralization of Western man's world encouraged an attitude of "indifference to the feelings of natural objects."

*The science of ecology is only the most recent and perhaps the most dramatic and sub-versive manifestation of the impact of modern science upon Western man's largely distorted sense of self-impor-tance in the cosmos.*

**GEORGE SESSIONS**

To restore some bit of intrinsic value to nature, White suggested that the modern world might be well advised to return to the medieval world-view of Saint Francis of Assisi, whose "view of nature and man rested on a unique sort of pan-psychism of all things animate and inanimate, designed for the glorification of their transcendent Creator." All things are revered by God and therefore they should also be revered by man. "Francis tried to depose man from his monarchy over creation and set up a democracy of all God's creatures."

Sessions considers the Franciscan world-view to be an ethical improvement upon both of the traditional Judeo-Christian models of the man-nature relationship: the exploitation model and the stewardship model.

But a closer look at the Franciscan ethic reveals that it contains difficulties which stem from an ecologically naive view of the world. For on this view, each individual entity (whether man, chipmunk, or rock) is apparently envisioned to be of equal worth "in the sight of God." It provides no basis for an adjudication of the conflicts which inevitably arise—for example, who or what has a "right" to eat whom, and upon what basis this is to be decided. Predation is an inevitable fact of biological life. If all individuals are to be accorded equal worth, the problem of predation is left unsolved (for humans: other animals appear to be largely unencumbered with these kinds of "problems").

*Sometimes truth comes riding into history on the back of error.*

**REINHOLD NIEBUHR**

Furthermore, it is not made clear how rocks and the "less articulate" forms of life are to participate, either directly or indirectly, in the universal democratic process.

But most seriously, this solution misleadingly focuses attention on the "rights" of individual entities (a distinctively Western humanistic preoccupation), thus obscuring the crucial ecological point that the environmental crisis is not primarily the result of a threat to the continued existence of *individual entities* as such, but to the *species diversity* so essential to the continued viable functioning of the earth's fragile *ecosystems*. In a very fundamental sense, the unit of ecological meaningfulness is the entire functioning interdependent ecosystem—or more generally, the ecosphere.

Other recent attempts have been made by philosophers and theologians to establish criteria for solving the ethical problem of "who may eat whom."

Professor Charles Hartshorne tackles the problem of the relative value of the inhabitants of our ecosphere by picturing a God who looks upon all his creation with "impartial delight." Hartshorne contends that "the ultimate value of human life, or of anything else, consists *entirely* in the contribution it makes to the divine life." Since God created all that exists, then everything is of some value to "the divine life"; but since God is essentially rational, then the more rational the creature is, the more valued it would be in God's eyes. The relative value of organisms and species is therefore established. Creatures that are very low on the sentient-rational scale are also very low in value; humans are of greatest value being highest on the sentient-rational scale. Nothing possesses intrinsic value, according to Hartshorne; something gains the quality of value only because God values it.

A contemporary theologian, Professor John Cobb, has attempted to establish *intrinsic* criteria by which various creatures in the ecosphere could be judged to be of relative value. Cobb suggests that "experiential states"—such as sensitivity, capacities for pleasure, abstract reasoning, and creativity—establish such a hierarchy of worth. Used with caution—since we aren't yet certain about the "experiential states" of all Earth's creatures—humans appear to be at the top of the scale. On such a quality-of-experience scale, those creatures at the top of the ladder would possess "rights" over the life and destiny of those creatures lower on the scale.

This analysis by Dr. Cobb seems to reflect with some accuracy the actual state of things in nature. Still, it may be risky to elevate evolution's apparent hierarchy into a normative ethical system and conclude that this is the way the value system *ought* to be. Cobb acknowledges the anthropocentric nature of the scale but suggests that this is inescapable since, after all, we humans are the ones engaged in the task of trying to make sense of the whole ecological/ethical problem.

Attempts such as these to establish a hierarchy for "the world of an individual or species" has drawn angry criticism from some ecophilosophers. Stuart Hampshire, for instance, believes all attempts to discern *intrinsic* qualities are off the mark because such attempts will always be designed to fulfill our own aristocentric needs. Such scales of value implicitly say that the creatures of earth are to be cherished to the degree they are most like humans and can minister to our needs. This utilitarian viewpoint, Hampshire writes, "places men at the very center of the universe, with their states of feeling as the source of value in the world." Then he asks a difficult question: "Is the destruction, for instance, of a species of animals to be avoided, as a great evil, only or principally because of the loss of pleasure that human beings may derive from the species? May the natural order be farmed by human beings for their comfort and pleasure without any restriction other than the comfort and pleasure of future human beings?"

*Another fundamental error [is] . . . the unnatural distinction Christianity makes between man and the animal world to which he really belongs. It sets up man as all important, and looks upon animals as merely things. . . . Christianity contains in fact a great and essential imperfection in limiting its precepts to man, and in refusing rights to the entire animal world.*

ARTHUR SCHOPENHAUER

## FRUIT AND RUBBER HARVEST ARE GIVEN TWICE TIMBER'S VALUE.
### *The New York Times/The Environment Tuesday, July 4, 1989*

Providing evidence that environmentalists and Brazilian officials say could slow the pace of large-scale clearing of tropical forests, a team of scientists has found that rain forests are worth more if left standing than if cut for timber or cattle grazing.

The study, reported in the current issue of the journal Nature, showed that revenues generated by harvesting edible fruits, rubber, oils and cocoa from 2.5 acres of tropical rainforest are nearly two times greater than the return on timber or the value of the land if used for grazing cattle. . . .

More than 28 million acres of forest and other woodlands are lost annually around the world, and at the current rate of deforestation it is projected that several countries, including El Salvador, Costa Rica, Nigeria and the Ivory Coast, will have destroyed all their forests in 30 years.

"The study indicates that deforestation is a bad investment," said Charles M. Peters of the Institute of Economic Botany at the New York Botanical Garden, who headed the three-year study.

"People who have wanted to save the forest using environmental arguments have not been very persuasive because many of these nations have a large debt," he said. "But these findings offer a very powerful argument for forest conservation." . . .

The new study showed that 12 products, primarily edible fruits and latex, found in one hectare, about 2.5 acres, of forest at the village of Mishana, in northeastern Peru near the Brazilian border, are worth $6,330 if sold in local markets over 5 years, with the cost of harvesting deducted from the market price.

The study also showed that the same land is used as a timber plantation would produce $3,184 over the same period, and that if converted to cattle pastures, it would be worth $2,960. . . .

"It appears that keeping it as managed forests has greater economic value," said Lester B. Lave, an economist and environmental expert at Carnegie-Mellon University in Pittsburgh.

"Brazil has a rapidly growing population and must look to the forest to provide them with a place of employment," he said. "Instead of cutting it and using it for farmland, they now might consider developing it as managed forests."

---

*In a typical ocean food-chain, tuna eats mackerel, mackerel eats smelt, smelt eats copepods, and copepods eat diatoms. "Or, stated in the reverse, 10,000 lb. of diatoms will make 1,000 lb. of copepods; 1,000 lb. of copepods will make 100 lb. of smelt; 100 lb. of smelt will make 10 lb. of mackerel; 10 lb. of mackerel will make 1 lb. of tuna; 1 lb. of tuna will make 0.1 lb. of man. It takes 10 lb. of food to make 1 lb. of the animal that feeds upon it. . . . "*

**MACGINITIE AND MACGINITIE**

George Sessions writes:

An ecological world-view has been unbelievably slow to dawn on modern Western man. Such a view of man and Nature has been intuitively obvious to ancient cultures, but modern Western man, even with all of his recent scientific sophistication, still seems to resist the full implications of the Copernican and Darwinian revolutions and an ecological view of man as continuous with, and fully dependent upon, the rest of Nature.

It is difficult to envision an adequate, or metaphysically appropriate, environmental ethics which does not *begin* by taking the *natural system* as ethically ultimate.

But "conventional wisdom" continues to view science primarily as a means of gaining control over a "hostile and alien" Nature. Nature is seen as a backdrop for society's ever-expanding ecologically suicidal way of life.

The attempt to "mine" Nature in order to satisfy apparently insatiable desires for material goods has objective limits—natural limits set by the delicate homeostatic equilibriums of ecosystem functioning. What is to be feared is that we have already surpassed these limits in some cases with future consequences we can only begin to guess.

Those who feel deeply about Spaceship Earth with all its sentient creatures are fortunate to have had a champion whose stature approaches that of a patron saint: Aldo Leopold, a forester who loved all forms of living things, cared for them, and—incredibly—foresaw the ecological consequences of our callous unconcern for the world we live in. His testament—"a powerful plea for a land ethic"—was published posthumously after his death in 1948.

In *A Sand County Almanac* Leopold pointed out that no viable ecospheric ethic could work "without love, respect, and admiration for the land, and a high regard for its value." Then he added, lest he be misunderstood, "I mean value in the philo-

sophical sense." For an ethic, he wrote, is "a process in ecological evolution."

An ethic, ecologically, is a limitation on freedom of action in the struggle for existence. An ethic, philosophically, is a differentiation of social from anti-social conduct. These are two definitions of one thing. The thing has its origin in the tendency of interdependent individuals or groups to evolve modes of co-operation. The ecologist calls these symbioses. Politics and economics are advanced symbioses in which the original free-for-all competition has been replaced, in part, by cooperation mechanisms with an ethical content. . . .

There is as yet no ethic dealing with man's relation to land and to the animals and plants which grow upon it. . . . The land-relation is still strictly economic, entailing privileges but not obligations.

All ethics so far evolved rest upon a single premise: that the individual is a member of a community of interdependent parts. . . . The land ethic simply enlarges the boundaries of the community to include soils, waters, plants, and animals, or collectively: the land. . . . In short, a land ethic changes the role of *Homo sapiens* from conqueror of the land-community to plain member and citizen of it.

*[Lamarck] formulated a number of very modern ideas: that you cannot attribute to any creature psychological capacities for which it has no organs: that mental processes must always have physical representation; and that the complexity of a nervous system is related to the complexity of mind.*

GREGORY BATESON

## COEXISTENCE—IN LIFE AND DEATH

Man used to regard himself as somehow apart from the animals and plants, following a set of rules that were different from those followed by the rest of nature. Then the study of comparative anatomy made him realize that he is similar in many

*When I'm near that animal, I know I'm in the presence of an intelligence. Namu, I wish I could understand your language, and your mind. I don't know, maybe one day we'll find a way. Maybe . . . maybe it'll be something more direct than words, maybe something as simple as touch—language of mutual trust.*

**Namu, the Killer Whale/NBC-TV**

*If we spoke a different language, we would perceive a somewhat different world.*

**LUDWIG WITTGENSTEIN**

*In sober truth, nearly all the things which men are hanged or imprisoned for doing to one another are nature's everyday performances. . . . All human action whatever consists in altering, and all useful action in improving, the spontaneous course of nature.*

**JOHN STUART MILL (1884)**

structural ways to the other animals. The study of physiology showed similar mechanisms of blood circulation, of muscle contraction, of digestion, and of other body functions. Comparative biochemistry demonstrated the basic similarity of chemical mechanisms, reaction sequences, and metabolic patterns in all living organisms. The study of evolution revealed that all these similarities were the consequences of a common origin.

The interrelatedness of life is now regarded as a part of the beauty and excitement of nature.

*Biology and the Future of Man*

Humans have had deep, ambivalent feelings about our kinship with the other animals. We have grudgingly accepted coexistence with them.

On the one hand, we are aware of striking similarities. Skeletal systems are structurally similar, even down to single bone shapes. The flesh that we carry is too much alike, and when cut we bleed red whether we be bird, beast, or man. Facial configurations are alike and sometimes appear like parodies of one another. We look into the eyes of animals and feel that we recognize. We know their inner worlds in the same way we know the inner worlds of other men. We empathize with their behavior, from the pain of a wounded deer to the playfulness of bear cubs and sea otters. We identify with the hunting instinct of a mother lioness as well as the fear-flight of the hunted antelope. We feel guilt when we have hurt an animal, just as we do if we have hurt another human being. All this gives us a queasy feeling. We do what we can to suppress it, yet the feeling of kinship remains.

It is precisely because the kinship was so obvious that we have protested so loudly that there is no kinship. People resent it, feeling that they are endowed with vastly superior qualities which make them unique and special. As evolutionary humans advanced they have felt the distance increasing between themselves and the other animals.

So, our kinship with animals has been an uncomfortable one. On the one hand we intuit the kinship and confess our commonality; on the other, we deny it vehemently and demean the animal world.

An awareness is just dawning in our brains of the *physical*/ecological relationships with the animals of our planet, but the *psychological*/ecological relationships are probably of equal importance, though to date they have been but little explored.

From the standpoint of other animals, the human is a killer to be feared. Early in his hominid evolution man learned to use weapons to kill for food. Although basically omnivorous, his appetites place him in a class with other killer-carnivores. But man has one behavioral pattern rarely found in the animal world: he kills for pleasure—for "sport"—even when his stomach is full. For this reason the animals of the world are realistic in their fear-response to humans. This combination of pleasure-killing and advanced killing technique renders man extremely dangerous.

But all this goes without saying; today we are all aware of it. But the question persists as to *why* man kills *for pleasure*. What is meant by "pleasure" in this context? How can one experience pleasure from the act of killing something? It's a question that needs an answer, and no trite appeal to "sportsmanship" or "stalking instinct" is quite sufficient.

## ANIMAL CONSCIOUSNESS

Do animals have minds? Are they conscious? Can they think?

Sensitive human beings have always empathized with nonhuman beings, but serious scientific effort to understand the minds of other animals has only just begun.

Why has this empathetic understanding been so long in coming? For one thing, we are xenophobic. We humans are not very good at empathizing with one another, never mind with creatures that differ from us. Our hominid ancestors undoubtedly thought less and intuited more; at any rate, our abilities to enter into others' experiences have dimmed, and our pets now read us much better than we read them.

Also western thinking about animals was derailed by some very influential thinkers, most notably Descartes. The physical body, he said, is merely a machine with mechanical motion. Our human bodies house a consciousness ("the ghost in the machine"), but animals are machines without consciousness or feelings. The fox caught in a trap cries in pain, but what we hear, Descartes says, is not evidence of pain at all; it is merely the sound of damaged machinery.

A third reason for our slow understanding is in how scientific research has been manifest. If "objective" data could not be obtained, then a field would not be considered a legitimate subject of inquiry. The behavioral school of psychology is a good example: since human experience was not measurable, it was ignored; ergo it did not exist.

Certain inferences are very convincing to sensitive observers, however. Animals' mental/emotional experiences often seem to match ours. They *experience* pleasures of many sorts: moods, fear, sexual feelings, hunger, confusion, agitation, aggressive urges, anger, pain. Our intuitions tell us that we have at least these experiences in common.

Early in our century the French philosopher Henri Bergson wrote and lectured with great energy in an effort to get people to realize that the essence of being alive is not biological process, but *experience*. In every animal's tiny niche evolution has developed capacities for experiencing so as to monitor the environment, and to thereby adapt, avoid pain, seek pleasure, and reproduce. To be a human being is to *experience* our existence moment by moment, to think, feel, fear, hope, dream, plan ahead, remember good things, and all. It is thus also for the hummingbird, the otter, the deer, and all other living things. (See pp. 222–225.) It is on the basis of this intuition—that many if not all animals can *experience* suffering—that an ethic must be grounded. Thusly Dr. Schweitzer insists that a truly ethical person will always include the plight of animals within the sphere of his moral concern. This is also one of the bases for the doctrine of *ahimsa* ("non-hurtfulness") of the Hindu, Buddhist, and (especially) Jain religions.

Experiencing, yes; but what about thinking? In 1976, with the publication of *The Question of Animal Awareness,* Donald Griffin began a lifelong exploration of animals' mental capacities. John Alcock, a professor of zoology at Arizona State University, comments on Griffin's explorations of animal thought processes.

Griffin acknowledges that no one has even begun to test the proposition that nonhuman animals think in a manner similar to that of human beings. . . . To persuade us that many animals are far more than "sleepwalkers" or robots, Griffin surveys at length three lines of evidence that to him are suggestive of

*CONTINUED*

*CONTINUED*

consciousness: (1) the ability of some animals to change their behavior adaptively under different and sometimes novel circumstances, (2) certain similarities in brain neural function between lower animals and humans, and (3) the complex communicative abilities of many species.

In 1992 Griffin published *Animal Minds* (University of Chicago Press). He gives many examples of complex behavior that could indicate that the animal is thinking about the consequences of its actions.

The ability of certain small birds to open milk bottles, the capacity of a Clark's nutcracker to remember where it has hidden on the order of a thousand small caches of seeds, the playful behavior of foxes with small prey, the cooperative hunting of lions, flexible communication in weaver ants, the skill pigeons exhibit in categorizing visual stimuli, the famous dances of honey bees, the honey guide's ability to lead humans and other animals to distant bee colonies, the "linguistic" feats of chimpanzees and gray parrots, the complex deceptive signaling of fireflies and mantis shrimps. . . .

Currently there exist two theories of consciousness. One theory holds that consciousness is a universal quality adapted by each species to its specific needs. A second theory, based on the contents of consciousness, concludes that consciousness is species specific. The consciousness of each species developed by evolution is aware of and monitors the specific stimuli in its environment needed for its survival. The role of consciousness is pragmatic, and its content for, say, a cat, would be very different from that of an eagle, a butterfly, an octopus, or a gorilla. What an ant is aware of in its environment differs enormously from what a squirrel is aware of; it literally *sees* a different world, and *thinks about* it differently. The consciousness of each species would therefore reflect the special environment in which it makes a living.

Griffin himself contributed greatly to this conclusion with his brilliant research on bat sonar. He showed that a little brown bat uses a highly complex perceptual apparatus that is qualitatively different from those possessed by humans and the vast majority of other animals. These bats detect and track down flying insects in complete darkness by producing volleys of ultrasound frequencies that the human ear is totally incapable of detecting.

Theorists sharing the sociobiological perspective contend that consciousness is evolution's tool for assuring the transmission of a species' genes. The ability on the part of any creature to think about its actions, anticipate their consequences, and plan accordingly (reflective consciousness) would have an advantage over an organism that merely responds to immediate stimuli (perceptual consciousness).

Consciousness of any sort would have enormous survival value, and undoubtedly evolution has supported the ability to think wherever the opportunity arises. But reflective consciousness would enable any species to jump light-years ahead in its ability to respond to, and then to manipulate, its environment. It would be a strange anomaly if evolution has not developed such a survival quality along varied limbs of the evolutionary tree.

*Excerpts:* JOHN ALCOCK
"Consciousness-Raising III,"
*Natural History* (September, 1992)

Man kills because there is something ultimate in what he is doing. When man kills he has in his hands the essence of life and death. Much of man's killing is done to affirm his own existence; it is a confirmation of his own still-being-alive. Man is the only animal that can reflect upon his own life *and death*. He alone can philosophize about it, question its meaning, and fear it ahead of time. Life and death are both mysteries, but while we have life it is death that haunts our living.

When one holds in his hand a pheasant, or kneels beside a bear or antelope, each of which, a few moments before, shared the impulse to live that is the essence of existence, he can feel for a moment that he has conquered life and in so doing has also conquered death. At that moment one becomes God: although he didn't give life, he has been able to take it away—as though "it" existed as an item of personal property—like a cherished memento or trinket—which the creature "owned." Indeed, to hold a dead animal *from which* one has taken life is to *possess* life. Primitive men often believed that they could accumulate more life by collecting life from those creatures they killed. Perhaps some of this feeling lingers in us; for by contrast, as a hunter stands holding a no-longer-living animal, he often uses the phrase that he "feels alive."

Not too long ago, human sacrifice was practiced in most religions, great and small. Sometimes members of other tribes, especially captured warriors, were sacrificed ritually to the god of the conquering tribe. Often this was a contractual obligation: the deity had helped them win in battle, so they offered a gift in return. Many tribes, however, sacrificed their own members. Instances of ritual killing are the Babylonian sacrifice of a surrogate king; the Canaanite primitial sacrifice of one's firstborn by bloodletting or "passing through fire"; the Egyptian, Assyrian, and Chinese practice of killing scores of attendants to serve the spirits of their royal masters in the next life. Abraham's near-sacrifice of his son Isaac presupposes the existence of the institution of ritual sacrifice.

*Death also provides a challenge and a test, particularly to men who must prove to themselves that they can face death and not run or flinch— the essence of bravery. Perhaps a person feels that he must conquer death through flaunting it, or at least through looking straight into its hollow eye sockets before he can feel man enough to live.*

THEODORE LIDZ

*In human history, we have learned (I hope) that the conqueror role is eventually self-defeating. Why? Because it is implicit in such a role that the conqueror knows ex cathedra, just what makes the community clock tick, and just what and who is valuable, and what and who is worthless, in community life. It always turns out that he knows neither.*

**ALDO LEOPOLD (1948)**

*The trees and rocks will teach thee what thou can'st not learn from human teachers.*

**SAINT BERNARD OF CLAIRVAUX**

*We plant trees to benefit another generation.*

**CAECILIUS STATIUS**

In one form or another, human sacrifice has been practiced in almost every ancient culture known to man.

At some point, however, sensitivity to suffering deepens, and ways are devised to avoid human sacrifice. Historically, the story of the sacrifice of Isaac by Abraham was understood by ancient Hebrews to be the origin of the ransom system. Make no mistake, one's firstborn belonged to the god Yahweh, but henceforth he could be "ransomed" with an ox, a ram, or perhaps a pair of doves. Similar animal substitutes are found elsewhere.

Eventually, in almost every tradition, ritual killing comes to an end, accompanied by appropriate theological rationale. In the Christian tradition, the sacrifice of God's only son was interpreted to be the final, complete sacrifice, replacing the Judaic sacrificial system; and the sacrifice of God's only son—which is parallel to the sacrifice of Abraham's only son—recurs eternally in the "Sacrifice of the Mass." In other religions, live sacrifices were replaced by the sacrifice of figurines, which were ritually broken, or by wood or paper substitutes bearing names, which were buried or burned.

Few places in the world today still witness blood sacrifices carried on for religious reasons.

Ordinary ethics seeks to find limits within the sphere of human life and relationships. But the absolute ethics of the will-to-live must reverence every form of life, seeking so far as possible to refrain from destroying any life, regardless of its particular type. It says of no instance of life, "This has no value." It cannot make any such exceptions, for it is built upon reverence for life as such. It knows that the mystery of life is always too profound for us, and that its value is beyond our capacity to estimate. . . . True, in practice we are forced to choose. At times we have to decide arbitrarily which forms of life, and even which particular individuals, we shall save, and which we shall destroy. But the principle of reverence for life is none the less universal.

ALBERT SCHWEITZER

Dostoevsky's psychology rests on a fundamental belief in the deep, ineradicable humanity of men. A logical, officially sanctioned decision to spill blood is reversible and remedial, if deep in a person's heart there is still a small spark of compassion. Sometimes a man is driven to things; he finds that he has to be inflexible. But it is important that he should keep the feeling that the circumstances that forced him to cruelty are themselves unnatural.

Permission to kill with the approval of one's conscience destroys the humanity of man.

PAVEL SIMONOV

*Mental health and the ultimate happiness of man consists in his active striving to understand his place in Nature through a scientific understanding of the interrelatedness of all aspects of the Universe.*

**GEORGE SESSIONS**

One of the most interesting things we humans do is to anthropomorphize all our animal kin, and we did this long before Walt Disney institutionalized the technique. We project our human qualities into nonhuman creatures; we think of them as though they have the same experiences we do. We endow them with our fears, angers, jealousies. In animated cartoons every animal we know—from mice to roadrunners, from dumb dogs to stammering pigs and elephants with outsized ears—feels human feelings.

We anthropomorphize (the word means "to make into human form," from the Greek *anthropos,* "human," and *morphos,* "form") for at least two reasons. (1) We can't help it. Since we experience only human experiences, it is inevitable that we would project our experience onto other creatures. (2) We want other creatures to be like us. The more humanoid they are the better we feel about them and can relate to them.

Look at the matter in another way: How could we *not* project our experiences into our fellow creatures? If we look into the eyes of a baby seal or hear the cry of a dog in pain—even though we can't know for sure what the animal is experiencing—it's difficult not respond as though the animals feel what we would be feeling were we in their place. We empathize through our own experience to theirs, and in fact it may be that our intuition here is closer to the truth than our solipsistic skepticism.

## "No Man Is an Iland"

Humankind has been a part—but only a part—of the evolutionary/ecological system. We may soon be the controller of all our planet's life and the determiner of its destiny, but what we will control will be a complex system of interrelationships, and we humans will remain a part of the system.

It is easy for one to feel lonely in the midst of a crowd; it is easy to feel alienated in a world to which one is deeply related. We may never realize the existence of the multitudinous tie-lines that connect us to the world we live in.

"No man is an Iland, intire of itself," wrote John Donne. Each is a part of the whole, subject to the same physical forces that move the atoms and the planets. We are composed of the same fivescore elements that make up the seas and rocks, trees and stars. We are subject to the same protoplasmic processes found throughout the animal kingdom. The same neural events explode in all our brains, and our physical being is determined by a DNA code system identical to that which guides the replication of all animals and plants. Most profoundly, we share the will-to-live with every living creature.

We are part of an awesome protoplasmic venture.

### Reflections

1   What are your thoughts on our recent recognition that humans are a part of the whole evolutionary/protoplasmic venture, and that, in a sense, we can claim "to be one" with plants, animals, and perhaps larger processes? Do you have a philosophic response to this concept?

2   Do you agree that we humans harbor a deep ambivalence about our kinship with other animals, perhaps because we feel that close tie and fear it?

3   Pages 444–445. contain an important realization—that we anthropomorphize our animal kin. What does it mean to say that we "anthropomorphize" other beings? Why do we engage in anthropomorphic imaging since, after all, it involves a fallacy?

4   The question persists as to why man kills for pleasure. What would be your answer to this "strange and dangerous quality" that *Homo sapiens* appears

*(Continued on p. 451)*

*Don't take man too seriously, even when orienting him among the animals and plants on this local planet; and certainly not when comparing him with possibilities elsewhere in the richly endowed Metagalaxy.*

             **Harlow Shapley**

*Short then is the time which every man lives, and small the nook of the earth where he lives. . . .*

             **Marcus Aurelius**

*Our climb to the top has been a get-rich-quick story, and, like all nouveaux riches, we are very sensitive about our background.*

             **Desmond Morris**

# ALBERT SCHWEITZER

## *Reverence for Life*

In his *Memoirs of Child-hood and Youth,* Albert Schweitzer writes that his early years were dominated by a deep awareness of two things: the happiness of his childhood and the over-whelming amount of pain he saw around him.

As far back as I can remember I was saddened by the amount of misery I saw in the world around me. . . . One thing that specially saddened me was that the unfortunate animals had to suffer so much pain and misery. The sight of an old limping horse, tugged forward by one man while another kept beating it with a stick to get it to the knacker's yard at Colmar, haunted me for weeks.

It was quite incomprehensible to me—this was before I began going to school—why in my evening prayers I should pray for human beings only. So when my mother had prayed with me and had kissed me good-night, I used to add silently a prayer that I had composed myself for all living crea-tures. It ran thus: "O, heavenly Father, protect and bless all things that have breath; guard them from all evil, and let them sleep in peace."

As he matured it became clear to him that his good fortune in having a rel-atively happy youth was not to be taken for granted. "Whoever is spared personal pain must feel himself called to help in diminishing the pain of others. We must all carry our share of the misery which lies upon the world." So, at the age of twenty-one, still a college student, he vowed to devote his life till he was thirty to the ministry, to medical science, and to music. This was to be a time of both preparation and personal fulfillment, and he would accomplish all he could in these fields. Then, when he turned thirty, he would devote the rest of his life, in some way, to the service of humanity. Exactly what direction this service would take, he didn't yet know. Several life-affirming years would have to pass before—as he put it—"a chain of cir-cumstances pointed out to me the road which led to the sufferers from leprosy and sleeping-sickness in Africa."

Albert Schweitzer was born January 14, 1875, in Kaysersberg, in the Upper Alsace, a region that forever teeters between France and Germany; and his native tongue was the Alsatian dialect of German. When he was a few months old the family moved to nearby Günsbach where, in the company of three sisters and one brother, he lived through "a delightful childhood."

His father was the pastor of the evangelical parish in predominantly Catholic Alsace. From him Albert inherited a love of music, a bright mind and a commitment to rational inquiry, a dedicated work ethic, and iron self-discipline. From his mother he inherited a natural reserve and a passionate temperament.

From very early on he displayed an unusual talent for, and sensitivity to, music. At the age of five his father had begun to teach him some music on the family's old square piano; at eight he began to play the organ; at nine he substituted for the church organist at a service. He discovered that he possessed an unusual gift for improvisation and playing melodies and harmony from memory. All his life beautiful music overpowered him; he experienced it so deeply and mystically that he would have to sit down or hold on to something lest he be overcome "from excess of pleasure." When, at sixteen, he heard Wagner's *Tannhäuser* for the first time, it was days before he could put his mind back on his studies.

His high school years were spent at Münster and Mülhausen. He had to walk two miles over the hills every morning and evening to and from the Münster school, and his love of nature blossomed. "This walk it was my delight to take by myself, without any of the other boys who also went to school at Münster, so as to indulge my thoughts." In love with the beauties of nature, he tried to vent his feelings in poetry and drawing, but he succeeded in expressing himself only through musical improvisation.

At eighteen Schweitzer passed his "leaving examination" at the gymnasium (high school) and headed for the university at Strassburg to study theology and philosophy. He pursued his career as an organist, came under the spell of Wagner's operas, studied hard, wrote voluminously, and, at twenty-three, passed his theological examination and headed for Paris to study piano and organ. He returned to Strassburg to complete his doctorate in philosophy, writing his dissertation on the language of Kant's *Critique of Pure Reason*. At twenty-four he received his doctorate and accepted a position as pastor of St. Nicholas Church in Strassburg. At twenty-five (in July 1900) he obtained a second doctorate (in theology) and joined the faculty of his university. He spent all his free time writing, developing his manuscripts for publication. His historical study of the Synoptic Gospels was becoming "a bulky volume," and he was planning a work on Bach, another on organ building, one on Saint Paul, and a study of the Philosophy of Civilization which would be a major exposition of his theory of ethics.

True to his commitment, Schweitzer had made his contribution to theological thought with a monumental work, *The Quest of the Historical Jesus* (1906). At the same time he had also been working on his commitment to music by writing, in French, a book on Bach. It was published in 1905. He also wrote an influential essay on organ-building.

The time had arrived to make the great transition to a life of service to humanity. Medical missionaries were urgently needed in the French Congo, so Schweitzer decided to go to Africa, not as an evangelist, but as a medical doctor. To that end, at the age of thirty, he undertook a three-year program of medical training to earn his M.D. degree. On Good Friday 1913, with Europe on the brink of war, Schweitzer and his wife—he had married Hélène Bresslau in 1912—left Günsbach for the French

*A man is ethical only when life, as such, is sacred to him, that of plants and animals as that of his fellow men. . . .*

*Many a time have I, with a feeling of shame, said quietly to myself over a grave the words which my mouth ought to have spoken to the departed, while he was still in the flesh.*

*Whoever is spared personal pain must feel himself called to help in diminishing the pain of others.*

*Humanitarianism consists in never sacrificing a human being to a purpose.*

*A good conscience is the invention of the devil.*

*Reverence for life is the highest court of appeal.*

*There slowly grew up in me an unshakable conviction that we have no right to inflict suffering and death on another living creature unless there is some unavoidable necessity for it, and that we ought all of us to feel what a horrible thing it is to cause suffering and death out of mere thoughtlessness.*

Congo. At Lambaréné on the Ogowe River Schweitzer settled into a small "hospital" constructed of corrugated iron and roofed with palm leaves. From his very first days he was beseiged by the sick who came to the hospital from up to two hundred miles away. The amount of suffering among the Africans was even greater than he had imagined.

War broke out in Europe in late summer of 1914, and, with only a year of service behind them, the Schweitzers were told they were prisoners of war and confined to the mission station. Work at the hospital was forbidden, and they were to have no contact with natives or other colonials. "So on the second day of my internment, still quite amazed at being able to sit down at my writing-table early in the morning as in the days before I took up medicine, I set to work on the Philosophy of Civilization.

◆

As Schweitzer reflected on the meaning of "civilization," what came clear to him is that the essence of civilization is the will toward ethical growth by both individuals and society. "The will to civilization is then the universal will to progress which is conscious of the ethical as the highest value for all." We may think that our being civilized is proven by our intellectual or material accomplishments, but it should be obvious that only human beings who have achieved a certain positive stability in their ethical relationships can fully enjoy the more material benefits of that civilization. Without that ethical foundation, the material blessings may exist, but a collective enjoyment of them *by individuals* is not possible. Ethics, therefore, is the glue that holds a civilization together and makes authentic progress possible. "Civilization I define in quite general terms as spiritual and material progress in all spheres of activity, accompanied by an ethical development of individuals and of mankind."

As of the summer of 1915,

*Slowly in our European thought comes the notion that ethics has not only to do with mankind but with the animal creation as well. This begins with St. Francis of Assisi. The explanation which applies only to man must be given up. Thus we shall arrive at saying that ethics is reverence for all life.*

*It is through the idealism of youth that man catches sight of truth. . . . If all of us could become what we were at fourteen, what a different place the world would be!*

*The ethic of Reverence for Life is the ethic of Love widened into universality. It is the ethic of Jesus, now recognized as a necessity of thought.*

Schweitzer had arrived at a clear philosophical solution to half the problem: he understood that the life-affirming values of Western civilization had weakened and taken the punch out of the worldview by which Western society actually lives. But something still eluded him. He was determined to hang on until his intellect could clearly see the connection between life-affirmation and some kind of ethical principle that would render it meaningful. Formal connections alone were inadequate; he longed for something firmer—something almost tangible —that would make his search intelligible.

After months of searching, he finally found what he sought. It was during a long boat trip upriver. "Late on the third day, at the very moment when, at sunset, we were making our way through a herd of hippopotamuses, there flashed upon my mind, unforeseen and unsought, the phrase, 'Reverence for Life.' The iron door had yielded: the path in the thicket had become visible. Now I had found my way to the idea in which world- and life-affirmation and ethics are contained side by side! Now I knew that the world- and life-affirmation, together with its ideals of civilization, is founded in thought." (See back to pp. 7–8.)

What does Schweitzer mean by "Reverence for Life"? One must start from the immediate data of experience. At the core of consciousness is the ever-present experience, "I am life which wills to live, in the midst of life which wills to live." This is a fact, an undeniable reality of my life. All my activities, awake and asleep, are designed to sustain the continuity of my self as a unitary life-form. I eat, work, rest, and grow in order to keep *my* self alive and functioning.

But in this will-to-live I am not alone. The most fundamental fact of life is that each single living organism on planet Earth, since Life's beginning, has shared with me the very same will-to-live. Whether for a microbe, a trilobite, a brontosaurian, or an Alsatian missionary, to live entails a continuous struggle to assure the survival of the self. I am a self in the midst of selves, a will-to-live in the midst of an infinite number of other wills-to-live.

Picture this scene on an African veld: A mother zebra stands in the open grassland with its young colt, grazing. A mother lioness flanked by three cubs lurks at the edge of the clearing, waiting for the right moment to stalk and kill the young zebra for food for her cubs. From an ethical standpoint, what is good for the zebras—the successful continuation of their wills-to-live—is bad for the lions; and what is good for the lions—obtaining food to nourish the continuity of their wills-to-live—is bad for the zebras. The only ethic that can be derived from such a scenario is one of pure relativism. What is good for one party is not good for the other, and vice versa; and there are no principles to be inferred that can ameliorate the facts of the situation and bring about a happy ending. The "evolutionary ethic" does not submit to our human sensitivities or accommodate our ethical ideals.

But human thought and feeling alter everything. The lion and zebra cannot develop ethical principles because they can't reflect on their behavior. They live instinctively, without reflective thought. Programmed by instinct to act in their own interests, they are oblivious to the needs of other selves. By contrast, we humans can reflect on our behavior and thereby transcend it. We can watch the lion-zebra struggle, think about it concretely and abstractly, feel the pain—and write books about it. We can imagine our human selves in similar competitive struggles; we can establish guidelines for behavior that will help us anticipate such predicaments, avoid them, and solve them when we must.

Reverence for life, then, means respecting the will-to-live of every living creature. Reverence for life includes *all* life. The Western philosophical tradition in ethics has failed because it did not extend its sphere of concern to other living creatures. Schweitzer blames our religious heritage for encouraging us to limit our empathy to our own kind when it is completely natural and human to feel compassion for the suffering of all living things. The individual who does not feel an animal's pain is not truly ethical. "A man is ethical only when life, as such, is sacred to him, that of plants and animals as that of his fellow-men, and when he devotes himself helpfully to all life that is in need of help."

Reverence for Life—"In that principle my life has found a firm footing and a clear path to follow."

War had broken out in Europe, and the Schweitzers—German citizens in French colonial territory—were confined to the hospital at Lambaréné until, in September of 1917, they were reclassified as prisoners of war and sent to France. In July 1918 they were exchanged for French prisoners and returned to their home at Günsbach.

For the next six years Schweitzer worked and wrote from his base in Alsace. In April 1924 he was back at Lambaréné. The corrugated-iron hospital was still standing, but virtually everything else had been reclaimed by the jungle. For a year he was a doctor in the morning and a "master-builder" the rest of the day. Within a year the medical center had grown so much that it was decided to move to a new location two miles upriver and to modernize the facilities. For the rest of his life he would spend a year or two working at Lambaréné, then journey to Europe to conduct a lecture-recital tour to raise funds for his work, then back to Lambaréné. The medical staff at the hospital was gradually augmented so that it ran smoothly without *Le Grand Docteur*.

In 1949 Schweitzer visited the United States for his only time to speak at the Goethe Centennial in Aspen, Colorado. In 1950 a poll was conducted among artists in eighteen countries and Schweitzer was named "The Man of the Century." He received numerous

*The mistake made by all previous systems of ethics has been the failure to recognize that life as such is the mysterious value with which they have to deal.*

*In the parable of Jesus the shepherd saves not merely the soul of the lost sheep but the whole animal.*

*To the man who is truly ethical all life is sacred, including that which from the human point of view seems lower in the scale.*

*Renunciation of thinking is a declaration of spiritual bankruptcy. . . . I therefore stand and work in the world as one who aims at making men less shallow and morally better by making them think.*

honorary degrees, including a doctorate in music from Edinburgh and three doctorates in law. He was elected to the prestigious French Academy in 1952 and received the Order of Merit from Queen Elizabeth in 1955. In October 1953, at the age of 78, he was awarded the Nobel Peace Prize; he used the proceeds to build a leprosy annex to his hospital.

Albert Schweitzer died at Lambaréné on September 4, 1965, and is buried under the Palm Tree above the Ogowe river beside Hélène, who died in 1959.

to possess? What do you think is meant by "pleasure" in this context? Is there a better name for it?

5   This chapter suggests (pp. 443–444) that much of man's killing is done to affirm his own existence; it is a confirmation of his still-being-alive. Do you agree? How would you put it?

6   Read the pungent description of Dostoevsky's psychology by Pavel Simonov (p. 444). Listen carefully to his meaning, then decide whether you agree with it.

7   Think about Schweitzer's Reverence for Life—a concept which he believed to be "the realistic answer to the realistic question of how man and the world are related to each other." How do you feel about this all-inclusive ethic?

6
4

## THE THEORETICAL LIFE

Plato once made the distinction between the practical life (*praktikos bios*) and the theoretical life (*theoretikos bios*). By the practical life Plato meant a life that is lived in terms of short-range goals, while the theoretical life is lived in terms of long-range goals. The theoretical life is in every way as "practical" (in the modern sense) as the platonic practical life, but it is planned and guided in terms of our deeper and more ultimate requirements rather than in terms of the immediate and often too-pressing needs and desires of today. The theoretical life is to be planned so that the future will be fulfilling when its time comes.

It was the task of philosophers, Plato believed, to think farther ahead to envision realistically the distant problems and goals that are as inevitable as tomorrow and that, in our prevision of them, determine profoundly the quality of the life we live today.

Is it a puerile truism or a refreshened insight to be reminded that the future will arrive—for us, for our children, for their children? Few of us would disagree with the notion that a life lived exclusively in terms of the next twenty-four hours would leave each of us in a pickle the following day. Wisely, therefore, we plan ahead—for hours, days, months (vaguely), and years (more vaguely). But we do plan. Only a fool would not plan for the good life, providing future-planning is a viable possibility.

Plato's point is that the better we envision wise and fulfilling futures for ourselves and our children, the better the chance of our dreams becoming realities. This same point is now being made by contemporary future-thinkers, including the veteran futurist Fred Polak: "In the act of searching out the road into the future, man crosses the frontiers of the unknown and raises Homo sapiens to a new level: the level of foresight and purposefulness. . . . In taking thought for tomorrow, man begins to create tomorrow."

*The future isn't what it used to be.*
ARTHUR C. CLARKE

*Each age has had its cherished superstitions. A new age dawns with their identification and rejection.*
DANIEL N. ROBINSON

Our histories are created for us by historians. Past events are resurrected from the record of past presents, selected because of their meaning and value, and summarized for us in history books. We can then see ourselves in the long perspective of our past.

Creation of our past is but one side of the story: our futures can be created in similar fashion. "Humans are time travelers, who chart their courses through time with maps of the future," writes Robert Bundy. Without the creation of our futures we can't know where we are going. We need to perceive ourselves in the light of optional futures fully as much as we need to know our pasts.

Heretofore, our futures have been created by our religions, by visionaries, utopians and anti-utopians, and by science-fiction writers. Only recently has futurism come into its own.

## RESEARCH INTO THE FUTURE

Until a few years ago "research into the future" was not a thinkable thought. Conceptually, its time had not yet arrived. Of course, this did not prevent human imagination from giving substance to our futures. Dreaming has always been a part of being human.

Human beings cannot live without hope, or face an empty future. Our great religions all envision a future time when the tragedy of earthly history will be replaced by, or be consummated in, a Reign of God, a Messianic Age, a Golden Age, a New Jerusalem. A blank future is intolerable. Even a frightening future is preferable to nothingness.

"We create our literary myths, legends, and epics of the future, not so that we will find our golden age, but because in the creation of utopian standards, we have created forms which make present action possible" (Hugh Duncan). The Garden of Eden in Western doctrine remains the archetype of the perfect human condition to which we will return . . . someday.

Another kind of inhabitable fantasy-world has entered the scene: literary utopias. Among them are Plato's *Republic*, Thomas More's *Utopia* (More coined the word from two Greek words, *ou-topos*, "no-where"), Voltaire's *Candide*, Campanella's *City of the Sun*, and H. G. Wells' *Modern Utopia*. These utopias were motivated in part by the perception of this world as essentially uninhabitable by sensitive spirits. If Racine is right that life is a comedy for the thinker, but a tragedy for one who feels, then utopias are attempts on the part of some sensitive thinkers to create in their minds, if not in this world, a place where life would be worth living.

In recent decades anti-utopias have largely replaced the utopias in our consciousness: Huxley's *Brave New World*, Orwell's *1984*, Bradbury's *Fahrenheit 451*, Ayn Rand's *Anthem*. These visions fell upon us with a shattering impact. Their shrill warning was heard by many because they warned of the totalitarian dangers. Much of their success was due to the fact that we recognized them to be future versions of conditions that we could already observe around us. These anti-utopias were fiction-worlds born from the minds of gifted seers who passed their scenarios on to us.

*To put finally to rest our Newtonian delusions, to renew our conception of nature as living, and so to see ourselves once more as living beings in a world of living beings, still constitutes the major task of philosophy in the twentieth century.*

**MARJORIE GRENE**

*"Perhaps what we need is a kick in our complacency to prepare us for what lies ahead."*

**"CAPT. JEAN-LUC PICARD"**
**Star Trek: The Next Generation**

*It is the business of the future to be dangerous; and it is among the merits of science that it equips the future for its duties.*

**ALFRED NORTH WHITEHEAD**

Serious research into the future began only some forty years ago, and as a discipline and worldwide movement it is about thirty years old. In 1964 a project called "Mankind 2000" attempted to sensitize the European populace to rapidly approaching global problems. The first World Future Research Conference was convened in Oslo in 1967. The Russians have several prestigious futures programs in operation. The Club of Rome was organized in 1968 for the purpose of alerting world leaders to the coming collision between soaring human population and economic growth.

In America a large number of future research organizations have been launched: the RAND Corporation, the Hudson Institute, The Commission on the Year 2000, the American Institute of Planners, and the World Future Society. Today most governments and large private industries have futures groups that carry on forecasting in special-interest fields.

Four things have conspired to bring about the rapid birth of the futures research movement.

*The military mind will be the curse of the race so long as there is a military . . . or will it be the salvation?*

**CHRISTOPHER ANVIL**

1. Techniques for forecasting developed almost overnight, largely because of the progress of science and technology. Compared with human behavior, technology is relatively predictable. Coupled with the burgeoning, microminiaturized computers, trend projections and correlations not previously possible suddenly became quick and easy. "Given his present state of knowledge, social as well as scientific and technological, man now has an enormously enhanced capacity to choose his future, both collectively and individually" (McHale).

2. A series of global events has scared us into thinking about the real possibility of world catastrophe: uncontrolled weapons escalation; polluted lakes, rivers, and skies; blackouts and brownouts; oil spills and the killing of the oceans; near extinction of many animals; defoliation, droughts, and possible ozone depletion; the hunger-zones of the world with growing populations and food shortages. Add to all this unstable governments, wobbly international currencies, economic troubles, global power struggles, and world leaders who command little or no confidence—put all this together and there is little wonder that, in the minds of many, a spectre of doom hovers over a shrinking world.

*Our world is now future-oriented, you see, in the sense that the rate of change has become so rapid that we can no longer wait until a problem is upon us to work out the solution. If we do, then there is no real solution, for by the time one has been worked out and applied, change has progressed still further and our solution no longer makes sense at all. The change must be anticipated before it happens.*

**ISAAC ASIMOV**

3. There has developed a rapid realization that all the countries of the world are now so interdependent in fundamental ways that problems can only be understood and dealt with in terms of world systems. Energy problems are global. Pollution obeys no political checkpoints. The world is one system economically. Any war now affects all nations. Movements that flare up in remote corners rapidly ignite tensions around the world. Communications are global and instant. In a word there will no longer be any really significant local problems. The serious challenges of the next fifty years will all be global in nature, and localistic or nationalistic mobilization cannot hope to change the course of such worldwide threats.

4. It has become clear that we are still thinking within frameworks from the past, and they no longer work. The idea that any one nation can go it alone for its food, energy, and basic materials is not true any more. The belief that wars can be won is a myth; in nuclear wars there are no winners. The idea

of "manifest destiny" is history. And the "rugged individualism" that once moved men and mountains and bred pioneers who held themselves beholden to no one—all this is gone.

This, then, is the goal of futures research: to establish organizations—political, economic, industrial, academic, and more—that will previse the nature of these problems and have on the drawing boards contingency plans for facing them; and to have on a stand-by basis international organizations ready to give counsel and guidance to the power-movers when the time comes that world leaders can no longer ignore the problems.

So futurists and futurism were born. In 1945 Arthur C. Clarke began to describe in detail specific upcoming technological events. In 1958 Robert Jungk began talking about "early warning systems" that would study the long-range consequences of uncontrolled technologies. By 1960 Fred Polak had begun to clarify how our visions of the future help us to achieve the futures we envision; and Herman Kahn had begun to develop complex "scenarios" of alternative futures and to analyze systematically the events that might actually bring them about. In 1963 Dennis Gabor wrote of "inventing" our futures and then creating means of arriving at our inventions.

In 1963 Buckminster Fuller began to make us dream with a colorful stream of futuristic images, holistic programs, and novel hardware—the boldest display of concrete previsions since Leonardo da Vinci, with whom he is often compared. By 1965 Bertrand de Jouvenel was turning out treatises on humanistic elements in future planning ("the intellectual construction of a likely future is a work of art"). By 1966 Marshall McLuhan, with cryptic phrases and lilting puns, was warning us that new communications media—the media themselves, that is, quite apart from their content—would revolutionize our world-views and lifestyles. By 1968 Erich Jantsch was engaged in "integrative forecasting" to determine the technological impact on social and human institutions.

Also in 1968 Paul Ehrlich jolted a complacent society by pointing out the inevitable consequences of unchecked population growth. And in 1970 Alvin Toffler described the "future shock" that awaits us: "We cannot create a sane social system until technology is tamed, the educational system revolutionized, and future-consciousness injected into our political lives."

Just because the problems are so new and our thinking is so outdated, it is the consensus among futurists that mankind now stands at the threshold of the most critical period of human history. There is a near-unanimous feeling that the next fifty years will constitute a transition period that will write the future of man, one way or the other. Their deepest fear derives from the fact that the dangerous problems are all global while humankind's mental machinery is still fueled by past ideas that no longer burn. Our concepts remain essentially local, regional, tribal, and nationalistic. This is not a matter of irrelevant patriotism, for realistic loyalties promote cohesive bonds and foster shared visions and goals. It is rather that aristocentric myths prevent an accurate understanding of the nature of the global problems that threaten us and make it impossible to set in motion the forces that could be effective against these large-scale problems.

*The world's biggest problems today are really infinitesimal: the atom, the ovum, and a bit of pigment.*

HERB CAEN

*There was once a time when I wrote of colonies on the Moon, and the only place I could have such outlandish nonsense published was in science fiction magazines. Now I write of colonies on the Moon in very much the same way—and the articles are published by* The New York Times.

ISAAC ASIMOV

A recent report of the Club of Rome was issued in a volume entitled *Mankind at the Turning Point* (1974). Derived from a massive accumulation of data, conclusions were clear: we face an urgent need for a thoroughgoing restructuring of our conceptual frameworks, basic assumptions, and a reorientation of values—if we are to survive the next fifty years.

1. A *world consciousness* must be developed through which every individual realizes his role as a member of the world community.
2. A *new ethic in the use of material resources* must be developed that will result in a style of life compatible with the oncoming age of scarcity. One should be proud of saving and conserving rather than of spending and discarding.
3. An *attitude toward nature must be developed based on harmony rather than conquest*. Only in this way can man apply in practice what is already accepted in theory—that is, that man is an integral part of nature.
4. If the human species is to survive, man must develop a *sense of identification with future generations* and be ready to trade benefits to the next generations for the benefits to himself. If each generation aims at the maximum good for itself, Homo sapiens is as good as doomed. One futurist commentator, Howard Didsbury, summarized the mood of the report: "Enlightened self-interest dictated by necessity may tend to make clear mankind's ultimate choices: cooperation or destruction. If cooperation is chosen it may 'lead to the creation of a new mankind.' Should mankind choose the alternative, all is silence."

## THE FUTURISTS AND THE FUTURE

Looking ahead for decades and centuries, there is no single world-picture on which all futurists agree, although there is remarkable agreement on many points. Futurists' visions will depend partly upon their specialties and partly upon their personal feelings of optimism or pessimism about the operations of "human nature" past and present. Moreover, whether a futurist is essentially negative or positive depends somewhat on whether his or her picture of the future is a short-range or long-range vision. In general, the short-range futurists concentrate on the looming problems that could engulf us and tend to be less cheery about the decades immediately ahead. The middle- and long-range futurists tend to be far more optimistic because of that widely held intuition that *if* mankind can make it through the next fifty years then the most distant future is practically unlimited in its promise of progress, human growth, and personal fulfillment.

**ALVIN TOFFLER** With the publication of *Future Shock* in 1971 Alvin Toffler reached international prominence as a futurist. Since then he has edited *The Futurists* (1972) and written *The Eco-Spasm Report* (1975) and *The Third Wave* (1980). He is essentially a short-range futurist (relatively, that is) who is especially knowledgeable about socioeconomic trends.

As a futurist Toffler is acutely aware of two essentially human problems that threaten all global economic and political processes during the next few decades.

*It's a poor sort of memory that only works backward.*
LEWIS CARROLL
**Through the Looking-Glass**

*Anyone who wishes to cope with the future should travel back in imagination a single lifetime—say to 1900—and ask himself just how much of today's technology would be, not merely incredible, but incomprehensible to the keenest scientific brains of that time.*

ARTHUR C. CLARKE

First: *Lack of future-consciousness.* Instead of anticipating the problems and opportunities of the future, we lurch from crisis to crisis. The energy shortage, runaway inflation, ecological troubles—all reflect the failure of our political leaders at federal, state, and local levels to look beyond the next election. Our political system is "future-blind." With but few exceptions, the same failure of foresight marks our corporations, trade unions, schools, hospitals, voluntary organizations, and communities as well. The result is political and social future shock.

Second: *Lack of participation.* Our government and other institutions have grown so large and complicated that most people feel powerless. They complain of being "planned upon." They are seldom consulted or asked for ideas about their own future. On the rare occasions when they are, it is ritualistic rather than real consultation. Blue-collar workers, poor people, the elderly, the youth, even the affluent among us, feel frozen out of the decision process. And as more and more millions feel powerless, the danger of violence and authoritarianism increases. Moreover, if this is true within this country, it is even more true of the world situation in which the previously powerless are demanding the right to participate in shaping the global future.

In *Future Shock* Toffler massively documented his thesis that world economic conditions are out of control, are accelerating, and are being faced only with outmoded myths and methods. He pointed out that, almost without exception, those dealing with these gigantic "economic" problems know nothing but economics; whereas the actual problems are interdisciplinary by nature and can't even be understood, let alone solved, by narrow-range economics specialists.

The giant economic forces of our time have become tails wagging the dogs. Many economic systems, especially the multinational corporations, are more powerful than the nations they use as bases of operation. Such nations are, in effect, "colonies" of such transnational powers. And all these economic processes are moving faster than we can understand or cope with.

Toffler therefore suggests alternative approaches for facing a world that has "gone random" and is running out of control. One solution is long-range planning. We need to think big and to think boldly.

Futurism differs from planning, if one wishes to make that distinction, by reaching beyond economics to embrace culture, beyond transportation to include in its concerns family life and sex roles, beyond physical and environmental concerns to include mental health and many other dimensions of reality. It reaches beyond the conventional time frame of the industrial style planner toward longer, ten-, twenty-, or thirty-year speculative horizons, without which the short-range plans make little sense. Furthermore, it seeks radical new ways to democratize the process—not merely because that is good, just, or altruistic, but because it is necessary: without broad-scale citizen involvement, even the most conscientious and expertly drawn plans are likely to blow up in our faces.

These accelerating out-of-control global economic movements are scary, to be sure, but, Toffler adds, we are faced with "an awesome but exhilarating task that few generations in human history have ever faced: the design of a new civilization."

ARTHUR C. CLARKE Serious scientific forecasting had its first futurist in Arthur C. Clarke, a scientist-writer equally renowned for his science fiction. In

*Most intellectual problems are, ultimately, problems of classification and nomenclature.*

S. I. HAYAKAWA

*We live now on a satellite adrift in space—why would man not make more satellites to his taste if it came within his means?*

RON BRACEWELL

*On a single day in 1988 scientists recorded 6,000 manmade forest fires burning in the Amazon rainforest. The consequences to the forest and to the world are devastating.*

*Sixty acres every minute of every day are destroyed in the Amazon basin.*

*We lose one hundred species of plants and animals every day in the Amazon.*

*The survival of indigenous people is intimately linked to the survival of their environment. The Indian is the guardian of the forest. Protecting one will protect the future.*

JEAN-PIERRE DUTILLEUX

## IF THE FOREST DIES. . .

There is so much smoke all the animals are dying. The rivers are dying as well. That is why I am very worried about my people. My spirit is always warning me that when the forest is all destroyed there will be no more shade. There will be very strong winds. The sun will get very hot. And it will be difficult to breathe. Then everybody will die. Not just the Indians. Everybody will die. This is my concern. I am warning you. You have to think. You have to change your ideas. Leave the jungle alone.

CHIEF RAONI

The jungle is a fantastic green, magical, cathedral-like thing. It has changed my life. The feeling I get when I am there is that we 'civilised' people are a bit lost. We are confused about who we are, what we are doing. The Indians don't have any such confusion. They have a way of life in harmony with the environment. What I hope to do is make the rainforest real to the rest of the world, to give it a human face.

STING

Futurists are alarmed by what is seen as a lack of personal participation in decisions affecting our future because we feel individually impotent. We feel powerless to initiate change: "Nothing I can do will make any difference."

There are, however, notable exceptions to this nihilism. *Some* individuals *are* making a difference. Public attention to human and environmental issues is increasing as consciousness-raising organizations proliferate (such as Amnesty International, Greenpeace, World Wildlife Fund, Nature Conservancy, The Cousteau Society). Political leaders and respected figures in the arts and

Sting and filmmaker Jean-Pierre Dutilleux discuss demarcation proposal with Chief Raoni (center) and another tribal leader.

CONTINUED

Sting to Chief Raoni: "The white man has no real home. He is lost in a world that he doesn't understand. He has ceased to communicate with the spirits of the earth and the forest, the river and the air, so he is alone. Unhappy, he searches for happiness and when he sees happiness in others he becomes angry and wants to destroy it because inside he is empty. I am not a politician, I am only a singer, but many people listen to me. I promise you that whenever I can speak on your behalf I will do so. I shall tell your story to whomever I can because you are the only protectors of the forest and if the forest dies then so does the earth. Even a white man can understand this."

entertainment fields are aggressively articulating their concerns. Great numbers of people are newly inspired to participate.

The formation of the FUNDACAO MATA VIRGEM and the work it has set out to accomplish is a case in point. At issue is the deforestation of the Brazilian rainforest and the protection of its inhabitants.

Take a look at the key players. There is Raoni, a warrior chieftain of the Megkronotis, a Kayapó tribe. The invasion of his jungle world began in the fifties: burning, logging, mining, ranching. He sees his homeland being destroyed, his people displaced and killed. He seeks only to preserve a way of life that has been followed for thirty thousand years. He does what he can. The Brazilian government doesn't lack policies, just the will to carry them out. Little change takes place.

1973. Enter player number two, Jean-Pierre Dutilleux, a young Belgian filmmaker and photojournalist dedicated to documenting the plight of indigenous people around the world. He will become a most valuable friend. He journeys into the rainforest and meets Raoni. He is deeply moved by what he sees. In 1976 he returns to the Amazon and films *Raoni*, documenting the horrors that have fallen on the Kayapó. His film is celebrated worldwide and receives an Academy Award nomination. Raoni becomes an international symbol of native peoples' right to determine their own destiny. Jean-Pierre and Raoni unite to marshal support. In 1980 Raoni requests that a natural preserve be established. He and Jean-Pierre organize the cooperation of other tribal leaders and create a draft of the proposed area. There is much enthusiasm among Brazilian artists, writers, and environmentalists, but the group doesn't possess enough influence to impress the government. A high-profile spokesperson is needed.

December, 1987. Enter player number three—Sting. An internationally

CONTINUED

CONTINUED

renowned singer-songwriter, he is an intelligent, sensitive man with a deep abhorrence of cruelty. His human concerns and gentle ideals are apparent in his lyrics. He is a natural. He accompanies Jean-Pierre into the Amazon jungle where he talks with Raoni and experiences the continuing devastation. He pledges his help. The cast is complete.

Spring, 1988. Sting's involvement receives worldwide media attention. *Vogue* (June, 1988) publishes Sting's Amazon journal accompanied by Jean-Pierre's revealing photos. It is read in forty countries. Raoni appears with Sting at the opening of the Amnesty International world tour in São Paulo. Sting tapes a 60-second television appeal in seven languages, seen throughout the world. Multitudes begin to care.

February, 1989. Sting and Dutilleux meet with President José Sarney, calling on him to support the founding of FUNDACAO MATA VIRGEM (The Rainforest Foundation, Inc.), and to authorize a demarcation of the proposed preserve. The president expresses his concern and promises an in-depth study. Sting

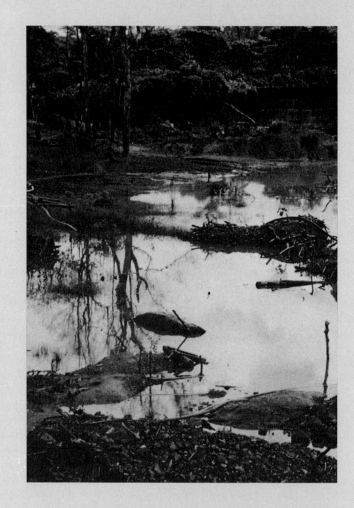

CONTINUED

CONTINUED

and Dutilleux attend the first meeting of indigenous people and pledge their solidarity with the struggle of the Kayapó. Sting puts his career on hold and devotes all his time to the Foundation. It becomes a reality in March. Its goals are (1) to preserve areas of the Amazon rainforest surrounding the last remaining Indian tribes; (2) to promote worldwide awareness of the Amazon rainforest, its inhabitants, and the consequences of its destruction; (3) to encourage the inclusion of environmental studies in education curricula throughout the world. A tour is organized to raise public awareness and funds. The campaign includes meetings with President Mitterand of France, Pope Jean-Paul II, the Prince of Wales, and other heads of state. The entourage visits seventeen countries and receives enormous media attention. Their efforts continue.

Three unlikely allies. Each brought something special. Each needed the others. Each contributed his gift, his strength, his concern, his genius: Raoni's primitive eloquence, Jean-Pierre's quiet determination, Sting's willingness to give a hundred percent of himself to the project. The group hopes the success of their endeavor may provide inspiration for others who seek to improve the human condition.

BARBARA TAYLOR CHRISTIAN

Further: *Jungle Stories—The Fight for the Amazon,* by Sting and Jean-Pierre Dutilleux (London: Barrie and Jenkins; Canada: Little, Brown, and Co.; 1989).

Permission to use text and photographs is hereby acknowledged: The Rainforest Foundation, Inc., Dept. 0101, Los Angeles, CA 90084-0101. Special thanks to Kate Priest and Jean-Pierre Dutilleux. Photo credits: Map session, Guy Weber; Sting and Raoni and devastated forest, Jean-Pierre Dutilleux.

---

1945 he presented a remarkably accurate and detailed description of radio and television communications satellites (and has regretted ever since not attempting to patent "an idea whose time had come"—and he didn't recognize it!). Another futurist, John McHale, makes the significant comment that "Clarke has been consistently more accurate in his prophecies than many of his fellow scientists and science-fiction writers." His major futurist writings are *Profiles of the Future* (1963), *Voices from the Sky* (1965), and *The Promise of Space* (1967). Whether his science-fiction classic *Childhood's End* should also be included among his prophetic visions remains a tantalizing question.

Clarke contends that there are two good reasons for believing that the future will not much resemble the present. One is that known trends are accelerating on all fronts and in a relatively short time the world will be almost unrecognizable to those of us living today.

But there is a stronger reason: the pace of *unpredictable breakthroughs* is also accelerating, and these are the true causes of quantum leaps in progress. A few past unforeseen discoveries are: X-rays, nuclear energy, radio, television, photography, sound recording, quantum mechanics, relativity, transistors, and lasers. There can be little doubt that such unpredictables will continue, and these unexpected jumps will propel us into unexpected worlds.

What about the foreseeable events of the future?

*Someday is too far away. . . .*
*(Master Charge TV commercial)*

*Someday may be too late. . . .*
*(Kodak TV commercial)*

By permission of John Hart and Field Enterprises, Inc.

For the 1990s, Clarke foresees a fairly complete understanding of the links in life's chain; and the first knowledge of gravity waves. During the 1990s will come the practical use of nuclear fusion, the application of bionics, and true artificial intelligence.

During the first quarter of the twenty-first century, Clarke envisions our colonizing the planets and their satellites; breaking the secret of matter at the subparticle level and understanding the fundamental nature of matter and energy; storing man's vast accumulation of knowledge in a world library; and the practical use of robots, for home or office. Weather control will be advanced and interstellar probes will have been sent on their way.

Before mid-century is reached, Clarke believes that electronic contact will have been made with extraterrestrial intelligences (ETs); and in human society genetic engineering will be generally practiced.

*The only certainty in [the] remote future is that radically new things will be happening.*
FREEMAN DYSON

Clarke declines to peer beyond the year 2100, but during the second half of the twenty-first century some of the more auspicious realities will be the control of gravity and planetary engineering (the greening of Mars, the cooling of Venus), and the design and creation of life-forms in the laboratory. As for space travel, we will have achieved velocities near the speed of light, and interstellar voyages will have begun. Near the end of the twenty-first century two world-shattering events are likely: direct contact with ETs and the achievement of virtual immortality for mankind.

Of all these achievements, three will probably be more future-transforming than the rest: gravity control, immortality, and exchanges with ETs.

On gravity: Clarke-the-scientist is not sure that gravity control can be accomplished, but he has an intuition that there has to be some way. He elaborates in detail on the benefits of gravity control if it could be achieved, but then he demurs: "It may seem a little premature to speculate about the uses of a device which may not even be possible, and is certainly beyond the present horizon of science. But it is a general rule that whenever there is a technical need, something always comes along to satisfy it—or to bypass it. For this reason, I feel sure that eventually we will have some means of either neutralizing gravity or overpowering it by brute force."

On immortality: "Death—like sleep—does not appear to be biologically inevitable. . . . Because biological immortality and the preservation of youth are such potent lures, men will never cease to search for them. . . . It would be foolish to imagine that this search will never be successful, down all the ages that lie ahead."

Clarke notes that traditionally—for very good reasons—we think of the mind, the brain, and the body as "going together," necessarily. But this natural "triad" may not be indivisible. It just may be that the entire human body—*except the brain*—can be bionically replaced, so that the brain could continue to live on in the fullness of personality for hundreds of years. Beyond this bionic stage, however, Clarke has envisioned the theoretical means by which *the mind alone* could exist without brain. That is, the mind—with all its capacities, its perceptions, memories, and awareness—may then exist independent of the physical encumbrance of brain-matter.

HERMAN KAHN In the early 1960s Herman Kahn gained wide attention for his analyses of the consequences of possible thermonuclear war. In 1961 he published *On Thermonuclear War* which became the prototype for Stanley Kubrick's character, Dr. Strangelove. He followed in 1962 with *Thinking About the Unthinkable*. In 1967 he co-authored *The Year 2000*. Kahn is essentially a short-range analyst who specialized first in politico-military scenarios involving weapons, resources, logistics, and the like; but in the late 1960s he turned to the analysis of the world's not-too-distant socioeconomic and political leadership problems.

During his first "think tank" period as an expert in military strategy and weapons design, Kahn's logic went like this: There is strong probability that thermonuclear war will occur *at some time* in the future since it is difficult to believe that war can be successfully evaded forever by such erratic plays as bargaining talks, diplomatic trade-offs, détentes, summit maneuvers, arms sales, power balancing, treaties, or whatever. Therefore, Kahn asks what exactly would happen if war should occur. He projected detailed "scenarios" of possible results. In actual wars, there would be "degrees of awfulness" depending upon the weapons used, strategies employed, and states of preparedness. Kahn's conclusions were largely responsible for America's emphasis upon civilian defense programs during the early 1960s.

Kahn's blunt realism provoked outraged responses, especially from church groups, and he was criticized by laymen and experts alike for his heartless, inhuman analyses of "the unthinkable."

It is therefore significant that the hardminded realist of the 1960s later became optimistic about the prospects for world peace and prosperity for the era that lies ahead: "I think there are good prospects for what the Europeans would call la *belle époque* . . . a worldwide period of growth, trade, peace, and prosperity on the whole, and a time, generally speaking, of optimism about the future."

Kahn, working with the Hudson Institute, which he founded, has analyzed

AMERICAN BUSINESSMAN: *(touring Japan):* "Are you operating on a five-year plan?"

JAPANESE BUSINESSMAN: *"We are operating on a 250-year plan."*

AMERICAN: *"(!) How do you operate on a 250-year plan??"*

JAPANESE: *"Very patiently."*
**The CBS Evening News**

*Man will not ultimately be content to be parasitic on the stars but will invade them and organize them for his own purposes.*

J. D. BERNAL

in depth the economic resources of the world today, and he is adamant about what he sees: "Are we running out of energy? The answer is absolutely no. No way. Are we running out of resources? Absolutely not. No way. Are we running out of the ability to feed people from a technological and economic point of view? Absolutely not. No way. Can we retain clear air and clear water and a reasonably aesthetic landscape? Absolutely."

Kahn points out that our water and air are far cleaner today than a decade ago. We Americans, however, love to worry. Our environmental and pollution problems are essentially solved. We have cleaned up the Willamette River and Lake Erie, and many species of fish, long gone, have returned to the Hudson and the Thames. "Many mistakes and setbacks will certainly occur. But ten or fifteen years from now, almost certainly by the year 2000, it is very likely that we will look back with great pride on our accomplishments. We will breathe the clean air, drink directly from the rivers, and smile with pleasure at the aesthetic landscape. . . . In any reasonable historical perspective, that outcome will be termed a clear win for environmental protection."

Furthermore, our energy problems are best thought of as passing socioeconomic adjustments rather than as portents of major cataclysms. We may well go through seasons of energy conservation or be forced to modify our lifestyles. But in the long run the promise is hopeful: the use of solar energy will increase; with safeguards nuclear fission will continue to meet our needs; and nuclear fusion "has never appeared more promising."

After exhaustive analysis of the world's present condition in terms of population, food, energy, and materials resources, Kahn summarizes: "All in all, we remain optimistic about the potential of man's future. We can only hope that he does not throw away this potential through foolish political behavior or misplaced concern about non-existent or badly formulated growth issues." In general, "things are going rather well."

*Ask a new question and you will learn new things.*

GEORGE GREENSTEIN

*You can never plan the future by the past.*

EDMUND BURKE

## A NEW KIND OF REALISM

Our views of the human drama, both past and future, have generally been determined by temperament and/or religious doctrine. Very few philosophies (or theologies) of history have been developed from an objective assessment of historical facts. Our stance usually turns on our feeling for "human nature"; if we trust human initiative, then we tend to have an optimistic outlook on history; if we distrust it, we tend toward pessimism.

But a new kind of realism has recently emerged. Based on a more objective assessment of empirical data, this realism attempts to project a variety of scenarios in the hope we can face them and solve them in time.

SIR FRED HOYLE    There has never been a time during his adult life when Fred Hoyle did not "think big." The universe, nothing less, has constituted his thought-world since his professional life began. When he turned his attention to man's unholy condition, it was inevitable that his viewpoint would be cosmic. Hoyle's best-known writings are in astrophysics and cosmology. His principal futurist work is *Encounter with the Future* (1965).

Hoyle describes and diagrams the general timeline that he believes most likely for the next five thousand years. He assumes the inevitability of thermonuclear war. Hoyle's model is planned around mathematical probabilities regarding population expansions and depletions of various raw materials. He considers it nearly impossible at this late date for us to harness our reproductive energies and reduce birthrates to the level of deathrates. On the contrary, he believes, birthrates will continue almost exponentially and deathrates will diminish. But a point will be reached at which the world population will have neither living room nor adequate food; the world's organizational systems will suddenly disintegrate, followed by a sharp decrease in populations. Famines and plagues might play a part in this process, but Hoyle is fairly sure that nuclear wars will be the primary instrument of depopulation.

The ultimate outcome of this series of population growths and collapses will be the emergence of superior human qualities, including an average I.Q. of perhaps 150. This will in fact be a new species of human being wise enough, finally, to stop the oscillations and stabilize human existence at a more mature level. But only through a continuing experience of consummate tragedies can mankind prepare its fundamental nature for a more civilized phase of human (or post-human) existence.

Let me then outline in a few words, by way of conclusion, what the broad history of our species is going to be over the next five thousand years, give or take a millennium.

I think that at present we are in the first big expansion phase. This first phase is specially important. It possesses assets—coal, oil, etc.—that will not be repeated again. In return for the consumption of these assets it must establish a body of knowledge around which future civilizations will be able to build themselves. Without the establishment of this body of knowledge I do not believe our species will have more than a few centuries of existence ahead of it.

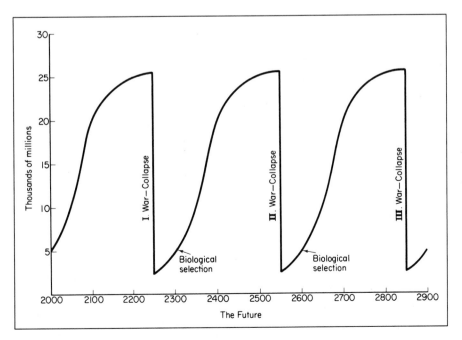

*Man, the sentient species of a small planet circling a small sun in a dim backwater of the galaxy, is about to undertake the breath-taking adventure of re-creating himself. By tinkering with the mechanisms of his heredity, he plans to improve on nature's designs. He believes he can learn to change any part of his body's engineering: his susceptibility to disease, his height and intelligence and beauty, the very span of his life. After two billion years of evolution by trial and error, we now stand at the beginning of humankind's next phase: the Second Genesis.*

**Max Gunther**

*The earth's population is not increasing exactly at a geometrical rate. Actually it is a bit faster; the rate of population increase is itself proportional to the population. If this rate could continue, the population would become infinite in a finite time. The present growth formula leads to an infinite population in 2026 A.D.—in fact, on Friday, November 13, a day dubbed "doomsday."*

**George O. Abell**

I think there will be a series of organizational breakdowns, or catastrophes, occasioned by overpopulation. This will lead to the sawtooth-shaped population curve [in the diagram]. During the beginnings of the reexpansion phases there will be selection for greater sociability and for higher intelligence. The degree of selection in any one cycle need not be dramatically large because the effects of the repeated cycles are cumulative. Indeed, I expect the number of cycles—the number that occurs before they are damped away—to be determined by how much selection occurs per cycle. If this is large, the number of cycles will be small—and vice versa, the net effect being the same.

The ultimate outcome I believe will be a highly sociable, highly intelligent creature. With this, I would consider a new species to have arrived. It will have its own problems, no doubt, but they will not be as elementary as those with which we are faced today.

SIR FRED HOYLE

NUCLEAR WINTER AND MEGADEATH Scientists have been turning their attention to the question of exactly what would happen if a nuclear war should occur. In 1981 Paul Crutzen and John Birks raised the question of how much smoke would be generated by the fires that would follow a nuclear burst. Based on a scenario with an exchange of 5,742 megatons, their calculations indicated that sufficient carbon would rise into the lower atmosphere to block 90 percent of the sunlight from reaching the earth's surface.

In 1983 a major report was published detailing for the first time a wide range of inevitable effects of a nuclear Armageddon. This study is known as the TTAPS study, after the last initials of the five scientists who wrote it: Richard Turco, Brian Toon, Thomas Ackerman, James Pollack, and Carl Sagan. Numerous subsequent studies have augmented and—unfortunately—confirmed the predictions of the TTAPS group.

The scientists calculated what would happen in a variety of scenarios with varying megatonnage and targets. They concluded that even in the event of a relatively light yield, the volume of dust lofted into the atmosphere would be enormous (100,000 tons for each megaton), followed by raging fires producing carbon clouds. The dust and soot would encircle the northern hemisphere within days of the detonation. Black carbon is an efficient filter and would screen the sunlight from reaching the earth's surface; the amount of sunlight at the surface would immediately drop to one percent of normal. Virtually all green-plant photosynthesis would stop and plant life would die. Without light and heat from the sun, temperatures at the surface of the earth would drop below freezing.

Further studies have shown that there would be a climatic inversion. Air layers that normally rise over the tropics and blow northward would cease; instead, the subtropical air layers would rise and blow southward, carrying the carbon-dust clouds into the equatorial regions and southern hemisphere. Thus within a few days of the first detonations, a filtering layer of carbon-dust would cover the earth, leaving it dark and frozen. This would be "nuclear winter."

Best estimates are that a billion people would be killed in the first exchange, and another billion injured. But all society's systems (economic, medical, logistic, communications) would have been destroyed, so that most of those who survived the first exchange would perish in a few weeks. Thus, a nuclear war would directly kill about two billion human beings.

*Think? Why think! We have computers to do that for us.*

JEAN ROSTAND

*Mere opinion remains opinion no matter how many share it. . . . [However] the public comes to conclude that a widespread belief expresses a veritable law of nature.*

DANIEL N. ROBINSON

Continued filtering of sunlight and lack of photosynthesis would mean that no crops or feed for animals could be grown, and most living things throughout the world that survived the initial holocaust would starve or freeze to death. For the first time the specter is raised of the extinction of the human race, and perhaps the extinction of all life on earth.

What would all this mean? Humans have always reflected on suffering and death, and grown from their reflections. But after nuclear war and megadeath there would be no one left to reflect. The protoplasmic venture would be finished, the magnificent experiment done. There would be nothing more to be said, and no one to say it.

The possibility that the earth, poisoned by radioactivity, would lie fallow for thousands of years is not out of the question. But sometime, in some distant future, life—tenacious, irrepressible life—would develop again from simple protocells, and in a million or a billion years, the evolutionary story would be told once again.

## A SPECIAL KIND OF HOPE

Optimism and pessimism are opposites, referring to contrasting sets of expectations. But realism and hopefulness are not opposites. Authentic realism always contains an element of hope since it is an attempt to face and solve problems *in order to move on* to a better condition.

There is a deliberateness in this realistic hopefulness. We must maintain hope to live. If, as individuals, we have joyous experiences to look forward to, then we awaken each day with energy, eager to work toward those experiences; but if we awaken to the prospect of unrelenting pain, then our dread can send us back to bed in an effort to return to sleep. What is true for individuals is true for society as a whole.

The hopeful futurists such as McCall and Bradbury are fully aware of the threats that face the human race. They are not avoiders, or escapists. "When I

Four stages in the Nuclear Winter projection: nuclear detonations, massive fire and smoke, a smoke-enshrouded Earth, a dead planet. Paintings by Jon Lomberg.

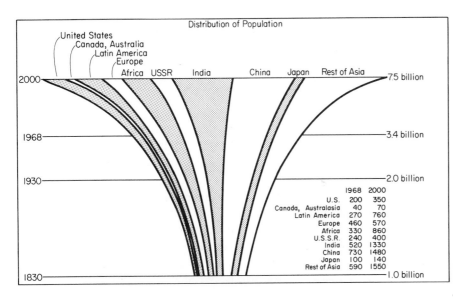

Distribution of Population

United States
Canada, Australia
Latin America
Europe
Africa   USSR      India        China    Japan    Rest of Asia

2000 ——————————————————————————————— 7.5 billion

1968 ——————————————————————————————— 3.4 billion

1930 ——————————————————————————————— 2.0 billion

|  | 1968 | 2000 |
|---|---|---|
| U.S. | 200 | 350 |
| Canada, Australasia | 40 | 70 |
| Latin America | 270 | 760 |
| Europe | 460 | 570 |
| Africa | 330 | 860 |
| U.S.S.R. | 240 | 400 |
| India | 520 | 1330 |
| China | 730 | 1480 |
| Japan | 100 | 140 |
| Rest of Asia | 590 | 1550 |

1830 ——————————————————————————————— 1.0 billion

*Politics is no longer the art of
the possible. It is now more
the art of attempting to avoid
the inevitable.*

JOHN McHALE

think about nuclear warfare," says McCall, "I can start sounding kind of dismal, but that isn't my fundamental personality—or my feeling about the future. In my work, what I *think about* is the promise of the future." Similarly, Bradbury says, "I see all the things the pessimists see, but I choose to *behave* anyway!"

ROBERT T. McCALL  "I see a very bright future for us all," says Robert McCall, and he has been painting his visions of our future since the early 1960s when he was commissioned to paint futuristic spacecraft for *Life* magazine and then the famous poster of the space wheel for the movie *2001: A Space Odyssey*. As director of the Air Force's art program, he became intimately familiar with the machineries of air and space, and his paintings are respected for their realism and technical authenticity. He has documented America's space program for NASA and chronicled the history of man's conquest of space in countless paintings, drawings, postage stamps, and murals—most notably in the towering mural for the Smithsonian Air and Space Museum. His books include *Our World in Space* and *Vision of the Future*.

McCall's paintings depict scenarios in which mankind has successfully realized the promise of technology. It is a world where human beings have solved their major problems and learned peace. They have beautified the environment, designed habitats for intelligent living, and can pursue their dreams.

"I want people to trust technology. I trust it. I'm not worried about it. I'm not fearful that it will get out of hand. I'm intrigued by the joyous vision of where we can go with technology and want to say something about it in my paintings. We humans will be in charge of technology; technology will not be in charge of us."

"In my paintings I describe the wonderful possibilities that the future holds for us. The only thing that will stop us from accomplishing those things is total annihilation, and I don't think that will ever happen. I have a conviction about that. Of course, I know that wars have occurred throughout history; that's recorded, and many of us have lived through war. But I don't see the human species being destroyed. I see us going on, inevitably."

"Some people suggest that if we are obsessed with tragedy, then that's what we'll get. Or if we image joyful things, then that's what we'll get. This is easy to say, and there's probably some truth in it. But the fact is that people who persistently image joyful things are probably joyful people; and people who image dismal things are dismal already."

In 1984 McCall painted a mural for Disney World's EPCOT center (below). The vast panorama is a celebration of the milestones in man's progress in civilization.

The left panel of the tableau shows mankind's earlier monuments: Egyptian pyramids, the Acropolis, Swayambhu temple, and the Kamakura Buddha. The central panel depicts more recent landmarks: Taj Mahal, Eiffel Tower, the American shrines.

On the third panel of the great painting looms a "dream metropolis" of the future, a city quite beyond present imagination, with "surprises at every turn." This panel, says McCall, is "symbolic of our move into space, a movement that will grow in intensity in the decades ahead. The time is not far off when thousands of people will be living semi-permanently in space."

The Prologue and the Promise. The McCall mural (19' x 70') at Disney World's EPCOT Center, by Robert McCall and Louise McCall.

"Vertical cities like this allow us to build up rather than spreading out; we can preserve the Earth and its beauty and ecology. And the floating city concept allows for that, too, since you're not scarring the surface of the Earth at all. You're floating just above it, and the earth is there to enjoy. The floating cities would make it possible for the Earth to stay green, to have parks and forests to beam down to."

In this sweeping view of history, time's arrow—and our eyes—move from left to right. What might the next scene be?

"I could paint a fourth panel. It would depict man's establishment of himself in outer space, in earth orbit, and then the colonization and settlement of the solar system. On that panel I would paint great power-stations in orbit two or three hundred miles above the earth beaming microwave energy to the earth's surface. Space habitats, designed for comfortable and fulfilled living. Colonies on the moon and Mars; settlements on the moons of Jupiter and Saturn; mining outposts on the asteroids. The solar system will be ours."

"Wherever we find ourselves, we'll still be striving for the same thing in our lives. We'll want to achieve our goals, and grow. We're going to fall in love, and we're going to have progeny, and we'll want to care for them and see them grow up whole and energetic and prosperous. All these things will remain constant. We'll see that they get done. Wherever we are we'll design our habitats and lifestyles so these essential good things will continue. Life in the space habitats will be idyllic, as lovely as the most scenic spots on Earth, because *we will make it that way.* Wherever we go, we will repeat what we love here on earth."

What about a next panel? Is there a fifth panel—?

"Yes. Deep Space. We *will* go there, *inevitably.*"

RAY BRADBURY A sense of the future permeates the pages of about everything Ray Bradbury has written. After enjoying the novels, plays, poems, and 350 short stories that Bradbury has penned during the last forty years, a reader retains a picture-filled memory of having visited the future: fiery starbound rockets, wispy aliens with gold-coin eyes, home-sick visitors on a drizzly Venusian landscape, and other strange people and stranger planets.

Bradbury has never attempted to become an "early warning system" for specific dangers. He is a raconteur, a teller of tales, a spinner of far-distant fantasies. Still, scattered through his writings are warnings of what the future might hold if things go wrong. In *Fahrenheit 451*, for instance, we glimpse a society

*In the coming world the capacity to face the new appropriately is more important than the ability to know and repeat the old.*

CARL ROGERS

*When a distinguished but elderly scientist states that something is possible, he is almost certainly right. When he states that something is impossible, he is very probably wrong.*

ARTHUR C. CLARKE
*(Clarke's Law)*

in which reading is banned and literature is burned. It is therefore a world without ideas, peopled with wax-tablet brains on which a Big Brotherly television can easily write its own embalmed image. No ideas, no creativity, no growth.

There runs through Bradbury's writings the theme of machines-gone-astray. A nursery, activated by the thought-wishes of the playing children, runs amok and takes on a horrifying life of its own. A robot police car patrols a darkened city watching for any hint of nonconformist behavior. Bradbury was a critic of Stanley Kubrick's motion picture *2001: A Space Odyssey* not merely because the mellow-voiced computer HAL-9000 became paranoid but because the men and women of the entire space venture had already lost their humanness and behaved like their machines.

Bradbury thinks not in terms of decades or centuries—the "practical life"—but in terms of thousands or millions of years—the "theoretical life." He is a harbinger of the great things that are in store for the human race.

His visions are metaphors. There are sophisticated machineries that allow one to face death, and then to die, over and over again, as often as needed, until at last one can accept life. There is a robot foster mother created in the perfect image of the children's needs who comes into their lives with just the right amount of caring. There is a Mister-George-Bernard-Shaw robot that will forever carry on learned dialogues about the Universe and its multifarious contents, and discourse on their meaning.

In one of his short stories, Bradbury tells of a time-traveler of the late twentieth century who voyages "upstream through the centuries" and sees our future. He beholds the inevitable consequences of man's fear and self-hatred: a barren Earth. We mushroomed our cities, burned the forests, poisoned the atmosphere, polluted the oceans, and melted the records of humanity's greatness. As a species entrusted with the flame we failed, and we took all earth's living things with us. We killed life; and we died.

So the time-traveler returns to our time with memories of our future nightmare—and lies. What he tells us is that we made it through all right and that a glorious future awaits us. For if he had told us of the bleakness he truly saw, then all mankind would have given up and longed for death.

So the time-traveler reports that we successfully charted a path through our nuclear adolescence and went on to great things. "We did it! The future is ours. We rebuilt the cities, freshened the small towns, cleaned the lakes and rivers . . . stopped the wars . . . colonized the Moon, moved on to Mars, then Alpha Centauri. We cured cancer and stopped death. We did it. . . .

"The world went mad with joy. It ran to meet and make that future. . . . "

Was the Royal Lie really necessary?

Yes, says the time-traveler. "Because I was born and raised in a time, in the Sixties, Seventies and Eighties, when people had stopped believing in themselves. I saw that disbelief, the reason that no longer gave itself reasons to survive, and was moved, depressed and then angered by it.

"Everywhere, I saw and heard doubt. Everywhere, I learned destruction. . . . Nothing was worth doing. Go to bed at night full of bad news at eleven, wake up in the morn to worse news at seven."

"Not only the Four Horsemen of the Apocalypse rode the horizon to flight themselves on our cities but a fifth horseman, worse than all the rest, rode with

*The dangers that face the world can, every one of them, be traced back to science. The salvations that may save the world will, every one of them, be traced back to science.*

ISAAC ASIMOV

them: Despair, wrapped in dark shrouds of defeat, crying only repetitions of past disasters, present failures, future cowardices.

"Bombarded by dark chaff and no bright seed, what sort of harvest was there for man in the latter part of the incredible Twentieth Century?

"So the self-fulfilling prophecies were declared; we dug our graves and prepared to lie down in them."

We wept at the grave of our children, and the child was us."

The time-traveler, therefore, tells us the Great Lie to save us. But is it truly a lie?

"You see the point, don't you . . . ? Life has *always* been lying to ourselves! As boys, young men, old men. As girls, maidens, women, to gently lie and prove the lie true. To weave dreams and put brains and ideas and flesh and the truly real beneath the dreams. Everything, finally, is a promise. What seems a lie is a ramshackle need, wishing to be born."

Says Bradbury: "The thing that I have against the negative futurists of the last thirty years is that they're all changing their minds now. And what you want to say to them is 'Dammit, why did you depress us in the first place? Where were you when we needed you? You almost destroyed us during the Flower Period a few years ago.' Some of them wanted to scare the devil out of us, and they did. But too often they scare all hope out of us and no one does anything."

Bradbury's previsions of Man's journey—on which he has just embarked—are magnificent dreams, filled with the excitement of discovery and the adventure of the unknown. A million years, a billion years, and more—until humanity is immortal and has graced the stars.

What of Man, ultimately—"this strange, weeping, laughing animal who awakens from monkey dreams to find himself almost Man? What is this remarkable thing that we are?"

In phrases reminiscent of Shaw: "We are something that's becoming itself. We are matter and force that does not know itself, changing ourselves, during the long night of the universe, into imagination and will. Willing ourselves to survive." This is what humans have been doing for millions of years and will continue to do for more millions of years. "Man will not die . . . ever. Hate as we often hate ourselves, yet we love ourselves more and the gift given us to live one time in a Universe as brutal, stunning, and nightmarish as it is beautiful. Oh, then again beautiful beyond our powers to say."

## MANY FUTURES: A COMMON VISION

Images of the future serve many purposes. The images so far described have been employed primarily to forecast threatening global problems and to set up the machinery through which they may be effectively met and solved. This is one function of future-images. But there is another.

Today's world has come unglued, unraveled. The old loyalties no longer bind, and the countless collectivities have fragmented, traveled, intermixed, interwoven. Out of this new mixture is emerging a new world. It isn't born yet, and it may remain in labor for another fifty years, perhaps a hundred. Barring

*History is a nightmare from which I am trying to awake.*

**JAMES JOYCE**

catastrophe, however, it will be born. We can be fairly sure of that, for lack of alternatives.

There is a pressing need for a sense of global identity and a shared vision of the future—a reason to exist. It is this profoundly human need that futurists have been watching and diagnosing, like physicians. The illness is clear enough, but the prescription is not at all clear as yet.

Robert Bundy writes:

> The West has lost any reason for being. Simply to further develop scientific and technological tools for their own sake, or to increase our mastery over nature, or to further expand the consumptive society, with its hedonistic license, cannot provide the motive power for a civilization. Some deeper spiritual center and transcendent values are required.
>
>  This loss of a reason to go on means we have no inspiring image of the future, no dominant vision within whose embrace different expectations can survive and draw strength, no overarching dream capable of infusing all of us with hope and giving us courage to confront and cope with our awesome problems.

A shared vision of our common future is therefore enormously important. Bundy notes that "positive images tell of another and better world in a coming time. They infuse people with the foreknowledge of a destiny of happiness, and thus engender the courage to confront and solve the problems facing civilization. Negative, pessimistic images work in the opposite way and may forecast a period of cultural decline and breakdown. . . . Without a living image of the future a society can become doomed to a rootless vacuum" and "condemned to disappear."

Bundy concludes:

*There is a vast difference between letting changes occur under the impact of technological advances and choosing the changes we want to bring about by our technological means.*

BERTRAND DE JOUVENEL

> Western civilization is passing away. So be it. This does not mean that our total inheritance from the past or our leadership potential for the future are lost. It does mean that many of the central dogmas and visions that drove Western civilization forward do not have a prominent place in the future. What does have a place in the future are: (1) the shared conviction that new magnetic images of the future can be born, (2) people who are united by common beliefs necessary for survival and development within a global perspective, and (3) groups that share across their boundaries while, as always, they remain separated by particular visions they are free to follow as long as others may also follow their visions.

## REFLECTIONS

1   Recall the statement that opens this chapter: That we create the past and can also create alternative futures; and that we need both past and future to see ourselves in perspective. How much value is there in this way of looking at ourselves and our place in time?

2   Of the various alternative futures suggested here as real possibilities, which one(s) do you think are most likely to transpire? Why?

3   As you ponder the future, are you personally trusting and optimistic or wary and pessimistic? Do your own experiences and feelings tend to color the optional futures which you can imagine? (Do you think personal

experiences may have colored the views of professional historians and professional futurists?)

4   What is your response to some of the specific events enumerated in this chapter as virtual certainties for the future? Are you eager to see some of these events and conditions materialize? Are there some that you fear? Would you want to live with them? Do you think that our great-grandchildren will be able to accept and live with them?

5   Ponder the sequence of maps on p. 313. Do you think this is a likely prediction of what will happen? (Apologies to Herr Rorschach, but *what is it* that's going to happen?)

6   What is your response to Sir Fred Hoyle's projection of the future? Can you see what his long-range optimism is based on? Do you think there is a probability that Hoyle's vision will actually happen?

7   Would you like to live in a space colony? What kind of a life do you think you would live there? Would you enjoy it more or less than living on Spaceship Earth? Can you tell why?

# MICROCOSM
# MACROCOSM
# COSMOS

*There is today—in a time when old beliefs are withering—a kind of philosophic hunger, a need to know who we are and how we got there. There is an ongoing search, often unconscious, for a cosmic perspective for humanity.*

<small>CARL SAGAN</small>

# 7₁

## MAY 28, 585 B.C.

Philosophy and science were born together in 585 B.C.—on May 28 at 6:13 p.m. (Milesian Standard Time); for at that instant an eclipse began in the Ionian city of Miletus, a solar eclipse that had been *predicted* by a philosopher named Thales. We have no evidence that Thales established the exact time of the event. This precise date has been calculated by modern astronomers, and if Thales had even come close—within a day or a week—he would have done well. But the significant point is that he had become aware of the regularities of nature on the basis of which he had made a prediction. However elementary this may seem, it is the dim recognition of what we now know as Natural Law.

## THE NATURE OF EMPIRICAL KNOWLEDGE

Thales (c. 585 B.C.)

*This is a world of pure mathematics, and when we penetrate to the bottom of it, that's all it will be.*

JOHN A. WHEELER

Our knowledge of nature and its "laws" derives from two distinct kinds of epistemic operations: empirical observation and rational system-building. Thus we have empirical knowledge and rational (or a priori) knowledge. Both present problems not yet solved.

Suppose you took a Jovian philosopher to a baseball game. He is a handsome humanoid with shining eyes. Having recently arrived from Jupiter, and being ever-alert to adventures of the mind, he watches the game with eager awareness. Since he has never seen a baseball game, you begin to explain the rules to him. He declines the offer and tells you he would prefer to figure out the rules for himself. And so, through all nine innings, you let him watch the action.

As he observes the players, he notes their patterns of movement; they perform the same motions over and over again. A player walks up to a particular spot and tries to hit a small, round object that another player throws at him (no,

*Philosophy is written in the vast book which stands open before our eyes, I mean the universe; but it cannot be read until we have learnt the language and become familiar with the characters in which it is written.*

GALILEO

*We are free to choose which elements we wish to apply in the construction of physical reality. The justification of our choice lies exclusively in our success.*

ALBERT EINSTEIN

he throws it past him). If the man with the stick swings and misses three times, the hand of the man dressed in black goes up and the man with the stick walks away looking either sad or angry. But if he hits the round object with the stick, he starts running, always in the same direction, toward another man.

And so, little by little, the "rules of the game" are inferred and reconstructed as the visitor from Jupiter watches the players' consistent, repeated patterns of behavior.

The "rules of the game" exist in the players' heads, and they play by them. The players know the rules because they have read them or have grown up with them, but our extraterrestrial epistemologist must *infer* the rules by watching behavior—that is, by watching matter-in-motion.

By the end of the second inning, he has some rough ideas of a few consistencies. By the fifth, he has added several more consistencies to his mental list and refined some previous observations. By the end of the game—Jovian genius that he is—he has been able to understand and jot down a set of rules that describes much of the players' actions.

After the game, the Jovian checks his list of inferred rules with you and you find that he has indeed discovered most of the rules that you know about baseball.

Now, he never *saw* the rules; he *created* the rules *in his mind* because they seemed to describe consistently the behavior of the players. All that he actually observed, of course, was players-in-motion.

Our minds operate in similar fashion to formulate "scientific laws." They are the "rules of the game" that we have inferred. We often deceive ourselves by thinking that we have observed the rules, whereas the fact is that we created them to account for consistencies *that we remembered* while watching matter-in-motion. We never observe the "law of gravity" or the "inverse-square law" which describes the propagation of light, or the "laws" of mass-energy transformation. All the "laws" of physics are created in our minds; all this is *empirical* knowledge.

Scientists who work with submicroscopic entities are at a special disadvantage since they never even get to see matter-in-motion. They must create the "rules of the game" by observing only secondary traces (streaks on photographic plates, for example) left by particles of matter. In other words, particle physicists must create in their minds pictures of the matter as well as the principles of motion that describe the behavior of such matter.

All empirical knowledge is hypothetical and merely probable. That is, it consists of operational hypotheses that we continue to use as long as they are consistent with our observations.

Plants need sunlight to grow. Gray whales migrate in March. Robins lay blue eggs. Scandinavians have blond hair. Water will conduct electricity if salt is dissolved in it. Light travels at 186,000 miles per second. Water cannot flow uphill. A lunar month is 27 days, 7 hours, 43 minutes. Tornadoes never occur in December. A fire will not burn without oxygen. Whale sharks are harmless to man.

All these things we know from repeated experience. But do we know them for sure? *All* robins' eggs are blue, someone might argue; he has investigated countless nests and noted thousands of robins' eggs—all pale blue. That seems to settle the matter. Still, can one be absolutely positive that some berserk robin hasn't laid a bright purple egg in a nest somewhere?

No empirical knowledge is ever certain. *To every statement one can imagine an exception.* One can easily imagine a gray whale deciding not to migrate in March, or a tornado tearing across Kansas in December, or a whale shark mistaking a man for a rather large tidbit of plankton. If one can imagine an exception to the statement, then it is obviously not *necessary* knowledge; it is only *contingent* knowledge with a probability of being correct. This is true of all the Natural Laws of physics that we have formulated to describe matter-in-motion.

This is also why, in the social sciences, we must employ statistics to establish the "coefficient of correlation" so that we can figure the probability of correctness of any hypothesis. What we determine is the number of cases out of a hundred in which the hypothesis would hold true.

*The laws of mathematics and logic are true simply by virtue of our conceptual scheme.*

W. V. QUINE

## THE NATURE OF A PRIORI KNOWLEDGE

A second kind of knowledge about the natural world is rational or a priori knowledge. It has baffled philosophers from the beginning and still puzzles us to the point of irritation.

We know certain *necessary* truths, it seems, to which *we cannot imagine exceptions.* Seven plus five equals twelve—now, always, and everywhere. Parallel lines in the same plane will never intersect. The area of a circle can be determined with the formula $\pi r^2$. The angles of a triangle always add up to 180°.

Now, are these truly universal truths? The rationalist answers yes. Can one conceive, in his wildest imagination, any exception to these statements? Can we imagine two parallel lines intersecting? or $7 + 5 \neq 12$? or a triangle's angles not totaling 180°? No, we can't.

Here, then, lie the foundations of the "exact sciences": all known systems of mathematics, geometry, and logic.

How many robins' eggs would we have to examine to be sure that *all* robins' eggs are blue? Obviously, all of them: every egg ever laid. How many triangles do we have to investigate to be sure that they all contain angles totaling 180°? Only a few. The rationalist argues that once we understand the nature of the knowledge we are dealing with, then we don't have to ponder any more triangles at all. We know a priori (that is, without further empirical observation) that the angles of *all* triangles will total 180°. And what about $7 + 5 = 12$? Is this true for this and all imaginable universes? It would seem to be.

If an ornithologist reported the discovery of a clutch of bright purple robins' eggs, we might believe him. We would have no *logical* reason to disbelieve him. But if a geometrician reported that he had spotted a circle somewhere in Antarctica whose diameter was greater than its circumference, we might think he had stayed out in the snow too long. We would disbelieve him on *logical* grounds.

Therefore, it is clear that we are dealing with two distinctly different kinds of knowledge about nature, and the way they apply to the external world is different.

*Reason is the substance of the universe. . . . The design of the world is absolutely rational.*

G. W. F. HEGEL

The problem with empirical knowledge is that we can never be absolutely sure of anything. Sometimes we can't even be sure how uncertain we should be! We must always ask: Do we have sufficient experience of an event to be reasonably (operationally) sure? Most of our "scientific laws" continue to work, but then we are reminded of some "laws" that have recently been abandoned.

The more theoretical problem of a priori knowledge haunts our intellects. Why is it that mathematical knowledge describes so accurately the operations of nature? Why does $7 + 5 = 12$? Could it be that we can develop a coherent mathematical system in our minds which, by some sort of coincidence, applies to the natural world? Or does nature really operate on inherently perfect mathematical principles? How do we know there are not exceptions to nature's mathematical system?

We are still mystified at the relationship between our magnificent mental system and the equally magnificent natural system—both of which seem to be perfect mathematical systems in harmony with one another.

Or is our problem defined incorrectly? Why does $2 + 2 = 4$? Is it because we say so? Is this formula—$2 + 2 = 4$—an eternal truth because we have constructed a logical system that is internally coherent? Or is it because this operation describes real operations in nature? The pragmatist contends that we keep on using the formula only because it keeps on working; but the rationalist is not satisfied with such an answer. He argues that two plus two *must* equal four, anywhere in the universe; it is a cosmic truth, not a pragmatic model.

## OTHER WAYS OF KNOWING?

When it is said that there are two ways of knowing the natural world, this claim has a decidedly Western sound. It is a Western assumption that the subject is the knower and that nature is the object known. If the relationship is *defined* this way, then the foregoing elucidation of the problems involved between subject and object should be fairly accurate and not without meaning.

But we might wonder whether there are other ways of knowing. Is it a true and final fact that man is the experiencing subject and the real world is the experienced object, and that the two are distinct, separate entities? Or might there be a "field interaction" that would render false the subject-object dichotomy? Perhaps man's knowing is more immersed in the "object" than he thinks and his separateness is merely an illusion. Perhaps the processes of knowing are but part of a larger process. Or perhaps there are other *ways* of knowing realities.

A Western philosopher who was convinced there is a better way was Henri Bergson. He contended that the only true method of "doing metaphysics"—knowing the real world as it actually is—is through "intuition," a kind of "intellectual empathy." The rational mind is far too occupied with static concepts and mental filing systems to be able to perceive the ever-changing *process* we call "nature." Nature is pure duration, with no stops and starts, absolutes, or quantification. Man can only know nature by putting aside the intellect and intuiting directly the flowing reality of which he is a part.

Those familiar with Eastern modes of experience are aware that this is a meaningful way of knowing reality. Buddhism, for instance, explicitly rejects the subject-object dichotomy as dangerously false. The goal of Zen meditation is satori, a sort of "flash of realization" that man is one with reality and not separate from it. It is a sensitive, totalic awareness of being a part of nature. Subject and object merge into one, or better, they are at last perceived as always having been one.

## REALITIES BEYOND APPEARANCES

Man has been disturbed by the natural world into which he is born and in which he has to live. It is clear to him that things are not quite what they seem.

There are life-giving forces that make things grow, and all living things are in a condition of constant change. There are forces that shake the ground and belch up cinders and ash through the mountaintops. There are forces that rumble in a rainstorm and crackle across the sky in streaks of light. There are insidious forces that make one hurt inside and burn with heat and die. There are roots and insects and animals and seeds that give off juices which can kill.

Ancient man wondered about these things. Obviously there were all sorts of *realities beyond appearances*. They could be felt. They could be benevolent, but more often they were hostile and harmful. What were these forces—these invisible, capricious powers?

Today, of course, we know that the ancient intuition was correct: there are indeed forces beyond appearances. We must admire ancient men for making as much sense of their world as they did.

Sir Arthur Eddington illustrates the difference between macrocosmic reality as we experience it and some of the "realities beyond appearances."

The learned physicist and the man in the street were standing together on the threshold about to enter a room.

The man in the street moved forward without trouble, planted his foot on a solid unyielding plank at rest before him, and entered.

The physicist was faced with an intricate problem. To make any movement he must shove against the atmosphere, which presses with a force of fourteen pounds on every square inch of his body. He must land on a plank travelling at twenty miles a second round the sun—a fraction of a second earlier or later the plank would be miles away from the chosen spot. He must do this whilst hanging from a round planet head outward into space, and with a wind of ether blowing at no one knows how many miles a second through every interstice of his body. He reflects too that the plank is not what it appears to be—a continuous support for his weight. The plank is mostly emptiness; very sparsely scattered in that emptiness are myriads of electric charges dashing about at great speeds but occupying at any moment less than a billionth part of the volume which the plank seems to fill continuously. It is like stepping on a swarm of flies. . . .

Happily even a learned physicist has usually some sense of proportion; and it is probable that for this occasion he put out of mind scientific truths about astronomical motions, the constitution of planks and the laws of probability, and was content to follow the same crude conception of his task that presented itself to the mind of his unscientific colleague.

Particle streaks. Photo courtesy of NAL.

*Some of the ablest men in the world at present regard matter as merely a special type of undulatory disturbance.*

J. B. S. HALDANE

*In so far as mathematics is about reality, it is not certain, and in so far as it is certain, it is not about reality.*

ALBERT EINSTEIN

*Sir Arthur Eddington has calculated that the number of particles in the universe is $2.36216 \times 10^{79}$, or, in round numbers, $2^{264}$.*

## THIS WORLD OF OURS—WHAT IS IT?

The very first Greek philosophers asked questions, not about man, but about the world in which they lived. They knew nothing of the basic elements (hydrogen, oxygen, and so forth) or natural law ("physics"—the science of matter-in-motion) as we do. But sensing man's perilous (mis)understanding of his world, they asked questions, and asked them in a new way.

What is this "matter" of which everything is made? Is everything made of some single substance which we know (like water, air, or fire)? Or is it made of some unknown substance that under certain conditions turns into the water, air, and fire of experience?

And what are the forces that activate matter into motion? The winds blow, lightning fells the giant pine, crops grow and die. What are the forces behind all this? Is it a single force or many? Could the force be "divine" or "mental"? Could it be *alive*? Is it *outside* matter? (Zeus doesn't really hurl the thunderbolt of lightning.) Or *inside* matter? (Thales pondered magnets and decided their forces were internal; he concluded that they must have "souls.")

These first philosopher-scientists phrased such questions as best they could. In all, they were asking but two fundamental questions: (1) What is everything made of? (2) What are the forces that cause motion? There must be a lesson in all this. Our present accumulation of scientific knowledge about the natural world is nothing less than staggering, yet what are the fundamental questions we are asking today? *(1) What is everything made of? (2) What are the forces that cause motion?*

But it would be misleading to leave the matter here. As of the last decade of the twentieth century, we have traveled a long journey in our understanding of the substances that make up the realm of the physically real. We may still use the same sentences, but we aren't asking the same questions. Today, when we ask "What is everything made of?" our minds jump to a vast accumulation of exciting information to shape our answers.

You're taking a walk along the beach and pick up a wave-washed pebble. It's milky white and shiny. What is it? What is it made of? The *name* (symbol) for it is "quartz," but this conventional name tells us nothing. So, what is it, really?

The first step in finding out must be taken at *the molecular level of organization*. A molecule is a group of atoms of two or more basic elements bound tightly together so that they behave as a single unit. Every molecule of the same "species" is made up of the same proportions of the same elements. A molecule of water, for example, is composed of two atoms of hydrogen and one atom of oxygen ($H_2O$); every water molecule on Earth and throughout the universe is constructed in just this way.

This is the first level of organization that gives the world its consistencies and enables us to make sense of it. Just as all molecules of water are the same, so are all the molecules of sugar, alcohol, salt, methane, silver iodide, ammonia, insulin, formaldehyde, carbon dioxide, and countless other substances that affect our lives. We can name, define, and discover their qualities ("water molecules are wet"), and exploit them because their components and qualities are

## The Periodic Table of Elements

"What is the world made of?" This question has bothered man since the beginning of human inquiry. Thales thought the world was nothing but water. Anaximenes reasoned that it was all air. Heraclitus said it was fire. Empedocles and Aristotle decided it was a blend of Fire, Earth, Air, and Water.

At the atomic level, we now know what "the world" is made of. The entire universe and everything in it—including ourselves—is composed of about a hundred basic elements. When the "Periodic Table of Elements" was devised by Dmitri Mendeleev in 1871, even in its incomplete form it began to reveal numerous secrets regarding the orderly relationships within Nature. Today the philosophic implications are staggering.

Each element is determined solely by the number of protons it contains in its nucleus (carbon has six protons, for example; gold has 79). As the elements were arranged in the Table according to the number of each element's protons, then groups of elements with strikingly similar characteristics were seen. The columns to the left of the zigzag line tend to be metals; those to the right are nonmetals. The helium group (vertical column at right) consists of inert gases that refuse to react with other elements; but the volatile elements of the fluorine group react with almost any element they touch. The way all these elements combine to produce other substances is determined by the number of electrons that swirl in shells around the nucleus.

Today it's fashionable to take all this knowledge for granted, but this is the kind of understanding that would have made the first philosopher-scientists jubilant with excitement.

### Periodic Table of Elements

| 1 | 2 | 3 | 4 | 5 | 6 | 7 | 8 | 9 | 10 | 11 | 12 | 13 | 14 | 15 | 16 | 17 | 18 |
|---|---|---|---|---|---|---|---|---|---|---|---|---|---|---|---|---|---|
| Hydrogen<br>1 **H**<br>1.008 | | | | | | | | | | | | | | | | | Helium<br>2 **He**<br>4.003 |
| Lithium<br>3 **Li**<br>6.939 | Beryllium<br>4 **Be**<br>9.012 | | | | | | | | | | | Boron<br>5 **B**<br>10.81 | Carbon<br>6 **C**<br>12.01 | Nitrogen<br>7 **N**<br>14.01 | Oxygen<br>8 **O**<br>16.00 | Fluorine<br>9 **F**<br>18.99 | Neon<br>10 **Ne**<br>20.18 |
| Sodium<br>11 **Na**<br>22.99 | Magnesium<br>12 **Mg**<br>24.31 | | | | | | | | | | | Aluminum<br>13 **Al**<br>26.98 | Silicon<br>14 **Si**<br>28.09 | Phosphorus<br>15 **P**<br>30.97 | Sulfur<br>16 **S**<br>32.06 | Chlorine<br>17 **Cl**<br>35.45 | Argon<br>18 **Ar**<br>39.95 |
| Potassium<br>19 **K**<br>39.10 | Calcium<br>20 **Ca**<br>40.08 | Scandium<br>21 **Sc**<br>44.96 | Titanium<br>22 **Ti**<br>47.90 | Vanadium<br>23 **V**<br>50.94 | Chromium<br>24 **Cr**<br>52.00 | Manganese<br>25 **Mn**<br>54.94 | Iron<br>26 **Fe**<br>55.85 | Cobalt<br>27 **Co**<br>58.93 | Nickel<br>28 **Ni**<br>58.71 | Copper<br>29 **Cu**<br>63.55 | Zinc<br>30 **Zn**<br>65.37 | Gallium<br>31 **Ga**<br>69.72 | Germanium<br>32 **Ge**<br>72.59 | Arsenic<br>33 **As**<br>74.92 | Selenium<br>34 **Se**<br>78.96 | Bromine<br>35 **Br**<br>79.90 | Krypton<br>36 **Kr**<br>83.80 |
| Rubidium<br>37 **Rb**<br>85.47 | Strontium<br>38 **Sr**<br>87.62 | Yttrium<br>39 **Y**<br>88.91 | Zirconium<br>40 **Zr**<br>91.22 | Niobium<br>41 **Nb**<br>92.91 | Molybdenum<br>42 **Mo**<br>95.94 | Technetium<br>43 **Tc**<br>(99) | Ruthenium<br>44 **Ru**<br>101.1 | Rhodium<br>45 **Rh**<br>102.9 | Palladium<br>46 **Pd**<br>106.4 | Silver<br>47 **Ag**<br>107.9 | Cadmium<br>48 **Cd**<br>112.4 | Indium<br>49 **In**<br>114.8 | Tin<br>50 **Sn**<br>118.7 | Antimony<br>51 **Sb**<br>121.8 | Tellurium<br>52 **Te**<br>127.6 | Iodine<br>53 **I**<br>126.9 | Xenon<br>54 **Xe**<br>131.3 |
| Cesium<br>55 **Cs**<br>132.9 | Barium<br>56 **Ba**<br>137.3 | Lanthanide series<br>57–71 | Hafnium<br>72 **Hf**<br>178.5 | Tantalum<br>73 **Ta**<br>180.9 | Tungsten<br>74 **W**<br>183.9 | Rhenium<br>75 **Re**<br>186.2 | Osmium<br>76 **Os**<br>190.2 | Iridium<br>77 **Ir**<br>192.2 | Platinum<br>78 **Pt**<br>195.1 | Gold<br>79 **Au**<br>197.0 | Mercury<br>80 **Hg**<br>200.6 | Thallium<br>81 **Tl**<br>204.4 | Lead<br>82 **Pb**<br>207.2 | Bismuth<br>83 **Bi**<br>209.0 | Polonium<br>84 **Po**<br>(210) | Astatine<br>85 **At**<br>(210) | Radon<br>86 **Rn**<br>(222) |
| Francium<br>87 **Fr**<br>(223) | Radium<br>88 **Ra**<br>(226) | Actinide series<br>89–103 | Rutherfordium<br>104 **Rf**<br>(260) | | | | | | | | | | | | | | |

**Lanthanide series**

| | | | | | | | | | | | | | | |
|---|---|---|---|---|---|---|---|---|---|---|---|---|---|---|
| Lanthanum<br>57 **La**<br>138.9 | Cerium<br>58 **Ce**<br>140.1 | Praseodymium<br>59 **Pr**<br>140.9 | Neodymium<br>60 **Nd**<br>144.2 | Promethium<br>61 **Pm**<br>(145) | Samarium<br>62 **Sm**<br>150.4 | Europium<br>63 **Eu**<br>152.0 | Gadolinium<br>64 **Gd**<br>157.3 | Terbium<br>65 **Tb**<br>158.9 | Dysprosium<br>66 **Dy**<br>162.5 | Holmium<br>67 **Ho**<br>164.9 | Erbium<br>68 **Er**<br>167.3 | Thulium<br>69 **Tm**<br>168.9 | Ytterbium<br>70 **Yb**<br>173.0 | Lutetium<br>71 **Lu**<br>175.0 |

**Actinide series**

| | | | | | | | | | | | | | | |
|---|---|---|---|---|---|---|---|---|---|---|---|---|---|---|
| Actinium<br>89 **Ac**<br>(227) | Thorium<br>90 **Th**<br>(232.05) | Protactinium<br>91 **Pa**<br>(231) | Uranium<br>92 **U**<br>238.0 | Neptunium<br>93 **Np**<br>(237) | Plutonium<br>94 **Pu**<br>(242) | Americium<br>95 **Am**<br>(243) | Curium<br>96 **Cm**<br>(247) | Berkelium<br>97 **Bk**<br>(247) | Californium<br>98 **Cf**<br>(249) | Einsteinium<br>99 **Es**<br>(254) | Fermium<br>100 **Fm**<br>(253) | Mendelevium<br>101 **Md**<br>(256) | Nobelium<br>102 **No**<br>(256) | Lawrencium<br>103 **Lr**<br>(257) |

always the same. Many millions of these molecular compounds are produced by nature, and millions more are now produced in our chemical laboratories.

So, what is the quartz made of? It is composed of molecules of the elements silicon and oxygen (silicon dioxide, $SiO_2$).

Next down, we come to *the atomic level of organization.* An atom is an exceedingly complex little system that behaves quite autonomously and follows its own set of rules. It consists of an incredibly small (but very heavy) nucleus of protons and neutrons and a shell of as many as a hundred electrons orbiting the nucleus more than a hundred million billion times each second. The atom is tiny—less than a hundred millionth of an inch in diameter. And the dog definitely wags the tail: more than 99.9 percent of the mass of the atom is found in its nucleus; the rest (less than .1 percent) is in its electrons. If an atomic nucleus were the size of a baseball, then the electron(s) would be the size of pinhead(s) orbiting about a mile away.

From this insight into the atom, two conclusions have produced major changes in the way we think about matter and the world. (1) Everything in the universe is in motion at very high speeds ("relativistic speeds"), and there is *nothing* that is not in motion. *Nothing* is at rest anywhere in the cosmos. (2) In the final analysis nothing is really solid. Everything is composed of atoms, and the atom is mostly space dominated not by solid pieces of matter but by powerful nonmaterial force fields.

It is the atom that gives the rich distinctive qualities to the elements as we experience them: gold, copper, sulfur, chromium, lead, uranium, carbon, helium, and so on. All the basic elements are now known to us, and they total about a hundred. They can be arranged in the Periodic Table of Elements according to their weights. (This is how we know that all the elements in the universe have been discovered: there are no gaps or blanks in the Periodic Table.) Everything in the universe is composed of the atoms of these few elements arranged in various molecular combinations.

So, what is the quartz pebble made of? It is composed of molecules of the elements silicon and oxygen that are composed of atoms made of protons, neutrons, and electrons.

Next down, things get more complicated.

When the Greek philosopher Democritus first theorized that all matter was composed of atoms, he pictured little indivisible pieces of solid matter and called them "atoms," from the Greek *a-tomé,* "uncuttable." This image of the atom prevailed in scientific thinking well into the nineteenth century. Then it was discovered that the uncuttable atom had parts. But these parts were still thought of as tiny solid pieces of charged matter which in turn might be made up of even smaller solid pieces of charged matter, and so on, perhaps infinitely. New discoveries soon destroyed this picture of the atom and its constituents. At the subatomic level there are no pieces of solid matter, or solid pieces of anything. The notion of "solid matter" as we know it at the experiential level ceases to exist and is replaced by points of energy and coherent force fields.

With the development of high-energy research tools it was found that the atom is nothing less than a three-ring circus with its wild-animal acts and high-wire performances all going on at the same time. The heart of the atom seemed

*Reality is the real business of physics.*

ALBERT EINSTEIN

*Physics tells us much less about the physical world than we thought it did.*

BERTRAND RUSSELL

*The notion that matter is something inert and uninteresting is surely the veriest nonsense. If there is anything more wonderful than matter in the sheer versatility of its behavior, I have yet to hear tell of it.*

SIR FRED HOYLE

to be an endless wellspring of quirky particles, so disparate and chaotic that they made no sense at all.

Today, after three or four decades of phenomenally successful probing, we know that the nucleus of the atom is composed of protons and neutrons orbiting a nuclear center in tightly organized shells. It is spherical or distorted into the shape of a football or doorknob. Its basic particles, proton and neutron, are essentially the same particle in different energy states, bound together by a charged particle called a pion. The exchange of pions creates the strong nuclear force that binds the atomic nucleus together.

Much more has been revealed by the high-energy particle accelerators ("atom smashers"). A whole family of particles exists that are subject to the strong nuclear force, and another family subject only to the weak force. All particles, it seems, have antiparticles; so there exist antiprotons, antielectrons (called positrons), and antineutrinos. To date more than two hundred particles have been discovered in experiments, and several hundred more have been postulated in theory but have yet to be discovered in reality.

So, until the early 1960s chaos reigned. Then in 1964 a theory was devised that began to account for the activity in this little three-ring circus. This "quark" theory was devised to explain the behavior of all the particles in the nucleus subject to the strong force. All the hundreds of particles that have been discovered in the heart of the nucleus can be explained as combinations of quarks and antiquarks. The proton and neutron, for instance, are made up of three quarks each. Even the pion is made up of two quarks.

At first all this was only theory. Then in 1968 the first quarks were found in accelerator experiments. By 1984 a total of six quarks had been found and their basic properties known.

This is *the quark level of organization*. So, what is the quartz made of? It is composed of molecules of the elements silicon and oxygen that are composed of atoms made of protons, neutrons, and electrons that, in turn, are composed of various combinations of quarks. Everything in the universe can finally be explained in terms of combinations of quarks and their force fields.

Is this the end of the story? No one knows. It is turning out that the quark story is not really simple after all. Each quark, it has been discovered, comes in three "brands" (physicists say three "colors"), so there are really eighteen quarks. But since each quark has an antiquark, one can think in terms of thirty-six quarks. Moreover, theorists have had to postulate the existence of eight "gluons" that are carriers of the binding charge between quarks. The theories that have made sense of this complex world are called quantum

Polymethylene crystals, magnified 37,000 times, show that nature grows both "left-handed" and "right-handed" spiral designs.

electrodynamics (QED) and quantum chromodynamics (QCD), and both theories have been marvelously successful in bringing order out of chaos.

But intensive search continues for ever more fundamental constituents of matter. Physicists keep hoping that they will finally arrive at rock-bottom reality and know at last what the universe is made of. Maybe there is such a resting place, but in their more dismal moments physicists sometimes fear that the levels might continue on ad infinitum, and the search for reality may never end. What can be said at present is that, although there are theories that proceed beyond quarks, there is no evidence that any further levels exist.

*No development of modern science has had a more profound impact on human thinking than the advent of quantum theory. . . . The distress which this reorientation caused continues to the present day. Basically physicists have suffered a severe loss: their hold on reality.*

BRYCE DEWITT AND
NEILL GRAHAM

## THE DEMATERIALIZATION OF MATTER

"What is everything made of?"

Werner Heisenberg has written that, to such a question,

the final answer will more closely approximate the views expressed in Plato's *Timaeus* than those of the ancient materialists. . . . The elemental particles of present day physics are more closely related to the Platonic bodies than they are to the atoms of Democritus.

The elemental particles of modern physics, like the regular bodies of Plato's philosophy, are defined by the requirements of mathematical symmetry. They are not eternal and unchanging, and they can hardly, therefore, strictly be termed real. Rather, they are simple expressions of fundamental mathematical constructions

## MATHEMATICS AND ETERNAL TRUTHS

Mathematics is, I believe, the chief source of the belief in eternal and exact truth, as well as in a supersensible intelligible world. Geometry deals with exact circles, but no sensible object is *exactly* circular; however carefully we may use our compasses, there will be some imperfections and irregularities. This suggests the view that all exact reasoning applies to ideal as opposed to sensible objects; it is natural to go further, and to argue that thought is nobler than sense, and the objects of thought more real than those of sense-perception. Mystical doctrines as to the relation of time to eternity are also reinforced by pure mathematics, for mathematical objects, such as numbers, if real at all, are eternal and not in time. Such eternal objects can be conceived as God's thoughts. Hence Plato's doctrine that God is a geometer, and Sir James Jeans' belief that He is addicted to arithmetic. Rationalistic as opposed to apocalyptic religion has been, ever since Pythagoras, and notably ever since Plato, very completely dominated by mathematics and mathematical method.

The combination of mathematics and theology, which began with Pythagoras, characterized religious philosophy in Greece, in the Middle Ages, and in modern times down to Kant. . . . I do not know of any other man [Pythagoras] who has been as influential as he was in the sphere of thought. . . . The whole conception of an eternal world, revealed to the intellect but not to the senses, is derived from him. . . .

BERTRAND RUSSELL

which one comes upon in striving to break down matter ever further, and which provide the content for the underlying laws of nature. In the beginning, therefore, for modern science, was the form, the mathematical pattern, not the material thing. And since the mathematical pattern is, in the final analysis, an intellectual concept, one can say in the words of Faust, *"Am Anfang war der Sinn"*—"In the beginning was the meaning."

Matter has been dematerialized, not just as a concept of the philosophically real, but now as an idea of modern physics. Matter can be analyzed down to the level of fundamental particles. But at that depth the direction of the analysis changes, and this constitutes a major conceptual surprise in the history of science. The things which for Newton typified matter—e.g., an exactly determinable state, a point shape, absolute solidity—these are now the properties electrons do not, because theoretically they cannot, have. . . .

 The dematerialization of matter encountered in this century . . . has rocked mechanics at its foundations. . . . The 20th century's dematerialization of matter has made it conceptually impossible to accept a Newtonian picture of the properties of matter and still do consistent physics.

NORWOOD RUSSELL HANSON

## FORCE FIELDS AND PHILOSOPHIC INTERESTS

If ultimate reality turns out to be a series of waves or vibrating superstrings, then we can turn to our other fundamental question: "What are the forces that cause motion?" We have traveled far since Thales first asked questions about motion and change, but we are far from the end of the journey. Today there are four known forces that cause motion.

 One is gravity. When we lift an arm, walk, or stumble and fall, we discover our conditioning to the earth's gravity field. Enough is known about its operation to enable us to orbit satellites, calculate the trajectory of lunar missions, and describe the orbits of the planets. In fact, gravitational interaction is the best described of the known forces.

 However, the nature of gravity remains a mystery. Current theory assumes that gravity takes wave form as particles called "gravitons," and strong sources of gravity waves seem to be located in the heart of our Milky Way galaxy. Also it is of interest to note that gravity seems to be the only force that is irreversible: it always attracts and never repels. Once gravity waves are better understood, and when and if gravitons are detected, it will be interesting to find out whether our notions about antigravity forces are science or fiction.

 A second force is the electromagnetic, and this, like gravity, is familiar at the experiential level of reality. It operates on particles that have electric charge or that possess a magnetic field. The interaction of magnets and iron, the combining of atoms into molecules, and the transmission of signals along a neural pathway to the brain, through the air to a TV set, or along a wire to a videophone—all these are electromagnetic interactions. Because it manifests itself in so many forms at the macrocosmic level, and because of its great versatility, this is the force we have been able to put to practical use serving human needs.

 Two other forces are found at the subatomic level. One force—the strong interaction—holds together the nucleus of the atom. Since the nuclear protons

*Just as Newton shattered the medieval crystal spheres, modern quantum theory has irreparably smashed Newton's clockwork. We are now certain that the world is not a deterministic mechanism.*

NICK HERBERT

*The knowledge of science fails in the face of all ultimate questions.*

KARL JASPERS

*I think it is safe to say that no one understands quantum mechanics. Do not keep saying to yourself, if you can possibly avoid it, "but how can it be like that?" because you will go "down the drain" into a blind alley from which nobody has yet escaped. Nobody knows how it can be like that.*

RICHARD FEYNMAN

are all positively charged, they would violently repel each other. Despite this, the nucleus holds together. Therefore, some force, incredibly strong, acts to overcome the electromagnetic repulsion and binds from a few to several hundred protons and neutrons together into an ordered nucleus. This strong interaction is about a hundred times stronger than electromagnetic forces.

The second subatomic force—the weak interaction—operates on a family of particles that includes electrons, muons, tauons, and nutrinos. This is no longer considered a fourth separate force since it has been shown that the weak nuclear force is a manifestation of the electromagnetic force. It is now called the electroweak force.

Several philosophic questions come to mind in relation to our reflections on matter and force.

(1) Are these the only forces at work in our universe or might there be more, perhaps of a different kind? (2) Have our notions of reality been affected by our deeper knowledge of nature? (3) Can we make any meaningful inquiries at this point into the origins of matter/motion?

Admittedly, dealing with such questions may be quite beyond our present capacities. Our fragmentary understanding leaves much to be desired. However, in the larger perspective of our quest for knowledge, we have been approaching reality objectively for only a short time. Our questions are really just beginning, and we may have to wait for answers.

Are these physical forces the only activating principles at work in our world? Do these four known sources, interacting with energy/matter, account for all the objects/events in the cosmos? Or must we postulate other forces? What about the order and "design" of nature? or the aggregates of matter that constitute living cells? or complex life systems? or the delicate operations of mind and consciousness? Can *all* these things be accounted for by the four known physical interactions?

As one scans the panorama of human experience, it appears that there are at least three other forces that have been believed to exist. To think of them as causative forces parallel to the physical forces, we might call them (1) mind-force, (2) spirit-force, and (3) god-force.

Many would contend that there is sufficient evidence in experience to warrant the hypothesis of some sort of mind-force. Evidence might come from telepathy, psychokinesis, or clairvoyance. If such events are actual—and present evidence is highly inconclusive—all attempts to reduce such events to known physical forces (for example, very short electromagnetic wavelengths) have failed. Of course, this might be the result of inadequate scientific technique. Those who have had experiences that they have interpreted as ESP events are convinced that mind-force is real.

Spirit-force has been postulated from the beginning of humanity to account for a multitude of experiences, from the blowing wind (*pneuma* in Greek and *ruaḥ* in Hebrew mean both "wind" and "spirit") to emotional disturbances. We are convinced now that most of these events experienced by prescientific man can be accounted for by physical or psychological principles. Still, when one hears reports of poltergeists that bang on doors and knock vases off shelves, one may be tempted to give second thought to the idea of a spirit-force.

Apart from religious belief derived from authority, is there any evidence for the existence of a god-force? In all of mankind's religions there have been mystics who claim that their lives have been touched by a god-force; they have seen the supernatural in visions or had their bodies healed by the divine. A large number of these experiences can be explained psychologically, so the problem would be to determine whether there are events that cannot be so explained and that necessitate the hypothesis of a god-force.

These forces—if they exist—have never been neatly separated in man's experience, nor can they be now. (It has only been in our century, of course, that the four physical interactions have been distinguished as separate forces.) Whether such metaphysical forces exist remains an open question. Care must be used to apply "Occam's razor": the principle that calls for the simplest explanation and precludes hypothesizing any force that the evidence does not demand.

How have our notions of reality been affected by current concepts of matter/motion?

There has been a strong temptation on the part of some philosophers—especially those inclined to make their philosophy a religion—to think of reality in degrees. That is, they considered some objects/events to be "more real" than others. Precisely what the terms "more real" or "less real" could mean is not always made clear. Generally, this world—the macrocosmic world of experience—was considered unreal; therefore, it was not to be valued. Plato was convinced that this world of particular things is an imperfect reflection of the perfect abstract "forms"; qualitatively it is not up to standard and therefore should not be taken too seriously. This world is made of matter, and matter is always imperfect. It resists shaping, like thick clay resists sculpturing. Only the eternal verities of mathematics or the "forms" of Goodness, Truth, and Beauty are truly real.

Similar concepts are to be found in the philosophies of the Gnostics, Neoplatonists, and Thomas Aquinas. The Hindu system of Shankara is even less equivocal: *everything* in this world is *maya* ("illusion"); it is merely a mirage and only Brahman is real.

Unless—for religious reasons—one has a need to declare this world "unreal," current thought tends to accept all levels of existence as equally real. We are gradually moving away from two extremes that have prevailed in the past: the idealism that considered macrocosmic experience as more real than, say, atomic interactions; and the overreaction of a scientism that held that physics provides the only true picture of reality.

There seems to be no good reason not to accept all objects/events in the external world as equally real, and this must include the full range from "point-events" of energy—whatever they are—to the grandest cosmological operations involving billions of galaxies.

There may be one qualification to all this. As indicated earlier, it is too soon to tell for sure what "matter" is. When physicists write that particles cannot "strictly be termed real" and may turn out to be something like "mathematical principles," then we may have to rethink the nature of ultimate reality at this particle or subparticle level.

Or is the problem merely semantic? "Ultimate reality" may eventually turn out to be nonmaterial, but would that necessarily mean that it is "less real"?

*Mathematics may be defined as the science in which we never know what we are talking about nor whether what we say is true.*

BERTRAND RUSSELL

*The true lover of knowledge is always striving after being. . . . He will not rest at those multitudinous phenomena whose existence is appearance only.*

PLATO

*What has been thought of as a particle will have to be thought of as a series of events. The series of events that replaces the particle has certain important physical properties, and therefore demands our attention; but it has no more substantiality than any other series of events that we might arbitrarily single out. Thus "matter" is not a part of the ultimate material of the world, but merely a convenient way of collecting events into bundles. . . .*

BERTRAND RUSSELL

## What Is the Origin of Matter?

In the history of ideas, certain questions have to wait before they can be asked. One such question (the most obvious of all) was so overwhelming that it was asked and immediately tucked away, never to be taken seriously again. The question: What is the origin of matter?

The problem has been ignored because it seemed insoluble; a simple creationist answer appeared the only one possible. When did the universe begin? What created matter? Or from what was matter created? "God created the universe and set matter in motion." And the little girl who persisted—"Then who made God?"—we brushed aside.

Her question is legitimate. Philosophers have long pointed out that the creationist answer is no answer at all. It was merely a deus ex machina like that employed by Greek tragedians to unravel a tangled plot. The deity dropped in from above the stage and, by divine fiat, set everything right. To say that *X* created *Y*—or *G* created *M*—*ex nihilo*, "out of nothing," is merely to *define* the question as being off-limits to serious inquiry.

At this early stage of inquiry into the origin of matter only a few promising lines of thought have been developed. In his "steady-state" theory of the universe, Sir Fred Hoyle assumed that matter is being created continually in space out of nothing, but he never attempted a serious explanation of how this might happen. Hoyle did little more than pose the problem.

> Matter is capable of exerting several types of influence—or fields as they are usually called. There is the nuclear field that binds together the atomic nuclei. There is the electro-magnetic field that enables atoms to absorb light. There is the gravitational field that holds the stars and galaxies together. And according to the new theory there is also a creation field that causes matter to originate.

To this last statement, Hoyle adds: "Matter originates in response to the influence of other matter."

Matter-in-motion can create other matter; for matter-in-motion is energy, and energy can be transformed into more matter. Therefore, in theory, if we can imagine the universe beginning with even a very small amount of matter—perhaps just a few atoms—in a state of acceleration, then we can logically describe how all the matter in the universe might have come into existence. Each bit of matter traveling at high speeds can be transformed into more matter.

Today we can (almost) create matter in our laboratories. In a phenomenon known as "pair-creation," physicists can create electrons in the vacuum of the accelerator, that is, out of nothing. They have also succeeded in creating pairs of positive and negative protons out of nothing. Weisskopf states that, in his opinion, this represents the actual creation of matter.

Electrons can also be created from photons of light. The interesting point is that light does not have mass, while electrons have. Photons (with a rest mass of zero) are massless energy; at the speed of light the photons can be transformed into mass according to the mass-energy transformation equation: $E = mc^2$.

What does all this mean? One implication seems to be that questions about the origin of matter are not wholly out of order. Nevertheless, at the present time

---

*Physical things are those series of appearances whose matter obeys the laws of physics.*

Bertrand Russell

*There is a famous anecdote about Laplace's submitting to the Emperor Napoleon a copy of his* System of the World. *Napoleon asked him what was the place of God in the system. Laplace answered: "Sir, I do not need this hypothesis." It is interesting to note that Laplace, who did not need the hypothesis of God in his book on astronomy, needed a Superior Intelligence in his formulation of the principle of causality. . . .*

Philipp Frank

really convincing answers are lacking. In all cases physicists began their experiments with something (not "nothing"), and they had at their disposal sophisticated scientific equipment with which they could accelerate particles into higher energy states. Theoretically, we can imagine a universe empty of all mass but a single, lonely electron, plus some force that can push that electron into relativistic speeds, then we can logically account for all the rest of the matter in the entire universe. But what that "Prime Mover" might be still bothers us.

The best we can do at present is to hold on to the question and not be lured into thinking it has been answered. We will probably have to rephrase the question numerous times before an answer begins to come. Indeed, it might be found in some different frame of reference altogether.

## REFLECTIONS

1 Reflect on the snowflakes and other illustrations of natural objects/events throughout the chapter. What can you infer about "nature" from their common patterns?

2 Why was Thales's prediction of the eclipse so important that we date the beginnings of philosophy and science from this event? (Recall earlier comments about Thales on pp. 22–24)

3 We possess two clear-cut kinds of knowledge about the real world—empirical knowledge and a priori knowledge. Clarify the working of each and then go to the question raised on p. 482. Can you think of any further *ways* of knowing reality? Might Bergson's notion of intuitive knowledge be correct?

4 Summarize—briefly, and very carefully, in your own words—exactly what the Jovian philosopher saw and did as he watched the baseball game. In fact, did he *see* the baseball game at all? What is the role of memory in the construction of knowledge? Now, how does this analogy apply to our knowledge of (a) the natural world, (b) human behavior, and (c) the personality of another individual?

5 Now, when all is said and over with, isn't it true that all robins' eggs are blue? What's the hassle all about? Why make such a big deal of something that everyone knows?

6 Note the comment on p. 482: The "theoretical problem of a priori knowledge haunts our intellects. Why is it that mathematical knowledge describes so accurately the operations of nature?" What is the best answer you can give to this puzzle?

7 Whether or not you have ever studied physics or chemistry, spend some time pondering and just enjoying the Periodic Table of Elements (p. 485). This table shows how incredibly far we have come since the first philosopher-scientists began to inquire into the nature of the "world-stuff"—matter. Note the many varieties of order evident in the Periodic Table. What is your philosophic response to the varieties of relationships and patterns to be found here—that is, in "nature"? Do you think you can share Sir Fred Hoyle's feeling (see marginal quote on p. 486) about the fascination of pure matter?

*(CONTINUED ON P. 498)*

*At the basis of the whole modern view of the world lies the illusion that the so-called laws of nature are the explanation of natural phenomena.*
LUDWIG WITTGENSTEIN

*Rationalism is an adventure in the clarification of thought.*
ALFRED NORTH WHITEHEAD

*We believe in the possibility of a theory which is able to give a complete description of reality, the laws of which establish relations between the things themselves and not merely between their probabilities.*

ALBERT EINSTEIN

# PYTHAGORAS

## *The Universe Is Made of Numbers*

Pythagoras was the thinker who first proved that knowledge of the world is possible. He was a Greek philosopher . . . and mathematician, astronomer, physicist, musician, teacher, monastic, mystic, feminist, psychotherapist, seer, and cult leader . . . which indicates only that he was an unusual human being with a bright mind, a zest for life, and a passion to understand the world.

Pythagoras was born on the beautiful Aegean island of Samos about 580 B.C. He was the son of Mnesarchus, an engraver of gems, probably an affluent aristocrat and landowner. Pythagoras lived at the right time and place for intellectual growth. First, he was given the finest formal education available in gymnastics, music, mathematics, and what was known of the natural sciences. Second, he lived at a geographic crossroads where ideas from the East—Mesopotamia, Persia, India, and perhaps China—were beginning to flow into the Mediterranean world. Third, a new scientific outlook was emerging in the Ionian cities, and Pythagoras was thor-

oughly trained to see and think as a scientist. Finally, he traveled widely in Egypt, tradition says, where he learned geometry and astronomy, and also some cultural lore from the priests; and to Phoenicia, Chaldea, Arabia, and perhaps India. All in all, Pythagoras was fortunate intellectually: he had ample experiences, observations, questions, and ideas, that are the ferment of philosophy.

Around the age of fifty he returned home from his travels and found that Samos had been usurped by the tyrant Polycrates. So Pythagoras, and probably a few followers, emigrated westward to Italy and settled at a health spa known as Crotona. There he founded one of the great schools of antiquity.

His school was an institution of learning and a sanctuary for the cultivation of the spirit. It was housed in a sprawl of buildings extensive enough to accommodate hundreds of students. Members took vows of loyalty and adhered to strict rules. They shared property, ate meals together, wore a distinctive white garb, and were known for their quiet lives, modest behavior, and solemn decorum.

Members were divided into two

groups: the "outsiders" (*exoterici*), who studied "in silence" during a five-year probationary period; and the "insiders" (*esoterici*), who were admitted to the secrets of the cult and permitted to listen to the teaching of Pythagoras himself. Pythagoras was one of the first feminists. He admitted women to his school equally with men and saw to it that they were given the same basic education—philosophy, mathematics, music, and the arts; but in addition they were given vocational training in the care of the home and family.

If we can believe later historians, it is not difficult to reconstruct a day in the life of the Pythagorean community.

On awakening, members practiced memory exercises, attempting to recall exactly the events of the day before, in sequence; then the day before that, and so on. This practice was probably connected to the Pythagorean belief that all learning is recollection—that is, remembrance of truths known by the soul from previous lifetimes—and was doubtless designed to perfect the memory so that it could better apprehend the eternal truths.

Each member then went on a solitary morning walk. Members valued solitude and silence and practiced both throughout the day. This early morning stroll helped them to maintain personal harmony and to cope with the stressful demands of the world.

Members then attended classes. They studied and discussed the subjects they were taking, the doctrines of the cult, and the regulations that governed their living together. After another walk, they devoted an hour or so to health care. They would "compete at wrestling in the gardens and groves or at high-jump with leaden weights in their hands, while others would practice the art of pantomime."

They lunched on bread and honey. Afternoons were filled with more studies. Toward evening they enjoyed a promenade, two or three together walking along the streets or through the countryside. They marched in cadence, "walking in graceful rhythm together," so as to maintain harmony in all things. Supper was taken in small groups and consisted of maize, bread, raw and cooked vegetables and herbs, some meat, and a small amount of wine.

After the evening meal, libations were offered to the gods. Animal sacrifices were prohibited by the Pythagoreans, who believed that animals and humans alike share "the privilege of having a soul." The community worshiped Apollo the Life-Giver, but other gods and demons were honored, and the ceremonies included magical rites and divination.

Evening was a social time, but not for idle chatter. Members read and discussed in groups, with younger members reading what the older members chose. As the evening drew to a close more libations were offered, and one of the elders gave a short talk or homily. At bedtime, members donned "pure white night-garments" and slept in "pure white beds." "By such disciplines," a later Pythagorean wrote, they "sought to arrange their lives entirely for the purpose of following God."

Hovering over the community was the philosopher himself, a power and final authority, a felt presence, a god incarnate—a Christ-figure. Pythagoras was a tall man, always dressed immaculately in a white robe. Some of his followers were convinced that he worked magic and performed miracles. It was reported (by Aristotle) that the citizens of Crotona thought of him as a manifestation of Apollo and thought he possessed a "golden thigh," which he displayed at the Olympian games. He lived simply and ate abstemiously—little more than bread and honey, some vegetables, and a little wine. He loved mathematics, astronomy, and music, and all three became elements of his mystical religion.

Pythagoras was married, probably late in life, to a Crotonan woman named Theano. A daughter, Damo, became caretaker of her father's secret writings, and a son, Telauges, succeeded his father as head of the Pythagorean community.

*Above all, have respect for yourself.*

*After going to bed do not allow sleep to close your eyelids until you have first examined all your actions of the day, asking yourself: Wherein have I done amiss? What have I omitted that ought to have been done? If you find on reflection that you have done anything amiss, be severe with yourself; if you have done anything good, rejoice. (From the Pythagorean* Golden Verses)

*[The Pythagoreans] say that at the center there is fire, the earth being in effect one of the planets, which moves in a circle about the center and thus produced night and day. They hold the theory that there is another earth, behind and facing this one, which they call the counter-earth.*

ARISTOTLE

*Assist a man in lifting a burden, not in laying it down.*

*Let no swallows nest on your roof.*

✦

*Reason is immortal, all else mortal.*

*In Hades, [a Pythagorean philosopher] said, referring to the unseen after-world, the uninitiated will be dreadfully unhappy, for they will be constantly occupied pouring water from a leaky pitcher into a leaky sieve.*

PLATO
*Gorgias*

*By healing your soul you will thereby deliver it from all evils, from all afflictions.*

*[The Pythagoreans] construct the entire visible universe out of numbers—not numbers in the abstract, but spatially extended units of magnitude.*

It was Pythagoras who discovered nature's modus operandi: mathematics. "The language of nature is mathematics," as Galileo later phrased it. This is one of humanity's great discoveries; it made possible the science of physics and the development of our technological civilization. Bertrand Russell once wrote that Pythagoras was "intellectually one of the most important men that ever lived, both when he was wise and when he was unwise."

The story is told of Pythagoras's passing by a blacksmith shop and hearing from inside the ringing of hammers pounding on the anvils. The blows produced a variety of pitches. Pythagoras went inside to watch and observed that the lower notes were produced by the heavy hammers, the higher notes by the lighter hammers. Pythagoras had already experimented with the measuring of weights and knew that the weight of any object can be broken into fractional units and described mathematically. He had probably also worked with stringed instruments and knew that harmonic intervals are determined by the length of the vibrating string and can be expressed in precise ratios with abstract numbers. Now it dawned on him that all natural objects had their own vibrations and that the entire universe of matter-in-motion had a mathematical structure. Everything in the cosmos is vibrating, he concluded, as though the world is a great orchestra and every material object is an instrument in that orchestra, giving off its own musical pitch. Anvils, bells, cymbals, and pounding drums; the tinkle of porcelain shattering; the ring of the sculptor's chisel against marble; the boom of a volcano erupting; and even the planets orbiting through the night skies —everything vibrates and makes music. Pythagoras coined the phrase "the music of the spheres" and claims to have actually heard such music.

This was an important intellectual event: the movement from singular objects/events to universal mathematical generalizations. This discovery provoked in Pythagoras a life-long love affair with abstract mathematics and geometry and facilitated numerous discoveries. He discovered several geometrical theorems, tradition tells us, the most famous still bearing his name—the "Pythagorean Theorem": the sum of the squares of the sides of a right triangle is equal to the square of the hypotenuse. (We are told that Pythagoras was so elated by this discovery that he made a thank-offering to the gods.) He also worked with square roots and discovered that $\sqrt{2}$ is an inexpressible number. (Its existence became one of the secrets of the Pythagorean cult, since it wasn't supposed to exist; and the records tell of the excommunication of one of its members for betraying the existence of this "irrational" number.) He was intrigued by an arrangement of ten dots in triangular form, called a *tetractys*, which became a religious symbol; those joining the community took an oath on the tetractys: "I swear by Him who reveals Himself to our minds in the tetractys, which contains the source and roots of everlasting nature"—that is, the secret of immortality. It is not impossible that Pythagoras had stumbled on a psychic symbol (called a *shri yantra* in Tibetan Buddhism), a symbol of unity and wholeness employed in meditation.

The other Ionian philosophers had sought to discover what substance the world is made of—such as water, air, fire, or something else. But Pythagoras concluded that reality is not a substance but a formal structure that can be expressed in pure numbers. "The whole of modern physics, with its mathematical theories of light, radiation, atomic structure, and so forth, is a continuation of the same line of thought and a vindication of the Pythagorean point of view" (R. G. Collingwood). The approach of modern physics is still that of Pythagoras: what the universe is "made of" is of secondary importance; what we seek is a quantification of the "vibrations" of whatever the substantial entities are.

Since these mathematical patterns of change can be apprehended by the human mind, knowledge of the world is truly possible. This is the philosophical significance of Pythagoras's discovery.

Pythagoras was not only a scientist and mathematician; he was also a mystic and redeemer. He sought the secret of living for himself and his followers; and he seems to have developed one of history's earliest intellectually coherent "ways of liberation."

The key was *harmonium,* "harmony." Any structure is in a state of harmony if all its parts "vibrate" together. The cosmos is a harmonious whole, Pythagoras believed. "They supposed the whole heaven to be a *harmonia* and a number," wrote Aristotle. Similarly, the soul—a sort of mini-cosmos—can enjoy a state of harmony when all its parts work together. Most of the time the soul—imprisoned in the physical body, juggling an ever-changing blending of opposites—has a difficult time coordinating all its parts.

Pythagoras taught that this present lifetime is but a short interlude in a long journey of the soul. Each soul is reincarnated repeatedly into material form; and in each incarnation the body (*sôma*) again becomes the prison of the soul (*sêma*). After each lifetime the soul descends to Hades, where it undergoes a purging of its sin; then it returns to Earth and once more becomes re-incarnate in its prison house.

The goal of life is to put a stop to this round of rebirth—the "wheel of things," as Pythagoras phrased it. This can be achieved by striving for a virtuous life, which to the Pythagoreans meant a harmony of soul—a soul in tune with itself and with the cosmos. The truly harmo-nious soul will not be returned for rebirth but will become forever a part of the divine world-soul.

How can this harmony be achieved? First, through meditation on cosmic harmony. When we become absorbed into the cosmic vibrations and partake of its harmony, we are able to identify our soul with the cosmos. Second, by living a well-balanced life (in terms of diet, exercise, and good habits) and keeping the components of the soul properly attuned. This was the reason-for-being of the Pythagorean community: to provide a closed environment free of stress, with time for quietude, where healthful habits and routines could be practiced.

Thus, "the music of the spheres" and the harmony of the soul can become one.

Pythagoras lived to be at least eighty years old. The local populace of Crotona became incensed at the political activities of the Pythagoreans, who were authoritarian in their philosophy of power, believing that those with true knowledge should rule. The Crotonans were decidedly democratic and perceived the cult as a threat. Mobs stormed the monastery, burned it, killed a large number of the community (forty, by one report), and drove away the rest.

Pythagoras was forced to flee. Chased by assailants, he came to a patch of beans, against which the Pythagoreans had a taboo. He halted, "declaring that he would let himself be killed rather than reveal the secret doctrines" of the community. They killed him. The date was about 497 B.C.

The Pythagorean community endured for only about a century longer and then vanished from history.

8  Ponder Heisenberg's and Hanson's statements on p. 488 (see also Russell's remark on p. 491, marginal quote). Can you restate in your words what you think they mean when they all contend that, in the twentieth century, "matter has been dematerialized"? What might be some of the philosophic consequences of this achievement?

9  Note the four known physical forces, the forces that "perform the work" of the universe by keeping "matter in motion." Besides these basic four, do you have any evidence that there are any forces at work in the universe?

10  Spend some time—perhaps a lot of time—reflecting on Zeno's paradoxes on motion. Take any one and analyze the argument to the point where you understand his logical errors (if there are any).

11  Criticize the argument that God must have created matter because the assumption that matter has existed through all eternity is an illogical assumption. Therefore, there *must* have been a "first cause"—which is God (p. 492). Refer to the "cosmological argument" for God on pp. 572–573.

12  Have you personally speculated on the problem of the origin of matter? Are you willing to do so now? What questions can you think of to initiate inquiry? To whom might we turn for hard data that would help us phrase our questions in an intelligible fashion?

# TIME/SPACE

# 7.2

## WE LIVE IN A RELATIVISTIC UNIVERSE

We live in a relativistic universe. The Newtonian universe that existed till the beginning of the twentieth century was one in which conventional physics adequately described matter-in-motion. But a relativistic universe is one in which matter is in motion at very great speeds. When velocities are sharply increased some strange things begin to happen. Such high velocities, we now know, are the general rule at both the microscopic and cosmological scales of physical reality. It is primarily at the macroscopic level of experience that Newtonian theories still operate.

Since Albert Einstein published his paper on special relativity in 1905, our understanding of our universe and our place in it has undergone continual revision. It may not seem at first glance that relativistic notions affect our routine behavior, but the fact is that we are immersed in relativistic events. For instance, light photons striking our retinas can be described only in relativistic terms, and the very atoms that compose our bodies are themselves in motion at these high velocities.

Beyond all this, the significant fact is that a new world-view was born with special relativity. It has gradually become part of our consciousness.

Relativistic phenomena astound the layman, excite the physicist, and boggle the mind of the philosopher. In fact, the physicists don't even pretend to understand much of what they describe; they go their way developing pragmatic equations without worrying very much whether their formulas describe realities presently accessible to experience.

At the microscopic level, common sense is offended. "Almost all the 'great principles' of traditional physics turn out to be like the 'great law' that there are always three feet to a yard; others turn out to be downright false." So observes Bertrand Russell.

*I cannot believe that God plays dice with the cosmos.*
ALBERT EINSTEIN

*"After a while one begins to think that space and time are not quite real."*
RICHARD BACH
*"Chang," Jonathan Livingston Seagull*

Particles can be accelerated so as to increase their energy and when "smashed" each resulting particle will weigh as much as the original particle. Also there is discontinuity: a particle observed at one place will be subsequently observed at another place without having moved through any point to get there. Even the concept of time reversal is used by some physicists to explain particle behavior.

Equally strange events are occurring at the cosmological level. Einstein's equations predict that as objects move at very high speeds (near the speed of light), time slows down, mass increases, and length decreases (at least, that's the way we would observe and measure them). Also the universe may be curved (positively or negatively, but as yet we don't know which), and Einstein thought in terms of "curved space."

If time is real, there may indeed be time anomalies; and if space is real, there could be space anomalies. That is, events have been observed for which hypotheses of time/space anomalies would be workable explanations.

Other unbelievable goings-on have been observed for some time. Quasars, for instance, generate far more energy than present physical theory can explain, and pulsars are probably the long-predicted neutron stars—stars in the throes of death—whose matter weighs billions of tons per cubic inch. Now astronomers are developing models of "black holes" where the gravitational attraction of a collapsing neutron star would be so great that no light could escape from it.

Another incredible fact is that our relativistic world-view was developed within the mind of one man.

A galaxy in the constellation Centaurus (NGC 5128), a source of intense radio noise and (perhaps) the actual collision of two galaxies. Reproduced courtesy of the Hale Observatories.

What Einstein did was not a formal accomplishment. He did not approach the problem from the standpoint of finding some mathematical equation which will describe a certain group of phenomena. Something much more fundamental was at stake, namely, the critical evaluation of the cultural foundation of theoretical physics. Certain things which were always taken for granted, were put under scrutiny and their falseness proved. This was no longer mere physics and mathematics. . . . Here started that dogged uphill fight of Einstein which lasted ten years and which is perhaps unparalleled in the entire history of the human mind; a fight which did not arise from any experimental puzzle of the mind.

CORNELIUS LANCZOS

*I maintain . . . that the transient now with respect to which the distinction between the past and the future of common sense and psychological time acquires meaning has no relevance at all apart from the egocentric perspectives of a conscious (human) organism and from the immediate experiences of that organism.*

ADOLF GRÜNBAUM

## THE SPECIAL THEORY OF RELATIVITY

According to Einstein's theory, no material object can travel faster than the speed of light (which is about 186,000 miles per second). Relativistic phenomena become measurable around 10 percent of the speed of light.

At these velocities, three significant things begin to happen to all objects in motion, including human beings: (1) time slows down, (2) the mass of objects increases, and (3) the length of objects (measured parallel to the plane of motion) decreases.

Take, for instance, the phenomenon known as "time dilation." The measurement of time—and perhaps the actual "flow" of time—is strictly relative—relative, that is, to the standpoint of the observer. Two travelers moving in different reference systems at high speeds relative to each other would *measure* time differently, and both would be right.

The "twin paradox" apparently illustrates actual realities. Imagine twin brothers twenty years old, one of whom becomes an astronaut. He takes a journey through space to a planet orbiting the star Rigil Kent (which is also known as Alpha Centauri, the nearest star to us after the sun), which is about four light-years distance. His spaceship travels at 148,000 miles per second. At that speed (which is four-fifths of the speed of light), according to all the clocks on this spaceship—calendars, wristwatches, atomic clocks, heartbeats—his experience of time would slow to three-fifths of its normal rate *as observed and measured by his twin brother on earth*. He would therefore make the journey to Rigil Kent in three years and the return trip in three years, the entire roundtrip taking six years. But while he was on the six-year journey his twin brother on earth would age ten years. From his earthbound viewpoint, he would measure his space-traveling brother's journey taking five years out and five years back—ten years according to his calendars and clocks.

And both measurements are correct. There is no suggestion that one measurement is the correct one and the other is distorted or illusory. Both are true. The astronaut would experience the passing of only six years and he would age only six years. But according to his stay-at-home brother, the space journey would have taken ten years and he himself would have aged a full ten years.

Time, therefore, is relative. It looks as though it's not merely a matter of the way we observe objects in motion. It appears that these phenomena are real. They take place within the objects themselves.

Albert Einstein (1879–1955)

*The idea that time can vary from place to place is a difficult one, but it is the idea Einstein used, and it is correct—believe it or not.*

RICHARD FEYNMAN

## The Message from Planet X

There is no absolute time throughout the universe by which absolute simultaneity can be measured. Absolute simultaneity of distant events is a meaningless concept.

How radical this notion is can be seen by a thought experiment in which vast distances and enormous speeds are involved. Suppose that someone on Planet X, in another part of our galaxy, is trying to communicate with the earth. He sends out a radio message. This is, of course, an electromagnetic wave that travels through space with the speed of light. Assume that the earth and Planet X are ten light-years apart, which means that it takes ten years for the message to travel to the earth. Twelve years before a radio astronomer on earth receives the message, the astronomer had received a Nobel Prize. The special theory permits us to say, without qualification, that he received this prize *before* the message was sent from Planet X.

Ten minutes after receiving the message, the astronomer sneezes. The special theory also permits us to say, without qualification, and for all observers in any frame of reference, that the astronomer sneezed *after* the message was sent from Planet X.

Now suppose that sometime during the ten-year period, while the radio message was on its way to the earth (say, three years before the message was received), the astronomer fell off his radio telescope and broke a leg. The special theory does *not* permit us to say without qualification that he broke his leg before or after the sending of the message from Planet X.

The reason is this. One observer, leaving Planet X at the time the message is sent and traveling to the earth with a speed judged from the earth to be slow, will find (according to his measurements of the passing of time) that the astronomer broke his leg *after* the message was sent. Of course he will arrive on earth long after the message is received, perhaps centuries after. But when he calculates the date on which the message was sent, according to his clock, it will be earlier than the date on which the astronomer broke his leg. On the other hand, another observer, who also leaves Planet X at the time the message is sent, but who travels very close to the speed of light, will find the astronomer broke his leg *before* the message was sent. Instead of taking centuries to make the trip, he will make it in, say, only a a trifle more than ten years as calculated on the earth. But because of the slowing down of time on the fast-moving spaceship, it will seem to the ship's astronaut that he made the trip in only a few months. He will be told on earth that the astronomer broke his leg a little more than three years ago. According to the astronaut's clock, the message was sent a few months ago. He will conclude that the leg was broken years before the message left Planet X.

If the astronaut traveled as fast as light (of course this is purely hypothetical; not possible in fact), his clock would stop completely. It would seem to him that he made the trip in zero time. From his point of view the two events, the sending of the message and its reception, would be simultaneous. *All* events on earth during the ten-year period would appear to him to have occurred before the message was sent. Now, according to the special theory there is no "preferred" frame of reference: no reason to prefer the point of view of one observer rather than another. The calculations made by the fast-moving astronaut are just as legitimate, just as "true," as the calculations made by the slow-moving astronaut. There is no universal, absolute time that can be appealed to for settling the differences between them.

Martin Gardner
*The Relativity Explosion*

The relativity of time measurement was a cornerstone of Einstein's system. In 1905 it was only theory, but we now have evidence to support it. According to predictions, all physical, chemical, and biological processes would begin to slow down when achieving relativistic speeds, and this is exactly what we find. In the accelerators, atomic particles (pions and others) have been pushed to high speeds and then subjected to high-energy collisions with other particles. When thus "smashed" these particles disintegrate at known rates. At high velocities, however, these particles disintegrate considerably more slowly, and the rate of disintegration is in exact agreement with Einstein's predictions. This means the "time experience" of the particle has slowed down to a fraction of what it was at rest.

The fact of time dilation is also supported by more recent observations of naturally occurring (nonlaboratory) phenomena. Cosmic rays from outer space continually collide with the gaseous molecules in the earth's upper atmosphere and break those molecules into component particles. One such particle, the mu-meson or muon, has a lifetime of only two microseconds (two millionths of a second). Should a muon be knocked from an atom and continue to travel near the speed of light, it could cover a distance of only a few hundred feet. Yet large quantities of muons are detected on the surface of the earth more than six miles from their collision points. But how can muons travel six miles in two microseconds? Only two answers seem possible. One is that the muons are traveling faster than the speed of light. But according to relativity theory this is impossible; nothing in the universe can travel faster than the speed of light. The other answer is that the muons do in fact disintegrate in two microseconds according to *their* time scales, but they have a longer life span (and can therefore travel farther) according to *our* time measurements. Just as in the "twin paradox," the muon's time-experience (two microseconds) remains unchanged; but to an outside observer its time appears to have slowed down, and therefore it is observed to travel immense distances in its short two-microsecond lifetime.

Saxon and Fretter comment that it took forty years for scientists to find direct empirical confirmation of the Special Theory of Relativity formulated by Einstein in 1905, "but physicists believed it implicitly from the outset because of its internal consistency and because a very substantial body of indirect evidence was gradually amassed."

A good deal of science fiction involving space travel (*Planet of the Apes*, for example, in which the astronauts jump ahead in time some two thousand years) embodies principles that are not at all fictional, but plausible science. According to present understanding it is quite possible to move forward in time. How far forward one might travel depends solely on the speed one can attain. (Note figures in box on top of the next page.)

There may be some semantic confusion in the phrase "we can move into the future." No object—astronaut, particle, or whatever—can move into *its own future*. The personal experience of time always remains constant. The "future" that we can "move into" is the future of the other reference system (the earth's, that of the twin who stayed at home, that of the scientist who measures the muon), simply because your time has slowed down and, relatively, their time has speeded up. Experientially, no matter what relativistic speeds we may attain, each singular lifetime is lived in the same old way.

Special relativity also predicts that mass will increase and length will

*The issue is whether causality is an ultimate principle or merely a substitute for statistical regularity.*

HANS REICHENBACH

*The search for ultimate reality, then, is a natural and necessary part of man's being. We need to realize that this kind of concern is part of what it means to be human. We also need to realize, however, that while some kind of commitment is inevitable, a final answer to this question can never be given, for man is limited, he is finite; he can never be expected to know all. In short, he is encapsulated, and for him to know the infinite is impossible by definition.*

JOSEPH ROYCE

| TIME DILATION AND SPACE TRAVEL | | |
|---|---|---|
| Speed of spaceship relative to earth in terms of the speed of light *(c)* | Factor by which crew's time slows down compared to earth time | Number of years of crew time required for round-trip journey to a star 100 light-years away |
| 0.9999 | 70.712 | 2.8 |
| 0.98 | 5.025 | 40.6 |
| 0.95 | 3.203 | 65.7 |
| 0.90 | 2.294 | 96.9 |
| 0.75 | 1.512 | 176.4 |
| 0.50 | 1.155 | 346.4 |
| 0.10 | 1.005 | 1990.0 |

*It is estimated there may be 135,000,000,000 stars in the Galaxy, and there may be as many as 100,000,000,000 other galaxies distributed through space. Astronomers are generally convinced that there are innumerable worlds on which life might develop.*

ISAAC ASIMOV

*One of our problems is trying to figure out which is up and which is down.*

JOHN YOUNG
*(from Apollo X spacecraft)*

decrease. These two ideas have also been accepted from the beginning by most physicists, and the former has been empirically verified. Again, in the accelerators, the mass of high-speed particles increases so much that adjustments must be made in the magnetic fields that drive and guide the particles. The increase in mass would otherwise fling them outside the magnetic holding field.

To date no empirical evidence has been found to substantiate the prediction about decrease in length, yet there seems to be no reason to doubt it as part of the relativistic package.

There is disagreement among physicists as to the philosophic implications of such relative measurements. The problem is whether these phenomena are real—that is, whether the object actually undergoes these changes—or whether the changes are merely observational phenomena.

One school of thought holds that these phenomena take place only from the standpoint of an observer in one reference system who is watching objects in another system moving at high speeds. In other words, they are observational, and the thought experiment involving the light-clock appears to imply that they are perceptual only.

In the diagram, the light-clocks are on two spaceships moving at high speeds relative to one another, speeds not far short of the speed of light. What would a passenger on each spaceship see if he could observe the light-clock on the other spacecraft?

Light-clock *A*, on your ship, just sits there, blinking. The top bulb sends a beam of light down to the photoelectric cell, which in turn triggers the bottom bulb, which sends a beam of light to the cell at the top; so down and up the light-beams go.

There is an identical light-clock *(B)* on the other spaceship. As it passes, what would you see? You would perceive a much longer beam of light than is emitted by your own clock, which (to you) is at rest. So the light-beam on the other spaceship travels farther *in the same period of time* as your light-beam. This could have two explanations: either the light of the other light-clock is moving faster or time has slowed down. The former is impossible, according to relativity, since the speed of light is a constant; it always travels at 186,000 mps. Therefore, what you are witnessing is a slower movement of time on the other spaceship compared with the movement of time according to your clock.

But ask: What would the passengers on the other spaceship see as they watch your clock pass by? They would see precisely what you see, only reversed. To you, *his* time has slowed down; to him, *your* time has slowed down.

This sort of thought experiment seems to indicate that the whole matter of relativity is merely perceptual. Einstein's equations describe nothing more than the way we would measure things that move very fast relative to our point of observation.

But other physicists are not so sure. Some are convinced that such phenomena are not perceptual, but real, that they really happen to objects. It would seem that the increase in particle mass in the accelerators and the slow-down of decay time in the disintegration of pions is not merely a matter of measurement, but is an event that the particle actually undergoes. If this is not the case, then why the adjustments that are necessary in the magnetic fields?

The same dilemma applies to time. Saxon and Fretter candidly write that to understand relativistic phenomena, "we must realize that time dilation is a property of time itself, not of any particular clock."

At present the puzzle does not appear to be solvable.

Light clocks redrawn from David S. Saxon and William B. Fretter, *Physics for the Liberal Arts Student.*

*Perhaps the most majestic feature of our whole existence is that while our intelligences are powerful enough to penetrate deeply into the evolution of this quite incredible Universe, we still have not the smallest clue to our own fate.*

SIR FRED HOYLE

## TIME IN PHYSICAL THEORY

Is time real? Does time exist in the real world, or is time merely an experience? The majority of philosophers and psychologists (as opposed to physicists) have held that time is an experience only. It is our experiencing of the continuum of our flow of consciousness. If there were no consciousness there would be no experience of time, and therefore there would be no time. Time, they have contended, is in no sense a property of the real world.

To be sure, there are sequences of events in the real world, and it appears that certain events must happen before other events. The concept of causality

Zeno (c. 450 B.C.)

## ZENO'S LOGICAL PARADOXES

For almost 2500 years philosophers and mathematicians have had fun with—and suffered sheer anguish from—the logical paradoxes of a philosopher named Zeno. About 450 B.C. Zeno made a trip to Athens from his home town of Elea in Italy and presented a series of paradoxes to a gathering of eminent thinkers. Socrates was in the audience and engaged him in a discussion of some of his arguments. Zeno's aim was to show that some of our common assumptions about motion, space, and time appear to lead us into contradictions.

His most famous argument is the story of a handicap race between Achilles and a tortoise. If the tortoise begins the race some distance ahead of Achilles, then by the time Achilles reaches the point where the tortoise *was,* the tortoise, however pokey, will have moved ahead a ways. Again, when Achilles reaches the point where the tortoise *was,* the tortoise will still be ahead, though the distance between them is forever closing. Therefore Achilles can never overtake the tortoise.

Zeno argued that motion is an illusion: If an object moves, then it must move either in the place where it is or in some place where it is not. But obviously it cannot move where it is not; it should be equally obvious that it cannot move where it is. Therefore, concludes Zeno, it cannot move, and motion does not exist.

Another of his paradoxes has to do with space. If space *is,* it will be *in* something; for everything that *is* is in something; and to be in something is to be in space. Space then will be in space, which will be in another space, and so on ad infinitum. Therefore space does not exist.

(Stephen Hawking, the Cambridge cosmologist, poses a similar paradox when he entitled his bestselling book *A Brief History of Time.* By definition the word "history" refers to something that has endured for some period *in time.* This implies that time has endured in time, which has endured in time, which has endured in time, and so on. Which is the point Zeno was making: Time, therefore, is not real.)

Another of Zeno's paradoxes involves the racetrack: A runner cannot reach the end of the raceway until he has reached the half-way mark; but he can't reach the half-way mark until he has first reached half-way to the half-way mark (the "quarter-way" mark), and so on, ad infinitum. Conclusion: the runner can never even begin the race, and motion is therefore an illusion.

A similar point is made in Zeno's famous paradox of the arrow: At any instant, an arrow in flight occupies a space equal to itself, and therefore is at rest. This holds true of the arrow at any instant of its alleged flight through the air. At *every* instant it is at rest, and you can't derive motion from a series of rest stops, no matter how many. Therefore the arrow cannot move, and motion doesn't exist.

We may intuit or *feel* that Zeno's arguments are wrong; but achieving intellectual clarity as to where and why they are wrong may require some time. Is Zeno right, for instance, when he argues that everything that exists "exists in something"? For something to exist, does it have to exist in space? (What about ideas, pain, love, and dreams? They exist, don't they? Of course they do. But where? Answer: In my (spaceless) experience.) Moreover, what is space? Is space real? Isn't space nothing other than my mind's concept for the volume of nothingness between real objects? And what of the arrow? We know full well from experience that arrows fly through the air all the time and hit or miss their targets. So Zeno must be setting a mind-trap or playing a word-game (and he is!); but we must persist with intellect until we see clearly what the trap is and to understand the word-game.

CONTINUED

Zeno was one of the truly great Greek minds. He invented arguments, notes Bertrand Russell, "all immeasurably subtle and profound, to prove that motion is impossible. . . . From him to our own day, the finest intellects of each generation in turn attacked the problems, but achieved, broadly speaking, nothing." Although Zeno's paradoxes have now been solved mathematically and logically, they remain so intriguing that new volumes about them appear almost annually.

has meaning as these events take place in sequence. There is a "before" and "after," which are real. But these are merely events, and events are matter-in-motion; and there is no ingredient called "time" involved in such processes.

If this is the case, then before consciousness came into being, events took place over the billions of years. Atoms interacted and the forces of the universe moved matter about, but no time was involved in these events.

On the other hand, physicists are almost equally split on the reality of time. There are many who hold—and Einstein himself held—that time is in some sense a feature of the real world. Clocks and relativistic physics do not merely measure the flow of our conscious experience; they measure time itself.

Will man ever be able to move back and forth in time? Any answer to this depends in part on the reality of time. Our popular notions of "time travel" have been derived largely from science fiction and TV programs, and a recent book entitled *Psychic Visits to the Past* states:

Commonly we think of ourselves as captives of time, caged in the present, moving toward the future at a set speed, with the past forever behind us. But this illusion swiftly fades as we begin to investigate the experiences of those with the psychic ability to move back and forth through time with seeming ease.

What exactly a dematerialized psyche can do cannot at present be described by a scientist, but if we remain in the realm of matter-in-motion, we can get some tentative answers. Our best knowledge at present indicates that we can move forward in time, but never backward in time. If we could travel just short of the speed of light—say, at a speed of 185,000 mps—it would be quite possible in one lifetime to move millions of years ahead in time. But moving backward in time appears to be an impossibility. The heroes of science fiction can move up and down the corridors of time, with or without a time-machine, tampering with historic events along the way; but it looks at present as though any "journey into the past" will be confined to fantasy.

## SPACE IN PHYSICAL THEORY

Is space real? Does space exist in the real world or is space only in our heads? Immanuel Kant was one of the first epistemologists to make the unequivocal statement that both time and space are aspects of the mind. They are "modes of perception," that is, structures of consciousness through which we experience

*Hitherto people have looked upon the Principle of Causality as a proposition which would in the course of years admit of experimental proof with an ever-increasing exactitude. . . .*

*Now Heisenberg has discovered a flaw in the proposition. . . . The principle of causality loses its significance as an empirical proposition.*

*Causality is thus only conceivable as a Form of the theoretical system.*

ALBERT EINSTEIN

*The objective world simply is, it does not happen. Only to the gaze of consciousness, crawling upward along the life-line of my body, does a section of this world come to life as a fleeting image in space which continuously changes in time.*

HERMANN WEYL

the real world. They are a priori and develop in minds through experience, but they are not derived from any experience of real time or space. Kant contended that it is impossible for us to do any thinking about real objects without the *concepts* of time and space. We can think of nothing in the real world without the idea of a space in which we can relate objects; mentally, objects "occupy" space: they are so many feet apart or they move at a certain speed through space. But space exists only in our concepts.

The same view can be taken of time. We cannot experience an object without having it "endure" in our consciousness. As we watch an object its existence persists "in time"; that is, it endures in our consciousness. Obviously, we could not perceive an object if this experience of duration were not so structured. Therefore, time and space are both in our minds as perceptual necessities. They are in no way a part of the external world.

How far does space extend? For hundreds of years people have puzzled over this question. We want to know how big the universe really is. If our universe curves back on itself and is therefore a finite universe, we want to know what lies "beyond" or "outside" this universe. How far *can* space extend?

If "space" is defined as the absence of everything, then it is "nothing." We are therefore asking how far "nothing" extends, and this turns out to be a false question. Our thinking about the "extension of the universe" becomes a conceptual problem and not a problem about anything real.

Can we use such expressions as "empty space" or "objects in space"? According to Einstein himself (and he seems to be agreeing with Kant) such concepts are essential to our thinking. Mathematicians are aware that they must use symbolic concepts even though they refer to nothing real: irrational numbers, imaginary numbers, the square root of minus one, and so forth. The idea of "empty space" is such a necessary concept.

We can think of an "empty box," which means that "nothing" is in the box. But how can *nothing* be *in* a box? If we are interested in knowing how much matter (such as three bushels of grain) we might place in the box, then the question is meaningful. Space is a potential. Similarly, we can think of the universe as a large box and ask how much matter could be placed in this hypothetical "empty space." How much space is there between the universes, and is it empty? Such concepts, Einstein has written, are mental tools, but necessities nevertheless.

It would appear at present that space is indeed "nothing." If we say there is space between any two objects, then we are saying that there is "nothing" between them. It is doubtful that space has any real status.

Is it possible for anything to exist "outside" space and time? Apart form theological assumptions, it is difficult to give meaning to such a question. Since we exist *in* space and time (or space and time exist *in* us), it is questionable whether we could know if anything exists "beyond" space and time. It is conceivable that there might be space anomalies—"holes in space"—or time anomalies—"time warps." Such ideas, however, are meaningless unless one assumes that time and space are real.

To conclude that anything, including deity, could exist outside of time would be a problematic concept. If time is merely an experience (which it most likely is), then to state that something can exist outside time is to say that it can

*In the inescapable flux, there is something that abides; in the overwhelming permanence, there is an element that escapes into flux.*

Alfred North Whitehead

*Does the harmony which human intelligence thinks it discovers in Nature exist apart from such intelligence? Assuredly no. A reality completely independent of the spirit that conceives it, sees it or feels it, is an impossibility. A world so external as that, even if it existed, would be forever inaccessible to us. What we call "objective reality" is, strictly speaking, that which is common to several thinking beings and might be common to all; this common part . . . can only be the harmony expressed by mathematical laws.*

Jules Henri Poincaré

exist outside of consciousness. This, of course, is a truism (except for Bishop Berkeley). To say that God existed before time is to say he existed before consciousness which, again, is quite possible. So we arrive at a theological statement that cannot be proved or disproved; that God alone existed, and therefore (providing he is conscious), time existed only in the consciousness of God. This is a standard orthodox concept of Western theology. It is not an empirical statement and rests upon numerous unexaminable presuppositions.

### REFLECTIONS

1 This chapter begins, "We live in a relativistic universe." What is meant by this?

2 Einstein's work has been hailed as a landmark accomplishment by the human mind. How so? What is so important about the *way* Einstein went about developing his theories?

3 The "twin paradox" is the most famous prediction of Einstein's Special Theory of Relativity and has been imaginatively explored by science-fiction writers: "time travelers," "time tunnel," *The Time Machine, Planet of the Apes,* and countless others. If Einstein's calculation is in fact true, do you understand what it predicts and—since it batters down our "common sense"—can you accept it and live with it?

4 Analyze and enjoy the story of "The Message from Planet X" (p. 502). Do you understand how simultaneity is a fallacy when applied to reference systems moving at high speeds relative to one another? What philosophic implications do you see in this relativistic concept?

5 When you reflect on the nature of time—such as moving backward and forward in time, or wondering how many dimensions time has—is it possible that you may be engaging in "the fallacy of the spatialization of time"—that is, thinking of time in terms of space? Can you think of despatialized time—pure time?

6 Ponder Zeno's argument (see marginal quote on p. 506) that space doesn't exist. Could he be right? If space *does* exist, does that make his argument wrong? If space *doesn't* exist, does that make his argument right?

7 Ancients and moderns alike have asked, "What is beyond space?" or "How far does space extend?" How would you answer such questions?

8 By way of summarizing, is time real (p. 505)? Is space real (p. 507)?

# COSMOS

# 7₃

## ANCIENT COSMOLOGIES

Ancient humans lived very close to the stars. Their lives were much affected by them, especially by the steady points of light that wandered through the star fields as though they were alive. They might in fact be the bright bodies of the gods themselves playing beneath the blue-black firmament, gods such as Jupiter, Venus, and Mars.

People felt themselves enclosed in a finite container of some sort: a box, or a valley with an inverted clay bowl arching overhead, or a flat disk under a giant crystalline dome. When thinkers tried to make sense of their cosmos they saw different things.

Egyptians thought of their flat earth as the floor of a rectangular box. Some saw also a flat sky that extended away to the distant corners of the box; but others saw a bowl-shaped sky supported around the rim by a range of mountains surrounding the world like a great wall. The stars were burning lamps suspended high above from the roof or dome.

Babylonians knew their flat earth to be a round disk of land floating in a vast sea. Beyond this sea mountains rose to support the dome holding aloft the heavens. These heavens were the dwelling place of the gods and were strictly off-limits to mortals; man's sole domain was his circular disk of earth. He could neither visit the outer corners of earth nor gaze upon the abode of the immortal gods.

The ancient Hebrews saw above them a gigantic bowl of beaten metal (like the "brazen heaven" of Homer's *Iliad*) that separated the lower from the upper waters. This "firmament" was shot through with small holes through which the waters could shower upon the earth. The sun and moon were attached to the vaulted firmament and appeared to roll across it each day. The firmament was held up around the edge by a great range of mountains ("pillars of the sky"). An ocean of water extended around the sides of the inverted bowl and down under the earth. High above the water dwelt God and the Host of Heaven. Beneath the flat surface on which the people lived "roots of earth" plunged deep into the abysmal waters. Also under the earth, near its center, there existed an enormous cavern called *sheol* where (some said) the ghost-shades of men slept after death.

The night could be quiet, but it was the raging, blinding fireball by day that dominated the lives of people.

To Egyptians the sundisk that scorched the desert and brought green life to the meandering Nile was the god Amon-Ra, floating across the liquid sky in a barge. He passed into the Valley of the Gods at sunset and emerged from the valley at dawn.

Mesopotamians saw the eastern gates opening each morning and Shamash the sun god racing out in a great chariot drawn by wild asses. The sun was one of the chariot's burning orange-bright wheels. At sunset Shamash exited through the western gates and all through the night drove his chariot along a dark tunnel under the mountainous edge of the universe, emerging again from the eastern gates at dawn.

To early Greeks, Helios arose daily out of the eastern sea in a quadriga drawn by four white stallions. As he lifted his fiery chariot into the sky the stars were scattered and dove into the sea. In late afternoon he approached the western boundaries of the earth, and far-away peoples living too near the edge would be singed by the heat of his chariot.

To the ancients the universe was closed, and they felt a kind of security in knowing that. There was continuous interaction among the gods, the evil spirits, and humans who wandered the flat earth. Generally, good things went on above, bad things went on below, and man knew that his place was somewhere in the middle.

Hebrew cosmos. Noteworthy in this cosmology is *sheol*, a dank cavern beneath the surface of the flat Earth where the ghost-shades of the dead will spend eternity in sleep. While this indicates the concept of an afterlife, *sheol* is not at this stage of Hebrew thought a place of punishment; but in later Judaic cosmology, under Zoroastrian influences, *sheol* was transmuted into the familiar hell of burning fires.

Egyptian cosmos, showing the goddess Nut, her body dotted with stars, bending in a giant arch over Earth, represented by a reclining figure wearing a skin of leaves. The sun moves across the sky above the goddess in a heavenly barge.

## TODAY'S UNIVERSE

As the twentieth century wanes, what do you and I see when we look up at the stars?

We know, first and last, that we are looking *out into space* and *back in time.* Whenever we look at any object in space we are also looking into the past: about $1^1/4$ seconds into the past when looking at the nearest natural object (our moon); about 9 minutes back in time to the nearest star (our sun); about 4 years back in time to the second nearest star (Alpha Centauri); about 2 million years into the past when gazing at our nearest neighbor galaxy (Andromeda). And with the aid of telescopes we can peer into time past some 12 billion years. The farther we look out in space, the farther we are looking back in time.

Astronomers today share a unique kind of excitement because there exists a real possibility that we may be looking far enough into the past to see events that took place near the time of origins—the creation of our universe. Evidence indicates that such a beginning occurred between 12 and 25 billion years ago, and some of the objects we are now seeing (notably the quasars) are probably phenomena that happened shortly after that beginning.

Conceptualizing the size of the universe as we know it today strains our imaginations. Indeed, one may have to live with incredible concepts for a time before they can become believable.

Our solar system is composed of our star/sun and nine orbiting planets, plus assorted planetoids, asteroids, and comets. If we take the orbit of the planet Pluto as the outside limit of our solar system, then it is about $7^1/_2$ billion miles (or 11 light-hours) in diameter. This local system is our home, our "front yard," incredibly small on a cosmic scale. The nearest star to our sun is a little more than 4 light-years away (about 26 trillion miles). Our Milky Way galaxy is about a hundred thousand light-years across, and our solar system moves within

*Everything indeed, everything visible in nature or established in theory, suggests that the universe is implacably progressing toward final darkness and decay.*

LINCOLN BARNETT

This woodcut depicts man's restless curiosity to know what "the heavens" are really like. Here a man has traveled to the edge of the uiniverse and poked his head through the firmament; he beholds the machinery that moves the heavenly bodies. This is precisely what *Homo scientificus* has succeeded in doing.

*For myself, I find it hard to accept the big-bang theory. I would like to reject it. How can I believe such a naive theory that says there was a finite time only twice as long as the age of our earth, [when] the universe was vastly different from its present state—a red hot ball? I much prefer Mr. Hoyle's more subtle steady-state. But I have to face the facts, as a working physicist. The evidence mounts up, experiment after experiment, [and] at least suggests that the clear predictions of the most naive theory—the big-bang— are coming true.*

PHILIP MORRISON

one spiral arm of our galaxy, some thirty thousand light-years from its center. We are really quite far out and not even in the central plane.

Furthermore, our galaxy is a part of a larger system. Some two dozen galaxies move together in what is known as the "local group." These include the Andromeda galaxies and the Magellanic clouds.

Photographs taken with very long exposures through giant telescopes reveal billions of galaxies extending in all directions. Many are spiral-shaped like our Milky Way, but they also come in many other shapes and sizes. Sometimes as many as several hundred galaxies appear together on a single photographic plate spanning but a few minutes of arc across the sky. The largest radiotelescopes now reach out more than 10 billion light-years—and the galaxies keep on going.

It is not impossible that we may be part of a "metagalaxy," a cluster of hundreds or thousands of galaxies spiraling together in what might look like our own Milky Way magnified a million times.

## THE EXPANDING UNIVERSE

Modern cosmology is based on a single discovery made by Dr. Edwin Hubble in 1929. That discovery was that the universe is expanding. With refined photographic equipment we can see literally billions of galaxies—"island universes"—and judging from the "red shift" (the Doppler effect) in their spectra, they all appear to be moving away from us at constant speeds. This expansion is the fundamental fact which any and all cosmological theories are obliged to explain.

In your mind's eye draw an imaginary sphere one mile in diameter and fill it with quarters and half-dollars floating about a foot apart. These coin-disks are the galaxies of our perceptual universe. If we locate ourselves at the center of this imaginary sphere, then what we observe is that all these coin-galaxies are receding from us. Those nearer to us are moving slower; the farther away they are the greater their speed of recession from us. Out near the edge of the sphere their velocities are nearing the speed of light. When, all around the inside surface of the sphere, the galaxies reach that speed, they become invisible. Each galaxy emitting light in our direction at 186,000 miles per second, but moving away from us at 186,000 mps, would cross over the threshold of perception. Light would require infinite time to reach us; hence, it becomes invisible. This is the edge of our "perceptual universe." All galaxies reaching the speed of light would vanish from sight.

These perceptual limits we must accept, but we can't avoid wondering what lies beyond perception. If we exist in a pulsating universe, then we wonder how far the galaxies continue beyond that perceptual threshold before they begin their long journey back to the center. How much of the pulsating bubble can we actually see? Are there other bubble-universes? If so, how many? Could they possibly extend to infinity? How much space exists between the bubble-universes?

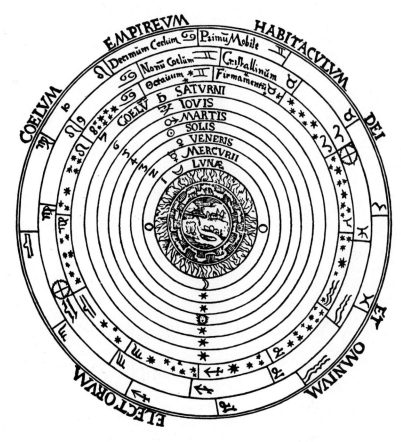

A medieval diagram of the geocentric (Ptolemaic) universe. With Earth at the center, the other members of the solar system move in concentric orbits. Diagram from Peter Appian's *Cosmographia* (1539).

*Next pages:* In contrast with the fanciful ancient cosmologies, here is the universe as we know it today. These dust clouds, stars, star clusters, and much more are merely a fraction of our own Milky Way galaxy. The smaller, dark globules in the photograph are dense masses of gas and dust that are contracting into stars; that is, new stars are continually being born out of such insterstellar matter. This is a photograph of the Star Queen nebula (M16) in the constellation Serpens.

## THE BIG-BANG MODEL

At present we can do little more than develop models that are coherent extensions of our theories about the closer parts of the universe that lie within our range of perception.

The big-bang theory holds that all of the matter in the universe was pulled together by gravity into one huge, hot ball—a "primordial atom"—several hundreds of light-years in diameter. As gravitational forces increased, the ball became ever more condensed. Pressure and temperature reached enormous levels. As contraction continued, there occurred a gravitational collapse

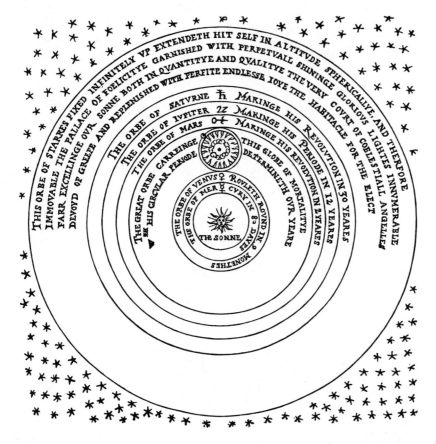

The heliocentric (Copernican) cosmos as drawn by Thomas Digges in 1576. In the center of the system is "the sonne," and the other heavenly bodies—though, strangely, not the stars—revolve in circular orbits around the sun. Notice, however, that the moon revolves around the earth.

amounting to an implosion. The outer layers rushed inward until they reached a critical point at which the massive cosmic ball exploded. This is the "big bang."

Matter was flung outward in all directions. Great clouds of gases and dust formed. Stars condensed from the dust clouds and pulled one another closer into clusters; great accumulations of matter began swirling as galaxies. This vast hodgepodge of exploded matter continued—and still continues—to journey outward from the scene of the explosion.

According to this picture, there was but a single explosion and since that time the universe has been "running down." From the time of the explosion the second law of thermodynamics (entropy) operates to dissipate energy. Living things exist only during this interim period while the fires are still burning. After that all the galaxies, stars, and planets will grow cold and die; they will float outward forever into the distance reaches of space. There will be no more heat and no more light.

## THE PULSATING MODEL

The pulsating model concurs with the big-bang model that matter was shot outward in all directions by a cosmic explosion. However, the total gravitational attraction of all the mass in the universe is so great that the universe cannot "escape from itself." That is, the gravitational pull of the universe's mass is greater than the force of the explosion. Galaxies traveling outward will gradually slow down—as though there were an elastic net around the entire universe—and reverse their direction, moving back toward the center from which they were exploded. As all mass converges, it becomes again a primordial hot ball. The dynamics repeat themselves and another big bang sends matter on its way through space. Calculations indicate that explosions occur at intervals of about 80 billion years. After each explosion galaxies, stars, and planets are born and life emerges, perhaps throughout the universe. But ultimately the stars grow old, life dies, and all matter contracts again into a hot ball.

Thus, the universe "pulsates," from explosion to explosion. A pulsating universe is anything but dead; it is a live, eternal universe, building up energy and dissipating it randomly only to build up energy again, losing nothing. Its perpetual processes are inherent and irrevocable.

We are now at a point in time about 20 billion years after the last big bang. The universe is still rapidly expanding. Some 20 billion years from now most of the galaxies will have stopped receding and begun their return journey. In 60 billion years another explosion will start the cycle again, and, perhaps, some 80 billion years hence, countless living beings will look up at the stars at night and wonder what it's all about.

It is interesting how closely the pulsating-cosmos theory resembles the teleocosmologies of some of mankind's religions. According to Hindu mythology, the god Shiva spins out the universe while he dances; when the Lord of the

*The deflation of some of our more common conceits is one of the practical applications of astronomy.*

CARL SAGAN

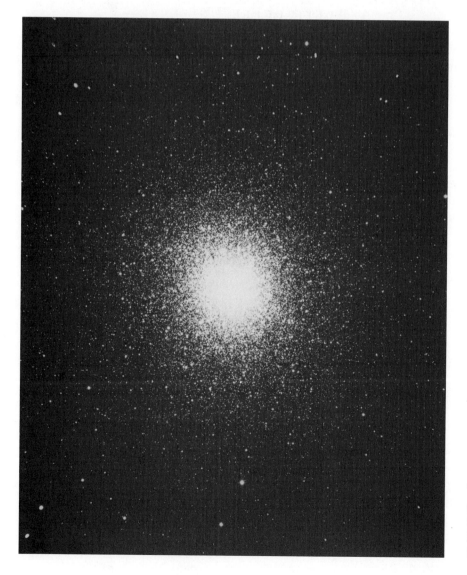

*I think the universe is slowing down. In fact, it is slowing down so fast that sometime in the future the expansion of galaxies will cease and contraction begin. . . . The galaxies will coalesce with one another and finally merge once again into a primeval fireball.*

ALLEN SANDAGE

The impressive Hercules globular cluster (M13) containing some 10,000 stars. Photo courtesy of the Hale Observatories.

Dance tires, his creative activity wanes, the universe runs down, all life vanishes, and there is quiescence until Shiva revives and begins dancing again. This cosmic cycle, billions of years long, repeats itself eternally.

Similar also is the Norse cycle, which ends in the Doom of the Gods (the *Götterdämmerung*), when the forces of chaos will inaugurate the final battle. In stunning contrast to most religious teleocosmologies, the battle will be fought in vain. The valiant warriors of Valhalla, and even the gods themselves, will be crushed, and all life will be extinguished. Earth and cosmos will be consumed by fire. Then, after a long while, a new earth will be born, and order will be restored by the sons of Odin and Thor. Mankind too will be generated again from a human couple who will have survived the conflagration. Thus, after a fiery end, the cycle of life begins again.

## A MULTIBUBBLE UNIVERSE—?

*I always felt that man is a stranger on this planet, a total stranger. I always played with the fancy: maybe a contagion from outer space is the seed of man. Hence, our prior occupation with heaven—with the sky, with the stars, the gods—somewhere out there in outer space. It is a kind of homing impulse. We are drawn to where we come from.*

ERIC HOFFER

Recent cosmologists are beginning to envision the possibility that the universe may consist not merely of a single pulsating bubble, but several bubbles or perhaps an infinite number. All that we can perceive is a portion of our own bubble-universe, but if there is one pulsating bubble, then why not more? If matter should extend infinitely, then the dynamics of pulsation must operate everywhere in similar fashion.

This multibubble universe is more gigantic than anything the human mind has heretofore tried to comprehend. Yet the more knowledge we obtain the more credible a multibubble cosmology becomes. The fact of the matter is that there is a feeling of aristocentrism about the notion that there is but a single bubble-universe—namely *ours*.

---

### AND THEN WHAT HAPPENED?

There is an amusing short tale by the Irish writer Lord Dunsany (in his book *The Man Who Ate the Phoenix*) in which Atlas explains to Dunsany what happened on the day when science made it no longer possible for mortals to believe in the old Greek model of the universe. Atlas admits that he had found his task rather dull and unpleasant. He was cold, because he had the earth's South Pole on the back of his neck, and his hands were always wet from the two oceans. But he remained at his task as long as people believed in him.

Then the world, Atlas says sadly, began to get "too scientific." He decided he was no longer needed. So he just put down the world and walked away.

"Yes," Atlas says. "Not without reflection, not without considerable reflection. But when I did it, I must say I was profoundly astonished; utterly astonished at what happened."

"And what did happen?"

"Simply nothing. Simply nothing at all."

MARTIN GARDNER
*Relativity for the Million*

# DO WE LIVE IN A CURVED UNIVERSE?

One aspect of the theory of relativity is that space is "curved" and that therefore we live in a "curved universe." Einstein suggested that the total gravitational force of all mass produces a universe that must be understood in terms of "curved space geometry." All objects moving in such a universe—from massive pulsars to massless photons—would follow curved trajectories. Whether the universe is curved positively or negatively (or not curved at all) has not yet been established. If negatively curved, it is an "open" universe; mass moving along gravitational lines of force would exit from our universe and vanish. But if positively curved—and there seems to be increasing direct evidence that it is—then it is a "closed" universe curving back on itself. Mass (and photons of light) would curve in great circles through the gestalt gravitational fields.

If positive curvature is real, then visual displacement of distant objects may be far greater than we have thought. Nothing in the heavens would be where we presently "see" it. Light emitted by objects will have been bent in its journey to us. Out near the edge of our perceptual universe, where galaxies are receding from us at great speeds, the objects we observe may now exist in some other part of the universe altogether; indeed, they may not now exist at all. Moreover, the speeds we observe may represent their velocities billions of years ago. Where such objects are located now, and what their velocities are, we cannot be sure. We find ourselves caught in a frustrating but exciting quandary.

We are beginning to get an idea of our place in the cosmic picture, but undoubtedly some shattering discoveries—always the unexpected—are still in store for us.

*"One ought not to grumble at Heaven that things happen according to its Way (Tao). . . . When stars fall or the sacred tree groans, the people of the whole state are afraid. They ask, "Why is it?" I answer: There is no reason. This is due to a modification of Heaven and Earth, to the mutation of Yin and Yang. . . . If people pray for rain and get rain, why is that? I answer: There is no reason for it. If people do not pray for rain, it will nevertheless rain."*

**HSÜN TZU (c. 250 B.C.)**

## REFLECTIONS

1   There is one single idea which, if we could assimilate it deep into our consciousness, can change the way we perceive the universe. When looking at all heavenly objects, "we know, first and last, that we are looking *out into space* and *back in time.*" Next time you have a clear sky and a little time, recall this fact as you gaze at each star or planet with new space/time eyes.

2   Reflect on, and just appreciate, the ancient cosmologies. In general, what do you think of the accomplishments of these prescientific minds in ordering their perceptions of their universe?

3   Browse through the pages of this and the following chapter and gaze empathetically into the photographs of the stars, galaxies, and other deep-space objects that populate our universe. Move *into* the pictures . . . and *out into* the universe. Can you comprehend its vastness? What do you feel as you ponder a universe of such dimensions?

4   "Modern cosmology is based on a single discovery"—that we live in an expanding universe (p. 514). What does that mean? What is expanding? Where are we located in this expanding model?

5   Review each of the cosmologies currently considered viable. Do you understand the general dynamics of the big-bang and pulsating theories? Do you understand what kind of evidence astronomers are now seeking that would make possible a final determination of which theory is correct?

6    As you think of the cosmologies most widely held by scientists today, which would you prefer to believe in? Or live in? Which would be the most comforting and secure?

7    If we are living in a pulsating universe, then the probability is very high that life develops throughout the universe and exists for lengthy durations after each big bang. What does this possibility do to your thinking about the nature of life? about God? and the universe? about yourself? about the purpose of life?

8    What is meant by Einstein's phrase that "space is curved"? If, by definition, space is "nothing," then how can "nothing" be curved? (See p. 521.)

9    Martin Gardner's account (from Lord Dunsany) of how Atlas "just put down the world and walked away" is a charming parable; and, as with all parables, the meaning remains implicit. Make explicit what the story says to you.

The Whirlpool galaxy (NGC 5194) in the constellation Canes Venatici, with a smaller satellite galaxy attached to the end of one of the large galaxy's two arms. Photo courtesy of the Hale Observatories.

# GALILEO GALILEI

## *"The Noblest Eye Is Darkened"*

Galileo became the founder of modern physics because he possessed one rare and simple gift: he could see.

He lived in an era when reality was prescribed, not perceived. Descriptions of the real world were supplied by Great Authorities, and when you looked at the world you were required to see what you were told was there to be seen; no more, no less.

Galileo protested in anger, saying in effect: "I will do my own seeing! I will see for myself whatever exists to be seen."

This stance might be called the "Galileian Principle"—the declaration that we will allow no intervention in our interpretation of our own experience. But such arrogance—the conviction that we can see for ourselves—was quite enough to threaten the Great Authorities and ignite the flames of the Inquisition.

Galileo's father, Vincenzio Galilei, was a well-educated Florentine musician who sought to grace his son with all the qualities of a Renaissance man; he tutored him in Latin and Greek, mathematics and music (lute and organ), drawing and painting. His mother, Giulia Am-

mannati, was intelligent and educated but touchy and difficult; she bequeathed obstinacy and competitiveness to her offspring. Galileo, born in 1564, was the first of their seven children.

At ten he entered the monastery school of Vallombrosa; for five years he was immersed in Latin classes and Italian literature. At seventeen he enrolled at the University of Pisa. He displayed an aptitude for the sciences but he had a passion for mathematics, which remained the first love of his life.

One day he went to meditate in the cathedral of Pisa. A large, hanging, oil-burning chandelier had been pulled over to one side for lighting and once lit had been released to swing back and forth. Galileo observed that each swing took precisely the same amount of time, no matter how wide the arc of the swing. To make sure of this he timed the swings by his own pulsebeat. He then went home, constructed two pendulums of the same length, set them swinging in various arcs, and timed them. However wide the arc, the swings took the same time. Galileo had discovered "isochronism," which he proceeded to quantify and describe with mathematics. This was a quiet beginning for the science of physics—the study of matter-in-motion.

While at Pisa Galileo developed a reputation for articulate dissent. He made a perfect nuisance of himself by challenging his teachers' authoritarian pronouncements and arguing incessantly with them, for which he was nicknamed "the wrangler." It is not surprising that he left the university without a degree.

In 1592 he was appointed to the University of Padua, where for eighteen years he taught mathematics and geometry, mechanics (physics), and astronomy. His spacious home accommodated boarders; his doors were open to friends and a steady flow of visitors. He shared his innovative ideas with all who would converse with him. All things mechanical intrigued him, and he loved to putter around and make gadgets in his well-stocked workshop.

Galileo was a man of medium stature, heavy set, not unattractive. He could be charming or abrasive, depending on mood more than circumstance. He possessed a rare intellect (estimated I.Q. 185) and a razor-sharp tongue, which he used to cajole friends, awe students, entertain public audiences, season conversations with wit, and make fools of detractors. He was a gifted writer. Without his enormous literary talent we would not have masterworks from his pen—and neither would he have been in constant trouble.

Early in July of 1609 Galileo heard rumors about a magnifying instrument developed by a Dutch lensmaker. The few people who had seen it considered it merely a novelty, but with characteristic insight Galileo obtained the instrument and converted what was regarded as a toy into a major instrument for the acquisition of scientific knowledge.

In January 1610, shivering in the wintry cold, Galileo turned his telescope on Jupiter and saw "three little stars, small but very bright" on either side of the planet. Three nights later he recognized what they were: orbiting moons. "What we are seeing with our own eyes are four starlets which revolve around Jupiter, just as the Moon revolves around the Earth, and all of them together trace out a grand revolution around the Sun in the period of twelve years."

What Galileo had seen, rightly interpreted, would demolish the entire geocentric world-view, and the tyranny of the Aristotelian/Ptolemaic dogma would be broken. He published his discoveries in a small Latin pamphlet, which he called *Sidereus Nuncius—Message from the Stars*. It immediately produced a swell of both accolades and anger. A copy was sent to the great German astronomer Johannes Kepler, who hailed it as epoch-making. Galileo was invited to Rome, where he was wined and dined. There he won the respect, if not the affection, of the Jesuit astronomers and was inducted into a prestigious academy of science.

But his enemies also increased in number and fervor. Books and articles appeared branding his discoveries the fantasies of a heretic. In 1613 he published three letters on sunspots and again offended the Aristotelian scientists, who knew that the sun, being perfect, could not have "spots." In the same year he also wrote a letter setting forth his opinions on the proper relationship of religion and science; it was circulated among faculty members at the University of Pisa. Within a few months this letter had found its way to those heading the Inquisition in Rome and was being scrutinized for heretical opinions. The Pope appointed a special commission to investigate the matter, and on March 5, 1616, the Holy Office published its official position:

> The view that the sun stands motionless at the center of the universe is foolish, philosophically false, and utterly heretical, because contrary to Holy Scripture. The view that the earth is not the center of the universe and even has a daily rotation is philosophically false, and at least an erroneous belief.

Galileo had been working for some years on a monumental book comparing

*The book of Nature is written in the language of mathematics.*

*I do not feel obliged to believe that the same God who has endowed us with sense, reason, and intellect has intended us to forgo their use.*

*We must deal with the real world, and not one on paper.*

*Without mathematics, one wanders about in a dark labyrinth.*

the two world-views, and it was published in 1632 with the title *Dialogue Concerning the Two Great World Systems —Ptolemaic and Copernican.* It took him five years to write it, but it was the culmination of a lifetime of insightful seeing and brilliant theorizing—a masterpiece.

Galileo had discovered that the world of matter-in-motion is a simple system that can be described with mathematics. He discovered this through his own experiments—by timing a swinging chandelier, by dropping cannonballs from the Tower of Pisa, for instance.

Moreover, he saw—as did the ancient Greeks—that just a few observations give us universal knowledge. Just a few demonstrations of uniform acceleration give us knowledge of *all* falling objects in the whole universe. Picture him: Galileo working in his laboratory in Padua, developing formulas for understanding the most distant reaches of the cosmos. Terrestrial dynamics and cosmic dynamics are one. This was a disturbing discovery because cosmic knowledge had heretofore been held in protective custody within the sanctuary of sacred theology.

Galileo belonged to his time, of course. He was not an agnostic; he never questioned the existence of God. He believed that God had created the world on a mathematical model. But what delighted Galileo and dismayed the theologians was the claim that our human knowledge is the same as God's knowledge. Mathematical understanding is perfect understanding, Galileo had seen, whether found in God's mind or ours.

What all this comes down to is that God reveals himself in two ways: through scripture *and* through nature. And while scriptural revelation is obscure, ambiguous, even cryptic—just listen to the theologians argue ad infinitum over its interpretation—nature's revelation has the clarity and certainty of mathematical precision and is, therefore, a superior kind of knowledge. When Galileo took the next logical step and said that Holy

Writ should be corrected by natural knowledge, that his reasoning was dangerous became only too clear. This position was Galileo's own "protestant" revolt against the tyranny of arbitrary authority.

Galileo's greatest contribution to science was in method. With rare insight he studied the dynamic motions of worldly as well as heavenly objects, attempting to quantify them—to express all his observations mathematically. This was the true beginning of the science of physics as we know it today.

Galileo's philosophical importance is that he separated two different worlds of reality and began to write an "instruction manual" for one of them: the real world, the world-out-there, the beautifully ordered cosmos of matter-in-motion, which operates according to mathematical principles. Such qualities as number, motion, figure, magnitude, position—the so-called primary qualities—all belong to this real world. The "instruction manual" for the operation of this world is the textbook of physics.

The other world—the human world, the world-in-here—is composed of colors, tastes, sounds, odors—the so-called secondary qualities—as well as feelings, opinions, values, spiritual events, and other experiences. Galileo considered this experiential world to be so chaotic that no "instruction manual" could be written for it.

In August 1632 the office of the Inquisition banned sale of the *Dialogue,* and existing copies were confiscated. Galileo was ordered to Rome to stand trial. The warrior's strength was gone, but he was still stubborn. On April 12, when examined by the Dominican inquisitor, he stated that his book had been properly licensed by the authorities and that he had held and discussed the Copernican view as theory and not fact, as he had been directed in 1616.

The Pope personally ordered strong action against Galileo—that he be further questioned under threat of torture, that if he still remained recalcitrant he was to be interrogated before a plenary session of the Holy Inquisition, and that he be imprisoned or silenced.

On June 21, 1633, Galileo stood before the Inquisition. The judges implored him to confess honestly his true views. His devious reply was that he had never been a Copernican. The threat of torture was used, but he continued to hold that, ever since he had been warned some nineteen years earlier, he had considered the Copernican view to be false. He was lying, of course; they knew he was lying. He was ushered back to his room.

The following day, June 22, 1633, he was returned to the great hall of the Inquisition. The judges and cardinals were present in full regalia. He was sentenced to life imprisonment according to the pleasure of the Holy Office. He was handed a written formula of confession, forced to kneel and recite:

I, Galileo Galilei . . . arraigned personally before this tribunal and kneeling before you . . . swear that I have always believed, do now believe, and by God's help will for the future believe, all that is held, preached and taught by the holy Catholic and Apostolic Roman Church. But whereas . . . after an injunction had been judicially intimated to me by this Holy Office, to the effect that I must altogether abandon the false opinion that the sun is the centre of the world and moves . . . I wrote and printed a book in which I discuss this doctrine already condemned. . . .

Therefore . . . I abjure, curse, and detest the aforesaid errors and heresies, . . . and I swear that in the future I will never again say or assert, verbally or in writing, anything that might furnish occasion for a similar suspicion against me. . . .

After the trial Galileo was eventually allowed to return to his villa near Florence, where he remained for the rest of his life, under house arrest. He could wander in his garden, study, receive friends, and teach his students; but he could not leave the premises. His favorite daughter, Maria Celeste, came to live with him and, for a few months, helped to restore life. But his health continued to fail and was severely aggravated by his daughter's death in 1634.

In 1637 came the final irony—the loss of his eyesight. In despair he cried, "These heavens, this earth, this universe, which by wonderful observation I had enlarged a thousand times . . . are henceforth dwindled into the narrow space which I myself occupy." When his old friend Castelli heard of his blindness, he wrote: "The noblest eye is darkened which nature ever made, an eye that had seen more than the eyes of all that are gone and that had opened the eyes of all men to come."

Even then the fire was not entirely gone. Though forbidden to publish, he completed a giant opus entitled *Dialogues Concerning Two New Sciences*, which laid the philosophical foundations of modern physics. Friends smuggled it out to Holland, where it was published in 1638. The Dutch government awarded him a gold chain to honor his many contributions, but the Inquisition denied him permission to accept it.

By November 1641 his strength was gone, at last. Always a faithful Catholic, he received the last sacraments of the church. He died on January 8, 1642, at four o'clock in the morning, in the arms of his disciples.

*ON GALILEO (by his friend Castelli when he heard of Galileo's blindness): The noblest eye is darkened which nature ever made, an eye that had seen more than the eyes of all that are gone and that had opened the eyes of all men to come.*

# 7 4

## WE ARE NOT ALONE

Only a few years ago the attitude of the scientific community toward the existence of life on other worlds was an unyielding skepticism. In 1934 the British
astrophysicist Sir Arthur Eddington could summarize the scientific consensus
this way:

> Within our galaxy alone there are perhaps a thousand million stars as large and as
> luminous as the sun; and this galaxy is one of many millions which formed part of
> the same creation but are now scattering apart. Amid this profusion of worlds there
> are perhaps other globes that are or have been inhabited by beings as highly devel-
> oped as Man; but we do not think they are at all common. The present indications
> seem to be that it is very long odds against a particular star undergoing the kind of
> accident which gave birth to the solar system.

During the 1950s several renowned astronomers were giving serious
thought to the possibility that life is a common cosmic occurrence. It was no
longer believed that the creation of our solar system was a once-in-a-billion
accident resulting from a near-collision with a passing star. The accident theory of Sir James Jeans was rapidly replaced by the hypothesis that solar systems
condense from the same "nebula" of gaseous and dusty cloud-matter from
which the star condenses, and at the same time. This model—the "nebular
hypothesis"—is almost universally accepted today. The conclusion, therefore,
is that planetary systems similar to our own are scattered throughout the universe and orbit their home stars in the same way that Sol's nine planets swirl
around their sun. Other worlds exist on which life might well evolve and
develop.

One of the first astronomers to conclude that other-worldly life must exist
was Harlow Shapley. In 1957 Shapley wrote that he was convinced that

*Sometimes I think we're*
*alone. Sometimes I think*
*we're not. In either case, the*
*thought is staggering.*

**BUCKMINSTER FULLER**

*The earth is the cradle of*
*mankind, but one cannot live*
*in the cradle forever.*

**TSIOLKOVSKY**

Harlow Shapley (1885–1972)

*The trouble with living on a planet is that it tends to make most of the inhabitants think small.*

LARRY NIVEN

Martian landscape from Viking 1 Lander. Meteorology boom, which supports Viking's miniature weather station, cuts through the picture's center.

sentient organisms, the product of biochemical evolution, must be a common occurrence in the universe. From general considerations of planetary origins and the evolution of chemical compounds on a cooling planet's surface, we concluded first that not less than a hundred million "high life" locations exist, and the number is probably more like a hundred trillion. Secondly, that there is no reason not to believe that the biochemical evolution on, let us say, one half of the suitable planets has equalled or attained much greater development than here. Thus, in answer to an earlier question, we have decided that *we are not alone* in this universe. . . .

There are good grounds for believing that the development of life-forms through an evolutionary process is a universal operation. Assuming this to be so, Shapley attempted to calculate the probabilities of evolvement of intelligent life.

Life *on* stars seems to be out of the question because of their high temperatures, so life would most likely arise in planetary systems associated with stars. Such planets would have to move in stable, near-circular orbits that would avoid great temperature extremes. Some sort of atmosphere, the presence of some free water, and somewhat constant radiation levels might also be requisites. Within these broad parameters for tolerable conditions, it appears likely that some form of life will inevitably develop.

Shapley makes the conservative guess that perhaps one star in a thousand has a planetary system; and that perhaps one in a thousand systems has a planet with just the right temperature tolerances for life; then of these planets perhaps only one in a thousand has sufficient quantities of air and water to transform organic molecules into protoplasm.

Using these figures Shapley estimated that only one star in a trillion ($10^{12}$) has a planet that meets all the requirements. The odds against life-supporting environments seem overwhelming. Still, if the total number of stars in our universe is about a hundred billion billion ($10^{20}$), then the number of planets with conditions suitable for the growth of life comes out to be a hundred million ($10^{20} \div 10^{12} = 10^{8}$). And "this is a minimum," Shapley concluded, not too happily: "Personally I would recommend . . . its multiplication by at least a thousand times, possibly by a million."

$N = R_* f_p n_e f_l f_i f_c L$  Since Harlow Shapley completed his calculations, significant advances have been made in many of the sciences relevant to the question of extraterrestrial life—in biochemical evolution, microbiology and genetics, radioastronomy, communication theory and technology, and many others. An enormous amount of thought has been given to the subject, and estimates have been refined.

Two astronomers from Cornell University, Frank Drake and Carl Sagan, developed an equation for calculating the number of communicating civilizations that may exist in our Milky Way galaxy at the present moment in time. (After all, if we want to communicate, we want to communicate now!) Here is their formula:

$$N = R_* f_p n_e f_l f_i f_c L$$

In this equation, the number of such advanced civilizations $N$ is assumed to be the function of seven variables:

$R_*$ = the number of stars that are born each year in our Milky Way galaxy (a good estimate: ten per year)

$f_p$ = the average number of planets orbiting each star (on the average: about one)

$n_e$ = the number of such planets that have a life-sustaining environment (again, probably about one per planetary system)

$f_l$ = the number of such congenial planets on which life actually evolves (again: probably one. The consensus among biologists is that life will eventually evolve in just about any congenial site, given enough time.)

*In our time this search [for extraterrestrial life] will eventually change our laws, our religions, our philosophies, our arts, our recreations, as well as our sciences. Space, the mirror, waits for life to come look for itself there.*

**RAY BRADBURY**

$f_i$ = the number of these life-bearing planets that evolve intelligent life (the probable number: one. The reasoning is the same as for $f_j$: given sufficient time, intelligence will almost always evolve.)

$f_c$ = the number of intelligent life-forms that develop a communications technology (a conservative guess: perhaps 1 percent)

$L$ = the average lifetime of such a communicating civilization. (Here we're stumped and can make only feeble guesstimates. We know of only one such civilization: our own. If *we* make it through the next couple of centuries, how long will *our* "communicating civilization" last?)

Substituting these figures for the symbols in the Drake/Sagan equation, we get:

$$N = 10 \times 1 \times 1 \times 1 \times 1 \times 1/100 \times L$$

or

$$N = 1/10 \times L$$

*If we establish contact with extraterrestrial life it will reveal to us our true place in the universe, and with that will come the beginning of wisdom.*

ISAAC ASIMOV

The conclusion, therefore, is that the number of civilizations in our galaxy with whom we could communicate at the present time is one-tenth the mean lifetime of such a technological civilization. If scientific societies such as ours last, say, two hundred years after they reach the technological stage, then one-tenth of two hundred is twenty. There are only twenty possible contacts in our galaxy of over a hundred billion stars. We might as well give up hope of finding other intelligent life in the biocosmos and learn to live with our loneliness.

But *if* civilizations survive their crisis transitions and last for millions of years—and a plausible argument can be made that, having survived a technological infancy (rather like a three-year-old child playing with a hand grenade), then civilizations continue to exist almost forever—then there exist thousands or millions of extraterrestrial societies right now. The figure could be one-tenth of a million or one-tenth of a billion; but in any case, our attempt to make contact across the light-years of space would not be undertaken in vain.

Man has probably reached a point in his relationship to the biocosmos from which there is no turning back. Peter Angeles makes the point: "If extraterrestrial intelligence is never found at any time in the universe, the quest will still go on; there will always remain a possibility in an infinite universe that extraterrestrial intelligence exists *somewhere,* or did exist *somewhere,* or will come into existence *somewhere.* In an infinite universe the biocosmic belief cannot be eradicated."

## A COSMIC CONTEXT FOR MANKIND

Carl Sagan reminds us that all human societies, like human infants, begin their lives in an egocentric condition. "A human infant begins to achieve maturity by the experimental discovery that he is not the whole of the universe. The same is true of societies engaged in the exploration of their surroundings." Maturity must include the continuing reassessment of oneself in relation to one's world and to the component parts of that world.

*The universe is old, the race of man young. There may be . . . must be . . . other races out there—or even closer to home. . . .*

ROGER ZELAZNY

The need to understand our place in the scheme of things has taken on a special meaning because of humankind's problematic future on this world and the probable existence of life on other worlds. In the words of Nobel laureate

George Wald, "We need some widely shared view of the place of Man in the Universe."

The search for extraterrestrial life should be seen as a natural, normal next step in the "reality adjustments" we make in our relationships. Such adjustments continue on all fronts: in man's relationship to man, in our ecological ties with other fauna and flora that share our planet, and with the life-sustaining physical elements of our environment. We live in times of change; vital information about ourselves and our world is acquired faster than we can process it. We urgently need to know where we stand so that we can make sound survival judgments and behave appropriately.

"There is today," notes Sagan, "—in a time when old beliefs are withering—a kind of philosophical hunger, a need to know who we are and how we got here. There is an ongoing search, often unconscious, for a cosmic perspective for humanity."

*A one-planet deity has for me little appeal.*
HARLOW SHAPLEY

From the time of their joint beginnings, philosophy and science have worked together to achieve a more realistic picture of humankind—of our origins, our nature, and our destiny.

Sagan: "We are aware of our deep connection, both in form and in matter, with the rest of the universe. The cosmos revealed to us by the new advances in astronomy and biology is far grander and more awesome than the tidy world of our ancestors. And we are becoming a part of it, the cosmos as it is, not the cosmos of our desires."

Our religious myths reveal that we humans want desperately to be participants in a meaningful biocosmic program. The chances are strong that we are in fact participants, and always have been. In the not too distant future, we may at last discover what that "scheme of things" might be.

## OUR EXPANDING CONSCIOUSNESS

Isaac Asimov has drawn up a short history of cosmic measurements showing "the successive enlargement of man's picture of the universe."

500 B.C.: 5,000 miles (the distance across the known universe: a flat disc-shaped earth with a vaulted dome. The calculator: Hecataeus of Miletus)

225 B.C.: 8,000 miles in diameter (a spherical earth. The calculator: Eratosthenes of Cyrene)

150 B.C.: 480,000 miles (an imaginary sphere including the moon. The calculator: Hipparchus of Nicaea)

1671: 1,800,000 miles (diameter of the known universe: the solar system as far out as Saturn. The calculator: Giovanni Cassini)

1704: 6 million miles (diameter of the known universe derived from the orbit of Halley's Comet. The calculator: Edmund Halley)

1840: 320 trillion miles or 54 light-years (diameter based on the known distance to the star Vega. The calculator: Friedrich von Struve)

1906: 55,000 light-years (diameter of hypothetical disc-like galaxy. The calculator: Jacobus Kapteyn)

1920: 330,000 light-years (diameter of Milky Way galaxy. The calculator: Harlow Shapley)

*I have declared infinite worlds to exist beside this our earth. It would not be worthy of God to manifest Himself in less than an infinite universe.*
GIORDANO BRUNO (1548-1600)

1923: 5.4 million light-years (a spherical universe including the newly recognized Andromeda galaxy. The calculator: Edwin Hubble)

1940: 400 million light-years (the known universe including galaxies observed to be 200 million light-years away from us. The calculator: Milton Humason)

1963: 2 billion light-years (after discovery of the first quasar by Maarten Schmidt)

1973: 24 billion light-years (based on measurement of the most distant object observed in the universe as of this date, a quasar known as OH471).

This list is more than a compendium of figures. It is a metaphor for the expansion of our consciousness. As our world-view has grown so has our perception of the parts—religious, ethical, esthetic, epistemological, and so forth—that make up that world-view.

Larry Niven hits the mark when he points out that planet dwellers riding along on a cosmic pinpoint tend to think small. We can't deny our history: tunnel-vision has plagued our perceptions. Today we are challenged *to see* the universe as it really is. This gigantic bubble-cosmos is there and it undoubtedly contains all forms of life, and when we discover our cosmic context then our primitive world-views will turn into new visions. Then we will belong to a bio-cosmos.

*The APCD predicts no smog again tomorrow . . . Birmingham, Alabama, has had an air pollution crisis this week . . . The planet Mars today had a violent dust storm, and it'll take at least 10 days to clear . . . On the moon the low tonite will drop to 307 degrees below zero, and tomorrow it'll climb all the way up to an afternoon high of 273 degrees above zero . . . The astronauts will stir up some more dust tomorrow cruising around in the moon buggy, so there'll be light to moderate eye irritation on the moon.*

KELLY LANGE
*KNBC News*

## PHILOSOPHIC CONSEQUENCES

What will it mean if we establish contact with extraterrestrial intelligences (ETs)? Since we have misgivings about our own future on earth, perhaps the realization that *they exist* will be the most significant message. George Abell, an astronomer, suggests that we should be jubilant if we "discover even *one* other

Artist's conception of ground level view of Cyclops system antennas. Photo courtesy of NASA, Ames Research Center, Moffett Field, California.

civilization that has endured for tens of thousands of years; at least if those fellows made it, perhaps there is hope for us!"

Psychological impact upon us will be deep. Of special importance is how we think and feel about ourselves. In terms of evolution, it was probably inevitable that one single species would win out over all others on earth in the survival game; and for humans the evolvement of the capacity for abstract reasoning gave us the edge. But it's lonely at the top!—far lonelier than we now admit to ourselves—and this "ontological loneliness" is surely the motivating drive behind much human behavior for which we commonly give other facile explanations: the destructive competition within our own species (wouldn't this competitive animosity be redirected if we were having to relate with several different kinds of peer-intelligent life-forms?); our cruelty to other forms of life (that is, our general lack of empathy and respect for other living things); our preoccupation with the noise of communication (words, speeches, dialogues, and other "silence breakers") as compared with communication itself; and a variety of problems in our relationships with one another (for instance, individual alienation and the resulting pressures we place on others "to end our loneliness"). If we were forced to relate to peers or superiors—forced to understand, empathize, tolerate, respect—then our individual and collective self-images would probably undergo rapid change.

Religious ideas would also change. In a biocosmos of populated planets with varied rotation times ("days") and revolution periods ("years"), severe strain would be placed on doctrines and dogmas that tie Ultimate Reality to earth functions. For instance: *sacred space* (*ge*ography: "holy ground," holy cities: Mecca, Jerusalem, Benares; temples, shrines, the "Holy of Holies"); *sacred time* (sabbaths, Holy Days, Holy Weeks, sacred festivals); *sacred languages* (Sanskrit, Arabic, Hebrew, or "King James English"); *sacred foods* (corn in the Eleusinian and Osirian mysteries, Eucharistic bread and wine, "kosher" foods); *sacred teleocosmic dramas* that depend upon the earth history ("Adam and Eve and the Snake," Faithful Remnants and Chosen People, the New Jerusalem, the "End of the World"); and *our anthropomorphic images* of the deities (note Michelangelo's frescoes on the ceiling of the Sistine Chapel).

Our ethical and esthetic notions will be threatened. We will be forced into asking new kinds of questions. Would ETs be "persons" or "selves"? Would they have a serious "right to life"? On what criteria might they be defined as worthy of our moral concern? What is the role of empathy in moral considerations? Could we empathize with them? What if—because of their appearance —we couldn't empathize with them? What if—because of *our* appearance— they couldn't empathize with us? (Is empathy learned or inherent?)

Imagine ETs engaging in behavior that, to our way of thinking, is clearly immoral: ritual flagellation of themselves to develop "moral qualities"; indiscriminate sex with countless variations on a theme by de Sade; the practice of "emotional violence" to maintain "survival readiness"; and so on. The more humanoid they appeared to us, the more easily we would become offended by behavior that, if *we* indulged in it, would be defined and felt as immoral.

Given such ethical situations, what are our capacities for rapid redefinition of "right" and "wrong"? What might be their capacities for rapid redefinition? Could we develop a calculus of "minimal reaction" that would guide human

ASTRONAUT ED MITCHELL: *You develop an instant global conciousness, a people orientation, an intense dissatisfaction with the state of the world and a compulsion to do something about it.*

ASTRONAUT RUSTY SCHWEICKART: *I'm not the same man. None of us are.*

behavior toward ETs so that, as with other life-forms on earth, we would inflict the least possible harm? Could we communicate such a calculus to them? Would a biocosmic perspective serve to clarify the pragmatic character of moral codes? How might humans respond to a truly advanced morality? (What is "a truly advanced morality"?)

On one point there is universal agreement among scientists: whatever ETs look like, they will *not* look like us. They will not be humanoid. "The biology on other planets is of course expected to be different from our own because of the statistical nature of the evolutionary process and the adaptability of life." This conclusion, written by Frank Drake and Carl Sagan, opens the door to every plausible organismic configuration imaginable to the human mind.

In hundreds of his stories, Ray Bradbury has described scenarios in which man and ETs confront each other and find themselves caught in sundry dilemmas. His science-fiction settings can serve as thought experiments that prevision the ethical and esthetic problems of actual encounter.

In a *Life* magazine article Bradbury painted verbal pictures of how extraterrestrials might appear. Among the beings that he conjured were creatures that live in very thick atmospheres and have extremely small bodily openings to cut down on intake; and creatures that live in very thin atmospheres and have "mouths and nose vents like barn doors."

Bradbury warns:

> To the lonely space man, an alien woman with the above features would hardly be attractive. Right here, the entire field of esthetics looms before us. Astronautical history may depend on those concepts of beauty and utility our men take along as unacknowledged cargo to the stars. Countless books will have to be written under the general title: *Esthetics and Etiquette for Other Worlds.* Otherwise, we are in danger of mistaking a rough skin for a rough mind, a third eye for an evil eye, a cold hand for a cold and hostile heart.

*I think there is no question that we live in an inhabited universe that has life all over it.*

GEORGE WALD

## MAN AND COSMOS: ADJUSTING OUR RELATIONSHIPS

What is man's place in the cosmos? As a better understanding of our universe has been growing, old perspectives have become obsolete. New answers are more realistic, but they are sometimes more painful.

Man has undergone three agonizing decentralizations. We have waged a steady struggle *against* decentralization, but at the same time—paradoxically—our accumulating knowledge has gradually forced us to abandon all illusions about our centrality.

**1. The Cosmological Decentralization** The *cosmological decentralization* was the first painful reassessment of man's place in the scheme of things. The evidence began to mount that the geocentric picture of our solar system was in error and that the earth is not the center of all Creation as people had hoped and religion had held. Early in the seventeenth century the Copernican theory gained ground with the observations of Galileo and the mathematical calculations of Kepler and Brahe. The battle raged between those

*For the first time in the history of our species, we have devised the tools—unmanned space vehicles and large radio telescopes—to search for extraterrestrial life. I would be very ashamed of my civilization if, with these tools at hand, we turned away from the cosmos.*

CARL SAGAN

who would defend man's right to be the center of the cosmos and those who, consenting to fact, were beginning to consider the heliocentric theory. The latter theory—that the earth orbits around the sun—had been known since ancient times, and when Copernicus (1473-1543) reintroduced it there was little stir. But as evidence in support of it mounted, bitterness increased.

It was Galileo Galilei, a teacher of geometry and astronomy at the University of Padua, who suffered most from resistance to heliocentrism. With a naive optimism, Galileo published his theories and invited scholars and churchmen to check his evidence supporting the heliocentric theory. He did not foresee the hostile reaction he would receive. When he invited a certain professor of philosophy to look through his telescope and see for himself the moons of Jupiter, the professor merely laughed and declined. He knew, from logic alone, that Jupiter could not have moons, and he knew on theological grounds that the earth was the center of the universe.

A similar argument was put forth by a Florentine astronomer named Francesco Sizzi. In a famous polemical passage he reasoned:

> There are seven windows in the head: two nostrils, two eyes, two ears, and a mouth. So also in the heavens there are two favorable stars, two unfavorable, two luminaries, and Mercury alone undecided and indifferent. From all this, and from other such natural phenomena, such as the seven metals, etc., all too pointless to enumerate, we can conclude that the number of planets is necessarily seven.
>
> Furthermore, the [alleged] satellites [of Jupiter] are invisible to the naked eye, and therefore can have no influence on the earth, and therefore would be useless, and therefore do not exist.
>
> Besides all this, the Jews and other ancient peoples as well as modern Europeans have always divided the week into seven days and have named them after the seven planets. Now if we [like Galileo] increase the number of planets, this whole and beautiful system falls to the ground.

Following this first cosmological displacement, two others have taken place, minor by comparison.

The first occurred early in this century when it was discovered by astronomers that our solar system is not central to our Milky Way galaxy. Rather, it is located in a spiral arm, and this is indeed the periphery—the "south forty"—of our island universe.

The second displacement took place during the 1930s when it was established that the Milky Way galaxy is only one of many island universes. We are but one of a local cluster of some two dozen galaxies; and we are an infinitesimal part of a universe composed of billions of galaxies. Our Milky Way is not central in any way that we can see, except to us.

In theory, there could be a fourth cosmological displacement: the discovery that our bubble-universe is only one of many. While much can be said for the theory, whether other pulsating universes exist is quite beyond our knowing. However, there seems to be no good reason *not* to believe that there are pulsating bubbles scattered in all directions through the universe. To cling to the belief that there is but a single bubble-universe rings now like another aristocentric claim. Cosmologically, we are part of the universe, which undoubtedly extends farther than we can ever know.

*It seems always great to me when God's world gets a little bigger and when I get a somewhat more true view of my place and my smallness in that universe. The growing awareness of cosmic cohabitation is enormously important to me, and it fits well into a growing knowledge of God's world.*

KRISTER STENDAHL

*Consider the question of whether earth is the only haven for intelligent life in the universe. It is very unlikely that such is the case. On the contrary, the number of planets in the universe capable of sustaining life is believed to be enormous, perhaps as many as $10^{22}$, which is about a million times greater than the total number of individual cells in the human body.*

SAXON AND FRETTER

**2. The Biological Decentralization** Man has also undergone a *biological decentralization.* We have considered ourselves superior to all other living creatures and believed we possessed a divine mandate to conquer, domesticate, or kill the "lower" animals. Moreover, there was a qualitative difference between man and the animals: the former had a soul, while the latter did not.

Charles Darwin brought the simmer to a boil. Shortly after his publication in 1859 of *Origin of Species,* the battlelines were drawn. The notion that man was not created as man—in distinctive Homo sapient form—and placed in the Garden by God himself; the idea that humans might have developed over great spans of time from primitive animal creatures that were distinctly unhuman— this was an insult comparable to the cosmological decentralization.

The climax of the battle might be thought of as the "monkey-trial" in Dayton, Tennessee, in 1925. The young science teacher, John Scopes, was indicted in a test case for teaching evolution in the local high school. By the time defense attorney Clarence Darrow had shown the fallacy of the arguments against evolution and had placed William Jennings Bryan, the prosecuting attorney, on the stand, the trial had become a worldwide spectacle. Darrow lost the case, legally; but time has shown that the principle of intellectual freedom was the real victor. Since the Scopes trial we have been less disturbed that our remote ancestors might have been something less than "human."

We are now undergoing another phase of the biological decentralization: it is a reassessment of our ecological status. Although our pride seems less involved in this process, we are realizing that man is but part of a system. By some criteria, we can claim to be a superior part of the system. We are having to admit, however, that we can't exist without the system, nor can we proceed to do whatever we wish to the fauna and flora around us. To survive we must bow to the balancing mechanisms at work within the ecosystem. Man is not the system; we did not *make* the system. We *belong* to it.

**3. The Psychological Decentralization** Man is also undergoing a *psychological decentralization.* It is probably just beginning.

Until the present time nothing has challenged man's *intellectual* superiority: our capacities for abstract reasoning, communicating, knowledge-storage, and culture. These were clearly supreme. But if man must confront other intelligent forms of life, this could turn out to be the most painful "rite of passage" we will ever face. (The only greater ego-pain I can imagine would be the utterly shattering realization that the human race is irrevocably bound for extinction.)

There is some likelihood that we are nearing such a confrontation. We are beginning to consider the possibility that other forms of intelligent life may exist on earth. Many of the higher primates have greater intellectual skills than we thought. Dolphins of course, come to mind. They may possess an intelligence as great as man's but so different that we underestimate it because we don't understand it. It may turn out to be a complex intelligence deserving our sincere respect.

Our most severe reassessment of mankind will come if and when we confront extraterrestrial intelligence. Almost inevitably, *they* will contact *us,* which means that they will be far advanced compared to us. Their intelligence may be superior to man's—perhaps an I.Q. of 250 is merely bright normal to them. By

*What is the ultimate truth about ourselves? Various answers suggest themselves. We are a bit of stellar matter gone wrong. We are physical machinery—puppets that strut and talk and laugh and die as the hand of time pulls the strings beneath. But there is one elementary inescapable answer. We are that which asks the question. Whatever else there may be in our nature, responsibility towards truth is one of its attributes.*

SIR ARTHUR EDDINGTON

*Once the human species has initiated the search for other life in the universe, the search can never end; for until we find it, there will always be the possibility that it exists; and the search will never end until we find it.*

PETER ANGELES

comparison—however much it may hurt—the only appropriate stance for man may be one of humility.

It is often noted that science-fiction writers have prepared us, for more than a half-century now, for "future shock." Perhaps they have extended our horizons in preparation for a confrontation with intelligence so it might be less of a shock. One cannot but wonder when/if this rather ultimate "decentralization" will occur and how severe its affects may be upon man's opinions of man.

The *Pioneer* and *Voyager* planetary probes, mankind's first interstellar travelers, carry plaques and records indicating the planet of their origin and bearing pictures of the beings that inhabit it. The striking fact is *the explicit assumption* that other intelligent creatures might someday intercept the probe and wonder who sent it hurtling through space.

All these decentralizing crises that man has experienced are religious in nature, for they deal with the ultimate question of man's place in the universe and our relationships within it.

It has heretofore been a role of Western religion to affirm man's worth. Man feels inferior enough as it is. The preservation by religious institutions of the convictions that man is only just lower than the angels and that we are, in fact, children of God has undoubtedly been both comforting and healing. Man might not have survived the struggle without the sense of worth and purpose such beliefs have given us.

Nevertheless, as a child grows he realizes that he must compromise his ego-centered nature if he is to live in the world of men. Man's decentralizations are part of our growth as a cultured species; it is a part of our humanization. To face realistically one's place in the scheme of existence offers us yet another chance to adjust to "the world as it is." For some, accepting realities is more fulfilling than defending therapeutic beliefs. We can feel better about ourselves and others when we no longer have a need for aristocentric myth.

*The receipt of an interstellar message would be one of the major events in human history, and the beginning of the deprovincialization of our planet.*

CARL SAGAN

## REFLECTIONS

1 In only a couple of decades scientists have done a remarkable about-face on the question of the existence of life on other planets. Carl Sagan, an exobiologist and philosopher, has written extensively on man's need of, and search for, a "cosmic context" within which we could better understand ourselves. Are you in essential agreement with Sagan's assessment of this human venture?

2 What do you think of Larry Niven's sage-like comment (see marginal quote on p. 530) that the trouble with people who live on planets is that they "tend to think small"? Is this a truism, or an adage you could store for later use?

3 The Florentine philosopher, Francesco Sizzi, has become famous (or infamous) for his reply to Galileo. After your first chuckle, what did you think of his stand and the way he rationalized it?

4 What do you think of the intent of the Drake/Sagan formula? Although some of the quantities are not yet known with precision, what is the general message of the equation itself? On reflection, what do you think of "the L-factor"?

5  Reflect on the impact upon our thinking and feeling of the discovery of the existence of extraterrestrial life and intelligence. What is your evaluation of the implications suggested in this chapter? Can you think of other eventual changes in the way we think and feel if we do live in a true biocosmos?

6  Phrase in your own personal way your response to the question, "What is man's place in the cosmos?" (Maybe you can be specific by focusing on man's relationships to component elements of the universe—such as our earth, other human beings, other living creatures, extraterrestrial intelligence, and so forth—and then formulating a general answer.)

7  Put into your own words the three decentralizations that Western man has experienced. If taken seriously, how do you think these new perspectives would affect (1) our self-image as individuals? and (2) mankind's collective image of itself?

8  Note the statement on p. 540: "All these decentralizing crises which man has experienced are religious in nature. . . ." Is this meaningful? Do you agree? Why or why not?

9  What do you think of the afterthoughts by Astronauts Mitchell and Schweickart on how their space voyages changed their lives (see marginal quote on p. 535)?

10  What do you think of the proverb-like saying by Tsiolkovsky (see marginal quote on p. 529)?

# CARL SAGAN

## *The Spaceship of the Imagination*

*The cosmos is all there is or ever was or ever will be.*

*In the deepest sense, the search for extraterrestrial intelligence is a search for who we are.*

I

He stands on a rocky cliff by the sea. Waves churn below and seagulls skim the breakers. He wears an orange windbreaker.

"The Cosmos is all there is or ever was or ever will be. Our feeblest contemplations of the Cosmos stir us . . . we know we are approaching the greatest of mysteries."

He plucks a dandelion seed from a crevice in the rock and lets it dance away in the wind.

"Come with me," he beckons.

For years to come, Carl Sagan will be known as the eloquent tourguide who lectured us and dreamed us through the light-years of space and time in his thirteen-part television series *Cosmos*. Backed by a gifted team of filmmakers and scientists, and with dazzling special effects, the dandelion seed is transformed into "the spaceship of the imagination," and Sagan shows us the wonders of the universe.

"In the last few millennia we have made the most astonishing and unexpected discoveries about the Cosmos and our place within it. . . ."

Sagan invites us to share his knowledge and excitement; and this "personal voyage" truly becomes the grandest of adventures. Before it is over he shows us supernovas, pulsars, black holes, star clusters, exploding galaxies, the big bang, other worlds where intelligent life might be found—and countless other cosmic and historical events.

"They remind us that humans have evolved to wonder, that understanding is a joy, that knowledge is prerequisite to survival."

◆

II

Sagan leans against a stop sign, watching a police officer give out a ticket, listening to railcars roaring past. He wears the same orange windbreaker.

"I lived here . . . in Brooklyn. . . . I knew my immediate neighborhood intimately—every candy store, front stoop, backyard, empty lot, and wall for playing Chinese handball. It was my whole world."

In winter, he recalls, he could see the stars. "I looked up at them and wondered what they were." His friends told him "they were lights in the sky." Since he already knew that, he went to the library and found a book on stars. "I opened the book breathlessly right there in the library and the book said something astonishing—a very big thought. Stars, it said, were suns, but very far away. The sun was a star, but close up.

"I was ignorant . . . but I could tell that if the stars were suns they had to be awfully far away, farther away than 86th street, farther away than Manhattan, farther away, probably, than New Jersey.

"This just blew my mind. Until then, my universe had been my neighborhood. Now I tried to imagine how far away I'd have to move the sun to make it as faint as a star. I got my first sense of the immensity of the universe. I was hooked."

Sagan decided then and there that he would become an astronomer.

"But," his worried grandfather asked, "how will you make a living?"

Carl Sagan was born in Brooklyn in 1934, of an American-born mother and an emigrant Russian father, a cloth cutter in the garment industry. His parents expected their son to follow the family vocation, but they had the wisdom to support his own gifts and intellectual interests. "As a child it was my immense good fortune to have parents and a few good teachers who encouraged my curiosity." So he grew up under the city lights, playing handball, devouring science fiction, and dreaming of other worlds "fabulously unlike Brooklyn."

After high school, Sagan headed directly for a career in science. In 1951, at sixteen, he entered the University of Chicago on a scholarship. Nine years later he emerged with four degrees in science, including a Ph.D. in astronomy and astrophysics. He was twenty-six.

While in graduate school at Berkeley and Stanford, Sagan sensed the far-ranging implications of the work of the biochemists. At twenty-two he wrote his first technical paper on "Radiation and the Origin of the Gene"; and this has been followed by more than three hundred articles and a dozen books, most of them related to the biochemistry of life-origins. Sagan is preeminently an exobiologist.

"Science is a joy," says Sagan, "and it belongs to everyone. It is not just something for an isolated, remote elite. It is our birthright."

## III

In tropical southern India, inside a temple dedicated to Shiva, Sagan walks among some very old bronze statues of Hindu gods.

"The most elegant and sublime of these bronzes is a representation of the creation of the universe at the beginning of each cosmic cycle, a motif known as the Cosmic Dance of Shiva."

Sagan describes the blackened-bronze figure standing in a circle of flame: Shiva as Nataraja, dancing the Cosmic Dance of creation and destruction. His right hand holds a drum, symbolizing creation; his left hand holds a torch of flame, representing the conflagration that will finally destroy the universe. "Creation and Destruction."

Sagan emerges from the dark interior of the temple and sits in the warm sun. In a niche in the temple wall above him is a gray stone statue of the ever-popular Ganesha, the elephant-headed god of prosperity and enlightenment.

"The most sophisticated cosmological ideas came from Asia, and particularly from India," Sagan ponders aloud. "Most cultures imagine the world to be only a few hundred generations old. Hardly anyone guessed that the cosmos might be far older. But the ancient Hindus did." The Hindu cosmic cycle of 8.64 billion years—about half the actual age of our universe—is "a kind of premonition of modern astronomical ideas"—especially the theory of the oscillating universe.

Music from a village festival drifts through the palm trees.

"The big bang," he notes, "is modern scientific myth. It comes from the same human need to solve the cosmological question."

*Whether we are alone in the cosmos is something I dearly want to know.*

*Something like the processes that on earth led to man must have happened billions of other times in the history of our galaxy. There must be other starfolk.*

ENCYCLOPAEDIA GALACTICA: ENTRY
WORLD: *806.4615.0110*
*Civilization Type: 1.0 J.*
*Society Code: 4G4, "Humanity."*
*Star: G2V, r = 9.844 kpc, θ = 00°05'24", φ = 206°28'49".*
*Planet: third, a = 1.5×10¹³ cm,* $M = 6 \times 10^{27}$ *g, R = 6.4 ×* $10^8$ *cm, p = 8.6 × 10⁴ s, P = 3.2 × 10⁷ s.*
*Extraplanetary colonies: none*
*Planet age: 1.45 × 10¹⁷ s.*
*First locally initiated contact: 1.21 × 19⁹ s ago.*
*Receipt first galactic nested code: application pending.*
*Biology: C, N, O, S, H₂O, PO₄.*
*Deoxyribonucleic acid.*
*No genetic prosthesis.*
*Mobile heterrotrophs, symbionts with photosynthetic autotrophs. Surface dwellers, monospecific, polychromatic O₂ breathers. FE-chelated tetrapyroles in circulatory fluid.*
*Sexual mammals.*
*m ≈ 7 × 10⁴g, t ≈ 2 × 10⁹s.*
*Genomes: 4 × 10⁹*
*Technology: exponentiating/ fossil fuels/nuclear weapons/ organized warfare/ environmental pollution.*
*Culture: ~ 200 nation states, ~ 6 global powers; cultural and technological homogeneity underway.*
*Prepartum/postpartum: 0.21 [18], Individual/communal: 0.31 [17], Artistic/technological: 0.14 [11] Probability of survival (per 100 yr): 40%.*

*I believe that a thousand years from now our descendants will look back on our time and marvel that in so critical, confused, and dangerous an age we were able to avoid self-destruction and take decisive steps to understand that vast cosmic ocean of which we are a tiny part.*

*We live in an age where the fundamental questions— about the nature of matter, the origin of life and consciousness and intelligence, the beginnings and ends of worlds and universes—are being approached rigorously and scientifically. We have an opportunity to satisfy that passion to know.*

*We have always watched the stars and mused about whether there are other beings who think and wonder. In a cosmic setting vast and old beyond ordinary human understanding, we are a little lonely.*

*It may be that we are very much like the inhabitants of, let's say isolated valleys in New Guinea, who communicate with their neighbors by runner and drum, and who are completely unaware of a vast international radio and cable traffic over them, around them, and through them.*

The philosophic enterprise that Sagan is conducting is a part of what he calls "cosmic consciousness-raising." For our era, science—or more exactly, the scientific way of thinking—is the source of the fundamental data of consciousness. It alone can give us an understanding of the realities of our universe. After millennia of mythology, it is now possible for the mind of man to enter realistically into the fabric of the universe and to involve itself, in a liberating way, with the events of the cosmos.

Intelligibility becomes a function of the interaction between the self and the world. In his work, Sagan is facilitating this interaction of selves with a newly discovered cosmos. He is guiding us through an odyssey that can resurrect all our rationalities and all our sentiments. "In *Cosmos*, we have tried to speak not just to the mind but also to the heart." From physics and chemistry to the music of the spheres and the poetry of our souls, *nothing is to be left out*. Our total humanness is to be expressed and reaffirmed.

## IV

Sagan walks to the helm of "the spaceship of the imagination." At the console he reaches upper left and punches up a monitor showing the Milky Way galaxy; at upper right is a readout screen for displaying information on each world and its life-forms.

"Advanced technological civilizations would know about many worlds," he explains. A great blue-white spiral galaxy comes up on the screen at the front of the spaceship.

"Perhaps they would share their findings, assembling some vast repository of the knowledge of countless worlds. They might compile an Encyclopaedia Galactica.

"Perhaps someday there will be an entry in the Encyclopaedia Galactica for our planet or perhaps, even now, there exists a planetary dossier . . . a listing for 'Earth.' What do they know about us?"

WORLD: 806.4615.0110
Civilization Type: 1.0 J
Society Code: 4G4, "Humanity". . .
   Technology: Exponentiating
   Fossil fuels/nuclear weapons
   Organized warfare
   Environmental pollution . . .
   Probability of survival (per 100 yr): 40%

The Encyclopaedia Galactica is Sagan's way of imaging "a cosmic context for mankind." We have an essential longing to know where we fit into the scheme of things.

Meanwhile, until such evidence is obtained, we must think in cosmic terms. The truth, notes Sagan, is that we have moved in a cosmic perspective since our presapient beginnings. "The deepest cosmological questions are embedded in human folklore and myth, superstition and religion." We have *assumed* that a relationship with heavenly beings exists.

"We have always watched the stars and mused about whether there are other beings who think and wonder. In a cosmic setting vast and old beyond ordinary human understanding, we are a little lonely."

The search for a cosmic context for mankind has began and cannot end until that context is known.

"In the deepest sense," writes Sagan, "the search for extraterrestrial intelligence is a search for who we are."

# OF
# ULTIMATE
# CONCERN

*We have seen the highest circle of spiraling powers. We have named this circle God. We might have given it any other name we wished: Abyss, Mystery, Absolute Darkness, Absolute Light, Matter, Spirit, Ultimate Hope, Ultimate Despair, Silence.*

NIKOS KAZANTZAKIS

*We are all children in a vast kindergarten trying to spell God's name with the wrong alphabet blocks.*

TENNESSEE WILLIAMS

**8**₁

## RELIGION AS A SEARCH FOR MEANING

Religion is man's involvement in the meaning of his existence, and the depth of one's involvement is the depth of his religion. It is participation in life in a special way for a special purpose. Religion is our attempt to find a meaningful relatedness to all the significant events of human experience. It is, as Paul Tillich phrased it, "our ultimate concern for the Ultimate."

Sometimes one finds definitions of religion that take into account only a particular set of answers to man's ultimate questions. Accordingly, religion is defined as belief in the supernatural, belief in spirits, or belief in One God; or an anthropologist might define religion as man's ritualistic expression of socially accepted beliefs and values.

But such definitions of religion miss the point. Religion is not to be defined in terms of the *answers* that human beings give—for they are legion—but rather in terms of the *questions* that we ask. The particular local and cultural answers to which a single religious society commits itself tell us much about the group; but it is in our agonized questioning that we discover the universal religious condition of all human beings.

Indeed, the atheist who feels no necessity to hypothesize an Omnipotent Deity to account for the machinations of the universe is making an observation fully as ultimate, and fully as religious, as the theist who protests that the universe cannot be understood apart from belief in God.

Religion is not to be confused with the various forms of intellectualization that follow religious experience.

As time passes and people find that they share similar convictions, doctrines develop. A *doctrine* is a formal interpretation of religious experience. Its purpose is to crystallize and preserve the fundamental elements of an experience, and to make it possible for those within the group to communicate

*There are many paths to God, my son. I hope yours will not be too difficult.*
LEW WALLACE
*Ben Hur*

*Let the one who puts a jinx on the village die. Let him die, he who thought evil thoughts against us. Also give us fish.*

*Wapokomo prayer*

concerning the nature of the experience. A doctrine is a social phenomenon. Those with similar beliefs are saying they belong together as part of the believing group; more than that, they are attempting to participate in the religious experience that the doctrine refers to.

As a religious institution develops, leaders emerge who are empowered to distinguish between true and false doctrines. Thus, they proclaim dogmas. A *dogma* is a doctrine that is supposed to have universal acceptance by all believers. It is a closed issue. It must be accepted as true if the particular benefits offered by the religion are to be attained.

A *creed* also is a formalization arising from religious experience. The term *creed* is from the Latin *credo*, "I believe," and a creed thus functions to distinguish believers from nonbelievers. Creeds in the form of short, capsule statements of essential beliefs are often used as membership cards and passwords.

Lastly, *theology* is the intellectualization of the totality of one's religion. Traditionally, the theologian belongs to a particular religion. He is not a "philosopher of religion" who studies, with an eye to objectivity, the religious experience of all mankind; rather, he is a believer who stands within the "circle of faith," attempting to update and reinterpret the meaning of the faith for the people of his own time. Thus a Muslim theologian speaks to Muslims, a Catholic theologian speaks to Catholics, and so on.

This traditional role, however, is presently being broken and broadened. Many of today's theologians are making statements of ultimate concern that apply to all human beings and not merely to the members of a particular group. This change contains profound implications for the future of parochial religion.

## THE ANTHROPOMORPHIC SPIRITS

Primitive people lived out their lives in a world of aggressive natural forces: rainstorms, floods, forest and veld fires, locusts and famine, illness, pain, and death. Most of these forces were hostile—they were "evil." But there were friendly forces, too: rain for crops, life-generating energies that brought new lambs to their flocks and new children to their families and clans, sun to make their corn grow, good winds to sail their outriggers, good conditions that filled their nets with fish. These forces were aggressive; they took the initiative; the storms, floods, and forest fires came whether they liked it or not.

These are impersonal, illusive, inconceivable forces. What caused them? What are the causal energies behind the raging hurricane or the silent, burning disease?

As we have seen, all that man can know is our own experience. We experience our consciousness, our feelings, our will, our ideas. We also experience a self that we do not identify with our bodies, so we conclude that our essence is not body but "soul."

Therefore, of necessity, the universe about us is conceived within the limits of our own experience. We cannot negotiate with unseen forces; we cannot even think about the inconceivable. Yet conceive them we must, for we cannot escape negotiating with them.

Therefore, to understand and negotiate with the forces that be, we think of

*All phases of becoming are subject to arrest. . . . Infantilism in religion results in an arrest due to the immediate needs for comfort and security or self-esteem. . . . We find many personalities who deal zealously and effectively with all phases of becoming except the final task of relating themselves meaningfully to creation. For some reason their curiosity stops at this point.*

GORDON ALLPORT

*All religions pronounce the name of God in their particular language. As a rule it is better for a man to name God in his native tongue rather than in one that is foreign to him.*

SIMONE WEIL

## Can Religion Be Defined?

Religion is one's attitude toward whatever he considers to be the determiner of destiny.

James Bissett Pratt

Religion is man's ultimate concern for the Ultimate.

Paul Tillich

Religion is the ritual cultivation of socially accepted values.

John Fischer

Religion, as a minimum, is the belief in spiritual beings.

E. B. Tylor

Religion is a propitiation of, and dependency on, superior powers which are believed to control and direct the course of nature and human life.

Sir James G. Frazer

Religion is *concern* about experiences which are regarded as of supreme value; *devotion* towards a power or powers believed to originate, increase, and conserve these values; and some *suitable expression* of this concern and devotion, whether through symbolic rites or through other individual and social conduct.

Edgar S. Brightman

Religion consists in the perception of the infinite under such manifestations as are able to influence the moral character of man.

Max Müller

A religion, on its doctrinal sides, can thus be described as a system of general truths which have the effect of transforming character when they are sincerely held and vividly apprehended.

Alfred North Whitehead

Religion is a belief in an ultimate meaning of the universe.

Alfred R. Wallace

Religion is a theory of man's relation to the universe.

S. P. Haynes

Religion is our feeling about the highest forces that govern human destiny.

John Morely

Religion is a sense of the sacred.

Sir Julian Huxley

Religion is (subjectively regarded) the organization of all duties as divine commands.

Immanuel Kant

*Continued*

them as consciousnesses with minds, wills, appetites, and emotions. Through a complex linguistic history, we have come to call them *spirits,* and they come in many forms: demons, evil spirits, ancestral ghosts, angels, gods and goddesses, kami, jinn, and so on.

These spirits are like man, enough like us so that we can talk with them. We can cajole, threaten, complain, and bargain with them. We can understand why at times they behave with consistency (for we do) or become capricious and unpredictable (we are occasionally that way with members of our families).

"O, Great Motage, Protector of humble men, Descendant of the Great Fish, Father of the most Terrible Volcano and Devourer of all enemies, we humbly beg your leave to join with the Methodists."

We can bribe them into doing us favors; we can offer them gifts of varying worth. More sophisticated spirits are believed to respond to higher, subtler forms of sacrifice: the sacrifice of one's will in obedience, or of earthly pleasures, or of one's ego.

These are profound processes, developed over long periods of time. They arise from man's deepest needs to survive the onslaught of the aggressive forces of nature and society. During more peaceful times, though, these personified forces can help man achieve fulfilling goals; they enable us to "grow in spirit" and become more stable, confident, and loving—a being at peace with one's self.

What motivates man to colonize the universe with spirits like ourselves? *Survival.* The whole purpose of religion is to work out a "saving" relationship. In Judeo-Christian terms this relationship is known as "justification"—getting into a "right relationship with God." But it can be universalized: the goal of religion is to get into a right relationship with Shiva, with Allah, with Isis, with Christ, with Mithras, with Amitabha Buddha—all so that the desired end might be attained. And that end is to survive—that is, to find "salvation."

An interesting phenomenon often overtakes the spirits if they live a long while. They frequently become a part of a "theological complex," a system so grandiose that they are no longer accessible to the masses of people and cannot meet their daily needs. In the Greek and Roman religions the gods became so engrossed with the affairs of state that they were no longer meaningful to the common person. During the empire the great gods of the Roman pantheon were functionaries of state ceremonies, to be worshiped by emperors and other dignitaries. So distant had they become that the farmer and merchant had long since forgotten them.

And so, the great gods were replaced by godlets, by the lares and penates who still had plenty of time to take care of the mortals' mundane affairs. Pomona would look after their fruit trees, Mellona their beehives, Epona their horses, Juventa their children; and two-faced Janus still had time to act as sentinel over their doors, looking after all who went in or came out of their houses.

This is a common development. Whenever the deities become too great, too important—too distant in their transcendent glory—to take care of man's immediate concerns, then lesser spirits inevitably replace them and carry on their ministrations. They may be called angels, guardian spirits, genii, lares and penates, saints, bodhisattvas, or avatars of Vishnu. But in all cases, they are concerned, responsive, and available in time of need.

*In a maritime community depending on the products of the sea there is never magic connected with the collecting of shellfish or with fishing by poison, weirs, and fish traps, so long as these are completely reliable. On the other hand, any dangerous, hazardous, and uncertain type of fishing is surrounded by ritual. . . . Coastal sailing as long as it is perfectly safe and easy commands no magic. Overseas expeditions are invariably bound up with ceremonies and ritual.*

**E. B. TYLOR**

*The AMA [American Medical Association] urges you to let the faith that nourishes you grow strong, for faith is a physician. . . .*

**TV Commercial**

## PRAYER

In the year 204 B.C. Scipio Africanus sailed from Sicily to attack Hannibal's forces at Carthage. Just before the great expedition sailed, Scipio stood on his flagship at dawn and, after the herald had ordered silence, offered his prayer.

Ye gods and goddesses, who inhabit the seas and the lands, I supplicate and beseech you that whatever has been done under my command, or is being done, or will later be done, may turn out to my advantage and to the advantage of the people and the commons of Rome, the allies, and the Latins who by land or sea or on rivers follow me, [accepting] the leadership, the authority, and the auspices of the Roman people; that you will support them and aid them with your help; that you will grant that, preserved in safety and victorious over the enemy, arrayed in body and laden with spoils, you will bring them back with me in triumph to our homes; that you will grant us the power to take revenge upon our enemies and foes; and that you will grant to me and the Roman people the power to enforce upon the Carthaginians what they have planned to do against our city, as an example of [divine] punishment.

Was Scipio's prayer answered? He shortly destroyed two great armies of Carthaginians and Numidians and went on to a decisive defeat of Hannibal in a battle near Zama on October 19, 202 B.C. There was a tradition that Scipio was a favorite of the gods and was therefore in intimate communication with them. How does one determine whether prayers are answered if not in terms of results?

*O millet, thou hast grown well for us; we thank thee, we eat thee.*

**Ainu prayer**

πνεῦμα, ατος, τό, (πνέω) *a blowing*, πνεύματα ἀνέμων Hdt., Aesch.: alone, *a wind, blast*, Trag., etc.   **2.** metaph., θαλερωτέρῳ πν. with more genial *breeze* or *influence*, Aesch.; λύσσης πν. μάργῳ Id.; πν. ταὐτὸν οὔποτ' ἐν ἀνδράσιν φίλοις βέβηκεν *the wind* is constantly changing even among friends, Soph.   **II.** like Lat. *spiritus* or *anima, breathed air, breath*, Aesch.; πν. βίου *the breath* of life, Id.; πν. ἀθροίζειν to collect *breath*, Eur.; πν. ἀφιέναι, ἀνιέναι, μεθιέναι to give up *the ghost*, Id.; πνεύματος διαρροαί the *wind-pipe*, Id.   **2.** *that is breathed forth, odour, scent*, Id.   **III.** *spirit*, Lat. *afflatus*, Anth.: *inspiration*, N.T.   **IV.** *the spirit* of man, Ib.   **V.** *a spirit*; in N.T. of *the Holy Spirit*, τὸ Πνεῦμα, Πν. ἅγιον :— also of *angels*, Ib.:—of *evil spirits*, Ib.   Hence

πνευμᾰτικός, ή, όν, *of spirit, spiritual*, N.T.

πνεύμων, ονος, ὁ, (πνέω) *the organ of* breathing, *the lungs*, Lat. *pulmo*, Il., Plat.: mostly in pl., Trag.; πνεῦμ' ἀνεὶς ἐκ πλευμόνων Eur.

πνεῦν, Dor. poët. for ἔπνεον, impf. of πνέω.

πνευστιάω, *to breathe hard, pant*, Arist.; Ep. part. πνευστιόων, Anth.

ΠΝΕ'Ω, Ep. πνείω, Ion. impf. πνείεσκον: f. πνεύσομαι, Dor. πνευσοῦμαι: aor. 1 ἔπνευσα: pf. πέπνευκα:— Like other dissyll. Verbs in -έω, this Verb only contracts εε, εει :—*to blow*, of wind and air, Od., Hdt., Att.; ἡ πνέουσα (sc. αὔρα) *the breeze*, N.T.   **II.** *to breathe, send forth an odour*, Od.:—c. gen. *to breathe* or *smell of* a thing, Anth.   **III.** of animals, *to breathe hard, pant, gasp*, Il., Aesch.   **IV.** generally, *to draw breath, breathe*, and so *to live*, Hom.; οἱ πνέοντες = οἱ ζῶντες, Soph.   **V.** metaph., c. acc. cogn. *to breathe forth, breathe*, μένεα πνείοντες breathing spirit, of warriors, Il.; so, πῦρ πν. Hes.; φόνον, κότον "Αρη Aesch.; so, πνέοντας δόρυ καὶ λόγχας Ar.; Ἀλφειὸν πνέων, of a swift runner, Id.   **2.** μέγα πνεῖν to be of a high *spirit, give oneself airs*, Eur.; τόσονδ' ἔπνευσας Id.:—also, with a nom., as if it were the wind, μέγας πνέων Id.; πολὺς ἔπνει καὶ λαμπρὸς ἦν Dem.

Note the variety of different, but associated, meanings attached to the Greek word *pneuma* and its related forms.

*"The priest—he used to read from the Moslem* Quran, *and the Hindu* Gita, *moving from one to the other as if it mattered not which was being read as long as God was being worshipped."*

**Gandhi (the motion picture)**

*"Captain Pike has his illusions, and you, Captain Kirk, have your realities. May you find your way as pleasant."*

**"THE MENAGERIE" Star Trek**

## SPIRIT-POSSESSION

Spirits "possess" or "inhabit" people. Man has always been quite sure of this since we intuit ourselves to be a "spirit inside a body." If one's own being is a dualism of essence and matter—soul and body—then it is only reasonable that other spirits, too, might inhabit our bodies.

This phenomenon — "spirit-possession" — has been the universal means of accounting for the complexities of human behavior. Not only does possession explain the various forms of "insanity" and certain symptoms of illness (epileptic attacks, for instance) that we observe in others; it also accounts for the strange feelings we find inside ourselves: dizziness, fevers, pains, convulsions. And almost all states of religious consciousness can be thus explained: ecstatic trances, visions, "conversions," "speaking in tongues," oracular prophecies, and so on. Negatively, if possessed by a bad spirit (by a demon, a witch, a jinn, or by "sin"), we can point to the cause of the evil things we do. On the other hand, when possessed by helpful spirits (Vohu Manah, the Holy Spirit, the Spirit of Allah), then we can do good things and even accomplish feats that otherwise would have been quite beyond our capability.

From earliest times special techniques have been known for exorcizing demons—for depossessing one of a bad spirit. Likewise, techniques have been used for inducing possession by good spirits. To be possessed by the "Holy Spirit" is the most valued of human experiences according to Zoroastrians, Christians, and Muslims. In some groups such a blessing would be proven by intense emotion (the "strange warming of the heart" described by John Wesley), "speaking in tongues" (among Pentecostals), or an egoless consciousness (among Catholic mystics).

People have always had experiences that they invest with ultimate significance, and often such events—from acts of courage and moments of love to visions and esthetic "highs"—effect drastic changes in our lives.

We preserve the essence of an experience by reflecting on it, conceptualizing and labeling it. As time passes, the mind "processes" the experience; it interprets it. Interpretations necessarily make use of available theological ideas and linguistic tools. What the experience "means" is therefore culturally relative, though we are not usually aware of this fact.

When attempting to understand a religious experience, there are two *kinds* of interpretations to be taken into account. One is given to the event by the experiencer himself. It will develop within the framework of his personal religious beliefs, and it is this interpretation that gives the experience meaning and affects his life.

Another interpretation, equally valid, must be made by a knowledgeable analyst or scientist. The experience may be explained in terms of motivations, emotional needs, or altered physiological states and body chemistry. Although the objective account does not pretend to include the meaning that the experience holds for the experiencer, it provides a valuable perspective for understanding one aspect of the event.

## THE FUNCTION OF MYTH

All religion is expressed in myth. A myth is a story involving the supernatural that is accepted by members of a specific social group—a clan, a tribe, an ethnic group, a religious community large or small, a nation—that explains the origin, significance, or meaning of an event. When that story is believed in, it becomes true; and when it becomes true through belief, it is then religion. All myths are true for those who believe in them.

Believers generally know, and are committed to, the myths of a single tradition. In philosophy of religion, however, our goal is to achieve a synoptic overview of the human race's whole mythic enterprise; similar stories from many traditions are collected and studied together to discover if there are deeper levels of meaning than is apparent from the stories themselves. The goal is to make explicit what has heretofore been implicit in the myths.

The popular connotation of myth as a false account is irrelevant here and must be totally cleared away. Since the time of the ancient Greeks the word "myth" has been a technical term, and it does not carry the implication that a story is not based in reality or fact and is therefore "a figment of imagination." This negative use of the term functions primarily to derogate others' beliefs and has no place in critical philosophy.

"Myth" derives from the Greek *muthos* (Latin *mythos*) and refers to the story that is embodied in the spoken part of a religious ritual, as distinct from the *dromenon,* the acted-out part of the ritual. All religious drama contains both story and action. What goes on in the action part you could know only if you were there to see it; but the spoken story can be told and retold down through the ages quite apart from the drama and its religious meaning.

Myths don't involve the question of truth at all. Myths just are. Like trees, planets, doorknobs, time, and history, myths simply exist. Is a doorknob true? The question is absurd. So also for myth. We can inquire into the function of a doorknob, of course; and we can also reflect on the role and significance of myth in our lives.

Throughout the twentieth century a picture of myth and its function has been emerging. E. B. Tylor (*Primitive Culture*) and Sir James Frazer (*The Golden Bough*) were among the first to discern recurring ideas and themes; and both came to believe that myths reveal universal patterns or "laws" through which the human psyche manifests itself. Sigmund Freud (*Totem and Taboo*) and C. G. Jung (*Man and His Symbols*) added to our understanding of the subconscious materials that express themselves in universal symbols, images, motifs, and themes.

The greatest illumination into myth has come from the scholarship of

*In the nineteenth century the problem was that* God is dead; *in the twentieth century the problem is that* man is dead. *Man is surely at least on the critical list.*

ERICH FROMM

*The priest smiled. "What man who has lived for more than a score of years desires justice, warrior? For my part, I find mercy infinitely more attractive. Give me a forgiving deity any day."*

ROGER ZELAZNY
*Lord of Light*

Joseph Campbell (*Hero with a Thousand Faces, The Masks of God* in four volumes; and recently Bill Moyers' videotaped interviews with Campbell and the published transcript, both entitled *The Power of Myth*). Campbell opened three doors for us into the world of mythology:

1. He has shown that myths play a vital role in the collective life of mankind. They are not just classical folktales or delightful stories. Myths nourish mankind's collective spiritual life, and the society that loses its capacity for myth is empty, soul-less. In trying to apprehend the significance of myths clinical definitions are all but useless; it is this life-giving function we must seek to understand.

2. Campbell has also shown that it is in our myths that we can discover mankind's deepest, most honest assessment of the human condition. Myths reveal why the human condition is intolerable, why we are compelled to alter our perception of it, and how, in all our religions, we humans have gone about doing just that—in order to render an uninhabitable condition as tolerable as humanly possible.

3. Campbell documented and clarified the one great theme that dominates all mythology: the hero's journey. This is the master-myth: virtually all mythic stories illustrate one or more stages of this odyssey, which is a symbolic account of the psychic journey made by each human being in his or her lonely passage from birth to death and beyond.

The story of Demeter and Persephone is a classic example of myth and illustrates its symbolic nature.

The story of the Eleusinian mystery has come down to us in a long epic poem called the "Homeric Hymn to Demeter." This drama was one of the favorite religious stories of the Greek world, and for over a thousand years the little town of Eleusis, fourteen miles west of Athens, gave to worshipers a very personal drama of salvation.

The beautiful Persephone, daughter of Demeter and Zeus, was gathering flowers in the meadow one beautiful spring day—"roses and crocuses and beautiful violets, irises also and hyacinths and narcissi." As she reached to pick an especially beautiful flower, the earth suddenly opened and from the nether world sprang Pluto, riding in a chariot. The "wide-pathed earth yawned" and the god of Hades "caught her up reluctant in his golden car and bore her away lamenting" into the dark world of the dead.

From a distance her mother heard her cries, but nowhere could Demeter find her daughter. For nine days she wandered over the Earth, searching. Then Helios revealed to Demeter what had happened. Furious that Zeus had conspired in her daughter's captivity, she left the home of the gods on Olympus and wandered in the world of man. At the town of Eleusis, although in disguise, she was treated with love; so it was there that she decided to live.

Eventually she revealed to the Eleusinians her true identity and asked that they build her a temple. When it was finished, she enclosed herself in her new home and sought revenge on Zeus. She decreed a "most dreadful and cruel year for mankind over the all-nourished earth. . . . In the fields the oxen drew many a curved plough in vain, and much white barley was cast upon the land without

*We have art that we do not die of the truth.*

FRIEDRICH NIETZSCHE

News item: *This is the first step in the investigation into the bridge disaster. A public hearing will be held . . . next week. The cause may never be learned, but as Assemblyman "Smith" put it, "This bridge collapse was not an act of God. Someone is responsible."*

**KNBC News**

*Spirit of this place, we give thee tobacco; so help us, save us from the enemy, bring us wealth, bring us back safely.*

**Iroquois Indian prayer**

avail." One by one the gods entreated her to give nourishment to the earth again, but she vowed not to relent until she had Persephone with her again.

Finally Zeus commanded the Keeper of the Dead to return Persephone to the world of the living. Crafty Pluto "secretly gave her sweet pomegranate seed to eat" before allowing her to return to the bright world of sunshine. Therefore part of her belonged to the nether world, and she was obliged to spend a third part of every year in the lower world with her husband Pluto, reigning as queen of Hades; the other two-thirds she could spend with her mother and the gods and men. So Demeter, with divine justice, allowed the earth to come alive for two-thirds of each year, and allowed it to die for a third season.

Before returning to Olympus, Demeter taught her divine mysteries to the gentle people of Eleusis—"awful mysteries which no one may in any way transgress or pry into or utter." All who were willing to study, purify themselves, and go through the solemn and sacred rites could share in those divine mysteries.

Annual ceremonies began with an elaborate parade from Athens and continued for nine days at Eleusis. Each member participated, around the clock, in profoundly moving spiritual scenes. They drank a sacred drink and thereby infused into their mortal bodies the immortality promised by the divine mythos. They became actors, each one of them, as the sacred story was gradually revealed and reenacted and as the gods were brought to life again in the religious drama. Each member participated in personal teleocosmic salvation events and possessed a faith which carried him or her forward into the Unknown.

Myths such as the Eleusinian perform numerous functions: they explain natural events, provide a feeling of control over the uncontrollable, and reduce the threat of the unknown. They express our fears, longings, dreams, and requirements for existing in the human condition. They provide social coherence and cultural continuity, and when recounted in drama, song, dance, and around the campfire, they make for lively entertainment.

At one level the Eleusinian myth accounts for the cycle of the seasons. Spring is the time of fertility when crops grow and meadows turn green again; but summer and fall soon follow, and the winter kills all. Why? Because Persephone, who *is* life-energy, must die to this world for a season. The myth also puts death in its perspective: there can be no spring without winter, no day without night, no birth without death. The cycle of life is a whole; it does not come in parts.

Though myths are symbolic, their message and meaning is personal. The descent of Persephone into Hades is a symbolic death, but she is rescued to live again in the sunlight in an eternally recurring spring. This is a universal theme. In Mesopotamia the god Tammuz dies but is sought and found in the underworld by Ishtar who loved him. A similar story is told of Adonis who is found by Aphrodite, of Osiris and his resurrection by Isis, of the Shinto kami god Izanami who is pursued into the nether regions by her husband Izanagi. In every case the hero-god is persistently sought by someone who loved him, and that love insures that the hero/heroine is not lost to death but will return to life, inevitably. Persephone's annual death to Hades is a sacrifice, and because she dies and returns, all life will be renewed. Her death and return strips away the pain and fear of death for all believers. These are personal reassurances.

*If God did not exist it would be necessary to invent him.*
**VOLTAIRE**

*If there were not a Devil, we would have to invent him.*
**OSCAR WILDE**

*Great Quahootze! Let me live, not be sick, find the enemy, not be afraid of him, find him asleep, and kill many of him.*

***Nootka Indian prayer***

In the history of religions a myth is a social phenomenon. However, if a story performs the same functions for a single individual, then the word "myth" is still viable; here, too, it does not carry any implication of being false or "merely imagination."

Viktor Frankl recounts a conversation between himself and a rabbi.

He had lost his first wife and their six children in the concentration camp of Auschwitz where they were gassed, and now it turned out that his second wife was sterile. I observed that procreation is not the only meaning of life, for then life in itself would become meaningless, and something that in itself is meaningless cannot be rendered meaningful merely by its perpetuation. However, the rabbi evaluated his plight as an orthodox Jew in terms of despair that there was no son of his own who would ever say *Kaddish* [prayer for the dead] for him after his death.

But I would not give up. I made a last attempt to help him by inquiring whether he did not hope to see his children again in Heaven. However, my question was followed by an outburst of tears, and now the true reason of his despair came to the fore: he explained that his children, since they died as innocent martyrs, were found worthy of the highest place in Heaven, but as for himself he could not expect, as an old sinful man, to be assigned the same place. I did not give up but retorted, "Is it not conceivable, Rabbi, that precisely this was the meaning of your surviving your children; that you may be purified through these years of suffering, so that finally you, too, though not innocent like your children, may *become* worthy of joining them in Heaven? Is it not written in the Psalms that God preserves all your tears? So, perhaps none of your sufferings were in vain." For the first time in many years he found relief from his suffering, through the new point of view that I was able to open up to him.

When the *Apollo XIII* spacecraft was some fifty-six hours into its flight to the moon, an explosion in an oxygen tank blew open quad four of the service module.

| | |
|---|---|
| APOLLO. | OK, Houston, we've had a problem here. . . . We've had a main-B buss interval. |
| HOUSTON. | Roger, main-B interval. OK, stand by Thirteen. We're looking at it. |
| APOLLO. | OK, right now, Houston, the voltage is looking good. And we had a pretty large bang associated with the caution and warning there. . . . And we've got a main buss-A interval, too, showing. . . . |
| HOUSTON. | Stand by, Jim. . . . Thirteen, Houston. We'd like you to attempt to reconnect fuel cell one to main-A and fuel cell three to main-B. Verify that quad-delta is open. |
| APOLLO. | OK, Houston . . . I tried to reset, and fuel cells one and three are both showing gray flags. But they're both showing zip on the flows. |
| HOUSTON. | We copy. Thirteen, Houston, we'd like you to open circuit [to] fuel cell one. Leave two and three as is. |
| APOLLO. | OK, I'll get to work on that. |

A day later, after the spacecraft had looped around the moon and was limping homeward to earth, a course correction was necessary.

| | |
|---|---|
| HOUSTON. | Apollo Thirteen now 5,426 nautical miles out from the moon, traveling at a speed of 4,552 feet per second. . . . Less than thirty seconds away. . . . The engine is on. Stand by. . . . Ground confirms ignition. |
| APOLLO. | We're burning. Forty percent. |

*What we need is well-informed blind belief.*
*"Professor Harry Wolper"*
*Creator*

*The world is now without mysteries.*
PIERRE BERTHELOT (1885)

| | |
|---|---|
| HOUSTON. | Houston copies. Attitude looks good at this point. . . . One minute now into the burn. . . . We've gained 451 feet per second at this time. . . . All systems are looking good. Coming up on three minutes. . . . The on-board display shows less than a minute to go in the burn now. . . . Coming up on four minutes into the burn. . . . Ten seconds to go. |
| APOLLO. | Shut-down. |
| HOUSTON. | Roger, shut down. . . . The engine is off. We are at 79 hours 32 minutes into the flight. . . . 5,707 nautical miles out from the moon at this time. |
| APOLLO. | I'd say that was a good burn. |

The president proclaimed Sunday, April 19, a national Day of Thanksgiving for the safe return of the astronauts. Earlier in the week the California state senate had swiftly passed a resolution urging citizens to join in praying for the safe return of the *Apollo XIII* crew. Senator Murphy said he had learned that when you're in trouble it is wise not only to look around but to look up as well.

Frank Reynolds reported on ABC television: "In Rome the pope prayed, for which we are grateful; and in South Africa a witch doctor did the same thing, and we are grateful for that too."

The dean of a major metropolitan cathedral prayed: "We give thanks to Almighty God for the safe return of our astronauts. . . . We praise Thy Holy Name that Thou hast conducted in safety through the vast vistas of space, Thy servants James, Frederick, and John, and to return them to this good Earth, our home, where Thy children dwell."

Much later a newsman asked the astronauts if they were aware of the Infinite looking over them. Jack Swigert replied: "If you're asking me if I prayed, I certainly did. And I have no doubt that perhaps my prayers and the prayers of the rest of the people contributed an awful lot to getting us back."

*We would be a lot safer if the Government would take its money out of science and put it into astrology and the reading of palms. I used to think that science would save us. But only in superstition is there hope. I beg you to believe in the most ridiculous superstition of all: that humanity is at the center of the universe, the fulfiller or the frustrater of the grandest dreams of God Almighty. If you can believe that and make others believe it, human beings might stop treating each other like garbage.*

KURT VONNEGUT, JR.

*The lonelier I am, the more of a recluse I become, the greater is my love of myths.*

ARISTOTLE

## TELEOCOSMIC DRAMAS

People have rarely been able to shake the feeling that they are participants in a sweeping drama or a teleological universe and that their lives are a vital part of its plot and program. After all, our macrocosmic existence has a sort of storyline: we are born and proceed psychophysiologically through a series of "dramatic" developmental phases—childhood, adolescence, the stages of adulthood, and so on. All living things around us seem to share this developmental sequence. Even "nature" itself goes through a birth-life-death cycle: spring-summer-winter, dawn-day-night, the lunar phases. "Everything has a pattern"; it must also have meaning.

Of even greater significance is the fact that man is not alone. We exist in a universe filled with supernatural spirits with perhaps a Supreme Spirit, and these beings have human characteristics: they play, they fight, they needle one another and us with prankster-jokes, they scheme (note the Greek Olympians). They carry on a colorful social life with human beings (note, for instance, the love life of the shepherd god Krishna), and thus we humans become a part of their plans. We may even become the central concern or the principal characters in the ongoing cosmic drama.

*Saint Augustine was asked by a scoffer what God was doing before He created the world. Replied the great theologian: "He was busy creating hell for people who ask foolish questions."*

Our search for meaning is so intense that we are always more than willing to be cast in whatever teleocosmic dramas may exist.

Teleocosmic programs have existed in all of man's religions, from the simplest to the most sophisticated; and they have been developed in infinite detail by the Riddle-challenging minds of theologians and philosophers. Since our need to *interpret* everything is irrepressible, our selective interpretation of the events of life commonly take on a teleological structure. Somewhere we will find the basis for a story-line, a plot, a plan, and apocalyptic dramas, a goal-directed scheme, even a conspiracy (recall the Book of Job, for instance).

By merely being born we have been cast in the play, and our roles are to be taken seriously, for how well we perform our given roles affects the quality of our lives and determines our destiny. Little wonder, then, that we attempt again and again to clarify the teleocosmic plot so that we can better understand and play our roles.

The teleocosmic dramas most familiar to us are theological and have their origins in the Western religions: Zoroastrianism, Judaism, Christianity, and Islam. These Western dramas are *linear* and *historical.*

## APOCALYPTIC DRAMAS

*Joseph Campbell's life work was to seek out the themes common to all myths that reveal the human psyche's need for profound principles to live by.*
*Moyers: "You're talking about a search for the meaning of life?" I asked.*
*Campbell: "No, no, no," he said. "For the experience of being alive."*

**BILL MOYERS**
***The Power of Myth***

*I do not fear the habits, the politics, or the religion of any man anywhere in the world as long as he lives with an awe of God.*

**POPE JOHN XXIII**

We saw in an earlier chapter (5-1) that the metaphor of the drama has been used by philosophers of history to try to interpret the meaning and goal of human history (if either in fact exists). Just as a drama may move from the opening curtain through three or four acts that are subdivided into several scenes, and with a named *dramatis personae* who move the suspenseful plot through its tangles to the denouement, the unraveling of the plot, and a final curtain—this way of interpreting history provides us with a teleocosmic storyline in which we can participate, individually and collectively.

This metaphorical interpretation of history-as-drama has been developed to its highest point in the Western family of religions. The metaphor called for a moment in time for the opening curtain—such as 4004 B.C. (Archbishop Ussher's calculation) or 5737 B.C.E. (the Judaic calculation)—and a set moment for the descent of the final curtain—A.D. 156, 732, 1946, 1984, 2001, or 2026. Various elements of the plot along the way have been mapped out. Therefore, one's role in the drama should, in principle, be knowable; and if we can understand the plot, determine which scene we are currently playing, and read the signs of the times, then we'll know what is expected by the Playwright. By a correct reading of the plot (especially if we have a script) we'll know when the denouement is destined to occur.

These are personal linear-historical dramas, directed from above. They are, in the fullest sense, apocalyptic dramas, since much of the program—the background scenario, the props, the stagehands, as well as the Director—are off-stage, *above* space and time, carrying on the drama; while we humans are *in* space and time, moving along from scene to scene, playing out the story.

The teleocosmic drama held in common by the Western family of religions has its origins, as we would expect, in the world-view of the parent: Zoroastrianism.

Here the battlefield metaphor is first developed by the founder Zoroaster (c. 660 B.C.), and the teleocosmic drama—not unlike *Macbeth* or *Richard III*—is the account of a great battle. When this world was created by the Divine Mind, hosts of heavenly creatures of light also come into being: a Holy Spirit through whom the God of Light works his will; plus the Amesha Spentas (Immortal Holy Ones) and Yazatas (Angels), all led by Ahura Mazda, the Creator and Wise Lord of this world and the final judge and redeemer of history.

The evil counterparts are the daevas led by the supreme evil spirit, Angra Mainyu, the Lord of Darkness. Human history is a battlefield confrontation of the evil forces and heavenly forces, led by the "generals" Spenta Mainyu and

### "IT WAS A GOOD PLAY. . . ."

Finding Dr. Faustus in his study, Mephistopheles recounted to him the story of creation.

The endless praises of the choirs of angels had begun to grow wearisome; for, after all, did he not deserve their praise? Had he not given them endless joy? Would it not be more amusing to obtain undeserved praise, to be worshipped by beings whom he tortured? He smiled inwardly, and resolved that the great drama should be performed.

For countless ages the hot nebula whirled aimlessly through space. At length it began to take shape, the central mass threw off planets, the planets cooled, boiling seas and burning mountains heaved and tossed, from black masses of cloud hot sheets of rain deluged the barely solid crust. And now the first germ of life grew in the depths of the ocean, and developed rapidly in the fructifying warmth into vast forest trees, huge ferns springing from the damp mould, sea monsters breeding, fighting, devouring, and passing away. And from the monsters, as the play unfolded itself, Man was born, with the power of thought, the knowledge of good and evil, and the cruel thirst for worship. And Man saw that all is passing in this mad monstrous world, that all is struggling to snatch, at any cost, a few brief moments of life before Death's inexorable decree. And man said: "There is a hidden purpose, could we but fathom it, and the purpose is good; for we must reverence something, and in the visible world there is nothing worthy of reverence." And Man stood aside from the struggle, resolving that God intended harmony to come out of chaos by human efforts. And when he followed the instincts which God has transmitted to him from his ancestry of beasts of prey, he called it Sin, and asked God to forgive him. But he doubted whether he could be justly forgiven, until he invented a divine Plan by which God's wrath was to have been appeased. And seeing the present was bad, he made it yet worse, that thereby the future might be better. And he gave God thanks for the strength that enabled him to forgo even the joys that were possible. And God smiled; and when he saw that Man had become perfect in renunciation and worship, he sent another sun through the sky, which crashed into Man's sun; and all returned again to nebula.

"Yes," he murmured "it was a good play; I will have it performed again."

FROM BERTRAND RUSSELLS' *Mysticism and Logic*,
Doubleday Anchor, 1957, pp. 44–5.

Angra Mainyu. In this aeons-long struggle man is caught up in a cosmic conflagration and must decide, of his own free will, on which side he will take this stand.

For man, just as for the spiritual forces, the war is essentially a moral struggle. The individual has but one chance—one lifetime—during which to determine his or her destiny. Professor Robert Smith describes the scene in this fashion:

> The cardinal Zoroastrian moral principle that each man's soul is the seat of the war between good and evil sets the stage for man's plight. This war in the breast is of critical importance as the supreme Ahura Mazda is not unopposed in creation. Over against Asha (the Truth) is Druj (the Lie). Truth is confronted with Falsehood, Life with Death. The Good Spirit is opposed by the Bad Spirit. On this earthly battlefield, Angra Mainyu is set over against Spenta Mainyu in dualistic fashion. One must feel that they are co-equals in this earthly battle. However, the capacity of Angra Mainyu for mischief is boundless and the evil power he possesses is many times multiplied by the demons he creates to assist him. Without man's active participation on the side of Ahura Mazda, the world will not be a "brighter place to live" and man will not "be like God." Consequently, even in the working out of the Zoroastrian doctrine that the ultimate victory will be Ahura Mazda's, the first duty of every right-thinking man is to oppose and win the battle here and now.

And so, the battle progresses down through human history, man's only weapons being Truth and Righteousness, assisted by Good Thoughts, Good Words, and Good Deeds. Each is to "fight all the enemies of Good Mind as though they were his own enemies and as if he were the only warrior upon the battlefield."

All battles come to an end eventually, and the victorious vanquish the losers. Whole armies win and lose battles, but in the final analysis, all armies are composed only of individual soldiers. So, prior to any battle's final outcome, each soldier carries on his own personal struggle to the death, or life. So also for Zoroaster's spiritual warriors.

For the first time in world religion, the concept of eschatology dominates. The drama of individual judgment—a single scene, perhaps, in the great cosmic battle—occurs. If a warrior falls in battle, then his judgment takes place on the fourth day after his death. For three nights the soul of the dead sits at the head of its former body, meditating on its past deeds, words, and thoughts. During this time the soul is comforted (if it has been a righteous soul) by good angels, or tormented (if it has been wicked) by demons.

On the fourth day the soul makes its way to the Chinvat Bridge. There the soul holds the scales for the final weighing of merits and demerits. Judgment is rendered and sentence passed; the soul then walks onto the Bridge. The Zoroastrian text called the *Bundahishn* describes what then takes place in the center of the Bridge.

> There is a sharp edge which stands like a sword; . . . and Hell is below the Bridge. Then the soul is carried to where stands the sharp edge. Then, if it be righteous, the sharp edge presents its broad side. . . . If the soul be wicked, that sharp edge continues to stand edgewise, and does not give a passage. . . . With three steps which it (the soul) takes forward (evil thoughts, evil words, evil deeds) it is cut down from the head of the Bridge, and falls headlong into Hell.

*Faith brings us to truth; philosophy makes us grasp it; ethics makes us practice it; and ritual makes us one with it.*

JAGMANDERLAL JAINI

*Imagine how the Christian conscience would react to the idea that, behind the scenes, God and the Devil were the closest friends but had taken opposite sides in order to stage a great cosmic game. Yet this is rather much how things stood when the Book of Job was written, for here Satan is simply the counsel for the prosecution in the court of Heaven, as faithful a servant of the court as the advocatus diaboli at the Vatican.*

ALAN WATTS

When (the righteous soul) takes a step over the Chinvat Bridge, there comes to it a fragrant wind from Paradise, which smells of musk and ambergris, and that fragrance is more pleasant to it than any other pleasure.

When it reaches the middle of the Bridge, it beholds an apparition of such beauty that it hath never seen a figure of greater beauty. . . . And when the apparition appears to the soul, (the soul) speaks thus: "Who art thou with such beauty that a figure of greater beauty I have never seen?"

The apparition speaks (thus): "I am thine own good actions. I myself was good, but thine actions have made me better."

And the apparition embraces the soul, and they both depart with complete joy and ease into Paradise.

But if the soul be that of a wicked man . . . there blows to him an exceedingly foul wind from Hell [and] it sees an apparition of such extreme ugliness and frightfulness that it hath never seen one uglier and more unseemly. . . .

She speaks (thus): "I am thine own bad actions. I myself was ugly, and thou madest me worse day after day, and now thou hast thrown me and thine own self into misery and damnation, and we shall suffer punishment till the day of Resurrection."

And the apparition embraces it, and both fall headlong from the middle of the Chinvat Bridge and descend to Hell.

*An admirable piece of work infinitely more complex than the usual feminist novel. Gail Goodwin gives the devil his due, and he turns out to be, at least half the time, female.*

**JANET GARDNER**
*(from a book review of Violet Clay)*

The cosmological structure of the Zoroastrian drama was adopted by its offspring. Many elements were revised, but most remained intact just as they came from Zoroastrianism. In late Judaic theology, the archangels and angels fought on behalf of Yahweh and constituted the Forces of Light; while demons and evil spirits led by Satan made up the Forces of Darkness.

Hebrew religion had its own heritage before it was infused (after the sixth century B.C.) with Zoroastrian elements. That drama was now combined with the battlefield metaphor.

The Judaic teleocosmos began in the Garden of Eden. This was paradise and the tenants were perfect, companions and children of God. This is the opening scene of the drama, and the final scene is a return to Eden—to paradise and perfection. By the time the concept had been filled out with details the Hebrews had ceased to be a wandering tribe and had become a nation. The final scene of the plot was therefore envisioned as a "messianic age" in which the nation Israel, or at least a faithful Remnant, would reign supreme over all the earth. Truly it would be a paradise, for peace would be forever and prosperity would surpass belief. As one fragment of late Jewish literature put it, every grapevine

*Every person acquires the stature of the enemy he wrestles with.*

**NIKOS KAZANTZAKIS**

would bear a thousand clusters, and every cluster would bear a thousand grapes, and every grape would yield a gallon of wine.

Between these opening and closing scenes lies human existence as we know it, with suffering and death. It is only too likely that this is the only condition evolutionary man has ever known; but we find profound satisfaction in the conviction that there was a time when everything was all right and that we can anticipate a future setting in which all will be made right again.

Being a child of Judaism and a grandchild of Zoroastrianism, Christianity adopted about the same beginning to the teleocosmic drama—the garden paradise of Eden—and developed further the metaphor of the cosmic battlefield. Christians, however, added a new element. Along the timeline of human existence, there came a moment when life was suddenly given meaning by the intervention of the Creator deity himself. Until the advent of the redeemer god, the Christ, human suffering had been pointless; it counted for nothing. But after his appearance, human suffering became a "trial by fire" to create spiritually worthy souls who, collectively, would compose a "communion of saints" to bear witness until they could join together in the Kingdom of God. Nevertheless, human suffering will continue until the final act of the drama, when the Reign of God begins with the Parousia, the Return of the Messiah. "For the Lord himself, at the summons, when the archangel calls and God's trumpet sounds, will come down from heaven, and first those who died in union with Christ will rise; then those of us who are still living will be caught up with them on clouds into the air to meet the Lord, and so we shall be with the Lord forever" (I Thess. 4:16f.).

For early Christians (and adventist groups of any century) this is the joyous fulfillment of God's plan. With a climactic crescendo—full orchestra and chorus—it closes out the tragic drama and opens the Reign of God.

## FINAL CURTAIN—END OF DRAMA

THE ESCHATON In linear historical plots, we find that believers almost universally conclude that they are living near the end of the play. Their hope is that the dramatic last scene will be acted out during their lifetime. The history of apocalyptic thinking suggests that there are clearly identifiable psychological factors that make us want to live at the climax of the historical drama. We want to know, deep in our bones, that the bloody period of man's agony is about over; that peace, justice, and goodwill are about to prevail; that in our own lifetimes we can enjoy a modicum of happiness, To live prior to the denouement of the drama leaves me in a suspended state—like leaving an exciting motion picture before the ending.

Man is a creature of hope, and his teleocosmic dreams almost always foresee a future time when life will be good again and there will be no more fear, pain, loneliness, and death. It is here that man reveals his deepest pessimism. He intuits that he cannot bring about such conditions by himself, so he envisions supernatural beings who will appear on earth at their appointed times to call a drumroll for the last act of the teleocosmic drama.

Judaism looks forward to the coming of the *Messiah* (the "Anointed One").

---

*The current wave of interest in the occult is partly a way of saying that there is more to the world than the gods of science have let us know about. This isn't to say that the old gods are being restored; the new spirituality is as anti-institutional church as it is anti- or post-scientific. It is to say that we now know that there are more things in heaven and earth than are dreamt of in your philosophies, Aristotle, Thomas, and Newton.*

**EDWARD B. FISKE**

Ekam sat, viprā bahudhā vadanti. *(Truth is One; sages call it by various names.)*

**Vedic text**

*One who has experienced this will understand something of it; it cannot be more clearly expressed, since all that comes to pass in this state is so obscure. I can only say that the soul feels close to God and that there abides within it such a certainty that it cannot possibly do other than believe.*

**SAINT THERESA OF AVILA**

According to one interpretation, the nation Israel will be established by God as the Chosen Light to the gentiles to rule over them forever. According to another interpretation, the Son of Man will appear to usher in a spiritual Messianic Age.

Christians came to believe that *Jesus the Christ* (again, the specially "Anointed One") will return and supervise the Last Judgment, the separation of the righteous from the wicked. He will represent God himself when the Reign of God begins.

In Buddhism, *Maitreya* is at present a Buddha-in-the-making, waiting to come to earth in due time to inaugurate the final age and bring peace. In Hinduism, a messiah named *Kalki* will make his appearance on a white horse and brandishing a flaming sword. This savior, the tenth avatar of Vishnu, will save the righteous and destroy the wicked at the end of the fourth (hopelessly depraved) world period.

In Zoroastrianism, a messiah called *Soshyans* will appear in the final days and preside over a general resurrection. A flood of molten metal will pour across the earth purging the wicked of their evil but bathing the righteous in soothing balm. Ahura Mazda will hurl the Evil One, Ahriman, into a lake of fire, and the saved will then dwell together in a new heaven and a new earth, enjoying eternal peace. (Incidentally, in this particular drama, adults will remain forever at the age of forty and children at fifteen.)

In Islam, the Shi'ites await a messianic figure entitled the *Mahdi* to complete the task, begun by Muhammad, of carrying the message of salvation to all mankind. This "Divinely Guided One" will usher in a period of peace before the end of the world and the onset of the Last Judgment.

## UNITY IN DIVERSITY: ALL RELIGION IS ONE

There is a minority report within man's religions that contends that all religions are one. Most have said this because they wanted it to be so, but some of these claims are the result of personal experience with many religious faiths.

We are not today at the point of knowing whether "all religions are one." Certainly the various gods are thought to possess different characteristics. They behave differently and demand different responses from their worshipers.

Yet when people have experienced a religious odyssey, they commonly emerge with a feeling of oneness. It could be that our ultimate experiences are similar but become distorted in the process of interpretation. It might also be that certain universal psychophysical processes operate to produce similar experiences. Among these may be alpha rhythms and methods of self-hypnosis.

It may also be that one finds what one looks for. If he or she wishes to find the differences in the many religions of man, they can be found; but if one searches for similarities underlying man's religious approaches to the Riddle of Life, they too are there and can be found.

One of the more successful attempts to clarify the "highest common factors" contained in man's great religions has been called "the Perennial Philosophy." Aldous Huxley described four such elements from which we might infer that, however varied the paths we travel, man's religious quest is quintessentially One.

*Indeed, I do not forget that my voice is but one voice, my experience a mere drop in the sea, my knowledge no greater than the visual field in a microscope, my mind's eye a mirror that reflects a small corner of the world, and my ideas—a subjective confession.*

CARL G. JUNG

*Without God, we cannot. Without us, God will not.*

SAINT AUGUSTINE

1. This world as we conceptualize and experience it is a manifestation of a greater reality, a "Divine Ground of Being." All the realities of experience, both mental and material, are merely "bits and fragments" of that Ultimate Reality. They constitute only limited, angular glimpses of that Divine Ground.

2. Human beings can acquire knowledge *about* that Divine Ground, but such knowledge is relatively unimportant. Of greater significance is the fact that we can enter into a direct intuitive knowledge of it, a knowledge involving our whole being and not merely our conceptualizing intellects. This is a mystical knowing that unites the knower with the Known, or the known with the Knower.

3. In his very nature, man is a duality. We are composed of ephemeral elements (body, ego-self, data bits, memory) and eternal essence (soul, atman, "divine spark"). The ephemeral elements are temporal and temporary, but the eternal essence can become One with the Divine Ground of Being.

4. The singular goal of human existence on earth is for each individual to come to know the eternal essence of his being and to identify it more and more closely with the Divine Ground of all Being.

Huxley considered the Perennial Philosophy to be one of the great insights in the history of human understanding, and his judgment is still shared by many present-day philosophers of religion. Huxley's previsions are clear and strong:

> In existing circumstances there is not the slightest chance that any of the traditional religions will obtain universal acceptance. Europeans and Americans will see no reason for being converted to Hinduism, say, or Buddhism. And the people of Asia can hardly be expected to renounce their own traditions for the Christianity professed, often sincerely, by the imperialists who, for four hundred years and more, have been systematically attacking, exploiting and oppressing, and are now trying to finish off the work of destruction by "educating" them. But happily there is the Highest Common Factor of all religions, the Perennial Philosophy which has always and everywhere been the metaphysical system of the prophets, saints and sages. it is perfectly possible for people to remain good Christians, Hindus, Buddhists or Moslems and yet to be united in full agreement on the basic doctrines of the Perennial Philosophy.

> There was a man who worshiped Shiva but hated all other deities. One day Shiva appeared to him and said, "I shall not be pleased with thee so long as thou hatest the other gods." The man was inexorable. After a few days Shiva again appeared to him and said, "I shall never be pleased with thee so long as thou hatest." The man kept silent. After a few days Shiva again appeared to him. This time he appeared as Harihar, namely, one side of his body was that of Shiva, and the other side that of Vishnu. The man was half pleased and half displeased. He laid his offerings on the side representing Shiva, and did not offer anything to the side representing Vishnu. Then Shiva said, "Thy bigotry is unconquerable. I, by assuming this dual aspect, tried to convince thee that all gods and goddesses are but various aspects of the one Absolute Brahman."

RAMAKRISHNA

*When hope is taken away from a people, moral degeneration quickly follows.*

PEARL S. BUCK

*It's not surprising, Sir. Sharing an orbit with God is no small experience.*

*"Counselor Troi"*
*Star Trek/TNG*

The Muslim mystic Ibn Arabi is quoted as saying:

> There was a time when I took it amiss in my companion if his religion was not like mine, but now my heart admits every form. It is a pasture of gazelles, a cloister for monks, a temple for idols, a Ka´aba for the pilgrim, the tables of the Law, and the scared book of the Quran. Love alone is my religion, and whithersoever man's camels turn, it is *my* religion and *my* faith.

## REFLECTIONS

1  This chapter offers a working definition of "religion" as "man's involvement in the meaning of his existence." After reflection on this definition along with others on pp. 551-552, develop the best definition you can of religion as you personally understand it. Can you defend, rationally and empirically, each part of your definition?

2  Note the anthropologist Tylor's observation of the use of ceremonies and ritual by maritime communities (see marginal quote on p. 553). What inference can you make from such religious practice?

3  How would you respond to the question asked in the Box on p. 553: "How does one determine whether prayers are answered if not in terms of results?" Was Scipio's prayer answered?

4  Recall your reflections upon the story of the Indian physicist/priest (p. 3) who described the eclipse in terms of celestial mechanics and then proceeded to chant to the goddess Kali to make the eclipse go away. Is there a similar incompatibility of world-views in the story of the *Apollo XIII* explosion and the subsequent behavior of astronauts and others (pp. 558-559)? Can you apply the conclusions you reached regarding the Indian's dilemma to the Apollo incident?

5  Study the many varied meanings attached to the Greek word *pneuma* in ancient times (p. 554-Box). What can you conclude from a comparison of the multiple English translations of this one word?

6  What is the function of the concept of "spirit-possession"?

7  Understanding the more technical usage of the word *myth* is important. So, what psychological and epistemic function does *myth* refer to? What about the beliefs held by the rabbi described by Frankl—would you call these beliefs myths? What exactly are you saying about his beliefs?

8  What are your thoughts and second-thoughts after reading the list of future saviors (pp. 564–565)?

9  After your first startled reaction to Kurt Vonnegut's plea on p. 559 (see marginal quote) can you bring yourself to agree with him? Can you at least build a hypothetical case for what he is saying?

10  List some of the human needs that are met by teleocosmic dramas. Could we live without such dramas? Would our lives be richer without them or impoverished without them?

## ULTIMATE
## REALITY

8
2

## ULTIMATE QUESTIONS

The Ethiopians make their gods black-skinned and snub-nosed; the Thracians say theirs have blue eyes and red hair. If oxen and horses had hands and could draw with their hands and make works of art just as men do, then horses would draw their gods to look like horses, and oxen like oxen—each would make their bodies in the image of their own.

XENOPHANES

*Non ridere, non lugere, neque detestari, sed intelligere. Not to laugh, not to lament, not to curse, but to understand.*
BARUCH SPINOZA

The questions that we ask about Ultimate Reality are always phrased in terms of our own particular world-view, of course; and the questions that have meaning to a Hindu or Buddhist may be meaningless to a Christian or Muslim. Problems about Ultimate Reality cannot be made intelligible apart from the thought framework within which they are posed.

The questions we in the West ask are deceptively simple: Does God exist? What is he like? How can we know what he wants of us?

In Eastern religion, the Hindu might ask: What is the true nature of the Ultimate Reality that lies beyond the gods? Is the world of physical matter merely illusion? How can I attain liberation from the round of rebirths? The Buddhist might ask: Is it really true, as the Buddha claimed, that to exist is to suffer? If so, how can I escape suffering and attain enlightenment?

Other, Far Eastern worshipers might ask: What is the true way of life—the Tao? How can I best seek the Tao so that my life may be peaceful and full? What does Heaven want of me?

Philosophy is neither theology—which attempts to make religion intellectually meaningful—nor evangelism—which attempts to persuade others to believe. Rather, philosophy's concerns are primarily metaphysical and epistemological. *Metaphysical:* What is Ultimate Reality? How many orders of reality

*Most intellectual people do not believe in God, but they fear him just the same.*
WILHELM REICH

exist? Is there a supernatural order of reality? Do deities and spirits exist? Does God exist? In fact, what exactly is meant by such terms? *Epistemological:* Can we humans who belong to the natural order know that which belongs to the supernatural order? If so, how? Does God (or do the gods) "reveal"? Does he reveal a person (as some Christian theologians claim) or a data content? How can we be sure about the source of supernatural fact-claims mediated through human beings?

## THE PROBLEM OF DIVINE KNOWLEDGE

The images of deity that men hold are largely the product of particular circumstances of time and place. Western religions of Near Eastern origin conceive deity as male. We ask if *he* exists and we speak of a *father*-god. The majority of men, however, have imagined their deities to be feminine, and to these goddesses they have prayed for intercession, tender care, love, and life-generating energies.

The Judeo-Christian God is necessarily masculine since our god-concepts originated in the Bedouin sheikdoms that wandered out of the Arabian desert into the Fertile Crescent. The gods of these nomadic clans were modeled after the sheik chieftain. They were strongly masculine deities, associated with the aggressive forces of nature—volcanoes, earthquakes, storms—and with intertribal battles. Rarely, if ever, does the concept of a female deity evolve in a Bedouin society with patriarchal dominance. The early Hebrew god Yahweh exhibits the characteristics of the sheik chieftain. He is authoritarian in monitoring the loyalty pledged to him by his followers. He is stern, demanding, and quick to punish backsliding. He is a "jealous God" who will tolerate no competition from other gods. This early Hebraic world was patriarchal and the survival qualities necessary in a deity were authority and firmness; he must be quick to anger and of mighty power in battle. The blood covenant binding the deity to his tribe (Exodus 24:4–8) is basically Bedouin: he will be their leader and protector as long as they obey and "keep the covenant."

By contrast, where sprawling vineyards cover the hillsides and the valleys shelter fields of grain and fruit trees, here we are more likely to find the goddesses and their consorts. In gentler climes and social settings, the qualities associated with feminine roles—love, fertility, nurturance—are more valued than the fearsome, bellicose qualities of the desert deities. These female deities are at once Earth Mothers, fertility goddesses, and sacred virgins. As Earth Mothers they generate the life-giving forces that underlie the birth and growth of all living things. As fertility goddesses they symbolize conception, and by means of mystery rites, temple prostitution, and spring festivals, they can be persuaded to stimulate fertility in man's clans, flocks, and crops. As eternal virgin goddesses their primary purpose is to symbolize purity and to merit the devotion of mortal men.

When deities are considered to be male, then they frequently mate with mortal women. Zeus was forever entangled in amorous affairs, and the shepherd-god Krishna spent much of his time in the company of beautiful milkmaids. In Zoroastrian myth, the seed of Zoroaster, preserved for thousands of years in a crystal-pure lake, will impregnate three virgins who are to appear at intervals of three thousand years; they will give birth to the savior gods for each period of human history, the last being Soshyans, who will inaugurate the Last Judgment.

In Buddhist myth, a male Bodhisattva (savior-being) placed his reflection in the womb of Queen Maya. In her tenth month of pregnancy she gave birth to the Buddha from her right side. Her case was both a virgin conception and a virgin birth. We can follow the sequence of historical development by inverting this order of thinking: Buddhist apologists began with the undeniable facts of the Buddha's existence and his birth from a mortal mother. Since the Buddha's paternity was known (from doctrinal tradition) to have been divine, the supernatural parent must, of course, be male. This is a rather obvious line of logic. In similar fashion, the Holy Spirit that impregnated the Virgin Mary must be conceived in human minds as an aspect of the masculine Father-God.

This enigma—the virgin conception by Mary—has produced more doctrines and convened more councils than any other event in Western history. The idea of a male deity mating with a mortal maiden to produce what would logically be a God-man—half God, half man—is a common enough motif in man's religions, but the soteriological complexities of the Christian version required centuries of analysis and debate. Is this "son of God" himself man or God or both? Throughout the first four centuries of Christianity there were churchmen who held that he was *solely* God or *solely* man, but the doctrine that he was both God and man finally prevailed. This conclusion, however, merely posed further problems. If he was both, then how did his divine nature relate to his human nature? And what was the relationship of the divine nature in Jesus to the divine nature in the Father? (The Council of Nicea settled these questions in A.D. 325; the churchmen reaffirmed his dual nature and concluded that the divine nature in the Son and the Father were "in essence" the same.) What about will? If he was both God and man, did he have two distinct wills? (This problem—the "monothelite" controversy—was settled at a council in Constantinople in A.D. 681: Jesus has two wills, the divine and the human, but the human will was subservient in all things to his divine will.) And what of Mary? If Jesus was wholly God as well as wholly man, does this

> *It both is and is not; neither is, nor is not.*
>
> THE BUDDHA

> *Not female, nor yet male is it, neither is it neuter. Whatever body it assumes, through that body it is served.*
>
> *The Upanishads*

*The rash assertion that "God made man in His own image" is ticking like a time bomb at the foundations of many faiths, and as the hierarchy of the universe is disclosed to us, we may have to recognize this chilling truth: if there are any gods whose chief concern is man, they cannot be very important gods.*

ARTHUR C. CLARKE

not mean that Mary was the mother of God? (The Council of Ephesus in A.D. 431 answered yes. She is properly designated *Theotokos,* "the bearer of God.") (Saint Jerome, who is best known for his translation of the Scriptures into Latin [the *Vulgate*], had a friend named Paula whose daughter Eustochium took the vows of a nun and thus became "a bride of Christ." Jerome considered Mary to be the Mother of God, and he habitually addressed Paula as the mother-in-law of God. This is not the only case, however, where a god had a mother-in-law. Demeter, for instance, was Pluto's mother-in-law after Persephone became the bride of the king of Hades.)

When we find ourselves theologically entangled in mundane human relationships such as these, it is easy to lose our philosophical perspective. But if we can survive the subtleties of such debates, we may feel that our anthropomorphizing has gone too far. Xenophanes observed very early that "mortals suppose that the gods have been born, that they have voices and bodies and wear clothing like men"; he complained that "Homer and Hesiod attributed to the gods all sorts of actions that when done by men are disreputable and deserving of blame—such lawless deeds as theft, adultery, and mutual deception."

The supernatural figures of our great living religions may be ethically and spiritually nobler, but their anthropomorphic qualities are just as human as those shared by the Olympian gods and goddesses.

Much thought has been given to the problem of divine knowledge by other Western philosophers who were aware of our anthropomorphic manner of thinking.

Philo of Alexandria (fl. c. A.D. 40) contended that *no* qualities conceivable by the human mind can be attributed to God. God, that is, cannot be *thought* about. Whenever we think we are thinking about God, we are merely "deifying" human qualities. All we can do, Philo concluded, is to say what God is not.

Around the year A.D. 500 an anonymous writer called Pseudo-Dionysius (his writings were for a time attributed to a certain Dionysius mentioned by Saint Paul) decided that there are two ways of knowing God. Following the positive way, we can collect the qualitative concepts that we apply to man—man is good, wise, loving, alive, and so forth—and attribute these qualities in their ultimate form to the divine nature. That is, God is perfect goodness, wisdom, love, being, and so on. Since God is perfect, we can be sure that we are correct in attributing perfect qualities to God even though we cannot ourselves *conceive* these perfect qualities. (What exactly is "perfect wisdom" or "perfect being"?) But there is a second way of knowing—the negative way. We can collect in our minds all the qualities that we are sure God cannot possess: God is not corporeal matter; he is not evil; he cannot hate, cheat, deceive, and so on. By a process of "remotion" all these qualities are removed from our thinking about God. Thus, as we proceed to subtract all qualities that God cannot possess, we are left with an increasingly accurate nonconcept of God. By the "darkness of unknowing" we can arrive at a mystical notion of what God in fact is.

*In the multiplicity of his gods man does not merely behold the outward divinity of natural objects and forces but also perceives himself in the concrete diversity and distinction of his functions. . . . Over and over again we thus find confirmation of the fact that man can apprehend his own being only insofar as he can make it visible in the image of his gods. . . .*

ERNST CASSIRER

*There is no Hindu and there is no Muslim.*

GURU NANAK

## ARGUMENTS FOR THE EXISTENCE OF GOD

**1. THE COSMOLOGICAL ARGUMENT** In our Western philosophical tradition, there have been several attempts to prove, rationally or empirically, that

God exists. At least three are noteworthy. These are the cosmological, ontological, and teleological arguments for the existence of God.

The *cosmological argument* was first stated by Aristotle and further developed by Thomas Aquinas (1225–1274). The argument attempts to prove logically that there must be an "unmoved mover" and that such a force is in fact what we have thought of as God.

We live in a world of matter-in-motion. This is an obvious empirical fact. Aquinas observed that if an object is at rest, then it is not in motion; but any object at rest is potentially in motion. Motion is the actualized potential of a particular object. All objects at rest are potentially in motion, but no object will be activated into motion unless it is caused to move by something that is actually moving. No object at rest can be activated by another object at rest, nor can an object at rest set itself in motion. This means simply that every object in motion was set in motion by something else; but that something else must have been set in motion by something before it, and so on. Therefore we are confronted with an infinite series of objects, each of which actualizes the potential motion of the next in the series. But if we attempt to account for motion by going back in our minds in an infinite regression, we find ourselves in a logical contradiction—a dead end. Something *must* start the series, and this something, from a purely logical standpoint, must be something without an antecedent activator. Such an activator must necessarily be pure actuality and not potential. Whatever this pure actuality is, it is the "unmoved mover" which, writes Thomas, "everyone understands to be God."

*Man has never been the same since God died,*
*He has taken it very hard.*
*Why, you'd think it was only yesterday*
*The way he takes it.*
  EDNA ST. VINCENT MILLAY
  *"Conversation at Midnight"*

*Every saint has a past and every sinner a future.*
  OSCAR WILDE

**2. THE ONTOLOGICAL ARGUMENT** The *ontological argument* was developed by Anselm of Canterbury (1033–1109). Anselm is sometimes called the father of Scholastic philosophy, that movement of the twelfth and thirteenth centuries which rekindled intellectual activity in the West after the Dark Ages. Saint Anselm was a devoutly religious Benedictine monk whose writings, debates, and pastoral leadership greatly influenced his time.

While Thomas's cosmological argument for God is founded upon an empirical observation of matter-in-motion, Anselm's argument has no such empirical referent. It attempts to prove God's existence from the nature of thought alone. For several weeks Anselm had been convinced that such a proof might be possible. He devoted much thought and prayer to it and finally, late one night during vigils, his proof of God's existence stood clearly before his mind. Anselm was sure that he knew, by thought alone, that God exists—indeed, that God *has* to exist. Here is his argument:

The mind has a concept of a Being than which nothing greater can be conceived. This Being, than which nothing greater can be conceived, must exist in reality as well as in thought. For if it existed only in thought (subjectively), then it would be possible for the mind to conceive of an even greater being who exists in reality (objectively) as well as in thought, and this being would be greater. But this is impossible. Therefore, this Being, than which nothing greater can be conceived, must exist in reality as well as in thought. And this Being is God.

Anselm was elated that he could prove rationally what he already knew to be true. To his proof, he appended a thankful prayer to God "because through

*Faith is best defined as expecting the best until the worst has been proved.*
  GERALD ENSLEY

your divine illumination I now so understand that which, through your generous gift, I formerly believed. . . ." He continued: "So truly dost thou exist, O Lord God, both in thought and in fact, that it is impossible for the minds of Thy creatures not to know of Thine existence."

**3. THE TELEOLOGICAL ARGUMENT** The *teleological argument* for the existence of God is based on the apparent order and design of nature and cosmos, and on the purposive nature of evolution.

From earliest times man has wondered about the cyclical motions of the stars and planets, the endless rounds of days and seasons, the consistency of nature's operations, and the rhythmic patterns of order in the world about him. Greek thinkers used the word *logos* (literally, "word") to account for this order. This logos might be thought of as a kind of "world reason," an organizing force, possibly emanating from a divine mind, which binds all the dynamic elements of nature into a working order.

Today, of course, we know that the cosmos has more order than the ancients could have imagined, an order that can be described in terms of mathematical equations, physical and chemical formulas, and psychobiological processes. Living organisms have distinctive metabolic and life-cycle rhythms, largely determined for each by an incredibly complicated DNA code. Sub-atomic studies have revealed the complex configurations of energy patterns. We also know that cosmic processes—involving suns, galaxies, and perhaps even the pulsating universe itself—run through ordered sequences resembling birth, life, and death.

The question: Can all this beautiful harmony exist apart from an ordering intelligence, a mind that would be the creator and sustainer of this order? The Stoics, among others, drew a simple analogy. The human mind is fundamentally an organizer: it orders, systematizes, labels, and stores bits of experience for later use. Our minds order our experiences of reality. Likewise, there must be a Cosmic Mind pervading reality itself and operating toward similar ends. The ordered world as we know it cannot be accounted for apart from the ordering of a Cosmic Intelligence.

The teleological argument—as the word *teleology* indicates—has to do with direction or destiny; and it was the development of life and the movement of evolution that seemed to demonstrate most clearly the possibility of a directive intelligence.

This argument was given careful scrutiny by the biologist Lecomte du Noüy in his book *Human Destiny.* Du Noüy calculated that according to the laws of probability the emergence of living organisms from inorganic molecules would have been less than one in a hundred billion. He concludes that life could only begin through an act of a purposive intelligence, and that the movement of evolution is, in his word, "telefinalistic."

> *Man needs the unfathomable and the infinite just as much as he does the small planet which he inhabits.*
>
> **DOSTOEVSKY**

Telefinality orients the march of evolution as a whole and has acted, ever since the appearance of life on earth, as a distant directing force tending to develop a being endowed with a conscience, a spiritually and morally perfect being. To attain its goal, this force acts on the laws of the inorganized world in such a way that the normal play of the second law of thermodynamics is always deflected in the same direction, a direction forbidden to inert matter and leading to ever greater dissymmetries, ever more "improbable" states.

## THE DEATH(S) OF GOD(S)

Is God dead? Friedrich Nietzsche believed so.

Have you not heard of that madman who lit a lantern in the bright morning hours, ran to the market place, and cried incessantly, "I seek God! I seek God!" As many of those who do not believe in God were standing around just then, he provoked much laughter. Why, did he get lost? said one. Did he lose his way like a child? said another. Or is he hiding? Is he afraid of us? Has he gone on a voyage? or emigrated? Thus they yelled and laughed. The madman jumped into their midst and pierced them with his glances.

"Whither is God" he cried. "I shall tell you. *We have killed him*—you and I. All of us are his murderers. . . . God is dead. God remains dead. And we have killed him. How shall we, the murderers of all murderers, comfort ourselves? What was holiest and most powerful of all that the world has yet owned has bled to death under our knives. Who will wipe this blood off us? What water is there for us to clean ourselves? What festivals of atonement, what sacred games shall we have to invent? Is not the greatness of this deed too great for us? Must not we ourselves become gods simply to seem worthy of it? There has never been a greater deed; and whoever will be born after us—for the sake of this deed he will be part of a higher history than all history hitherto."

Here the madman fell silent and looked again at his listeners; and they too were silent and stared at him in astonishment. At last he threw his lantern on the ground, and it broke and went out. "I come too early," he said then; "my time has not come yet. This tremendous event is still on its way, still wandering—it has not yet reached the ears of man. . . ."

It has been related further that on that same day the madman entered divers churches and there sang his *requiem aeternam deo.* Led out and called to account, he is said to have replied each time, "What are these churches now if they are not the tombs and sepulchers of God?"

Friedrich Nietzsche (1844–1900)

*Even for a god there is a point of no return. . . .*

**Star Trek**, NBC-TV

*Almost all philosophers have confused ideas of things. They speak of material things in spiritual terms, and of spiritual things in material terms.*

**BLAISE PASCAL**

Nietzsche and others have presaged the death of God. But what does such a statement mean? A modern death-of-God theologian, William Hamilton, rhetorically asks, "Is there really an event properly called 'the death of God'? Or is the current chatter enveloping the phrase simply another of the many non-events afflicting our time?" He answers: "No. The death of God has happened. To those of us with gods, and to those without. To the indifferent, the cynical and the fanatical. God is dead, whatever that means."

To Nietzsche it meant that the very concept of God as traditionally conceived in Western thought no longer has the power, as it once did, to transform human life. Belief in a God is still held by individuals, and countless others pay lip service to god doctrines. But these beliefs no longer do what beliefs are supposed to do: to grip one's very existence with ultimate truths; to establish one firmly in a meaningful teleocosmic plan; to transform character and hence the quality of one's whole life; to make one feel special and of

---

### "Clearly I Miss Him . . ."

"But if I live later, I will try to live in such a way, doing no harm to any one, that it will be forgiven."

"By whom?"

"Who knows? Since we do not have God here any more, neither His Son nor the Holy Ghost, who forgives? I do not know."

"You have not God any more?"

"No. Man. Certainly not. If there were God, never would He have permitted what I have seen with my eyes. Let *them* have God."

"They claim Him."

"Clearly I miss Him, having been brought up in religion. But now a man must be responsible to himself."

"Then it is thyself who will forgive thee for killing."

"I believe so," Anselmo said.

Ernest Hemingway
*For Whom the Bell Tolls*

---

infinite worth; to provide secure and final answers to questions about living and dying.

World-views have changed. Spirits and demons have died: we now account for human behavior in terms of operant conditioning and motivation. The Devil has died: a "devil" is nothing more than a mental abstraction that we have personified and objectified. And a capricious, all-too-human deity can no longer command our devotion. We have seen too many gods; our anthropomorphic habits are too obvious to be brushed aside. God, too, is dead.

*Politics and religion are obsolete; the time has come for science and spirituality.*

Vinobe Bhave

If we scan the pantheon of man's divinities, we discover deicides without end. Sooner or later, it seems, all the gods of men die.

There was a time when Egyptian fellahin knew that King Osiris weighed the hearts of men before they could enter into his kingdom, and Isis the Queen was a benefactress to all—revealing laws, rendering justice, calming the sea, timing the harvests, and persuading men and women to love each other.

The sky god Varuna was able to see into the hearts of his Aryan worshipers and cast away their sins. The redeemer god Balder returned each spring to the snow-laden northland and brought with him light and warmth. The mystery gods Dionysus, Orpheus, and Mithras promised immortality to all who pledged their loyalty and performed the proper rites. From his temple on the slopes of Mount Parnassus the bright sun-god Apollo offered divine wisdom and worldly counsel to faithful pilgrims.

*Now that Starglider has effectively destroyed all traditional religions, we can at last pay serious attention to the concept of God.*

Arthur C. Clarke
*"Dr. Choam Goldberg"*
*The Fountains of Paradise*

The beautiful virgin goddess Artemis protected wandering children and assuaged the pain of women in childbirth. Persephone brought health and prosperity to her devotees, then led them down to the nether realm where she was queen. The virgin Athena, proud and protective, was close to the hearts of her Athenian worshipers.

The virgin-born Quetzalcoatl who, in Nahuatl mysteries, was a man become god, presented himself as an example of man's purest aspiration, having burned himself in a fire to purge away his sin. Lord Mazda proffered aid and eternal life to righteous Zoroastrians who believed in Spenta Mainyu (the Holy Spirit) and in the Amesha Spentas (the Immortal Ones—angel-like beings and divine messengers).

As long as there were followers who believed in them, all these gods and goddesses could transform lives. But when, with the passing of the centuries, there were no longer any believers, then no more lives were transformed, no more guilt forgiven, no more souls saved.

In the pantheon of deceased gods and goddesses are enshrined the most awesome names ever uttered by the suppliant voices of mortal men and women: Adonis, Aphrodite, Apollo, Aton, Bacchus, Balder, Cybele, Demeter, Diana, Dionysus, El, Fortuna, Gaia, Hel, Hercules, Indra, Ishtar, Isis, Janus, Jupiter, Marduk, Mars, Nanna, Orpheus, Osiris, Persephone, Quetzalcoatl, Rudra, Saturnus, Shamash, Tammuz, Thor, Uranus, Varuna, Venus, Wotan, Xochipilli, Zagreus, Zeus. . . .

One of the tasks of a theologian is to update the faith and make it intelligible to his contemporaries. Numerous attempts have been made to deal with the problem of God-knowledge in modern terms. A notable example is that of Dr. Paul Tillich.

Tillich contended that we cannot *know* anything about God, but this limitation does not prevent God's working in our lives. Knowing about him and experiencing him are hardly the same. God is "the ground of our being." We exist, and objects exist; but "existence" is a human category of thought, and God is beyond existence. He is pure being itself.

But, Tillich notes, we are caught in a human predicament that we had best accept. It is true that we cannot conceive the inconceivable or speak the unspeakable. But if we think or speak at all, then we must think in concepts and speak with language symbols. Therefore, we must continue to do just this, but with the full understanding that our thoughts and words refer to nothing whatever that is real. There is nothing to be gained by fighting our predicament, says Tillich. Rather, we must accept it and live within its confines. Let's continue to speak of God as "he" (or in other traditions as "she" or "it"); we can continue to think of God as "knowing," "seeing," "hearing," "loving," and so on. These are pragmatic modes of thinking and feeling. Man is a symbolic creature, and we can live with our condition providing we don't confuse symbol and reality. Such words as *God* and *he* are indispensable as symbols, but we must never mistake them for realities.

The only "God" that "exists" is beyond the gods of man. Since all our thinking ultimately is symbolic, Christians can continue to think of the Christ as the "new man" described by Paul, the whole man whose existence and essence have become one. He symbolizes the ultimate possibilities for each of us. It is only by accepting these symbols for what they truly are—as ontological aspects of the human condition—that we can come to terms with our existence and express our "ultimate concern for the Ultimate."

*We must be brave enough to declare that every culture must create its own God idea rather than rely upon outworn tradition.*

JOSHUA LOTH LIEBMAN

Carl Gustav Jung (1875–1961)

*Cause me to pass from the unreal to the real, from darkness to light, from death to immortality.*
**Brihadaranyaka I.3/28**

Religious experience is absolute. It is indisputable. You can only say that you have never had such an experience and your opponent will say: "Sorry, I have." And there your discussion will come to an end. No matter what the world thinks about religious experience, the one who has it possesses the great treasure of a thing that has provided him with a source of life, meaning and beauty and that has given a new splendor to the world and to mankind. He had pistis [faith] and peace. Where is the criterium by which you could say that such a life is not legitimate, that such experience is not valid and that such pistis is mere illusion? Is there, as a matter of fact, any better truth about ultimate things than the one that helps you to live?

CARL G. JUNG

## REFLECTIONS

1    How do philosophical concerns with religion differ from theological and evangelical concerns (p. 569)?

2    We could analyze ad infinitum "the problem of divine knowledge" and the way we anthropomorphize our deities. We have created literally millions of gods and goddesses "in the image of man" (and woman). No thinker has expressed the problem better than the Greek philosopher Xenophanes (p. 569). Is the human habit of anthropomorphizing a new insight for you, or have you previously worked through the problem? Do you still accept a deity image with anthropomorphic qualities? If you answer Yes, then how do you reconcile your imagery with our anthropomorphic predicament?

3    Analyze critically the cosmological argument developed by Aristotle and Aquinas (pp. 572–573). What are the basic assumptions upon which the argument rests? What are its logical fallacies, if any? After analysis, does it remain to you a persuasive argument for the existence of God?

4    Analyze critically the ontological argument of St. Anselm (p. 573). What implicit assumptions are behind the argument? What are its major fallacies? In the final analysis, what is its persuasion power to you personally?

5    Analyze critically the teleological argument for God's existence (pp. 574–575). What fallacies are involved in this argument, if any? Where would you go for hard data to help clarify the question and to answer it? Is the argument convincing?

6    On the subject of "the death of God," read again pp. 575–577. What are the death-of-God theologians saying to us? (Try to avoid easy, simplistic answers.) Are they correct, in your opinion? How could you check their fact-claims or value judgments to decide if they are correct?

7    What is your assessment of the conviction of Dr. Carl Jung, the Swiss depth-psychologist (p. 578), that "religious experience is absolute. It is indisputable. . . ."?

8    To the best of your knowledge, and after pondering this chapter, what is the nature of Ultimate Reality? Can it be described in mere human words? Is

it material? Is it natural but nonmaterial? Is it personal (that is, person-like)? Does it take the form of deity? If so, do you think this deity has particular characteristics such as masculinity or femininity? What kinds of *human experiences* might be interpreted as indicators of the existence and/or nature of this Ultimate Reality? (Take care, all along the way, to offer rational arguments or empirical evidence in support of your ideas; or, if this is not possible, then label carefully which ideas are personal beliefs.)

# THOMAS MERTON

## *The Other Side of Kanchenjunga*

On October 15, 1968, Thomas Merton, an American Catholic monk from a Trappist monastery in Kentucky, began a spiritual journey. "I am going home," he wrote in his journal, "to a home where I have never been in this body. . . ."

In actual fact, he was sitting in a Pan Am jet on the runway of the San Francisco International Airport waiting for takeoff. Destination: Southeast Asia. It was early morning, with the taxiing planes performing a "slow ballet of big tail fins in the sun."

The moment of take-off was ecstatic. . . . We left the ground—I with Christian mantras and a great sense of destiny, of being at last on my true way after years of waiting and wondering and fooling around. May I not come back without having settled the great affair.

This trip would carry him—while still "in the body"—through unscheduled adventures in India, Sri Lanka, and Thailand. In Bangkok the great affair would be settled.

The world first knew of Thomas Merton in 1948 when his autobiographical novel, *The Seven Storey Mountain*, revealed who he was and how he became a Trappist.

"In a year of a great war and down in the shadow of some French mountains on the border of Spain, I came into the world"—1915. "That world was the picture of Hell, full of men like myself, loving God and yet hating Him; born to love Him, living instead in fear and hopeless self-contradictory hungers."

His parents were artists—strong-willed, independent, avant-garde—and they shaped their son's inner world before their early deaths, his mother when he was six, his father when he was fifteen. From both came a Dionysian drive "for work and vision and enjoyment of expression." His mother was filled with "insatiable dreams" and a "great ambition after perfection"; she was "worried, precise, quick, critical of me, her son," and intellectually demanding. She kept a detailed diary in which she chronicled her son's every move.

Merton's youth was disturbed and unhappy. Out of a loneliness that was to haunt him all his life he very early began to write down his thoughts and feelings. By the time he was eight he had written three "novels."

His late teens took an Augustinian turn: wild revelries and continuous affairs. While he was attending Cambridge a young woman bore him a son; Merton abandoned both, and they were later killed in an air raid in London. He contributed bawdy sketches to school papers, and once became a barker for a sleazy sideshow.

By his early twenties Merton's psyche was a raging fire. Driven by enormous guilt, confusion, and loneliness, fueled by boundless energies, creative urges, and an intense longing for love, beauty, and perfection, Merton had arrived at the classical spiritual condition for "the making of a monk." Although he converted to Catholicism at twenty-three, much of the next two years seems to have been spent in confession. Still, the love affairs and wild parties and miserable hangovers continued.

The turning point came in December 1941—the week the world exploded at Pearl Harbor. Thomas Merton renounced that world and entered the Trappist Abbey of Our Lady of Gethsemani.

The Trappists were (and still are) one of the world's most severely ascetic communities. They are a reform branch of the Cistercian Order (a reform branch of the Benedictines), founded at La Trappe in France in 1664. The monks of Gethsemani call themselves the Order of Cistercians of the Strict Observance (they sign "OCSO" after their names) and have developed a lifestyle more austere even than that of their forefathers.

Their days are lived in terms of prayer, work, and silence. They arise at 2 a.m. for prayer, meditate or read till 5:30, offer more prayers at 7:45 and 11:00, observe vespers at 4:30, listen to a reading at 6:10, and retreat to bed at 7:00 p.m. They subsist on a meager vegetarian diet. Labor consists of hoeing, cutting, and threshing in the monastery's orchards and fields; tending livestock; and making repairs. They live in silence; all communication is managed with some four hundred basic gestures in sign language.

Merton's first years at Gethsemani were relatively happy, even though the physical labor, fasting, and scanty diet often left him weak. Separated from the world, his spirit found a modicum of peace, and he began the long process of healing. He was allowed to live in a "hermit hatch" a half-mile from the monastery.

He wrote continually and passionately, and in his seventh year as a monk he published *The Seven Storey Mountain*. To everyone's surprise, it soared upward on the best-seller lists, and the author was hailed as a new Augustine—"the most significant spiritual leader in America"—and more. Overnight fame and admiration came from the world to this world-renouncing monk. Soul-mates, would-be disciples, and notables made their way to the hermit hatch, and Merton's solitude was lost. Still, he continued producing poetry, essays, and novels and carried on a voluminous correspondence. His writings would eventually be collected into more than forty volumes.

In the summer of 1968, Merton was invited to attend an interfaith conference in Bangkok, Thailand. For a decade he had been studying Eastern literature and religion and had long felt a kinship with other "contemplatives" who had withdrawn from the world to give their spiritual lives highest priority. (It was a Hindu monk who first persuaded him to read St. Augustine's *Confessions*.) He corresponded with Theravada monks, Tibetan rimpoches ("spiritual masters"), Hindu swamis, and Taoist and Confucian priests. He developed a warm friendship with Daisetz Suzuki, the famed Zen master, and felt especially close to Zen. In 1965 he published *The Way of Chuang Tzu*, an interpretation of the Chinese sage whose teachings struck a responsive chord in Merton. Chuang Tzu had written: "The effect of life in society is to complicate and confuse our existence,

*No one is so wrong as the man who knows all the answers.*

*What is important is not liberation from the body but liberation from the mind. We are not entangled in our own body but entangled in our own mind.*

*Our real journey in life is interior; it is a matter of growth, deepening, and of an ever greater surrender to the creative action of love and grace in our hearts.*

*Every moment and every event of every man's life on earth plants something in his soul. . . . Most of these unnumbered seeds perish and are lost, because men are not prepared to receive them.*

*We can help one another to find out the meaning of life, no doubt. But in the last analysis the individual person is responsible for living his own life and for "finding himself." Others can give you a name or a number, but they can never tell you who you really are. That is something you yourself can only discover from within.*

making us to forget who we really are by causing us to become obsessed with what we are not." To that Merton had responded: "I think I may be pardoned for consorting with a Chinese recluse who shares the climate and peace of my own kind of solitude, and who is my own kind of person."

His flight from San Francisco carried him first to Bangkok, where he experienced first-hand the "other world" he knew so well from books and letters, and then to Calcutta—"the big, beat-up, teeming, incredible city. People!" The next stop was Dharamsala to meet with the Dalai Lama, the Tibetan leader in exile. Merton held long conversations with a teacher of Tantric Buddhism, who urged him to find a guru to pursue enlightenment. Merton wrote in his journal: "At least he asked me if I were willing to risk it and I said why not? . . . I would like to learn something by experience and it does seem that the Tibetan Buddhists are the only ones who at present have a really large number of people who have attained to extraordinary heights in meditation and contemplation." His time with the Dalai Lama was immensely rewarding; of special value was their exchange of ideas on methods of meditation. Easily and naturally Merton moved into the Buddhist experience. The Dalai Lama called him a *geshe*, a "learned lama."

Merton traveled next to Darjeeling in northeastern India, overshadowed to the north by the breathtaking Himalayan range and the peak of Kanchenjunga. On the way he visited with a Buddhist teacher, Chatral Rimpoche, and discussed meditation and the difficulty of attaining "perfect emptiness." Merton recalled:

The unspoken or half-spoken message of the talk was our complete understanding of each other as people who were somehow *on the edge* of a great realization and knew it and were trying, somehow or other, to go out and get lost in it—and that it was a grace for us to meet one another. . . . He told me, seriously, that perhaps he and I would attain to complete Buddhahood in our next lives, perhaps even in this life, and the parting note was a kind of compact that we would both do our best to make it in *this* life. . . . He was surprised at getting on so well with a Christian and at one point laughed and said, "There must be something wrong here!"

In Sri Lanka Merton talked with hermits living in caves near Kandy, then journeyed to Polonnaruwa. Here, at last, there was a gathering together of all the scattered pieces in the spiritual vision of this Western trespasser. In a natural grassy amphitheater, a massive outcropping of granite has been carved into four great statues of the Buddha. "The whole thing is very much a Zen garden . . . and the great figures, motionless, yet with the lines of full movement, waves of vesture and bodily form, a beautiful and holy vision." What these figures meant is not easily expressed either *by* a Western poet or *for* Western readers. "Polonnaruwa was such an experience that I could not write hastily of it and cannot write now, or not at all adequately."

I am able to approach the Buddhas barefoot and undisturbed, my feet in wet grass, wet sand. Then the silence of the extraordinary faces . . . questioning nothing, knowing everything, rejecting nothing, the peace . . . that has seen through every question without establishing some other argument. For the doctrinaire, the mind that needs well-established positions, such peace, such silence, can be frightening. . . . I don't know when in my life I have ever had such a sense of beauty and spiritual validity running together in one aesthetic illumination. . . . I know and have seen what I was obscurely looking for. I don't know what else remains, but I have now seen and have pierced through the surface and have got beyond the shadow and the disguise.

Thomas Merton represents for the modern world a new stage of maturity in religious understanding—a new spirit in dialogue and a new way of listening. It is worth noting that he did not arrive at this stage from an assumption that "all religions are One" (he thought that cliché rather useless) or through an intellectual comparison of doctrinal similarities.

It is characteristic of Merton's approach to Eastern thought that he did not so much reach out for contact with other traditions, but rather went so deeply into his own that he could not help discovering the common roots. A strange journey indeed: the traveler, instead of going abroad, digs into the ground on which he stands, but digs so deep that he comes out in China.

DAVID STEINDL-RAST

What Merton gradually came to see is not an uncommon realization for seekers: that experience opens the avenues of communication, whereas belief closes them off; that experience encourages dialogue, whereas belief encourages pronouncement; and that whereas experience leads to empathy and appreciation, commitment to doctrinal formulas produces antipathy and disparagement.

Merton found that those who enter into a "dialogue of experience" can share and learn from one another.

This inclusive view made it impossible for him to deny any authentic scripture or any man of faith. Indeed, he discovered new aspects of truth in Hinduism and Buddhism, in Zen, and in Sufi mysticism. His lifelong search for meditative silence and prayer was found not only in his monastic experience but also in his late Tibetan inspiration.

AMIYA CHAKRAVARTY
In the Preface to *The Asian Journal*, vii

In just this way, Merton pondered the stone Buddhas of Polonnaruwa. His spiritual security could allow these new symbols to produce fresh illuminations.

From Sri Lanka Merton flew back to Bangkok. On the morning of December 10, 1968, he spoke to a gathering of monks and clerics on "Marxism and Monastic Perspectives." He spoke casually and with humor, noting that both monk and Marxist believe that "the claims of the world are fraudulent," and his speech concluded with a call for empathy for other religions and an openness to the "painfulness of inner change."

Shortly after lunch Merton returned to his guest cottage to rest. When he failed to reappear, his friends went to his cottage and found him lying on the floor, with an electric fan, still spinning, across his chest. He had been accidentally electrocuted.

A few weeks earlier, during a visit to the forested tea country of Assam, Merton had stood looking at the snow-covered peak of Kanchenjunga. He wrote in his journal: "Last night I had a curious dream about Kanchenjunga. I was looking at the mountain and it was pure white, absolutely white, especially the peaks that lie to the west. And I saw the pure beauty of their shape and outline, all in white. And I heard a voice saying—or got the clear idea of: 'There is another side to the mountain.'"

Thomas Merton had climbed the peak alone, as all must. The seeker—whether he be Buddhist, Christian, Hindu, Jew, Muslim, Jain—must find his own path. It takes enormous courage and, perhaps, a special grace to see that *there is* another side. "There is another side of Kanchenjunga and of every mountain. . . ."

# 8 3

## ALL GRAVES ARE WRONG

"You been up to the grave yet?" asked the hunter, as if he knew I would answer yes.

"No," I said.

That really surprised him. He tried not to show it.

"They all go up to the grave," he said.

"Not this one."

He explored around in his mind for a polite way of asking. "I mean . . . " he said, "Why *not?*"

"Because it's the wrong grave," I said.

"All graves are wrong graves when you come down to it," he said.

"No," I said. "There are right graves and wrong ones, just as there are good times to die and bad times."

He nodded at this. I had come back to something he knew, or at least smelled was right.

*O great Nzambi, what thou hast made is good, but thou hast brought a great sorrow to us with death. Thou shouldst have planned in some way that we would not be subject to death. O Nzambi, we are afflicted with great sadness.*

**Congo funeral chant**

"Sure, I knew men," he said, "died just perfect. You always felt, yes, that was good. One man I knew, sitting at the table waiting for supper, his wife in the kitchen, when she came in with a big bowl of soup there he was sitting dead and neat at the table. Bad for her, but, I, mean, wasn't that a good way for him? No sickness. No nothing but sitting there waiting for supper to come and never knowing if it came or not. Like another friend. Had an old dog. Fourteen years old. Dog was going blind and tired. Decided at last to take the dog to the pound and have him put to sleep. Loaded the old blind tired dog on the front seat of his car. The dog licked his hand, once. The man felt awful. He drove toward the pound. On the way there, with not one sound, the dog passed away, died on the front seat, as if he knew and, knowing, picked the better way, just handed over his ghost, and there you are. That's what you're talking about, right?"

I nodded.

"So you think that grave up on the hill is a wrong grave for a right man, do you?"

"That's about it," I said.

"You think there are all kinds of graves along the road for all of us?"

"Could be," I said.

"And if we could see our life one way or another, we'd choose better? At the end, looking back," said the hunter, "we'd say, hell, *that* was the year and the place, not the *other* year and the other place, but that one year, that one place. Would we say that?"

"Since we have to choose or be pushed finally," I said, "yes."

"That's a nice idea," said the hunter. "But how many of us have that much sense? Most of us don't have brains enough to leave a party when the gin runs out. We hang around."

"We hang around," I said, "and what a shame."

We ordered some more beer.

RAY BRADBURY
"The Kilimanjaro Device"

*Millions long for immortality who do not know what to do with themselves on a rainy Sunday afternoon.*

SUSAN ERTZ

No problem in the human condition has been subject to man's creative imagination more than the prospect of one's own cessation. Ernest Becker writes that "the idea of death, the fear of it, haunts the human animal like nothing else; it is the mainspring of human activity—activity designed largely to avoid the fatality of death, to overcome it by denying in some way that it is the final destiny for man."

There is no experience that so forces even the most unphilosophic among us into philosophizing. Plato viewed the philosophic life as a rehearsal for death. "To philosophize," wrote Montaigne, "is to learn to die." Schopenhauer summarized it all: "Death is the true inspiring genius, or the muse of philosophy. . . . Indeed, without death men could scarcely philosophize at all."

There is significant variation in how far each of us will go to avoid facing the fact that we must die. The evidence for postmortem consciousness is ambiguous, which only adds to our need to relieve anxiety about nonexistence and to mitigate the agony we associate with dying. Our minds create elaborate myths to allay our anguish over this event. Yet it is a universal event and a basic function of the cosmos.

It is difficult to define "death" except in arbitrary terms. "A person is dead when his heart stops"—we have long believed. But this age-old criterion is obsolete now that medical science can sustain a body's physical processes,

*While I thought I was learning how to live, I was learning how to die.*

LEONARDO DA VINCI

including a beating heart, for months or years by artificial means. If the machines are shut down, the heart stops. Was the individual alive while the heart was beating?

Brainwaves are a better indicator, for to exist as a human person is to have a mind. Without the possibility of consciousness, there is no person; there exists only a physical organism that has lost its potential as a person. Therefore, when all the brainwaves are flat on the electroencephalograph, we conclude that the person is dead.

Yet even this is not accurate. Cases are known in which brain waves were nonexistent for many hours (that is, the person potential apparently ceased to exist), but the individuals were ultimately restored to full health, physically and mentally.

Another test of life/death is the brain's utilization of oxygen. If no oxygen is being used, brain cells are dying. When sufficient cells die (and this occurs within minutes of the onset of oxygen deprivation), then the brain reaches a point of irreversibility. At that point in time the person can be pronounced "dead."

How arbitrary and loose are our definitions, yet how crucial! At present, we can agree upon certain working definitions of "life" and "death" without having the foggiest notion of what *life* (and its absence, *death*) really is.

*He always knew he would die young. Therefore, he saw as much beauty as he could.*

RICHARD JANARO

## DEATH—A NONEXPERIENCE

We cannot experience death, although in our fear and confusion we may not know this to be so. Death can never be experienced because death is the *cessation* of experience. Wittgenstein's pungent logic helps: "Death is not an event in life. Death is not lived through." We may be able to experience *dying* to some degree. If one believes he is dying and indeed he is, he may be able to experience a progression of dying events. But if one is convinced he is dying, but in fact he is not (that is, he recovers), then he has not experienced dying. One can be sure he is experiencing dying only if he dies; hence—from a strictly logical point of view—no one can ever be sure that he is having such an experience.

Thanatologists—that is, philosophers of the death event—make a helpful distinction between the unique inner experience—the cessation of consciousness—and the outer experience—the termination of physiological processes. The latter we obtain through observation of the death events of others. We can watch the gradual deterioration of life processes and then their actual termination, and we say *this* is the end of life: *this* is death.

Within ourselves, all we experience is the onset of the cessation of consciousness. This is often a gradual process, beginning long before the termination of our physiological processes. Most individuals subside into an unconscious state or coma at some point before death occurs, so they don't experience the later (and possibly eventful) stages leading to the death event.

Which of these events do we fear and so desperately try to avoid? Or do we fear both? Would we really care about the termination of our physiological processes if we could be assured that the cessation of our consciousness would *not* follow?

*Death is the true inspiring genius, or the muse of philosophy. . . . Indeed, without death men could scarcely philosophize.*

ARTHUR SCHOPENHAUER

### MINER'S REQUEST
#### *Find Proof of Man's Soul*

PHOENIX (UPI)—An obscure Arizona miner named James Kidd was a man concerned with the human soul.

In a handwritten will dated in 1946 he said:

"After my funeral expenses have been paid and $100 (given) to some preacher of the Gospel to say farewell at my grave, sell all my property, which is all in cash and stocks and have this balance money go into a research of some scientific proof of a soul of the human body which leaves at death."

*"There ain't no word in Sioux for goodbye."*

**"WALTER CROW HORSE"**
*Thunderheart*

Will of James Kidd.
Reproduced courtesy of Clerk of the Superior Court, Phoenix.

Kidd was last seen in 1949 when he apparently left to work on two mining claims. He was 70 and a year after his disappearance he was declared legally dead. His will was filed for probate in 1964.

He left a checking account of $4,100.66 at the time of his disappearance, and he owned stocks worth more than $100,000 which have nearly doubled because of dividends and other earnings.

A Miami man who knew Kidd said the miner had always talked about the supernatural and, despite the fact he never went to church, believed in the existence of a human soul which could be photographed as it left the body.

CONTINUED

The court hearings on the will begin here before Maricopa County Superior Court Judge Robert L. Myers.

UPDATE: The case of the James Kidd will was closed on January 30, 1973, and the estate was awarded to the American Society for Psychical Research. Since that time ASPR research has concentrated on two hypotheses: "that some part of the human personality is capable of operating outside the living body on rare occasions"—that is, a temporary out-of-body experience (OBE); and "that it may continue to exist after the brain processes have ceased and the organism is decayed"—that is, permanent immortality.

Six OBE projects have been conducted. An OBE "fly-in" and an attempt to correlate OBEs and apparitions both supported the OBE hypothesis, but other interpretations (e.g. ESP) are possible. Perceptual experiments with OBEs and psychophysiological studies of subjects gave similar results: evidence in harmony with OBE hypothesis but other explanations possible. Instrumental recordings (i.e. photos) and a test of mediums gave negative results.

As for the second hypothesis, deathbed studies of apparitions, visions, hallucinations, etc. (reported by attending doctors and nurses) supported the conclusion that "some of the dying patients indeed appeared to be already experiencing glimpses of ecsomatic existence." But again, other interpretations can't be ruled out; so these results "should not be taken as a final balance of evidence for or against survival." Masses of data are still being processed.

*ASPR Newsletter*, Numbers 22, 24, and July 1976.

---

We do not fear death itself, and death—the cessation of consciousness—is nothing to be feared. Each night when we enter sleep we experience the cessation of consciousness; this is an experience which probably resembles the final cessation followed by death. Each night we die, literally. (But we awaken again. There is no wonder that sleep has become a synonym for death and that we universally picture ourselves waking from it.)

Three distinct kinds of fear are associated with death, and one of them—fear of suffering—is realistic. One does not live for very long before learning that pain and grief are companions of death. As children we see animals in pain before they die; throughout life we witness the agony of individuals caught in war, accidents, and disease. The constant association of pain and death never ceases. It becomes difficult for us to *think* of death without *feeling* the fears we have been conditioned to associate with it.

Another kind of fear, less common, results from confusion. For instance, a teenaged girl awoke repeatedly with nightmares about death, and her terror became so intense it dominated her waking hours as well. When her ideas of death were explored with a therapist, it was discovered that what she really feared was being buried alive. That is, the body in her dreams would in fact be dead, but she was unable to separate the idea of consciousness from the buried corpse. Well-known stories by Edgar Allen Poe and others supply ideas that can grow into such nightmares. When the fallacy of identification was recognized, the girl's "fear of death" gradually diminished.

*I don't mind dying. I just don't want to be there when it happens.*

WOODY ALLEN

*While we are reasoning concerning life, life is gone; and death, though perhaps they receive him differently, yet treats alike the fool and the philosopher.*

DAVID HUME

> ## VICTORIES AGAINST DARKNESS
>
> Death plays an important part in each day of my life. I have worked half in shadow, half in sun all of my life. When I put my new book *The Halloween Tree* (a history of Death in the world, really) in the mail eight weeks ago, I cried half-aloud: "There you are, Death, one up on you again!" My books are victories against darkness, if only for a small while. Each story I write is a candle lit for my own burial plot which it may take some few years to blow out. More than many writers, I have known this fact about myself since I was a child. It puts me to work each day with a special sad-sweet-happy urgency.
>
> RAY BRADBURY

## FEAR OF NONBEING

Another kind of death anxiety is all-pervasive. This is the universal fear: the fear of nonexistence. It is not fear of possible punishment in some hell or purgatory; nor is it merely a fear of the unknown. Rather, we experience a relentless anguish about nonexistence itself. We fear the *experience* of *nonbeing*, not recognizing that this is a contradiction in terms. However, a rational response to a nonrational fear is no solution.

We can remind ourselves that we already know "the experience of nonexistence." Most of us were not alive, say, two hundred years ago, but it didn't bother us then, nor does it concern us now. And, barring a scientific breakthrough, most of us will not be alive two hundred years hence. But *this* bothers us. The possibility of nonexistence in the future can disturb us, while nonexistence in the past doesn't.

Why?

*In a certain sense the whole of mythical thought may be interpreted as a constant and obstinate negation of the phenomenon of death. By virtue of this conviction of the unbroken unity and continuity of life myth has to clear away this phenomenon. Primitive religion is perhaps the strongest and most energetic affirmation of life that we find in human culture.*

ERNST CASSIRER

*Valhalla* (Norse): the great hall of immortality where warriors await the call of Odin to join in the final battle (the Götterdämmerung). *Elysium* (Greek): a place at the end of the earth on the banks of the river Oceanus where perfect happiness rewards those favored by the gods. *Paradise* (Persian): a lush, green park that serves as a temporary resting place for righteous souls awaiting the final resurrection. *Gardens of Delight* (Islamic): a place of reward for the faithful of Allah where, robed in silk and brocade, they are given all earthly delights imaginable. *Heaven* (Christian): the abode of God where the righteous dead will dwell together in perfect happiness in God's presence after the Last Judgment. *Svarga* (Vedic): a joyful place high above the world, bathed in flute song, where, for the faithful, the good things of this life will continue forever. *Isatpragbhara* (Jain): the heaven at the very top of the universe whither the pure consciousnesses of the righteous will rise and enjoy perfect bliss. *Isles of the Blest* (Orphic): the mystic Greek isles where the purified, now free from rebirth, will be rewarded with eternal happiness. *Kingdom of Osiris* (Egyptian): an oasis in the western desert with lush vegetation where the souls of the blessed will forever rest under spreading shade trees. *House of Song* (Zoroastrian): a place

*We know what fear is. We live
with it all of our lives. Only
the dead are without fear.*

**The Magnificent Seven**

*What the hell happened to
the last fifty years?*

**Forever Young**

somewhere among the stars beyond the Chinvat Bridge where the righteous will
enjoy perfect happiness in their companionship with one another.

Our endless contemplation of various heavens and hells reflects the conviction that we do not really die. Deep within we intuit that we are immortal.
Actually, we are split by an ambivalence about the mystery of death. On the one
hand, we know we will die, and as a social convention we confess this to others;
but on the other hand, each of us has an instinctlike resistance: "It can't actually happen *to me.*"

Generally, man does not identify the self/essence with one's physical body.
When we look at others, we see bodies, of course; we perceive physical organisms. But when we look into another's eyes, we see not merely the working parts
of a transducer (cornea, iris, and so forth); we "see" a person. As we watch facial

## LAST FLIGHT

The following letter is by Flying Petty Officer First Class Isao Matsuo of the 701st
Air Group. It was written just before he sortied for a kamikaze attack. His home
was in Nagasaki Prefecture.

28 October 1944

Dear Parents:

Please congratulate me. I have been given a splendid opportunity to die.
This is my last day. The destiny of our homeland hinges on the decisive battle in
the seas to the south where I shall fall like a blossom from a radiant cherry tree.

I shall be a shield for His Majesty and die cleanly along with my squadron
leader and other friends. I wish that I could be born seven times, each time to
smite the enemy.

How I appreciate this chance to die like a man! I am grateful from the depths
of my heart to the parents who have reared me with their constant prayer and tender love. And I am grateful as well to my squadron leader and superior officers
who have looked after me as if I were their own son and given me such careful
training.

Thank you, my parents, for the 23 years during which you have cared for me
and inspired me. I hope that my present deed will in some small way repay what
you have done for me. Think well of me and know that your Isao died for our country. This is my last wish, and there is nothing else that I desire.

I shall return in spirit and look forward to your visit at the Yasukuni Shrine.
Please take good care of yourselves.

How glorious is the Special Attack Corps' Giretsu Unit whose *Suisei*
bombers will attack the enemy. Movie cameramen have been here to take our pictures. It is possible that you may see us in newsreels at the theater.

We are 16 warriors manning the bombers. May our death be as sudden and
clean as the shattering of crystal.

Written at Manila on the eve of our sortie.

Isao

Soaring into the sky of the southern seas, it is our glorious mission to die as
the shields of His Majesty. Cherry blossoms glisten as they open and fall.

INOGUCHI AND NAKAJIMA
*The Divine Wind*

expressions, we "see" in others what we feel in ourselves: a self or soul that dwells in the body but that is not part of it. Our experience of consciousness feels like a "spirit" that dwells inside a "house," and various religious traditions refer to the coming and going of one's "spirit" into and out of the body. It "inhabits" a body. Indeed, several spirits may inhabit a body, simultaneously or in turn.

The Greeks developed the belief that the human spirit is free and of great value, while the body, quite a separate entity, is of little importance. The spirit can leave the body and wander where it wills. Some of the Greek philosophers held that the soul can be truly free only when the body-prison dies and releases it. The Greeks, therefore, had no strong feelings about mutilation or cremation. They felt concern if the corpse could not be given proper rites without which the soul could not find release; and it was especially tragic when Greek sailors were lost at sea and could never be given proper burial. Nevertheless, the body as such was of little worth.

*Each of us should write our own epitaph, so that we will state to ourselves simply how it is we want to be remembered.*

**ROY MENNINGER**

Our Judeo-Christian psyche-ology ("soul-ology") has been less dualistic. Jews and Christians distinguished between spirit and body, but they could never think of them as separable entities; therefore, after death reassembly of bodily materials is necessary for survival. The Hebrew could not imagine spirit wandering about without a body. For the Hebrew, as for the Egyptians, Sumerians, and others, mutilation of the body is a tragic misfortune, for we must carry into the next life whatever scars we acquire in this life.

Jesus uttered words to the effect that if your eye or hand causes you to sin, then destroy it, for "it is better for you to get into the Kingdom of God with but one eye than to be thrown into Gehenna with both eyes. . . . " (Mark 9:47). These words were not meant symbolically; they reflect the late Judaic notion that we take into the next life whatever scars we sustain in this one. When Jesus reappeared to his disciples after the discovery of the empty tomb, he was seen to bear on his spirit-body the wounds of the crucifixion.

In the Egyptian tomb of Menena, some culprit regained entrance to the burial chamber of this nobleman and mutilated the freshly painted frescoes. The faces of Menena and his family were chiseled away to ensure that they would go faceless into the next life.

Fresco on wall of the tomb of a nobleman, Menena, at Royal Thebes. The fresco retains its vivid colors after 3,500 years. Note that the faces and parts of the bodies of Menena and his family have been chiseled away, thus ensuring that the soul of each would enter the next life faceless and maimed, a misfortune for an Egyptian, who believed that we carry into the next life the scars acquired in this one.

## "THE DENIAL OF DEATH"

In Western thought we have strong religious reassurance that we will survive physical death. Orthodox doctrine denies that we die. The recorded fact-claim that Jesus awakened after physical death and promised us that we shall do the same is part of our Western theology of history. We have inherited a specific interpretation of the death event: there is no death of the self, and physical death is merely an event in a continuing drama.

Since these various antideath concepts are part of our own teleocosmic world-view, it is easy to avoid the feeling of certainty that death, in fact, awaits each of us. The idea of total oblivion has not been widely held or seriously faced.

Our difficulty in accepting the finality of death can be seen in a simple analysis of our linguistic utterances. Our talk about death generally occurs in two ways: we speak of our own death as "my death" and of the death of others as "your death." As I sit behind my typewriter thinking about death, it is rather easy to contemplate "your death." I read about the death of others in the morning newspaper; I saw it on the late news on television; it was vividly portrayed in a recent film I saw. Occasionally I see the death of others on the highway as I hurriedly drive by on the other side of the road. Perhaps I am one of those rare persons who has been with someone who died. In such an instant I observe "your death" as the cessation of respiration and heartbeat, in short, the termination of bodily process. But "my death" is a completely different matter. Not only is it impossible for me to observe, I have great difficulty thinking about it and imagining what it is like. How does one contemplate one's own nonbeing? It was this question that led Freud to postulate that every person, in his unconscious mind, is convinced of his own immortality. In observing his patients Freud discovered that denial functions as a coping mechanism enabling patients to handle their anxiety about their own death. Every time we attempt to contemplate our own death, Freud noted, we do so as spectators, that is, we are unable to think about or imagine our own nonbeing. What Freud described clinically was the overwhelming difficulty we have in thinking about death as a personal experience, death in its interiority.

The starting point is to investigate the nature of our experience as we think about and attempt to contemplate our own death. What is involved in my own experience (and I assume your own experience as well)? The first thing I am aware of is ambiguity. When I recognize my own mortality and finitude and the fact that my death is a reality, I feel helpless, even frustrated, that I can do nothing about it. I feel trapped by some power, some force I do not fully understand and cannot avoid. In her clinical experience Elisabeth Kübler-Ross has found that many of her terminally ill patients think of death as an uncontrollable, powerful force that comes upon them and about which they can do nothing. One patient said, "Right now I feel strong and well, but I know I have something growing inside of me that is beyond my control." It is this sense of "no exit," no way out of an existence in which death is the end, that gives rise to the basic ambiguity regarding the human condition.

RICHARD DOSS

When attempting to face the fact of death, the ever-present television screen is no help. It blurs the distinction between the living and the dead by holding before us an illusion of immortality. Television has been called "the great immortalizer." Each day we watch innumerable figures who, we have been told, are no longer alive. Yet obviously they live. They are alive before our eyes. The (alleged) fact that some physical organism no longer exists in space/time seems to make little difference.

From the time we enter formal education the great men of history live on in our books and our minds. They are as alive as others we read about who may or may not be alive. We don't (and can't) make any clear distinction between the living and the no-longer living. Is George Washington dead? Not to millions of school children. Is Martin Luther King dead? John Kennedy? Dwight Eisenhower? Spencer Tracy? Marilyn Monroe? Clark Gable? John Wayne? Anwar Sadat? We see them all on TV occasionally.

We see Robert Kennedy's victory speech at the Ambassador Hotel, over and over again. . . .

For those who can't believe in the true survival of consciousness the human mind has rationalized a variety of comforting alternatives. They allow us to retain the feeling that *something of us* is left after we cease to exist.

*Biological immortality* stresses the continuity of germ plasm from parent to offspring. *Social immortality* reminds us that we will linger in the memories of others for the good we do. *Moral immortality* holds that while we may be forgotten, we can add our small contribution to the continuing moral development of the human species. *Life-cycle immortality* suggests that energy is never lost but is conserved in other living things: from life to dust and to life again.

In the genre of science fiction, we can comfort ourselves with quasi-immortal states such as *cryonic suspension* ("freeze now, thaw later" or, in Alan Harrington's phrase, "freeze-wait-reanimate") or *total transplants* whereby a continually renewed physical organism can sustain indefinitely an individual consciousness. Scientists are also researching the mechanics of *regeneration*, which operate so well for some lower creatures such as starfish and lobsters.

But all such notions are consolation prizes rather than immortalities. They are designed to ease the pain of loss—the loss of conviction that consciousness survives death.

Does true immortality—the survival of a conscious self—really exist? Is there any conceivable way that there could be a continuity of conscious experience after the termination of our physical processes? What arguments—rational or empirical—might convince us that such continuity does indeed take place?

## ARGUMENTS FOR IMMORTALITY

The strongest *rational argument for immortality* is based on belief in the goodness of God. This is an "if . . . then" kind of argument: *If* God exists and *if* he is good, *then* immortality must necessarily exist.

According to this reasoning, it is unthinkable that God would create purposive beings who dream dreams and have the capacity for unlimited growth, only to let all this come to nothing. Could a good God *not* make provision for the fulfillment of these dreams and the actualization of this potential? The fact is

*Consider how that past ages of eternal time before our birth were no concern of ours. This is a mirror which nature holds up to us of future time after our death.*

LUCRETIUS

*When one has lived as long as I have, it's a serious matter to die. Every year one puts out new roots.*

DAVID LINDSAY
*Voyage to Arcturus*

*To be man is to strive to be God.*

JEAN-PAUL SARTRE

Judgment scene before King Osiris. The dog-headed god Anubis is weighing the heart of the deceased—Princess Entiuny—against a symbol for truth; if judged worthy, her spirit can pass on into the western paradise, the Kingdom of Osiris. The goddess Isis, sister of Osiris and compassionate interceder, stands behind the princess.

*Belief in immortality secures a bond of union between the living and the dead, which is a fact of immense importance for the continuity of culture and for the safe keeping of tradition.*

ASHLEY MONTAGU

*You bury only my body, not me.*

SOCRATES

*Well, really, Crito, it would be hardly suitable for a man of my age to resent having to die.*

SOCRATES

that man barely begins to understand life and to grow during his short lifetime. Most of us just begin to touch our dreams and solve some problems—and it's over. This would surely be an agonizing joke for a compassionate God to play on his children.

Therefore, there must exist an afterlife where man's self/essence can continue to grow. How great such a growth potential would be, especially if released from the impediments of the physical body, we can only imagine.

The American Personalist philosopher, Edgar Brightman, considered this to be the strongest argument for immortality. To his way of thinking there is no strong argument for immortality apart from the existence of God; but granting God's existence, then there exists no weighty argument *against* immortality.

The strongest *empirical evidence for immortality*—and it may seem strange to some—is from seances during which contact is allegedly established with discarnate spirits.

It would not be far wrong to say that "special effects" and/or hypnosis is involved in 95 percent of all mediumistic activity; and therefore perhaps 5 percent of seances are free of fraud and demonstrate authentic phenomena. Now, within this 5 percent, the great majority of happenings can be accounted for with known psychological principles or telepathic hypotheses. This leaves only a small part of 1 percent that necessitate hypotheses assuming something like discarnate spirits. Within this very small percentage of cases, interesting but problematic events occur. For instance, the "discarnate spirits" frequently reveal information that no one present could possibly know. It has been suggested that there is a "collective subconscious" or a "superconsciousness" that is tapped by the mind of the medium; and while such a theory is not beyond the realm of possibility, the hypothesis of the existence of discarnate spirits seems at present a simpler and better explanation.

It is somewhere within this small percentage of spiritualistic phenomena that empirical data might be found to support the idea of a continued consciousness after physical death. At present we have no verified data in this area, and much more research is needed.

### THE HEART OF HELLAS
#### *Epitaphs*

*My name is*—What does it matter?—*My
Country was*—Why speak of it?—*I
Was of noble birth*—Indeed? And if
You had been the lowest?—*Moreover, my life
Was decorous*—And if it had not been so,
What then?
                *and I lie here now beneath you—*
Who are you that speak?
To whom do you speak?

PAULUS SILENTIARIUS

#### *Epitaph of an Abstainer*

Remember Euboulos the sober, you who pass by,
And drink: there is one Hadês for all men.

LEONIDAS OF TARENTUM

#### *Epitaph of a Slave*

Alive, this man was Manês the slave: but dead,
He is the peer of Dareios, that great King.

ANYTE

#### *Epitaph of a Young Man*

Hail me Diogenês underground, O stranger, and pass by:
Go where you will, and fairest fortune go with you.
In my nineteenth year the darkness drew me down—
And ah, the sweet sun!

ANONYMOUS

#### *Epitaph of a Sailor*

*Tomorrow the wind will have fallen
Tomorrow I shall be safe in harbor
Tomorrow*
        I said:
                and Death
Spoke in that little word:
The sea was Death.
                O Stranger
This is the Némesis of the spoken word:
Bite back the daring tongue that would say
        *Tomorrow!*

ANTIPHILOS OF BYZANTIUM

DUDLEY FITTS (translator)<br>*Poems from the Greek Anthology*

## ARGUMENTS AGAINST IMMORTALITY

The strongest *rational argument against immortality* derives from empirical observations that man has a profound "instinct" to stay alive. We are terrorized by this final unknown, this "great Perhaps," as Rabelais put it; and along with this ultimate fear goes man's incredible power of imagination. We can create an endless variety of concepts to meet our emotional needs. Therefore, with a simple formula—man's intense need plus his and her ever-fertile imagination—we may be able to explain to our satisfaction all of man's dreams of immortality: subtle imagery of blissful spirits, teleocosmic schemes of reincarnation, myths without end about heavens and hells and how we can get there, or stay out. As one surveys the range of man's fantasies about postmortem life, it seems that they just might be our most lavish creative productions. Man dreams of a paradise, but this life is anything but a paradise. There must be a paradise somewhere. . . .

This is a rational argument, but it is founded upon empirical observation and possesses considerable coherence; while it *proves* nothing, as an inductive hypothesis it is formidable.

The strongest *empirical evidence against immortality* is the observation—apparently without exception—that the termination of physical processes is soon followed by the cessation of consciousness as measured on EEGs and other instruments. That is, our bodies die and we have no evidence—unless the "discarnate spirits" are real—that consciousness continues in any form. We have no scientific knowledge at present that would be compatible with the continuation of consciousness; just the reverse, in fact: our best scientific knowledge is only compatible with the cessation of consciousness.

We could argue that, from the cessation of brainwaves on an electroencephalograph, we cannot validly infer that consciousness ceases. This is strictly true. Yet no alternative inference seems better. We can *think of* such things as "organized electromagnetic fields" or "vibration patterns" that somehow sustain themselves without underlying physical systems, but do we have any dependable evidence at present that would lead us to believe such concepts refer to anything real? Since there appears to be a one-to-one causal relationship between brainwaves and consciousness, there is logical justification for inferring the end of experience from the termination of the brain's electrical activity.

## THE FUTURE OF DEATH

How we perceive "the problem of death" depends partly upon the attitude options open to us at any particular time and place. Mankind's general stance toward death has wavered between a stubborn denial and a grudging submission. Our religious myths deny the death of the personal self while confirming the intolerable anxiety and pain of physical death.

Western man has long attempted to see death in new ways, and, thanks to recent investigations, death is now perceived as the terribly complex and

*The bullfight is a miniature of life. Death is a part of life, and it is an integral part of the bullfight. As in life, death hovers; it is inevitable, if not for the man, certainly for the bull. And in life, each of us must eventually die. One of the things the matador is saying when he fights bravely is that the way we die is important, or, that what is really important is how we live.*

**JOSEPH ROYCE**

*This is the great error of our day in the treatment of the human body that physicians separate the soul from the body.*

**PLATO**

ambiguous event that it is. From the nihilistic angle, the shriek of Ivan Ilytch paints the horror of facing one's own death at the end of a meaningless life. But Albert Camus goes further: "Because of death, human existence has no meaning. All the crimes that man could commit are nothing in comparison with that fundamental crime which is death."

By contrast, a more positive feeling is expressed by those who see death as the singular event that puts one's life in perspective and acts as the ultimate source of its meaning. Without death, they contend, our lives would be meaningless. The length of one's lifetime is irrelevant. If one lives a life filled with good experiences, then fifty years of meaningfulness is a full measure; but if one's life is meaningless, then five hundred years would be hell.

A brand new kind of vision has recently emerged: a prolongation of life that borders on immortality. For as long as we humans defined ourselves as "mortal men" condemned to a death condition with "no exit," it was impossible for us to dream of alternatives. We could not allow ourselves to think that there might be an "exit." When we want very, very much something that is wholly beyond our reach, it is too painful to dream of possessing it; but given the remotest chance of grasping it, then we dream. *More* life—in quality perhaps, but certainly in quantity—may be (*may* be) within reach.

Science has extended the life expectancy of an individual in the Western world by about twenty-five years during the last century; and there is every reason to expect this trend to continue. How long might a lifetime become if we could solve the secret of aging? Or if we could learn how to transplant all human vital organs or replace them with synthetic surrogates? Or discover a chemistry that will prevent senility and loss of memory? Or develop a eugenics technology that would pair genetic factors that sharply increase human longevity? Recent trends in microbiology and related fields enable us to take some of these possibilities seriously for the first time.

A blunt defiance of death is now coming from some quarters. Alan Harrington, author of *The Immortalist*, takes an unequivocal stand: "Death is an imposition on the human race, and no longer acceptable. Man has all but lost his ability to accommodate himself to personal extinction; he must now proceed physically to overcome it. In short, to kill death: to put an end to his own mortality as a certain consequence of being born."

*If I were given the choice of how long I should like to live with my present physical and mental equipment, I should decide on a good deal more than seventy years. But I doubt whether I should be wise to decide on more than three-hundred years. Already I am very much aware of my own limitations, and I think that three-hundred years is as long as I should like to put up with them.*

SIR FRED HOYLE

Je m'en vay chercher un grand Peut-être. (*I am going to seek a great Perhaps.*)

RABELAIS
(*from his deathbed*)

*From a ninety-year-old woman: "I'm looking forward so much to the next life. If it weren't for that I'd have nothing at all to look forward to."*

**ANNE CHRISTIAN**

*Death does not carry a passport.*

**ANWAR SADAT**

*My death does not belong to me—it is the outer limit of my consciousness, the last of my possibles. The meaningless-ness of death for me is summed up in the phrase that "my death is the one moment of my life which I do not have to live." My death is not for me but for others; it is not my concern, but the concern of others who will notice it and need to deal with it. . . .*

**JOSEPH MIHALICH**

Current reassessment of man's place in a biocosmos of living creatures is another helpful perspective. Whether or not we succeed in the near future in making contact with extraterrestrial intelligences (ETIs), this "cosmic context for man" has become a coherent world-view within which we can rethink the nature and destiny of man. In this perspective we are faced with *a new kind of question* about death.

Q  Suppose we should discover that ETIs actually exist who enjoy life spans of three hundred years, or five hundred years, or a thousand. Might we then come to feel that man's life span of three score years and ten is wholly intolerable?

Q  How might we humans feel if ETIs are enabled to fulfill their plans and dreams to a degree that has heretofore seemed unthinkable to us? Could we continue to accept docilely the early and frustrating curtailment of our dreams?

Q  In terms of our self-esteem, could we continue to tolerate a seventy- to eighty-year life span? Wouldn't all our deaths then be viewed as premature?

Q  How long might we want to live *under present conditions* if we discover that some ETIs live for hundreds or thousands of our earth years?

Q  What grounds do we have for assuming that death events as we know them are cosmic universals? Perhaps our notions are based solely on local and contingent examples.

Q  Is it remotely conceivable that there may be forms of "process termination" other than death as we know it?

Q  Wouldn't higher life-forms at least attempt to establish control over both the time and the conditions of life termination?

Q  Wouldn't such control in fact be merely an extension of scientific and medical goals now on our human drawing boards?

Q  If such control could be accomplished by man, how might it affect the whole intent and meaning of human existence?

Q  If we could live for two thousand years, would our present profound need for immortality be assuaged? What would we want *then?*

In a science-fiction classic, *Time Enough for Love*, Robert Heinlein has successfully captured the painful contrast between the near-immortal members of the Howard families and the short-lived "ephemerals"—that is, us. The Howards are normal earthlings who find that they live for centuries as a result of a natural genetic mutation. The oldest member of the clan, Lazarus Long, reminisces about one short period of his long life, a very happy time spent with a short-lived ephemeral, Dora.

Dora is the only woman I ever loved unreservedly. I don't know that I can explain why. I did not love her that way when I married her; she had not had a chance as yet to teach me what love can be. Oh, I did love her, but it was the love of a doting father for a favorite child or somewhat like the love one can lavish on a pet.

I decided to marry her not through love in any deepest sense but simply because this adorable child who had given me so many hours of happiness wanted something very badly—my child—and there was only one way I could give her what she wanted and still please my own self-love. So, almost coldly, I calculated the cost and decided that the price was low enough that I could let her have what she wanted. It could not cost me much; she was an ephemeral. Fifty, sixty, seventy, at the most eighty years, and she would be dead. I could afford to spend that trivial amount of time to make my adopted daughter's pitifully short life happy—that's how I figured it. It wasn't much, and I could afford it. So be it.

***

I decided that the husband of an ephemeral had to *be* an ephemeral, in every way possible to him. The corollaries to that decision caused us to wind up in Happy Valley.

Happy Valley—The happiest of all my lives. The longer I was privileged to live with Dora, the more I loved her. She taught me to love by loving me, and I learned—rather slowly; I wasn't too good a pupil, being set in my ways and lacking her natural talent. But I did learn. Learned that supreme happiness lies in wanting to keep another person safe and warm and happy, and being privileged to try.

And saddest, too. The more thoroughly I learned this—through living day on day with Dora—the happier I was . . . and the more I ached in one corner of my mind with certain knowledge that this could be only a brief time too soon over when it *was* over, I did not marry again for almost a hundred years. Then I did, for Dora taught me to face up to death, too. She was as aware of her own death, of the certain briefness of her life, as I was. But she taught me to live *now,* not to let anything sully *today* . . . until at last I got over the sadness of being condemned to live.

## DEATH—VERSUS LIFE

Clearly, *how* one dies is very important—while one is still alive. We want assurance that our death will be dignified; that the conditions of termination will be surrounded by respect and honor; that it will not be degrading to ourselves or loved ones; that it will not be an unplanned, messy kind of death. We want to feel sure that it will not result from ignominious causes; from cowardice, foolish anger, or stupidity. And certainly not least, we want the assurance that our last experience of consciousness will not be dominated by physical pain or emotional anguish.

There are two central questions involved in facing our own death: the questions of what we can leave behind and what we can take with us. It has been written that we must develop convictions and feelings about each of these questions if we are to face our own cessation with any sense of peace.

But some say that the better question is: What can I do with the days I have left to make life really worthwhile?

## REFLECTIONS

1    "All graves are wrong when you come right down to it" (pp. 585–586). How do you respond to the point Bradbury is making?

2    How would you answer the question: "Would we really care about the termination of our physiological processes if we could be assured that the cessation of our consciousness would *not* follow?" (p. 587).

3    "The possibility of nonexistence in the future can disturb us, while nonexistence in the past doesn't." Why?

4    This "fear of nonexistence" is widely dealt with in existential literature, and many philosophers are convinced that this fear is one of the powerful driving forces behind much human behavior. So, what exactly is meant by the "fear of nonexistence" (or "nonbeing")? Is the concept meaningful to you personally?

*Que acreditó su ventura,*
*Morir cuerdo y vivir loco.*
*(For if he like a madman*
*    lived,*
*At least he like a wise one*
*    died.)*

**CERVANTES**
**Don Quixote's Epitaph**

*When my time comes, I hope no one drains my veins of their sustaining fluid and fills them with formaldehyde, then wastes me by putting me in a concrete box in the ground for eternity. Rather, just a simple pine box with an acorn on top of it. Find a place where a tree is needed and return me to nature. When the acorn grows, I can nourish it and give back in some measure what I've taken. Maybe someday kids can crawl in my branches or a raccoon might curl up in my trunk or the larks can sing out from my leaves. At any rate, I would rather let an oak tree be my epitaph than a marble slab be my tombstone.*

**MIKE ROYKO**

*Fruit must fall from the tree.*
**JERRY HUNTER**

5    Three kinds of fear commonly associated with death are described on pp. 589–590 of this chapter. Are these descriptions accurate, in your judgment? Have any of these fears (or others) been a significant part of your experience? How have you dealt with them?

6    Think a while about the James Kidd will (pp. 588–589). Do you think there is any empirical evidence for the existence of a "soul"? Do you think there could be? If so, what kind of evidence? How would you go about gathering evidence? That is, what path might you follow if you really wanted to "show cause" why you should receive the James Kidd estate?

7    Review and clarify in your own mind the empirical and rational arguments presented in this chapter for and against immortality (pp. 595–598). Which of these arguments are most persuasive? On the basis of these four arguments, what is your conclusion regarding the existence of personal immortality?

8    Answer the following question as precisely as you can, but first give careful attention to the definition of each term in the question: "Where do you think we will go after we die?" (If you think that fallacious or meaningless words are used here, then rephrase the question until you get it to produce results.)

9    Evidence would seem to indicate that the preponderance of human beings can't face death without myth. Myths that attend upon death, its meaning, and its aftermath are legion in all religions. In your opinion, could mankind face death without myth? (What is meant by *myth* in such a question?) What do you think the experiential consequences might be?

*There are many forms of life in space. Many forms of death, too.*

**Space: 1999**

"I cannot see what lies ahead. Will you walk with me?" Photo courtesy of John Reseck

# OMAR KHAYYAM

## *"One Thing at Least Is Certain—This Life Flies"*

"In the city of Balkh, on the street of the slave-sellers, in the house of Amir Abu Sa'd" —so the story goes, and the storyteller is Nizam of Samarkand—"I had joined the crowd of happy guests. In the course of our friendly conversations, I heard Omar say, 'My grave will be in a spot where the trees will shed their blossoms on me twice in each year.'

"Which seemed to me impossible —for there is but one springtime. Still, I knew that he never spoke idle words.

"Then, in the year 530—it being some years since the great man had veiled his countenance in the dust—I came to Nishapur; and I went to visit his grave on the eve of Friday, taking with me a guide to lead me to the tomb. He brought me to the Hira cemetery. I turned to the left and his tomb lay at the foot of a garden wall, over which hung the flowering branches of pear-trees and peach-trees. On his grave had fallen so many flower-petals that his dust was covered beneath them.

"Then I remembered what he had said in the city of Balkh, and I fell to weeping. Because, on the face of the whole Earth, I had found no one to compare with him.

"May Allah have mercy upon him!"

Omar Khayyam was a mathematician, astronomer, and poet born at Nishapur in the extreme northeastern corner of Persia. He lived from about A.D. 1038 (A.H. 432 by the Moslem calendar) to A.D. 1123 (A.H. 517). The word *khayyam*, which means "tentmaker," was the profession of his father Ibrahim and possibly his also by inheritance. He was apparently schooled in his home city and was recognized for his talents from his earliest years. He became court astronomer to King Malikshah, who placed him in charge of an observatory —"House of the Stars"—and gave him a royal stipend in gold. For decades, free of material worries, he labored lovingly on his star charts (he reformed the calendar), geometry (he wrote a commentary on Euclid), and mathematics (his works include *Treatise on Algebra*); and he composed elegant poetry. He was respected by his fellow scientists, esteemed by the king, worshiped by his devoted followers, and hated by religious leaders.

This is virtually all we know about

Omar Khayyam's *life*. Of Omar's mind and heart we know considerably more. By common consent he was the greatest thinker of his time, possessing an extra-ordinary mind that soared high above those of his contemporaries. What is remarkable is that Omar was both a brilliant mathematician ("left brain") and a brilliant poet ("right brain"); it is unusual to find the analytical intellect living in harmony with the romantic intuitions of the poet.

He spent his life, says his translator Edward FitzGerald, "busied in winning knowledge of every kind." Al-Qazwini says that Omar was "versed in all kinds of philosophy and mathematics." He studied Greek philosophy and expounded it; he pondered Avicenna's thought system and criticized it. He experimented with algebraic equations and geometric constructions five hundred years ahead of his time. He had a superb memory: he once reproduced a book almost word for word after reading it through seven times.

Omar's clear intellect brought him into direct conflict with the entrenched religious establishment. Despite the influx of Greek ideas and the rational ferment created by an impending enlightenment, Shi'ite orthodoxy remained extremely repressive. New ideas were fought down, often violently, and the variety of politico-religious sects emerging were at one another's throats.

Such repression was intolerable to Omar, who proceeded to speak his mind fearlessly. He criticized bigotry, superstition, and mindless adherence to custom. As a scientist, he was offended when narrow-minded individuals held to beliefs that contradicted the simplest rational observations. He abrasively carried on running battles with an ignorant clergy who refused to consider any idea not sanctioned by scripture or tradition. As a result, he was denounced as the "arch-freethinker" of his time and warned to "bridle his tongue."

Omar's outspokenness brought criticism and reprisal. He was challenged by the Sufis and marked by the Assassins. The Sufi Razi derides him as "an unhappy philosopher, atheist, and materialist," citing two of his verses to prove the extent of his "confusion and error." He was disliked by al-Ghazzali and deplored by al-Qifti for his rationalism, whose "inward meanings are to the Law stinging serpents," filled with malice. The great poet Jalalu'd-Din Rumi complained that many had turned to Greek philosophy because of Omar: "How long [will you study] this philosophy of the Greeks? Study instead the philosophy of the Faithful!" Al-Qazwini tells of a certain theologian who came to Omar privately in the early morning for lessons in philosophy but in the evening denounced him from the pulpit as a "freethinker and atheist."

In Persia Omar's claim to fame has always been his achievements in mathematics and astronomy, but in the West he is loved for his poetry. In it he confided his passion and his pain.

In *The Rubaiyat of Omar Khayyam* each rubaiyah is a self-contained epigram expressing a complete thought. Its lines follow the rhyme scheme *aaba*, the third line lending a suspense that is resolved with the finality of the last line. Rubaiyat were written by everyone who could hold a pen, from toddlers to the most exquisite laureates. Over a thousand have been attributed to Omar, though a majority of these were probably penned by other poets.

In twelfth-century Persia these rubaiyat served a special purpose: freedom of expression. Since one might pay a dear price for such expression, the rubaiyat, with their veiled allusions, offered protection from inquisitors. While other verse forms might tell stories or embody religious ideas, the rubaiyat contained the more authentic feelings and ideas of its author and thus became a very personal medium of expression. The most unorthodox ideas could be given innocuous interpretations so as to offend no one.

What we find in Omar's rubaiyat, which were not written for publication, is the thought of a vigorous "freethinker"

*The Wine of Life keeps oozing drop by drop,*
*The leaves of Life keep falling one by one.*

*Ah, make the most of what we yet may spend,*
*Before we too into the Dust descend; . . . .*

*"While you live,*
*Drink! for, once dead, you never shall return."*

*Into this Universe, and Why not knowing*
*Nor Whence, like Water willy-nilly flowing;*
*  And out of it, as Wind along the Waste,*
*I know not Whither, willy-nilly blowing.*

*Ah, my Beloved, fill the Cup that clears*
*TO-DAY of past Regrets and future Fears:*
*  To-morrow!—Why, To-morrow I may be*
*Myself with Yesterday's Sev'n thousand Years.*

*Come, fill the Cup, and in the fire of Spring*
*Your Winter-garment of Repentance fling:*
*  The Bird of Time has but a little way*
*To flutter—and the Bird is on the Wing.*

*A Book of Verses underneath the Bough,*
*A Jug of Wine, a Loaf of Bread—and Thou*
*  Beside me singing in the Wilderness—*
*Oh, Wilderness were Paradise enow!*

*Not one returns to tell us of
the Road,
Which to discover we must
travel too.*

*I sent my Soul through the
Invisible,
Some letter of that After-life
to spell:
    And by and by my Soul
return'd to me,
And answer'd "I Myself am
Heav'n and Hell."*

*The Moving Finger writes;
and having writ,
Moves on: nor all your Piety
nor Wit
    Shall lure it back to cancel
half a Line,
Nor all your Tears wash out a
Word of it.*

who is fighting stupidity and hypocrisy. They are the outpourings of a soul undergoing great personal struggle. Further, they express outrage toward Time and Fate and the absurd futility of the human dream. Omar's cry of agony comes from the fact that his mind clearly sees that religion's preachments about life and death are wrong; but, try as he will, he cannot drive through to any comforting solution of his own. His lines are bitterest when he sees Fate canceling all that he has cherished: the splendor of marble palaces, the beauty of the rose, the laughter and the love of a lover. He rages, he ridicules, he tries to celebrate; but in the end, he despairs. In this life, while "the Moving Finger writes," there can be no peace.

Omar is in love with life—an emotion that most religions strongly discourage. His mind is filled with images of beautiful things: fields of golden grain, red roses and purple hyacinths, flowing water, wind, snow in the desert, caravans, books, merriment with friends, music and song, lips he has kissed and tresses caressed, a jug of wine, a potter thumping his clay, a muezzin chanting from the minaret. . . .

But a shadow darkens the splendor of all he sees. A rose is a rose, Omar reminds himself; the moon is the moon; his lover is his lover. But he utterly fails, for a rose is not a rose but a loveliness that blossoms today, then wilts tomorrow and dries into dust. And his lover, beside him now "singing in the wilderness"— tomorrow his lover, too, will be dust beneath the rose bush. And the moon—

Yon rising Moon that looks for us
    again—
How oft hereafter will she wax and
    wane
How oft hereafter rising look for us
Through this same Garden—and for
    one in vain!

A rose is not a rose for Omar; it is a rose-in-time. *Time* is the enemy. He rages at it for what it does to us—bringing us life and beauty and dreams, then coldly quenching that beauty and killing the dreams. Time brings, and it takes away. Time destroys all, in time. Like a pre-Einsteinian relativist, he knows that realities exist only in a four-dimensional space-time equation. He can't perceive a rose as just a rose, though Heaven knows he tries. He *is* a realist.

The Wine of Life keeps oozing drop by
    drop,
The Leaves of Life keep falling one by
    one.

Omar therefore tries to fall back hard upon the present—

Ah, my Beloved, fill the Cup that
    clears
TO-DAY of past Regrets and future
    Fears: . . .

But this doesn't work very well. "Live for today—it's all we have." It's a bit like saying forget the world, go lie on the beach, and hear only the joyous sounds of the sea—while your heart is breaking. True, you may long with all your heart to accomplish it, to pretend that what is isn't so, to convince yourself that in a few days, or weeks, or years, time will have taken care of it all and the hurt will be gone—which it will, and you know this. But as often as your mind whispers the wish, the rest of your being cries out that what is is what is. And the pain lingers.

This is what it means to be human: to know that all you have is the present moment, the Now; but to be aware during all your Nows that the time will come, too soon, when the Now is over—and then?

Oh, threats of Hell and Hopes of
    Paradise!
One thing at least is certain—*This*
    Life flies,
One thing is certain and the rest is
    Lies;
The Flower that once has blown
    for ever dies.

One begins to sense a refreshing candor reading through Omar's quatrains. He states simply what many of us have wanted to say. He reproves the cosmos and whatever runs it. "I won't capitulate. . . . No self-respecting human soul would live life as it is Given. It humiliates our hopes and devastates our dreams." This is blunt thinking, and we may prefer our philosophers to be more ambiguous. Sometimes Omar is ambiguous, sometimes he isn't.

In the final analysis, Omar Khayyam came to terms with death—specifically his own death—on his own terms. His religious traditions supplied him with a full set of assumptions preparing a believer for death and the afterlife. But these assumptions didn't satisfy Omar, who proceeded to work out his own realities about death, in his own way, with courage and candor. Omar blasphemes because he must, but he blasphemes on our behalf.

The analytic philosopher may want to argue that there is something wrong with Omar's questions; his assumptions are faulty and his logic is flawed. Were he a biologist or physicist, and not a poet, he might have thought in terms of chemical processes and sequences of causal events. But in the last analysis, Omar may be right: he speaks our pain for us, crying out against the Tyranny of Time.

Not a few scholars have suggested that Omar's ideas should be heard with common sense: that our picture of him must not be one of an unkempt drunkard by the wayside but rather of a quiet sage living his daily rounds, watching the stars, drawing circles with his compass, drinking with his friends. Not that his pain was not deep; his quatrains are certainly not cold equations. But for Omar, as for the rest of us, life must still be lived hourly, and with whatever gusto an old "freethinker" can muster.

It is pleasant to believe that Omar's despair might have been eased by a modicum of wit—which we know he possessed, for we are told that Omar one day came upon some bricklayers repairing the academy of Nishapur. They were having trouble with a donkey, loaded down with bricks, that was refusing to enter the building, despite kicking and prodding. Omar laughed, and going up to the donkey, whispered in its ear:

O lost and now returned, *'yet more astray'*
Thy name from men's remembrance passed away,
Thy nails have now combined to form thy hoofs,
Thy tail's a beard turned round the other way!

Without further ado, the donkey trotted into the building, and the workmen asked Omar how he had persuaded the stubborn animal to move. He replied that in a previous life the donkey had been a lecturer at this very academy, and that, until it was recognized and acknowledged, it was unwilling to visit his old friends.

And if *you* saw a donkey acting like a jackass, could you resist the temptation to walk up to it and say *something* in its ear? Omar's laughter echoes through the centuries, though early writers, who had misplaced their sense of humor, missed Omar's delight and invested the account with weighty implications of strange powers and doctrines of reincarnation.

Today the grave of Omar Khayyam is known or visited by few. It is to be found four miles southeast of the town of Nishapur, adjacent to a mosque. Visitors, it is certain, would be welcome: should we in our joyous rounds reach the spot where he is dust, we are invited to have one on him, and "turn down an empty Glass!"

Dedicated to Dr. Robert W. Smith.

# 8 4

## THE KNOWLEDGE THAT HURTS MOST

Once there lived in the ancient city of Afkar two learned men who hated and belittled each other's learning. For one of them denied the existence of the gods and the other was a believer.

One day the two met in the market-place, and amidst their followers they began to dispute and to argue about the existence or the non-existence of the gods. And after hours of contention they parted.

That evening the unbeliever went to the temple and prostrated himself before the altar and prayed the gods to forgive his wayward past.

And the same hour the other learned man, he who had upheld the gods, burned his sacred books. For he had become an unbeliever.

KAHLIL GIBRAN

*Ever look at a male lion in a zoo? Fresh meat on time, females supplied, no hunter to worry about—he's got it made, hasn't he?* **Then why does he look bored?**

**ROBERT HEINLEIN**
*Glory Road*

The Don Juan of the Mind: no philosopher or poet has yet discovered him. What he lacks is the love of the things he knows, what he possesses is *esprit*, the itch and delight in the chase and intrigue of knowledge—knowledge as far and high as the most distant stars. Until in the end there is nothing left for him to chase except the knowledge which hurts most, just as a drunkard in the end drinks absinthe and methylated spirits. And in the very end he craves for Hell—it is the only knowledge which can still seduce him. Perhaps it too will disappoint, as everything that he knows. And if so, he will have to stand transfixed through all eternity, nailed to disillusion, having himself become the Guest of Stone, longing for a last supper of knowledge which he will never receive. For in the whole world of things there is nothing left to feed his hunger.

FRIEDRICH NIETZSCHE

*Does the grass bend when the wind blows upon it?*
**CONFUCIUS**

## WHAT *DID* I WANT?

*Philosophy is the highest music.*

PLATO

"... in New Orleans. On Bourbon Street."

"No, that's your dream. It's not mine."

"Well, then, what is yours?"

"I have no dream."

"How terrible for you!"

TENNESSEE WILLIAMS

**This Property Is Condemned**

New Zealand, maybe. The *Herald-Trib* had had the usual headlines, only more so. It looked as if the boys (just big playful boys!) who run this planet were about to hold that major war, the one with ICBMs and H-bombs, any time now.

If a man went as far south as New Zealand there might be something left after the fallout fell out.

New Zealand is supposed to be very pretty and they say that a fisherman there regards a five-pound trout as too small to take home.

I had caught a two-pound trout once.

About then I made a horrible discovery. I didn't want to go back to school, win, lose, or draw. I no longer gave a damn about three-car garages and swimming pools, nor any other status symbol or "security." There was *no* security in this world and only damn fools and mice thought there could be.

Somewhere back in the jungle I had shucked off all ambition of that sort. I had been shot at too many times and had lost interest in supermarkets and exurban subdivisions and tonight is the PTA supper don't forget dear you promised.

Oh, I wasn't about to hole up in a monastery. I still wanted—

What *did* I want?

I wanted a Roc's egg. I wanted a harem loaded with lovely odalisques less than the dust beneath my chariot wheels, the rust that never stained my sword. I wanted raw red gold in nuggets the size of your fist and feed that lousy claim jumper to the huskies! I wanted to get up feeling brisk and go out and break some lances, then pick a likely wench for my *droit du seigneur*—I wanted to stand up to the Baron and *dare* him to touch my wench. I wanted to hear the purple water chuckling against the skin of the *Nancy Lee* in the cool of the morning watch and not another sound, nor any movement save the slow tilting of the wings of the albatross that had been pacing us the last thousand miles.

I wanted the hurtling moons of Barsoom. I wanted Storisende and Poictesme, and Holmes shaking me awake to tell me, "The game's afoot!" I wanted to float down the Mississippi on a raft and elude a mob in company with the Duke of Bilgewater and the Lost Dauphin.

paper flower
paper bird
paper moon
who walks
the wild earth
any more ?

I wanted Prester John, and Excalibur held by a moon-white arm out of a silent lake. I wanted to sail with Ulysses and with Tros of Samothrace and eat the lotus in a land that seemed always afternoon. I wanted the feeling of romance and the sense of wonder I had known as a kid. I wanted the world to be what they had promised me it was going to be—instead of the tawdry, lousy, fouled-up mess it is. . . .

Maybe one chance is all you ever get.

ROBERT HEINLEIN
*Glory Road*

Who has not asked, "What am I doing here?" But what is the answer? *Socrates* believed that we are here to be happy and that the path of happiness is through knowledge, which leads to virtue, which leads to happiness. *Epicurus* taught that we are here to cultivate the pleasures of the mind—wisdom and understanding—but the Cyrenaic philosopher *Aristippus* became famous for teaching that we are here to cultivate pleasures, and the more the merrier (and those of the mind only as a last resort). A prophet from Nazareth, *Yeshua bar Yoseph*, suggested we are here to learn the qualities of faith and love toward one another so that we will merit membership in the Reign of God when it begins. Shortly after that, *Paul of Tarsus* preached that we are here to have faith in the Messiah so that our original sin could be washed away and we would be ready for the return of the Christ.

*Lao-tzu* apparently believed that we are here to seek the Tao and know the inner harmony of Nature's Way; but *Confucius* disagreed, declaring that we are here to discover the proper way to behave in our relationships with others. *The Buddha* taught that we are here to transcend *tanha*—the selfish craving that is the cause of human suffering—and enter the state of *nirvana*. *Shankara*, a Hindu mystic, was convinced that we are here to discover that this world is only *maya* ("illusion") and to realize that each of us is already one with Ultimate Reality.

*Muhammad* believed that we are here to render faithful obedience to Allah as revealed in the Quran. *John Calvin* told the Genevans that we are here solely to love God and so live a life of faith and discipline that we will "enjoy Him forever." But *Hegel*, being a philosopher on the rational side, wrote to persuade us that we are here to develop our capacity for reason and, in so doing, manifest the logic of the Absolute Mind in the movement of human (especially German) history.

## EXISTENCE AND THE REAL: PERSISTENT CONFUSION

It is impossible to define the purpose of life in a general way. "Life" does not mean something vague, but something very real and concrete, just as life's tasks are very real and concrete. They form man's destiny, which is different and unique for each individual. No situation repeats itself and each situation calls for a different response. Sometimes the situation in which a man finds himself may require him to shape his own destiny by action. Sometimes a man may be required simply to accept fate, to bear his cross.

When a man finds that it is his destiny to suffer, he will have to accept suffering as his task; his single and unique task. He will have to struggle for the realization that even in suffering he is unique and alone in the universe. No man can relieve him of his suffering, or suffer in his place. His unique opportunity lies in the way in which he bears his burden.

VIKTOR FRANKL

The central character of *Nausea*, Antoine Roquentin, enunciates Jean-Paul Sartre's reflections on the meaning of human existence.

Prior to these past few days, I had really never felt what it means "to exist." . . . Ordinarily, existence hides itself. It is here, round about us, within us: we are it, and

---

*If I had my life to live over again, I would have made it a rule to read some poetry and listen to some music at least every week. . . . The loss of these tastes is a loss of happiness, and may possibly be injurious to the intellect, and more probably to the moral character, by enfeebling the emotional part of our nature.*

CHARLES DARWIN

*Man is by nature a purposive creature, who develops neuroses when purpose is denied him.*

COLIN WILSON

*The true biologist deals with life, with teaming boisterous life, and learns something from it, learns that the first rule of life is living. The dryballs cannot possibly know a thing every starfish knows in the core of his soul and in the vesicles between his rays.*

JOHN STEINBECK

*If a patient [should ask] Frankl, "What is the meaning of life for me?" he is likely to get a Socratic answer: "What is the best chess move?"*

AARON UNGERSMA

## LESSONS

Charles Beard (1874–1948) was a renowned historian and economist. His colleague, George Counts, tells of a conversation they had in the autumn of 1931.

He and I were motoring over the hills of Connecticut in the vicinity of New Milford. Having been profoundly impressed by the vast range of his knowledge and thought, a range that seemed to embrace the entire human record from ancient times, I asked how long it would take him to tell all he had learned from his lifetime study of history. After contemplating the question a few moments he replied that he "thought" he could do it in "about a week." We drove on a short distance in silence. Whereupon he said he could probably do it in a day. After another brief pause, he reduced the time to half an hour. Finally, bringing his hand down on his knee, he said: "I can tell you all I have learned in a lifetime of study in just three laws of history. And here they are:

"First, whom the gods would destroy they first make mad."

"Second, the mills of the gods grind slowly, yet they grind exceedingly fine."

"Third, the bee fertilizes the flower that it robs."

About ten days later we took a stroll along Riverside Drive in New York City. Evidently he had been giving further thought to my question. At any rate, he said he would like to add a fourth law to his laws of history:

"When it gets dark enough you can see the stars."

GEORGE S. COUNTS
"Charles Beard, The Public Man,"
in Howard K. Beale (ed.)
*Charles A. Beard: An Appraisal*

*How terrifying and glorious the role of man if, indeed, without guidance and without consolation he must create from his own vitals the meaning for his existence and write the rules whereby he lives.*

THORNTON WILDER
*Julius Caesar*

*Those who have suffered much become very bitter or very gentle.*

WILL DURANT

we cannot speak two words without speaking of it, but in the end we never grasp it. . . . Existence is not something which can be thought from a distance: it overwhelms you brusquely. . . .

[Existence means nothing more than] to be here; existents appear, they are encountered, but they can never be inferentially deduced. I believe there are people who have understood this, but they have been trying to overcome this contingency by inventing a Necessary Being who causes himself (a *causa sui*). No Necessary Being, however, can explain existence. . . . There is not the least reason for our "being-there." . . . And I, too, am *"de trop"* [superfluous, unnecessary, absurd]. And yet people are trying to hide themselves behind the idea of law and necessity. In vain: every existent is born without reason, prolongs its existence owing to the weakness of inertia, and dies fortuitously.

JEAN-PAUL SARTRE

That Man is the product of causes which had no prevision of the end they were achieving; that his origin, his growth, his hopes and fears, his loves and his beliefs, are but the outcome of accidental collocations of atoms; that no fire, no heroism, no intensity of thought and feeling, can preserve an individual life beyond the grave; that all the labours of the ages, all the devotion, all the inspiration, all the noonday brightness of human genius, are destined to extinction in the vast death of the solar system, and that the whole temple of Man's achievement must inevitably be buried beneath the debris of a universe in ruins—all these things, if not quite beyond dispute, are yet so nearly certain, that no philosophy which rejects them can hope to stand. Only within the scaffolding of these truths, only on the firm foundation of unyielding despair, can the soul's habitation henceforth be safely built.

BERTRAND RUSSELL

## TRIVIALITIES

But wherein do such pronouncements about the absurdity of existence become statements about the real world? Are they not more on the order of reflexive value judgments that betray the inner world of the individuals who make them? After all, to say the world is meaningless is merely to say, "I find no meaning in it." Value judgments are personal responses, not scientific descriptions.

Much modern Western philosophy has contended that there are no real values and that, by a sort of hopeless *tour de force*, each of us must inject meaning into his own life. Existentialists such as Heidegger and Sartre have held that only a personal confrontation with death itself puts our lives in perspective but that this "flash of authenticity" cannot be made a part of our everyday

*When the universe has crushed him man will still be nobler than that which kills him, because he knows that he is dying, and of its victory the universe knows nothing.*
BLAISE PASCAL

### THE CREATIONS OF MY MIND

1.  With clarity and quiet, I look upon the world and say: All that I see, hear, taste, smell, and touch are the creations of my mind.

2.  The sun comes up and the sun goes down in my skull. Out of one of my temples the sun rises, and into the other the sun sets.

3.  The stars shine in my brain; ideas, men, animals browse in my temporal head; songs and weeping fill the twisted shells of my ears and storm the air for a moment.

4.  My brain blots out, and all, the heavens and the earth, vanish.

5.  The mind shouts: "Only I exist!

6.  "Deep in my subterranean cells my five senses labor; they weave and unweave space and time, joy and sorrow, matter and spirit. . . .

10.  "I impose order on disorder and give a face—my face—to chaos.

11.  "I do not know whether behind appearances there lives and moves a secret essence superior to me. Nor do I ask; I do not care. I create phenomena in swarms, and paint with a full palette a gigantic and gaudy curtain before the abyss. Do not say, 'Draw the curtain that I may see the painting.' The curtain IS the painting. . . .

13.  "I am the worker of the abyss. I am the spectator of the abyss. I am both theory and practice. I am the law. Nothing beyond me exists."

NIKOS KAZANTZAKIS
*The Saviours of God*

*If you are creating, how can you not feel alive?*
LORI VILLAMIL

consciousness. But this is questionable, for "there are states of consciousness that are not 'everyday consciousness' and which are not 'transcendental' either. These produce a definite sense of values and purpose." In saying this, perhaps Colin Wilson is closer to the truth, and he goes on:

> "Peak experiences" all seem to have the same "content": that the chief mistake of human beings is to pay too much attention to everyday trivialities. We are strangely inefficient machines, utilizing only a fraction of our powers, and the reason for this is our short sightedness. Koestler's "mystical" insight made him feel that even the threat of death was a triviality that should be ignored; "So what? . . . Have you nothing more serious to worry about?" Greene's whisky priest: "It seemed to him, at that moment, that it would have been quite easy to be a saint." Death reveals to us that our lives have been one long miscalculation, based on a triviality.

> A painter who is painting a large canvas has to work with his nose to the canvas, but periodically he stands back to see the effect of the whole. These over-all glimpses renew his sense of purpose.
> Man's evolution depends upon a renewal of the sense of over-all purpose. For several centuries now, the direction of our culture has been a concentration upon the minute, the particular. In the field of science, this has produced our present high level of technological achievement. In the field of culture, we have less reason for self-congratulation, for the concentration upon the particular—to the exclusion of wider meanings—has led us into a *cul de sac.* Yeats described the result as "fish gasping on the strand"—a minute realism that has lost all drive and purpose.

## WORK, WORK...TO KILL THE FLOWERS

In subjecting these views to the critical questioning that constitutes one important side of the philosophical task, we are, therefore, engaging in an experiment that is both very personal and at the same time "vicarious." We are not only taking the personal risk of having our views exposed as inadequate, but, since most of our views are also those of the vast majority of the rest of the people in our culture, it is the intellectual outlook of our whole culture that is here being put to the test. If we should suffer the collapse of some of our cherished beliefs (and the loss of a cherished belief does involve a painful sort of suffering), then it is not only for ourselves that we suffer, but for those many others in our culture who share those beliefs. It is only through such suffering, however, that human thought progresses.

But human thought does progress, and this is what makes the enterprise worthwhile. Many people must have suffered the kind of intellectual agony of which we have been speaking, during the long interval of time that separates us from our primitive ancestors; but there can be little doubt that our way of looking at the world—our world-view—is closer to the truth than the superstitious, animistic, magical views that they are known to have held. If our view is not the whole truth—and it would surely be presumptuous to say that it is—then let us press on toward that elusive goal as best we can. It is the lure of beliefs that are closer to the truth that beckons us on and leaves us dissatisfied with beliefs that are obviously short of that goal.

WILLIAM HALVERSON

Just when a humanlike consciousness—in the form of self-awareness—began, we cannot at present tell. Perhaps 2 million years ago, perhaps 14 million, perhaps more. But the question is academic. The significant thing is that

*I have the key to happiness: remember to be profoundly, totally conscious that you are.*
*I myself, sorry to say, hardly ever use this key. I keep losing it.*

EUGENE IONESCO

*In shallow ponds, even little fish can stir up a commotion. In the oceans, the largest whales make hardly a ripple.*

**Hindu proverb**

## GROWN-UPS ARE VERY STRANGE

When you can measure what you are speaking about, and express it in numbers, you know something about it; but when you cannot measure it, when you cannot express it in numbers, your knowledge is of a meager and unsatisfactory kind: it may be the beginning of knowledge, but you have scarcely, in your thoughts, advanced to the stage of science.

WILLIAM THOMSON, LORD KELVIN
*Popular Lectures and Addresses*

Grown-ups love figures. When you tell them that you have made a new friend, they never ask you any questions about essential matters. They never say to you, "What does his voice sound like? What games does he love best? Does he collect butterflies?" Instead they demand: "How old is he? How many brothers has he? How much does he weigh? How much money does his father make?" Only from these figures do they think they have learned anything about him.

ANTOINE DE SAINT-EXUPÉRY
*The Little Prince*

we are giving birth to, developing, flowering, a seed planted ages ago; and that this is a glorious flowering, whatever the pain we must pay for the seeds of such flowering. After flowering, most flowers die, though most plants do not die but continue to live and grow. This inevitable flowering of man's awareness is totally unavoidable, and like a flower that has gradually, slowly, grown from bud to its moment of opening to the world, there is no turning back; it is flower, or die.

*Many a time I have wanted to stop talking and find out what I really believed.*
**WALTER LIPPMAN**

Now the cello has stopped. All that can be heard is the ironic funeral march from the first symphony of Mahler. The girl is walking across the desert towards a hill, the only feature in the otherwise gently sloping terrain, apart from a black plume of smoke which is rising distantly in the air. As she gets nearer to this oily cloud of smoke, scurrying human activity can be seen on the ground beneath. Occasionally a gout of bright flame bursts along the ground, and more smoke is added to the cloud rising swiftly in the air. Now the camera, in a tracking shot, reveals a close-up of the girl's face as she walks along. At first lines of concentration furrow her forehead as she tries to make out what is going on, then the concentration is replaced by bewilderment, and then, a little later, by anger. Now the camera is static, and we see the whole scene as the girl walks up.

Men in shirt sleeves are rushing about, their faces grimy and shining with sweat. They look bewildered and panic-stricken, but this is obviously their normal state of mind. On their backs they carry the large chemical tanks of flamethrowers, and the straps have rubbed into their shoulders for so long that they are obviously in great pain. All around the ground is seared and black. It appears that nothing could possibly grow in such a devastated place, but straggly vegetation is visibly thrusting itself up through the soil. Every moment one of the strange plants is beginning to bloom. . . . A bud appears, almost instantaneously, and begins to open. Lush, coloured petals are visible, promising future beauty. But as soon as one of the men sees this he moves up and immerses the plant in a bath of flame from the nozzle of the weapon he is carrying. All that is left when the fire dies away is charred black soil. But after only a few seconds, pushing up through this inhospitable earth, can be seen a new plant.

The girl clearly doesn't like this place, but when one of the men comes close to her, a fevered expression on his face, she lightly touches his arm.

GIRL.  What is this? What are you doing?

MAN.  Killing them.

GIRL.  But—why?

MAN.  To stop them from growing. *(The man turns away to spread a carpet of flame, and then turns back to the girl.)* The only way is to kill them. If we weren't doing this good work they'd be spreading all over the desert.

GIRL.  But why do you want to stop them?

MAN.  We don't want these—these filthy blossoms all over the desert. For one thing they'd encourage laxness—all our men would be too lazy to do any useful work, like they're doing now.

GIRL.  But the only reason they're working is to kill the flowers.

MAN.  And besides which, we're used to the desert. When I see those disgusting petals coming out I feel a strange—tension inside me. What would happen if I gave way to that, and watched them evolving all the way? And anyway, why are you so interested? I don't like the kind of talk you're giving me.

GIRL.  It's just that I can't understand you. You're killing something that's beautiful and alive, something that can grow and give you pleasure. . . .

The man looks at the girl with a disgusted expression on his face, and quite deliberately spits at the ground by her feet. Then he turns back to his work. But just before his face goes out of frame his expression can be seen to change from one of disgust to an infinite sadness. The music fades.

LANGDON JONES
"The Eye of the Lens"

## THE WORLD-RIDDLE

Each man tries in his personal, and perhaps desperate, way to make this short life/time meaningful. We identify with the things of our universe that are comparatively timeless—with the rock-ribbed mountains, the washing oceans, the stars, with evolution, with life itself—to appropriate a little part of their time spans, their seeming immortality. Or we alleviate nonbeing by losing our selves within great causes and great principles and great people; or by becoming a part of the teleocosmic drama of our society and our religion.

Behind all this is the burden of our consciousness of death. We must attempt to be immortal, to be God, and to ease the dread of nonexistence.

But to strive to feel one with the stars—what is this but to die? Stars die. Earth's light will go out; life may dim and vanish, here. No matter: *we are* a part, an ever-so-tiny part, of the infinite program of the universe. I do not deceive myself into thinking I am buying time by longing for the suns or immersing myself in life. *I am* one with the stars. *I am* one with life. I identify, rightly, with all birth and all death of all time. And when I die, I shall not need to feel as

---

*Man can will nothing unless he has first understood that he must count on no one but himself; that he is alone, abandoned on earth in the midst of his infinite responsibilities; without help, with no other aim than the one he sets himself, with no other destiny than the one he forces for himself on this earth.*

JEAN-PAUL SARTRE

*"My soul, your voyages have been your native land!"*

NIKOS KAZANTZAKIS
*"Odysseus" The Odyssey*

*Wer immer streben sich bemüht,*
*Den können wir erlösen.*
*(Who strives always to the utmost, him can we save.)*

JOHANN WOLFGANG VON GOETHE

*"What is the Way [Tao]?" Nansen answered, "Your everyday mind is the Way." "How, then, does one get into accord with it?" "If you try to accord, you deviate." Life, he is saying, is not a problem, so why are you asking for a solution?*

ALAN WATTS

though I never was at all; but rather *that* I was, and that is enough. I was a part of it all. I remain a part of all past and all future. I am a moment within the energy systems of motion and life and purpose.

Does this ease my loneliness? Yes. All this follows naturally from the constantly expanding boundaries of my conscious relatedness: the finite self within the context of the infinite.

*What is the meaning of existence?*

*Earthrise.* Photo of the blue and white planet, Earth, by the first terran space travelers, December, 1968. Taken by the crew of Apollo VIII when they were 240,000 miles from home. Photo courtesy of NASA.

# NIKOS KAZANTZAKIS

## *"I Know Not If I Shall Ever Anchor"*

Now the day's work is done. "I collect my tools: sight, smell, touch, taste, hearing, intellect. Night has fallen . . . . I return like a mole to my home, the ground. Not because I am tired and cannot work. I am not tired. But the sun has set."

With these words Nikos Kazantzakis begins the story of his life, an adventure of the mind and spirit, an odyssey—an *ascent.*

Three thousand years ago the Greek poet Homer narrated the story of Odysseus the seafarer who left his homeland, fought great battles, sailed the Aegean isles, drank, loved, and returned home to betrayal and boredom, then set sail again to see and conquer a larger world that dreamers never know.

In 1938 Kazantzakis created a sequel to Homer's epic poem, beginning where Homer left off. Odysseus is still the hero; he returns home, slays his wife's paramours, regains his place of authority, fathers dull offspring, and becomes thoroughly bored with it all. So he gathers his followers, builds a boat, and sails away on a final great journey.

No map, no itinerary, no plan: an unscheduled voyage of freedom to explore the known world and to die in triumph, finally, in the Antarctic.

Does Odysseus find what he is seeking? No. Does he save his soul? No. Nor does it matter. Through the search itself he achieves a noble spirit. It matters not in the end that he is not delivered; he has battled through the seven levels of the soul to achieve himself. His God has been the search for God. "My soul," Odysseus cries out, "your voyages have been your native land!"

✦

Nikos Kazantzakis was born into the passionate peasantry of Crete and raised with fishermen, farmers, and shepherds. His father Michaeles was a burly patriot who grew a long black beard to mourn the loss of Cretan freedom to the Turks.

Nikos later wrote that he never felt any tenderness or love from, or for, his father—only fear. "The fear he called forth in me was so great that all the rest—love, respect, intimacy—vanished." "An oak he was, with a hard trunk, rough leaves, bitter fruit, and no flowers. . . . He ate up all the strength around him; in his shade every other tree withered. I withered. . . . He it was who reduced my blood to ink."

Nikos early displayed the qualities of the scholar he would become—observant, questioning, shy, creative, nonconforming; and Michaeles, bewildered, from afar watched his son grow. "My father was wild and uneducated, but he never denied me anything when it was a question of my intellectual development. Once I overheard him say to a friend when he was in a good mood, 'Who cares about the bloody vineyards, or the raisins, wine, and olive oil! Let the whole harvest turn into paper and ink for my son! I have faith in him.'"

By contrast Nikos' relationship with his mother, Marghi, was one of secure silence. Always a mysterious shadow, she told him of her home village, their ancestors, and sailing ships. "I had never seen my mother laugh; she simply smiled and regarded everyone with deep-set eyes filled with patience and kindness. She came and went in the house like a kindly sprite, anticipating our every need without noise or effort. . . ." Her world was composed of knitting socks, cleaning vegetables, talking with neighbors, caring for the children, and greeting her husband at the door.

"Both of my parents circulate in my blood, the one fierce, hard, and morose, the other tender, kind, and saintly. I have carried them all my days; neither has died. As long as I live they too will live inside me and battle in their antithetical ways to govern my thoughts and actions. My lifelong effort is to reconcile them so that the one may give me his strength, the other her tenderness; to make the discord between them, which breaks out incessantly within me, turn to harmony inside their son's heart."

His childhood was passed in the spartan villages and the bustling streets of Herakleion. At the age of five his mother placed a golden baptismal cross around his neck and his father marched him off—"like a small sacrificial vic-

tim"—to the local school run by Greek Orthodox priests. "You're going to learn to read and write here so you can become a man," his father explained. "Cross yourself."

Between switchings, he learned about geography, history, politics, Turks, Greeks, and Greek grammar; but religious history fascinated him above all. It was a marvelous fairy tale "with serpents who talked, floods and rainbows, thefts and murders. Brother killed brother, father wanted to slaughter his only son, God intervened every two minutes and did His share of killing, people crossed the sea without wetting their feet."

How all these marvelous things could have happened, "we did not understand. We asked the teacher, and he coughed, raised his switch angrily and shouted, 'Stop this impertinence! How many times do I have to tell you—no talking!'

"'But we don't understand, sir,' we whined.

"'These are God's doings,' the teacher answered. 'We're not supposed to understand. It's a sin!'

"We shrank into our desks and did not utter a sound."

Hatred between Greek and Turk flamed into bloodshed, and Michaeles sailed with his family to the island of Naxos where Nikos was enrolled in a school run by French Catholics. "Until this time Crete and Greece had been the confined arena in which my struggling soul was jammed; now the world broadened, the divisions of humanity multiplied, and my adolescent breast creaked in an effort to contain them all. Before this moment I had divined but had never known with such positiveness that the world is extremely large and that suffering and toil are the companions and fellow warriors not only of the Cretan, but of every man. . . ."

After the successful uprising of the Cretans against the Turks in 1897, Michaeles brought his son home to a free Crete and a passionate summer of

*I am a mariner of Odysseus with heart afire but with mind ruthless clear; not, however, of that Odysseus who returned to Ithaca and stayed there, but of that other Odysseus who returned, killed his enemies and, stifled in his native land, put out to sea once more.*

*All my life I struggled to stretch my mind to the breaking point, until it began to creak, in order to create a great thought which might be able to give a new meaning to life, a new meaning to death, and to console mankind.*

*Each man acquires the stature of the enemy with whom he wrestles. It pleased me, even if it meant my destruction, to wrestle with God.*

*I force my body to obey my soul, and thus I never tire.*

*God sits waiting at the end of every road.*

*I said to the almond tree, "Sister, speak to me of God." And the almond tree blossomed.*

*". . . The soul of man is an arrow: it darts as high as it can toward heaven but always falls back down again to earth. Life on earth means shedding one's wings."* [Jesus in The Last Temptation of Christ.]

freedom. His education continued, disrupted now only by the turbulent onset of adolescence. There awakened in him two clamoring beasts: that leopard, the flesh—relentless, hungry—and that eagle, the mind—insatiable and thirsty for understanding. For the moment, however, the mind soared ahead of the flesh. "I kept asking myself, How can people sing, how is it their hearts are not throbbing to learn what God's nature is, and where we come from, and where we are going."

Nikos completed his secondary education at the gymnasium in Herakleion, then sailed to Athens and spent a dismal four years pursuing a law degree at the university. But all his law courses failed utterly to nourish the needs of his mind or heart. He reminisces, sadly: "My heart breaks when I bring to mind those years I spent as a university student in Athens. Though I looked, I saw nothing. . . . In Crete I had risen in revolt against my destiny. I had given myself over to wine for one moment, touched the Irish girl for another moment. But this was not my road. . . ."

After university Nikos returned to Crete for a summer, and there he wandered the countryside, alone except for his books and notebooks. He had begun to feel the luminous satisfactions of writing. "Here is my road, here is duty." He was struggling with the ultimate themes of life and death. "Each man acquires the stature of the enemy with whom he wrestles. It pleased me, even if it meant my destruction, to wrestle with God."

◆

In the prologue to his autobiography, *Report to Greco*, Kazantzakis wrote that there are three kinds of souls: One kind of soul says "I am a bow in your hands, Lord. Draw me, lest I rot." A second kind says "Do not overdraw me, Lord. I shall break." But a third kind says "Overdraw me, Lord, and who cares if I break!"

Kazantzakis, of course, was a soul of the third kind.

These are the questions that haunted Kazantzakis' mind and heart for a lifetime: Who/What is God? What is Man's place in the world? What is the ultimate destiny of Mankind?

During his time in Paris, he had become acquainted with the ideas of two of the great Western philosophers, Nietzsche and Bergson. He was not merely influenced by them; he was overwhelmed and devastated. He wrote:

Indignation had overcome me in those early years. I remember that I could not bear the pyrotechnics of human existence: how life ignited for an instant, burst in the air in a myriad of color flares, then all at once vanished. Who ignited it? Who gave it such fascination and beauty, then suddenly, pitilessly, snuffed it out? "No," I shouted, "I will not accept this, will not subscribe; I shall find some way to keep life from expiring."

Kazantzakis fell under the spell of Nietzsche and made a pilgrimage to all the towns in Germany where the poet/philosopher had lived. Nietzsche's Dionysian vision of man shaping himself into the superman by sheer force of will and courage captured Kazantzakis' imagination and taught him that the only way one can be free is to struggle—to lose oneself in a cause, to fight fiercely for that cause without recoil, without fear, and without hope of reward.

But as the struggle continued, it was Bergson who was finally able to heal. Early on Kazantzakis had abandoned as too materialistic the anthropomorphic imagery of Christian tradition. Now he was moved by Bergson's Apollonian concept of an *élan vital*—a life-force that can manipulate and organize matter. Under Bergson's guidance, he came to think of God not as a person or a *persona* but as an elemental force field of living nature working to effect more complex organizations of matter, moving relentlessly and opportunistically to produce higher forms of life. God is not matter;

and the World/Cosmos is not (pantheistically) the "body of God." God, rather, is the antientropic life-force that organizes elemental matter into systems that can manifest ever more subtle and advanced forms of being and consciousness. We humans have our place as golden links in the chain of being that leads on toward forms of life yet undreamed of. Our lives develop meaning as we realize our selves as links in that chain.

Our duty is to try to find the rhythm of God's progression, and when we find it to adjust, as much as we can, the rhythms of our small and ephemeral life with his. Only thus may we mortals manage to achieve something immortal. . . . We all ascend together, swept up by a mysterious and invisible Urge. Where are we going? No one knows. Don't ask, mount higher! Perhaps we are going nowhere, perhaps there is no one to pay us the rewarding wages of our lives. So much the better! For thus may we conquer the last, the greatest of all temptations—that of Hope. We fight because that is how we want it. . . . We sing even though we know that no ear exists to hear us; we toil though there is no employer to pay us our wages when night falls.

Nietzsche showed Kazantzakis how to frame the question; Bergson pointed the way toward an answer. "My heart's calmness always returned when I went to hear Bergson's magical voice. . . . His words were a bewitching spell that opened a small door in the bowels of necessity and allowed light to pour in."

In the search for God, where does Kazantzakis come out? Not as a true believer. Not as a Marxist prophet. Certainly not as a saint. Not as a Christ redeemed by the cross or a Buddha delivered from the world of pain. And not as a lover of women or father to a family. None of these things matter: his kingdom is not of this world. Does it matter in the end

that—following in the wake of his mentor Odysseus—he does not *become* something, that he does not *arrive*, that he is not *transmogrified into spirit?* No. It matters not.

Homer's Odysseus went in search of his homeland; Kazantzakis' Odysseus sought God. "The first found his Ithaca, the second became the slayer of gods, searching for the true God." In the end, Kazantzakis knows that *he* is Odysseus but knows not if he will ever anchor in Ithaca—"unless Ithaca is the voyage itself."

◆

Nikos looked the way an ascetic Greek scholar should: tall, thin, angular, with piercing eyes and shaggy brows. He dressed simply in black suit and sailor's sweater. He ate sparingly, often working through days and nights and forgetting to eat. Each morning he rose at six o'clock and took a two-hour walk before breakfast.

He worked unceasingly. The last decade of his life was marked by an easing of inner conflicts and prolific writing. From 1948 to 1957 he produced eight books. By the age of 70 his novels had been translated into thirty languages, and he was famed throughout Europe and America, mostly in the latter from the movie version of *Zorba the Greek*.

He loved his solitude. His inner life was intensely emotional, but outwardly he appeared serene, as though he were occupied with higher tensions parallel to, but quite above, the human drama. He possessed "a spiritual and mental energy," a psychologist once told him, "quite beyond the normal." He loved the sea, music, the rain, traveling. He was honest, simple, direct, and without guile.

In 1953 Kazantzakis developed leukemia, but it had little immediate effect upon the pace of his life and work. He knew he had not finished his work; he had volumes to write; he needed more time. "I feel like doing what Bergson

*I see no reason why my grocer should be immortal. Or why I should. But I do see a reason why great souls should not die when they depart the flesh.*

*All of life is struggle.*

*Our lifetime is a brief flash, but sufficient.*

*We sing even though we know that no ear exists to hear us; we toil though there is no employer to pay us our wages when night falls.*

*As I watched the seagulls, I thought: "That's the road to take; find the absolute rhythm and follow it with absolute trust."*

*That which interests me is not man, nor the earth, nor the heavens, but the flame which consumes man, earth, and sky.*

*Each morning the world rediscovers its virginity. . . .*

*Every man has a cry, his cry, to sling into the air before he dies; let us waste no time, therefore, lest we be caught short. It is true that this cry may scatter ineffectually in the air, that there may be no ear either below on earth or above in heaven to hear it. No matter. You are not a sheep, you are a man, and that means a thing which is unsettled and shouts. Well then—shout!*

says—going to the street corner and holding out my hand to start begging from passers-by: 'Alms, brothers! A quarter of an hour from each of you.' Oh, for a little time, just enough to let me finish my work. Afterwards, let Charon come."

In 1957 he visited China on invitation of the government; against his doctor's advice he made the journey, wanting to see what changes had taken place since his visit two decades earlier. In Canton he received a smallpox vaccination to which he had an allergic reaction. He flew home via Tokyo, Alaska, and over the Pole to Denmark, and finally to Freiburg, Germany. Infection, temperature of 105°, flu, complications. He was visited in the University Clinic by Albert Schweitzer, the one man in all the world he most admired. Then, with his wife at his side, he "slept away, lovingly, beautifully, kindly, without complaint." He died October 26, 1957, four months before his 75th birthday.

Charon came at last.

Nikos Kazantzakis was inevitably controversial. Few understood him; passionate Greeks flew into a rage before attempting to understand. His thoughts were too subtle, his phrases too erudite, his allusions veiled, his words undefined (or redefined), his philosophical framework too ethereal for the popular reader.

Not being understood, he was misrepresented. Like Nietzsche he was attacked for what he had never said.

He was first accused of atheism by the Greek Orthodox Church in 1939 and a trial date was set, but he was never summoned. In 1953 the church fathers tried again, outraged by his imaginative treatment of Jesus in *The Last Temptation of Christ*. In 1954 the book was placed on the Index of forbidden books by the Roman Catholic Church. Kazantzakis telegraphed the Committee of the Index a line (in Latin) saying he would go "over their heads" and let the Lord himself be his judge. To the leaders of the Greek Church he wrote (in Greek): "Holy Fathers, you gave me a curse, but I give you a blessing. May your conscience be as pure as mine, and may you be as moral and as religious as I."

After Kazantzakis' death the archbishop of Athens refused to allow his body to lie in state (as was customary for renowned sons of Hellas) or to celebrate a funeral mass for him. At home in Crete he was given a Christian burial and his body was laid to rest by the great wall of the city where he was born.

On his tombstone in Herakleion are engraved the words: "I do not hope for anything. I do not fear anything. I am free."

For an answer which cannot be expressed the question too cannot be expressed. *The riddle* does not exist. If a question can be put at all, then it *can* also be answered. . . . For doubt can only exist where there is a question; a question only where there is an answer, and this only where something can be *said*. We feel that even if *all possible* scientific questions be answered, the problems of life have still not been touched at all. Of course there is then no question left, and just this is the answer. The solution of the problem of life is seen in the vanishing of this problem. (Is not this the reason why men to whom after long doubting the sense of life became clear, could not then say wherein this sense consisted?)

LUDWIG WITTGENSTEIN

The whole world is a circus if you look at it the right way. Every time you watch a rainbow and feel wonder in your heart. Every time you pick up a handful of dust and see not the dust but a mystery, a marvel there in your hand. Every time you stop to think "I'm alive! and being alive is fantastic!" Every time such a thing happens, you're a part of the circus of Dr. Lao.

*The Seven Faces of Dr. Lao*

# REFLECTIONS

1   Assuming that you have just read through this chapter—text, marginal quotations, vignettes, illustrations, and all—then your responses must be numerous, mixed, and fragmented. Without forcing coherence at this point, what are some of the most luminous meaning-events that linger in your mind? Ask yourself why each item is meaningful.

2   Ponder the quotation from Robert Heinlein (see marginal quote on p. 609). How would you answer his question, *"Then why does he look so bored?"*

3   What do you think of the point that Viktor Frankl is making on p. 611?

4   On p. 614 Colin Wilson scores a point that, for many of us, is quite meaningful. What does it say to you?

5   When you compare the statements by Lord Kelvin and Saint-Exupéry (p. 615-Box), what is your first (and most authentic?) response? Can these two points of view be reconciled? Is there room in your life for both?

6   Reflect at length, and with leisure, on the passage from Langdon Jones's "Eye of the Lens." Among several possible meanings, what do you think the author is saying?

7   Having arrived at this point—assuming that you have read through the entire textbook—how would you proceed now to answer such a question as "What is the meaning of life?" or "Why are we here?" Are such questions still meaningful questions? If you still feel a bit stymied by such a question, then study carefully, and with a good deal of time and reflection, just the marginal quotations in this final chapter—then return and attempt to answer the question again. Do this several times, if necessary. If no answer emerges, proceed to Postlude.

*We shall not cease from exploration
And the end of all our exploring
Will be to arrive where we started
And know the place for the first time.*

**T. S. ELIOT**
***Four Quartets***

Omnes Sancti Angeli et Archangeli, intercedite pro nobis. *All ye devoted bodhisattvas, who for us your fellow living beings and for our release have forborne, aeon after aeon, to enter into your rest, tarry with us, we beseech you, yet a little while longer.*

**ARNOLD TOYNBEE**

*May you find your path and follow it!*

***The Buddha***

*"I've traveled so far, and all I've done is come back home."*

**GANDHI** *(the motion picture)*

### POSTLUDE

*The Mahayanas tell the story of a sage*
*who once stood on a riverbank*
*looking across at the opposite shore.*
*Although the far side*
*was but dimly visible*
*through the river mists,*
*he could see that it was*
*unspeakably beautiful.*
*The hills were green*
*and the trees were all in blossom.*

*So he said to himself,*
*"I want to go there."*
*There was a raft tied*
*at the river's edge.*
*He untied the raft*
*and began to paddle*
*toward the distant shore.*

*The journey was long and hazardous*
*for the currents in midstream were swift.*
*The raging rapids tossed and turned the raft,*
*and he had to work with all his strength*
*to maintain his balance.*
*From the center of the river*
*both shores were lost from view,*
*and there were times when he was not sure*
*which way he was drifting.*
*But he continued paddling,*
*and in due time*
*he reached the far shore.*

*He got out of the raft and said,*
*"Ah, at last I am here.*
*It was a perilous journey,*
*but now I have reached nirvana."*
*He looked about him.*
*The hills were green*
*and the trees were all in blossom.*

*Then he turned around and looked back.*
*He could not see the opposite shore*
*whence he came.*
*Nor was there any river to be seen.*
*And there was no raft.*

# GLOSSARY

When making use of the following brief definitions of terms, note again what a definition is. Definitions are only *predictions of possible meanings* which words may be given in living contexts. Exact meanings can never be known apart from the concrete situation in which they are used. Therefore, think of the following definitions merely as openers. For further clarification, refer to the index and note specific contexts in which any particular term is used.

**absolute**   A concept of something which is assumed to be free of all qualifications. Whatever is absolute would be underived, complete, perfect, and unconditioned; as such, it could not be modified or changed in any way.

**abstraction**   A concept, developed in the mind, taking into account only selected characteristics of a set of objects which are thought of as belonging to the same class. Once the mind has created a generalized abstraction (not *this* painting by Gauguin but painting-in-general), the mind is freed from having to deal with particular objects.

**agnosticism**   In epistemology, a term (coined by Thomas Huxley) referring to the deliberate suspension of speculation and judgment about things which cannot be known (e.g., the afterlife or the supernatural). The word can be used to mean "I don't know" or "It cannot be known."

**ambiguous**   Refers to a word or other symbol which is given different meanings in different contexts. To say that a word is ambiguous often means that one is at a loss to interpret it correctly because one doesn't know the original context in which it was used.

**analytic**   (1) A twentieth-century philosophic movement whose main concerns are the logical analysis of language and the process of reasoning. (2) In epistemology, a particular kind of statement in which the predicate merely spells out what the subject implies (e.g., "A triangle has three angles"). An analytic statement says nothing about the real world.

**anthropomorphic**   Literally, "in the form of man." The projection of human qualities onto nonhuman objects (e.g., nature, animals, deities). For instance, the Greek gods and goddesses were anthropomorphic, possessing all the physical, mental, and emotional characteristics of mortals.

**antinomian**   Literally, "against the law." In the widest sense, refers to those who deliberately choose to exist outside the accepted BTF-patterns of their society. In Western religion, the word is often used to refer to religious groups which, considering themselves saved by their faith or special knowledge, hold that they are then above all laws and restrictions.

**apocalyptic**   A specific movement in Western religious thought and literature purporting to reveal the (heretofore hidden) divine plan of history. In the four great Western religions (Zoroastrianism, Judaism, Christianity, and Islam), apocalyptic literature moves within the framework of a cosmic battle taking place between the forces of Good and the forces of Evil, detailing dramatic events in the struggle, and revealing the future progress of the conflict to the eschaton or end-time. See TELEOCOSMOS.

**a priori**   In epistemology, a kind of knowledge not derived from, or dependent upon, experience. Rather, it is a universal and necessary knowledge, such as $7 + 5 = 12$. Kant held that time, too, is a priori; the mind *brings time to* its experience of objects/events and does not derive its notion of time from experience of anything in the real world. Time, that is to say, is *prior to* experience. (Don't confuse a priori knowledge with the notion of "innate ideas" which we are supposedly born with.)

**argument, philosophical**   A sort of dialectical conversation, carried on with others or oneself, by which one attempts to clarify his thinking, especially to clarify the validity of the fact-claims used to support particular ideas or statements. A philosophical argument is not an ego-argument.

**aristocentric**   Refers to an inordinate claim to a position of superiority, for oneself or one's group. From the Greek *aristos* (superlative of *agathos*, "good") meaning "the best of its kind" or "the most to be valued."

Aristocentric claims are most often made in behalf of one's ethnic group or "race," one's tribe or nation, or one's religion.

**atheism**    A denial of theism (a-theism); the explicit conclusion that God or gods do not exist. Often a positive statement that the hypothesis of supernatural beings is not required to account for anything observed in human experience.

**authoritarianism**    The claim on the part of an individual or institution to be a special source of trustworthy knowledge. In epistemology, the position that our most dependable information derives from, or is validated by, some particular authority. Contrasts with the position that knowledge is best validated by personal experience.

**authority**    In epistemology, one of the four basic sources of knowledge. Knowledge which we accept on the authority of others.

**autonomy**    The capacity for self-determination; the freedom to operate in terms of one's own volition. Also, functioning harmoniously as an integrated self rather than merely responding inconsistently to disparate environmental stimuli. "Autonomy means the capacity of the individual to make valid choices of his behavior in the light of his needs" (Gail and Snell Putney, *The Adjusted American*).

**axiology**    A branch of philosophy concerned with the study of values, their origin and nature.

**belief**    (Unthinking) acceptance of an idea or system of ideas—that is, "blind belief." As in "I *believe* it. Don't confuse me with the facts!" Contrasts with *faith*.

**biocosmos**    The conception of a universe which would include life as inherent and natural; that is, a cosmos in which life-forms are an integral factor in the overall process of cosmic evolution.

**biogenesis**    The general term for the study of the origin of life. There have been numerous biogenetic theories. ARCHEBIOSIS (chemical evolution) is the theory that life develops from inorganic compounds whenever conditions permit it, both on the earth and (probably) throughout the cosmos. PANSPERMIA (or transmission) suggests that life drifted to earth from some other world, perhaps in meteorites. SPONTANEOUS GENERATION suggests that fully developed species are produced from nonliving matter. HYLOZOISM is the theory that all matter is alive. CREATIONISM is the theory that life originates only through an act of the supernatural.

**Brahman**    A Hindu doctrine of absolute and supreme Reality, as compared with the unreal and illusory nature of this world; Ultimate Reality itself; pure being.

**BTF-patterns**    An abbreviation for behavior, thought, and feeling patterns, the basic elements which together constitute selves and societies.

**causality**    An assumption that certain events cause or produce subsequent events. This is an axiomatic assumption of naturalism and a working assumption of science: that nothing happens without prior cause and that the cause-effect principle applies universally.

**coherence-test**    A truth-test which states that any fact-claim which coheres with previously accepted facts can be considered to be true.

**concept**    A mental construct containing all the objects/events which one has classed together according to selected common properties; an abstraction. Contrast with PERCEPT: we have percepts of particular objects/events (*this* seashell, *this* panda, *this* orbit), while a concept is a generalized notion to which the singular object/events belong (seashell, panda, orbit). Most common nouns are employed as concepts.

**contextualism**    In ethics, the school of thought which holds that relevant ethical decisions can be made only within the context of a particular ethical problem where the unique factors of the situation can be taken into account. Contrast with ethical FORMALISM.

**contingent**    In epistemology, a hypothesis or conclusion which is not *necessarily* true. A conclusion which, being derived from empirical observation, is only probably true. All robins' eggs are *probably* blue, but they are not *necessarily* blue. Contrast with necessary knowledge. See DEDUCTION.

**correspondence-test**    A truth-test (developed primarily by Bertrand Russell) which can be used whenever empirical observation is possible. It states that if there is a high degree of correspondence between a (subjective) idea or statement and an (objective) object/event, then the concept can be considered true.

**cosmological argument**    An argument for the existence of God, first proposed by Aristotle and further developed by Aquinas. The argument is based on the assumption that causality is absolute and real. Every event must be preceded by another event which is its cause. But it is impossible to think of an infinite regress of causal events. Therefore, there must have been a first cause, an Uncaused Cause which started off this domino-chain of events; this First Cause is defined as God.

**cosmology**    The study of the nature and structure of the universe. Sometimes used to refer to the study of the origin of the universe, though more correctly this is termed *cosmogony*.

**cosmos**    From the Greek *kosmos*, "the world" or "the ordered universe." Refers to the entire universe considered as a single, harmonious order; a Gestalt world-system.

**creationism**  The theory that life originated through an act of the supernatural; carries the implication that life cannot originate through other means. (Theory is not limited to any particular account of life-origins).

**deduction**  In logic, the process of drawing out (explicating, making explicit) the implications of one or more premises or statements. Deductive conclusions necessarily follow from the premises. (All bitter fruit is poisonous. Manzanillas are bitter fruit. Therefore, manzanillas are necessarily poisonous.) In deductive logic, the conclusion can be valid (if it has been correctly inferred) and yet be false because the starting premises were false. But if the premises are true and the conclusion is correctly inferred, then the conclusion *must* be both valid and true.

**determinism**  The assumption or doctrine that every event in the universe has a prior cause and that all effects are at least theoretically predictable if all the causes are known.

**dialectic**  From the Greek *dialektike*, "to converse." The attempt to clarify thought and arrive at facts through a back-and-forth sort of conversation. See ARGUMENT. Also, a thought-process (associated with and propounded by Hegel) wherein ideas attempt to grow and complete themselves through a three-beat rhythm of thesis, antithesis, and synthesis; a back-and-forth progressive movement of thought.

**doubt, methodical**  A philosophical method of deliberately disbelieving any idea in order to force it to prove its truth-value with empirical facts and/or rational argument. A way of making fact-claims prove their credentials and of preventing them from being accepted uncritically. Methodical doubt is a helpful corrective to our tendency to take ideas for granted.

**dualism**  The view that there exist two related entities, neither of which can be reduced to or identified with the other. In psychology, dualism implies that mind and body are separate entities, different in kind, and that neither can be explained in terms of the other. Metaphysical dualism is the position that there are two orders of reality (usually assumed to be the natural and supernatural), each of which is a distinct and irreducible order.

**ecstasy**  Greek *ek-stasis*, "standing outside" (oneself). A mystical mode of consciousness found in almost every religion in which the self is considered to have been displaced by a possessing spirit (usually a good spirit) which brings about a trance or frenzied condition considered to have ultimate religious significance.

**egocentric illusion**  An epistemological condition: the fact that each of us perceives himself to be the hub and center of the cosmos, though in reality none of us is such a center. From a perceptual standpoint, the universe would appear to revolve around every perceiving creature, human and nonhuman alike.

**egocentric predicament**  A term coined by the American philosopher Ralph Barton Perry to describe the epistemological fact that each of us is limited to our own perceptual world and cannot move beyond perception to know what the real world is like as it exists apart from perception. Some extreme idealists (e.g., Berkeley) assess this predicament and proceed to the conclusion that the inexperiencible world doesn't exist. Realists usually accept the predicament as a nuisance but proceed to develop a structure of probable facts about the real world which (they assume) lies beyond direct perception.

**élan vital**  Literally, "vital impulse." Term used by Henri Bergson to refer to the impulse-to-life, which, he theorized, directs evolution upward toward the development of higher, more complex forms of life.

**empathy**  The capacity on the part of any creature—man or animal—to assess correctly what another creature is experiencing but without itself sharing the experience. Empathy implies understanding of, but not participation in, another's inner world.

**empirical**  In philosophy, the word *empirical* is used in at least two distinct ways. (1) It refers to knowledge acquired by our senses only. Any other knowledge (facts derived by reason, for instance) is not empirical. An "empiricist" would be one who tends to trust the senses (over reason) as our basic source of trustworthy information. In science, there is frequently the added implication that the sense data must be "public facts," that is, subject to repeated experiment and verification. (2) "Empirical" is often used to refer to *any* knowledge gained by *any* human experience (not merely sense experience). This wider definition would include dreams, emotions, religious experiences, and so on; any knowledge derived from these experiences would be called empirical.

**epistemic naivety**  The condition of one who accepts uncritically his own vast accumulation of data, not yet having come to terms with the contradictions, fictions, and fallacies which are to be found in any large accumulation of disparate fact claims.

**epistemic**  Shortened form of epistemological.

**epistemology**  Branch of philosophy which studies human knowledge. It analyzes the sources of knowledge, processes of thought, truth-tests, fact-claims, value-judgments, etc. A study of what we truly know and don't know.

**eschatology**    Literally, the doctrine of "last things." One's ideas regarding the final events at the "end of time." The Western Zoroastrian-Judaic family of religions holds that history will end through the intervention of supernatural forces. See TELEOCOSMOS and APOCALYPTIC.

**ESP**    Extrasensory perception. See PSI.

**essence**    The qualities without which any particular object/event would not exist or would be a distinctly different kind of object/event. The qualities necessary for anything to be what it is. (Existentialists are especially concerned to point out that objects may have essences, but that man does not.)

**ethnocentrism**    A sociological term referring to the universal tendency of social groups—tribes, nations, races, cultures, religions—to take their own superiority for granted. See ARISTOCENTRISM.

**ethics**    Branch of philosophy which analyzes notions of right and wrong in human relationships. Normative ethics attempts to establish ideals for intent and behavior. The field of ethics is theoretical, in contrast to morality, which refers to one's actual behavior relative to standards by which such behavior is judged to be right and wrong.

**etiology, etiological**    The study of the origins of things or the study of their causes.

**existence**    In existentialism, the word *existence* refers to one's experience of vivid, concrete reality in the living present. Often it carries the connotation of being profoundly aware that one is; that to exist is living in, emphasizing, experiencing fully, being intensely involved in the conscious present.

**existentialism**    School of philosophy emerging from the dehumanizing conditions of World War II, but having deep historical roots, especially in the writings of Søren Kierkegaard (1813–1855). Existentialism emphasizes the uniqueness and freedom of the individual person and argues that each person must take full responsibility for his own existence and to "create himself." Most existentialists hold that existence can have meaning only as one participates fully in life. A central motif in existential thought is "the individual versus the crowd."

**fact**    An idea or statement about which one can feel a high degree of certainty *because,* having been doubted and then subjected to logical and empirical analysis, it still stands.

**fact-claim**    Any idea submitted as a candidate for consideration as an item of human knowledge. In epistemology, a fact-claim becomes a fact only after it has been carefully checked with the truth-tests and logical analysis and has passed muster; only then does it deserve to be called a "fact."

**faith**    In philosophical usage, the capacity which enables one to act upon the best facts that he possesses, although they are incomplete and there is no signed guarantee of satisfactory results. In a general sense, faith is the courage to proceed to live—to exist as fully as possible—in terms of possibilities and probabilities rather than absolutes and certainties. Contrast with BELIEF.

**fallacy**    An error in reasoning. In logic, a conclusion arrived at by means of inaccurate reasoning. A logical mistake.

**fatalism**    The doctrine that every event of our lives is *pre*-determined and that no amount of effort on our part can change anything or make any difference. The source of the predetermination is usually attributed to some vaguely conceived notion of natural causation, though it can be attributed to divine causes. (Originally "fatalism" was inflicted by the three Greek Fates or goddesses of destiny.) Fatalism can be both a mood and a rationalization for submission to conditions over which one feels he has no control.

**finite**    Limited. In theology, a limited deity; one that is not omnipotent.

**formalism**    In ethics, the position that there are universal ethical standards that apply to all men; such "laws" are often believed to have been revealed by a deity. Formalistic ethics contrasts with both RELATIVISM and CONTEXTUALISM, which hold that no such universal laws exist.

**free will**    The theory that man's will is free to make authentic choices that are not predetermined; an affirmation that man's feeling of freedom is accurate and that our choices made between options are genuine decisions. Free will is the doctrine that, somehow, the human consciousness is not subject to the same causal principles which the scientist assumes to operate in the rest of the physical world. Some solution to the controversy over free will versus determinism is a precondition to any discussion of ethics and responsibility.

**god**    Roughly synonymous with Ultimate Reality or Ultimate Being. In philosophy the existence of a deity would be a hypothesis developed to account for empirical data or to be supported by rational arguments. It would not be, as in religious systems, the object of uncritical belief.

**hedonism**  In ethics, the doctrine that pleasure is the ultimate goal of life which does and should determine our behavior. Philosophical hedonists (e.g., Bentham and Mill) held that man labors under "two sovereign masters": pleasure and pain. Life should be devoted to the avoidance of pain and the augmentation of pleasure, for self and others.

**hominid** *(Hominidae)*  Scientific classification of the evolutionary branch that includes the three great apes (chimpanzees, gorillas, orangutans) and humans. In taxonomy the *Hominidae* constitute a family.

**hominoid** *(Hominoidae)*  Scientific classification of the evolutionary branch that includes the great apes (hominids plus gibbons) and humans. In taxonomy the *Hominoidae* are a superfamily.

**hylozoism**  Theory held by the earliest Greek philosophers that all matter is alive or in some way possesses life.

**idealism**  Idealism is the theory that reality is primarily mental rather than material; it consists of mind (or Mind), minds, ideas, or selves. There are numerous brands of idealism, no two quite alike. Plato was an idealist since he believed that "ideas" exist in the cosmos quite apart from brains. Christians are similarly idealistic if they believe that "ideas" or "eternal verities" exist in the mind of God. George Berkeley was an idealist since he believed that only minds (God's and ours) exist. G. W. F. Hegel was an idealist because he believed the Absolute Mind (a superlogical God of sorts) permeates human activity and that we can "think God's thoughts." Mary Baker Eddy, the founder of Christian Science, was an idealist because she believed that we all exist within the Mind of God, the only Reality. Eastern religions such as Hinduism and Buddhism are idealisms since they hold that life's true purpose (for instance, Zen *satori*, "awareness," or the trance-state of *nirvana*) is achieved only through an odyssey of the mind. Shankara's teaching that this world is maya ("illusion"), "comparable to foam, a mirage, a dream," makes this interpretation of Vedanta the Eastern world's most extreme philosophical idealism.

**imply**  To make statements from which logical inferences can be drawn, but without explicitly stating them. The process of drawing out implications is termed INFERENCE. In everyday usage there is much confusion between *infer* and *imply*. See LOGIC.

**induction**  In logic, the process of developing generalized explanations, hypotheses, or laws from a collection of facts. Induction is the commonest of our daily procedures for gathering knowledge. It includes the hasty generalizations we are prone to make based upon very limited experience (that is, an inadequate collection of related facts). Inductive conclusions are never necessary (as are deductive conclusions), but only probable. See DEDUCTION, CONTINGENT.

**inference**  An idea which the mind is forced to create after having seen the implications of certain propositions. One infers—draws out, makes explicit—what is implied in a set of premises. The branch of philosophy called logic studies the rules by which we can infer ideas correctly from given premises.

**intuition**  (1) A source of knowledge—ideas, remembered facts, hypotheses, solutions to problems—which seem to emerge from the subconscious mind, apparently produced through activity of the subconscious before appearing in the light of consciousness. See pp. 186f. (2) Term used by Henri Bergson to describe the only method he believed could give us an accurate understanding of reality; a process of "intellectual empathy" through which we can understand the duration or unbroken continuum which in fact constitutes physical reality.

**invalid**  (in·val´id, not in´va·lid)  Refers to an idea which has not been inferred correctly; a fallacious conclusion produced by faulty reasoning.

**logic**  Branch of philosophy defined as the study of valid inference; systematic analysis of the correct and incorrect processes of reasoning.

**macrocosm**  Refers to man's particular vantage point as he views, and attempts to comprehend, the universe. The macrocosm is man's experiential level of reality as he looks up and down, so to speak: up at cosmic realities (cosmos) and down at microscopic realities (microcosm). Without the aid of instruments man is caught at the macrocosmic level since neither cosmos nor microcosm is directly perceivable.

**materialism**  The doctrine that everything in the universe is nothing other than various manifestations of matter-in-motion, and, in theory, can be reduced to, and explained by, principles of causality. All the objects/events for which we have such diverse labels—matter, mind, energy, life, and perhaps spirit—are only variant forms of matter-in-motion.

**maya**  The Hindu doctrine that this world is unreal; it is mere illusion. All we know are the illusory surface appearances of things. If the material world is unreal, only Brahman or Ultimate Reality is truly real.

**metaphysics**  A branch of philosophy concerned with what actually exists, that is, with what the true nature of things really is. Traditionally, metaphysics has been divided into two subbranches: ONTOLOGY, the study of being, and COSMOLOGY, the study of the cosmos (cosmology is now generally thought of as a branch of astronomy). See ONTOLOGY.

**monism**    Any world-view which purports to reduce all existence to a single order of reality; the doctrine that there is but one order of reality, whether it be mind (which would be called "psychical monism") or matter-in-motion ("naturalistic monism"), or some other kind of reality.

**moral**    Refers to the way one overtly behaves in his relationships with others. In the most general sense, moral behavior is intended to produce, somewhere, somehow, constructive results; immoral behavior is intended to produce destructive results. Contrast with ETHICS, which is the theoretical study of ideal (normative) relationships.

**mystic**    One who seeks or one who experiences dissolution of ego-self and separateness and feels that his being has merged or become united with Deity, Ultimate Reality, or Nature.

**mysticism**    The school of religion which values the mode of consciousness in which the ego-self is lost and an experience of oneness with Ultimate Reality is attained. Epistemologically, the mystic commonly claims that only through a mystical experience—as opposed to rational or empirical inquiry—can reality be known.

**myth**    A story or account, by definition involving some element of the supernatural, which is accepted by a community as a satisfactory answer to, or explanation of, some meaningful question or experience. Historically, myths are held collectively by religious communities, tribes, nations, or the like; but a story can perform the same function for an individual, in which case use of the term *myth* is justifiable.

**naive realism**    The uncritical acceptance of one's sense data as representing accurately the nature of the real world; a sort of "blind faith" in what one's senses seem to tell him.

**naturalism**    The world-view which holds that there is but a single order of reality, that of matter-in-motion. Naturalism, by definition, excludes the existence of a "super-natural" order of reality.

**nihilism**    In epistemology, the doctrine that nothing is knowable, or is worth knowing; the contention that all knowledge is illusory, relative, and meaningless. Similarly, in ethics, nihilism is the doctrine that all moral judgments are irrational, relative, and, finally, meaningless. In a word, nihilism is the belief that there is no knowledge, no value, and no meaning that is of any real worth to man.

**nirvana**    A mode of consciousness valued by the Buddhist and Hindu as the supreme goal of human existence. Literally, "extinction of consciousness," but better conceived as a state of consciousness described as an experience of wholeness, peace, and joy. In Hindu and Buddhist doctrine this mode of consciousness will continue after death for one who has reached the point of liberation *(moksha)* from the Wheel of Karma—the "round of rebirths."

**objective**    Refers to whatever exists in the real world apart from our perception of it. Having to do with the perceived object as opposed to the perceiving subject. See SUBJECTIVE.

**Occam's razor**    (Also called the Principle of Parsimony.) One of the fundamental principles of scientific method. It states that, all else being equal, the simplest explanation is the best. That is, in developing inductive hypotheses, the simplest hypothesis which accounts for all relevant data is most likely to be true. Named after the scholastic philosopher William of Occam, who phrased it: "The number of entities should not be needlessly increased."

**ontological argument**    A logical argument for the existence of God developed by Saint Anselm of Canterbury (1033–1109). Anselm attempted to prove the existence of God from the nature of thought alone.

**ontology**    From the Greek *ontos,* "being," and *logos,* "study of." Branch of philosophy which studies the nature of reality or being, especially as applied to living things. The term ontological is commonly used to emphasize the fact that some specific quality is an inescapable aspect of life itself. The fear of death, for instance, is said to be ontological since there is no way—short of the extinction of consciousness—to escape the fear. We could repress it, but the fear would remain a part of our being, buried precariously in the unconscious, where it can become a powerful but unrecognized cause of puzzling behavior.

**panpsychism**    The doctrine that everything is composed of, or contains, mind or "soul" *(psyche)*. Some Western thinkers have speculated that the binding forces within atoms might be, in some way, the operations of mind.

**panspermia**    The biogenetic theory that life may have developed on earth after having been transferred from other worlds, perhaps by meteorites. See BIOGENESIS.

**pantheism** The doctrine that God is All. Pantheists usually hold that God is in all matter or that the totality of all matter is "the body of God."

**paradox** A condition where two mutually exclusive ideas or statements appear to be true; and until the arrival of further data or some sort of resolution, both ideas or statements must be accepted and acted upon.

**parsimony, principle of** See OCCAM'S RAZOR.

**percept** The first-stage result of the mind's organization of sense data. The mind perceives a concrete object—*this* coin or *this* car—which remains in consciousness as an unnamed, singular object. A percept (or perception) is what is given in consciousness, the object of cognition. Contrast with CONCEPT, in which objects are mentally classed with other objects, and the mind henceforth thinks of the class rather than the object. Contrast also with SENSE DATUM, a raw, unorganized sense-response.

**philosophy** The love of wisdom. From Greek *philein* ("to love") and *sophia* ("wisdom"). Philosophy comprises several distinct disciplines or methods which have in common the goal of improving upon the condition of human knowledge and our knowledge of the human condition.

**pluralism** The world-view holding that there exist more than two orders of reality, each of which is distinct and irreducible. For instance, if one believes that the universe is composed of matter, mind, spirit, and divine-essence, then he would be a pluralist. Compare with MONISM and DUALISM.

**pragmatic-test** The truth-test (developed primarily by William James) which states that if an idea or statement "works"—that is, brings about desirable results—then the idea or statement can be considered true. James held that the truth-value of any idea is to be judged in terms of the results it can produce.

**pragmatic paradox** A human condition in which an idea must be believed to be true in terms of correspondence—that is, one must be convinced that some object/event exists as a real entity—before the idea can be considered to be true on the pragmatic-test. For example, one must believe that immortality exists as a real event (which, one must believe, could be empirically checked, under the right conditions, with the correspondence-test) before the belief in immortality can produce positive results in his life. If he believed it to be true solely on the pragmatic-test, it would in fact *not* be true because it wouldn't "work."

**pragmatism** An American school of philosophy associated mainly with William James and John Dewey. One of its central themes is that philosophy should be put to work solving the more pressing human problems instead of preoccupying itself in metaphysical speculations. See p. 86. According to the pragmatists, truth is tentative and forever changing; truth is the quality of whatever ideas "work" at the present time.

**precognition** Having knowledge of an event supposedly before it happens. See PSI.

**predestination** A theological term referring to divine predeterminism. The doctrine that God has already determined (at least) whether each human soul will be saved or lost, or (at most) that every singular event of existence will occur as planned. A "hard" predestination logically excludes the possibility of free will.

**predicament** A problem condition to which, by definition, there is no solution; a situation which must be accepted. One may be able to deal productively with problems arising from a predicament (e.g., *fear* of nonbeing), but not with the predicament itself (that each of us faces nonbeing).

**premise** In logic, an idea or statement which, along with other ideas or statements, can lead to a conclusion. In reasoning, a premise is a starting statement, an opener.

**primal freedom** Freedom from subjective limitations, thereby enabling one to make authentic choices; freedom from primal limitations.

**primary qualities** In epistemology, the qualities, according to John Locke, which inhere in real objects: e.g., weight, motion, shape, extension. Compare with SECONDARY QUALITIES.

**PSI** Refers to all parapsychological or "paranormal" experiences. Among them: TELEPATHY, the sending of messages (ideas and/or feelings) from one mind to another; CLAIRVOYANCE, the mind's "seeing" an object/event at a distance; PSYCHOKINESIS (PK), "mind over matter," the power of the mind to influence the behavior of objects; PRECOGNITION, knowledge of an event (supposedly) before it takes place. ESP (extrasensory perception) is a rough synonym for PSI, though we do not know at present whether such experiences (if they do in fact occur) are truly *extra*sensory

**psyche** Greek word meaning "soul"; usually thought of as a substantialized, objectified form of the self, though in earlier times and other places the word has been given a bewildering variety of meanings.

**psychokinesis** The power of the mind to influence directly the behavior of objects/events. See PSI.

**rational**    Roughly synonymous with "reasonable"; having the capacity to engage in reasoned inquiry.

**rationalism**    In epistemology, a philosophical tradition that holds that our most dependable information derives from reason rather than from empirical observation. A rationalist is one who trusts reason more than the deceptive "rabble of the senses."

**rationalize**    The process of developing reasons ("rationales") for holding certain beliefs or performing certain actions—reasons which are not the true reasons but which are more acceptable than the true reasons. One who is subjectively naive will thus delude himself as well as others; one who is subjectively aware may reserve his rationales only for others. By definition, a rationalization is a fallacy engaged in out of need to defend one's thoughts, feelings, or actions. (Don't confuse with RATIONALISM.)

**real, realism**    Among the most important terms in philosophy. To be real is to exist apart from perception. If I state that the teakwood figurine of the Buddha on my desk is "real," then I am stating the belief that the figurine exists as a "thing-in-itself" quite apart from my perception of it; if I were not perceiving it in any way whatsoever, it would still exist. (This position is *material realism,* and modern use of the term is often restricted to this meaning, *real* therefore refers to material objects or the physical world in general.) If I should go further and claim that the Cosmic Buddha exists, quite apart from my perception of him (or It), then this is a *theological realism.* If I claim that beauty exists in the orchid or rainbow, apart from my perception (that is, I close my eyes but I am convinced that "beauty" still remains in the rainbow), then I am an *esthetic realist.* Lastly, if I claim that right and wrong (or Good and Evil) actually exist in the real world, then I am a *value realist* or an *ethical realist.*

In common parlance we speak of dreams, headaches, fears, bad vibrations, etc. as "real." "They are *my* realities," we contend. "Don't tell me my head doesn't hurt. My headache is real!" But the headache is not real, as the term is used in philosophy; the headache certainly does not exist apart from your perception of it.

**reality**    In epistemology, the totality of all things that exist apart from perception. The real world. See REAL, REALISM. In social science, a fabric of BTF-patterns shared by members of a particular society; all that is *considered* to be real by that social group.

**reason**    One of many kinds of thinking (others being remembering, daydreaming, intuiting, dreaming, etc.).

The mental process of using known facts to arrive at new facts. In logic, the activity of inferring conclusions from premises.

**relativism**    In ethics, the belief, based on empirical observation, that what is considered to be right and wrong differs from one society to another and from one person to another. The term usually implies that there are no universal codes of right and wrong. Contrast with FORMALISM. (Don't confuse with Einstein's RELATIVITY.)

**relativity**    In physics, Albert Einstein's theories of special (1905) and general (1916) relativity. Roughly, a system of mathematics and physics which predicts the behavior of matter-in-motion at high speeds. (Don't confuse with ethical RELATIVISM.)

**samadhi**    Literally, "concentration"; a form of meditation. In Hinduism and Buddhism, a trancelike mode of consciousness wherein the mind achieves a blissful, contentless, transpersonal state; the attainment of *atman,* or authentic self-essence.

**satori**    In Zen Buddhism, the "moment of awakening" when a mediator realizes the illusory nature of self and separateness; a holistic feeling of mystical oneness.

**Scholasticism**    A movement in Western ecclesiastical history beginning c. A.D. 1100 and flowering during the thirteenth century, resulting from the recovery of the Greek classics and the revitalized use of rational inquiry following the Dark Ages. A period of renewed intellectual activity within the framework of the accepted truths of medieval Catholic religion. Among the great Scholastic philosophers (the "schoolmen") were Anselm of Canterbury, Bernard of Clairvaux, Peter Abelard, Albertus Magnus, and Thomas Aquinas.

**Scholastic method**    Specifically, the use of reason by the Scholastic philosophers, not to discover truth but to explore, explicate, and defend *known* (i.e., revealed) truths. The truths themselves were not subject to doubt or inquiry.

**secondary freedom**    The capacity to make genuine choices without being limited by external restrictions (e.g., economic, social, political). Contrast secondary limitations (which are objective) with primal limitations (which are subjective). See PRIMAL FREEDOM.

**secondary qualities**    According to John Locke, qualities which do not inhere in objects/events but are subjective sensations (e.g., color, sound, taste) Compare with PRIMARY QUALITIES.

**self**    The conscious subject which experiences, designated by "I" or "ego." The word has frequently been used to refer to some unknown entity which unifies the data of consciousness into a coherent, operational system. Self, however, may be better conceived as the coherent system rather than some hypothetical unifying entity. An ambiguous and problematic concept.

**self-determination**    In psychology and ethics, the position that one's personal BTF-patterns have antecedent causes, but that such causes may reside within oneself and not in the environment. We can become "self-caused." Self-determination is a middle position between an extreme free will position which denies determinism and a behavioristic position which denies free will.

**semantics**    Broadly, the study of meaning. A study of the total response of the human organism to symbols of all sorts (words, signs, gestures, etc.). In a narrow sense, the study of words and their meanings.

**sensation**    The immediate response of the senses to stimuli. A synonym for SENSE DATUM. (*Sensation* does not refer to emotional responses.)

**sense data**    Immediate sensory responses as registered in consciousness—patches of color, bits of sound—which are synthesized by the mind into the perception of an object. Sense data (singular, *datum*) are the first raw materials of experience which make their way from our sense receptors to the interpretive areas of the brain, where they are organized into perceptions of particular objects.

**skepticism**    In epistemology, an attitude of doubt; either a deliberate methodical doubt to force fact-claims to prove themselves or a general doctrine of philosophical agnosticism, a sincere doubt that accurate knowledge is possible.

**solipsism**    The doctrine that only "I" (the solipsist, of course) exist. A logical (but quite illogical) inference from the conclusion that all we can truly know are our own experiences.

**soul**    Roughly, a substantialized, objectified notion of the self. See PSYCHE.

**subjective**    Refers to the subject which experiences, as opposed to the object which is experienced. The term refers to the location of events which constitute the experiencing process (subjective), as opposed to the events which belong to the real world (objective).

**substance**    The ultimate "stuff" (Greek *physis*) of which any object is made; the underlying reality to which primary qualities adhere. The word *substance* is a label applied to the *assumption* that there is a continuing essence in any object which remains immutable through all ephemeral changes in its "perceivable" qualities.

**summum bonum**    In ethics, the Ultimate Good of

human existence; that is, the final goal toward which all our endeavors should be directed. Various such goals have been proposed: happiness, pleasure, self-actualization, ethical love, soul-salvation, etc.

**supernatural**    An order of reality above and outside the natural order. In philosophy, the supernatural is not the object of religious belief; supernaturalists would contend that it is necessary to postulate such an order to account for the complex data of experience. Contrast with NATURALISM; see also MONISM, DUALISM.

**sympathy**    Literally, "to suffer with" another. The capacity not merely to understand what another is experiencing (which is EMPATHY), but the actual duplication, so to speak, in one's own experience of what another is experiencing.

**synoptic**    From the Greek *sun-optikos*, "seeing the whole together" or "taking a comprehensive view." The attempt to achieve an all-inclusive overview of one's subject matter and to see all its parts in relationship to one another.

**Tao**    In Chinese religion, "The Way"; a sort of cosmic pathway that lies between or within the interactions of the energy-modes Yang and Yin. To discover the Tao is to begin to live in perfect harmony with self and cosmos.

**teleocosmos**    From the Greek *teleos*, "finished" or "complete" implying purposive design and goal-directed movement; and *kosmos*, "an ordered universe." A world-view with a program which moves with direction and purpose, and in which man plays a major role. The most noteworthy teleocosmic world-views belong to man's religions and resemble cosmic dramas in structure, including a full cast of characters—protagonists and antagonists, gods and demons, supporting roles and bit players—and carefully designed plots leading to a dramatic climax and a dénouement. Man's role is the central element of teleocosmic dramas, though this fact may be obscured by large-scale cosmic events which occur as the drama unfolds.

**teleological argument**    An argument for the existence of God based on the apparent purposive nature of evolutionary movement and/or the design and order of the universe. Order implies an orderer; design implies a designer. The American Personalists considered this to be the strongest empirical argument for the existence of God.

**teleology**    From the Greek *teleos*, "finished" or "complete." The theory that deliberate purposive activity, rather than mere chance, is involved in some process. The interpretation of any series of events—such as an organism's growth, evolution, or human history—as expressions of purposeful movement; goal-directed, as though planned out and guided toward a present end or ideal.

**telepathy**    Communication of mind with mind via supposedly extrasensory media. See PSI.

**theism**    Belief in gods or God. Often used to mean belief in a specific Western doctrine of an omnipotent, omniscient, and personal deity. Contrast with ATHEISM, the denial that gods or God exists.

**theology**    The rational organization of religious beliefs and practices in order to render them logically coherent and meaningful. Theology is an intellectual discipline in contrast to religion which involves one's whole being.

**time dilation**    A phenomenon predicted by Albert Einstein's special theory of relativity: for any object moving at great velocities (relative to the speed of light) time would slow down.

**truth**    "Truth is the approximation of thought to reality" (Brand Blanshard). Truth is a quality possessed by ideas and statements, a quality which is of value to a philosopher only after having been carefully checked with one or more of the truth-tests. The notion of an ethereal, nonspecific (and untestable) truth is meaningless.

**valid**    In logic, a technical term referring to a conclusion which has been correctly inferred from specific premises. Validity is the property of an idea or statement which has been correctly derived by logical inference.

**vitalism**    The doctrine that a "life principle" must suffuse itself (or be injected) into inorganic matter before life-processes can begin. What this "vital" element might be is usually unspecified, but it is often associated with the supernatural.

**world-view**    In a broad sense, one's philosophy of life; an all-inclusive, coherent way of looking at life and the cosmos. From the German *Weltanschauung*, a sort of unconscious, totalic fabric into which one incorporates all his experiences and through which he sees the world.

# CREDITS

## I TEXT REFERENCES

### INTRODUCTION

**xix** Excerpt from *A Concise Introduction to Philosophy*, by William Halverson, pp. 18f. Copyright © 1981 by William Halverson. Reprinted by permission of McGraw-Hill, Inc.

### PART I  THE FINE ART OF WONDERING

**1** Ray Bradbury, "The Nefertiti-Tut Express," from *ExtraTerrestrial Intelligence*, ed. James L. Christian (Prometheus Books, 1976), p. 8.

### CHAPTER 1–1  THE WORLD-RIDDLE

**4** Alexei Panshin, *Rite of Passage* (Ace SF, 1968), p. 252.

**5** From *The Little Prince* by Antoine de Saint-Exupéry. Copyright © 1943 and renewed 1971 by Harcourt Brace & Company, and reprinted by permission of the publisher.

**6** Viktor E. Frankl, *MAN'S SEARCH FOR MEANING* (Washington Square, 1963), pp. 167f. Copyright © 1959, 1962, 1984, 1992 by Viktor E. Frankl. Reprinted by permission of Beacon Press.

**7** From *Out of My Life and Thought* by Albert Schweitzer. Translated by C. T. Campion. Copyright © 1935, 1949, 1961 by Henry Holt & Company, Inc. Reprinted by permission of Harcourt Brace & Company.

**8** Abraham Maslow. Reprinted from *Psychology Today* magazine, August 1970, p. 16. Copyright © Sussex Publishers, Inc. Reprinted with permission from *Psychology Today* magazine.

**9** Gordon Allport. From Frankl, *MAN'S SEARCH FOR MEANING* (Washington Square, 1963), pp. ix-xiii. Copyright © 1959, 1962, 1984, 1992 by Viktor E. Frankl. Reprinted by permission of Beacon Press.

**11** Desmond Morris, *The Naked Ape* (McGraw-Hill, 1967), pp. 187, 189, 156, 159.

**12** Konrad Lorenz. Excerpt from *On Aggression* by Konrad Lorenz (Bantam, 1967), p. 233. Copyright © 1963 by Dr. G. Borotha Schaeler Verlag Wien; English copyright © 1966 by Konrad Lorenz; copyright © by Deutscher Taschenbuch Verlag GMBH and Co., Munchen. Reprinted by permission of Harcourt Brace & Company.

**12** Jacques Cousteau. From "The Undersea World of Jacques Cousteau: The Night of the Squid," ABC-TV, telecast April 12, 1970.

**13** Abraham Maslow, *New Knowledge in Human Values* (Harper, 1959), pp. 123, 126.

**13** René Dubos, *The Torch of Life* (Pocket Books, 1962), p. 15. Copyright © 1962 by Pocket Books, Inc. Credo Perspectives, planned and edited by Ruth Nanda Anshen. Reprinted by permission of Pocket Books, a division of Simon & Schuster, Inc.

**14** From "The Sands of Time" by Robert Wright and George Forrest. Copyright © 1959 by Robert Wright and George Forrest. Reprinted by permission of Frank Music Corp.

**14** Program notes by E. C. Stone for the London recording of Richard Strauss' *Also Sprach Zarathustra* by the Vienna Philharmonic Orchestra, conducted by Herbert von Karajan. (Final italics added.)

### CHAPTER 1–2  THE SPIRIT OF PHILOSOPHY

**21** Socrates. Plato, *The Apology*, in *The Last Days of Socrates*, translated by Hugh Tredennick (Penguin Classics, 1954; rev. ed. 1959), pp. 49–52. Copyright © 1954, 1959, 1969 by Hugh Tredennick. Reprinted by permission of Penguin Books, Ltd. (The opening line of Socrates' defense is from the Jowett translation.)

**24** Thomas: John 20:24–29. Paul: 1 Corinthians 1:20; Colossians 2:8; Galatians 3:28.

**25** St. Augustine. Philip Schaff, *History of the Christian Church*, Vol. III, *Nicene and Post-Nicene Christianity* (Eerdmans, 1950 [1910]), pp. 998, 1004.

**25** St. Anselm. Schaff, *History*, Vol. V, *The Middle Ages* (1949 [1907]), pp. 600f.

**25** Abelard. Schaff, *History*, Vol. V, pp. 622–624.

**28** Paul Tillich, *Dynamics of Faith* (Harper, 1957), pp. 31f.

**29** René Descartes, *Meditations*, 1: "Things We May Doubt."

**32** From the transcript of a television play, *Dr. Einstein before Lunch*, by Ernest Kinoy, produced by The Jewish Theological Seminary of America on NBC-TV (5-20-73).

### CHAPTER 1–3  HOW TO PHILOSOPHIZE / CRITICAL ANALYSIS

I am especially indebted to my colleague, Professor Robert Putman, a Socratic scholar, for his assistance with this chapter.

**45** Jean Brun, *Socrates* (Walker, 1962), p. 21.

### CHAPTER 1–4  HOW TO PHILOSOPHIZE / SYNOPTIC SYNTHESIS

**61** William Halverson, *A Concise Introduction to Philosophy*, pp. 18f. See page xix above.

**72** Brand Blanshard, "Limited Minds and Unlimited Knowledge." An address to the University Class at Bucknell University. From the *Bucknell University Bulletin*. Used by permission.

**73** R. Buckminster Fuller, "Technology and the Human Environment." From Robert Disch (ed.), *The Ecological Conscience: Values for Survival*, pp. 175f. Copyright © 1970. Reprinted by permission of Prentice-Hall, Inc., Englewood Cliffs, N.J.

**74** Isaac Asimov, *VIEW FROM A HEIGHT* (Lancer, 1974), pp. 7–10. Copyright © 1963 by Isaac Asimov. Used by permission of Doubleday, a division of Bantam Doubleday Dell Publishing Group, Inc.

### CHAPTER 1–5  THE WAYS OF PHILOSOPHY

**85** Erich Fromm, *Marx's Concept of Man* (Frederick Ungar, 1961), p. 3.

**85** Louis Untermeyer, *Makers of the Modern World* (Simon & Schuster, 1955), p. 26.

**88** Thomas Merton, *The Way of Chuang Tzu* (New Directions, 1965), p. 10. Copyright © 1965 by the Abbey of Gethsemani.

**89** Excerpt from *WITTGENSTEIN AND MODERN PHILOSOPHY* by Justus Hartnack (Doubleday Anchor, 1965), pp. 4f, 8. Translation © 1965 by Methuen & Company, Ltd. Reprinted by permission of Doubleday, a division of Bantam Doubleday Dell Publishing Group, Inc.

### PART II  THE CONDITION AND THE ODYSSEY

**99** William Halverson, *A Concise Introduction to Philosophy*, pp. 18f. See page xix above.

### CHAPTER 2–1  PREDICAMENT / ILLUSION

In Part II of this book my indebtedness to others is especially great. The concept of the egocentric illusion (Chapter 2–1) is to be found, in various contexts, throughout the writings of Arnold Toynbee; though I alone am responsible for this elaboration of the idea. Chapters 2–2, 2–3, and 2–4 were enriched by concepts and material from Barbara Taylor Christian. I have incorporated many of her observations dealing with personality and growth.

**104** "The Prayer of the Little Ducks." From *Prayers from the Ark* by Carmen Bernos de Gasztold, translated by Rumer Godden (Viking, 1962), p. 59. Copyright © 1962 by Rumer Godden. Reprinted by permission of Viking Penguin, a division of Penguin Books USA, Inc.

**106** Paul Horton and Chester Hunt, *Sociology* (McGraw-Hill, 1964), p. 91. Copyright © 1984 by Paul Horton and Chester Hunt. Reprinted by permission of McGraw-Hill, Inc.

**106** Milton Rokeach, *The Three Christs of Ypsilanti* (Knopf, 1964), pp. 4ff, 315, 313f.

**109** Horton and Hunt, *Sociology*, p. 86. See p. 106 above.

**112** Camus. From the preface to "The Myth of Sisyphus" in *THE MYTH OF SISYPHUS AND OTHER ESSAYS*, translated by Justin O'Brien. Copyright © 1955 by Alfred A. Knopf, Inc. Reprinted by permission of the publisher.

**113** Camus. From the preface to "The Stranger" in *LYRICAL AND CRITICAL ESSAYS*, edited and with notes by Philip Thody and translated by Ellen Conroy Kennedy. Copyright © 1968 by Alfred A. Knopf, Inc. Copyright © 1967 by Hanish Hamilton, Ltd. and Alfred A. Knopf, Inc. Reprinted by permission of Alfred A. Knopf, Inc.

## CHAPTER 2–2 SELF / AUTONOMY

**120** Arthur W. Combs (ed.), *Perceiving, Behaving, Becoming: A New Focus for Education* (ASCD 1962 Yearbook, Washington, D.C.), p. 84. Copyright © by the Association for Supervision & Curriculum Development.

**121** Erich Fromm, *The Art of Loving* (Bantam, 1963), pp. 49ff. Copyright © Harper & Row, Publishers, Inc.

**122** David Hume, *Treatise of Human Nature*, Book I, Part ii, Sec. 5.

**126** S. I. Hayakawa, "The Fully Functioning Personality," in *Symbol, Status, and Personality* (Harcourt, Brace & World, N.D.), pp. 51ff.

**127** James F. Masterson, *The Search for the Real Self* (The Free Press, 1988), quotations and paraphrases of pp. viif, 42–46.

**135** From James T. Baker, *Ayn Rand* (Twayne Publishers, 1987) p. 150.

## CHAPTER 2–3 CHANGE / GROWTH

**137** Excerpt from "The Young Monkeys" by Harry and Margaret Harlow in *Psychology Today* magazine, September 1967. Copyright © 1976 by Sussex Publishers, Inc.

**141** Rollo May, *Love and Will* (Norton, 1969), pp. 165ff.

**141** Gregory Bateson, "Language and Psychotherapy." Quoted from Alan Watts, *Psychotherapy East and West* (Mentor, 1961), p. 105.

**142** Desmond Morris, *The Naked Ape* (McGraw-Hill, 1967), Chapter IV, "Exploration."

**143** Combs, *Perceiving, Behaving, Becoming*, pp. 141f. See page 120 above.

**144** Alexei Panshin, *Rite of Passage* (Ace SF, 1968), pp. 241ff. Copyright © 1968 by Alexei Panshin.

**150** From *THE MADMAN* by Kahlil Gibran. Copyright © by Kahlil Gibran and renewed 1946 by the Administrators C.T.A. of Kahlil Gibran Estate and Mary G. Gibran. Reprinted by permission of Alfred A. Knopf, Inc.

## CHAPTER 2–4 LIFE / TIME

**157** William Shakespeare, *As You Like It*, Act II, Sc. 7, lines 144ff.

**161** From *Developmental Psychology Today: An Introduction* (CRM Books, Del Mar, California), p. 383. Copyright © 1970 by CRM, Inc.

**166** Hudson Hoagland, "Some Biochemical Considerations of Time," and Roland Fischer, "Biological Time," in Dr. J. T. Fraser (ed.), *Voices of Time* (George Braziller, 1966), pp. 325 and 360, respectively. Copyright © 1966 by J. T. Fraser.

**169** Sheldon Harnick, "Sunrise, Sunset . . ." from *Fiddler on the Roof*. Copyright © 1964 by The New York Times Music Corporation (Sunbeam Music Division). All rights administered by the New York Times Music Corporation. Used by permission.

**170** Erik H. Erikson, "A Healthy Personality for Every Child," in Robert H. Anderson and Harold G. Shane (eds.), *As the Twig Is Bent* (Houghton Mifflin, 1971), pp. 136f.

**171** *Newsweek*, January 3, 1972, p. 56.

**171** Leo Tolstoy, *The Death of Ivan Ilytch*, translated by Aylmer Maude (Oxford). Quoted from Joseph Royce, *The Encapsulated Man* (Van Nostrand, 1964), pp. 108f.

## PART III THE REAL WORLD: KNOWING AND UNKNOWING

**179** Buckminster Fuller. See page 73 above.

## CHAPTER 3–1 KNOWLEDGE

**187** J. Samuel Bois, *The Art of Awareness* (William C. Brown, 1973).

## CHAPTER 3–2   SENSES / REALITY

**198** Lincoln Barnett, *The Universe and Dr. Einstein* (Mentor, 1952), pp. 123f.

**205** Buckminster Fuller, "This is the New Invisible World," *TV Guide*, February 6–12, 1970, p. 9.

**205** Voltaire. Quoted from W. Lambert Gardiner, *Psychology: The Story of a Search* (Brooks/Cole, 1970), p. 139.

**205** Quoted with permission of Professor Courtland Holdgrafer.

**205** David Hume, *A Treatise of Human Nature*, Book I, Part iv, Sec. 1.

## CHAPTER 3–3   THE PRAGMATIC MIND

**215** S. I. Hayakawa, *Language in Thought and Action* (Harcourt, 1963). Copyright © 1978 by Harcourt Brace & Company. Reprinted by permission of the publisher. These sections on abstracting and classifying are indebted to Chapters 10, 11, and 12 of Dr. Hayakawa's semantics text. The story of the village animals is a paraphrase of the account found on pages 214f.

**218** Hayakawa, *Language in Thought and Action* (Harcourt, 1963), p. 216. See p. 215 above. (Original italics removed.)

## CHAPTER 3–4   TRUTH

**230** For Charles S. Peirce's original article "How to Make our Ideas Clear," see Walter G. Muelder and Laurence Sears, *The Development of American Philosophy* (Houghton Mifflin, 1940), pp. 341ff.

**230** John J. McDermott (ed.), *The Writings of William James* (Modern Library, 1968), p. xxi. The introduction to this anthology contains an excellent brief biography of James.

**231** William S. and Mabel Sahakian, *Realms of Philosophy* (Schenkman, 1965), p. 41.

## PART IV   THE INNER WORLD: THE FANTASTIC JOURNEY

**241** Nikos Kazantzakis, *The Saviors of God* (Simon and Schuster, 1960), pp. 47f.

## CHAPTER 4–1   PSYCHE / SOMA

**243** R. D. Laing, *The Politics of Experience* (Ballantine, 1967), p. 26.

**245** William James. Quoted from Charles T. Tart (ed.), *Altered States of Consciousness* (John Wiley, 1969), p. 21.

**245** Carlos Castaneda, *The Teachings of Don Juan: A Yaqui Way of Knowledge* (Ballantine, 1969).

**246** Milton H. Erickson, "A Special Inquiry with Aldous Huxley into the Nature and Characteristics of Various States of Consciousness," in Tart, *Altered States of Consciousness*, pp. 45–71. See page 245 above.

**248** Erich Fromm, D. Suzuki, and di Martino, "Zen Buddhism and Psychoanalysis," (Allen & Unwin, 1960). Quoted from Tart, *Altered States of Consciousness*, p. 490. See page 245 above.

**249** From a lecture by Terry Allen and used with his permission. Requested credit line: "Our Oneness— Mother the Earth . . . Father the Universe."

## CHAPTER 4–2   PAST / PRESENT / FUTURE

**259** R. M. MacIver, *The Challenge of the Passing Years: My Encounter with Time* (Simon & Schuster, 1962), p. xxiii. (Italics added.)

**259** A. Cornelius Benjamin. Excerpt from A. Cornelius Benjamin, "Ideas of Time in the History of Philosophy," in J. T. Fraser (ed.), *Voices of Time* (George Braziller, 1966), p. 4. Copyright © 1966 by J. T. Fraser. Reprinted by permission of Dr. J. T. Fraser.

**260** Friedrich Waismann, "Analytic-Synthetic," in Richard M. Gale (ed.), *The Philosophy of Time* (Doubleday Anchor, 1967), pp. 55f.

**263** St. Augustine, *Confessions*, Book XI. (Any edition.)

**264** Jean Piaget, "Time Perception in Children."

**264** *Sir Isaac Newton's Mathematical Principles of Natural Philosophy and His System of the World*, translated by Andrew Motte (University of California Press, 1947), p. 6. Quoted from Fraser, *Voices of Time*, p. 18.

**265** Immanuel Kant, *Critique of Pure Reason*, translated by F. Max Müller (Doubleday Anchor, 1966), pp. 29ff.

**265** A. Cornelius Benjamin. Quoted from Fraser, *Voices of Time*, p. 22. See page 259 above.

**266** Arthur C. Clarke, *Profiles of the Future* (Bantam, 1964), p. 138.

**266** J. B. Priestley, *Man and Time* (Dell, 1968), pp. 205, 288.

**267** Louise Robinson Heath, *The Concept of Time* (University of Chicago Press, 1936), p. 199.

**268** William James, *Psychology, Briefer Course* (Holt, 1892), p. 280.

**268** Paul Fraisse, *THE PSYCHOLOGY OF TIME*, translated by Jennifer Leith (Harper, 1963), pp. 84f. Copyright © 1963 by Paul Fraisse. Reprinted by permission of HarperCollins Publishers, Inc.

**271** Eric Berne, *Games People Play* (Grove, 1964), p. 178.

**272** Carl Rogers, "Toward a Theory of Creativity." From Carl Rogers, *On Becoming a Person* (Houghton Mifflin, 1961), pp. 353f.

## CHAPTER 4–3 FREEDOM / CHOICE

**275** Carl R. Rogers and Barry Stevens, *Person to Person: The Problem of Being Human* (Real People Press, 1967), p. 47.

**276** St. Paul. See Romans 7:15–24.

**277** Peter L. Berger, *Invitation to Sociology: A Humanistic Perspective* (Doubleday Anchor, 1963), p. 176.

**279** Bruno Bettelheim, "Joey: A 'Mechanical Boy,'" in *Frontiers of Psychological Research* (Freeman), pp. 223–229. Reprinted from *Scientific American*. Original article dated March 1959.

**279** B. F. Skinner, *Beyond Freedom and Dignity* (Knopf, 1971). For similar ideas presented in fiction form see Skinner's *Walden Two* (Macmillan, 1948).

**282** Rogers and Stevens, *Person to Person*, p. 50. See page 275 above.

**282** Robert D. Cumming (ed.), *The Philosophy of Jean-Paul Sartre* (Modern Library, 1966), p. 233.

**284** William Barrett, *Irrational Man* (Doubleday Anchor, 1962), pp. 241f.

## CHAPTER 4–4 SYMBOLS / COMMUNICATION

**293** Edwin A. Burtt, *MAN SEEKS THE DIVINE* (Harper, 1957), pp. 137f. Copyright © 1957 by Harper & Row Publishers, Inc.; copyright © 1964 by Edwin Arthur Burtt. Reprinted by permission of HarperCollins Publishers.

**294** J. Samuel Bois, *The Art of Awareness* (William C. Brown, 1973).

**294** Leland E. Hinsie and Robert Jean Campbell, *Psychiatric Dictionary* (Oxford, 1960).

**295** Reuben Abel, *Man Is the Measure* (Macmillan, The Free Press, 1976), p. 84.

**296** J. B. Priestley, *Man and Time* (Dell, 1968), pp. 227f. Copyright © 1989 by J. B. Priestley. Reprinted by permission of Outlet Book Company, Inc.

**297** From *Psychic Discoveries Behind the Iron Curtain* by Sheila Ostrander and Lynn Schroeder (Bantam, 1971), pp. 33ff. Copyright © by Sheila Ostrander and Lynn Schroeder. Published by Prentice-Hall, Inc., Englewood Cliffs, New Jersey.

## PART V COEXISTENCE: MAN'S LOVE / HATE CONDITION

**301** Snell Putney and Gail J. Putney, *The Adjusted American: Normal Neuroses in the Individual and Society* (Harper Colophon, 1966), p. 3.

**301** R. D. Laing, *The Politics of Experience* (Ballantine, 1967).

## CHAPTER 5–1 HISTORY / MEANING

**303** Arnold J. Toynbee, *A Study of History*, 12 vols. (Oxford, 1934–1961).

**307** Rosalind Murray (Toynbee), "Long Centuries Grown Cold." Quoted from Arnold Toynbee, *A Study of History* (Oxford University Press, 1954), Vol X, p. 140.

**310** Edward Hallett Carr, *What is History?* (Vintage, 1961).

**315** Will Durant, *The Story of Civilization*, Vol. IV, pp. 343f. The quotations are from Will and Ariel Durant, *The Lessons of History* (Simon & Schuster, 1968), p. 100.

**316** Will Durant, *The Story of Civilization*, Vol. IV, *The Age of Faith* (Simon & Schuster, 1950), pp. 343f.

## CHAPTER 5–2 LAWS / CONSCIENCE

**326** Martin Luther King, Jr. Quoted from Milton Mayer, *On Liberty: Man v. the State* (Center for the Study of Democratic Institutions, 1969), p. 5.

**326** Henry David Thoreau. Quoted from Paul Kurtz (ed.), *American Thought before 1900* (Macmillan, 1966), p. 312.

**326** Martin Luther. Quoted from Joseph Fletcher, *Situation Ethics* (Westminster, 1966), p. 62.

**326** Lewis F. Powell, Jr. Quoted from Milton Mayer, *On Liberty: Man v. the State*, p. 5. See above, this page.

**326** Immanuel Kant. Quoted from Milton Mayer, *On Liberty: Man v. The State*, p. 78. See above, this page.

**328** Quoted from the television series "The Bold Ones," NBC-TV.

**329** *Sicut universitatis conditor*, Ep. 1.401 (October, 1198). From Henry Bettenson (ed.), *Documents of the Christian Church* (Oxford, 1947), pp. 157f.

**330** *Unam sanctam.* From Henry Bettenson (ed.), *Documents of the Christian Church*, pp. 161ff, 157f. See above.

**331** Socrates. Plato, *Crito*, in *The Last Days of Socrates*, translated by Hugh Tredennick (Penguin, 1959), pp. 89ff. See page 21 above.

**332** "Obedience to Authority," by Stanley Milgram, in *TV GUIDE*, August 21, 1976. Copyright © 1976 by News America Publishing, Inc., Radnor, Pennsylvania. Reprinted with permission from *TV Guide* magazine.

**334** Joseph Klausner, *Jesus of Nazareth* (Beacon, 1964), pp. 371, 376, 226, 376.

**334** Plato, *The Phaedo*, from *The Great Dialogues of Plato*, translated by W. H. D. Rouse (Mentor, 1956), p. 521.

## CHAPTER 5–3  POLITICAL PHILOSOPHY / THE USER-FRIENDLY GOVERNMENT

**346** St. Paul. Romans 7:15-25.

**346** Niccolò Machiavelli, *Discourse upon the First Ten Books of Livy*, bk I, ch. 3.

**349** Proverbs 10:6, 12:21, 10:27.

**351** Will and Ariel Durant, *The Lessons of History* (Simon & Schuster, 1968), pp. 101–102.

## CHAPTER 5–4  LIFESTYLES

**353** Ruth Benedict, *Patterns of Culture* (Mentor, 1948), p. 2.

**354** Narration from the television series *Primal Man*,

Part 2: "The Battle for Dominance." David Wolper Productions. Dialogue is from filmed experiments at Stanford University by Philip Zimbardo. See also Philip Zimbardo, "The Psychological Power and Pathology of Imprisonment," a statement prepared for the U.S. House of Representatives Committee on the Judiciary, Subcommittee No. 3: Hearings on Prison Reform, San Francisco, October 25, 1971.

**358** Carlos Castaneda, *The Teachings of Don Juan: A Yaqui Way of Knowledge* (Ballantine, 1969). Originally published by the University of California Press.

**358** Paul Horton and Chester Hunt, *Sociology* (McGraw-Hill, 1964), p. 88. See page 106 above.

**359** Paul Kurtz (ed.), *American Thought before 1900* (Macmillan, 1966), pp. 15f.

**361** Henry David Thoreau. Quoted from Peyton E. Richter (ed.), *Utopias: Social Ideals and Communal Experiments* (Holbrook, 1971), p. 65.

## CHAPTER 5–5  ETHICS / CHOICES

**363** From *THE MADMAN* by Kahlil Gibran. See page 150 above.

**364** From *A Concise Introduction to Philosophy* by William Halverson, pp. 254ff. See page xviii above.

**365** Bonhoeffer. Quoted from Joseph Fletcher, *Situation Ethics* (Westminster, 1966), p. 33. Also note Bonhoeffer's *Letters and Papers from Prison* (Macmillan, 1953).

**365** Kahane. Quoted in *Playboy*, October 1972, p. 69.

**369** For a readable account of the "Categorical Imperative," see Lewis White Beck's translation of Kant's *Critique of Practical Reason* (Bobbs-Merrill Library of Liberal Arts, 1956). For a modern formulation of ethical formalism, see Walter G. Muelder, *Moral Law in Christian Social Ethics* (John Knox, 1966).

**371** For discussions of contextualism, see Joseph Fletcher's books *Situation Ethics* (Westminster, 1966) and *Moral Responsibility* (Westminster, 1967); and for a critical debate of contextualism and formalism, see Harvey Cox (ed.), *The Situation Ethics Debate* (Westminster, 1968).

**373** "High Chaparral," NBC-TV. David Dortort, Executive Producer in association with the National Broadcasting Company. Reprinted with permission.

**376** Albert Schweitzer, *The Teaching of Reverence for Life* (Holt, 1965).

## PART VI THE PROTOPLASMIC VENTURE

**383** Sheila Ostrander and Lynn Schroeder, *Psychic Discoveries Behind the Iron Curtain* (Bantam, 1971). See page 297 above.

## CHAPTER 6–1 LIFE

**392** Irene Kiefer, "Proving We Are the Stuff of Which Stars Are Made," *The Smithsonian* magazine, May 1972, pp. 50f. Copyright © 1972 The Smithsonian Institution. Reprinted by permission of *The Smithsonian.*

**394** John Keosian, *The Origin of Life* (Reinhold, 1964), p. 47.

**399** From *Biology and the Future of Man* by Philip Handler (Oxford, 1970), p. 504. Copyright © 1970 by Oxford University Press, Inc. Reprinted by permission.

**400** Spencer D. Pollard. *Science News*, April 8, 1972, p. 228. Reprinted by permission of *Science News* and the correspondent.

**403** Sir Julian Huxley, *EVOLUTION IN ACTION* (Mentor, 1957), p. 13. Copyright © 1953 by Julian S. Huxley. Reprinted by permission of HarperCollins Publishers.

**403** René Dubos, *The Torch of Life*, pp. 50f. See page 13 above.

**404** Philip Handler, *Biology and the Future of Man*, pp. 488f. See page 399 above.

**404** Harry Overstreet, *The Enduring Quest* (Norton, 1931), pp. 234f.

## CHAPTER 6–2 HUMANS

**411** Sir James G. Frazer, *Folklore of the Old Testament* (Macmillan, 1923), pp. 3ff. Reprinted by permission of Trinity College, Cambridge.

**416** Desmond Morris, *The Naked Ape* (McGraw-Hill, 1967), p. 48.

**417** Philip Handler, *Biology and the Future of Man*, p. 928. See page 399 above.

**420** From "Monkeys, Apes and Man," a National Geographic Special, CBS-TV, telecast October 12, 1971. (Italics added.) Copyright © 1971 by The National Geographic Society. Printed by permission of The National Geographic Society.

**421** Konrad Lorenz, *On Aggression* (Bantam, 1967), pp. 233, 230. See page 12 above.

**421** Ashley Montagu, *On Being Human* (Hawthorn, 1966), pp. 101, 97, 96.

**422** Sir Julian Huxley, *EVOLUTION IN ACTION* (Mentor, 1957), page 9. See page 403 above.

**423** Philip Handler, *Biology and the Future of Man*, p. 492. See page 399 above. (Final italics added.)

## CHAPTER 6–3 EARTH

**429** From *Out of My Life and Thought* by Albert Schweitzer. See page 7 above.

**429** *Poems from the Greek Anthology*, translated by Dudley Fitts, p. 114. Copyright © 1938, 1941, 1956 by New Directions Corporation. Reprinted by permission of New Directions Publishing Corporation.

**430** Dorothy Lee, *Freedom and Culture* (Prentice-Hall, 1959), pp. 163f.

**433** "Prior Possession." Reprinted by permission of Robert Baker.

**435** George S. Sessions, "Panpsychism versus Modern Materialism." Paper delivered at the Conference on "The Rights of Non-Human Nature" at Pitzer College, Claremont, California, April 18, 1974. See also George S. Sessions, "Anthropocentrism and the Environment Crisis" in the *Humboldt Journal of Social Relations* (Vol. 2, Fall/Winter, 1974). Reprinted by permission of the author.

**439** Philip Handler, *Biology and the Future of Man*, p. 491. See page 399 above.

**444** Albert Schweitzer, "The Ethics of Reverence for Life," in *Christendom*, Vol. 1, No. 2 (Winter 1936). Quoted from Charles R. Joy (ed.), *Albert Schweitzer: An Anthology* (Harper, 1947), p. 270.

**444** Pavel Simonov, "Dostoevsky as a Social Scientist," *Psychology Today*, December 1971, p. 104.

## CHAPTER 6–4 FUTURE

**465** Herman Kahn. *The Futurist*, October 1975, p. 232. Reprinted from *The Futurist*. A Journal of Forecasts, Trends and Ideas About The Future, published by the World Future Society.

**458** Alvin Toffler, *The Eco-Spasm Report* (Bantam, 1975), p. 101. Copyright © 1975 by Alvin Toffler.

Used by permission of Bantam, a division of Bantam Doubleday Dell Publishing Group, Inc.

**459** Arthur C. Clarke, *Profiles of the Future* (Bantam, 1964), pp. 56, 207.

**460** "If the forest dies . . ." Reprinted by kind permission of Barbara Taylor Christian.

**463** McHale's comment on Clarke. John McHale, *The Future of the Future*, p. 275.

**466** Fred Hoyle, *Encounter with the Future* (Trident, 1965), Chapter II, "The Anatomy of Doom." Credo Perspectives, planned and edited by Ruth Nanda Anshen. Copyright © 1965 by Fred Hoyle. Reprinted by permission of Simon & Schuster, Inc.

**470** From a conversation with Robert McCall, January 1984.

**471** Ray Bradbury. Quoted from James L. Christian (ed.), *ExtraTerrestrial Intelligence* (Prometheus, 1976), p. 12. Poem quoted from *Why Man Explores*, a symposium held at California Institute of Technology on July 2, 1976, sponsored by NASA/Langley Research Center, televised by PBS. Poem reprinted by permission of Ray Bradbury.

**474** This selection first appeared in the book by Robert Bundy (ed.), *Images of the Future: The Twenty-first Century and Beyond* (Prometheus, 1976), p. 232.

**474** Robert Bundy (ed.), *Images of the Future*, p. 235. See above.

## PART VII  MICROCOSM / MACROCOSM / COSMOS

**477** Carl Sagan. From the television series *Cosmos*.

## CHAPTER 7–1  NATURE

**479** Account of the baseball game taken from *The Memoirs of Professor R. Kulashto* (Ganymede Press, A.D. 2068), pp. 291ff.

**483** Sir Arthur Eddington. Quoted from Harry Overstreet, *The Enduring Quest* (Norton, 1931), pp. 27ff.

**488** Bertrand Russell, *A History of Western Philosophy* (Allen & Unwin, 1946), pp. 48, 55f.

**488** Werner Heisenberg, "From Plato to Max Planck," in *The Atlantic Monthly*, November 1959, p. 113. Copyright © 1959 by The Atlantic Monthly Company,

Boston, Mass. Reprinted by permission of Prof. Heisenberg.

**489** Norwood Russell Hanson, "The Dematerialization of Matter." Quoted from Paul R. Durbin, O.P., *Philosophy of Science: An Introduction* (McGraw-Hill, 1968), p. 103.

**492** Fred Hoyle, *Frontiers of Astronomy* (Mentor, 1957), p. 303.

**492** Victor Weisskopf, "Elementary Particles," in Samuel Rapport and Helen Wright (eds.), *Physics* (Washington Square, 1965), p. 215n.

## CHAPTER 7–2  TIME / SPACE

**501** Cornelius Lanczos, "Einstein and the Role of Theory in Contemporary Physics," *American Scientist*, 1959. Quoted from Joseph Royce, *The Encapsulated Man* (Van Nostrand, 1964), p. 64.

**502** Martin Gardner, *The Relativity Explosion* (Vintage, 1976), pp. 45ff. Copyright © 1976 Martin Gardner and reprinted with his permission.

**503** David S. Saxon and William B. Fretter, *Physics for the Liberal Arts Student* (Holt, 1971), pp. 164f. (See p. 164n.)

**506** For more on Zeno's word games, see Wesley C. Salmon (ed.), *Zeno's Paradoxes* (Bobbs-Merrill Library of Liberal Arts, 1970).

**507** Gracia Fay Ellwood, *Psychic Visits to the Past* (Signet, 1971). Quotation from back cover.

## CHAPTER 7–3  COSMOS

**520** Martin Gardner, *The Relativity Explosion* (Vintage, 1976), p. 192. See page 502 above.

## CHAPTER 7–4  BIOCOSMOS

**529** Sir Arthur Eddington, *New Pathways in Science* (University of Michigan Press, 1959), p. 309.

**529** Harlow Shapley, *Of Stars and Men* (Washington Square, 1960), pp. 133f, 67. Copyright © by Harlow Shapley.

**533** Isaac Asimov, *Of Matters Great and Small* (ACE, 1976), pp. 19–34.

**536** Ray Bradbury, "The Search for Extraterrestrial Life," *Life* magazine, October 24, 1960.

**537** Francesco Sizzi is quoted in Oliver Lodge, *Pioneers of Science* (1893), p. 106.

## PART VIII  OF ULTIMATE CONCERN

**547** Tennessee Williams, *Suddenly Last Summer*.

**547** Nikos Kazantzakis, *The Saviors of God* (Simon & Schuster, 1960), p. 101.

## CHAPTER 8–1  OF ULTIMATE CONCERN

**553** Scipio's prayer. Frederick C. Grant (ed.), *Ancient Roman Religion* (Bobbs-Merrill Library of Liberal Arts, 1957), p. 159.

**558** Viktor Frankl, *Man's Search for Meaning* (Washington Square, 1963), pp. 189f. See page 6 above.

**561** Quoted from Bertrand Russell, *Mysticism and Logic* (Doubleday Anchor, 1957), pp. 44f.

**562** Robert W. Smith, *Concepts of Man, Soul, and Immortality in the Gathas of Zarathustra* (1976). Reprinted by permission of the author.

**562** *Sardar Bundahishn*, 95.5–20.

**565** Aldous Huxley, *The Perennial Philosophy* (Harper, 1945).

**566** Swami Abhedananda (comp.), *The Sayings of Ramakrishna* (Vedanta Society, 1903), p. 54. Quoted from John B. Noss, *Man's Religions* (Macmillan, 4th ed., 1969), pp. 226f.

**567** Ibn Arabi. G. F. Moore, *The History of Religions* (Scribner's, 1919), p. 450.

## CHAPTER 8–2  ULTIMATE REALITY

**573** This wording of St. Anselm's "Ontological Argument" follows closely the text of Philip Schaff, *History of the Christian Church*, Vol. V, *The Middle Ages* (Eerdmans, 1949 [1907]), pp. 601ff.

**574** Lecomte du Noüy, *Human Destiny* (Longmans, Green, 1947), p. 87.

**575** From *The Portable Nietzsche*, translated by Walter Kaufmann (Viking, 1954), pp. 95f. Copyright © 1954, 1968, 1977, by The Viking Press, Inc.

Reprinted by permission of Viking Penguin, a division of Penguin Books USA, Inc.

**576** Ernest Hemingway, *For Whom the Bell Tolls* (Scribner's, 1940), p. 41.

**576** Carl G. Jung, *Psychology and Religion* (Yale University Press, 1938), pp. 113f.

## CHAPTER 8–3  DEATH / IMMORTALITY

**585** From "The Kilimanjaro Device" in Ray Bradbury's *I Sing the Body Electric!* (Bantam, 1971), pp. 3ff. Reprinted by permission of Don Congdon Associates, Inc. Copyright © 1965 by Ray Bradbury.

**588** James Kidd will reproduced courtesy Clerk of the Superior Court, Phoenix.

**588** "Miner's Request: Find Proof of Man's Soul," UPI report.

**590** Ray Bradbury in a letter to the author, April 22, 1972.

**592** Last Flight. Rikihei Inoguchi and Tadashi Nakajima with Roger Pineau, *The Divine Wind* (Bantam, 1960), pp. 178f. Reprinted by permission of Roger Pineau and the United States Naval Institute.

**594** Richard W. Doss, "Life and Death in the Biocosmos." From James L. Christian (ed.), *Extra-Terrestrial Intelligence* (Prometheus, 1976), p. 218. Used by permission.

**597** *Poems from the Greek Anthology*, trans. Dudley Fitts, pp. 126, 116, 106, 108, 107. See page 429 above.

**600** See appendix to James L. Christian (ed.), *Extra-Terrestrial Intelligence* (Prometheus, 1976), pp. 295ff.

**600** Robert Heinlein, *Time Enough for Love* (Putnam's, 1976), p. 326. Copyright © 1973 by Robert A. Heinlein. Reprinted by permission of G. P. Putnam's Sons.

**604** See *Rubaiyat of Omar Khayyam*, translated by Edward FitzGerald. Any edition.

## CHAPTER 8–4  MEANING / EXISTENCE

**609** From *THE MADMAN*, by Kahlil Gibran. See page 150 above.

**609** Friedrich Nietzsche. Quoted from Erich Heller, "The Modern German Mind: The Legacy of Nietzsche," in Thomas J. J. Altizer (ed.), *Toward a New*

*Christianity: Readings in the Death of God Theology* (Harcourt, 1967), p. 103.

**610** Robert Heinlein, *The Glory Road* (Berkley Medallion, 1970), pp. 34ff. Copyright © 1963 by Robert Heinlein.

**611** Viktor Frankl, *Man's Search for Meaning*, pp. 122ff. See page 6 above.

**611** Jean-Paul Sartre, *La Nausée* (Gallimard, 1938), pp. 162f. The English translation used here is by Kurt F. Reinhardt in his *Existentialist Revolt* (Frederick Ungar, 1952), p. 157.

**612** Bertrand Russell, *Mysticism and Logic* (Doubleday Anchor, 1957), pp. 45f.

**612** George S. Counts, "Charles Beard, The Public Man," in Howard K. Beale (ed.), *Charles A. Beard: An Appraisal* (Octagon, 1976).

**613** Nikos Kazantzakis, *The Saviors of God* (Simon & Schuster, 1960), pp. 47f.

**614** Colin Wilson, *Introduction to the New Existentialism* (Houghton Mifflin, 1966), pp. 151, 154.

**614** William Halverson, *A Concise Introduction to Philosophy* (Random House, 1967), pp. 215f.

**615** Langdon Jones, "The Eye of the Lens," in Michael Moorcock (ed.), *The Best SF Stories from New Worlds, No. 6* (Berkley Medallion, 1971), pp. 69f. Reprinted by permission.

**615** These extracts from William Thomson and Saint-Exupéry are quoted from W. Lambert Gardiner, *Psychology: The Story of a Search* (Brooks/Cole, 1970), p. 189, and the flash of insight that juxtaposed these two quotations must be credited to Professor Gardiner.

**623** Ludwig Wittgenstein, *Tractatus Logico-Philosophicus* (Routledge & Kegan Paul, 1960), 6.5, 6.51, 6.52, 6.521.

**623** From the motion picture *The 7 Faces of Dr. Lao* (1964).

# II   ILLUSTRATIONS

## INTRODUCTION

**xviii** Owl on a silver tetradrachm of Athens, minted in the reign of Hippias, c. 516 B.C.

**xx** *The Dropouts* by Howard Post. Copyright © 1969 The United Features Syndicate Inc., and used with their permission.

**xxi** *Peanuts* by Charles M. Schulz. Copyright © 1968 The United Features Syndicate Inc., and used with their permission.

## PART I   THE FINE ART OF WONDERING

**xxiv** John Fry, Dallas

## CHAPTER 1-1   THE WORLD-RIDDLE

**4** Auguste Rodin, *The Thinker*. Ink drawing by Charles Gottlieb. From *A Study of History*, Vol. 12, by Arnold J. Toynbee. Galaxy Edition, 1964. Reprinted by permission of Oxford University Press, Inc.

**5** *Where Do We Come From? What Are We? Where are We Going? (D'où venons-nous? Que sommes-nous? Où allons-nous?)* (1897) by Paul Gauguin, French, 1848–1903. Oil on canvas. 139.1 × 374.6 cm ($54 \frac{3}{4}'' \times 147 \frac{1}{2}''$). Tompkins Collection. Courtesy, Museum of Fine Arts, Boston.

**7** *Castle of the Pyrenees* by René Magritte (1959). Copyright © 1985 by Georgette Magritte. Reproduced by permission.

**8** Abraham Maslow. Courtesy *Psychology Today* magazine.

**9** Viktor Frankl. Courtesy USIU (United States International University), San Diego.

**9** *Calvin and Hobbes* by Bill Watterson. Copyright © 1986 by Bill Watterson. Distributed by Universal Press Syndicate. Reprinted by permission. All rights reserved.

**14** Andrew Wyeth, *Christina's World*, (1948). Courtesy of the Museum of Modern Art, New York.

## CHAPTER 1-2   THE SPIRIT OF PHILOSOPHY

**26** *The Ancient of Days* (1794), by William Blake. Copyright © The Whitworth Art Gallery, University of Manchester, England.

**29** *Calvin and Hobbes* by Bill Watterson. Copyright © 1986 by Bill Watterson. Distributed by Universal Press Syndicate. Reprinted by permission. All rights reserved.

## CHAPTER 1–3  HOW TO PHILOSOPHIZE / CRITICAL ANALYSIS

**46** Editorial cartoon by Frank Interlandi. Copyright © 1976 by *The Los Angeles Times.* Reprinted by permission.

## CHAPTER 1–4  HOW TO PHILOSOPHIZE / SYNOPTIC SYNTHESIS

**62** Zen Garden. Photograph by René Burri, Magnum.
**65** *Continuel Lumière Mobile,* 1963, by Julio Le Parc. Aluminum and wood, 15' square. Courtesy Denise-René Gallery, Paris.
**67** *Frank and Ernest.* Reprinted by permission of NEA, Inc.
**72** Shri Yantra reprinted from S. Vernon McCasland, Grace E. Cairns, and David C. Wu, *Religions of the World* (Random House, 1969).
**74** Photo courtesy Isaac Asimov.

## CHAPTER 1–5  THE WAYS OF PHILOSOPHY

**91** Copyright © Joseph Ferris. Reprinted by permission.

## PART II  THE CONDITION AND THE ODYSSEY

**98** John Fry, Dallas.

## CHAPTER 2–1  PREDICAMENT / ILLUSION

**103** Reprinted by permission of *Saturday Review.*
**104** *The Little Ducks.* Drawing by Jean Primrose. Reprinted by permission of the Viking Press, Inc.
**109** *Soldier Joe.* Drawing copyright 1944, renewed © 1972 by Bill Mauldin. Reprinted by permission of Bill Mauldin.

## CHAPTER 2–2  SELF / AUTONOMY

**116** Copyright © Joseph Ferris. Reprinted by permission.

**117** Zen Oxherding Pictures. Originally drawn by the Zen Master Kakuan (c. A.D. 1100–1200), who also wrote the verse and prose comments for each picture. These woodblock prints are by the Zen artist Tomikichiro Tokuriki. From Paul Reps, *Zen Flesh, Zen Bones* (Doubleday Anchor, N.D.), pp. 136–155. Reprinted by permission of Charles E. Tuttle, Tokyo.

## CHAPTER 2–3  CHANGE / GROWTH

**137** Courtesy Dr. Harry Harlow and the University of Wisconsin Primate Laboratory.
**138** Courtesy of the University of Wisconsin Primate Laboratory.
**139** Edvard Munch, *The Scream.* National Gallery/Art Resource, Oslo.
**142** Chambered Nautilus. Courtesy the American Museum of Natural History.
**142** David Park, *Standing Couple* (1958). Courtesy of the Krannert Arts Museum, University of Illinois.
**145** *Passing the Buck,* by Dick Sargent. Reprinted by permission of *The Saturday Evening Post.* Copyright © 1954 The Curtis Publishing Company. Photo courtesy Dr. Maurice Riseling, Laguna Niguel, California.
**146** Pablo Picasso. Courtesy the Museum of Modern Art, New York.
**149** *Peanuts* by Charles M. Schulz. Copyright © 1960 United Features Syndicate, Inc. Used by permission.
**150** *Ziggy.* Copyright © Ziggy and Friends, Inc. Distributed by Universal Press Syndicate. Reprinted with permission. All rights reserved.

## CHAPTER 2–4  LIFE / TIME

**159** Nat Farber/*Life Magazine.* Copyright © Time, Inc. Reprinted by permission.
**164** Copyright © by Sidney Harris/*American Scientist* magazine. Reprinted by permission of Sidney Harris.
**173** Drawing by Abner Dean, from *What Am I Doing Here?* Copyright © 1947 by Abner Dean. Reprinted by permission of the artist.

## PART III  THE REAL WORLD: KNOWING AND UNKNOWING

**178** John Fry, Dallas

## CHAPTER 3–1   KNOWLEDGE

**182** Richard Lippold, *Variation Number 7: Full Moon* (1949–1950). Brass rods, nickel-chromium, and stainless steel wire, $10' \times 6' \times 6'$. Courtesy of the Museum of Modern Art, New York.

**184** *Calvin and Hobbes* by Bill Watterson. Copyright © 1987 by Bill Watterson. Distributed by Universal Press Syndicate. Reprinted by permission. All rights reserved.

**184** Cartoon by Boris Drucker. Copyright © 1976 by *Playboy* magazine.

**185** *Peanuts* by Charles M. Schulz. Copyright © 1965 United Features Syndicate, Inc. Used by permission.

## CHAPTER 3–2   SENSES / REALITY

**197** Bridget Riley, *Current* (1964). Courtesy of the Museum of Modern Art, New York. Philip Johnson Fund.

**200–204** Electromagnetic spectrum diagram developed by Ronald L. Smith, former director of Tessman Planetarium, Rancho Santiago College.

**206** Cartoon by Henry Martin. Copyright © 1971 by *Saturday Review.*

## CHAPTER 3–3   THE PRAGMATIC MIND

**214** Drawing by Abner Dean from *What Am I Doing Here?* Copyright © 1947 by Abner Dean. Reprinted with permission of the artist.

**215** Courtesy Dr. S. I. Hayakawa.

**216** Village animals redrawn from S. I. Hayakawa, *Language in Thought and Action*, p. 214. Copyright © 1963 by Harcourt Brace Jovanovich. Redrawn with permission.

**219** Cartoon by Dennis Renault. Used by permission.

**221** Sky maps by John Polgreen from *The Sky Observer's Guide*. Copyright © 1959, 1965 by Western Publishing Company, Inc.

## CHAPTER 3–4   TRUTH

**228** Lord Russell. Photo Lotte Meitner-Graf, London.

## PART IV   THE INNER WORLD / THE FANTASTIC JOURNEY

**240** John Fry, Dallas

## CHAPTER 4–1   PSYCHE / SOMA

**248** Electroencephalograms courtesy of Jay W. Klug, Department of Experiential Physiology, Veteran's Administration Hospital, Sepulveda, California.

## CHAPTER 4–2   PAST / PRESENT / FUTURE

**261** Salvador Dali, *The Persistence of Memory*. Courtesy of the Museum of Modern Art, New York.

**262** *Calvin and Hobbes* by Bill Watterson. Copyright © 1987 by Bill Watterson. Distributed by Universal Press Syndicate. Reprinted by permission. All rights reserved.

**269** *Dennis the Menace* by Hank Ketcham. Copyright © North America Syndicate. Used by permission of Hank Ketcham and North America Syndicate.

**272** Monument Valley. *Arizona Highways*, June 1972, pp., 18f. Reproduced courtesy of the photographer, Dick Dietrich.

## CHAPTER 4–3   FREEDOM / CHOICE

**279** Photo courtesy of Dr. B. F. Skinner

**282** Photo courtesy of Dr. Carl Rogers.

**284** *Calvin and Hobbes* by Bill Watterson. Copyright © 1985 by Bill Watterson. Distributed by Universal Press Syndicate. Reprinted by permission. All rights reserved.

## CHAPTER 4–4   SYMBOLS / COMMUNICATION

**288** Cartoon by Sidney Harris/*American Scientist* magazine. Reprinted by permission of Sidney Harris.

**290** *B.C.* by Johnny Hart. Used by permission of Johnny Hart and Field Enterprises.

**291** *Peanuts* by Charles M. Schulz. Copyright © 1967 by United Features Syndicate, Inc. Used by permission.

## PART V COEXISTENCE: MAN'S LOVE/HATE CONDITION

**300** John Fry, Dallas.

## CHAPTER 5–1 HISTORY / MEANING

**308** Pablo Picasso, *Guernica*. Copyright © 1985 S.P.A.D.E.M., Paris/V.A.G.A., New York.

## CHAPTER 5–2 LAWS / CONSCIENCE

**327** Silver denarious of the Roman Emperor Tiberius (A.D. 14–37). This is the type of tribute coin shown to Jesus.

## CHAPTER 5–3 POLITICAL PHILOSOPHY / THE USER FRIENDLY GOVERNMENT

**342** Machiavelli. From The Bettmann Archive.
**346** Hobbes. From The Bettmann Archive.
**347** Rousseau. From the Bettmann Archive.
**348** Locke. From The Bettmann Archive.

## CHAPTER 5–4 LIFESTYLES

**357** *Calvin and Hobbes* by Bill Watterson. Copyright © 1986 by Bill Watterson. Copyright © 1986 by Bill Watterson. Distributed by Universal Press Syndicate. Reprinted by permission. All rights reserved.
**360** Paul Klee, *Senecio*. Copyright © 1981 by ADAGP, Paris. Used by permission.

## CHAPTER 5–5 ETHICS/ CHOICES

**375** *Calvin and Hobbes* by Bill Watterson. Copyright ©

1987 by Bill Watterson. Distributed by Universal Press Syndicate. Reprinted by permission. All rights reserved.

## PART V THE PROTOPLASMIC VENTURE

**382** John Fry, Dallas

## CHAPTER 6–1 LIFE

**388** Photo courtesy of Dr. Stanley Miller.
**389** Photo courtesy of Dr. Stanley Miller.
**390** Photo of microsphere courtesy of Dr. Sidney Fox.
**401** Dolphins. Redrawn from a drawing by Sarah Landry. From *Sociobiology,* by Edward O. Wilson (The Belknap Press of Harvard University Press, 1975).
**402** Photograph by Leonard Lee Rue III. Reproduced courtesy of the National Audubon Society/Photo Researchers.

## CHAPTER 6–2 HUMANS

**419** Illustration by James Bama for the cover of *The Naked Ape,* by Desmond Morris. Reprinted by permission of Dell Publishing Company, Inc.
**423** Paul Reps, *Zen Telegrams* (Charles E. Tuttle, 1959), p. 39. Reprinted by permission of Charles E. Tuttle, Tokyo.

## CHAPTER 6–3 EARTH

**433** Redrawn from a drawing by Charles W. Schwartz. From *A Sand County Almanac* by Aldo Leopold. Copyright © 1949 by Oxford University Press, Inc. Reproduced by permission.
**434** *Calvin and Hobbes* by Bill Watterson. Copyright © 1987 by Bill Watterson. Distributed by Universal Press Syndicate. Reprinted by permission. All rights reserved.
**435** Paul Reps, *Zen Telegrams,* p. 97. See page 423 above.
**443** *Calvin and Hobbes* by Bill Watterson. Copyright © 1985 by Bill Watterson. Distributed by Universal

## CHAPTER 6–4    FUTURE

**455** *Arizona Metropolis 3000* A.D. by Robert T. McCall. Reproduced by courtesy of the artist.

**460** Photograph by Guy Weber. Used by permission of The Rainforest Foundation.

**461** Photograph by Jean-Pierre Dutilleux. Used by permission of The Rainforest Foundation.

**462** Photograph by Jean-Pierre Dutilleux. Used by permission of The Rainforest Foundation.

**464** *B.C.* by Johnny Hart. Used by permission of Johnny Hart and Field Enterprises.

**467** Population expansion redrawn from Fred Hoyle, *Encounter with the Future* (Trident, 1965), p. 32. Redrawn by permission of Simon & Schuster, Inc.

**469** The Nuclear Winter Scenario. Illustrations Copyright © 1983 by Jon Lomberg and used by permission of the artist.

**469** Population distribution redrawn from Philip Handler (ed.), *Biology and the Future of Man* (Oxford, 1970), p. 898.

**470** Photo courtesy of Robert McCall.

**471** Robert McCall and Louise McCall, *The Prologue and the Promise.* Reprinted by permission of the artists.

**472** Ray Bradbury. Photo by Thomas Victor. Reprinted by permission of Ray Bradbury.

## PART VII    MICROCOSM / MACROCOSM / COSMOS

**476** John Fry, Dallas

## CHAPTER 7–1    NATURE

**483** Particle streaks. Reproduced courtesy NAL (National Accelerator Laboratory), Batavia, Illinois.

**487** Reproduced courtesy E. I. duPont de Nemours & Co. (Inc.) Wilmington, DE 19898. From Cyril Ponnamperuma, *The Origins of Life* (Dutton, 1972), p. 104.

## CHAPTER 7–2    TIME / SPACE

**500** Reproduced courtesy of the Hale Observatories.

**505** Light-clocks redrawn from David S. Saxon and William B. Fretter, *Physics for the Liberal Arts Student* (Holt, 1971), p. 165. Redrawn by permission of Holt, Rinehart and Winston, Inc.

## CHAPTER 7–3    COSMOS

**512** Hebrew cosmos redrawn from S. H. Hooke, *In the Beginning,* Vol VI of *The Clarendon Bible* (Oxford, 1947), p. 20. Redrawn by permission.

**513** Egyptian cosmos from Oliver Lodge, *Pioneers of Science* (Dover, 1960). Reprinted by permission.

**514** The Geocentric Cosmos. Woodcut from John C. Brandt and Stephen P. Maran, *New Horizons in Astronomy* (Freeman, 1972), p. 82. Reprinted by permission.

**516–517** The Star Queen Nebula (M16) in the constellation Serpens. Photo courtesy of the Hale Observatories.

**518** The Heliocentric cosmos. From John C. Brandt and Stephen P. Maran, *New Horizons in Astronomy,* p. 82. See page 514 above.

**519** The Globular Cluster M13 in the constellation Hercules. Photo courtesy of the Hale Observatories.

**522** The Whirlpool Galaxy M51 in the constellation Canes Venatici. Photo courtesy of the Hale Observatories.

## CHAPTER 7–4    BIOCOSMOS

**530** Martian landscape. Photo courtesy of NASA.

**534** Cyclops array. Photo courtesy of NASA/Ames Research Center, Moffett Field, California.

**538** The Rosette Nebula (NGC 2237) in the constellation Monoceros. Photo courtesy of the Hale Observatories.

## PART VIII    OF ULTIMATE CONCERN

**546** John Fry, Dallas

## CHAPTER 8–1 OF ULTIMATE CONCERN

**552** Cartoon by Clayton D. Powers, *Esquire* (December 1965), p. 213. Copyright © 1965 by Esquire, Inc. Reprinted by permission of *Esquire* magazine.

**561** Detail of painting of Adam and Eve by Lucas Cranach the Elder. Lee Collection, Courtauld Institute Galleries, London. Adam looks rather puzzled, doesn't he?

**563** *Calvin and Hobbes* by Bill Watterson. Copyright © 1972 by Bill Watterson. Distributed by Universal Press Syndicate. Reprinted by permission. All rights reserved.

## CHAPTER 8–2 ULTIMATE REALITY

**578** Carl G. Jung. From the Bettmann Archive.

## CHAPTER 8–3 DEATH / IMMORTALITY

**585** "The Grim Reaper" in Ingmar Bergman's motion picture *The Seventh Seal.* Copyright © 1960 by Ingmar Bergman. From *Four Screenplays by Ingmar Bergman.* Reproduced by permission of Simon & Schuster, Inc.

**591** King David weeping after having been told of the death of his son (2 Samuel 19:1). In the background, Joab, the general of David's army who killed him. Painting by Guy Rowe. From *In Our Image* by Houston Harte (Oxford, 1949). Reproduced courtesy of Houston Harte.

**599** *Calvin and Hobbes* by Bill Watterson. Copyright © 1986 by Bill Watterson. Distributed by Universal Press Syndicate. Reprinted by permission. All rights reserved.

**602** Photo courtesy of the photographer, John Reseck.

## CHAPTER 8–4 MEANING / EXISTENCE

**610** Paul Reps, *Zen Telegrams*, p. 81. See page 423 above.

**617** Earthrise. Photo courtesy of NASA.

# INDEX TO MARGINAL QUOTES

# NAME/SUBJECT INDEX